Happy Birthday

Tsippy Donny & Dafna

Jerusalem

A NEIGHBORHOOD STREET GUIDE

CHANOCH SHUDOFSKY

JERUSALEM: A NEIGHBORHOOD STREET GUIDE

Published by DEVORA PUBLISHING COMPANY

Cover and Book Design: Benjie Herskowitz

Translated by Adele Shudofsky

Production Manager: Daniella Barak

Photography: Government Press Office, Ginzach Kiddush Hashem, Yaakov Levine, Aryeh Shudofsky

Soft Cover ISBN: 978-1-934440-25-4

Email: sales@devorapublishing.com
Web Site: www.devorapublishing.com

Printed in Israel

In memory of my dear brother
NOAM z"l

For his devotion to
religious Zionist education
and love of Israel

Table of Contents

Note regarding listings of neighborhood names:

Diagonal line / separates two official names.

Parentheses ( ) denote an alternate informal name.

Brackets [ ] denote the translation of the name.

Introduction

As I visited each one of the neighborhoods in Jerusalem looking at the names of the streets, I started to imagine an historic meeting between King David, the Commander-in-Chief of the army, and David Marcus, soldier and first general of the Israel Defense Force. I pictured a meeting in the neighborhood of Komemiyut/Talbieh, at the intersection of Zeev Jabotinsky Street and Haim Arlosoroff Street, a real-life meeting between the founder of the Revisionist movement and one of the leaders of the Labor movement in the Land of Israel, and another meeting between the visionary of the Jewish state, Binyamin Zeev Herzl, and the founder of the State of Israel, David Ben-Gurion. Entirely imaginary, yes, but true according to the layout of Jerusalem's streets, because the streets do meet.

My interest in the street names impelled me to try to find a guide to the streets of Jerusalem arranged by neighborhoods, but without success. After an extended search, I discovered only one book about the streets of the capital, arranged alphabetically, but which was last printed in 1988, 19 years ago!

In order to fill the void, I decided that since that was the case, why shouldn't I myself write an updated book on the 2,500 streets, squares, thoroughfares, boulevards and alleyways of the city, by neighborhoods, for both the local citizen and the tourist. I set myself the goal of publishing a guide in two parts: an updated, alphabetical guide to the streets and a guide describing the neighborhoods in Jerusalem, arranged alphabetically, including a listing of the streets in each neighborhood, with the addition of maps, a list of sites of interest, walking tour routes and more.

The book "Jerusalem: A Neighborhood Street Guide" constitutes an historic journey through the history of the Jewish People. The names of the streets and neighborhoods are historic way stations extending from the period of the Bible, right up to our own days, to those very people and events that brought about the establishment of the State of Israel.

With all that I read and all my walking from neighborhood to neighborhood, I learned to recognize at close range how modern Jerusalem developed. Each neighborhood that was founded had its own special character, since its residents brought with them the particular national dress and way of life of the country from which they came. New neighborhoods were not easily established. Under Turkish rule, it was impossible for foreigners to acquire land to build houses, and if they did finally get permission and built, they were faced with the great danger of living outside the protective walls of the Old City. As a result, those early neighborhoods were built in the shape of a square, with the houses attached to one another on both sides and doorways facing in, the backs of the houses on each side of the square forming a single, protective wall toward the outside. The neighborhood entrances were iron gates that were kept locked at night. In every neighborhood a synagogue was built, and in the middle of the central courtyard was a cistern to catch rainwater. The houses were built of strong stone, and the British authorities for the most part required building houses of Jerusalem stone in order to preserve the special character of the city.

The names of the neighborhoods were not given at random, but rather they portrayed the uniqueness of each neighborhood. There are names which are Biblical in origin and express the yearning of the founders: Yegiy'a Kapayim ("fruit of our labor"), Mea She'arim ("one hundredfold"), Talpiot ("ramparts"). Names of other neighborhoods are based on personal names: Yemin Moshe ("Moshe's right hand"), Beit David ("the House of David"), Mahane Yehuda ("Yehuda's encampment").

There are neighborhoods whose names symbolize the country of origin of the founders: Shchunat HaBucharim ("neighborhood of the Bucharans"), Batei Kollel Varsha ("Kollel Warsaw houses"), HaMoshava HaGermanit ("the German Colony"); there are neighborhoods whose names are purely symbolic: Ahva ("brotherhood"), Beit Yisrael ("the House of Israel"), Komemiyut ("independence"); and yet other neighborhoods which are named for their geography: Ramot Allon ("Allon heights"), Yefei Nof ("beautiful view"), Har Nof ("mountain view") and the like.

Likewise, Jerusalem's street names, which appear to us as one whole historic fabric, are drawn from diverse sources, like famous personalities from the Bible: judges, kings and prophets; from the Middle

Ages: Sa'adia Gaon, Ibn 'Ezra; from the initials of their names: RaSH"I, RaMBa"M, and more; rabbis: Salant, Kook, Harlap; Zionist leaders: Herzl, Sokolow, Ruppin, and more; religious texts: Mesilat Yesharim ("Path of the Righteous"), Pri Hadash ("New Fruit"), HaTurim ("Columns"); and others: gentiles who were Lovers of Zion (Hovevei Tzion): Balfour, Eliot, Patterson; well-known places: 'Emek Refaim, HaShiloah, Hevron, Beit Lehem; fighting units and places connected with Israel's military campaigns: HaPaLMa"H, HaGaDN"A, Mehalkei HaMayim ("the water distributors"), Ma'avar HaMitla ("Mitla Pass"), 'Etzion Gever; plants and trees: Afarsemon ("persimmon"), Dagan ("grain"), HaEzov ("hyssop"), HaSigalit ("violet") and more.

The street names in each of the various Jerusalem neighborhoods are focused for the most part around a common theme: in Geulim/Bak'a the streets are named for the tribes of Israel and prominent judges in the Bible. In Mahane Yehuda the street names are the names of fruits that are sold there in the market. In Mea She'arim the streets bear the names of Torah scholars. In 'Ir Ganim the streets are named for wildflowers. In Ramat Eshkol the streets are called by names connected with the Six Day War.

In this book I have gathered information and knowledge about the individuals, events and places after which are named the streets that we cross every day without paying any attention to the source of the name. I recommend that every Israeli and every tourist walk through those same neighborhoods and streets where I walked, and as they do so to discover and soak up the rich past that I discovered and absorbed on my walks throughout this magical city – ***Yerushalayim***.

Chanoch Shudofsky
Jerusalem, February, 2008

How to Use the Guide

The first part of the Guide is an alphabetical list of the street names, arranged according to the first letter in the name: the person's family (last) name, acronyms (initials of a person's name) according to the first letter in them, names of books, places, events, organizations and the like, all appearing in alphabetical order according to the first letter in the name. Hebrew names beginning with "Ha-", "the" in Hebrew, will be found under the letter "H" (HaMehanechet, HaSatat). Arabic street names beginning with "El-", "the" in Arabic, are listed under the letter "E" (e.g. El-Akhtal, El-Bustami). Next to the name appear the name of the neighborhood in which the street is located and the page number on which it appears in the second section. In square brackets following the name, in bold type, is the designation of the name as boulevard, square, steps, lane or other non-street. If a translation of the name is shown, it appears in square brackets, not in bold type. The first section of the Guide serves as a cross-reference to the second section, that of the neighborhoods.

In the second section, the major part of the Guide, are listed alphabetically the neighborhoods to be found within the municipal boundaries of the city of Jerusalem, and for each neighborhood the streets in it are listed. In the description which begins each neighborhood listing is a short historical introduction, including the boundaries of the neighborhood (the surrounding neighborhoods or major streets which form the boundaries) and sites of interest, as well as the details of the theme or themes that the street names have in common, such as famous people, prophets of Israel, flowers, fruits, spices, historical events and the like.

In the first line appears the name of the street. If the name is that of a person, the dates of birth and death of the individual may appear. Likewise, the names of the cross-streets at the two ends or bordering streets are given, and then the map coordinates of the street, to aid in locating the street on the attached map. Although some streets do not appear on the map, the reader can still find the actual street by means of the map coordinates and cross-streets. The lines following this give a short explanation about the man, woman, book, fruit or the like that is the source for the name. If the street crosses more than one neighborhood, the street listing appears in each of the neighborhoods, but the explanatory paragraph appears only in the neighborhood that comes first alphabetically in this section. The other neighborhoods in which the street occurs are referenced each time.

For the reader's information, dates are noted in this way: dates before the common era are shown as BCE; dates of the common era up to the year 1000 CE have the notation CE; dates more recent than 1000 CE have no notation.

Also, when a particular street ends outside the neighborhood under discussion, in the listing of cross-streets or bordering streets the route of the street appears like this: named first is the cross-street or bordering street from which the street begins, then the cross-street at the end that is still within the neighborhood, then comes the cross-street where the street finally ends ("ends at"). For example: "Korei HaDorot" in Arnona is shown with the route: "Revadim – Siegfried Moses and ends at 'Ein Gedi".

Thanks and Appreciation

Upon completing the writing, I wish to thank a number of people with whose help and because of whom I have reached this point. First, my thanks to Ziva Amishai-Meisels, who, during the course of a conversation with me, planted the idea in my head that I myself should write a book on the neighborhoods and streets of Jerusalem, instead of looking for someone else to do it.

My thanks also to Dorin Schrecki who faithfully typed the entire Hebrew book from my handwritten (!) manuscript; to Yaacov Peterseil, president of Devora Publishing, who welcomed my manuscript with enthusiasm and was prepared to publish it without delay, which forged between us a strong and lasting connection; to Avner Zecharia of the Committee on Jerusalem Street Signs, who explained to me why certain names were given to certain streets in the city; to the staff of the Jerusalem municipal archive who made available to me important information regarding the street names; special thanks to the many long-time residents of Jerusalem who, in the course of my walking around the city streets, were good enough to give me a great deal of information about the streets and neighborhoods in which they live, out of their great love for the city.

Thanks and gratitude also to my family who helped with the production of the book; heartfelt thanks to my dear children – Tova and Yaakov, Shira and Shalom, Avigayil and Aryeh, who encouraged me and gave me constant support and always expressed their pride in me as I related the day-to-day progress of the writing; particular thanks from the depths of my heart to my dear wife – Adele – for her incredible dedication and commitment in translating the text into English and for the help, patience and devotion she demonstrated toward me in every step of the process of writing the Guide.

The Streets in Alphabetical Order

A

'Abadi, Yitzhak, see the neighborhood of Giv'at HaVradim/Shikun Rassco, page 209
Abba Berdiczew, see the neighborhood of Tzameret HaBira, page 505
Abba Uri [Lane], see the neighborhood of Bayit VaGan, page 126
'Abd el-Hamid Suman, see the neighborhood of Beit Hanina, page 139
'Abd el-Rahman Dajani, see the neighborhood of Beit Hanina, page 139
Abeles, Walter, Dr., see the neighborhood of Talpiot, page 490
Abir Ya'akov, see the neighborhood of Neve Ya'akov, page 392
Abohav, Yitzhak, Rabbi, see the neighborhood of Bayit VaGan, page 126
Abohav, Yitzhak, Rabbi, see the neighborhood of Ramat Sharett, page 424
'Aboud, Haim Shaul, Rabbi, see the neighborhood of Beit Yisrael, page 147
Abrabanel, Don Yitzhak, see the neighborhood of Rehavia, page 447
Abramsky, Ya'akov David [Square], see the neighborhood of Shikun HaBa"D, page 481
Abu Bakr e-Sadiq, see the neighborhood of Bab e-Zahara, page 101
Abu Firem el-Hamdani, see the neighborhood of Wadi el-Joz, page 506
Abu Madi, see the neighborhood of Beit Hanina, page 139
Abu Rabay'a, Muhamad Hamdan, see the neighborhood of Talpiot Mizrah, page 497
Abu Tamam, see the neighborhood of Beit Hanina, page 139
Abu Tor, see the neighborhood of Giv'at Hanania/Abu Tor, page 207
Abu 'Ubayda, see the neighborhood of Bab e-Zahara, page 101
Abula'fia, David [Square], see the neighborhood of Kiryat Moshe, page 296
Abula'fia, Haim, Rabbi, see the neighborhood of Mishkenot Yisrael, page 359
Adahan, Yihye, see the neighborhood of Morasha/Musrara, page 361
Adam, see the neighborhood of Talpiot Mizrah, page 497
Adam, Yekutiel, Aluf, see the neighborhood of Pisgat Zeev Ma'arav, page 412
Adam, Yekutiel, Aluf, see the neighborhood of Shu'afat, page 485
'Adani, Shlomo, Rabbi, see the neighborhood of Beit Yisrael, page 148
'Adani, Shlomo, Rabbi, see the neighborhood of Sha'arei Pina, page 470
Adler, Shaul, Dr., see Mid-Town, page 346
Admon ben Gadai, see the neighborhood of Batei Perlman/'Ir Shalom, page 120
Admoni, Elimelech, see the neighborhood of Yemin Moshe, page 513
Admor Rabbi Shlomo, see the neighborhood of Beit Yisrael, page 148
Adoniyahu HaCohen, Rabbi, see the neighborhood of HaBucharim, page 255
Afarsemon, see the neighborhood of Gilo, page 191
Afodi, see the neighborhood of Rehavia, page 447
AGa"N, Rabbi, see the neighborhood of Beit David/Beit HaRav Kook, page 132

Albright, William, see the neighborhood of Kiryat Aryeh, page 282
Alexandrion, see the neighborhood of Gonenim/Katamonim Bet, Gimel, Dalet, page 245
Alfandari, Shlomo El'azar, Rabbi, see the neighborhood of Mahane Yehuda, page 321
Alfandari, Shlomo El'azar, Rabbi, see the neighborhood of Mekor Baruch, page 339
Alfandari, Shlomo El'azar, Rabbi, see the neighborhood of Ohel Shlomo, page 399
Alfandari, Shlomo El'azar, Rabbi, see the neighborhood of Ruhama, page 459
Alfasi, Yitzhak, Rabbi, see the neighborhood of Rehavia, page 447
Alfiye, Meir, Rabbi [Square], see the neighborhood of Giv'at Shaul, page 228
Alfiye, Meir, Rabbi [Square], see the neighborhood of Har Nof, page 259
Alfiye, Yitzhak, Rabbi, see the neighborhood of Bayit VaGan, page 126
Algazi, Yom Tov, Rabbi, see the neighborhood of Yegiy'a Kapayim, page 510
Al-Hakari, see the Moslem Quarter, page 364
Alharizi, Yehuda, see the neighborhood of Rehavia, page 447
'Ali Ibn Abu Taleb, see the neighborhood of Bab e-Zahara, page 101
'Aliyat HaNo'ar, see the neighborhood of Ramot Allon, page 432
Al-Jabsha, see the Christian Quarter, page 154
Alkabetz, Shlomo, Rabbi, see the neighborhood of Giv'at Shaul, page 229
Alkahi, Mordechai, see the neighborhood of Talpiot Mizrah, page 497
Alkala'i, David [Square], see the neighborhood of Giv'at Shapira/French Hill, page 225
Alkala'i, Yehuda, Rabbi, see the neighborhood of Komemiyut/Talbieh, page 311
Al-Khanaqa, see the Christian Quarter. Page 154
Al-Kirami, see the Moslem Quarter, page 364
Allenby, Edmund [Square], see the neighborhood of Romema, page 453
Allon, Gedalia, see the neighborhood of the German Colony, page 177
'Alma, see the neighborhood of Nahlat Ahim/Nahlaot, page 372
'Alma, see the neighborhood of Sha'arei Rahamim (Sha'arei Yeshu'a), page 473
Almaliah, Avraham, see the neighborhood of Gonenim/Katamonim Het, Tet, page 249
Almog, see the neighborhood of Gilo, page 192
Almushnino, Moshe, Rabbi, see the neighborhood of Ramat Shlomo/Rechess Shu'afat, page 427
Al-Natar, see the neighborhood of Beit Safafa, page 143
Al-'Omari, see the Moslem Quarter, page 364
Alroi, David, see the neighborhood of Gonen/Katamon HaYeshana, page 236
Al-Sa'adiya, see the Christian Quarter, page 154
Alsheikh, Moshe ben Haim, see the neighborhood of Ahva, page 90
Altman, Aryeh, see the neighborhood of Pisgat Zeev Mercaz, page 402
Aluf Simhoni, Asaf, see the neighborhood of Kiryat Shmuel, page 301
Aluf Yohai bin Nun, see the neighborhood of Giv'at Beit HaKerem, page 201
Aluf Yohai bin Nun, see the neighborhood of Ramat Beit HaKerem, page 416

'Alwan, Shabtai, Rabbi, see the neighborhood of Mahane Yehuda, page 321
'Alwan, Shabtai, Rabbi, see the neighborhood of Ohel Shlomo, page 399
'Amasa, see the neighborhood of Manhat/Malha, page 329
Amatzia, see the neighborhood of the Greek Colony, page 251
Amdursky, Yerahmiel, see the neighborhood of HaBucharim, page 255
'Amiel, Moshe Avigdor, Rabbi, see the neighborhood of Kiryat Moshe, page 296
'Aminadav, see the neighborhood of Giv'at Hanania/Abu Tor, page 207
Amir, see the neighborhood of Yefei Nof, page 508
'Amos, see the neighborhood of Kerem Avraham, page 280
'Amram Gaon (ben Sheshna), see the neighborhood of Giv'at Shaul, page 229
'Am Ve'Olamo, see the neighborhood of Giv'at Shaul, page 229
'Anatot, see the neighborhood of Nahlat Tzion, page 383
Angel, Shlomo [Square], see the neighborhood of Giv'at Shaul, page 229
Angel, Vidal, Rabbi [Steps], see the neighborhood of Kiryat Moshe, page 296
Anielewicz, Mordechai, see the neighborhood of Kiryat HaYovel, page 286
'Antebbe, Avraham (Albert), see the neighborhood of Nahlat Tzadok, page 381
'Antebbe, Avraham (Albert), see the neighborhood of Sha'arei Hesed, page 468
Antigonus (Ish Socho), see the neighborhood of Gonenim/Katamonim Aleph and Vav, page 242
Antokolsky, Mordechai (Mark), see the neighborhood of Nahlat Tzadok, page 381
Antokolsky, Mordechai (Mark), see the neighborhood of Neve Betzalel, page 389
Antokolsky, Mordechai (Mark), see the neighborhood of Sha'arei Hesed, page 468
Antonia, see the Moslem Quarter, page 364
Anusei Mashhad, see the neighborhood of Talpiot Mizrah, page 497
'Arad, see the neighborhood of Manhat/Malha, page 329
Aranne, Zalman [Square], see the neighborhood of Giv'at HaMivtar, page 204
Aranne, Zalman [Square], see the neighborhood of Ramat Eshkol, page 421
Ararat, see the Armenian Quarter, page 93
Aravna HaYevusi, see the Jewish Quarter, page 270
Arazi, Reuven, see the neighborhood of Pisgat Zeev Mizrah, page 407
Arbel, see the neighborhood of Kerem/Beit Avraham, page 278
Archie Sherman [Square], see the neighborhood of Talpiot Mizrah, page 497
Arest, Avraham, see the neighborhood of Pat, page 400
Argov, Eli'ezer, see the neighborhood of Ramat Sharett, page 424
Ari BeMistarim, see the neighborhood of Ramot Allon, page 432
Ariel, see the neighborhood of Romema, page 454
Ariel, Thomas [Boulevard], see the neighborhood of Beit HaKerem, page 134
Aristobulus, Yehuda, see Mid-Town, page 346
Arlosoroff, Haim, Dr., see the neighborhood of Komemiyut/Talbieh, page 311
Arlosoroff, Haim, Dr., see the neighborhood of Rehavia, page 447
Armenian Patriarchate, see the Armenian Quarter, page 93
Armoza, Eliyahu [Square], see the neighborhood of Kiryat HaYovel, page 286
Arnon, see the neighborhood of Zichron Yosef, page 522
Arnon, Ya'akov, see the neighborhood of Ramat Beit HaKerem, page 416

Artom, Elia Samuele, see the neighborhood of Kiryat Ta'asiyot 'Atirot Mada'/Har Hotzvim, page 304
Aryeh ben Eli'ezer, see the neighborhood of Gilo, page 192
Arzei HaBira, see the neighborhood of Ma'alot Dafna/Arzei HaBira, page 316
Asa, see the neighborhood of the Greek Colony, page 252
'Asael, see the neighborhood of Giv'at Hanania/Abu Tor, page 207
Asaf, Gavriel [Square], see the neighborhood of Gonen/Katamon HaYeshana, page 236
Asaf, Simha, Rabbi [Square], see the neighborhood of Komemiyut/Talbieh, page 311
A-Saraye, see the Moslem Quarter, page 364
Ashbel, Sara and 'Aminadav [Square], see the neighborhood of Kiryat HaYovel, page 286
Ashberg, Eli Mordechai, Rabbi, see the neighborhood of the German Colony, page 177
Asher, see the neighborhood of Geulim/Bak'a, page 185
Ashkenazi, Betzalel, Rabbi, see the neighborhood of Beit Yisrael, page 148
Ashkenazi, Betzalel, Rabbi, see the neighborhood of HaBucharim, page 255
Ashtori HaParhi, Rabbi, see the neighborhood of Ahva, page 90
Asirei Tzion, see the neighborhood of Ramot Allon, page 432
Astora Meir, see the neighborhood of Neve Ya'akov, page 392
'Atarot, see 'Atarot -Industrial Zone, page 99
Atun, Ben Tzion, Rabbi, see the neighborhood of Sanhedria HaMurhevet, page 465
Auerbach, Moshe [Square], see the neighborhood of Giv'at Shapira/French Hill, page 225
Auerbuch, Efraim, Rabbi, see the neighborhood of Beit Yisrael, page 148
Auerbuch, Efraim, Rabbi, see the neighborhood of Sha'arei Pina, page 470
Auster, Daniel [Square], see the neighborhood of Rehavia, page 448
Avi Yona, Michael, see the neighborhood of Holyland Park, page 262
Avi'ad, see the neighborhood of Giv'at Mordechai, page 214
Avida', Yehuda Leib Zlotnick, Rabbi, see Mid-Town, page 346
Avidani, Hacham 'Eluan [Square], see the neighborhood of Zichron Yosef, page 522
Avidar, Yosef, see the neighborhood of Giv'at Massua, page 211
Avi'ezer Yellin, see the neighborhood of Ramot Allon, page 432
Avigad, Nahman, see the neighborhood of Neve Shaanan, page 391
Avigayil, see the neighborhood of Giv'at Hanania/Abu Tor, page 207
Avigdori, Shneur, Dr., see Mid-Town, page 346
Avigur, Shaul, see the neighborhood of Homat Shmuel/Har Homa, page 264
Avinadav, see the neighborhood of HaBucharim, page 255
Avisar, David, see the neighborhood of Mahane Yehuda, page 321
Avishai ben Tzruya, see the neighborhood of the Greek Colony, page 252
Avital, see the neighborhood of Mekor Haim, page 343
Avizohar, Yehoshu'a, see the neighborhood of Beit HaKerem, page 135
Avizohar, Yehoshu'a, see the neighborhood of Giv'at Beit HaKerem, page 202

Avizohar, Yehoshu'a, see the neighborhood of Ramat Beit HaKerem, page 416
Avner ben Ner, see the neighborhood of the Greek Colony, page 252
'Avodat Yisrael, see the neighborhood of Batei Kollel Warsaw/Nahlat Ya'akov, page 115
'Avodat Yisrael, see the neighborhood of Even Yehoshu'a, page 170
Avraham MiSlonim, see the neighborhood of Mea She'arim, page 336
Avramsky, Yehezkel, Rabbi, see the neighborhood of Ahva, page 90
Avtalyon, see the neighborhood of Geulim/Bak'a, page 185
Ayala, see the neighborhood of Gilo, page 192
Ayalon, David, see the neighborhood of Manhat/Malha, page 329
'Azaar, Shmuel, see the neighborhood of Talpiot Mizrah, page 497
'Azaria, see the neighborhood of the Greek Colony, page 252
'Azriel Hausdorf, see the neighborhood of Giv'at Shaul, page 229
Azulai, 'Akiva, see the neighborhood of Giv'at Shaul, page 229

B

Ba'al HaSheiltot, see the neighborhood of Giv'at Shaul, page 229
Ba'al HaTanya, see the neighborhood of Mea She'arim, page 336
Ba'al Or Sameiah, see the neighborhood of Kiryat Aryeh, page 282
Ba'al Or Sameiah, see the neighborhood of Ma'alot Dafna/Arzei HaBira, page 316
Ba'alei Melacha, see Talpiot-Industrial Zone, page 494
Bab-e-Nebi Daud, see the Armenian Quarter, page 93
Bachar, Nissim, see the neighborhood of Nahlat Tzion, page 383
Bachar, Nissim, see the neighborhood of Zichron Yosef, page 522
Bacher, Binyamin Zeev, Dr., see the neighborhood of the German Colony, page 177
Bachi, Roberto, see Giv'at Shaul- Industrial Zone, page 234
Badhav, Yitzhak, Rabbi [Steps], see the neighborhood of Yemin Moshe, page 513
Badr, see the neighborhood of Beit Hanina, page 139
Baha e-Din, see the neighborhood of Bab e-Zahara, page 101
Baharan, Shlomo Zalman, Rabbi, see the neighborhood of Batei Werner/Ohalei Moshe, page 123
Baharan, Shlomo Zalman, Rabbi, see the neighborhood of Bnei Moshe/Neve Shalom, page 152
Baharan, Shlomo Zalman, Rabbi, see the neighborhood of Mea She'arim, page 336
Bajaio, Haim, Rabbi, see the neighborhood of the German Colony, page 177
Bakshi, Aharon [Square], see the neighborhood of HaBucharim, page 255
Bakshi-Doron, Ben-Zion, Rabbi [Square], see the neighborhood of Komemiyut/Talbieh, page 312
Balaban, Meir, see the neighborhood of Neve Ya'akov, page 393
Balfour, Arthur James, Lord [Road], see the neighborhood of Giv'at Ram, page 218
Balfour, Arthur James, Lord, see the neighborhood of Komemiyut/Talbieh, page 312

Balfour, Arthur James, Lord, see the neighborhood of Rehavia, page 448
Banai, Eliyahu Ya'akov, see the neighborhood of Mahane Yehuda, page 321
Bani Omaya, see the neighborhood of Wadi el-Joz, page 506
Bank Yisrael, see the neighborhood of Giv'at Ram, page 218
Bar Giora, see the neighborhood of Mekor Baruch, page 339
Bar Kochva, Shim'on, see the neighborhood of Giv'at Shapira/French Hill, page 225
Bar Kochva, Shim'on, see the neighborhood of Tzameret HaBira, page 505
Bar Lev, Haim [Boulevard], see the neighborhood of Giv'at HaMivtar, page 204
Bar Lev, Haim [Boulevard], see the neighborhood of Giv'at Shapira/French Hill, page 225
Bar Lev, Haim [Boulevard], see the neighborhood of Kiryat Aryeh, page 282
Bar Lev, Haim [Boulevard], see the neighborhood of Nahlat Shim'on, page 376
Bar Lev, Haim [Boulevard], see the neighborhood of Sheikh Jarrah, page 478
Bar Nisan, see the neighborhood of Gonen/Katamon HaYeshana, page 236
Bar Niv, Zvi [Square], see the neighborhood of Gonen/Katamon HaYeshana, page 236
Bar Yohai, Shim'on, see the neighborhood of Gonenim/Katamonim Het, Tet, page 249
Bar Zakai, Yeshayahu, Rabbi (Bardaki), see the neighborhood of Sha'arei Hesed, page 468
Bar'am, Moshe [Road], see the neighborhood of Pat, page 400
Bar'am, Moshe [Road], see Talpiot-Industrial Zone, page 494
Baradnov, Yirmiyahu, see the neighborhood of Pisgat Zeev Ma'arav, page 412
Barak (ben Avino'am), see the neighborhood of Geulim/Bak'a, page 186
Bar'am, Ruti [Boulevard], see the neighborhood of Talpiot, page 490
Bar'am, Ruti [Boulevard], see the neighborhood of Talpiot Mizrah, page 497
Baranowicz [Lane], see the neighborhood of Giv'at Shaul, page 230
Barazani, Moshe, see the neighborhood of Talpiot Mizrah, page 497
Bar-Ilan (Berlin), Meir, Rabbi, see the neighborhood of HaBucharim, page 255
Bar-Ilan (Berlin), Meir, Rabbi, see the neighborhood of Mahanayim, page 318
Bar-Ilan (Berlin), Meir, Rabbi, see the neighborhood of Tel-Arza, page 503
Barkai, see the Jewish Quarter, page 270
Barkali, Shaul, see the neighborhood of 'Ein Kerem, page 163
Barkuk, see the Moslem Quarter, page 364
Barnett, Zerah, Rabbi, see the neighborhood of Har Nof, page 259
Bar-On, Uri, see the neighborhood of Pisgat Zeev Mercaz, page 402
Baruch, Marco, see the neighborhood of Kiryat HaYovel, page 286
Baruch, Natan [Square], see Mid-Town, page 347
Baruch, Shmuel, Rabbi, see the neighborhood of Beit Ya'akov, page 146
Baruch, Shmuel, Rabbi, see the neighborhood of Mahane Yehuda, page 321
Baruch, Shmuel, Rabbi, see Mid-Town, page 347
Baruch, Shmuel, Rabbi, see the neighborhood of Sha'arei Tzedek, page 475
Baruch, Shmuel, Rabbi, see the neighborhood of Shevet Tzedek/Shchunat HaPahim, page 480
Baruch, Shmuel, Rabbi, see the neighborhood of Zichron Yosef, page 522

Baruch, Ya'akov, Rabbi [Square], see the neighborhood of Mahane Yehuda, page 321
Baruchi, Yehoshu'a, see the neighborhood of Gilo, page 192
Baruchof, Mashiah, see the neighborhood of Mahane Yehuda, page 321
Baruchof, Mashiah, see Mid-Town, page 347
Bar-Yakar, Dov [Lane], see the neighborhood of Neve Ya'akov, page 393
Barzilai, Yehoshu'a, see the neighborhood of Talpiot, page 490
Basel, see the neighborhood of Kiryat Moshe, page 296
Basravi, Betzalel, see the neighborhood of Pisgat Zeev Mercaz, page 402
Bassan, Yitzhak, see the neighborhood of Ramat Eshkol, page 421
Bat Sheva', see the neighborhood of Giv'at Hanania/Abu Tor, page 207
Batei Hornstein, see the neighborhood of Batei Hornstein/Kollel Volyn, page 108
Batei Mahse, see the Jewish Quarter, page 271
Batei Mahse [Square], see the Jewish Quarter, page 271
Batei Warsaw, see the neighborhood of Batei Kollel Warsaw/Nahlat Ya'akov, page 116
Baum, Shlomo, see the neighborhood of Homat Shmuel/Har Homa, page 264
Bavli, Hana, see the neighborhood of Pisgat Zeev Mizrah, page 407
Baybars, see the neighborhood of Sheikh Jarrah, page 478
Bayit VaGan, see the neighborhood of Bayit VaGan, page 126
Bazak, Betzalel, see the neighborhood of Giv'at Mordechai, page 214
Bazak, Betzalel, see the neighborhood of Nayot, page 357
Bazov, David, Rabbi, see the neighborhood of Ramot Allon, page 433
Beer Mayim Haim, see the neighborhood of Bayit VaGan, page 126
Beer Sheva', see the neighborhood of Nahlat Tzion, page 383
Be-eri, see Mid-Town, page 347
Beerot Yitzhak, see the neighborhood of Gonen/Katamon HaYeshana, page 236
Begin, Menahem [Boulevard], see the neighborhood of Holyland Park, page 262
Beilis, Mendel, see the neighborhood of Ramot Allon, page 433
Beirav, Ya'akov ben Haim, Rabbi, see the neighborhood of Mishkenot Yisrael, page 359
Beit David [Lane], see the neighborhood of Nahlat Shiv'a, page 378
Beit El, see the Jewish Quarter, page 271
Beit Eshel, see the neighborhood of Gonen/Katamon HaYeshana, page 236
Beit Fagi, see the neighborhood of E-Tur, page 168
Beit Ha'Arava, see the neighborhood of Arnona, page 96
Beit Ha'Arava, see the neighborhood of Talpiot, page 490
Beit HaBad, see the Christian Quarter, page 154
Beit HaBad, see the Moslem Quarter, page 364
Beit HaDfus, see Giv'at Shaul-Industrial Zone, page 234
Beit HaHaim [Square], see the neighborhood of Sanhedria, page 463
Beit HaKerem, see the neighborhood of Beit HaKerem, page 135
Beit HaKnesset [Lane], see the neighborhood of Nahlat Shiv'a, page 378
Beit Hanina Road, see the neighborhood of Beit Hanina, page 139
Beit HaShoeiva, see the Jewish Quarter, page 271

Beit HaYotzer, see Talpiot-Industrial Zone, page 494
Beit Hogla, see the neighborhood of Talpiot, page 490
Beit She'arim, see the neighborhood of Giv'at Shaul, page 230
Beit Tzur, see the neighborhood of Nahlat Tzion, page 383
Beit Tzuri, Eliyahu, see the neighborhood of Talpiot Mizrah, page 497
Beit Ya'akov, see the neighborhood of Beit Ya'akov, page 146
Beit Ya'akov, see the neighborhood of Mahane Yehuda, page 321
Beit Yisrael, see the neighborhood of Beit Yisrael, page 148
Beit Yitzhak, see the neighborhood of Har Nof, page 259
Beitar, see the neighborhood of Talpiot, page 490
Bek, Nissan, Rabbi, see the neighborhood of Mahanayim, page 318
Belza [Square], see the neighborhood of Kiryat Belz, page 283
Belzer, Yitzhak, Rabbi, see the neighborhood of Beit Yisrael, page 148
Ben 'Azai, see the neighborhood of Geulim/Bak'a, page 186
Ben 'Adaya, Shmuel, see the neighborhood of Wadi el-Joz, page 507
Ben 'Amram, David, see the neighborhood of Sha'arei Pina, page 470
Ben 'Attar, Haim, see the neighborhood of Ramot Allon, page 433
Ben AV"I, Itamar, see the neighborhood of Kiryat Shmuel, page 301
Ben AV"I, Itamar, see the neighborhood of Merhavia, page 344
Ben Baruch, Shalom, see Mid-Town, page 347
Ben Bava, Yehuda, see the neighborhood of Gonenim/Katamonim Hei and San Simon, page 247
Ben Dor, Yitzhak, see the neighborhood of Talpiot Mizrah, page 498
Ben Dov, Ya'akov, see the neighborhood of Mekor Haim, page 343
Ben Gamla, Yehoshu'a, see the neighborhood of Gonenim/Katamonim Aleph and Vav, page 242
Ben Gamliel, Shim'on, Rabbi (RaSHBa"G), see the neighborhood of Gonenim/Katamonim Aleph and Vav, page 242
Ben Gamliel, Shim'on, Rabbi (RaSHBa"G), see the neighborhood of Gonenim/Katamonim Bet, Gimel, Dalet, page 245
Ben Gavriel, Moshe, see the neighborhood of Talpiot, page 490
Ben-Gurion, David [Boulevard], see the neighborhood of Giv'at Shaul, page 230
Ben Hamu, Shim'on, see the neighborhood of Homat Shmuel/Har Homa, page 264
Ben Hefetz, Tovia, see the neighborhood of Gonenim/Katamonim Aleph and Vav, page 242
Ben Labrat, Dunash HaLevi, see the neighborhood of Rehavia, page 448
Ben Maimon, Moshe, Rabbi [Boulevard], see the neighborhood of Rehavia, page 448
Ben Matityahu, Yosef (Josephus Flavius), see the neighborhood of Ahva, page 90
Ben Matityahu, Yosef (Josephus Flavius), see the neighborhood of Kerem/Beit Avraham, page 278
Ben Matityahu, Yosef (Josephus Flavius), see the neighborhood of Mahane Yehuda, page 321
Ben Matityahu, Yosef (Josephus Flavius), see the neighborhood of Ruhama, page 459

Ben-Zvi, Yitzhak [Boulevard], see the neighborhood of Sha'arei Rahamim (Sha'arei Yeshu'a), page 473
Ben-Zvi, Yitzhak [Boulevard], see the neighborhood of Shevet Tzedek/Shchunat HaPahim, page 480
Ben-Zvi, Yitzhak [Boulevard], see the neighborhood of Zichron Ya'akov, page 521
Ben-Zvi, Yitzhak [Boulevard], see the neighborhood of Zichron Yosef, page 523
Bereniki, see the neighborhood of Gonenim/Katamonim Hei and San Simon, page 247
Berger, Ya'akov, see the neighborhood of Gonenim/Katamonim Het, Tet, page 249
Bergman, Eli'ezer, Rabbi, see the neighborhood of Bayit VaGan, page 126
Berlin, Haim, Rabbi, see the neighborhood of Kiryat Shmuel, page 301
Berman, Ya'akov, Rabbi, see the neighborhood of Gilo, page 192
Bernstein, Peretz, see the neighborhood of Ramat Sharett, page 424
Betesh, Shim'on, Dr., see the neighborhood of Mekor Haim, page 343
Betzalel ben Uri, see the neighborhood of Batei Kollel Minsk/Beit HaLevi, page 111
Betzalel ben Uri, see the neighborhood of Batei Kollel Munkacs, page 112
Betzalel ben Uri, see the neighborhood of Knesset Yisrael, page 309
Betzalel ben Uri, see Mid-Town, page 348
Betzalel ben Uri, see the neighborhood of Nahlat Ahim/Nahlaot, page 372
Betzalel ben Uri, see the neighborhood of Nahlat Tzion, page 383
Betzalel ben Uri, see the neighborhood of Sha'arei Rahamim (Sha'arei Yeshu'a), page 473
Betzalel ben Uri, see the neighborhood of Zichron Ahim, page 516
Betzalel ben Uri, see the neighborhood of Zichron Ya'akov, page 521
Betzalel ben Uri, see the neighborhood of Zichron Yosef, page 523
Beyt, Shmuel (Hans), see the neighborhood of Bayit VaGan, page 126
Beyt, Shmuel (Hans), see the neighborhood of Giv'at Mordechai, page 215
Beyt, Shmuel (Hans), see the neighborhood of Ramat Beit HaKerem, page 416
Bialik, Haim Nahman, see the neighborhood of Beit HaKerem, page 135
Bianchini, Angelo Levi, see Mid-Town, page 348
Bibas, Yehuda, Rabbi, see the neighborhood of Shevet Tzedek/Shchunat HaPahim, page 480
Bichacho, Avraham, Rabbi [Lane], see the neighborhood of Nahlat Shiv'a, page 379
Bikur Holim, see the Armenian Quarter, page 93
Bikur Holim, see the Jewish Quarter, page 271
BIL"U, see the neighborhood of Gonen/Katamon HaYeshana, page 237
Bin Nun, Yehoshu'a, see the neighborhood of Gonenim/Katamonim Aleph and Vav, page 242
Bin Nun, Yehoshu'a, see the neighborhood of the Greek Colony, page 252
Binat Yissachar, see the neighborhood of Kiryat Belz, page 283
Bir e-Sabil, see the neighborhood of Shu'afat, page 485
Bir Nballa Road, see the neighborhood of Beit Hanina, page 139
Birkat Avraham, see the neighborhood of Ramat Shlomo/Rechess Shu'afat, page 427

Birnbaum, Natan, see the neighborhood of Zichron Moshe, page 518
Bisan, see the neighborhood of Beit Hanina, page 139
Bitzur, Yehoshu'a, see the neighborhood of Giv'at Massua, page 212
Blau, Moshe, Rabbi, see the neighborhood of Sanhedria, page 463
Bleicher, see the neighborhood of Mea She'arim, page 336
Blilius, Simcha (Sima), see the neighborhood of Zichron Moshe, page 518
Blumenfeld, Yehuda (Kurt), see the neighborhood of Kiryat HaYovel, page 286
Blumenthal, Avraham Yohanan, Rabbi [Square], see the neighborhood of Geula, page 182
Bnayahu ben Yehoyada', see the neighborhood of the Greek Colony, page 252
Bnei Beteira, see the neighborhood of Gonenim/Katamonim Hei and San Simon, page 247
Bnei Brit, see the neighborhood of Bnei Moshe/Neve Shalom, page 152
Bnei Brit, see Mid-Town, page 348
Bo'az, see the neighborhood of Geulim/Bak'a, page 186
Bodenheimer, Max Isidor (Yitzhak), see the neighborhood of Kiryat HaYovel, page 286
Boehm, Aryeh, see the neighborhood of Pat, page 400
Boehm, Yohanan [Square], see the neighborhood of Kiryat Shmuel, page 301
Bolivia, see the neighborhood of Kiryat HaYovel, page 286
Bonaventura, Enzo Yosef, Prof., see the neighborhood of Talpiot Mizrah, page 498
Bonei HaHoma, see the Jewish Quarter, page 271
Borj Laqlaq Road/Shvil HaHasidut, see the Moslem Quarter, page 364
Borochov, Dov Ber, see the neighborhood of Kiryat HaYovel, page 286
Bosem, see the neighborhood of Gilo, page 192
Bosmat [Lane], see the neighborhood of Gilo, page 192
Botta, Paul Emile, see Mid-Town, page 348
Botta, Paul Emile, see the neighborhood of Yemin Moshe, page 513
Bourla, Yehuda, see the neighborhood of Giv'at Ram, page 219
Bourla, Yehuda, see the neighborhood of Nayot, page 387
Bourla, Yehuda, see the neighborhood of Neve Shaanan, page 391
Bracha Tzefira, see the neighborhood of Ramat Sharett, page 424
Brachyahu, Aharon Michel, see the neighborhood of Beit HaKerem, page 135
Brand, Aharon, Dr., see the neighborhood of Har Nof, page 260
Brandeis, Louis, see the neighborhood of Romema, page 454
Brandwin, Yosef Shmuel, Rabbi, see the neighborhood of Pisgat Zeev Mizrah, page 407
Brazil, see the neighborhood of Kiryat HaYovel, page 286
Brenner, Yosef Haim, see the neighborhood of Komemiyut/Talbieh, page 312
Breuer, Yitzhak, Rabbi, see the neighborhood of Bayit VaGan, page 126
Brim, Yehoshu'a, Rabbi, see the neighborhood of Ramat Shlomo/Rechess Shu'afat, page 427
Brodetsky, Zelig Moshe [Road], see the neighborhood of Giv'at Ram, page 219
Brodi, Haim, Rabbi, see the neighborhood of Kiryat Shmuel, page 301
Broshi, Zalman [Steps], see the neighborhood of Romema, page 454

Brown, Eliyahu, see the neighborhood of Ramot Allon, page 433
Bruchiali, Aryeh [Square], see the neighborhood of Pisgat Zeev Mizrah, page 407
Bruria, see the neighborhood of Gonenim/Katamonim Aleph and Vav, page 243
Bruskina, Masha, see the neighborhood of Pisgat Zeev Mizrah, page 407
Buber, Martin (Mordechai), see the neighborhood of Mount Scopus, page 369
Bublik, Gedalia, see the neighborhood of Ramot Allon, page 433
Bulgaria [Square], see the neighborhood of Talpiot Tzafon, page 502
Bustenai ben Hanina, see the neighborhood of Gonen/Katamon HaYeshana, page 237
Buxbaum, Mordechai, see the neighborhood of Ramat Shlomo/Rechess Shu'afat, page 427
Buzaglo, Ashriel, see the neighborhood of Talpiot-Industrial Zone, page 494

C

Camon, see the neighborhood of Gilo, page 192
Carlebach, Yosef, Rabbi, see the neighborhood of Talpiot, page 490
Casa Nova, see the Christian Quarter, page 154
Caspi, Mordechai, see the neighborhood of Talpiot Tzafon, page 502
Cassuto, Moshe David, Rabbi, see the neighborhood of Bayit VaGan, page 127
Chasanowich, Joseph, see the neighborhood of Mea She'arim, page 336
Chelouche, Yosef, Rabbi, see the neighborhood of Shevet Tzedek/Shchunat HaPahim, page 481
Chile, see the neighborhood of Kiryat HaYovel, page 286
Chile [Square], see the neighborhood of Komemiyut/Talbieh, page 312
Chopin, Frederic, see the neighborhood of Kiryat Shmuel, page 301
Christian Quarter Road, see the Christian Quarter, page 154
Churchill, Winston [Boulevard], see the neighborhood of Mount Scopus, page 369
Clermont-Ganneau, Charles, see the neighborhood of Sheikh Jarrah, page 478
Cohen, Binyamin [Square], see the neighborhood of Ramot Allon, page 433
Cohen, Ephraim, see the neighborhood of Zichron Moshe, page 518
Cohen, 'Eli, see the neighborhood of Gonen/Katamon HaYeshana, page 237
Cohen, Ya'akov [Square], see the neighborhood of Mahane Yehuda, page 321
Colombia, see the neighborhood of Kiryat Menahem, page 294
Conder, see the neighborhood of Bab e-Zahara, page 101
Corazin, see the neighborhood of Nahlat Ahim/Nahlaot, page 372
Corazin, see the neighborhood of Sha'arei Rahamim (Sha'arei Yeshu'a), page 473
Cordovero, Moshe, Rabbi, see the neighborhood of Giv'at Shaul, page 230
Costa Rica, see the neighborhood of 'Ir Ganim Aleph, page 267
Costa Rica, see the neighborhood of 'Ir Ganim Gimel, page 268
Cremieux, Yitzhak Adolphe, see the neighborhood of the German Colony, page 177

D

Dagan, see the neighborhood of Gilo, page 192
Dahiyet el-Barid, see the neighborhood of Dahiyet el-Barid, page 160
Dahomey, see the neighborhood of 'Ir Ganim Bet, page 268
Dahomey, see the neighborhood of Kiryat Menahem, page 294

Dakar [Lane], see the neighborhood of Giv'at Shapira/French Hill, page 225
Dalman, see the neighborhood of Bab e-Zahara, page 102
Dalton, see the neighborhood of Nahlat Tzion, page 383
Damascus Gate, see the Christian Quarter, page 155
Damascus Gate, see the Moslem Quarter, page 367
Damascus Gate [Square], see the Moslem Quarter, page 367
Dan, see the neighborhood of Geulim/Bak'a, page 186
Daniel, see the neighborhood of Morasha/Musrara, page 361
Dar e-Salam, see the neighborhood of Shu'afat, page 485
Darom, see Mid-Town, page 348
Daskal, see the neighborhood of Ramat Denya, page 418
David, see the Armenian Quarter, page 93
David, see the Christian Quarter, page 155
David Hafetz [Square], see the neighborhood of HaBucharim, page 255
David HaMelech, see the neighborhood of David's Village-Mamilla, page 161
David HaMelech, see the neighborhood of Komemiyut/Talbieh, page 312
David HaMelech, see the neighborhood of Mahane Yisrael, page 326
David HaMelech, see Mid-Town, page 348
David HaMelech, see the neighborhood of Yemin Moshe, page 513
David HeHazan, Rabbi, see the neighborhood of HaBucharim, page 255
Davidson, Yisrael, see the neighborhood of Nayot, page 387
Davidson, Yisrael, see the neighborhood of Neve Granot, page 390
Davidson, Yosef [Square], see the neighborhood of Nayot, page 387
Dayan, Aryeh Leib, Rabbi, see the neighborhood of Beit Yisrael, page 148
Deedes, Wyndham, see the neighborhood of the German Colony, page 177
Degania, see the neighborhood of Yefei Nof, page 508
Degel Reuven, see the neighborhood of Kiryat Moshe, page 296
Degel Reuven, see the neighborhood of Maimon (Shchunat HaPo'el HaMizrahi), page 328
De-Haas, Ya'akov, see the neighborhood of Ramot Allon, page 433
De Lima, Nehemia, see the neighborhood of Ramot Allon, page 434
della Pergola, Refael, see the neighborhood of Gilo, page 192
della Rosa, Haim, Rabbi [Square], see the neighborhood of Mekor Baruch, page 339
Denya [Square], see the neighborhood of Beit HaKerem, page 135
Derech 'Anatot, see the neighborhood of Shu'afat, page 485
Derech 'Aza, see the neighborhood of Rehavia, page 448
Derech Beit Horon, see 'Atarot-Industrial Zone, page 99
Derech Beit Lehem, see the neighborhood of the German Colony, page 177
Derech Beit Lehem, see the neighborhood of Geulim/Bak'a, page 186
Derech Beit Lehem, see Talpiot-Industrial Zone, page 494
Derech Binyamina, see the neighborhood of 'Ein Kerem, page 164
Derech Gan HaHayot, see the neighborhood of Manhat/Malha, page 329
Derech HaAhayot, see the neighborhood of 'Ein Kerem, page 164
Derech HaHoresh, see the neighborhood of Ramot Allon, page 434
Derech HaIlanot, see the neighborhood of 'Ein Kerem, page 164

Derech Ha'Ofel, see the City of David, page 158
Derech Ha'Ofel, see the Moslem Quarter, page 365
Derech Har HaZeitim, see the neighborhood of Bab e-Zahara, page 102
Derech Har HaZeitim, see the neighborhood of Sheikh Jarrah, page 479
Derech HaSela', see the neighborhood of 'Ein Kerem, page 164
Derech HaShiloah, see the City of David, page 158
Derech HaTatzpit, see the neighborhood of 'Ein Kerem, page 164
Derech Hevron, see the neighborhood of Arnona, page 96
Derech Hevron, see the neighborhood of Geulim/Bak'a, page 186
Derech Hevron, see the neighborhood of Giv'at HaMatos, page 203
Derech Hevron, see the neighborhood of Giv'at Hanania/Abu Tor, page 207
Derech Hevron, see the neighborhood of Homat Shmuel/Har Homa, page 265
Derech Hevron, see the neighborhood of Talpiot, page 490
Derech Hevron, see the neighborhood of Talpiot Tzafon, page 502
Derech Karmit, see the neighborhood of 'Ein Kerem, page 164
Derech Ma'ale Adumim, see the neighborhood of Giv'at Shapira/French Hill, page 225
Derech Ma'ale Adumim, see the neighborhood of Tzameret HaBira, page 505
Derech Ramallah, see 'Atarot-Industrial Zone, page 99
Derech Ramallah, see the neighborhood of Beit Hanina, page 140
Derech Ramallah, see the neighborhood of Dahiyet el-Barid, page 160
Derech Shu'afat, see the neighborhood of Shu'afat, page 485
Derech Sorek, see the neighborhood of 'Ein Kerem, page 164
Derech Yeriho, see the City of David, page 158
Derech Yeriho, see the neighborhood of E-Tur, page 168
Derech Yeriho, see the Moslem Quarter, page 365
De Rossi, see the neighborhood of Ramat Beit HaKerem, page 416
Di Zahav, see the neighborhood of Ramat Eshkol, page 421
Di Zahav, Ephraim [Square], see Mid-Town, page 348
Dinowitz, Gittel, see the neighborhood of Mahane Yehuda, page 322
Dinowitz, Gittel, see the neighborhood of Ohel Shlomo, page 399
Dinur, Ben Tzion, Prof., see the neighborhood of Ramat Beit HaKerem, page 416
Diskin, Yehoshu'a Leib, Rabbi, see the neighborhood of Kiryat Wolfson, page 306
Diskin, Yehoshu'a Leib, Rabbi, see the neighborhood of Sha'arei Hesed, page 468
Disraeli, Benjamin, see the neighborhood of Komemiyut/Talbieh, page 312
Divrei Haim, see the neighborhood of Kiryat Belz, page 283
Divrei Yeruham, see the neighborhood of Bayit VaGan, page 127
Dominican Republic, see the neighborhood of 'Ir Ganim Bet, page 268
Dor Dor VeDorshav, see the neighborhood of the German Colony, page 177
Doreish Tov, see the neighborhood of Kiryat Zanz, page 307
Dorot Rishonim, see Mid-Town, page 348
Dostai (ben Rabbi Yehuda), Rabbi, see the neighborhood of Gonenim/Katamonim Aleph and Vav, page 243
Dostrovsky, Aryeh, Dr., see the neighborhood of Talpiot, page 491
Dov Yosef, see the neighborhood of Gilo, page 193

Dov Yosef, see the neighborhood of Pat, page 400
Dover Shalom, see the neighborhood of Kiryat Belz, page 284
Dovev Meisharim, see the neighborhood of Tel-Arza, page 503
Drezner, Yehiel, see the neighborhood of Talpiot Mizrah, page 498
Druk, Shlomo Zalman, Rabbi, see the neighborhood of Ramat Shlomo/Rechess Shu'afat, page 427
Dubnow, Simon, see the neighborhood of Komemiyut/Talbieh, page 312
Duchan, Moshe [Square], see the neighborhood of Rehavia, page 448
Duga, Shlomo, see the neighborhood of Gilo, page 193
Dultzin, Aryeh, see the neighborhood of Giv'at Massua, page 212
Dung Gate, see the Jewish Quarter, page 271
Du-Nuwas, Yosef, see Mid-Town, page 349
Dushinsky, Yosef Zvi, Rabbi, see the neighborhood of Sanhedria HaMurhevet, page 465
Duvdevani, Baruch, see the neighborhood of Bayit VaGan, page 127
Dvash, see the neighborhood of Gilo, page 193
Dvir, see the neighborhood of Nahlat Tzion, page 383
Dvora HaNevia, see the neighborhood of Batei Perlman/'Ir Shalom, page 120
Dvora HaNevia, see the neighborhood of Mea She'arim, page 336
Dvoretz, Yisrael Zissel, Rabbi [Square], see the neighborhood of Giv'at Shaul, page 230
Dvoretz, Yisrael Zissel, Rabbi [Square], see the neighborhood of Kiryat Moshe, page 296

E

Ebner, Meir, see the neighborhood of Kiryat HaYovel, page 286
E-Dahr, see the neighborhood of Shu'afat, page 485
E-Darj, see the neighborhood of Shu'afat, page 485
Edelman, Mordechai, see the neighborhood of Beit Yisrael, page 148
'Eden, Shmuel, see the neighborhood of Pisgat Zeev Ma'arav, page 412
Efrata, see the neighborhood of Talpiot, page 491
Ehrenfeld, Nahum, see the neighborhood of Pisgat Zeev Mercaz, page 402
Ehud (ben Gera), see the neighborhood of Geulim/Bak'a, page 186
Eig, Alexander, see the neighborhood of Ramot Allon, page 434
Eilat, see the neighborhood of Nahlat Tzion, page 383
'Ein Gedi, see the neighborhood of Talpiot, page 491
'Ein Kerem, see the neighborhood of 'Ein Kerem, page 164
'Ein Kerem [Square], see the neighborhood of 'Ein Kerem, page 164
'Ein Rogel, see the neighborhood of Giv'at Hanania/Abu Tor, page 207
'Ein Tzurim [Boulevard], see the neighborhood of Talpiot, page 491
'Ein Ya'akov, see the neighborhood of Mea She'arim, page 336
'Einayim LaMishpat, see the neighborhood of Mazkeret Moshe, page 333
Einstein, Albert, Prof. [Square], see the neighborhood of Komemiyut/Talbieh, page 312
Eitan, see 'Atarot-Industrial Zone, page 99
El-'Abbas, see the neighborhood of Beit Hanina, page 140

El-Adib As'ef, see the neighborhood of Sheikh Jarrah, page 479
El-Akhtal, see the neighborhood of Bab e-Zahara, page 102
El-'Arbi, see the neighborhood of Beit Hanina, page 140
El'asa, see the neighborhood of Sanhedria, page 463
El-Asfahani, see the neighborhood of Bab e-Zahara, page 102
Elashvili, Shabtai [Square], see Romema-Industrial Zone, page 457
El-Asma'i, see the neighborhood of Shu'afat, page 485
El'azar, David, see the neighborhood of Neve Ya'akov, page 393
El'azar, Yehuda, Rabbi [Square], see the neighborhood of Ramot Allon, page 434
El'azar HaMacabi, see the neighborhood of Mekor Baruch, page 340
El-Banias, see the neighborhood of Beit Hanina, page 140
El-Banji, see the neighborhood of Beit Hanina, page 140
El-Bukhturi, see the neighborhood of Beit Hanina, page 140
El-Bustami, see the Moslem Quarter, page 365
El-Butma, see the neighborhood of Beit Safafa, page 144
Eldad, Yisrael (Sheib), see the neighborhood of Talpiot, page 491
El-Dawar el-Awal, see the neighborhood of Beit Safafa, page 144
El-Farabi, see the neighborhood of Shu'afat, page 485
El-Hajaj ibn Yusef, see the neighborhood of Shu'afat, page 485
El-Halsa, see the neighborhood of Beit Hanina, page 140
Elhanan, Yitzhak, Rabbi, see the neighborhood of Komemiyut/Talbieh, page 312
El-Harami, Shukri, see the neighborhood of Dahiyet el-Barid, page 160
El-Hardob, see the neighborhood of E-Tur, page 168
El-Hilal, see the neighborhood of Beit Hanina, page 140
'Eli HaCohen, see the neighborhood of Shikun HaBa"D, page 482
'Eli HaCohen, see the neighborhood of Tel-Arza, page 503
Eliach, Shlomo Yosef, see the neighborhood of Neve Ya'akov, page 393
'Eliash, Mordechai, see the neighborhood of Batei Goral/Mishkenot HaTeimanim, page 107
'Eliash, Mordechai, see Mid-Town, page 349
Eliav, Ya'akov, see the neighborhood of Giv'at Shaul, page 230
Eliel Dror, see the neighborhood of David's Village-Mamilla, page 161
Eliel Dror, see the neighborhood of Yemin Moshe, page 513
Eli'ezer [Park], see the neighborhood of Rehavia, page 448
Eli'ezer HaGadol (ben Hyrcanus), Rabbi, see the neighborhood of Gonenim/Katamonim Aleph and Vav, page 243
Eli'ezer HaGadol (ben Hyrcanus), Rabbi, see the neighborhood ofGonenim/Katamonim Bet, Gimel, Dalet, page 246
Eli'ezri, Shmuel, Rabbi, see the neighborhood of Bayit VaGan, page 127
Eli'ezrov, Shlomo Yehuda Leib, Rabbi, see the neighborhood of Mahanayim, page 319
Elifaz (HaTeimani), see the neighborhood of Mahanayim, page 319
Eliot, George, see Mid-Town, page 349
Elisha', see the neighborhood of Morasha/Musrara, page 361
Elitzur, Yehuda, see the neighborhood of Pisgat Zeev Mizrah, page 407

El-Zeitoun, see the neighborhood of Beit Safafa, page 144
Em HaBanim, see the neighborhood of Ramot Allon, page 434
'Emanuel Noah, Mordechai, see the neighborhood of the German Colony, page 177
'Emek HaTeimanim, see the neighborhood of 'Ein Kerem, page 164
'Emek Refaim, see the neighborhood of the German Colony, page 178
'Emek Refaim, see the neighborhood of the Greek Colony, page 252
Emet LeYa'akov, see the neighborhood of Batei Werner/Ohalei Moshe, page 123
Emuna [Square], see the neighborhood of Shikunei Shmuel HaNavi, page 483
E-Nabi Shu'eib, see the neighborhood of Bab e-Zahara, page 102
E-Nahada, see the neighborhood of Beit Safafa, page 144
E-Nakhil, see the neighborhood of Beit Hanina, page 140
Ephraim, see the neighborhood of Geulim/Bak'a, page 186
Epstein, Ya'akov Nahum, Rabbi, see the neighborhood of Kiryat HaYovel, page 287
Eptimus, see the Christian Quarter, page 155
E-Rahma, see the neighborhood of Beit Safafa, page 144
Eretz Hefetz, see the neighborhood of Ma'alot Dafna/Arzei HaBira, page 316
Eretz Hefetz, see the neighborhood of Shikunei Shmuel HaNavi, page 483
E-Safa, see the neighborhood of Beit Safafa, page 144
E-Sahl, see the neighborhood of Shu'afat, page 486
E-Shabi, see the neighborhood of Shu'afat, page 486
E-Sheikh, see the neighborhood of E-Tur, page 168
E-Shifa, see the neighborhood of Beit Safafa, page 144
Eshkol, Levi [Boulevard], see the neighborhood of Giv'at HaMivtar, page 204
Eshkol, Levi [Boulevard], see the neighborhood of Ma'alot Dafna/Arzei HaBira, page 317
Eshkol, Levi [Boulevard], see the neighborhood of Ramat Eshkol, page 421
Eshkoli, Aharon Zeev, see the neighborhood of Ramot Allon, page 434
Eshlag, Yehuda Leib, Rabbi, see the neighborhood of Beit Yisrael, page 149
Ester HaMalca, see the neighborhood of Geulim/Bak'a, page 187
E-Tabari, see the neighborhood of Wadi el-Joz, page 507
Ethiopia, see Mid-Town, page 349
E-Toota [Steps], see the Moslem Quarter, page 365
Ettinger, 'Akiva, see the neighborhood of Kiryat HaYovel, page 287
Ettinger, Yitzhak Zvi [Steps], see the neighborhood of Kiryat Shmuel, page 301
E-Tur, see the neighborhood of E-Tur, page 168
ETZe"L, see the neighborhood of Giv'at Shapira/French Hill, page 226
'Etz Hadar, see the neighborhood of Shikunei Shmuel HaNavi, page 483
'Etz Haim, see the neighborhood of Mahane Yehuda, page 322
'Etzion Gever, see the neighborhood of Ramat Eshkol, page 422
Even HaEZe"L, see the neighborhood of 'Ezrat Torah, page 173
Even Sapir, see the neighborhood of Nahlat Ahim/Nahlaot, page 373
Even Sapir, see the neighborhood of Zichron Ahim, page 516
Even Shmuel (Kaufmann), Yehuda, Dr., see the neighborhood of Ramot Allon, page 434
Even Shoshan, Avraham [Square], see Mid-Town, page 349

Even Sikra, see the neighborhood of Yemin Moshe, page 513
Even Yehoshu'a, see the neighborhood of Batei Wittenberg/Sha'arei Moshe, page 124
Even Yehoshu'a, see the neighborhood of Even Yehoshu'a, page 171
Even Yisrael, see the neighborhood of Even Yisrael, page 173
Even Yisrael, see the neighborhood of Mahane Yehuda, page 322
'Evrona, see the neighborhood of Ramat Eshkol, page 422
Evyatar HaCohen, see the neighborhood of HaBucharim, page 256
E-Zahara, see the neighborhood of Bab e-Zahara, page 102
'Ezer Yoldot, see the neighborhood of Ahva, page 90
'Ezer Yoldot, see the neighborhood of Batei Hornstein/Kollel Volyn, page 108
'Ezra, see the neighborhood of HaBucharim, page 256
'Ezra Refael, see the neighborhood of Nahlat Tzion, page 384
'Ezra Refael, see the neighborhood of Ohel Moshe, page 397
'Ezra Refael, see the neighborhood of Zichron Tuvia, page 520
'Ezrat Nashim [Square], see the neighborhood of Giv'at Shaul, page 231
'Ezrat Torah, see the neighborhood of 'Ezrat Torah, page 174
'Ezrat Yisrael, see the neighborhood of 'Ezrat Yisrael, page 175
'Ezrian, Nissim, see the neighborhood of Giv'at Shaul, page 231

F

Faatal, Hacham Avraham, see the neighborhood of Ramat Shlomo/Rechess Shu'afat, page 428
Faidi el-'Alami, see the neighborhood of Beit Hanina, page 141
Falk, Zeev, see the neighborhood of Homat Shmuel/Har Homa, page 265
Farbstein, Yehoshu'a, Rabbi, see Giv'at Shaul-Industrial Zone, page 234
Farbstein, Yehoshu'a, Rabbi see the neighborhood of Kiryat Moshe, page 297
Farhi, Haim, Minister, see the neighborhood of HaBucharim, page 256
Federman, David, see the neighborhood of Pisgat Zeev Mizrah, page 408
Feinstein, Meir, see the neighborhood of Talpiot Mizrah, page 498
Feldman, Moshe Zeev, Rabbi, see the neighborhood of Kerem Avraham, page 280
Felt, James [Lane], see the neighborhood of Yemin Moshe, page 513
Ferrera, Avraham, see the neighborhood of Holyland Park, page 263
Fichmann, Ya'akov, see the neighborhood of Giv'at HaVradim/Shikun Rassco, page 209
Fischer, Maurice, see the neighborhood of Pat, page 400
Fishel, Yisrael Aharon, see the neighborhood of HaBucharim, page 256
Fleg, Edmond [Lane], see the neighborhood of Neve Ya'akov, page 393
Florentin, David, see the neighborhood of Kiryat HaYovel, page 287
Flower Gate, see the Moslem Quarter, page 365
Flower Gate Road, see the Moslem Quarter, page 365
Frank, Zvi Pesah, Rabbi, see the neighborhood of Bayit VaGan, page 127
Frankel, Eliyahu, Dr. [Steps], see the neighborhood of Bayit VaGan, page 127
Frankfurter, Felix, see the neighborhood of Ramot Allon, page 434
Freier, Recha [Square], see the neighborhood of Gonen/Katamon HaYeshana, page 237

Freud, Sigmund [Square], see the neighborhood of the German Colony, page 178
Fridler, Yoel, see the neighborhood of Pisgat Zeev Mizrah, page 408
Friedman, David, Rabbi, see the neighborhood of Beit Yisrael, page 149
Frischmann, David, see the neighborhood of Giv'at HaVradim/Shikun Rassco, page 209
Frumkin, Gad, see Mid-Town, page 349
Funt, Yisrael, see the neighborhood of Neve Ya'akov, page 393

G

Gabai, Yosef, Rabbi, see the neighborhood of Kiryat Mattersdorf, page 293
Gad, see the neighborhood of Geulim/Bak'a, page 187
Gafni, Simha, see the neighborhood of Beit HaKerem, page 135
Gal, see the neighborhood of Pisgat Zeev Mercaz, page 402
Galaktion, Gala [Square], see the neighborhood of Kiryat Shmuel, page 301
Gal'ed, see the Jewish Quarter, page 271
Gamzon, Reuven (Robert) [Lane], see the neighborhood of Neve Ya'akov, page 393
Gan Daniel, see Mid-Town, page 349
Gani, Meir [Square], see the neighborhood of Ramat Sharett, page 424
Gaon, Moshe David, see the neighborhood of Batei Kollel Horodna/Damesek Eli'ezer, page 109
Gaon, Moshe David, see the neighborhood of Mahane Yehuda, page 322
Gaon, Moshe David, see the neighborhood of Sha'arei Shalom, page 474
Garami, Tzion, see the neighborhood of Pisgat Zeev Mizrah, page 408
Gargi, Matityahu, Rabbi [Square], see the neighborhood of Ma'alot Dafna/Arzei HaBira, page 317
Gaster, Moshe, Rabbi [Alley], see the neighborhood of the German Colony, page 178
Gat, Ben Tzion, see the neighborhood of Kiryat Moshe, page 297
Gedalyahu (ben Ahikam), see the neighborhood of Geulim/Bak'a, page 187
Gedera, see the neighborhood of Romema 'Ilit, page 456
Gedud Beit Horon [Square], see the neighborhood of Pisgat Zeev Mizrah, page 408
Gedud Ha'Avoda, see the neighborhood of Arnona, page 96
Gedud Hermesh, see the neighborhood of Pisgat Zeev Mercaz, page 403
Gedud Michmash, see the neighborhood of Pisgat Zeev Mercaz, page 403
Gedud Moriah [Square], see the neighborhood of Pisgat Zeev Mercaz, page 403
Gedud Tuvia [Square], see the neighborhood of the German Colony, page 178
Gelber, Edward, see the neighborhood of Ramat Denya, page 418
Gemul, see the neighborhood of Nahlat Shim'on, page 376
Geneo, David and Sons, see the neighborhood of Nahlat Shiv'a, page 379
Geoni, Ya'akov, see the neighborhood of Kiryat HaYovel, page 287
Gershon, Meir, see the neighborhood of Pisgat Zeev Mizrah, page 408
Gesher HaHaim, see the neighborhood of Mekor Baruch, page 340
Gesher HaHaim, see the neighborhood of Sha'arei Yerushalayim, page 477
Geva', see the neighborhood of Nahlat Tzion, page 384

Gezer, see the neighborhood of Nahlat Tzion, page 384
Gid'on (ben Yoash), see the neighborhood of Geulim/Bak'a, page 187
Gihon, see the neighborhood of Giv'at Hanania/Abu Tor, page 207
Gihon Square, see the City of David, page 158
Gil'adi, Yisrael, see the neighborhood of Talpiot, page 491
Giv'at Beit HaKerem, see the neighborhood of Giv'at Beit HaKerem, page 202
Giv'at Canada, see the neighborhood of Gilo, page 193
Giv'at HaYonim, see the neighborhood of 'Ein Kerem, page 165
Giv'at Moshe [Boulevard], see the neighborhood of 'Ezrat Torah, page 174
Giv'at Moshe [Boulevard], see the neighborhood of Mahanayim, page 319
Giv'at Shaul, see the neighborhood of Giv'at Shaul, page 231
Giv'on, see the neighborhood of Nahlat Tzion, page 384
Givton, Hanoch [Square], see the neighborhood of Beit HaKerem, page 135
Giza (Fleischman), see the neighborhood of Ramot Allon, page 434
Glueck, Nelson, Dr., see the neighborhood of Ramot Allon, page 435
Goetz, Meir Yehuda, Rabbi [Steps], see the Jewish Quarter, page 272
Goitein, Yehezkel David, see the neighborhood of Pisgat Zeev Mizrah, page 408
Gol, Bentzion, see the neighborhood of HaBucharim, page 256
Gold, Zeev, Rabbi, see the neighborhood of Giv'at Mordechai, page 215
Golda Meir [Boulevard], see the neighborhood of Kiryat Ta'asiyot 'Atirot Mada'/ Har Hotzvim, page 304
Golda Meir [Boulevard], see the neighborhood of Kiryat Zanz, page 307
Golda Meir [Boulevard], see the neighborhood of Ramot Allon, page 435
Goldberg, Ariela Deem [Plaza], see the neighborhood of Komemiyut/Talbieh, page 313
Goldberg, Leah [Lane], see the neighborhood of Neve Ya'akov, page 393
Goldblum, Natan [Square], see the neighborhood of Ramat Beit HaKerem, page 417
Goldknopf, Aryeh, Rabbi, see the neighborhood of Ramat Shlomo/Rechess Shu'afat, page 428
Goldman, Ya'akov, Rabbi [Square], see the neighborhood of the Russian Compound, page 461
Golei Kenya, see the neighborhood of Giv'at Shapira/French Hill, page 226
Golomb, Eliyahu, see the neighborhood of Gonenim/Katamonim Het, Tet, page 249
Golomb, Eliyahu, see the neighborhood of Holyland Park, page 263
Golomb, Eliyahu, see the neighborhood of Kiryat HaYovel, page 287
Golomb, Eliyahu, see the neighborhood of Manhat/Malha, page 329
Golomb, Eliyahu, see the neighborhood of Ramat Denya, page 419
Golomb, Eliyahu, see the neighborhood of Ramat Sharett, page 425
Gordon, Aharon David, see the neighborhood of Kiryat HaYovel, page 287
Goren, Shlomo, Rabbi [Steps], see the Jewish Quarter, page 272
Gottlieb, Maurycy, see the neighborhood of the German Colony, page 178
Graetz, Zvi Heinrich, Dr., see the neighborhood of the German Colony, page 178
Grajewski, Pinhas, see the neighborhood of Giv'at Shaul, page 231
Granados, Jorge Garcia, see the neighborhood of Ramat Denya, page 419

Granot, Avraham, Dr., see the neighborhood of Neve Granot, page 390
Granot, Avraham, Dr., see the neighborhood of Neve Shaanan, page 391
Greek Catholic Patriarchate, see the Christian Quarter, page 155
Greek Orthodox Patriarchate, see the Christian Quarter, page 155
Greenberg, Haim, see the neighborhood of Ramot Allon, page 435
Greenspan, Hershel (Zvi), see the neighborhood of Talpiot Mizrah, page 498
Greenwald, Meir, see the neighborhood of Kiryat HaYovel, page 287
Grininger, Paul, see the neighborhood of Pisgat Zeev Mizrah, page 408
Gross, (William) Zeev, see the neighborhood of Ramot Allon, page 435
Grossberg, Hanoch, Rabbi, see the neighborhood of Tel-Arza, page 503
Grossman, Meir, see the neighborhood of 'Ir Ganim Aleph, page 267
Grossman, Meir, see the neighborhood of Kiryat HaYovel, page 287
Gruenbaum, Yitzhak [Square], see the neighborhood of Giv'at Ram, page 219
Gruner, Dov, see the neighborhood of Talpiot Mizrah, page 498
Grusenberg, Oscar (Yisrael), see the neighborhood of the Russian Compound, page 461
Guatemala, see the neighborhood of Kiryat HaYovel, page 287
Gulak, Asher, see the neighborhood of Neve Ya'akov, page 394
Gvaryahu, Haim, see the neighborhood of Pisgat Zeev Mizrah, page 408
Gvirtzman, Moshe, see the neighborhood of Pisgat Zeev Mizrah, page 408

H

Ha'A"H, see the neighborhood of Morasha/Musrara, page 361
HaADeRe"T, see the neighborhood of Kiryat Shmuel, page 301
HaAdmor MiBelz, see the neighborhood of Sanhedria HaMurhevet, page 466
HaAdmor MiBoston [Steps], see the neighborhood of Har Nof, page 260
HaAdmor MiBoyan, see the neighborhood of Har Nof, page 260
HaAdmor MiGur, see the neighborhood of Sanhedria HaMurhevet, page 466
HaAdmor MiLubavitch, see the neighborhood of Ramat Shlomo/Rechess Shu'afat, page 428
HaAdmor MiRuzhin, see the neighborhood of Har Nof, page 260
HaAdmor MiSadgora, see the neighborhood of Ramat Shlomo/Rechess Shu'afat, page 428
HaAdmor MiVizhnitz, see the neighborhood of Sanhedria HaMurhevet, page 466
HaAdmorim MiLeiner, see the neighborhood of Sanhedria, page 464
HaAdrichal, see the neighborhood of Romema, page 454
HaAfarsek, see the neighborhood of Mahane Yehuda, page 322
HaAgas, see the neighborhood of Mahane Yehuda, page 322
HaAhim, see the Christian Quarter, page 155
HaAhim Lehren, see the neighborhood of Ramot Allon, page 435
HaAhim Roth [Square], see the neighborhood of Ramot Allon, page 435
HaAhot Yehudit, see the neighborhood of Gilo, page 193
Ha'Aliya, see the neighborhood of Giv'at Ram, page 219
HaAmarkalim, see the neighborhood of Ahva, page 90
Ha'Ameilim, see the neighborhood of Batei Milner/Agudat Shlomo, page 117
Ha'Ameilim, see the neighborhood of Beit Yisrael, page 149

HaAmoraim, see the neighborhood of Gonenim/Katamonim Aleph and Vav, page 243
HaAnafa, see the neighborhood of Gilo, page 193
HaAR"I, see the neighborhood of Kiryat Shmuel, page 302
HaAR"I, see the neighborhood of Merhavia, page 344
HaArazim, see the neighborhood of Yefei Nof, page 508
HaArba'a, see the neighborhood of Pisgat Zeev Mercaz, page 403
HaArbeli, Nitai, see the neighborhood of Gonenim/Katamonim Bet, Gimel, Dalet, page 246
HaArgaman, see Romema-Industrial Zone, page 457
Ha'Armonim, see the neighborhood of Mahane Yehuda, page 322
Ha'Asara [Lane], see the neighborhood of Giv'at Shapira/French Hill, page 226
HaAshurim (Dir el Siran), see the Armenian Quarter, page 94
Ha'Askan, see the neighborhood of Talpiot Mizrah, page 499
Ha'Atzmaut [Park], see Mid-Town, page 349
HaAvivit, see the neighborhood of 'Ir Ganim Bet, page 268
HaAyal, see the neighborhood of Manhat/Malha, page 330
HaBa"D, see the Jewish Quarter, page 272
HaBanai, see the neighborhood of HaPo'alim, page 258
HaBareket, see the neighborhood of Gilo, page 193
HaBaron Hirsch, Maurice de, see the neighborhood of Kiryat Moshe, page 297
HaBE'SH"T, see the neighborhood of Beit Yisrael, page 149
HaBikurim, see the Jewish Quarter, page 272
HaBonim HaHofshiim [Square], see Mid-Town, page 349
HaBracha [Alley], see the neighborhood of Ramat Shlomo/Rechess Shu'afat, page 428
HaBreicha, see the neighborhood of Yemin Moshe, page 513
HaBroshim [Ascent], see the neighborhood of Beit HaKerem, page 135
Habshush, Haim, Rabbi, see the neighborhood of Beit Yisrael, page 149
Habshush, Haim, Rabbi, see the neighborhood of Nahlat Zvi/Shchunat HaTeimanim, page 386
Habshush, Haim, Rabbi, see the neighborhood of Sha'arei Pina, page 471
HaBurskaim, see the Christian Quarter, page 155
HaCalanit, see the neighborhood of 'Ir Ganim Aleph, page 267
HaCarcom, see the neighborhood of 'Ir Ganim Aleph, page 267
HaCardo, see the Jewish Quarter, page 272
HaCarmel, see the neighborhood of Mazkeret Moshe, page 333
HaCarmel, see the neighborhood of Ohel Moshe, page 397
HaCarpas, see the neighborhood of Gilo, page 193
Hacham Avraham, see the neighborhood of Manhat/Malha, page 330
Hacham Shalom, see the neighborhood of Zichron Ya'akov, page 521
Hacham Shalom, see the neighborhood of Zichron Yosef, page 523
Hacham Shim'on, Rabbi, see the neighborhood of Mahanayim, page 319
Hacham Shmuel Bruchim, see the neighborhood of Tel-Arza, page 504
Hachmi, Yosef, see the neighborhood of Bayit VaGan, page 127
Hachnasat Orhim, see the neighborhood of Mea She'arim, page 336

Hachsharat HaYishuv [Plaza], see Mid-Town, page 350
HaCongress HaTzioni, see the neighborhood of Ramot Allon, page 435
HaDaf HaYomi, see the neighborhood of Ramot Allon, page 435
HaDafna, see the neighborhood of 'Ein Kerem, page 165
Hadash, Meir, Rabbi, see the neighborhood of Ramat Shlomo/Rechess Shu'afat, page 428
HaDekel, see the neighborhood of Mahane Yehuda, page 322
HaDishon, see the neighborhood of Manhat/Malha, page 330
HaDmumit, see the neighborhood of Gilo, page 194
HaDolev, see the neighborhood of Gilo, page 194
HaDov, see the neighborhood of Manhat/Malha, page 330
HaDudaim, see the neighborhood of Gilo, page 194
HaEgoz, see the neighborhood of Mahane Yehuda, page 322
HaERe"Z, see the neighborhood of Ohel Moshe, page 397
HaEshkol, see the neighborhood of Mahane Yehuda, page 322
HaEzov, see the neighborhood of Gilo, page 194
Hafetz Haim, see the neighborhood of Zichron Moshe, page 518
Hafez, Ibrahim, see the neighborhood of Shu'afat, page 486
Haflaa, see the neighborhood of Har Nof, page 260
Haft, Ya'akov [Square], see the neighborhood of Beit HaKerem, page 136
Haftzadi, Nahum, see the neighborhood of Giv'at Shaul, page 231
Haftzadi, Salah [Square], see the neighborhood of Zichron Yosef, page 523
HaGaDN"A', see the neighborhood of Gonen/Katamon HaYeshana, page 237
Hagai, see the neighborhood of Geula, page 182
HaGalgal, see Talpiot-Industrial Zone, page 494
HaGalil, see the neighborhood of Nahlat Ahim/Nahlaot, page 373
HaGal'init, see the neighborhood of Gilo, page 194
HaGanenet, see the neighborhood of Gilo, page 194
HaGaon MiTurda, see the neighborhood of Tel-Arza, page 504
HaGedud HaHamishi, see the neighborhood of Pisgat Zeev Mercaz, page 403
HaGedud Ha'Ivri, see the neighborhood of Gonen/Katamon HaYeshana, page 237
HaGedud HaShishi [Square], see the neighborhood of Pisgat Zeev Mercaz, page 403
HaGefen, see the neighborhood of Gilo, page 194
HaGeonim, see the neighborhood of Sha'arei Hesed, page 468
HaGesher HaHai [Square], see the neighborhood of Pisgat Zeev Mercaz, page 403
HaGilbo'a, see the neighborhood of Ohel Moshe, page 398
HaGitit, see the Jewish Quarter, page 272
Hagiz, Moshe, Rabbi, see the neighborhood of Zichron Moshe, page 518
HaGomeh, see the neighborhood of Gilo, page 194
HaGR"A, see the neighborhood of Kiryat Wolfson, page 306
HaGR"A, see the neighborhood of Sha'arei Hesed, page 468
HaGuy, see the neighborhood of Beit HaKerem, page 136
HaHa"I [Square], see the neighborhood of Manhat/Malha, page 330
HaHa"I [Square], see the neighborhood of Ramat Sharett, page 425

HaKorchim, see 'Atarot-Industrial Zone, page 99
HaKoreh, see the neighborhood of Gilo, page 195
HaKotel, see the Jewish Quarter, page 273
HaKuzari [Park], see the neighborhood of Rehavia, page 449
Halafta, Rabbi, see the neighborhood of Gonenim/Katamonim Aleph and Vav, page 243
HaLamed Hei, see the neighborhood of Gonen/Katamon HaYeshana, page 238
HaLevanon, see the neighborhood of Batei Kollel Munkacs, page 112
HaLevanon, see the neighborhood of Knesset Yisrael, page 309
HaLevanon, see the neighborhood of Mazkeret Moshe, page 333
HaLevi, Eli'ezer, see the neighborhood of Kiryat Moshe, page 297
HaLevi, Shlomo (Momo), see the neighborhood of Kiryat Ta'asiyot 'Atirot Mada'/ Har Hotzvim, page 305
HaLevi, Yehuda, Rabbi [Steps], see the Jewish Quarter, page 273
Halhul, see the neighborhood of Nahlat Tzion, page 384
HaLilach, see the neighborhood of 'Ir Ganim Aleph, page 267
HaLot, see the neighborhood of Gilo, page 195
Halperin, Michael [Square], see the neighborhood of Talpiot Mizrah, page 499
Halprin, Yisrael, see the neighborhood of Gonen/Katamon HaYeshana, page 238
HaMa'alot, see Mid-Town, page 350
HaMa'apilim, see the neighborhood of Giv'at Oranim, page 216
HaMa'apilim, see the neighborhood of Gonen/Katamon HaYeshana, page 238
HaMa'aravim, see the neighborhood of Mahane Yisrael, page 326
HaMa'aravim, see Mid-Town, page 350
HaMa'as, see 'Atarot-Industrial Zone, page 99
HaMaavak [Lane], see the neighborhood of Giv'at Shapira/French Hill, page 226
HaMa'ayan, see the neighborhood of 'Ein Kerem, page 165
HaMaBI"T, see the neighborhood of Ahva, page 90
HaMadpisim, see 'Atarot-Industrial Zone, page 99
HaMadrasa [Steps], see the Moslem Quarter, page 366
HaMadreigot, see the neighborhood of Nahlat Ahim/Nahlaot, page 373
HaMadreigot, see the neighborhood of Zichron Ahim, page 516
HaMagid, see the neighborhood of the German Colony, page 178
HaMahtarot, see the neighborhood of Talpiot Mizrah, page 499
HaMahteret HaYehudit BeTzarfat [Square], see Talpiot-Industrial Zone, page 494
HaMalach, see the Armenian Quarter, page 94
HaMalach, see the Jewish Quarter, page 273
HaMaLBI"M, see the neighborhood of Bayit VaGan, page 128
HaMalhin [Square], see the neighborhood of Ramot Allon, page 436
HaMamtzi, see the neighborhood of Homat Shmuel/Har Homa, page 265
HaMargalit, see the neighborhood of Gilo, page 195
HaMaronitim, see the Armenian Quarter, page 94
HaMarpe, see the neighborhood of Kiryat Ta'asiyot 'Atirot Mada'/Har Hotzvim, page 305

Hanan ben Avshalom, see the neighborhood of Batei Perlman/'Ir Shalom, page 120
Hananel ben Hushiel, Rabbi, see the neighborhood of Gonenim/Katamonim Hei and San Simon, page 248
Hanania, see the neighborhood of the German Colony, page 179
HaNasi, see the neighborhood of Kiryat Shmuel, page 302
HaNasi, see the neighborhood of Merhavia, page 344
HaNasi HaShishi [Boulevard] , see the neighborhood of Giv'at Ram, page 219
HaNayadot, see the neighborhood of Pisgat Zeev Mercaz, page 403
HaNegbi, Shabtai, see the neighborhood of Gilo, page 195
HaNehoshet, see 'Atarot-Industrial Zone, page 99
HaNeird, see the neighborhood of 'Ir Ganim Aleph, page 267
HaNesher, see the neighborhood of Gilo, page 195
HaNeTZI"V, see the neighborhood of Batei Broyde/Ohalei Ya'akov, page 105
HaNeTZI"V, see the neighborhood of Batei Kollel Minsk/Beit HaLevi, page 111
HaNeTZI"V, see the neighborhood of Batei Kollel Munkacs, page 112
HaNeTZI"V, see the neighborhood of Batei Rand, page 121
HaNeTZI"V, see the neighborhood of Knesset Yisrael, page 309
HaNeTZI"V, see the neighborhood of Mazkeret Moshe, page 333
HaNevel, see the Jewish Quarter, page 273
HaNeviim, see the neighborhood of Beit David/Beit HaRav Kook, page 132
HaNeviim, see the neighborhood of 'Ezrat Yisrael, page 175
HaNeviim, see Mid-Town, page 350
HaNeviim, see the neighborhood of Morasha/Musrara, page 362
HaNeviim, see the neighborhood of Zichron Moshe, page 518
Hanina, Rabbi [Lane], see the neighborhood of Gonenim/Katamonim Aleph and Vav, page 243
Hanina Mizrahi Steps, see the neighborhood of Beit HaKerem, page 136
HaNitzan, see the neighborhood of Giv'at Ram, page 220
Hanna, see the neighborhood of Shikun HaBa"D, page 482
HaNotrim, see the neighborhood of Gonenim/Katamonim Het, Tet, page 250
Hantke, Arthur (Menahem), see the neighborhood of Kiryat HaYovel, page 287
HaNurit, see the neighborhood 'Ir Ganim Gimel, page 269
Ha'Oferet, see 'Atarot-Industrial Zone, page 99
Ha'Oleh [Lane], see the neighborhood of Giv'at Oranim, page 216
Ha'Oleh [Lane], see the neighborhood of Gonen/Katamon HaYeshana, page 238
Ha'Omer, see the Jewish Quarter, page 274
HaOr, see the neighborhood of Romema, page 454
HaOren, see the neighborhood of 'Ein Kerem, page 165
HaPaLMa"H, see the neighborhood of Gonen/Katamon HaYeshana, page 238
HaPaLMa"H, see the neighborhood of Kiryat Shmuel, page 302
HaPaLMa"H, see the neighborhood of Merhavia, page 344
HaParsa, see Talpiot-Industrial Zone, page 494
HaPartizanim [Lane], see the neighborhood of Giv'at Shapira/French Hill, page 227
HaPisga, see the neighborhood of Bayit VaGan, page 128
HaPortzim, see the neighborhood of Gonen/Katamon HaYeshana, page 238

Har Nevo, see neighborhood of Ohel Moshe, page 398
Har Shefer, see the neighborhood of Ramat Eshkol, page 422
HaRa"N, see the neighborhood of Rehavia, page 449
HaRakah, see the neighborhood of Mea She'arim, page 337
HaRakefet, see the neighborhood of 'Ir Ganim Bet, page 268
HaRakevet [Road], see the neighborhood of the German Colony, page 179
HaRakevet [Road], see the neighborhood of Geulim/Bak'a, page 187
HaRakevet [Road], see the neighborhood of the Greek Colony, page 252
HaRakevet [Road], see the neighborhood of Mekor Haim, page 343
Harari, Shlomo, see the neighborhood of Pisgat Zeev Mizrah, page 409
Harari, Yehuda, see the neighborhood of Tzameret HaBira, page 505
HaRaSHDa"M, see the neighborhood of Bayit VaGan, page 128
Harashei Barzel, see Talpiot-Industrial Zone, page 494
HaRav Hen, Avraham, see the neighborhood of Kiryat Shmuel, page 302
HaRav Zvi Yehuda HaCohen Kook, see the neighborhood of Kiryat Moshe, page 297
HaRAVe"D [Alley], see the neighborhood of Rehavia, page 449
Harchavim, see the neighborhood of Mekor Haim, page 343
Harduf, see the neighborhood of Gilo, page 195
HaRechev, see Talpiot-Industrial Zone, page 495
HaReE"M, see the neighborhood of Sanhedria, page 464
HaRemachim, see the Moslem Quarter, page 366
HaReuveni, David, see the neighborhood of Giv'at Shaul, page 231
HaRiDBa"Z, see the neighborhood of Zichron Moshe, page 518
HaRikma, see Romema-Industrial Zone, page 457
Harkavi, Avraham Eliyahu, Rabbi [Lane], see the neighborhood of Kiryat Shmuel, page 302
Harlap, Ya'akov Asher, Rabbi, see the neighborhood of Kiryat Shmuel, page 302
Harlap, Ya'akov Asher, Rabbi, see the neighborhood of Merhavia, page 344
HaRoeh, see the neighborhood of Ramot Allon, page 436
HaRosmarin, see the neighborhood of Gilo, page 196
Harun e-Rashid, see the neighborhood of Bab e-Zahara, page 102
HaSadna, see Talpiot-Industrial Zone, page 495
HaSahlav, see the neighborhood of 'Ir Ganim Aleph, page 267
HaSalah, see the neighborhood of Rehavia, page 449
Hasan bin Tabet Ansari, see the neighborhood of Shu'afat, page 486
HaSanhedrin, see the neighborhood of Sanhedria, page 464
HaSatat, see the neighborhood of HaPo'alim, page 258
HaSavyon, see the neighborhood of 'Ir Ganim Bet, page 268
HaSayar, see the neighborhood of Pisgat Zeev Mercaz, page 404
HaSayeret HaYerushalmit, see the neighborhood of Pisgat Zeev Mercaz, page 404
HaSeifan, see the neighborhood 'Ir Ganim Bet, page 268
HaSha'ar [Lane], see the neighborhood of 'Ein Kerem, page 165
HaShaked, see the neighborhood of Mahane Yehuda, page 322
HaShalechet, see the neighborhood of 'Ir Ganim Aleph, page 268

HaShalom VeHaAhdut [Lane], see the neighborhood of Sanhedria HaMurhevet, page 466
HaShalshelet, see the Moslem Quarter, page 366
HaShayarot, see the neighborhood of Gonen/Katamon HaYeshana, page 238
HaShayish, see the neighborhood of Gilo, page 196
HaShazif, see the neighborhood of Mahane Yehuda, page 323
HaShikma, see the neighborhood of Mahane Yehuda, page 323
HaShiryonai, see the neighborhood of Pisgat Zeev Mercaz, page 404
HaShisha 'Asar, see the neighborhood of Pisgat Zeev Mercaz, page 404
HaShlihim, see the Christian Quarter, page 155
HaShminit, see the Jewish Quarter, page 274
HaSho'arim, see the Jewish Quarter, page 274
HaShofar, see the Jewish Quarter, page 274
HaShofet Binyamin, see the neighborhood of Ramat Denya, page 419
HaShomer, see the neighborhood of Gonenim/Katamonim Het, Tet, page 250
HaShu'al, see the neighborhood of Manhat/Malha, page 330
Hasidei Pinsk Karlin, see the neighborhood of Beit Yisrael, page 149
Hasidoff, Avraham, see the neighborhood of Giv'at Massua, page 212
HaSigalit, see the neighborhood of Gilo, page 196
HaSitvanit, see the neighborhood of Gilo, page 196
HaSlav, see the neighborhood of Gilo, page 196
HaSolelim, see the neighborhood of HaPo'alim, page 258
HaSoreg, see Mid-Town, page 350
Hasson, 'Uzi (Yehezkel), see Mid-Town, page 351
HaTa'asiya, see Talpiot-Industrial Zone, page 495
HaTahana, see the neighborhood of Yemin Moshe, page 514
HaTa"M Sofer, see the neighborhood of Sha'arei Hesed, page 469
HaTamid, see the Jewish Quarter, page 274
HaTamrukim, see 'Atarot-Industrial Zone, page 99
HaTapuah, see the neighborhood of Mahane Yehuda, page 323
HaTavlin, see the neighborhood of Gilo, page 196
HaTayasim, see the neighborhood of Gonen/Katamon HaYeshana, page 238
HaTe-ayna, see the neighborhood of Gilo, page 196
HaTecheilet, see Romema-Industrial Zone, page 457
HaTekufa, see the neighborhood of Giv'at HaVradim/Shikun Rassco, page 209
Hatem e-Tawi, see the neighborhood of Bab e-Zahara, page 102
HaTenufa, see Talpiot-Industrial Zone, page 495
HaTibonim, see the neighborhood of Rehavia, page 449
HaTikva, see the neighborhood of Yemin Moshe, page 514
Hativat 'Etzioni, see the Armenian Quarter, page 94
Hativat 'Etzioni, see the Jewish Quarter, page 274
Hativat Giv'ati, see the neighborhood of Pisgat Zeev Mercaz, page 404
Hativat HaNaHa"L, see the neighborhood of Pisgat Zeev Mizrah, page 409
Hativat Harel, see the neighborhood of Ma'alot Dafna/Arzei HaBira, page 317
Hativat Harel, see the neighborhood of Sanhedria, page 464

Hativat Harel, see the neighborhood of Shikunei Shmuel HaNavi, page 483
Hativat Yerushalayim, see the Armenian Quarter, page 94
Hativat Yerushalayim, see the Christian Quarter, page 155
Hativat Yerushalayim, see the neighborhood of David's Village-Mamilla, page 161
Hativat Yerushalayim, see the Jewish Quarter, page 274
Hativat Yerushalayim, see the neighborhood of Yemin Moshe, page 514
HaTnu'a HaTzionit [Square], see Mid-Town, page 351
HaTnu'a HaTzionit [Square], see the neighborhood of Rehavia, page 449
HaTomer, see the neighborhood of Yefei Nof, page 509
HaTotehan, see the neighborhood of Pisgat Zeev Mercaz, page 404
HaTupim, see the Jewish Quarter, page 274
HaTurim, see the neighborhood of Mekor Baruch, page 340
HaTurim, see the neighborhood of Sha'arei Yerushalayim, page 447
HaTut, see the neighborhood of Mahane Yehuda, page 323
HaTzabar, see the neighborhood of Gilo, page 196
HaTzadik MiTchechanov, see the neighborhood of Ramot Allon, page 436
HaTzalaf, see the neighborhood of 'Ir Ganim Aleph, page 268
HaTzalam Rahamim [Lane], see the neighborhood of Ramat Sharett, page 425
HaTzanhanim, see the Christian Quarter, page 155
HaTzanhanim, see Mid-Town, page 351
HaTzanhanim, see the neighborhood of Morasha/Musrara, page 362
HaTzanhanim, see the neighborhood of the Russian Compound, page 461
HaTzariah HaAdom, see the Moslem Quarter, page 366
HaTzayar Ya'akov Steinhardt, see the neighborhood of Yemin Moshe, page 514
HaTzayar Yossi, see the neighborhood of Ramat Denya, page 419
Hatzerot, see the neighborhood of Ramat Eshkol, page 422
HaTzfira, see the neighborhood of the German Colony, page 179
HaTzionut, see the neighborhood of Kiryat HaYovel, page 287
HaTziporen, see the neighborhood of Gilo, page 196
HaTzivoni, see the neighborhood of Gilo, page 197
Hatzor, see the neighborhood of Nahlat Ahim/Nahlaot, page 373
HaTzori, see the neighborhood of Gilo, page 197
HaTzuf, see the neighborhood of Gilo, page 197
HaTzvi, see the neighborhood of Romema, page 454
Ha'Ugav, see the Jewish Quarter, page 274
HaUman, see Talpiot-Industrial Zone, page 495
Hausner, Gideon, see the neighborhood of Bayit VaGan, page 128
Hausner, Gideon, see the neighborhood of Holyland Park, page 263
HaVa'ad HaLeumi, see the neighborhood of Bayit VaGan, page 128
HaVa'ad HaLeumi, see the neighborhood of Giv'at Mordechai, page 215
Havakuk, see the neighborhood of Sha'arei Pina, page 471
Havat HaLimud, see the neighborhood of Talpiot Mizrah, page 499
Havillo [Square], see the neighborhood of Nahlat Shiv'a, page 379
Haviv, Avshalom, see the neighborhood of Talpiot Mizrah, page 499
Haviv, Haim, Rabbi, see the neighborhood of Kiryat HaYovel, page 288

HaYa"D [Square], see the Jewish Quarter, page 274
HaYabok, see the neighborhood of Zichron Yosef, page 523
HaYa'en, see the neighborhood of Manhat/Malha, page 330
HaYarden, see the neighborhood of Talpiot, page 492
HaYarkon, see the neighborhood of Zichron Yosef, page 523
HaYarmuch, see the neighborhood of Zichron Yosef, page 523
HaYehudim, see the Jewish Quarter, page 274
Hayei Adam, see the neighborhood of Batei Kollel Warsaw/Nahlat Ya'akov, page 116
Hayei Adam, see the neighborhood of Batei Werner/Ohalei Moshe, page 123
Hayei Adam, see the neighborhood of Batei Wittenberg/Sha'arei Moshe, page 124
Hayei Adam, see the neighborhood of Bnei Moshe/Neve Shalom, page 152
Hayei Adam, see the neighborhood of Even Yehoshu'a, page 171
Hayei 'Olam [Lane], see the Jewish Quarter, page 275
HaYekev [Alley], see the neighborhood of 'Ein Kerem, page 165
HaYeshiva, see the neighborhood of Geula, page 182
HaYetzira, see 'Atarot-Industrial Zone, page 100
Hayot, Zvi Peretz, Rabbi, see the neighborhood of Neve Ya'akov, page 394
HaYotzek, see 'Atarot-Industrial Zone, page 100
HaYozma, see 'Atarot-Industrial Zone, page 100
HaZayit, see the neighborhood of Mekor Baruch, page 340
Hazaz, Haim [Boulevard], see the neighborhood of Giv'at Ram, page 220
Hazaz, Haim [Boulevard], see the neighborhood of Rehavia, page 450
HaZehavit, see the neighborhood of Gilo, page 197
Hazon Ish, see the neighborhood of Ramat Shlomo/Rechess Shu'afat, page 429
Hazon Tzion, see the neighborhood of Beit HaKerem, page 136
Hedva [Steps], see the neighborhood of Ramot Allon, page 436
Hefetz, Shma'aya Baruch [Square], see Mid-Town, page 351
HeHacham Levi 'Amram [Square], see the neighborhood of Gonenim/Katamonim Aleph and Vav, page 244
HeHalutz, see the neighborhood of Beit HaKerem, page 136
HeHalutz, see the neighborhood of Giv'at Beit HaKerem, page 202
HeHalutz, see the neighborhood of HaPo'alim, page 258
HeHarash, see the neighborhood of Mea She'arim, page 337
HeHaruv, see the neighborhood of Mahane Yehuda, page 323
HeHavush, see the neighborhood of Gilo, page 197
Heil HaAvir, see the neighborhood of Pisgat Zeev Mercaz, page 404
Heil HaHandasa, see the neighborhood of Morasha/Musrara, page 362
Heil HaKesher, see the neighborhood of Pisgat Zeev Mercaz, page 404
Heil HaRefua, see the neighborhood of Pisgat Zeev Tzafon, page 413
Heil Himush, see the neighborhood of Pisgat Zeev Mercaz, page 405
Heil Nashim (He"N), see the neighborhood of Gonen/Katamon HaYeshana, page 239
Heine, Heinrich, see the neighborhood of Yemin Moshe, page 514
Heivar, see the neighborhood of Sha'arei Pina, page 471
Heleni HaMalca, see Mid-Town, page 351

I

J

K

Kabak, Aharon Avraham, see the neighborhood of Beit HaKerem, page 137
Kadima, see the neighborhood of Ramot Allon, page 437
Kafah, Yihya, Rabbi, see the neighborhood of Sha'arei Pina, page 471
Kaf-Tet BeNovember, see the neighborhood of Gonen/Katamon HaYeshana, page 239
Kagan, Helena, Dr. [Ascent], see the neighborhood of Ramot Allon, page 437
Kahan, Haim, Rabbi, see the neighborhood of Pisgat Zeev Mizrah, page 409
Kahaneman, Yosef, Rabbi, see the neighborhood of Ramat Shlomo/Rechess Shu'afat, page 429
Kahanov, Moshe Nehemia, Rabbi, see the neighborhood of Sha'arei Hesed, page 469
Kala'i, Hanoch, see the neighborhood of Manhat/Malha, page 330
Kalcheim, 'Uzi, Rabbi, see the neighborhood of Ramat Shlomo/Rechess Shu'afat, page 429
Kalonymos, Rabbeinu, see the neighborhood of Ramat Shlomo/Rechess Shu'afat, page 429
Kamson, Ya'akov David, see the neighborhood of Ramot Allon, page 437
Kanaei HaGalil, see the neighborhood of Gonenim/Katamonim Bet, Gimel, Dalet, page 246
Kanfei Nesharim, see the neighborhood of Giv'at Shaul, page 231
Kanfei Nesharim, see Giv'at Shaul Industrial Zone, page 234
Kann, Jacobus [Square], see the neighborhood of Kiryat HaYovel, page 288
Kaplan, Eli'ezer, see the neighborhood of Giv'at Ram, page 220
Kariv, Yitzhak, see the neighborhood of David's Village-Mamilla, page 161
Kariv, Yitzhak, see Mid-Town, page 352
Karmon, Moshe, see the neighborhood of Beit HaKerem, page 137
Karni, Yehuda, see the neighborhood of Ramot Allon, page 437
Karnibad, Refael, see the neighborhood of Ramot Allon, page 437
Karo, Yosef, Rabbi, see the neighborhood of Beit Yisrael, page 149
Kashani, Eli'ezer, see the neighborhood of Talpiot Mizrah, page 499
Katz, Michel Leib, see the neighborhood of Morasha/Musrara, page 362
Katzenellenbogen, Refael HaLevi, Rabbi, see the neighborhood of HarNof, page 261
Katzenelson, Yitzhak, see the neighborhood of Giv'at HaVradim/Shikun Rassco, page 210
Katzir, Aharon, see the neighborhood of Giv'at Shapira/French Hill, page 227
Katzir, Aharon, see the neighborhood of Mount Scopus, page 370
Katznelson, Reuven [Square], see the neighborhood of Neve Ya'akov, page 394
Kaufmann, Yehezkel, see the neighborhood of Ramot Allon, page 438
Kav VeNaki, see the neighborhood of Mekor Baruch, page 340
Kedoshei Bavel, see the neighborhood of Talpiot Mizrah, page 499
Kedoshei Saloniki, see the neighborhood of Talpiot Tzafon, page 502
Kedoshei Struma, see the neighborhood of Manhat/Malha, page 330
Kedushat Aharon, see the neighborhood of Kiryat Belz, page 284

Kehati, Pinhas, Rabbi, see the neighborhood of Giv'at Shaul, page 231
Kehilat Ungvar, see the neighborhood of Ramot Allon, page 438
Kehilat Yehudei 'Amadiya [Square], see the neighborhood of Zichron Yosef, page 523
Kehilot SHU"M, see the neighborhood of Ramot Allon, page 438
Kehilot Ya'akov, see the neighborhood of Ramat Shlomo/Rechess Shu'afat, page 429
Kellner, Aryeh, see the neighborhood of Kiryat HaYovel, page 288
Keren HaYesod, see the neighborhood of Komemiyut/Talbieh, page 313
Keren HaYesod, see Mid-Town, page 352
Ketura [Lane], see the neighborhood of Gilo, page 197
Ketzi'a [Lane], see the neighborhood of Gilo, page 198
Kfar Bar'am, see the neighborhood of Nahlat Ahim/Nahlaot, page 373
Kfar 'Etzion, see the neighborhood of Arnona, page 96
Kfar 'Etzion, see the neighborhood of Talpiot, page 492
Kfar HaShiloah, see the neighborhood of Beit Yisrael, page 149
Kfar 'Ivri, see the neighborhood of Neve Ya'akov, page 394
Kfar Nahum, see the neighborhood of Kerem/Beit Avraham, page 278
Khalid ibn el-Walid, see the neighborhood of Bab e-Zahara, page 103
Khalif el-Baldi, see the neighborhood of Wadi el-Joz, page 507
Khalil e-Sakakini, see the neighborhood of Beit Hanina, page 141
Khlat Mash'al, see the neighborhood of Beit Hanina, page 141
Khlat Sinad, see the neighborhood of Shu'afat, page 486
Ki Tov, see the neighborhood of Tel-Arza, page 504
Kibutz Galuyot, see the neighborhood of Geulim/Bak'a, page 187
Kida [Lane], see the neighborhood of Gilo, page 198
Kikar HaHatulot, see Mid-Town, page 352
Kikar HaHerut – HaDavidka, see Mid-Town, page 352
Kikar HaKastel, see the neighborhood of 'Ein Kerem, page 166
Kikar HaShabbat, see the neighborhood of Batei Kollel Warsaw/Nahlat Ya'akov, page 116
Kikar HaShabbat, see the neighborhood of Beit Yisrael, page 150
Kikar HaShabbat, see the neighborhood of Geula, page 183
Kikar TZaHa"L, see the Christian Quarter, page 156
Kikar TZaHa"L, see Mid-Town, page 352
Kikar TZaHa"L, see the neighborhood of the Russian Compound, page 462
Kikar Tzarfat, see Mid-Town, page 352
Kikar Tzarfat, see the neighborhood of Rehavia, page 450
Kikar Tzion, see Mid-Town, page 352
Kimhi, Dov, see the neighborhood of Giv'at HaVradim/Shikun Rassco, page 210
Kineret, see the neighborhood of Kerem/Beit Avraham, page 278
King George (V), see the neighborhood of Mahane Yehuda, page 323
King George (V), see Mid-Town, page 352
King George (V), see the neighborhood of Rehavia, page 450
King, Martin Luther, see the neighborhood of the German Colony, page 179
Kiryat David Ben-Gurion, see the neighborhood of Giv'at Ram, page 220

Kiryat HaYovel, see the neighborhood of Kiryat HaYovel, page 288
Kiryat Mada‘, see the neighborhood of Kiryat Ta‘asiyot ‘Atirot Mada‘/Har Hotzvim, page 305
Kiryat Moshe, see the neighborhood of Kiryat Moshe, page 297
Kisei Rahamim, see the neighborhood of Pisgat Zeev Mizrah, page 409
Kiss, Naomi, see the neighborhood of Morasha/Musrara, page 362
Kisufim [Steps], see the neighborhood of Ramot Allon, page 438
Klausner, Yosef Gedalia, Dr., see the neighborhood of Talpiot, page 492
Klein, Shmuel, Rabbi, see the neighborhood of the German Colony, page 179
Kleinman, Moshe, see the neighborhood of Kiryat HaYovel, page 288
Knesset Mordechai [Lane], see the neighborhood of HaBucharim, page 256
Kol, Moshe, see the neighborhood of Ramat Beit HaKerem, page 417
Kol Yisrael Haverim (KY"H), see the neighborhood of Mahane Yehuda, page 323
Kolitz, Haim [Road], see the neighborhood of Giv‘at Massua, page 212
Kolitz, Haim [Road], see the neighborhood of Kiryat HaYovel, page 288
Kolitz, Haim [Road], see the neighborhood of Manhat/Malha, page 331
Kook, Avraham Yitzhak HaCohen, Rabbi, see the neighborhood of Beit David/Beit HaRav Kook, page 133
Kook, Avraham Yitzhak HaCohen, Rabbi, see Mid-Town, page 352
Korczak, Janusz, see the neighborhood of Kiryat HaYovel, page 288
Korei HaDorot, see the neighborhood of Arnona, page 97
Korei HaDorot, see the neighborhood of Talpiot, page 492
Koresh, see Mid-Town, page 352
Korot Ha‘Itim, see the neighborhood of Kiryat Moshe, page 298
Kosovsky, Haim Yehoshu‘a, Rabbi, see the neighborhood of Kiryat Moshe, page 298
Kotler, Aharon, Rabbi, see the neighborhood of Giv‘at Shaul, page 232
Kovner, Haim HaLevi [Lane], see the neighborhood of Nahlat Shiv‘a, page 379
Kovshei Katamon, see the neighborhood of Gonen/Katamon HaYeshana, page 239
Kraus, Gertrud, Prof., see the neighborhood of Giv‘at Massua, page 212
Kremenetzky, Johann-Yona, see the neighborhood of Kiryat HaYovel, page 288
Ktav Sofer, see the neighborhood of Giv‘at Shaul, page 232
Kubovy, Aryeh (Louis), Dr., see the neighborhood of Ramat Denya, page 419
Kuenka, Bentzion, Rabbi, see the neighborhood of Giv‘at Shaul, page 232
Kurz, Moshe Aryeh, Rabbi Dr., see the neighborhood of Talpiot Mizrah, page 499
Kushnir, Nisan, see the neighborhood of Ramot Allon, page 438
Kutscher, Yehezkel, see the neighborhood of Ramot Allon, page 438

L

Lachish, see the neighborhood of Nahlat Tzion, page 384
Lampronti, Yitzhak, Rabbi, see the neighborhood of Romema, page 455
Lankin, Eliyahu, see the neighborhood of Talpiot, page 492
Lankin, Eliyahu, see the neighborhood of Talpiot Mizrah, page 500
Lapian, Eliyahu, Rabbi, see the neighborhood of Ramat Shlomo/Rechess Shu‘afat, page 430

Lapidot, Gershom, Rabbi, see the neighborhood of Beit Yisrael, page 150
Laskov, Haim, see the neighborhood of Pisgat Zeev Mercaz, page 405
Latin Patriarchate, see the Christian Quarter, page 156
LaTzadik, Zvi [Ascent], see the neighborhood of Bayit VaGan, page 128
Lavi, Theodor, see the neighborhood of Ramot Allon, page 438
Layish, see the neighborhood of Gilo, page 198
Leder, Zelig, see the neighborhood of Beit Yisrael, page 150
Lederer, Moshe and Esther, see the neighborhood of Batei Kollel Ungarin/Nahlat Zvi, page 113
LeH"I, see the neighborhood of Giv'at Shapira/ French Hill, page 227
Leib Yaffe, see the neighborhood of Arnona, page 97
Leib Yaffe, see the neighborhood of Talpiot, page 492
Leibowitz, Zvi, see the neighborhood of Ramat Denya, page 419
Lempel, Hadassa (Helena), see the neighborhood of Mount Scopus, page 370
Lendner, Moshe Dov, see the neighborhood of Beit Yisrael, page 150
Leon, Ben Tzion, see the neighborhood of Pisgat Zeev Mizrah, page 409
Leshem, see the neighborhood of Gilo, page 198
Lev Ha'Ivri, see the neighborhood of Komemiyut/Talbieh, page 313
Levanon, Zvi, see the neighborhood of Pisgat Zeev Ma'arav, page 412
Levi, see the neighborhood of Geulim/Bak'a, page 187
Levi, 'Ovadia [Square], see the neighborhood of Bayit VaGan, page 128
Levi, Primo, see the neighborhood of Talpiot Mizrah, page 500
Levi Yitzhak of Berdichev, Rabbi, see the neighborhood of Even Yehoshu'a, page 171
Levi, Yitzhak [Square], see the neighborhood of Talpiot, page 492
Levi, Yitzhak 'Azaria [Square], see the neighborhood of Mahane Yehuda, page 323
Levi, Yosef, Rabbi [Square], see the neighborhood of Har Nof, page 261
Levin [Square], see the neighborhood of Shikun HaBa"D, page 482
Levin, Shmaryahu, Dr., see the neighborhood of Kiryat HaYovel, page 289
Levona, see the neighborhood of Gilo, page 198
Levush Mordechai, see the neighborhood of Geula, page 183
Lichtenstein, see the neighborhood of Homat Shmuel/Har Homa, page 265
Lichtman, Avraham David, see the neighborhood of Pisgat Zeev Ma'arav, page 412
Lifshitz, Aryeh [Square], see the neighborhood of Nahlat Ahim/Nahlaot, page 373
Lifshitz, Nahum, see the neighborhood of Geulim/Bak'a, page 187
Lilian, Ephraim Moshe, see the neighborhood of Giv'at Ram, page 220
Lincoln, Abraham, see Mid-Town, page 353
Lions Gate, see the Moslem Quarter, page 366
Lions Gate [Road], see the Moslem Quarter, page 366
Lipov, Dov [Square], see the neighborhood of Kiryat HaYovel, page 289
Lipsky, Louis, see the neighborhood of Ramot Allon, page 438
Lipzin, Sol, see the neighborhood of Homat Shmuel/Har Homa, page 265
Livne, see the neighborhood of Ramat Eshkol, page 422
Livneh, Eli'ezer, see the neighborhood of Neve Ya'akov, page 394
Livni, Eitan, see the neighborhood of Pisgat Zeev Mizrah, page 409

Lloyd George, David, see the neighborhood of the German Colony, page 179
Locker, Berl, see the neighborhood of Pat, page 400
Lod, see the neighborhood of Nahlat Ahim/Nahlaot, page 373
Lohamei HaGhetaot, see the neighborhood of Giv'at Shapira/French Hill, page 227
Lohamei HaGhetaot, see the neighborhood of Tzameret HaBira, page 505
Lohamei HaRova', see the Jewish Quarter, page 275
Lopes, Eliyahu, Rabbi [Ascent], see the neighborhood of Bayit VaGan, page 129
Lorch, Netanel, see the neighborhood of Giv'at Ram, page 220
Lunz, Moshe, see Mid-Town, page 353
Lupo, Shmuel, see the neighborhood of Talpiot Tzafon, page 502
Luria, Yosef, Dr., see the neighborhood of Arnona, page 97
Lutan, Giora [Square], see the neighborhood of Giv'at Ram, page 221
Lutz, Charles, see the neighborhood of Neve Ya'akov, page 394
Luz, Kadish, see the neighborhood of Ramat Denya, page 419
Luz, Kadish, see the neighborhood of Ramat Sharett, page 425

M

Ma'agal Beit HaMidrash, see the neighborhood of Beit HaKerem, page 137
Ma'agal HaNikba, see the neighborhood of 'Ein Kerem, page 166
Ma'aglei HaRI"M Levin, see the neighborhood of Sanhedria HaMurhevet, page 466
Ma'aglei Yavne, see the neighborhood of Gonenim/Katamonim Aleph and Vav, page 244
Ma'aglot HaRav Pardes, see the neighborhood of Neve Ya'akov, page 394
Ma'ale HaAchsaniya, see the neighborhood of 'Ein Kerem, page 166
Ma'ale HaBustan, see the neighborhood of 'Ein Kerem, page 166
Ma'ale HaMoeitza, see the neighborhood of 'Ein Kerem, page 166
Ma'ale HaOranim, see the neighborhood of Ramot Allon, page 429
Ma'ale HaShalom, see the City of David, page 158
Ma'ale HaShalom, see the Jewish Quarter, page 275
Ma'ale ShaZa"CH, see the Jewish Quarter, page 275
Ma'ale Yitzhak Shiryon, see the neighborhood of Rehavia, page 450
Ma'ale Yoav, see the City of David, page 159
Ma'ale Zeev, see the neighborhood of Gonenim/Katamonim Aleph and Vav, page 244
Ma'ale Zeev, see the neighborhood of Gonenim/Katamonim Hei and San Simon, page 248
Ma'alot Benny, see the Jewish Quarter, page 275
Ma'alot Dafna, see the neighborhood of Ma'alot Dafna/Arzei HaBira, page 317
Ma'alot 'Ir David, see the City of David, page 159
Ma'amadot Yisrael, see the Jewish Quarter, page 275
Ma'ane Simha, see the neighborhood of Kiryat Mattersdorf, page 293
Ma'ane Simha, see the neighborhood of Romema 'Ilit, page 456
Ma'ase Hoshev, see Talpiot-Industrial Zone, page 495
Ma'avar HaMitla, see the neighborhood of Ramat Eshkol, page 422

Macabi, Mutzerai [Square], see Mid-Town, page 353
Maccabee Salzburger [Square], see the neighborhood of the Greek Colony, page 252
Madreigot Gan 'Eden, see the neighborhood of 'Ein Kerem, page 166
Madreigot HaBatzir, see the neighborhood of 'Ein Kerem, page 166
Madreigot HaBikur, see the neighborhood of 'Ein Kerem, page 166
Madreigot HaKfar, see the neighborhood of 'Ein Kerem, page 166
Madreigot HaRomaim, see the neighborhood of 'Ein Kerem, page 166
Magein HaElef, see the neighborhood of Shikunei Shmuel HaNavi, page 484
Magnes, Yehuda Leib, Dr. [Boulevard], see the neighborhood of Giv'at Ram, page 221
Magnes, Yehuda Leib, Dr. [Square], see the neighborhood of Rehavia, page 451
MaHa"L, see the neighborhood of Kiryat Aryeh, page 282
MaHa"L, see the neighborhood of Sheikh Jarrah, page 479
Mahanayim, see the neighborhood of Mahanayim, page 319
Mahane Yehuda, see the neighborhood of Mahane Yehuda, page 323
Mahlouf, 'Adan, Rabbi, see the neighborhood of Ramat Shlomo/Rechess Shu'afat, page 430
Mahoza, see the neighborhood of Batei Kollel Ungarin/Nahlat Zvi, page 113
Mai Ziyada, see the neighborhood of Beit Hanina, page 142
Maimon, Yehuda Leib HaCohen (Fishman), Rabbi, see the neighborhood of Kiryat Moshe, page 298
Maimon, Yehuda Leib HaCohen (Fishman), Rabbi, see the neighborhood of Maimon (Shchunat HaPo'el HaMizrahi), page 328
Malachi, see the neighborhood of Geula, page 183
MaLa"L, see the neighborhood of the German Colony, page 179
Malchei Yisrael, see the neighborhood of Ahva, page 91
Malchei Yisrael, see the neighborhood of Geula, page 183
Malchei Yisrael, see the neighborhood of Kerem/Beit Avraham, page 278
Malchei Yisrael, see the neighborhood of Kerem Avraham, page 280
Malchei Yisrael, see the neighborhood of Mekor Baruch, page 340
Malki Tzedek, see the Jewish Quarter, page 275
Malki, Refael Mordechai, Rabbi, see the neighborhood of Yemin Moshe, page 514
Ma'mal El-Talj, see the neighborhood of Beit Safafa, page 144
Mamilla, see Mid-Town, page 353
Mani, Eliyahu, Rabbi, see the neighborhood of Mahane Yehuda, page 324
Mann, Yitzhak David, see the neighborhood of Giv'at Mordechai, page 215
Manne, Mordechai Zvi, see the neighborhood of Komemiyut/Talbieh, page 313
Ma'on, see the neighborhood of Nahlat Tzion, page 384
Ma'oz, see the neighborhood of Ramot Allon, page 439
Mapu, Avraham, see Mid-Town, page 353
Mara, see the neighborhood of Ramat Beit HaKerem, page 417
Marat, Zalman [Square], see the neighborhood of Yefei Nof, page 509
Marcus, David, see the neighborhood of Komemiyut/Talbieh, page 313

Margolin, Eli'ezer, see the neighborhood of Gonenim/Katamonim Het, Tet, page 250
Marj el-Muhur, see the neighborhood of Shu'afat, page 486
Marj ibn 'Amer, see the neighborhood of Beit Hanina, page 142
Marom Tzion, see the neighborhood of Bayit VaGan, page 129
Marton, Erno Yehezkel, see the neighborhood of Geulim/Bak'a, page 188
Marva, see the neighborhood of Gilo, page 198
Marzouk, Moshe (Gil), Dr., see the neighborhood of Talpiot Mizrah, page 500
Masaryk, Thomas, see the neighborhood of the German Colony, page 180
Masat Moshe, see the neighborhood of Giv'at Mordechai, page 215
Masharif, see the neighborhood of Shu'afat, page 487
Maslianski, Zvi, see the neighborhood of Ramot Allon, page 439
Mass, Reuven, see the neighborhood of Ramot Allon, page 439
Massuot Yitzhak, see the neighborhood of Arnona, page 97
Matityahu, see the neighborhood of Geulim/Bak'a, page 188
Matityahu, Moshe [Square], see the neighborhood of Nahlat Ahim/Nahlaot, page 373
Maunoury, Maurice Bourges, see the neighborhood of Pisgat Zeev Mizrah, page 409
Mawlawiya, see the Moslem Quarter, page 366
Maximus Tzayeg, Patriarch, see the neighborhood of Beit Hanina, page 142
Mazal Aryeh, see the neighborhood of Pisgat Zeev Tzafon, page 413
Mazal Dli, see the neighborhood of Pisgat Zeev Tzafon, page 413
Mazal Gdi, see the neighborhood of Pisgat Zeev Tzafon, page 414
Mazal Keshet, see the neighborhood of Pisgat Zeev Tzafon, page 414
Mazal Moznayim, see the neighborhood of Pisgat Zeev Tzafon, page 414
Mazal Shor, see the neighborhood of Pisgat Zeev Tzafon, page 414
Mazal Taleh, see the neighborhood of Pisgat Zeev Tzafon, page 414
Mazal Teomim, see the neighborhood of Pisgat Zeev Tzafon, page 414
Mazar, Binyamin, see the neighborhood of Mount Scopus, page 370
Mazia, Aharon Haim, Dr., see the neighborhood of Batei Goral/ MishkenotHaTeimanim, page 107
Mazia, Aharon Haim, Dr., see Mid-Town, page 353
Mazkeret Moshe, see the neighborhood of Mazkeret Moshe, page 333
Mazor, see the neighborhood of Sha'arei Tzedek, page 475
Mea She'arim, see the neighborhood of Batei Kollel Ungarin/Nahlat Zvi, page 114
Mea She'arim, see the neighborhood of Batei Kollel Warsaw/Nahlat Ya'akov, page 116
Mea She'arim, see the neighborhood of Batei Naitin, page 119
Mea She'arim, see the neighborhood of Batei Perlman/'Ir Shalom, page 120
Mea She'arim, see the neighborhood of Beit Yisrael, page 150
Mea She'arim, see the neighborhood of Geula, page 183
Mea She'arim, see the neighborhood of Mea She'arim, page 338
Mea She'arim, see the neighborhood of Nahlat Zvi/Shchunat HaTeimanim, page 386
Mea She'arim, see the neighborhood of Sha'arei Pina, page 471

Megadim, see the neighborhood of Yefei Nof, page 509
Meginei Yerushalayim, see the neighborhood of Giv'at Shaul, page 232
Mehalkei HaMayim, see the neighborhood of Gonen/Katamon HaYeshana, page 239
Meinertzhagen, Colonel Richard [Square], see the neighborhood of Sheikh Jarrah, page 479
Meir, Shmuel [Boulevard], see the neighborhood of Homat Shmuel/Har Homa, page 266
Meir, Ya'akov, Rabbi, see the neighborhood of Ahva, page 91
Meir, Ya'akov, Rabbi, see the neighborhood of Yegiy'a Kapayim, page 511
Meiron, see the neighborhood of Kerem/Beit Avraham, page 278
Meitiv Nagein, see the neighborhood of David's Village-Mamilla, page 162
Meitzarei Tiran, see the neighborhood of Giv'at HaMivtar, page 204
Mekor Haim, see the neighborhood of of Mekor Haim, page 343
Melamed [Square], see the neighborhood of Rehavia, page 451
Melavei HaShayarot [Square], see the neighborhood of Beit HaKerem, page 137
Meltzer, Feivel, see the neighborhood of Kiryat Moshe, page 298
Menahem Meishiv, see the neighborhood of Kiryat Zanz, page 307
Menahem Natan Auerbach, Rabbi, see the neighborhood of Kerem/Beit Avraham, page 278
Menashe, see the neighborhood of Geulim/Bak'a, page 188
Menashe ben Israel, Rabbi, see Mid-Town, page 353
Menashe Nehemia, see the neighborhood of Giv'at Massua, page 213
Mendele Mocher Sforim, see the neighborhood of Komemiyut/Talbieh, page 313
Mendelsohn, Eric, see the neighborhood of Ramot Allon, page 439
Menora, see Mid-Town, page 353
Meretz, David, Dr., see the neighborhood of Ramat Sharett, page 425
Meridor, Eliyahu, see the neighborhood of Pisgat Zeev Mizrah, page 410
Meshulam, Yitzhak [Square], see the neighborhood of Kiryat Moshe, page 298
Mesilat Yesharim, see the neighborhood of Batei Goral/Mishkenot HaTeimanim, page 107
Mesilat Yesharim, see Mid-Town, page 353
Mesilat Yesharim, see the neighborhood of Sukkat Shalom, page 488
Mevo Yitzhak, see the neighborhood of Kiryat Moshe, page 298
Mexico, see the neighborhood of Kiryat Menahem, page 294
Meyuhas, Yosef Baran, see the neighborhood of Batei Kollel Horodna/Damesek Eliezer, page 109
Meyuhas, Yosef Baran, see the neighborhood of Mahane Yehuda, page 324
Meyuhas, Yosef Baran, see the neighborhood of Sha'arei Shalom, page 474
Micha, see the neighborhood of Geula, page 183
Michaelson, Y. Z., Prof., see the neighborhood of Neve Shaanan, page 391
Michal HaCohen [Square], see the neighborhood of Nahlat Shiv'a, page 379
Michal, see the neighborhood of Sanhedria, page 464
Michlin, Michel Haim, Rabbi, see the neighborhood of Bayit VaGan, page 129

Michvar, see the neighborhood of Gonenim/Katamonim Hei and San Simon, page 248
Midbar Sinai, see the neighborhood of Giv'at HaMivtar, page 205
Mif'alot, see 'Atarot-Industrial Zone, page 100
Mifratz Shlomo, see the neighborhood of Giv'at HaMivtar, page 205
Mikve Yisrael, see the neighborhood of Ma'alot Dafna/Arzei HaBira, page 317
Milikowsky, Natan, Rabbi [Square], see the neighborhood of Bayit VaGan, page 129
MiLyzhansk, Elimelech, Rabbi, see the neighborhood of Ramot Allon, page 439
Minhat Yitzhak, see the neighborhood of Shikun HaBa"D, page 482
Minz, Benjamin, see the neighborhood of Ramot Allon, page 439
Minzberg, Yisrael Zeev, Rabbi, see the neighborhood of Bayit VaGan, page 129
Miriam HaHashmonait, see the neighborhood of Geulim/Bak'a, page 188
Mirski, Yitzhak, see the neighborhood of Ramot Allon, page 439
Misgav LaDach, see the Jewish Quarter, page 275
Mishael, see the neighborhood of the Greek Colony, page 253
Mishkan Shilo, see the neighborhood of Giv'at Beit HaKerem, page 202
Mishkan Shilo, see the neighborhood of Ramat Beit HaKerem, page 417
Mishkanot, see the neighborhood of Batei Goral/Mishkenot HaTeimanim, page 107
Mishkanot, see the neighborhood of Mishkenot Yisrael, page 359
Mishkelov, Menahem Mendel, Rabbi, see the neighborhood of Har Nof, page 261
Mishkenot Shaananim, see the neighborhood of Yemin Moshe, page 514
Mishmar Ha'Am, see the neighborhood of Gonen/Katamon HaYeshana, page 239
Mishmar HaGvul, see the neighborhood of Ramat Eshkol, page 422
Mishmarot, see the neighborhood of Morasha/Musrara, page 362
Mishmerot HaKehuna, see the Jewish Quarter, page 276
Mish'ol HaDekalim, see the neighborhood of Ramot Allon, page 439
Mish'ol HaHadas, see the neighborhood of Ramot Allon, page 440
Mish'ol HaKitron, see the neighborhood of Ramot Allon, page 440
Mish'ol HaKoranit, see the neighborhood of Ramot Allon, page 440
Mish'ol HaKurtam, see the neighborhood of Ramot Allon, page 440
Mish'ol HaMagalit, see the neighborhood of Ramot Allon, page 440
Mish'ol HaRotem, see the neighborhood of Ramot Allon, page 440
Mish'ol HaYa'ra, see the neighborhood of Ramot Allon, page 440
Mish'ol Moran, see the neighborhood of Ramot Allon, page 440
Mish'ol 'Uzrad, see the neighborhood of Ramot Allon, page 440
Mishpat Dreyfus, see the neighborhood of Ramot Allon, page 440
Mishteret HaYishuvim, see the neighborhood of Pisgat Zeev Mercaz, page 405
Miss Landau (Rina Yehudit), see the neighborhood of Giv'at Massua, page 213
MiTudela, Binyamin, see the neighborhood of Rehavia, page 451
Mitzpe, see the neighborhood of Nahlat Tzion, page 384
Mivtza Kadesh, see the neighborhood of Gonen/Katamon HaYeshana, page 239
Mizrahi, Yohanan Yosef, see the neighborhood of Beit Yisrael, page 150
Mo'adim [Steps], see the neighborhood of Ramot Allon, page 441
Moda'i, Yitzhak [Road], see the neighborhood of Manhat/Malha, page 331

N

Nahshon, see the neighborhood of Giv'at Hanania/Abu Tor, page 207
Nahum (HaElkoshi) , see the neighborhood of Geula, page 183
Nahum Ish Gamzu, see the neighborhood of Mea She'arim, page 338
Naiditsch, Yitzhak, see the neighborhood of Kiryat HaYovel, page 289
Naiman, Shmuel Gedalia, Rabbi, see the neighborhood of Neve Ya'akov, page 394
Najara, Yisrael, Rabbi, see the neighborhood of Giv'at Shaul, page 232
Nakar, Meir, see the neighborhood of Talpiot Mizrah, page 500
Nakdimon (ben Gurion), see the neighborhood of Gonenim/Katamonim Aleph and Vav, page 245
Na'omi, see the neighborhood of Giv'at Hanania/Abu Tor, page 208
Narkiss, Mordechai, see Mid-Town, page 354
Narkiss, Mordechai, see the neighborhood of Nahlat Ahim/Nahlaot, page 374
Narkiss, Mordechai, see the neighborhood of Neve Betzalel, page 389
Narkiss, 'Uzi, HaAluf [Road], see the neighborhood of Pisgat Zeev Ma'arav, page 412
Narkiss, 'Uzi, HaAluf [Road], see the neighborhood of Pisgat Zeev Tzafon, page 415
Narkiss, 'Uzi, HaAluf [Road], see the neighborhood of Shu'afat, page 487
Nataf [Lane], see the neighborhood of Gilo, page 198
Natan HaNavi, see the neighborhood of Morasha/Musrara, page 362
Natan, Shmuel, Rabbi, see the neighborhood of Giv'at Massua, page 213
Natanson, Isser, see the neighborhood of Pisgat Zeev Mizrah, page 410
Navon, Yosef, see the neighborhood of Mahane Yehuda, page 324
Navon, Yosef [Square], see the neighborhood of Giv'at Hanania/Abu Tor, page 208
Nayot, see the neighborhood of Nayot, page 388
Nayot, see the neighborhood of Neve Granot, page 390
Nedava, Yosef, see the neighborhood of Pisgat Zeev Mizrah, page 410
Neeman, Yehoshu'a Leib [Square], see the neighborhood of Bayit VaGan, page 129
Neftoah, see the neighborhood of Romema 'Ilit, page 456
Negba, see the neighborhood of Gonen/Katamon HaYeshana, page 239
Nehagei HaPradot [Lane], see the neighborhood of Tzameret HaBira, page 505
Nehama Leibowitz, Prof., see the neighborhood of Homat Shmuel/Har Homa, page 266
Nehar Prat, see the neighborhood of Zichron Ya'akov, page 521
Nehar Prat, see the neighborhood of Zichron Yosef, page 523
Nehemia (ben Hachalia), see the neighborhood of Kerem Avraham, page 280
Nehorai, see the neighborhood of Gonenim/Katamonim Aleph and Vav, page 245
Ne'im Zmirot, see the neighborhood of David's Village-Mamilla, page 162
Neot Deshe, see the neighborhood of David's Village-Mamilla, page 162
Nerot Shabbat, see the neighborhood of Ramot Allon, page 441
Netiv HaMazalot, see the neighborhood of Pisgat Zeev Tzafon, page 415
Netiv HaRakevel, see Mid-Town, page 354

Netiv Yitzhak, see the neighborhood of Mahane Yehuda, page 324
Netiv Yitzhak, see the neighborhood of Ohel Shlomo, page 399
Netiv Zahara Levitov, see the neighborhood of Gonen/Katamon HaYeshana, page 239
Netivei 'Am, see the neighborhood of Ramot Allon, page 441
Netter, Ya'akov (Charles), see the neighborhood of Kiryat Aryeh, page 282
Netter, Ya'akov (Charles), see the neighborhood of Ma'alot Dafna/Arzei HaBira, page 317
Netzivin, see the neighborhood of Batei Kollel Ungarin/Nahlat Zvi, page 114
Neve Shaanan, see the neighborhood of Neve Shaanan, page 391
Neve Ya'akov [Boulevard], see the neighborhood of Neve Ya'akov, page 394
Neve Ya'akov [Boulevard], see the neighborhood of Pisgat Zeev Tzafon, page 415
New Gate, see the Christian Quarter, page 156
Nezer, David, see the neighborhood of Bayit VaGan, page 129
Nibarta, see the neighborhood of Nahlat Ahim/Nahlaot, page 374
Nibarta, see the neighborhood of Zichron Ahim, page 516
Nicaragua, see the neighborhood of Kiryat Menahem, page 294
Nikanor, see the neighborhood of Gonenim/Katamonim Hei and San Simon, page 248
Nikova, Rina, see the neighborhood of Pisgat Zeev Mizrah, page 410
NIL"I, see the neighborhood of Gonen/Katamon HaYeshana, page 240
Nissan, Avraham, Dr. (Katznelson), see the neighborhood of Kiryat HaYovel, page 289
Nissenbaum, Yitzhak, Rabbi, see the neighborhood of Kiryat Moshe, page 298
Nissim, Yitzhak, Rabbi, see the neighborhood of Homat Shmuel/ Har Homa, page 266
Nitronai bar Hilai, see the neighborhood of Giv'at Shaul, page 232
Niv, David, see the neighborhood of Pisgat Zeev Ma'arav, page 412
Nof Harim, see the neighborhood of Yefei Nof, page 509
Nofech, see the neighborhood of Gilo, page 198
Nordau, Max, Dr., see the neighborhood of Romema, page 455
Nov, see the neighborhood of Nahlat Tzion, page 384
Novomeysky, Moshe, see the neighborhood of Ramat Sharett, page 425
Nuñez, Benjamin, see the neighborhood of Giv'at Massua, page 213
Nur e-Din, see the neighborhood of Bab e-Zahara, page 103
Nurail Hoda, see the neighborhood of Beit Hanina, page 142
Nuriel, Z., HaRav [Steps], see the neighborhood of Manhat/Malha, page 331
Nurok, Mordechai, Rabbi, see the neighborhood of Kiryat Moshe, page 299
Nurse Zelma (Meir), see the neighborhood of Giv'at Massua, page 213

O

Odem, see the neighborhood of Gilo, page 199
Ofira, see the neighborhood of Sanhedria, page 464
Ohalei Yosef, see the neighborhood of Mahanayim, page 319
Ohalei Yosef, see the neighborhood of Tel-Arza, page 504
Ohel Moshe, see the neighborhood of Ohel Moshe, page 398

Ohel Shlomo, see the neighborhood of Mekor Baruch, page 340
Ohel Yehoshu'a, see the neighborhood of Kiryat Belz, page 284
Oholiav (ben Ahisamach), see Romema-Industrial Zone, page 458
'Olei HaGardom, see the neighborhood of Talpiot Mizrah, page 500
Oliphant, see the neighborhood of Komemiyut/Talbieh, page 314
Olsvanger, 'Immanuel, see the neighborhood of Kiryat HaYovel, page 289
'Omar el-Khayam, see the neighborhood of Beit Hanina, page 142
'Omar ibn el-'As, see the neighborhood of Bab e-Zahara, page 104
'Omar ibn el-Khatab, see the Armenian Quarter, page 94
'Omar ibn el-Khatab, see the Christian Quarter, page 156
'Omar ibn el-Khatab [Square], see the Armenian Quarter, page 95
'Omer [Square], see the neighborhood of Giv'at HaMivtar, page 205
'Oneg Shabbat, see the neighborhood of Mea She'arim, page 338
Onkelos, see the neighborhood of Giv'at Shaul, page 232
Or HaHaim, see the Jewish Quarter, page 276
Ornstein, Yitzhak, Rabbi, see Mid-Town, page 354
'Othman ibn 'Afan, see the neighborhood of Bab e-Zahara, page 104
'Otniel ben Knaz, see the neighborhood of Geulim/Bak'a, page 188
Otzar HaGeonim, see the neighborhood of Neve Ya'akov, page 395
Otzar HaSfarim, see the neighborhood of Batei Kollel Ungarin/Nahlat Zvi, page 114
'Otzma, see 'Atarot-Industrial Zone, page 100
'Ovadia, see the neighborhood of Kerem Avraham, page 281
'Ovadia MiBartenura, see the neighborhood of Komemiyut/Talbieh, page 314
'Oved, see the neighborhood of Giv'at Hanania/Abu Tor, page 208
'Ozer, see the neighborhood of Beit Yisrael, page 150

P

Pagis, Dan, see the neighborhood of Pisgat Zeev Mizrah, page 410
Palombo, David, see the neighborhood of Ramat Beit HaKerem, page 417
PaLYa"M [Lane], see the neighborhood of Tzameret HaBira, page 506
Panama, see the neighborhood of Kiryat Menahem, page 294
Panigel, Refael Meir, Rabbi, see the neighborhood of Neve Ya'akov, page 395
Panim Meirot, see the neighborhood of Kiryat Mattersdorf, page 293
Panim Meirot, see the neighborhood of Romema 'Ilit, page 456
Pann, Abel, see the neighborhood of Ramat Denya, page 419
Paran, see the neighborhood of Giv'at HaMivtar, page 205
Paran, see the neighborhood of Ramat Eshkol, page 422
Parnes, see the neighborhood of Har Nof, page 261
Pat, Ya'akov, see the neighborhood of Gonenim/Katamonim Bet, Gimel, Dalet, page 246
Pat, Ya'akov, see the neighborhood of Gonenim/Katamonim Hei and San Simon, page 248
Pat, Ya'akov, see the neighborhood of Gonenim/Katamonim Het, Tet, page 250
Pat, Ya'akov, see the neighborhood of Pat, page 401
Patria, see the neighborhood of Manhat/Malha, page 331

Patterson, John Henry, see the neighborhood of the German Colony, page 180
Pazner, Haim, see the neighborhood of Pisgat Zeev Mercaz, page 405
Pe-at HaShulhan, see the neighborhood of Ahva, page 91
Peduyim [Steps], see the neighborhood of Ramot Allon, page 441
Peki'in, see the neighborhood of Kerem/Beit Avraham, page 279
Pele Yo'etz, see the neighborhood of Yemin Moshe, page 515
Peleg, Shneur, see the neighborhood of Talpiot, page 493
Peretz, see the neighborhood of Geulim/Bak'a, page 188
Perl, William, see the neighborhood of Pisgat Zeev Mizrah, page 410
Petah Tikva, see the neighborhood of Romema 'Ilit, page 457
Petah Tikva, see Romema-Industrial Zone, page 458
Petahia, see the neighborhood of Nahlat Shim'on, page 376
Petayya, Yehuda, Rabbi [Lane], see the neighborhood of Sanhedria HaMurhevet, page 466
Picard, Yehuda Leo, Prof., see the neighborhood of Homat Shmuel/Har Homa, page 266
Pick, Haim Herman, see the neighborhood of Kiryat Moshe, page 299
Pierre Koenig, General, see the neighborhood of of Mekor Haim, page 343
Pierre Koenig, General, see Talpiot-Industrial Zone, page 495
Pierre Mendes-France [Square], see the neighborhood of Yemin Moshe, page 515
Pierrotti, Ermat, see the neighborhood of Morasha/Musrara, page 362
Pikud HaMercaz [Square], see the neighborhood of Morasha/Musrara, page 363
Pineles, Shmuel, see the neighborhood of Pat, page 401
Pines, Yehiel Michel, see the neighborhood of Yegiy'a Kapayim, page 511
Pines, Yehiel Michel, see the neighborhood of Zichron Moshe, page 519
Pinkas, David Zvi, see the neighborhood of Giv'at Mordechai, page 215
Pinsker, Yehuda Leib (Leon), Dr., see the neighborhood of Komemiyut/Talbieh, page 314
Pirhei Hen, see the neighborhood of Yefei Nof, page 509
Pituhei Hotam, see the neighborhood of Ma'alot Dafna/Arzei HaBira, page 317
Pituhei Hotam, see the neighborhood of Shikunei Shmuel HaNavi, page 484
Plugat HaKotel, see the Jewish Quarter, page 276
Plugat HaTankim HaYerushalmit, see the neighborhood of Pisgat Zeev Mercaz, page 406
Plugat Yehonatan [Square], see the neighborhood of Giv'at Shaul, page 233
Plumer, Herbert Charles [Square], see the neighborhood of Yemin Moshe, page 515
Pnina, see the neighborhood of Tel-Arza, page 504
Po'alei Tzedek, see Talpiot-Industrial Zone, page 495
Polanski, Shim'on Aharon, see the neighborhood of Beit Yisrael, page 150
Polotzky, Ya'akov, see the neighborhood of Gilo, page 199
Polyakov, Shoshana, see the neighborhood of Kiryat Moshe, page 299
Porath, Yisrael, Rabbi, see the neighborhood of Ramot Allon, page 441
Porush, Shlomo Zalman, Rabbi, see the neighborhood of Sha'arei Hesed, page 469

Prag, Yitzhak, Rabbi, see the neighborhood of Zichron Moshe, page 519
Prawer, Yehoshu'a, see the neighborhood of Ramot Allon, page 441
Press, Yesha'yahu, see the neighborhood of Zichron Moshe, page 519
Pri 'Amal, see the 'Atarot Industrial Zone, page 100
Pri Hadash, see the neighborhood of Batei Hornstein/Kollel Volyn, page 108
Pri Hadash, see the neighborhood of Zichron Moshe, page 519
Propes, Aharon Zvi, see the neighborhood of Ramot Allon, page 441
Pu'a (Rakovsky), see the neighborhood of Giv'at Shaul, page 233
Pumbedita, see the neighborhood of Batei Kollel Ungarin/Nahlat Zvi, page 114

Q

Qaeb bin-Zuhair, see the neighborhood of Beit Hanina, page 142

R

Rab'a el-'Adawiyeh, see the neighborhood of E-Tur, page 168
Rabbeinu Gershom, see the neighborhood of HaBucharim, page 256
Rabbeinu Politi, see the neighborhood of Arnona, page 97
Rabbeinu Politi, see the neighborhood of Talpiot, page 493
Rabbeinu Tam, see the neighborhood of Yegiy'a Kapayim, page 511
Rabbi 'Akiva ben Yosef, see Mid-Town, page 354
Rabbi Aryeh (Levin), see the neighborhood of Mazkeret Moshe, page 333
Rabbi Aryeh (Levin), see the neighborhood of Mishkenot Yisrael, page 359
Rabbi Binyamin, see the neighborhood of Beit HaKerem, page 137
Rabbi Hanina (Ben Dosa), see the neighborhood of Gonenim/Katamonim Bet, Gimel, Dalet, page 246
Rabbi Meir, see the neighborhood of Gonenim/Katamonim Aleph and Vav, page 245
Rabbi Tzadok, see the neighborhood of Gonenim/Katamonim Het, Tet, page 250
Rabin, Hizkiyahu, Rabbi, see the neighborhood of Har Nof, page 261
Rabin, Yitzhak [Boulevard], see the neighborhood of Giv'at Ram, page 221
Rabinovich, Aharon, see the neighborhood of Kiryat HaYovel, page 289
RaDa"K, see the neighborhood of Komemiyut/Talbieh, page 314
RaDa"K, see the neighborhood of Rehavia, page 451
Raful, Avraham Harari, Rabbi, see the neighborhood of Pisgat Zeev Mizrah, page 410
Rahel Imeinu, see the neighborhood of the German Colony, page 180
Rahel Imeinu, see the neighborhood of Gonen/Katamon HaYeshana, page 240
Rahel Imeinu, see the neighborhood of the Greek Colony, page 253
Rahel Yanait [Square], see the neighborhood of Giv'at Ram, page 221
Rahmilewitz, Moshe, Dr., see the neighborhood of Pisgat Zeev Mizrah, page 410
Rahvat HaSha'an, see the neighborhood of Kiryat Wolfson, page 306
Rahvat HaSha'an, see the neighborhood of Sha'arei Hesed, page 469
Raik, Haviva [Lane], see the neighborhood of Kiryat Shmuel, page 303
Rajib Nashashibi, see the neighborhood of Sheikh Jarrah, page 479
Rakah, Yosef, Prof., see the neighborhood of Giv'at Ram, page 221
RaLBa"H, see the neighborhood of Ahva, page 91

Reuven, see the neighborhood of Geulim/Bak'a, page 189
Revadim, see the neighborhood of Arnona, page 97
Revadim, see the neighborhood of Talpiot, page 493
Revivim, see the neighborhood of Ramot Allon, page 442
Rimon, Yosef Zvi, see the neighborhood of Ramat Beit HaKerem, page 417
Ringelblum, Emanuel, Dr., see the neighborhood of 'Ir Ganim Aleph, page 268
Ringelblum, Emanuel, Dr., see the neighborhood of Kiryat HaYovel, page 290
Rishon LeTzion, see the neighborhood of Romema 'Ilit, page 457
Rivka, see the neighborhood of Geulim/Bak'a, page 189
Rivka, see Talpiot-Industrial Zone, page 495
Rivlin, Eli'ezer, see Mid-Town, page 355
Rivlin, Moshe [Steps], see the neighborhood of Kiryat Shmuel, page 303
Rivlin, Ya'akov Moshe [Square], see the neighborhood of Rehavia, page 452
Rivlin, Yosef, see the neighborhood of Nahlat Shiv'a, page 379
Roeh Tzon, see the neighborhood of David's Village-Mamilla, page 162
Rogel, Shlomo [Square], see the neighborhood of Bayit VaGan, page 130
Rokah, Y. L. [Square], see the neighborhood of Romema, page 455
Rokeah, Shim'on, see the neighborhood of Beit Yisrael, page 151
Romema, see the neighborhood of Romema, page 455
Ronen, Yoram, see the neighborhood of Giv'at Massua, page 213
Root, see the neighborhood of the German Colony, page 180
Rosanes, Shlomo, see the neighborhood of the German Colony, page 180
Rosen, Moshe, Rabbi [Square], see the neighborhood of Sanhedria HaMurhevet, page 466
Rosen, Pinhas, see the neighborhood of Ramat Sharett, page 425
Rosenblatt, Yosele, see the neighborhood of Ramot Allon, page 442
Rosenheim, Ya'akov, Rabbi, see the neighborhood of Bayit VaGan, page 130
Rosenstein, Dov [Lane], see the neighborhood of Pat, page 401
Rosenthal, Avraham, see the neighborhood of Mea She'arim, page 338
Rosh Pina, see the neighborhood of Romema 'Ilit, page 457
Rotenberg, Shmuel Aryeh, see the neighborhood of Kiryat Shmuel, page 303
Rotenstreich, Nathan [Square], see the neighborhood of Komemiyut/Talbieh, page 315
Rothschild, Edmond de, see the neighborhood of Giv'at Ram, page 221
Rothschild, James Armand de, see the neighborhood of Giv'at Ram, page 222
Rubin, Mordechai Leib, Rabbi, see the neighborhood of Ramot Allon, page 442
Rubinstein, Yitzhak, Rabbi, see the neighborhood of Kiryat HaYovel, page 290
Rubovitz, Alexander, see the neighborhood of Talpiot Mizrah, page 501
Ruppin, Arthur Shim'on [Road], see the neighborhood of Giv'at Ram, page 222
Ruppin, Arthur Shim'on [Road], see the neighborhood of Kiryat Wolfson, page 306

S

Sa'adia Gaon, see the neighborhood of Rehavia, page 452
Sa'adiya, see the Moslem Quarter, page 367

Sa'adon, Baruch [Square], see the neighborhood of Gonenim/Katamonim Bet, Gimel, Dalet, page 246
Sacher, Harry [Park], see the neighborhood of Giv'at Ram, page 222
Sachs, Moshe, Rabbi, see the neighborhood of Nahlat Shim'on, page 377
Sacks, Aryeh [Square], see the neighborhood of Giv'at HaVradim/Shikun Rassco, page 210
Sadan, Dov, see the neighborhood of Pisgat Zeev Mizrah, page 410
Salakh a-Din, see the neighborhood of Bab e-Zahara, page 104
Salant, Binyamin Beinush [Lane], see the neighborhood of Nahlat Shiv'a, page 379
Salant, Shmuel, Rabbi, see the neighborhood of Mea She'arim, page 338
Salman, Eliyahu, Rabbi, see the neighborhood of Zichron Ya'akov, page 521
Salman, Eliyahu, Rabbi, see the neighborhood of Zichron Yosef, page 523
Salmi el-Farsi, see the neighborhood of E-Tur, page 169
Salomon, Yoel Moshe, see the neighborhood of Nahlat Shiv'a, page 380
Samuel, Herbert, see Mid-Town, page 355
San Martin, Jose de, see the neighborhood of Gonenim/Katamonim Het, Tet, page 250
San Salvador [Square], see the neighborhood of Giv'at Massua, page 213
Sar Shalom [Steps], see the neighborhood of Kiryat Moshe, page 299
Saraf [Lane], see the neighborhood of Gilo, page 199
Sarei Yisrael, see the neighborhood of Mekor Baruch, page 341
Sarei Yisrael, see the neighborhood of Romema, page 455
Sarna, Yehezkel, Rabbi, see the neighborhood of Giv'at Mordechai, page 215
Sayeret Duchifat [Boulevard], see the neighborhood of Pisgat Zeev Mercaz, page 406
Sayeret Egoz [Square], see the neighborhood of Pisgat Zeev Mercaz, page 406
Sayeret Golani, see the neighborhood of Pisgat Zeev Mercaz, page 406
Sayeret Haruv [Square], see the neighborhood of Pisgat Zeev Mercaz, page 406
Sayeret Shaked [Square], see the neighborhood of Pisgat Zeev Mercaz, page 406
Schaulsohn, Shmuel A., Rabbi, see the neighborhood of Har Nof, page 261
Schechtman, Yosef, see the neighborhood of Ramot Allon, page 442
Schick, Conrad, see the neighborhood of Bab e-Zahara, page 104
Schiff, Avraham, Rabbi, see the neighborhood of Ramot Allon, page 442
Schiller, Shlomo, see the neighborhood of Beit HaKerem, page 137
Schlein, Shmuel, see the neighborhood of Beit HaKerem, page 137
Schmorak, Ephraim, Dr., see the neighborhood of Kiryat HaYovel, page 290
Schnirer, Sarah, see the neighborhood of Kiryat Belz, page 284
Schocken, Salman Shlomo, see the neighborhood of Mount Scopus, page 370
Schoenberger, Yosef, see the neighborhood of Ramot Allon, page 442
Schorr, Moshe, see the neighborhood of Ramot Allon, page 442
Schreiber, Yisrael, Rabbi, see the neighborhood of Ramot Allon, page 443
Schwartz, Armon [Square], see the neighborhood of Giv'at HaVradim/Shikun Rassco, page 210

Schwartz, Yehosef, Rabbi, see the neighborhood of Batei Kollel Horodna/ Damesek Eliezer, page 109
Schwartz, Yehosef, Rabbi, see the neighborhood of Mahane Yehuda, page 324
Schwartz, Yehosef, Rabbi, see the neighborhood of Sha'arei Shalom, page 474
Schwarzbard, Shalom, see the neighborhood of Pisgat Zeev Mercaz, page 406
Sdei HeMe"D, see the neighborhood of Ahva, page 91
Sderot Bloomfield, see the neighborhood of Yemin Moshe, page 515
Sderot HaMuzeonim, see the neighborhood of Giv'at Ram, page 222
Sderot HaUma, see the neighborhood of Giv'at Ram, page 222
Sderot HaUniversita, see the neighborhood of Giv'at Shapira/French Hill, page 227
Sderot HaUniversita, see the neighborhood of Mount Scopus, page 370
Sderot HaUniversita, see the neighborhood of Sheikh Jarrah, page 479
Segal, Moshe, Rabbi, see the Jewish Quarter, page 276
Segal, Moshe Zvi, Prof., see the neighborhood of Ramot Allon, page 443
Segulat Yisrael, see the neighborhood of Pisgat Zeev Mizrah, page 411
Selim Benin Lane, see the neighborhood of Giv'at HaVradim/Shikun Rassco, page 210
Selma Lagerloff [Steps], see the neighborhood of Giv'at HaVradim/Shikun Rassco, page 210
Semadar, see the neighborhood of Yefei Nof, page 509
Sereni, Enzo Haim, see the neighborhood of Kiryat HaYovel, page 290
Sfat Emet, see the neighborhood of Batei Kollel Horodna/Damesek Eliezer, page 109
Sfat Emet, see the neighborhood of Mahane Yehuda, page 324
Sfat Emet, see the neighborhood of Ruhama, page 460
Sfat Emet, see the neighborhood of Sha'arei Shalom, page 474
Sfinat Mefkure [Square], see the neighborhood of Ramot Allon, page 443
Shaag, Avraham Haim, Rabbi, see the neighborhood of Bayit VaGan, page 130
Sha'ar HaBarzel, see the Moslem Quarter, page 367
Sha'arei Hesed, see the neighborhood of Sha'arei Hesed, page 469
Sha'arei Mishpat, see the neighborhood of Giv'at Ram, page 222
Sha'arei Moshe, see the neighborhood of Batei Wittenberg/Sha'arei Moshe, page 124
Sha'arei Pina, see the neighborhood of Sha'arei Pina, page 471
Sha'arei Shamayim, see the neighborhood of Batei Milner/Agudat Shlomo, page 118
Sha'arei Shamayim, see the neighborhood of Beit Yisrael, page 151
Sha'arei Torah, see the neighborhood of Bayit VaGan, page 130
Sha'arei Tzedek, see the neighborhood of Mahane Yehuda, page 324
Sha'arei Tzedek, see the neighborhood of Sha'arei Tzedek, page 475
Sha'arei Yerushalayim, see the neighborhood of Kiryat Mattersdorf, page 293
Sha'arei Yerushalayim, see the neighborhood of Romema, page 455
Sha'arei Yerushalayim, see the neighborhood of Romema 'Ilit, page 457
Shabazi, Shalom ben Yosef, Rabbi, see the neighborhood of Nahlat Ahim/ Nahlaot, page 374

Shabazi, Shalom ben Yosef, Rabbi, see the neighborhood of Zichron Ahim, page 516
Shabtai, Hizkiyahu, Rabbi, see the neighborhood of Ramot Allon, page 443
Shadad (bin Awis), see the Moslem Quarter, page 367
SHaDa"L, see the neighborhood of Mahane Yehuda, page 324
Shadiker, Nahum, Rabbi, see the neighborhood of Neve Ya'akov, page 395
Shadmi, Nahum, see the neighborhood of Talpiot, page 493
SHaHa"L, see the neighborhood of Giv'at Mordechai, page 215
Shaham, Meir, see Mid-Town, page 355
Shahar, Haim Dov, see the neighborhood of Beit HaKerem, page 137
Shahor, Binyamin [Square], see the neighborhood of Ramot Allon, page 443
Shahrai, Alter Ya'akov, see the neighborhood of Bayit VaGan, page 130
SHa"I, see the neighborhood of Ramot Allon, page 443
Shaki, Ino, Prof., see the neighborhood of Ramat Sharett, page 425
Shalem, Natan, see the neighborhood of Beit HaKerem, page 137
Shalev, Yitzhak, see the neighborhood of Giv'at Massua, page 213
Shalom 'Aleichem, see the neighborhood of Komemiyut/Talbieh, page 315
Shalom VeTzedek, see the neighborhood of Pisgat Zeev Ma'arav, page 413
Shalom Yehuda, Avraham, see the neighborhood of Talpiot, page 493
Shalom Zohar [Square], see the neighborhood of Bayit VaGan, page 130
Shalom, Binyamin [Lane], see the neighborhood of Pisgat Zeev Mizrah, page 411
Shama'a, Eliyahu Yosef, see the neighborhood of David's Village-Mamilla, page 162
Shama'a, Eliyahu Yosef, see Mid-Town, page 355
Shamai, see Mid-Town, page 355
Shamai, see the neighborhood of Nahlat Shiv'a, page 380
Shamgar (ben 'Anat), see the neighborhood of Kiryat Belz, page 284
Shamgar (ben 'Anat), see Romema-Industrial Zone, page 458
Shami, Yitzhak, see the neighborhood of Nayot, page 388
Shamir, see the neighborhood of Gilo, page 199
Shams e-Din Asyuti, see the neighborhood of Wadi el-Joz, page 507
Shapira, Zvi Herman, see the neighborhood of Kiryat HaYovel, page 290
Sharabani, Yehoshu'a, Rabbi, see the neighborhood of Ramat Shlomo/Rechess Shu'afat, page 430
Shar'abi, Shlomo, Rabbi, see the neighborhood of Ahva, page 91
Sharef, Zeev, see the neighborhood of Pisgat Zeev Mizrah, page 411
Sharett, Moshe [Boulevard], see the neighborhood of Ramat Denya, page 419
Sharett, Moshe [Boulevard], see the neighborhood of Ramat Sharett, page 426
Shari, Reuven, see the neighborhood of Ramot Allon, page 443
Sharon, Avraham, see the neighborhood of Kiryat HaYovel, page 290
Shatner, Mordechai, see the Giv'at Shaul Industrial Zone, page 234
Shatz, Boris, see Mid-Town, page 356
Shaul HaMelech, see the neighborhood of Sanhedria, page 464
Shauli, Moshe Cohen, Rabbi, see the neighborhood of Neve Ya'akov, page 395
Shayeret Har HaTzofim [Boulevard], see the neighborhood of Mount Scopus, page 370

Shazar, Shneur Zalman [Boulevard], see the neighborhood of Giv'at Ram, page 222
Shazar, Shneur Zalman [Boulevard], see the neighborhood of Mahane Yehuda, page 325
Shazar, Shneur Zalman [Boulevard], see the neighborhood of Romema, page 455
Shealtiel, Aluf David, see the neighborhood of Giv'at Ram, page 223
Shear Yashuv, see the neighborhood of Ramot Allon, page 444
Sheetrit, Shalom Shmuel [Square], see the neighborhood of Giv'at Ram, page 223
Shefa' Haim, see the neighborhood of Kiryat Zanz, page 307
Sheikh 'Anbar, see the neighborhood of E-Tur, page 169
Sheikh Hasan, see the Moslem Quarter, page 367
Sheikh Jarrah, see the neighborhood of Sheikh Jarrah, page 479
Sheikh Lulu, see the Moslem Quarter, page 367
Sheikh Mahmud, see the neighborhood of Beit Safafa, page 145
Sheikh Rihan, see the Moslem Quarter, page 367
Shejrat a-Dur, see the neighborhood of Beit Hanina, page 142
Shem MiShim'on [Square], see the neighborhood of Ramot Allon, page 444
Shema'ya, see the neighborhood of Geulim/Bak'a, page 189
Shenhar, Yitzhak [Steps], see the neighborhood of Giv'at HaVradim/Shikun Rassco, page 210
Sheshet HaYamim, see the neighborhood of Giv'at HaMivtar, page 205
Sheskin, Ya'akov, see the neighborhood of the German Colony, page 181
Shevet Tzedek, see the neighborhood of Shevet Tzedek/Shchunat HaPahim, page 481
Shevo, see the neighborhood of Gilo, page 199
Shfar'am, see the neighborhood of Nahlat Ahim/Nahlaot, page 374
Shifra, see the neighborhood of Kiryat Moshe, page 299
Shilo, see the neighborhood of Nahlat Tzion, page 384
Shilo, Yigael, see the neighborhood of Giv'at Ram, page 223
Shim'on, see the neighborhood of Geulim/Bak'a, page 189
Shim'on HaMacabi, see the neighborhood of Mekor Baruch, page 341
Shim'on HaTzadik, see the neighborhood of Kiryat Aryeh, page 282
Shim'on HaTzadik, see the neighborhood of Ma'alot Dafna/Arzei HaBira, page 317
Shim'on HaTzadik, see the neighborhood of Nahlat Shim'on, page 377
Shim'oni, David, see the neighborhood of Giv'at HaVradim/Shikun Rassco, page 210
Shimron, Erwin Shaul [Square], see the neighborhood of Kiryat Shmuel, page 303
Shimshon, see the neighborhood of Geulim/Bak'a, page 189
Shimshon Refael (Hirsch), Rabbi [Square], see the neighborhood of Bayit VaGan, page 130
Shir LiShlomo, see the neighborhood of Ramat Denya, page 420
Shirat HaYam, see the neighborhood of Ramot Allon, page 444

Shvil HaHoma, see the neighborhood of 'Ein Kerem, page 166
Shvil HaShibolim, see the neighborhood of 'Ein Kerem, page 166
Shvil HaTzofit, see the neighborhood of 'Ein Kerem, page 167
Shvil HaTzukim, see the neighborhood of 'Ein Kerem, page 167
Shvil Tzukei HaYeshu'a, see the neighborhood of 'Ein Kerem, page 167
Shvut, see the Jewish Quarter, page 276
Silberg, Moshe, Prof., see the neighborhood of Ramat Denya, page 420
Silberg, Moshe, Prof., see the neighborhood of Ramat Sharett, page 426
Silman, Kaddish [Steps], see the neighborhood of Beit HaKerem, page 138
Silver, Abba Hillel, see the neighborhood of Ramot Allon, page 444
Siman Tov, Ya'akov, see the neighborhood of Ramat Beit HaKerem, page 417
Simhat HaCohen [Square], see the neighborhood of Bayit VaGan, page 130
Simon, Leo Aryeh [Road], see the neighborhood of Giv'at Ram, page 223
Simtat Ha'Atalef, see the neighborhood of 'Ein Kerem, page 167
Simtat HaBe-er, see the neighborhood of 'Ein Kerem, page 167
Simtat HaGiv'a, see the neighborhood of 'Ein Kerem, page 167
Simtat HaKashatot, see the neighborhood of 'Ein Kerem, page 167
Simtat Ha'Orev, see the neighborhood of 'Ein Kerem, page 167
Simtat HaTzaftzafa, see the neighborhood of 'Ein Kerem, page 167
Simtat HaYayin, see the neighborhood of 'Ein Kerem, page 167
Simtat Jimmy, see the neighborhood of the German Colony, page 181
Sirkis, Daniel, Rabbi, see the neighborhood of Kiryat Moshe, page 300
Siton, David [Square], see the neighborhood of Kiryat Shmuel, page 303
Siton, David [Square], see the neighborhood of Rehavia, page 452
Sivan, Shalom, see the neighborhood of Ramot Allon, page 444
Slonim, 'Azriel Zelig, Rabbi [Square], see the neighborhood of Shikun HaBa"D, page 482
Slonim, Yehuda Leib, Rabbi [Square], see the neighborhood of Har Nof, page 262
Smith, George Adam, see the neighborhood of Giv'at Shapira/French Hill, page 227
Smolenskin, Peretz, see the neighborhood of Komemiyut/Talbieh, page 315
Smuts, Jan (Yohanan), see the neighborhood of the German Colony, page 181
Sneh, Moshe, Dr., see the neighborhood of Neve Ya'akov, page 395
Snunit, see the neighborhood of Gilo, page 199
Sokolow, Nahum, see the neighborhood of Komemiyut/Talbieh, page 315
Soloveitchik, Yitzhak Zeev HaLevi, Rabbi, see the neighborhood of Zichron Moshe, page 519
Somech, 'Ovadia, Rabbi, see the neighborhood of Nahlat Tzion, page 385
Sonnenfeld, Yosef Haim, Rabbi, see the neighborhood of Batei Milner/Agudat Shlomo, page 118
Sonnenfeld, Yosef Haim, Rabbi, see the neighborhood of Beit Yisrael, page 151
Sorotzkin, Zalman, Rabbi, see the neighborhood of Kiryat Belz, page 284
Sorotzkin, Zalman, Rabbi, see the neighborhood of Kiryat Mattersdorf, page 293
Sorotzkin, Zalman, Rabbi, see the neighborhood of Kiryat Zanz, page 308

Spiegel, Sam [Alley], see Talpiot-Industrial Zone, page 495
Spitzer, Shmuel Zangwill, Rabbi, see the neighborhood of Batei Kollel Ungarin/ Nahlat Zvi, page 114
St. Dimitrios, see the Christian Quarter, page 156
St. Francis, see the Christian Quarter, page 156
St. George, see the neighborhood of Bab e-Zahara, page 104
St. George, see the Christian Quarter, page 156
St. Helena, see the Christian Quarter, page 156
St. James, see the Armenian Quarter, page 95
St. Mark, see the Armenian Quarter, page 95
St. Peter, see the Christian Quarter, page 157
Stern, Avraham (Yair), see the neighborhood of Kiryat HaYovel, page 290
Stern, Menahem [Square], see the neighborhood of Kiryat Shmuel, page 303
Stoyanovsky, Rivka, see Mid-Town, page 356
Straus, Nathan, see the neighborhood of Batei Kollel Warsaw/Nahlat Ya'akov, page 116
Straus, Nathan, see the neighborhood of Batei Wittenberg/Sha'arei Moshe, page 124
Straus, Nathan, see the neighborhood of Bnei Moshe/Neve Shalom, page 152
Straus, Nathan, see the neighborhood of Even Yehoshu'a, page 171
Straus, Nathan, see Mid-Town, page 356
Straus, Shmuel [Square], see the neighborhood of Morasha/Musrara, page 363
Struck, Hermann, see the neighborhood of Ramot Allon, page 444
Sukenik, Eli'ezer Lipa, see the neighborhood of Kiryat Aryeh, page 282
Sukkat Shalom, see the neighborhood of Sukkat Shalom, page 488
Sulam Ya'akov, see the neighborhood of Ramot Allon, page 444
Sultan Kotoz, see the neighborhood of Beit Hanina, page 142
Sultan Suleiman, see the neighborhood of Bab e-Zahara, page 104
Sultan Suleiman, see the Moslem Quarter, page 367
Szenes, Hannah, see the neighborhood of Kiryat HaYovel, page 290
Szold, Henrietta, see the neighborhood of Kiryat HaYovel, page 291
Szold, Henrietta, see the neighborhood of Kiryat Menahem, page 294

T

Tabenkin, Yitzhak, see the neighborhood of Neve Ya'akov, page 395
Tabi, see the neighborhood of Gonenim/Katamonim Aleph and Vav, page 245
Tadesky, Gad (Guido), see the neighborhood of Talpiot Mizrah, page 501
Taha Hussein, see the neighborhood of Beit Hanina, page 142
Tahkemoni, see the neighborhood of Kerem/Beit Avraham, page 279
Tahkemoni, see the neighborhood of Mekor Baruch, page 341
Tahon, Ya'akov, see the neighborhood of Kiryat HaYovel, page 291
Tajer, Shlomo uMoshe, see the neighborhood of Pisgat Zeev Mizrah, page 411
Talmudi, Avraham, see the neighborhood of HaBucharim, page 257
Tamir, Shmuel (Katznelson), see the neighborhood of Pisgat Zeev Ma'arav, page 413

Tamuz, Yitzhak HaCohen, Rabbi [Square], see the neighborhood of Nahlat Ahim/Nahlaot, page 374
Tanhuma, see the neighborhood of Gonenim/Katamonim Bet, Gimel, Dalet, page 246
Tanne, David [Square], see the neighborhood of Giv'at HaMivtar, page 205
Tanne, David [Square], see the neighborhood of Ramat Eshkol, page 423
Tarfon, Rabbi, see the neighborhood of Gonenim/Katamonim Hei and San Simon, page 248
TaRMa"V (1882), see the neighborhood of Nahlat Zvi/Shchunat HaTeimanim, page 386
TaRMa"V (1882), see the neighborhood of Sha'arei Pina, page 471
Tarshish, see the neighborhood of Gilo, page 199
TaSHBe"TZ, see the neighborhood of Mekor Baruch, page 341
TaSHBe"TZ, see the neighborhood of Sha'arei Yerushalayim, page 477
Tavin, Eli, see the neighborhood of Pisgat Zeev Darom, page 415
Tavor, see the neighborhood of Batei Broyde/Ohalei Ya'akov, page 106
Tavor, see the neighborhood of Batei Rand, page 121
Tavor, see the neighborhood of Knesset Yisrael, page 309
Tavor, see the neighborhood of Mazkeret Moshe, page 334
Tavor, see the neighborhood of Ohel Moshe, page 398
Tchernichovsky, Shaul, see the neighborhood of Giv'at HaVradim/Shikun Rassco, page 211
Tchernichovsky, Shaul, see the neighborhood of Kiryat Shmuel, page 303
Tchorz, Catriel, see the neighborhood of Ramat Beit HaKerem, page 417
Techeilet Mordechai, see Romema-Industrial Zone, page 458
Teima, see the neighborhood of Sha'arei Pina, page 471
Teko'a, see the neighborhood of Nahlat Tzion, page 385
Tel Hai, see the neighborhood of Gonen/Katamon HaYeshana, page 240
Temkin, Mordechai, see the neighborhood of Giv'at Oranim, page 217
Thelma, see the neighborhood of Ramat Beit HaKerem, page 418
The Mosque, see the neighborhood of E-Tur, page 169
Tiberias, see the neighborhood of Nahlat Ahim/Nahlaot, page 374
Ticho, Avraham, Dr. [Lane], see the neighborhood of Beit David/Beit HaRav Kook, page 133
Ticho, Avraham, Dr. [Lane], see Mid-Town, page 356
Tidhar, David, see the neighborhood of Ma'alot Dafna/Arzei HaBira, page 317
Tiferet Yerushalayim [Square], see the Jewish Quarter, page 276
Tiferet Yisrael, see the Jewish Quarter, page 277
Tiltan, see the neighborhood of Ramat Sharett, page 426
Timna', see the neighborhood of Ramat Eshkol, page 423
Tirosh, see the neighborhood of Gilo, page 199
Tirtza, see the neighborhood of Yefei Nof, page 509
Tlalim, see the neighborhood of Ramot Allon, page 444
Tobler, see the neighborhood of Bab e-Zahara, page 104
Toledano, Refael Baruch, Rabbi, see the neighborhood of Ramat Shlomo/ Rechess Shu'afat, page 430

Topaz, see the neighborhood of Gilo, page 200
Torah MiTzion, see the neighborhood of Romema, page 455
Torah Va'Avoda, see the neighborhood of Bayit VaGan, page 130
Torah Va'Avoda, see the neighborhood of Kiryat HaYovel, page 291
Torat Haim, see the neighborhood of Bayit VaGan, page 131
Torat Hesed, see the neighborhood of Kiryat Belz, page 284
Toren, Haim, see the neighborhood of Pisgat Zeev Mizrah, page 411
Tosefot Yom Tov, see the neighborhood of Giv'at Shaul, page 233
Totzeret, see 'Atarot-Industrial Zone, page 100
Touro, Yehuda, see the neighborhood of Yemin Moshe, page 515
Tov, Moshe Aharon, see the neighborhood of Ramat Beit HaKerem, page 418
Tovia ben Moshe HaCohen, see the neighborhood of Gonenim/Katamonim Bet, Gimel, Dalet, page 247
Truman, Harry, see the neighborhood of Ramot Allon, page 444
Trumpeldor, Yosef, see Mid-Town, page 356
Tschlenow, Yehiel, Dr., see the neighborhood of Kiryat HaYovel, page 291
Tunik, Yitzhak, see the neighborhood of Pisgat Zeev Mizrah, page 411
Tur-Sinai, Naphtali Herz (Torczyner), see the neighborhood of Kiryat HaYovel, page 291
Tusiya Cohen, Shlomo, see the neighborhood of Ramat Beit HaKerem, page 418
Tuval, see the neighborhood of Romema, page 455
Tzafririm, see the neighborhood of Ramot Allon, page 445
Tzalmona, see the neighborhood of Ramat Eshkol, page 423
Tzeelim, see the neighborhood of Gilo, page 200
Tzefania (ben Cushi ben Gedalia), see the neighborhood of Geula, page 184
Tzefania (ben Cushi ben Gedalia), see the neighborhood of Kerem Avraham, page 281
Tzemah, Shlomo, see the neighborhood of Yefei Nof, page 509
Tzeret, see the neighborhood of of Mekor Haim, page 343
Tzfat, see the neighborhood of Nahlat Ahim/Nahlaot, page 374
Tzidkiyahu, see the neighborhood of Geulim/Bak'a, page 189
Tzimuki, Aryeh [Square], see Mid-Town, page 357
Tzipora, see the neighborhood of Geulim/Bak'a, page 189
Tzipori, see the neighborhood of Nahlat Ahim/Nahlaot, page 375
Tzo'ar, see the neighborhood of Nahlat Tzion, page 385
Tzruya, see the neighborhood of Giv'at Hanania/Abu Tor, page 208
Tzur, Ya'akov, see the neighborhood of Giv'at Massua, page 213
Tzvia VeYitzhak, see the neighborhood of Gilo, page 200

U

'Ukba bin Nefa, see the neighborhood of Beit Hanina, page 142
Ulitzur, Avraham, see the neighborhood of Talpiot, page 493
Ulshan, Yitzhak, see the neighborhood of Ramot Allon, page 445
Um el-Samad, see the neighborhood of Shu'afat, page 487
Umru el-Qeis, see the neighborhood of Wadi el-Joz, page 507
Unterman, Isser Yehuda, Rabbi, see the neighborhood of Gilo, page 200

Upper Volta, see the neighborhood of Kiryat HaYovel, page 291
Uriel Tzimmer, see the neighborhood of Sanhedria, page 464
Uruguay, see the neighborhood of Kiryat HaYovel, page 291
Usha, see the neighborhood of Nahlat Ahim/Nahlaot, page 375
Ussishkin, Menahem Mendel, see the neighborhood of Nahlat Ahim/Nahlaot, page 375
Ussishkin, Menahem Mendel, see the neighborhood of Rehavia, page 452
Ussishkin, Menahem Mendel, see the neighborhood of Sha'arei Hesed, page 470
Ussishkin, Menahem Mendel, see the neighborhood of Zichron Ahim, page 516
'Uzia, see the neighborhood of the Greek Colony, page 253
'Uziel, Ben Tzion Hai, Rabbi, see the neighborhood of Bayit VaGan, page 131

V

Va'ad Arba' HaAratzot, see the neighborhood of Ramot Allon, page 445
Valero, Haim, see the neighborhood of Batei Kollel Horodna/Damesek Eliezer, page 109
Valero, Haim, see the neighborhood of Mahane Yehuda, page 325
Valero, Haim, see the neighborhood of Ruhama, page 460
Valero, Haim, see the neighborhood of Sha'arei Shalom, page 474
Vamshe, David, Rabbi [Square], see the neighborhood of Ramat Shlomo/Rechess Shu'afat, page 430
Van Paassen, Peer, see the neighborhood of Bab e-Zahara, page 104
Vardinon, see the neighborhood of Gilo, page 200
Vashitz, Efraim, Dr., see the neighborhood of Arnona, page 98
Ventura, Moshe, see the neighborhood of Pisgat Zeev Mizrah, page 411
Via Dolorosa, see the Christian Quarter, page 157
Via Dolorosa, see the Moslem Quarter, page 367
Victor veYulius, see the neighborhood of Neve Ya'akov, page 396
Vilnay, Zeev, see the neighborhood of Giv'at Ram, page 223
Vincent, Louis, see the neighborhood of Bab e-Zahara, page 104
Vital, Haim, Rabbi, see the neighborhood of Giv'at Shaul, page 233
Vitkon, Alfred, see the neighborhood of Ramot Allon, page 445

W

Wadi 'Abdallah, see the neighborhood of E-Tur, page 169
Wadi el-Joz, see the neighborhood of Wadi el-Joz, page 507
Wadi Umm el-'Amid, see the neighborhood of Beit Hanina, page 142
Wallach, Moshe, Dr., see the neighborhood of Romema, page 455
Wallenberg, Raoul, see Mid-Town, page 357
Wallenstein, Moshe Nahum, Rabbi, see the neighborhood of Ramot Allon, page 445
Warburg, Otto, Prof., see the neighborhood of Kiryat HaYovel, page 292
Washington, George, see Mid-Town, page 357
Wasserman, Pinhas, Rabbi, see the neighborhood of Neve Ya'akov, page 396
Wedgwood, Josiah Clement, see the neighborhood of the German Colony, page 181

Weingarten, David [Square], see the neighborhood of Kiryat Moshe, page 300
Weisberg, Haim, Dr., see the neighborhood of Bayit VaGan, page 131
Weiss, Ya'akov, see the neighborhood of Talpiot Mizrah, page 501
Weitz, Yosef [Road], see the Giv'at Shaul Industrial Zone, page 234
Weizmann, Chaim, Dr. [Boulevard], see the neighborhood of Giv'at Shaul, page 233
Wiener, Asher, see the neighborhood of Talpiot Mizrah, page 501
Wiener, Shim'on Dov, Dr. [Ascent], see the neighborhood of Ramat Eshkol, page 423
Wingate, Charles Orde [Square], see the neighborhood of Komemiyut/Talbieh, page 315
Winograd, Yitzhak, Rabbi, see the neighborhood of Neve Ya'akov, page 396
Wise, Stephen Shmuel, see the neighborhood of Giv'at Ram, page 223
Wise, Stephen Shmuel, see the neighborhood of Neve Shaanan, page 391
Wissmann, Leo, see the neighborhood of Bayit VaGan, page 131
WIZO [Square], see the neighborhood of Beit HaKerem, page 1388
Wolffsohn, David, see the neighborhood of Giv'at Ram, page 223
Women's League [Road], see the neighborhood of Giv'at Ram, page 224

Y

Ya'akovi, Yitzhak and Rahel [Plaza], see the neighborhood of Beit HaKerem, page 138
Ya'akovson, Binyamin Zeev, Rabbi, see the neighborhood of Kiryat Zanz, page 308
Ya'ari, Avraham, see the neighborhood of Gilo, page 200
Ya'betz, Zeev, Rabbi, see Mid-Town, page 357
Yad Harutzim, see the Talpiot-Industrial Zone, page 495
Yad Mordechai, see the neighborhood of Gonen/Katamon HaYeshana, page 240
Yadin, Yigael, see the neighborhood of Ramat Shlomo/Rechess Shu'afat, page 430
Yadin, Yigael, see the neighborhood of Shu'afat, page 487
Yadler, Ben Tzion, Rabbi [Lane], see the neighborhood of Sanhedria HaMurhevet, page 466
Ya'el, see the neighborhood of Geulim/Bak'a, page 189
Yaffe, Shmuel, see the neighborhood of Pisgat Zeev Mizrah, page 411
Yafo, see the neighborhood of Batei Kollel Horodna/Damesek Eliezer, page 109
Yafo, see the neighborhood of Batei Sa'idoff, page 122
Yafo, see the neighborhood of Beit David/Beit HaRav Kook, page 133
Yafo, see the neighborhood of Beit Ya'akov, page 146
Yafo, see the neighborhood of Even Yisrael, page 173
Yafo, see the neighborhood of 'Ezrat Yisrael, page 175
Yafo, see the neighborhood of Mahane Yehuda, page 325
Yafo, see the neighborhood of Mekor Baruch, page 341
Yafo, see Mid-Town, page 357
Yafo, see the neighborhood of Nahlat Shiv'a, page 380
Yafo, see the neighborhood of Ohel Shlomo, page 399

Yafo, see the neighborhood of Romema, page 456
Yafo, see the neighborhood of the Russian Compound, page 462
Yafo, see the neighborhood of Sha'arei Tzedek, page 475
Yafo, see the neighborhood of Sha'arei Yerushalayim, page 477
Yahadut Tzarfat, see the neighborhood of Nahlat Shiv'a, page 380
Yahalom, see the neighborhood of Gilo, page 200
Yahil, Haim, see the neighborhood of Gonenim/Katamonim Hei and San Simon, page 249
Yair (HaGil'adi), see the neighborhood of Geulim/Bak'a, page 190
Yakim, see the neighborhood of Nahlat Shim'on, page 377
Yakinton, see the neighborhood of Gilo, page 200
Yallon, Hanoch, see Mid-Town, page 357
Yam HaMelah, see the neighborhood of Talpiot, page 493
Yam Suf, see the neighborhood of Ramat Eshkol, page 423
Yam Suf, see the neighborhood of Sanhedria, page 465
Yam Suf, see the neighborhood of Sanhedria HaMurhevet, page 466
Yannai, Alexander, see Mid-Town, page 357
Yanovsky, Daniel, see the neighborhood of Talpiot, page 493
Yanovsky, Daniel, see the neighborhood of Talpiot Mizrah, page 501
Yanovsky, Daniel, see the neighborhood of Talpiot Tzafon, page 502
Yaqut el-Hamawi, see the neighborhood of Wadi el-Joz, page 507
Yasmin [Lane], see the neighborhood of Gilo, page 201
Yassky, Haim, Dr., see the neighborhood of Mount Scopus, page 371
Yatriv, see the neighborhood of Sha'arei Pina, page 471
Yatziv, see 'Atarot-Industrial Zone, page 100
Yefei 'Einayim, see the neighborhood of David's Village-Mamilla, page 162
Yefei Nof, see the neighborhood of Yefei Nof, page 510
Yefei Rom, see the neighborhood of Gilo, page 201
Yehezkel (ben Buzi HaCohen), see the neighborhood of Geula, page 184
Yehoash, see the neighborhood of the Greek Colony, page 253
Yehoshafat, see the neighborhood of the Greek Colony, page 253
Yehoshu'a, Ya'akov, see the neighborhood of Pisgat Zeev Mercaz, page 407
Yehoyariv, see the neighborhood of Nahlat Shim'on, page 377
Yehuda, see the neighborhood of Geulim/Bak'a, page 190
Yehuda HaMacabi, see the neighborhood of Mekor Baruch, page 341
Yehuda HaNasi, Rabbi, see the neighborhood of Gonenim/Katamonim Bet, Gimel, Dalet, page 247
Yehuda HaNasi, Rabbi, see the neighborhood of Gonenim/Katamonim Hei and San Simon, page 249
Yehudei Hungaria HaGedola [Square], see the neighborhood of BateiKollel Ungarin/Nahlat Zvi, page 114
Yehudit (Montefiore), see Mid-Town, page 357
Yehudit (Montefiore), see the neighborhood of Ruhama, page 460
Yeivin, Yehoshua H., see the neighborhood of Nayot, page 388
Yellin, Avino'am, see the neighborhood of Geula, page 184

Yellin, David, see the neighborhood of Batei Kollel Horodna/Damesek Eliezer, page 110
Yellin, David, see the neighborhood of Mahane Yehuda, page 325
Yellin, David, see the neighborhood of Ruhama, page 460
Yellin, David, see the neighborhood of Sha'arei Shalom, page 474
Yellin, David, see the neighborhood of Zichron Moshe, page 519
Yellin, Yehoshu'a [Lane], see the neighborhood of Nahlat Shiv'a, page 380
Yemima, see the neighborhood of Ramat Denya, page 420
Yemin Avot, see the neighborhood of Giv'at Shaul, page 234
Yemin Avot, see the neighborhood of Kiryat Moshe, page 300
Yemin Moshe, see the neighborhood of Yemin Moshe, page 515
Yesha'yahu, see the neighborhood of Batei Hornstein/Kollel Volyn, page 108
Yesha'yahu, see the neighborhood of Zichron Moshe, page 519
Yeshu'at Ya'akov, see the neighborhood of Mea She'arim, page 338
Yetziat Eropa, see the neighborhood of Manhat/Malha, page 331
Yiftah (HaGil'adi), see the neighborhood of Geulim/Bak'a, page 190
Yigal, see the neighborhood of Ramot Allon, page 445
YiK"A [Square], see the neighborhood of Giv'at Ram, page 224
Yirmiyahu (ben Hilkiyahu HaCohen), see the neighborhood of Romema, page 456
Yirmiyahu (ben Hilkiyahu HaCohen), see Romema-Industrial Zone, page 458
Yirmiyahu (ben Hilkiyahu HaCohen), see the neighborhood of Shikun HaBa"D, page 482
Yir-on, see the neighborhood of Nahlat Ahim/Nahlaot, page 375
Yisa Bracha, see the neighborhood of HaBucharim, page 257
Yishai, see the neighborhood of Giv'at Hanania/Abu Tor, page 208
Yismah Melech, see the neighborhood of David's Village-Mamilla, page 162
Yismah 'Ovadia [Square], see the neighborhood of Bayit VaGan, page 131
Yissachar, see the neighborhood of Geulim/Bak'a, page 190
Yitaron, see 'Atarot-Industrial Zone, page 100
Yitzhak HaNadiv, see the neighborhood of Mount Scopus, page 371
Yitzhak Sade, HaAluf, see the neighborhood of Gonenim/Katamonim Het, Tet, page 250
Yitzhar, see the neighborhood of Gilo, page 201
Yitzhari, Yihya, Rabbi, see the neighborhood of Sha'arei Pina, page 471
Yizhar, 'Armoni [Lane], see the neighborhood of Nahlat Ahim/Nahlaot, page 375
Yizhar, 'Armoni [Lane], see the neighborhood of Nahlat Tzadok, page 382
Yizra'el, see the neighborhood of Batei Kollel Minsk/Beit HaLevi, page 111
Yizra'el, see the neighborhood of Batei Kollel Munkacs, page 112
Yizra'el, see the neighborhood of Knesset Yisrael, page 310
Yoav, see the neighborhood of the Greek Colony, page 253
Yocheved, see the neighborhood of Geulim/Bak'a, page 190
Yoel, see the neighborhood of HaBucharim, page 257
Yohanan HaSandlar, see the neighborhood of Ahva, page 92

Yohanan MiGush Halav, see the neighborhood of the Russian Compound, page 462
Yona (ben Amitai), see the neighborhood of Geula, page 184
Yona, Jacques Carpas, Dr. [Square], see the neighborhood of Giv'at HaVradim/Shikun Rassco, page 211
Yonatan (Yehonatan), see the neighborhood of the Greek Colony, page 253
Yoni [Square], see the neighborhood of Gonen/Katamon HaYeshana, page 240
Yoram Katz [Lane], see the neighborhood of Gonen/Katamon HaYeshana, page 240
Yordei HaSira, see the neighborhood of Gonen/Katamon HaYeshana, page 240
Yosef Haim, Rabbi, see the neighborhood of Nahlat Tzion, page 385
Yosef Nasi, Don, see the neighborhood of Mekor Baruch, page 341
Yosha', Meir, see the neighborhood of Pisgat Zeev Mizrah, page 411
Yotam, see the neighborhood of the Greek Colony, page 253
Yotvata, see the neighborhood of Ramat Eshkol, page 423
Yovav, see the neighborhood of Manhat/Malha, page 331

Z

Zamenhof, Eli'ezer, see the neighborhood of Mahane Yisrael, page 327
Zamenhof, Eli'ezer, see Mid-Town, page 358
Zangwill, Israel, see the neighborhood of Kiryat HaYovel, page 292
Zarhi, Yisrael, see the neighborhood of Ramot Allon, page 445
Zaritsky, David, Rabbi, see the neighborhood of Ramot Allon, page 445
Zayid ibn Tabet, see the neighborhood of Shu'afat, page 487
Zayit Ra'anan, see the neighborhood of Kiryat Zanz, page 308
Zecharia, see the neighborhood of Kerem Avraham, page 281
Zecharia HaRofe, see the neighborhood of Nahlat Zvi/Shchunat HaTeimanim, page 386
Zecharia HaRofe, see the neighborhood of Sha'arei Pina, page 472
Ze'ira, Rabbi, see the neighborhood of Gonenim/Katamonim Aleph and Vav, page 245
Zeitlin, see the neighborhood of Ramat Denya, page 420
Zelnick, Mordechai HaLevi [Square], see the neighborhood of Bayit VaGan, page 131
Zemora, Moshe, see the neighborhood of the Russian Compound, page 462
Zer, Mordechai, see the neighborhood of Pisgat Zeev Mizrah, page 412
Zerubavel (ben Shealtiel), see the neighborhood of Geulim/Bak'a, page 190
Zevin, Shai, Rabbi, see the neighborhood of Neve Ya'akov, page 396
Zholti, Betzalel, Rabbi, see the neighborhood of Ramat Shlomo/Rechess Shu'afat, page 431
Zichron Tuvia, see the neighborhood of Zichron Tuvia, page 520
Zichron Ya'akov, see the neighborhood of Romema 'Ilit, page 457
Zilberstein, see the neighborhood of Pisgat Zeev Mercaz, page 407
Zion Gate, see the Armenian Quarter, page 95
Zion Gate, see the Jewish Quarter, page 277
Zion Gate [Square], see the Jewish Quarter, page 277

Ziv, Yosef, see the neighborhood of Tel-Arza, page 504
Zola, Emile, see the neighborhood of the German Colony, page 181
Zondek, see the neighborhood of Ramot Allon, page 446
Zuckerman, Baruch, see the neighborhood of Neve Ya'akov, page 396
Zusman, Yoel, see the neighborhood of Giv'at Ram, page 224
Zuta, Haim Leib, see the neighborhood of Beit HaKerem, page 138
Zvulun, see the neighborhood of Geulim/Bak'a, page 190

The Neighborhoods and their Streets in Alphabetical Order

Ahva

Name and establishment:

This neighborhood, located in the center of town north of the Zichron Moshe neighborhood, was founded in 1907 by the "Brotherhood Association", one of whose goals was mutual help among its members, and from here comes the name. When it was founded, they wanted to call it "The Gates of Brotherhood", as was written in its book of regulations, "...and we named the community The Gates of Brotherhood...because this undertaking was like a large gate open wide for us...and we actually made the effort to be and to live as its sons and builders, with love and brotherhood."

Its founders, the members of the association, were young Ashkenazic Jews, who came from the old Yishuv but didn't want to be dependent on charity but rather wanted to support themselves on their own. They wanted to combine the life of Torah with labor, and they built the neighborhood not for the sake of the redemption of the land but for the sake of the redemption of man, like the neighborhood of Yegiy'a Kapayim.

The residents today belong to the ultra-Orthodox community.

Boundaries:

North – Geula and Kerem Avraham

South – Zichron Moshe and the Schneller Orphanage

East – Batei Kollel Warsaw

West – Mekor Baruch

Sites: within its boundaries or nearby is the Mahane Yehuda Market, and at the center of the neighborhood stands the *Tiferet Zvi* Yeshiva.

Streets: the streets of this neighborhood are named after scholars, religious commentators of the Second Temple period and later, and books of religious law. The main street is HaAmarkalim (the administrators), and small side streets branch off from it.

The streets are:

Alsheikh, Moshe ben Haim (1507 – 1600)
'Ezer Yoldot – HaParhi – dead end **H11**

Author of a commentary on the Torah, one of the prominent interpreters and arbiters of Jewish law in Tzfat, one of the disciples of Rabbi Yosef Karo.

Ashtori HaParhi, Rabbi (1282–1355) Sholal – Malchei Yisrael **H11**

The first of the researchers of the Land of Israel, he devoted himself to this study. His book, Button and Flower, is considered the first of the books of research on Israel.

Avramsky, Yehezkel, Rabbi (1886 – 1976) HaParhi – Meir **H11**

A genius in Torah, commentator on the Tosefta, Jewish legal authority, he was a recipient of the Israel Prize in 1955.

Ben Matityahu, Yosef (Josephus Flavius) (1st cent. BCE and CE)
Malchei Yisrael – Yafo **G11**

A Cohen, commander of the Jewish army against the Romans at the end of the Second Temple period. He is considered the greatest Jewish historian of his generation. His important works: "Antiquities of the Jews" and "The Jewish Wars" (see the neighborhoods of Kerem/Beit Avraham, Mahane Yehuda, Ruhama, Yegiy'a Kapayim, Zichron Moshe).

'Ezer Yoldot Malchei Yisrael – Alsheikh **H11**

Midwives' assistance, named in honor of the association that provides assistance to midwives and for the institution of this name that is located on this street (see the neighborhood of Batei Hornstein/Kollel Volyn).

HaAmarkalim Meir – Ben Matityahu **G-H11**

The administrators, Jewish businessmen in the Diaspora who concerned themselves with Jewish settlement of the Land of Israel and raised funds for it. They were the founders of the neighborhood of Batei Mahse in the Old City.

HaMaBI"t (1504 – 1585) Meir – HaParhi **H11**

Acronym of Rabbi **M**oshe **b**ar-**Y**osef **T**rani, one of the foremost rabbis and arbiters of religious law among Sephardic Jewry. He was rabbi of the whole community of Tzfat.

Malchei Yisrael Sarei Yisrael – Straus **G-H11**

Kings of Israel, named for the kings of Israel in the Biblical period, when Jerusalem was the capital of their kingdom (see the neighborhoods of Geula, Kerem/Beit Avraham, Kerem Avraham, and Mekor Baruch).

Meir, Ya'akov, Rabbi (1856 – 1937) Malchei Yisrael – Sholal **H11**

Chief rabbi, the "Rishon LeTzion", of the Sephardic community in Jerusalem (see the neighborhood of Yegiy'a Kapayim).

Nafha, Yitzhak, Rabbi (2nd-3rd cent. CE) Meir – RaLBa"H **H11**

One of the foremost scholars of the Mishnaic period in Israel, as well as one of the great masters of Aggada. He is buried in Meiron.

Pe-at HaShulhan 'Ezer Yoldot – HaParhi **H11**

Named for the book of this name (1830) by the Ashkenazi Rabbi Yisrael ben Shmuel of Shklov. The book is a commentary on the Shulhan 'Aruch of Rabbi Yosef Karo and deals with religious laws connected with the Land of Israel. He was one of the disciples of the Gaon of Vilna and one of the leaders of the members of Kollel Perushim (followers of the Vilna Gaon) in Tzfat and Jerusalem.

RaLBa"H (1484 – 1545) Malchei Yisrael – HaAmarkalim **H11**

Initials of **R**abbi **L**evi **b**en **H**aviv, one of the premier rabbis of Jerusalem. He defended the authority of Jerusalem's rabbis and all the Jewish communities of the Land of Israel.

Reishit Hochma Meir – Alsheikh **H11**

Named for the book of morals written by Rabbi Eliyahu ben Moshe de Vidas (1550–1588). The name of the book is taken from a Biblical verse: "The beginning of wisdom is fear of God..." (Psalms 111:10). His book is the outstanding example of moral literature.

Sdei HeMe"D Ben Matityahu – Meir **G-H11**

Named after books on the subject of religious law by Rabbi **H**aim Hizkiyahu **Med**ini (1832 – 1904), rabbi, arbiter of religious law, and spiritual leader of Hebron and chief of its rabbis.

Shar'abi, Shlomo, Rabbi (1720 – 1777) Meir – RaLBa"H **H11**

One of the foremost rabbis of Yemenite Jewry. He founded the Kabbalist *Beit El* Yeshiva in the Old City of Jerusalem and served as its head.

Sholal, Yitzhak, Rabbi (d. 1527) Meir – Pri Hadash **H11**

The last *nagid* (community head) of the Jews of Egypt and the Land of Israel under Mameluke rule. He founded yeshivot for the study of Torah and religious learning.

Yohanan HaSandlar Meir – dead end **H11**

Called the "shoemaker", a famous scholar of the Mishna, buried, according to tradition, in Meiron.

Armenian Quarter [HaRova' HaArmeni]

Name and establishment:

This neighborhood, located in the southwestern part of the Old City between the Jaffa Gate and the Zion Gate, and extending along the western and southern sides of the walled city bordering the Jewish Quarter, is named for the Armenian Christians who lived there from earlier generations until today.

The Armenian Quarter is on the site of the western part of the "Upper City" of Second Temple times, where there were public buildings, the high priest's palace and Herod's palace. The Armenians first settled in this area in the fourth century CE, in the period of Byzantine rule. Here is the residential neighborhood and center of national-religious-cultural life of the Armenian community and the seat of the Armenian Orthodox Patriarchate of Jerusalem. At the end of World War I, thousands of refugees of the Turkish slaughter of Armenians arrived in Jerusalem, and most took up residence in this quarter.

The Armenians were pioneer photographers in Jerusalem, and the printing business in the Armenian Courtyard was one of the first in Jerusalem that published books on the Land of Israel in general and on Jerusalem in particular.

Boundaries:

North – the Christian Quarter
South – Mount Zion and the Ben Hinom Valley
East – the Jewish Quarter
West – Hutzot HaYotzer (Arts & Crafts Lane) and Yemin Moshe

Sites: within its boundaries or nearby are the Tower of David and its museum. At the center of this quarter, in the large Armenian Courtyard, is their first and holiest church in this neighborhood, the Church of St. James, built in the twelfth century, a convent, a museum and the printing shop.

Streets: the neighborhood streets are named for the nearby Christian churches and monasteries, and personalities and events connected with the Christian religion.

The streets are:

Ararat St. Mark – HaMalach **I13**

The mountain on which Noah's ark rested after the flood (Genesis 8:4). This mountain rises near the current border between Turkey and Armenia, and is sacred to Armenians.

Armenian Patriarchate *[HaPatriarch HaArmeni]*
El-Khatab – Zion Gate **I13**

Named for the seat of the Armenian Patriarch and the offices of the Armenian Orthodox community located on this main street of the quarter.

Bab e-Nebi Daud the southern Old City wall **I13**

The "Gate of the Prophet David", the Arabic name for the Zion Gate, from which a road leads to the tomb of King David on Mount Zion.

Bikur Holim Ararat – dead end **I13**

Visit to the sick. This street is the location of the old Bikur Holim Hospital, founded in 1837 by followers of the Gaon of Vilna, the *Perushim*, opponents of Hasidism, in order to provide medical assistance to Jews and thereby help them avoid seeking help from the nearby British missionary hospital. The hospital opened on this site in 1855, between the Jewish and Armenian Quarters. In 1924 most of the hospital departments were moved to the New City. The building was completely evacuated during the War of Independence in 1948 due to fear of being surrounded by Arabs, and the remaining departments were transferred to Nathan Straus Street in the center of the city (see the Jewish Quarter).

David Armenian Patriarchate – HaYehudim **I13**

The street begins at the Jaffa Gate and Tower of David and continues eastward in the direction of the Temple Mount. In the Middle Ages the

Jaffa Gate was called Bab Daud, David's Gate, named for King David (see the Christian Quarter).

HaAshurim [Dir el Siran] HaBa"D – HaMalach **I13**

The Assyrians, named for the Assyrian-Syrian Orthodox monastery on this street.

HaMalach HaBa"D – Ararat – HaBa"D **I13**

The angel. From the Arabic: el-Malach (see the Jewish Quarter).

HaMaronitim Armenian Patriarchate – St. Mark **I13**

The Maronites. Named for the Maronite Christian monastery located on this street.

Hativat 'Etzioni Zion Gate – Jaffa Gate **I13-14**

'Etzion Brigade, a brigade in the Israel Defense Force that fought in the War of Independence (1948) in the center of Israel (see the Jewish Quarter).

Hativat Yerushalayim Ma'ale HaShalom – Yafo **I13-14**

Jerusalem Brigade, a brigade in the IDF, made up of Jerusalemite soldiers, which fought in the Six Day War in the hills of Jerusalem and of Hebron (see the neighborhoods of the Christian Quarter, David's Village-Mamilla, the Jewish Quarter, Yemin Moshe).

Jaffa Gate [*Sha'ar Yafo*] western side of Old City wall **I13**

One of the eight gates in the wall surrounding the Old City. The western side of this wall continues northwest from the gate to Jaffa Road [Rehov Yafo], an important thoroughfare in the New City. The gate was constructed together with the wall in 1538 by Sultan Suleiman, at the beginning of Turkish rule in the Land of Israel. In 1898, to the right of the Jaffa Gate, a section of the wall was torn down for the visit of the German Kaiser Wilhelm II, to allow him entry by automobile. Inside the gate, to the right, is the fortress called the Tower of David (see the Christian Quarter).

'Omar ibn el-Khatab (592 – 644 CE)
Jaffa Gate – Armenian Patriarchate **I13**

The second caliph in Islam. During his rule, the Arabs captured Jerusalem; he visited and held his prayers nearby. A mosque erected later on the site where he prayed is named for him, the Mosque of 'Omar – today called the Dome of the Rock (see the Christian Quarter).

'Omar ibn el-Khatab [Square] (592 – 644 CE)
plaza inside the Jaffa Gate **I13**

(See 'Omar ibn el-Khatab.)

St. James Armenian Patriarchate – Ararat **I13**

The Christian equivalent of Jacob, one of the twelve apostles (disciples) of Jesus.

St. Mark HaBa"D – David **I13**

One of the twelve apostles of Jesus and one of the four Evangelist authors of the gospels in the New Testament.

Zion Gate [*Sha'ar Tzion*] southern side of Old City wall **I13**

One of the eight gates in the wall surrounding the Old City. This gate, in the southern part of the wall, leads onto Mount Zion, hence its name. The gate was constructed during the period of Turkish rule, in 1540, one of the two gates closest to the Jewish Quarter. Arabs call this gate Bab e-Nebi Daud, the Gate of the Prophet David, due to its proximity to King David's Tomb. In earlier generations, the Arabs called this gate Bab Kharat el-Yahud – the Gate of the Jewish Quarter (see the Jewish Quarter).

Arnona

Name and establishment:

This neighborhood, situated in southern Jerusalem between Talpiot and the road to Ramat Rahel, was founded in 1931. It was named for the first child born in the neighborhood: Arnona, who was named after the Arnon stream, which flows from the mountains of Moab to the Dead Sea, all of which are visible in the distance.

Until the Six Day War, the border between Israel and Jordan passed near this neighborhood. After the war, the neighborhood underwent rapid development, and new and luxurious apartments are being built here now.

Professor M.Z. Segal, a prominent Biblical scholar who served as one of the first lecturers at the Hebrew University, lived in this neighborhood for many years.

Boundaries:
North – Talpiot
South – Kibbutz Ramat Rahel
East – Kfar 'Etzion Street
West – Derech Hevron

Sites: within its boundaries or nearby is the sculpture "Olive Tree Pillars", standing at the end of Gedud Ha'Avoda Street, east of the entrance to Kibbutz Ramat Rahel.

Streets: the streets in this neighborhood are named for the settlements in the 'Etzion Bloc, a soldier, an educator, leaders of the Zionist movement and a book.

The streets are:

Beit Ha'Arava Revadim – Korei HaDorot **H17**

A pioneering village on the banks of the Jordan River and the Dead Sea that was destroyed in the War of Independence (see the neighborhood of Talpiot).

Derech Hevron [Hebron Road]
Hativat Yerushalayim – the city of Hebron **I14-F20**

Hebron is a city south of Jerusalem where the Machpela Cave – burial place of the Biblical forefathers – is located. For seven years it was also King David's first capital city. Hebron is one of the four Jewish holy cities in the Land of Israel, along with Jerusalem, Tiberias and Tzfat. The route of Derech Hevron extends from the north from Hativat Yerushalayim, a street near Har Tzion [Mount Zion], to the neighborhoods of Giv'at Hanania/Abu Tor, Geulim/Bak'a, Talpiot Tzafon, Talpiot, Arnona, Giv'at HaMatos, Homat Shmuel/Har Homa and comes to an end further south at Bethlehem and Hebron.

Gedud Ha'Avoda Leib Yaffe – Ramat Rahel **H18**

Labor legion, a pioneering organization, named after Yosef Trumpeldor, that was established in 1920. Its purposes were work, protection and co-operative settlement of the land in the form of *kibbutzim*. Its members were founders of Kibbutz Ramat Rahel.

Kfar 'Etzion Leib Yaffe – Siegfried Moses, ends at Klausner **I17-18**

A kibbutz south of Jerusalem, in the Hebron Hills. All of the 'Etzion Bloc (four communities – Kfar 'Etzion, Massuot Yitzhak, 'Ein Tzurim and Revadim) was conquered by the enemy during the War of Independence

(1948). The Bloc was retaken by the Israel Defense Force during the Six Day War (1967). Kibbutz Kfar 'Etzion was rebuilt, and some of the residents who returned are the children of the first residents, many of whom were murdered in 1948 (see the neighborhood of Talpiot).

Korei HaDorot Revadim – Siegfried Moses, ends at 'Ein Gedi **H-I17**

Named for a book on the history of generations of rabbis, written by Rabbi David Konforti (c.1618–1690). He was one of the rabbis of Saloniki (Greece) and one of the great historians of the sages of Israel (see the neighborhood of Talpiot).

Leib Yaffe (1875 – 1948)
Gedud Ha'Avoda – Siegfried Moses, ends at Klausner **I17-H18**

A Zionist activist, the director of Keren Hayesod in Jerusalem, an author and poet. He was killed in the War of Independence (see the neighborhood of Talpiot).

Luria, Yosef, Dr. (1871 – 1938) Leib Yaffe – dead end **H18**

An educator and author, he was deeply involved in the language controversy against those German-speaking Jews who advocated using German as the language of instruction in Jewish schools in the Holy Land in the early 1900's. He served as head of the teachers union and was head of the education department of the Zionist Organization.

Massuot Yitzhak Leib Yaffe – dead end **H18**

One of the four kibbutzim of the 'Etzion Bloc in the Hebron Hills that was captured by the enemy in the War of Independence. The Bloc was retaken by the Israel Defense Force in the Six Day War, and Massuot Yitzhak was rebuilt in a new location.

Moses, Siegfried (1887 – 1974) Korei HaDorot – Kfar 'Etzion **H-I18**

One of the leaders of the Zionist movement in Germany and one of the builders of the State (see the neighborhood of Talpiot).

Rabbeinu Politi (b. 1894) Beit Ha'Arava – 'Ein Tzurim **H17**

One of the most respected members of Sephardic Jewry in the city, he was a communal leader in Jerusalem and one of its builders (see the neighborhood of Talpiot).

Revadim Kfar 'Etzion – 'Ein Tzurim **H17-18**

One of the four communities of the 'Etzion Bloc in the Hebron Hills that was captured by the enemy in the War of Independence. The Bloc was retaken by the Israel Defense Force in the Six Day War, and Revadim was rebuilt in a new location (see the neighborhood of Talpiot).

Vashitz, Efraim, Dr. (1879 – 1945) Leib Yaffe – Luria **H18**

A doctor and member of the top leadership of the Jerusalem community during the British Mandate period.

'Atarot-Industrial Zone

Name and establishment:

The 'Atarot Industrial Zone is located at the northeast edge of the city, near the 'Atarot airport and the site of what was Moshav 'Atarot, originally called Kalandia, the same as the nearby Arab village. This area was secured by the IDF in the Six Day War (1967). The meaning of the name 'Atarot is not clear, but the residents explain that the source is from the word *'atara* meaning crown, as the hills surround the moshav like a crown.

Many different manufacturing businesses are located in this industrial area. Nearby highways lead north toward the airport and the city of Ramallah, south to Jerusalem and west, by way of Beit Horon, to the coastal plain.

The land on which Moshav 'Atarot was built was bought in 1912, and among the pioneers of 'Atarot was the immigrant Levi Skolnick, that is Levi Eshkol, who later became prime minister of Israel. From that same year until the War of Independence, various groups of young people lived in the moshav. However, with the outbreak of the War of Independence, they were forced to evacuate. The airport was reactivated after the Six Day War, but fell out of use in recent years. Part of the 'Atarot airport is on the property of Moshav 'Atarot, whose residential area nearby was populated for decades before the State was established.

Boundaries:

North – Ramallah
South – Ramat Shlomo
East – Neve Ya'akov
West – Kalandia Village

Sites: within its boundaries or nearby is the ‘Atarot airport, no longer in use.

Streets: the neighborhood streets are named for various kinds of industries.

The streets are:

‘Atarot Derech Beit Horon – Mif‘alot **H1**

Named for the old moshav on this site, the former airport and the present industrial center.

Derech Beit Horon [Beit Horon Road]
Derech Ramallah – Sha‘arei Yerushalayim **H-K1**

Named for the Biblical city Beit Horon, located west of this industrial area.

Derech Ramallah [Ramallah Road]
Derech ‘Uzi Narkiss – city of Ramallah **I1-3**

The road leading to the city of Ramallah (see the neighborhoods of Beit Hanina, Dahiyet el-Barid).

Eitan Yatziv – Yatziv **H1**

Named for the book *Derech Eitan* of Rabbi Avraham Joffen (1886-1970).

HaKorchim ‘Atarot – Yatziv **H1**

Binders, to designate the occupation of binding books.

HaMa‘as Mif‘alot – dead end **H1**

Another word for working or doing.

HaMadpisim ‘Atarot – Yatziv **H1**

Named for the printers of books in Israel.

HaMovilim Yatziv – HaNehoshet **H1**

To designate the work of transporting freight.

HaNehoshet HaKorchim – Mif‘alot **H1**

Copper, one of the materials used by manufacturers.

Ha‘Oferet ‘Atarot – Yatziv **H1**

Lead, another metal used by manufacturers.

HaTamrukim ‘Atarot – HaMa‘as **H1**

Cosmetics, to indicate one of the products of the manufacturing itself.

HaYetzira 'Atarot – Mif'alot **H-I1**

Work of art, to designate one of the areas of craftsmanship.

HaYotzek Yatziv – dead end **H1**

To designate the craft of metal-casting.

HaYozma Yatziv – Pri 'Amal **H-I1**

To designate a characteristic, initiative, needed by craftsmen, among others.

Mif'alot 'Atarot – Derech Ramallah **H-I1**

Another name for manufacturing businesses.

'Otzma Mif'alot – Mif'alot **H1**

Strength, to indicate the resources needed to carry out the work.

Pri 'Amal Totzeret – dead end **H1**

The fruit of labor, referring to the resulting products of work.

Totzeret 'Atarot – dead end **H-I1**

Product, referring to the material produced from labor.

Yatziv HaYotzek – dead end **H1**

To indicate the quality of stability or steadiness needed in carrying out various crafts.

Yitaron HaYozma – Totzeret **H1**

Gain, to indicate the benefit of doing work.

Bab e-Zahara

Name and establishment:

This large neighborhood, in the eastern part of Jerusalem, extends from the American Colony, a cluster of buildings that is today part of the neighborhood of Bab e-Zahara, to Herod's Gate, also called the Flower Gate, and it is from here that it takes its name: "Gate of Flowers". Nearly all of the residents are Muslim. This is one of the first Arab neighborhoods built outside of the walls of the Old City in the nineteenth century.

In the beginning of the eighteenth century, a renowned Muslim in Jerusalem, the Mufti Muhammed Alhalili, built a unique house outside the northern wall called Kes Alhalili, which stands today in the courtyard of the Rockefeller Museum, in an area called Karm e-Sheikh, over which the Muslim neighborhood of Bab e-Zahara extends today.

Boundaries:
North – the American Colony, Sheikh Jarrah
South – the Old City
East – Wadi el-Joz
West – Beit Yisrael

Sites: within its boundaries or nearby are found primarily elementary and high schools, among the most important of which is the Ashdayeh High School; Orient House, built in 1897 by Ismail Bech-Alhusseini for his family, but which is used today in its splendor as an office building; an American institution, the Albright Institute for Archeological Research; the Rockefeller Garden and the adjacent Rockefeller Museum.

Streets: the neighborhood streets are named after famous Muslim personages in Islamic history. The main street is Salakh a-Din (Saladin) Street.

The streets are:

Abu Bakr e-Sadiq Ibn 'Afan – Wadi el-Joz **I-J10**

The nickname of 'Othman bin 'Abdullah, one of the friends of the Prophet Muhammed and the first Muslim caliph (a street in the American Colony).

Abu 'Ubayda (d. 638 CE) Salakh a-Din – Ibn Jubeir **I11**

Abu 'Ubayda bin 'Abdullah bin el-Jarrah, a Muslim commander and conqueror of Syria, one of the friends of the Prophet Muhammed and his companion-at-arms in war (a street in the American Colony).

'Ali ibn Abu Taleb Salakh a-Din – El-Walid **I-J11**

The fourth caliph of Islam, son-in-law of the Prophet Muhammed, the legal heir to the founder of Islam and head of the Shi'ite sect of Islam.

Baha e-Din (17th cent.) Muhammed e-Salakh – dead end **J11**

Arab author from Persia (Iran) (a street in the American Colony).

Conder (1848-1910) Nablus Road – Dalman **I11**

Claude Reignier Conder, a researcher of the Land of Israel and Jerusalem (a street in the American Colony).

Dalman (1855 – 1944) Nablus Road – E-Nabi Shu'eib **I10**

Gustav Herman Dalman, a German author and geographical researcher of the Land of Israel and the folklore of its Arab residents, he wrote books on Jerusalem (a street in the American Colony).

Derech Har HaZeitim [Mount of Olives Road]
Nablus Road – Wadi el-Joz **J10**

Named after the mountain in this location (a street in the American Colony; see the neighborhood of Sheikh Jarrah).

El-Akhtal (640 – 710 CE) Ikhwan e-Safa – Nur e-Din **J11**

An Arab Christian poet who lived in the period of the Umayyad caliphs of Damascus.

El-Asfahani (12th cent.) Salakh a-Din – Harun e-Rashid **J12**

One of the great Muslim scholars.

El-Khariri (1054 – 1122) Ibn Batuta – El-Akhtal **J11**

Abu Muhammed el-Kassem el-Khariri, a Muslim author and linguist.

El-Mas'udi (10th cent. CE) Ibn Batuta – El-Asfahani **J11-12**

One of the great Muslim travelers.

El-Muqadasi, Muhammed (10th cent. CE)
Suleiman – Wadi el-Joz **J10-12**

One of the great Muslim geographers (see the neighborhood of Wadi el-Joz).

El-Ya'aqubi (d. 897 CE) Ikhwan e-Safa – Ibn Batuta **J11**

Arab historian and geographer.

E-Nabi Shu'eib Shimon HaTsadik – Dalman **I10-11**

The prophet Jethro, Moses' father-in-law, according to Muslim and Druze tradition (a street in the American Colony).

E-Zahara Harun e-Rashid – Salakh a-Din **J11**

The second name of Fatima, the daughter of Muhammed, the founder of the Islamic faith.

Harun e-Rashid (763 – 809 CE) Nur e-Din – Suleiman **J11-12**

One of the great caliphs of the 'Abbasid dynasty of Baghdad.

Hatem e-Tawi (6th cent. CE) Ikhwan e-Safa – Baha e-Din **J11**

Arab poet.

Ibn Batuta (1304 – 1377) Ibn Khaldun – El-Khariri **J11**

Muhammed bin 'Abdullah ibn Batuta, Arab geographer and traveler, the first to tour the Muslim lands.

Ibn Jubeir (1145 – 1217) Nablus Road – Baha e-Din **I11**

Abu Lehusin Muhammed bin Ahmed ibn Jubeir, Arab geographer and traveler; the journal of his travels is famous in Arab literature (a street in the American Colony).

Ibn Khaldun (1332 – 1406) Ibn Batuta – Abu Taleb **J11**

One of the great Muslim historians.

Ibn Khukal (10th cent. CE) El-Akhtal – dead end **J11**

Muslim geographer.

Ibn Sinna (980 – 1037 CE)
Salakh a-Din – El-Asfahani **J12**

Famous Arab philosopher and doctor.

Ikhwan e-Safa El-Muqadasi – Ibn Khaldun

A group of Arab scholars and philosophers called "the faithful brothers", from the city of Basra in Iraq, in the second half of the tenth century CE.

Khalid ibn el-Walid (d. 641 CE)
El-Muqadasi – Ibn Jubeir **J11**

Muslim commander, conqueror of the Land of Israel (a street in the American Colony).

Muhammed e-Salakh Abu Taleb – Abu 'Ubayda **I-J11**

Muslim educator.

Nablus Road [Derech Shchem]
Suleiman – the city of Nablus **I12-J10**

This road leads to Nablus (Shchem in Hebrew) and on to Damascus. Biblical Shchem was a city in the hills of Samaria (Shomron) that served as a center for the Israelites in the periods of the Biblical forefathers, Joshua, the Judges and the Kingship, and later a center for the Samaritan sect (see the neighborhood of Sheikh Jarrah).

Nur e-Din Harun e-Rashid – Suleiman **J12**

An Arab commander, he conquered Egypt from the Crusaders in the twelfth century.

'Omar ibn el-'As (7th cent. CE) Salakh a-Din – Nablus Road **I11**

An Arab commander and statesman, he took part in the conquest of the Land of Israel and Syria.

'Othman ibn 'Afan (567 – 656 CE) Wadi el-Joz – Ibn Jubeir **I-J11**

Caliph 'Othman, a Syrian caliph of the Umayyad family, set the text of the Koran (a street in the American Colony).

Salakh a-Din (d. 1193) the Flower Gate and Suleiman–Nablus Road **I-J11**

Saladin, sultan of Egypt and Syria, conquered the Land of Israel from the Crusaders in the twelfth century.

Schick, Conrad (1822 – 1901) Nablus Road – dead end **I12**

A German archeologist, he was the city engineer of Jerusalem at the end of the Ottoman regime.

St. George Nablus Road – Bar Lev **I11**

Named for the school found on this street, which is named after one of the Christian saints.

Sultan Suleiman (1495 – 1566) Nablus Road – Jericho Road **J12**

Nicknamed "the Magnificent", he was one of the great Turkish sultans and the builder of the walls of Jerusalem (see the Moslem Quarter).

Tobler (1806 – 1877) Nablus Road – E-Nabi Shu'eib **I10**

Titus Tobler, doctor, linguist, archeologist and researcher of the Land of Israel, he became famous for his archeological digs in Jerusalem (a street in the American Colony).

Van Paassen, Peer (d. 1968) Nablus Road – Bar Lev **I11**

One of the Righteous Gentiles who acted to save the Jewish people, he published a book that expressed his opposition to the British and his support of the Jewish people and the State of Israel (a street in the American Colony).

Vincent, Louis (1872 – 1960) Nablus Road – dead end **I11**

French archeologist and researcher of the Bible and of the history of Jerusalem (a street in the American Colony).

Batei Broyde/Ohalei Ya'akov

Name and establishment:

The neighborhood, in the center of town south of the neighborhoods of Mazkeret Moshe and Ohel Moshe and north of Nahlat Ahim/Nahlaot, was founded in the years 1902-1903. The official name is Ohalei Ya'akov. The neighborhood and the synagogue are called by the name of the benefactor Reb Ya'akov Yosef Broyde, from the city of Warsaw, Poland. A memorial plaque in his name is affixed to the wall of the study hall here.

Reb Ya'akov Broyde was one of the Lovers of Zion and head of the Zionist society "Menuha V'Nahala" which founded the village of Rehovot. He bought from the Jerusalem Community Council half the parcel of land for the neighborhood of Knesset Yisrael, and built the neighborhood there. A block of residential housing, in the form of a courtyard, it was intended only for scholars of the non-Hasidic community, who pray in the Ashkenazic manner. In other words, they were "Mitnagdim", as opposed to the nearby neighborhood of Batei Rand, where the Hasidim lived.

The entrance to this neighborhood is from Tavor Street. The gate faces north toward Mazkeret Moshe.

Boundaries: the houses of Batei Broyde extend between HaNeTZI"V and Tavor Streets.

North – Mazkeret Moshe and Ohel Moshe

South – Betzalel Street

East – Mishkenot Yisrael and Sukkat Shalom

Northwest – Mahane Yehuda Market

Sites: within its boundaries or nearby are the *Kehillat Ya'akov* Great Study Hall and the Mahane Yehuda Market.

Streets: the neighborhood streets bear place names connected to northern Israel.

The streets are:

HaNeTZI"V (1817 – 1893) Betzalel – Tavor **G12**

Acronym of **H**aRav **N**aftali **Z**vi **Y**ehuda **B**erlin, head of the famed Volozhin Yeshiva. One of the great arbiters of religious law in his generation (see the neighborhoods of Batei Kollel Minsk/Beit HaLevi, Batei Kollel Munkacs, Batei Rand, Knesset Yisrael, Mazkeret Moshe).

Tavor Shomron – 'Ezra Refael **G12**

Mount Tabor, rising between the Galilee and the Jezreel Valley (see the neighborhoods of Batei Rand, Knesset Yisrael, Mazkeret Moshe, Ohel Moshe).

Batei Goral/Mishkenot HaTeimanim

Name and establishment:

This neighborhood, in the middle of town, in the southern part of the Mishkenot Yisrael neighborhood, was established in 1884 for the Yemenite community. The name of the neighborhood is connected to the lottery (*goral* is "lot") that was conducted from time to time among those needing housing, and according to which the homes were given to the needy.

Rabbi Dr. Marcus Adler, the son of Rabbi Nathan Adler, the chief rabbi of the Jews of England, was visiting then in the Land of Israel and became aware of the problem of the Yemenite immigrants. When he returned to England, with the help of the London Jewish community, he began to collect money to build housing. Through a committee set up in Jerusalem, he bought the land near the neighborhood of Mishkenot Yisrael and built thirteen buildings on it, twelve of which were to serve as homes and the thirteenth for a house of prayer. Later, this too became a residential building, and above it was built the Goral Synagogue, the first Yemenite synagogue in Jerusalem. On the wall of the buildings is engraved a memorial text.

Boundaries:

The buildings border Mazia Street and to the south the neighborhood of Mishkenot Yisrael.

Sites: within its boundaries or nearby are the Goral Synagogue and the Mahane Yehuda Market.

Streets: the streets of the neighborhood are named for professional men.

The streets are:

'Eliash, Mordechai (1892 – 1950) Agrippas – Ben Yehuda **H12**

A jurist, politician and Israel's first ambassador to the United Kingdom (see the neighborhood Mid-Town).

Mazia, Aharon Haim, Dr. (1858 – 1930)
'Eliash – Mesilat Yesharim **G-H12**

A doctor, linguist and writer, he contributed to the improvement of sanitation in Jerusalem and the Land of Israel. One of the founders of the Committee on the Hebrew Language and one of the first to coin medical terms in Hebrew (see the neighborhood of Mid-Town).

Mesilat Yesharim Betzalel – Agrippas **G-H12**

Named for a book of ethics by **H**a**R**av **M**oshe **H**aim **L**uzzato – HaRaMHa"L (1707–1747). A Kabbalist and poet, he was known for his literary activity. He became immersed in study of the Kabbala in his youth in Italy. To avoid the threatened excommunication by the rabbis in Italy for teaching Kabbala, he immigrated to Israel and lived in Akko (see the neighborhoods Mid-Town, Sukkat Shalom).

Mishkanot Agrippas – Mesilat Yesharim **G12**

Named for the neighborhood of Mishkenot Yisrael (see the neighborhood Mishkenot Yisrael).

Shomron Agrippas – Mesilat Yesharim **G12**

The capital city of the kingdom of Israel, a hilly region in central Israel between Jerusalem and the Jezreel Valley (see the neighborhoods Batei Rand, Mishkenot Yisrael).

Batei Hornstein/Kollel Volyn

Name and establishment:

This neighborhood, in the center of town beside Yesha'yahu Street, past the Zichron Moshe neighborhood, was established in 1905 and named after its founder, the philanthropist Rabbi David HaCohen Hornstein. The neighborhood was built as two courtyards with thirty apartments, a study hall and a bathhouse for the Kollel Volyn men in Jerusalem.

The neighborhood residents are members of the ultra-Orthodox community.

Boundaries:

North – Geula

Southwest – Zichron Moshe

East – Yesha'yahu and Straus Streets

Streets: the neighborhood is built as two courtyards.

The streets are:

Batei Hornstein Yesha'yahu – 'Ezer Yoldot **H11**

Named for the neighborhood and its founder, Rabbi David HaCohen Hornstein.

'Ezer Yoldot Malchei Yisrael – Pri Hadash **H11**

(See the neighborhood Ahva.)

Pri Hadash Yesha'yahu – Ben Matityahu **H11**

Named for a book of critiques on the Shulhan 'Aruch, by Rabbi Hizkiya da Silva (1659 – 1698), a rabbi, arbiter of Jewish law, and head of a yeshiva in Jerusalem (see the neighborhood Zichron Moshe).

Yesha'yahu Malchei Yisrael – HaNeviim **H11**

Isaiah, one of the Major Prophets of Israel. He lived in Jerusalem and prophesied the redemption of the city (see the neighborhood of Zichron Moshe).

Batei Kollel Horodna/Damesek Eli'ezer

Name and establishment:

The neighborhood, located in the middle of town bordering the Mahane Yehuda neighborhood, was founded in 1892 by Rabbi Shimon Eli'ezer Kahane as a neighborhood for Jews from the city of Horodna. The neighborhood is also named after him. The Kollel, one of the first such enclaves in Jerusalem, was constructed in the form of two rows of houses, comprising thirty-four apartments and a large and beautiful synagogue. The buildings were intended as dwellings for the men of the Kollel, in order to enable them to live there free of charge for a number of years.

Boundaries:

North – Mekor Baruch

South – Mahane Yehuda Market

East – Mea She'arim

West – Ohel Shlomo, Sha'arei Tzedek

Sites: within its boundaries or nearby is the Mahane Yehuda Market.

Streets: the streets of the neighborhood are named for respected men and civic leaders of the Sephardic community in Jerusalem.

The streets are:

Gaon, Moshe David (1889 – 1958) Yehosef Schwartz – Meyuhas **G11**

A teacher, researcher of the history of Oriental Jews, and one of the honored leaders of the Sephardic community (see the neighborhoods of Mahane Yehuda, Sha'arei Shalom).

Meyuhas, Yosef Baran (1868 – 1942) Yafo – Yellin **G11**

Teacher, writer, civic leader and researcher of Sephardic and Arabic folklore, he was one of the founders of the village of Motza and one of the heads of the Sephardic community in Jerusalem (see the neighborhoods of Mahane Yehuda, Sha'arei Shalom).

Schwartz, Yehosef, Rabbi (1805 – 1866) Yafo – Yellin **G11**

A rabbi and arbiter of religious law, he was one of the major researchers of the Land of Israel in his generation (see the neighborhoods of Mahane Yehuda, Sha'arei Shalom).

Sfat Emet Ben Matityahu – Meyuhas **G11**

Named after the book by Hasidic master Rabbi Yehuda Leib Alter (1847 – 1905), the rabbi of the Gur Hasidim (see the neighborhoods of Mahane Yehuda, Ruhama, Sha'arei Shalom).

Valero, Haim (1845 – 1923) Yafo – Ben Matityahu **G11**

Born in Jerusalem, one of the foremost bankers in the city, president of the Sephardic community in the city and a member of the city council and the consular courts (see the neighborhoods of Mahane Yehuda, Ruhama, Sha'arei Shalom).

Yafo [Jaffa] **[Road]** Jaffa Gate – Weizmann Boulevard **F11-I12**

The main thoroughfare of the city, the central street in the New City. The street leads to the city of Jaffa, the port city of Jerusalem in ancient days (see the neighborhoods of Batei Sa'idoff, Beit David/Beit HaRav Kook, Beit Ya'akov, Even Yisrael, 'Ezrat Yisrael, Mahane Yehuda, Mekor Baruch, Mid-Town, Nahlat Shiv'a, Ohel Shlomo, Romema, Russian Compound, Sha'arei Tzedek, Sha'arei Yerushalayim).

Yellin, David (1854 – 1942)
Meyuhas – Ben Matityahu and ends at Yesha'yahu **G-H11**

An educator, linguist, researcher of the poetry of the Jews of Spain, one of the founders and the head of the Hebrew Language Committee, he invented new words, following the example of his contemporary Eli'ezer ben Yehuda. He was founder and director of the Hebrew Teachers Seminary, located today in Beit HaKerem, a member of the Jerusalem town council and deputy mayor during the period of the British Mandate, and he served as chairman of the National Committee and as president of the Elected Assembly of the Jews of the Land of Israel, as well as a professor at the Hebrew University (see the neighborhoods of Mahane Yehuda, Ruhama, Sha'arei Shalom, Zichron Moshe).

Batei Kollel Minsk/Beit HaLevi

Name and establishment:

This neighborhood, located in the middle of town between the neighborhood of Knesset Yisrael Bet (see the neighborhood Knesset Yisrael) and Betzalel Street, north of Nahlat Ahim/Nahlaot, was founded in 1897 by the Kollel of emigrants from the city of Minsk. The neighborhood is also called Beit HaLevi for the Zeldowitz family from Minsk, who were Levites. Those in charge of the Kollel acquired a field near the neighborhood of Knesset Yisrael and, with the help of the Zeldowitz family, put up a neighborhood with eighteen apartments on two floors for the poor of the Kollel. The houses were built in the form of a long railroad train, and the back side of the buildings faced toward Knesset Yisrael Bet. Today, long-time residents of Jerusalem live there.

The houses of Kollel Minsk are on HaNeTZI"V Street near Betzalel Street.

Boundaries:

North – Mazkeret Moshe

South – Betzalel Street and Nahlat Ahim/Nahlaot

East – Mishkenot Yisrael and Sukkat Shalom

Northwest – Mahane Yehuda Market

Sites: within its boundaries or nearby are the Gerard Behar community center and the Mahane Yehuda Market.

Streets: the street is named for one of the great arbiters of religious law.

The streets are:

Betzalel ben Uri Ben-Zvi – Mesilat Yesharim **G12**

Of the tribe of Judah, he was one of the Biblical builders of the Tabernacle in the desert. On this street is the renowned Betzalel School of Art (see the neighborhoods of Batei Kollel Munkacs, Knesset Yisrael, Mid-Town, Nahlat Ahim/Nahlaot, Nahlat Tzion, Sha'arei Rahamim, Zichron Ahim, Zichron Ya'akov, Zichron Yosef).

HaNeTZI"V (1817 – 1893) Betzalel – Tavor **G12**

(See the neighborhoods of Batei Broyde/Ohalei Ya'akov, Batei Kollel Munkacs, Batei Rand, Knesset Yisrael, Mazkeret Moshe.)

Yizra'el Betzalel – HaNeTZI"V **G12**

Jezreel, for the winter capital of the kings of Israel in the Jezreel Valley, today the name of a kibbutz (see the neighborhoods of Batei Kollel Munkacs, Knesset Yisrael).

Batei Kollel Munkacs

Name and establishment:

The neighborhood, located in the middle of town near the neighborhoods of Knesset Yisrael and Batei Rand, next to Betzalel Street, was founded in 1928. This neighborhood, numbering about thirty dwellings, was founded as a Kollel neighborhood of Jews from the city of Munkacs, in honor of Rabbi Meir Ba'al HaNess.

Boundaries:

North – Mazkeret Moshe

South – Betzalel Street and Knesset Yisrael and Batei Rand

East – Mishkenot Yisrael and Sukkat Shalom

Northwest – Mahane Yehuda Market

Sites: within its boundaries or nearby is the Mahane Yehuda Market

Streets: the streets of the neighborhood have names connected with northern Israel.

The streets are:

Betzalel ben Uri Ben-Zvi – Mesilat Yesharim **G12**

(See the neighborhoods of Batei Kollel Minsk/Beit HaLevi, Knesset Yisrael, Mid-Town, Nahlat Ahim/Nahlaot, Nahlat Tzion, Sha'arei Rahamim, Zichron Ahim, Zichron Ya'akov, Zichron Yosef.)

HaLevanon HaNeTZI"V – Rama **G12**

The first Hebrew newspaper in the Land of Israel, which appeared in 1863 in Jerusalem. It was named "Lebanon" for the coastal mountains north of Israel. (see the neighborhoods of Knesset Yisrael, Mazkeret Moshe).

HaNeTZI"V (1817 – 1893) Betzalel – Tavor **G12**

(See the neighborhoods of Batei Broyde/Ohalei Ya'akov, Batei Kollel Minsk/Beit HaLevi, Batei Rand, Knesset Yisrael, Mazkeret Moshe.)

Yizra'el Betzalel – HaNeTZI"V **G12**

(See the neighborhoods of Batei Kollel Minsk/Beit HaLevi, Knesset Yisrael.)

Batei Kollel Ungarin/Nahlat Zvi

Name and establishment:

This neighborhood, located in the center of town north of the Mea She'arim neighborhood and facing its middle gate, was founded in 1891 by the Jews of Hungary, the "Hungarian Kollel" known by its name, Kollel *Shomrei HaHomot* (guardians of the walls, or "Neturei Karta"). The official name of the neighborhood is "Nahlat Zvi", for the verse: "...I gave you a pleasing land, a heritage desired by a multitude of nations..." (Jeremiah 3:19) and after the name of the patron who donated the money for construction of the buildings, Rabbi Yitzhak Zvi Ratzesdorfer, from the city of Antwerp in Belgium.

The main stimulus to the expansion of the neighborhood began in 1891 when the philanthropist visited his teacher, Rabbi Yosef Haim Sonnenfeld, in the Old City. He acquired a parcel of land near Mea She'arim and built apartments for the poor students of the Kollel. What is characteristic of the planning of the neighborhood is the attempt to limit the expenses of constructing the apartment block. The outside walls were connected from one apartment to the next and thus came about the long row-houses built around a central courtyard, in which there were shared synagogues and houses of study, restrooms and water cisterns.

At the heart of the neighborhood was the study hall named for the Hatam Sofer, one of the great rabbis of Hungary, who was not fortunate enough to immigrate to Israel, although he planted in his disciples' hearts the commandment of settling in the Land of Israel and sent them to make their permanent residence here starting in the 1830s. Diaspora Jews helped in the construction of the houses and their names are commemorated on memorial stones affixed above or next to the entrance doors of the apartments in the neighborhood. On the gate into the neighborhood is carved: "Kollel Shomrei HaHomot of the Rabbi Meir Ba'al HaNess Charities".

Boundaries:

North – Shomrei Emunim Street and Beit Yisrael
South – Mea She'arim
East – Batei Naitin and Shivtei Yisrael Street
West – Geula

Sites: the Hatam Sofer Yeshiva and the Ktav Sofer Yeshiva

Streets: narrow lanes. A number of the streets are named for ancient cities and Talmudical academies in Babylonia.

The streets are:

Lederer, Moshe and Esther (20th cent.)
Mea She'arim – dead end **I11**

Named after Moshe Yehuda and Esther Lederer, among the first activists on behalf of Kollel Shomrei HaHomot in Europe at the time of the Holocaust and afterwards in the United States.

Mahoza Shivtei Yisrael – dead end **I11**

A city in Babylonia on the bank of the Tigris River. One of the centers of the Talmudical academies in Babylonia, along with Sura and Pumbedita.

Mea She'arim Straus – Shivtei Yisrael **H11**

Named for that neighborhood, it is the main street of the Mea She'arim neighborhood (see the neighborhoods of Batei Kollel Warsaw/Nahlat Ya'akov, Batei Naitin, Batei Perlman/'Ir Shalom, Beit Yisrael, Geula, Mea She'arim, Nahlat Zvi/Shchunat HaTeimanim, Sha'arei Pina).

Netzivin Mea She'arim – dead end **I11**

An ancient city on the bank of the Euphrates River in Babylonia.

Otzar HaSfarim Shivtei Yisrael – Netzivin **I11**

A bibliographical book by Yitzhak ben Ya'akov (1801 – 1863) that contains lists of thousands of books and periodicals that were printed up until 1863, including descriptions and contents.

Pumbedita Ktav Sofer Yeshiva – Spitzer **I11**

A city in Babylonia on the bank of the Euphrates River. One of the centers of the Talmudical academies in Babylonia, along with the academy at Sura. A community and spiritual center for the Babylonian Jews.

Shivtei Yisrael TZaHa"L Square – Pikud HaMerkaz Square – Shmuel HaNavi **I12**

Named for the twelve tribes of Israel (see the neighborhoods of Mea She'arim, Morasha/Musrara, Russian Compound).

Shomrei Emunim [keepers of the faith] Sonnenfeld – Shivtei Yisrael **I11**

Named for a book on Hasidism by the Hasidic master Rabbi Aharon Roth, known as Rav Ahrele (1894 – 1944). He started a Hasidic dynasty that fought against modernizations in religion. In his later years he lived and was active in the Land of Israel, especially Jerusalem.

Spitzer, Shmuel Zangwill, Rabbi (d. 1958) Mea She'arim – Shomrei Emunim **I11**

A civic leader among the ultra-Orthodox community in Jerusalem. Head of Kollel Ungarin.

Yehudei Hungaria HaGedola [Square] the plaza facing the Ktav Sofer Yeshiva **I11**

Named for the Hungarian Jews, the "Hungarian Kollel", who were the first residents in the neighborhood.

Batei Kollel Warsaw/Nahlat Ya'akov

Name and establishment:

The neighborhood, located in the middle of town west of Mea She'arim, was established in 1898 and named for the builders of the Warsaw Kollel who contributed money for the building. The neighborhood is also called "Nahlat Ya'akov" after the philanthropist Reb Ya'akov Shraga Tzenwurzel from Poland, who with his own money bought the parcel of land on which were built about forty apartments for the poor of the Kollel and two houses of study: Ohel Shmuel for the Hasidim and Ohel Yitzhak for the non-Hasidic community. Additional housing was built by Mr. Reisford of Warsaw on land bought from the adjacent Even Yehoshu'a neighborhood.

The entire neighborhood is one long block of attached houses, extending from Kikar HaShabbat eastward along Mea She'arim Street until the Mea She'arim neighborhood. The entrance to Batei Kollel Warsaw is from the Even Yehoshu'a side. The Kollel offices are located in the buildings on the incline on Straus Street going toward Kikar HaShabbat. A giant sign hangs above the office, announcing "Rabbi Meir Ba'al HaNess Fund–Poland Kollel."

On the gate that faces Malchei Yisrael Street is affixed a memorial plaque commemorating the deeds of the patron.

Boundaries:

North – Geula and Beit Yisrael
South – Even Yehoshu'a
East – Mea She'arim
West – Straus Street and Zichron Moshe

Sites: within its boundaries or nearby are two houses of study – Ohel Shmuel for Hasidim and Ohel Yitzhak for the non-Hasidim.

Streets: The one street of the neighborhood on which the houses are built is named for the neighborhood, and the parallel street is named for a Hasidic book.

The streets are:

'Avodat Yisrael Hayei Adam – Straus **H11**

Devotion, named for a Hasidic book by Rabbi Yisrael, the Maggid of

Kuzhinitz (1733-1813), that deals with homilies on the festivals and the Passover Haggada. He was known as a miracle-worker. A well-known prayerbook containing all of the prayers in a scientific edition is called "The Order of the Devotion of Israel" (see the neighborhood of Even Yehoshu'a).

Batei Warsaw Hayei Adam – Straus **H11**

Named after the neighborhood.

Hayei Adam Straus – Mea She'arim **H11**

Named for the book containing the laws of the Shulhan 'Aruch dealing with daily conduct, edited by Rabbi Abraham ben Yehiel Michal Danzig (1748 – 1820). He was one of the great arbiters of religious law in Lithuania (see the neighborhoods of Batei Werner/Ohalei Moshe, Batei Wittenberg/Sha'arei Moshe, Bnei Moshe/Neve Shalom, Even Yehoshu'a).

Kikar HaShabbat Straus at Yesha'yahu at Mea She'arim at Malchei Yisrael **H11**

The square where Sabbath observers gather to demonstrate against those who violate the Sabbath (see the neighborhoods of Beit Yisrael, Geula).

Mea She'arim Straus – Shivtei Yisrael **H11**

(See the neighborhoods of Batei Kollel Ungarin/Nahlat Zvi, Batei Naitin, Batei Perlman/'Ir Shalom, Beit Yisrael, Geula, Mea She'arim, Nahlat Zvi/ Shchunat HaTeimanim, Sha'arei Pina.)

Straus, Nathan (1848 – 1931) Yafo – Kikar HaShabbat **H11-12**

An American Jewish philanthropist, he built sheltered housing and soup kitchens for the poor and homeless in Jerusalem and with his own money built the Bikur Holim hospital on this street. He visited Israel several times. In 1920 he was appointed chairman of the American Jewish Congress and afterwards served as its president. He and his brothers were partners in the ownership of the giant New York department store chains Macy's and Abraham & Straus. The city of Netanya is named for him (see the neighborhoods of Batei Wittenberg/Sha'arei Moshe, Bnei Moshe/Neve Shalom, Even Yehoshu'a, Mid-Town.)

Batei Milner/Agudat Shlomo

Name and establishment:

This neighborhood, in the middle of town northeast of Mea She'arim on the street that leads to the Mandelbaum Gate, between Batei Kollel Ungarin/Nahlat Zvi and Shmuel HaNavi Street, was founded in 1892. At that time, the neighborhood consisted of 35 apartments built for the poor of Jerusalem by one of the prominent businessmen of the city name Rabbi Shlomo HaCohen Milner, and the neighborhood was named for him. The familiar and official name was Agudat Shlomo. Shlomo Milner learned the occupation of miller and became an expert. The name Milner means "miller," and he built a large flour mill on his property near Batei Wittenberg/Sha'arei Moshe.

During the War of Independence, the location of the neighborhood was strategic, facing the Mandelbaum crossing into Jordan. Even though it was in the line of fire at the front, and despite its being all that stood between the Jordanian army and Batei Kollel Ungarin, its residents did not abandon the neighborhood even in the most difficult days. Today, the neighborhood is run down and only a number of solitary apartments remain standing.

Boundaries:

North and east – Beit Yisrael

South – Mea She'arim

West - Geula

Sites: within its boundaries or nearby a synagogue was established for the Vizhnitz Hasidim, called Yeshu'at Yisrael, named after Rabbi Yisrael Hager, who was the head of the Vizhnitz Kollel at the beginning of the twentieth century.

Streets: the single street inside the neighborhood is named for the workshops on the street.

The streets are:

Ha'Ameilim Sonnenfeld – Sha'arei Shamayim **I11**

Named for the workshops, lumber and carpentry shops on this street (see the neighborhood of Beit Yisrael).

Sha'arei Shamayim Rapoport – dead end **I11**

A symbolic name, the gates of heaven (see the neighborhood of Beit Yisrael).

Sonnenfeld, Yosef Haim, Rabbi (1849 – 1932)
Mea She'arim – Yoel **H11**

The chief rabbi of Agudat Yisrael, the ultra-Orthodox community, and its spiritual leader. One of the builders of many neighborhoods in Jerusalem. One of the directors of the Diskin Orphanage and president of several public institutions in Jerusalem (see the neighborhood of Beit Yisrael).

Batei Naitin

Name and establishment:

This neighborhood, in the center of town opposite Mea She'arim and next to Batei Kollel Ungarin/Nahlat Zvi, was founded in 1903 and named for the American philanthopist Menahem Nathan. He was a Lover of Zion, and in his will he left money for the construction of dwellings in Jerusalem for scholars. The entry gate to the neighborhood is opposite Salant Street.

The neighborhood includes four rows of large buildings with two or three floors, in which every apartment is exactly like the others, so that they are all equal. Batei Naitin was a neighborhood whose apartments were intended solely for the poor, so they could live there for three years and then they would have to turn the apartments over to different tenants. Today's residents belong to the ultra-Orthodox community.

Boundaries:
North – Beit Yisrael
South – Mea She'arim
East – Shivtei Yisrael Street
West – Batei Kollel Ungarin/Nahlat Zvi

Sites: within its boundaries or nearby is the synagogue Zichron Menahem, named for its founder.

Streets: narrow lanes bordering with Mea She'arim Street at its eastern end.

The street is:

Mea She'arim	Straus – Shivtei Yisrael	**H11**

(See the neighborhoods of Batei Kollel Ungarin/Nahlat Zvi, Batei Kollel Warsaw/Nahlat Ya'akov, Batei Perlman/'Ir Shalom, Beit Yisrael, Geula, Mea She'arim, Nahlat Zvi/Shchunat HaTeimanim, Sha'arei Pina.)

Batei Perlman/'Ir Shalom

Name and establishment:

This neighborhood, in the middle of town on one narrow lane east of Mea She'arim, was founded in 1887 and built by a commercial company headed by the banker Ya'akov Frutiger. The original name of the neighborhood was 'Ir Shalom (city of Shalom/peace), named after Shalom Konestraum, a partner in the company and the power behind the construction. In 1892 Reb Elimelech Perlman, from one of the old families in the city, along with his relatives, bought all the "numbers" of the building plots in the neighborhood and built more buildings around it. The Perlman family began to do business in iron and building materials and opened the first store for these materials on lower Yafo near the wall. With time, the original name of the neighborhood was forgotten and the buildings came to be known as Batei Perlman.

Boundaries:

North – Batei Naitin and Batei Kollel Ungarin/Nahlat Zvi
South – HaNeviim Street
East – Morasha/Musrara
West – Mea She'arim

Streets: the streets of the neighborhood are named for Jerusalem judges.

The streets are:

Admon ben Gadai Mea She'arim – Dvora HaNevia **I12**

One of the (civil) decree judges in Jerusalem during the Second Temple period.

Dvora HaNevia (11th cent. BCE) HaNeviim – Salant **I12**

Deborah, judge, prophet and one of the central figures during the Biblical period of Judges: "And Dvora, a woman prophet, wife of Lapidot, judged Israel at that time" (Judges 4:4). (See the neighborhood of Mea She'arim.)

Hanan ben Avshalom Dvora HaNevia – Admon **I12**

One of the (civil) decree judges in Jerusalem during the Second Temple period.

Mea She'arim Straus – Shivtei Yisrael **H11**

(See the neighborhoods of Batei Kollel Ungarin/Nahlat Zvi, Batei Kollel Warsaw/Nahlat Ya'akov, Batei Naitin, Beit Yisrael, Geula, Mea She'arim, Nahlat Zvi/Shchunat HaTeimanim, Sha'arei Pina.)

Batei Rand

Name and establishment:

This neighborhood, in the center of town south of the neighborhoods of Mazkeret Moshe, Ohel Moshe and Mahane Yehuda, was founded in 1910 and named after the philanthropist and Hasid from the city of Zanz, Rabbi Mendel HaCohen Rand of Galicia, who donated the money to build the buildings.

After he immigrated to the Land of Israel, Mendel Rand lived in the Old City and built there a courtyard where he brought rabbis of the Zanz Hasidim and provided them with apartments rent-free. A few years later, after the neighborhood of Batei Broyde/Ohalei Ya'akov was built, where only Mitnagdim (religious Jews opposed to Hasidim) lived, Mendel Rand bought a large parcel of land near that neighborhood and ordered built a large two-story building, a magnificent synagogue and a ritual bath, only for Hasidim.

The main gate and the entrance to the neighborhood are from Tavor Street.

Boundaries:
North – Mazkeret Moshe and Ohel Moshe
South – Betzalel Street
East – Mishkenot Yisrael and Sukkat Shalom
Northwest – Mahane Yehuda Market

Sites: within its boundaries or nearby is the Mahane Yehuda Market.

Streets: the names of the streets are connected with northern Israel.

The streets are:

HaNeTZI"V (1817 – 1893) Betzalel – Tavor **G12**

(See the neighborhoods of Batei Broyde/Ohalei Ya'akov, Batei Kollel Minsk/Beit HaLevi, Batei Kollel Munkacs, Knesset Yisrael, Mazkeret Moshe.)

Shomron Agrippas – Mesilat Yesharim **G12**

(See the neighborhoods of Batei Goral/Mishkenot HaTeimanim, Mishkenot Yisrael.)

Tavor Shomron – 'Ezra Refael **G12**

(See the neighborhoods of Batei Broyde/Ohalei Ya'akov, Knesset Yisrael, Mazkeret Moshe, Ohel Moshe.)

Batei Sa'idoff

Name and establishment:

This neighborhood, in the middle of town, west of the Mahane Yehuda Market and near the building that was formerly Sha'arei Tzedek Hospital, was founded in 1911 by a Bucharan Jew named Yitzhak Sa'idoff. The buildings of Batei Sa'idoff, between Sha'arei Tzedek and Mani Streets, were rows of stores and workshops on the first floor, above which were dwellings. They were built to revive the area. Today, the entire structure is abandoned.

Boundaries:
North – Mekor Baruch
East – Mahane Yehuda Market
Southwest – Sha'arei Tzedek and the building that formerly housed Sha'arei Tzedek Hospital

Sites: within its boundaries or nearby are the Mahane Yehuda Market and the building that was formerly Sha'arei Tzedek Hospital.

Streets: the single street of the neighborhood is the city's main traffic thoroughfare.

The street is:

Yafo	Jaffa Gate – Weizmann Boulevard	**F11-I12**

(See the neighborhoods of Batei Kollel Horodna/Damesek Eli'ezer, Beit David/Beit HaRav Kook, Beit Ya'akov, Even Yisrael, 'Ezrat Yisrael, Mahane Yehuda, Mekor Baruch, Mid-Town, Nahlat Shiv'a, Ohel Shlomo, Romema, Russian Compound, Sha'arei Tzedek, Sha'arei Yerushalayim.)

Batei Werner/Ohalei Moshe

Name and establishment:

This neighborhood, located in the center of town near the neighborhoods of Mea She'arim and Even Yehoshu'a, was founded in 1902. It is named for the Jerusalem rabbi Moshe Mendel Werner, who built the neighborhood to be dedicated to housing for the poor. The money for the construction came from an inheritance left by an American relative, Rabbi Moshe Alexander, after whom the neighborhood is also named, Ohalei Moshe.

The residents of the neighborhood are religious Ashkenazic Jews.

Boundaries:

North – Mea She'arim Street

South – Even Yehoshu'a

East – Baharan Street and Mea She'arim

West – Hayei Adam Street

Sites: within its boundaries or nearby is the Manischewitz Yeshiva, founded by the Manischewitz brothers, owners of the matza factory in America.

Streets: the neighborhood streets are named for books of religious law.

The streets are:

Baharan, Shlomo Zalman, Rabbi (1838 – 1910)
Mea She'arim – Salant **H11**

One of the founders of Mea She'arim who bought and built his home on the first lot in the Mea She'arim neighborhood, he was a civic leader in Jerusalem and assisted on a voluntary basis in the financial management of the Mea She'arim Society (see the neighborhoods of Bnei Moshe/Neve Shalom, Mea She'arim).

Emet LeYa'akov Hesed LeAvraham – dead end **H11**

Named after a book of laws on the Torah, by Rabbi Yisrael Ya'akov Algazi (1680–1756), the Sephardic chief rabbi, leader of the rabbis of the Land of Israel.

Hayei Adam Straus – Mea She'arim **H11**

(See the neighborhoods of Batei Kollel Warsaw/Nahlat Ya'akov, Batei Wittenberg/Sha'arei Moshe, Bnei Moshe/Neve Shalom, Even Yehoshu'a.)

Hesed LeAvraham Baharan – Hayei Adam **H11**

Named after a book of commentary on the Zohar, by Rabbi Avraham ben Mordechai Azulai (1570–1643). He was a Kabbalist and one of the prominent commentators on the Zohar.

Batei Wittenberg/Sha'arei Moshe

Name and establishment:

This neighborhood, in the center of town near Mea She'arim and behind the Straus Street hospital, was founded in 1886 and named for the philanthropist Rabbi Moshe Wittenberg, president of the HaBa"D (Lubavitch) Hasidim in Jerusalem, who built the neighborhood. The original name of this neighborhood was Sha'arei Moshe.

The Batei Wittenberg/Sha'arei Moshe neighborhood is the first one built by private philanthropists wanting to perpetuate their own names by building homes for the sole use of the poor, who would live in them without charge and after three years switch with another group.

At the gate of the neighborhood on the side of Hayei Adam Street is affixed a memorial stone acknowledging the efforts of this patron in the following words: "The buildings are named Sha'arei Moshe. Built in 5646. For an eternal memory."

Boundaries:
North – Batei Kollel Warsaw/Nahlat Ya'akov
South – borders on Straus Street
East – Hayei Adam Street and Bnei Moshe/Neve Shalom
West – Even Yehoshu'a

Streets: the neighborhood is built as a large courtyard, like a box, that borders the central streets in the area.

The streets are:

Even Yehoshu'a Hayei Adam – Straus **H11**

Yehoshu'a's stone, named for the neighborhood and its founder, Yehoshu'a Helfman (see the neighborhood Even Yehoshu'a).

Hayei Adam Straus – Mea She'arim **H11**

(See the neighborhoods of Batei Kollel Warsaw/Nahlat Ya'akov, Batei Werner/Ohalei Moshe, Bnei Moshe/Neve Shalom, Even Yehoshu'a.)

Sha'arei Moshe Baharan – Hayei Adam **H11**

Named after the neighborhood and Rabbi Moshe Wittenberg (1825–1899), a philanthropist and one of the founders of neighborhoods in Jerusalem.

Straus, Nathan (1848 – 1931) Yafo – Kikar HaShabbat **H11-12**

(See the neighborhoods of Batei Kollel Warsaw/Nahlat Ya'akov, Bnei Moshe/Neve Shalom, Even Yehoshu'a, Mid-Town.)

Bayit VaGan

Name and establishment:

This neighborhood, in the western part of the city, was founded in 1921. The wish of its first residents was that they would have a garden next to the house, and hence its name, "house and garden". In addition, the goal of its founders was to establish a national-religious neighborhood and to increase the number of Jewish neighborhoods around Jerusalem. At the time of the establishment of the State, Bayit VaGan was the westernmost Jewish neighborhood in the city. The houses here are built descending the steep slopes like steps in accord with the topography. Three parallel central streets were laid out: HaPisga, Bayit VaGan and HaRav ‘Uziel Streets, while paths, lanes, ascents and steps connected them to one another.

During the War of Independence, battles raged there, and from the same area the Jewish fighters stormed and conquered the area to the west and south where the nearby neighborhoods of Kiryat HaYovel and Manhat/Malha were later built.

The many manufacturing plants that functioned in the neighborhood after 1940 moved out of the area over the years, except for the gigantic water reservoir from which water is pumped to all the Jerusalem neighborhoods. From 1956 educational, religious and other institutions began to be built here, such as important high schools like Himmelfarb and Boyer, veteran yeshiva high schools like Netiv Meir, Marom Tzion and Kiryat No‘ar, prestigious post-high school yeshivas and institutes of religious research like Yad HaRav Herzog and the Institute for Technology According to Halacha (religious law).

Today, the neighborhood residents are national-religious, but the area’s ultra-Orthodox population is growing.

Bayit VaGan is one of six garden neighborhoods built in the early twentieth century (see also the neighborhoods of Rehavia, Beit HaKerem, Talpiot, Kiryat Moshe and Mekor Haim).

Boundaries:

North – Ramat Beit HaKerem, Giv‘at Beit HaKerem, Beit HaKerem

South – Ramat Sharett, Ramat Denya, Manhat/Malha

East – Giv‘at Mordechai

West – Kiryat HaYovel, ‘Ein Kerem

Sites: within its boundaries or nearby are the Sha‘arei Tzedek Medical Center, Yad Sarah, Mount [*Har*] Herzl, Yad VaShem, Kiryat No‘ar (Youth Village), the Holyland Hotel and the new Herzl Museum.

Streets: the streets of the neighborhood are called by the names of great rabbis of Jerusalem, religious books, Lovers of Zion, leaders of the *Mizrahi* movement and the *Agudat Yisrael* movement, teachers, authors, commentators and archeologists. There are three central streets in the neighborhood: HaPisga, Bayit VaGan and HaRav ‘Uziel.

The streets are:

Abba Uri [Lane] (1891 – 1967) ‘Uziel – Bayit VaGan **D14**

One of the founders of Bayit VaGan and one of the first teachers in the Land of Israel.

Abohav, Yitzhak, Rabbi (14th cent.) Minzberg – Cassuto **C15**

A master of homiletics, learned in ethics, and a collector of Aggadic material. He was one of the first to gather and arrange the Aggada according to topics. He held an important place in the literature of popular ethics (see the neighborhood of Ramat Sharett).

Alfiye, Yitzhak, Rabbi (1878 – 1956) Bayit VaGan – Frank **D15**

One of the Jerusalem rabbis and one of its chief Kabbalists.

Bayit VaGan Herzl Boulevard – Rath **D14-15**

Named for the neighborhood, this is one of its three central streets.

Be-er Mayim Haim ‘Uziel – Bayit VaGan **D15**

Well of Living Waters, a book on the Torah by Rabbi Haim of Chernovitz (he died in 1818), one of the Hasidic leaders in the second generation after the Ba‘al Shem Tov. He became famous in Jerusalem for his religious essays.

Ben Nahum, Yitzhak, Rabbi (1923 – 1994)
Sha‘arei Torah – Torat Haim **C15**

He was one of the pillars of the Kurdish community and one of its senior rabbis. He was one of the founders of the religious and spiritual center for Jews from Kurdistan.

Bergman, Eli‘ezer, Rabbi (1798 – 1852)
HaPisga – Weisberg – dead end **C14**

One of the first *olim* (immigrants) from Germany in Jerusalem, and one of the most important rabbis.

Beyt, Shmuel (Hans) (1902 – 1948)
Herzl Boulevard – ShaHa”L **D13-14**

One of the educators of the young people who made aliya from Germany. He was killed while protecting a convoy bringing military equipment to Jerusalem while it was under siege during the War of Independence (see the neighborhoods of Giv‘at Mordechai, Ramat Beit HaKerem).

Broyer, Yitzhak, Rabbi (1883 – 1946) HaPisga – dead end **D14-15**

An author and ideologist, he was one of the leaders of the ultra-Orthodox community and president of the *Poalei Agudat Yisrael* movement (PAG"I).

Cassuto, Moshe David, Rabbi (1883 – 1951) Michlin – Silberg **D15**

A rabbi and Bible researcher and commentator, he was the spiritual leader of the Italian Jewish community. He was a professor at the Hebrew University of Jerusalem.

Divrei Yeruham Minzberg – dead end **D15**

Named for the book by Rabbi Yeruham Warhaftig (1874–1955). He was head of a yeshiva and one of the disciples of Rabbi Haim of Brisk. He received a prize from the Jerusalem municipality for his religious writings.

Duvdevani, Baruch (1917 – 1984)
Nezer David – dead end **D16-E15**

An educator, he was one of the organizers of *'aliya* (immigration) to Israel.

Eli'ezri, Shmuel, Rabbi (1905 – 1991) Shahrai – dead end **D14**

He was one of the first rabbis in the New City of Jerusalem. He was the first rabbi of the neighborhood and one of its founders. He worked hard on behalf of education for youth and served as an army chaplain for the Jerusalem district during the War of Independence.

Frank, Zvi Pesah, Rabbi (1873 – 1960) Sha'arei Torah – Rath **D15**

A rabbi and arbiter of religious law, he was the official rabbi of Jerusalem and was one of those who established the chief rabbinate of Israel.

Frankel, Eliyahu, Dr. [Steps] (1898–1974)
'Uziel – Bayit VaGan **D14-15**

He was a physician in the neighborhood.

Hachmi, Yosef (1887 – 1961)
Nezer David – dead end – Shahrai **D14-15**

He was a civic leader, a banker and a builder of Jerusalem.

HaHID"A (1724 – 1806) HaPisga – HaPisga **D14**

The initials of Rabbi **H**aim **Y**osef **D**avid **A**zulai, one of the great Kabbalists and arbiters of religious law. He published many books in all areas of Torah study, books of commentary and histories of the sages of Israel.

Haklai, Zeev (1910–1964) Shahrai – Herzl Boulevard – dead end **D13-14**

He was a teacher and educator of youth and worked to promote the immigration of youth to Israel.

HaMaLBI"M (1809 – 1880) HaPisga – Bayit VaGan **D14**

Rabbi **M**eir **L**eibush **b**en **Y**ehiel **M**ichal was a commentator on the Bible and preached the return to Zion.

HaPisga Herzl Boulevard – Alfiye – dead end **C14-D15**

Summit, one of the three central streets of the neighborhood. The street passes along the highest elevation in Jerusalem.

HaRaSHDa"M (1505 – 1589) HaPisga – Bergman **C14**

Rabbi **Sh**muel **di M**edina was one of the outstanding rabbis and arbiters of religious law in Saloniki (Greece) in the sixteenth century.

Hausner, Gideon (1916 – 1991) Avi Yona – Avi Yona **D-E16**

He was Israel's attorney general, prosecutor in the Eichmann Trial in Jerusalem, chairman of Yad VaShem and a government minister (see the neighborhood of Holyland Park).

HaVa'ad HaLeumi ShaHa"L – dead end **E14-15**

The National Committee, the leadership of the Jewish community in the Land of Israel during the period of British rule (see the neighborhood of Giv'at Mordechai).

Herzl Boulevard Shazar Boulevard – HaPisga **F11-D13**

Named after Dr. Binyamin Zeev (Theodor) Herzl (1860 – 1904), the visionary of the State of Israel. Following the trial of Alfred Dreyfus, a Jewish officer in the French army, Herzl concluded that there was no solution to anti-Semitism except the establishment of a Jewish state. He founded the World Zionist Congress and set up financial tools – the Jewish Colonial Trust and *HaKeren HaKayemet LeYisrael* (the Jewish National Fund). These instruments made possible the establishment of the State of Israel forty-four years after his death. His remains were brought to Israel in 1949 and buried on the mountain in Jerusalem that bears his name. This main street named for him passes on the north-west side of Bayit VaGan (see the neighborhoods of Beit HaKerem, Kiryat Moshe, Maimon, Yefei Nof).

LaTzadik, Zvi [Ascent] (1840 – 1906) Bayit VaGan – HaHID"A **D14**

Named after the book by Rabbi Zvi Michel Shapira.

Levi, 'Ovadia [Square] (1924 – 1981) Hachmi at Shahrai **D14**

A Jerusalem contractor and builder.

Lopes, Eliyahu, Rabbi [Rise] (1890 – 1938)
Bayit VaGan – HaHID"A **D14**

He was one of the important rabbis of Jerusalem and a founder of the Bayit VaGan neighborhood.

Marom Tzion HaPisga – HaHID"A **D14**

Named for the religious center for youth that is found on this street.

Michlin, Michel Haim, Rabbi (1867 – 1938) 'Uziel – Rath **D15**

He was a journalist, author and researcher of the Land of Israel.

Milikowsky, Natan, Rabbi [Square] (1879 – 1935)
Herzl Boulevard at Beyt **D13**

One of the foremost preachers of Zionism in the Jewish Diaspora.

Minzberg, Yisrael Zeev, Rabbi (1895 – 1962)
Divrei Yeruham – Aboab **D15**

He was one of the foremost rabbis of Jerusalem, the rabbi of the Old City until the War of Independence.

Mor, Ezrah [Square] (1912 – 1968) Bayit VaGan at 'Uziel **D14**

He was the Hagana commander of Bayit VaGan during the War of Independence, helped establish the Israel Police Force.

Mutzafi, Silman, Rabbi (1900 – 1975) Silberg – dead end **D15**

One of the foremost Kabbalists, he wrote various essays on Kabbala, Aggada and ethics.

Neeman, Yehoshu'a Leib [Square] (1900 – 1979)
LaTzadik at HaPisga **D15**

One of the first researchers of Jewish religious music.

Nezer, David (1887 – 1972) 'Uziel – Bernstein **D15-16**

Named after Rabbi David HaCohen, one of the prominent Jerusalem rabbis, an ideologist, and head of the *Mercaz HaRav* (Kook) Yeshiva. He was known by the nickname "the Ascetic" ("Nazir").

Rath, Meshulam, Rabbi (1875 – 1963) Michlin – Frank **D15**

He was a rabbi and arbiter of religious law and one of the founders of the *Mizrahi* movement. He was also a member of the chief rabbinate.

Rogel, Shlomo [Square] (1927 – 1990) Beyt at Avizohar **D13**

He was a scientist, professor of medicine and one of the most veteran cardiologists in Israel.

Rosenheim, Ya'akov, Rabbi (1870 – 1965)
HaPisga – Torah Va'Avoda **C-D14**

He was one of the spiritual leaders of the German Jewish community and a founder of the world *Agudat Yisrael* movement.

Shaag, Avraham Haim, Rabbi (1883 – 1958)
Bayit VaGan – HaHID"A **D14**

One of the founders of the *Mizrahi* movement in the Land of Israel, he was a member of the leadership of the National Committee and a member of the first Knesset (parliament).

Sha'arei Torah Ben Nahum – dead end **C14-15**

Gates of Torah, named after a religious publication by Rabbi Yitzhak HaCohen Feigenbod (1828–1911). He was one of the early Lovers of Zion.

Shahrai, Alter Ya'akov (1874 – 1937) Beyt – Hachmi **D13-14**

He was a writer, a journalist and a founder of the Community Council of Jerusalem, and its secretary during the British Mandate period.

Shalom Zohar [Square] (1936 – 1986) 'Uziel at Minzberg **D15**

He was the president of the Western community (Jews from North Africa) in Jerusalem.

Shimshon Refael (Hirsch), Rabbi [Square] (1808–1888)
Duvdevani at the Ulpana **E15**

A rabbi and author, he was the leader and ideologist of rigorously Orthodox Jewry in Germany in the nineteenth century.

Simhat HaCohen [Square] 'Uziel at Michlin **D15**

Named after the Kabbalist Rabbi Mass'ud HaCohen Alhadad, who headed the Beit El Hasidim in the Old City for twenty-four years (1903 – 1927). He made aliya from Morocco with his parents when he was very young. He lived a long life and died at the age of one hundred and seven, and he was buried on Har HaZeitim [the Mount of Olives].

Torah Va'Avoda HaPisga – Gordon **C14**

Torah and work. This street was named after a religious pioneering movement, one of whose founders and leaders was Rabbi Yesha'yahu

Shapira (1891–1945) (see the neighborhood of Kiryat HaYovel).

Torat Haim Ben Nahum – dead end **D15**

Torah of Life, named in honor of Rabbi Zerah Epstein (1872–1931), one of the great Torah scholars and a civic leader in Jerusalem. He was head of the *Torat Haim* Yeshiva, which in that period was located in the Old City.

'Uziel, Ben Tzion Hai, Rabbi (1880 – 1953)
Herzl Boulevard – Minzberg **D14-15**

He was appointed chief rabbi of Saloniki and later chief rabbi of Tel-Aviv and Jaffa, the Rishon LeTzion, chief rabbi of the Sephardic community in Israel. He also served as a delegate to Zionist Congresses, was one of the heads of the National Committee and one of the founders of the Religious Zionist movement. He was named an honorary citizen of the City of Tel-Aviv.

Weisberg, Haim, Dr. (1892 – 1959) HaPisga – Bergman **C14**

One of the founders of the Zionist movement in Hungary and one of the first organizers of the Hagana in Jerusalem (1921).

Wissmann, Leo (1906 – 1989) Shahrai – dead end **D14**

One of the pioneers of industry, named a *Yakir Yerushalayim*, Honored Citizen of Jerusalem.

Yismah 'Ovadia [Square] (1872 – 1952) Michlin at Rath **D15**

An arbiter of religious law, an author and judge who labored in Morocco for the benefit of the Land of Israel.

Zelnick, Mordechai HaLevi [Square] (1911 -1979)
Frank at Silberg **D15**

A community activist and one of the builders of Jerusalem.

Beit David/Beit HaRav Kook

Name and establishment:

This neighborhood, in the center of town, on the incline of HaRav Kook Street, was established in 1872 by the builder and philanthropist Rabbi David Reiss, and from here comes the name. The neighborhood was built by him for the benefit of poor scholars, so that they could live in the apartments free of charge for three years. The

Beit David neighborhood was the first offshoot of Nahlat Shiv'a, on the other side of Yafo. The entrance to it is from Dr. Ticho Lane, and it is a block of residential housing built as a square courtyard surrounded by ten two-story buildings. The apartments are all on the ground floor, and the second floor was built as a synagogue. On the northern wall is a memorial plaque in memory of David Reiss and his wife Mene.

In 1921 when Rabbi Avraham Yitzhak HaCohen Kook was chosen as chief rabbi of Jerusalem, he established his home and his office in this neighborhood. He lived there until his death in 1935, as is noted on the plaque attached to the house. In 1924 he founded the famous yeshiva, *Mercaz HaRav*, in the courtyard of his home, and it remained there until the 1960s, when it moved to a large, new building in the Kiryat Moshe neighborhood (see the neighborhood of Kiryat Moshe).

The neighborhood was recently renovated, and it is now home to art galleries and art shops.

Boundaries:
North – Rehov HaNeviim [Prophets Street] and Mea She'arim
South – Yafo and Kikar Tzion [Zion Square]
East and west – Mid-Town

Sites: within its boundaries or nearby are Ticho House, which is part of the Israel Museum, and HaRav Kook House (this was the name of part of Reiss House) – renovated and restored, and now a museum of his life.

Streets: the street alongside Beit David, HaRav Kook Street, is named after him.

The streets are:

AGa"N, Rabbi (1787 – 1848) Yafo – Straus **H12**

Initials of Rabbi **A**vraham Haim **Gagin**, the Sephardic chief rabbi and leader of Jerusalem rabbis, who was the first to be officially recognized in this position by the Turkish authorities, by royal decree (see Mid-Town).

HaNeviim Yafo – Damascus Gate **H-I12**

Prophets, named in honor of Israel's prophets, most of whom lived and prophesied in ancient Jerusalem (see the neighborhoods of 'Ezrat Yisrael, Mid-Town, Morasha/Musrara, Zichron Moshe).

Kook, Avraham Yitzhak HaCohen, Rabbi (1865 – 1935)
HaNeviim – Yafo **H12**

The first Ashkenazic chief rabbi of Israel, appointed during the period of the British Mandate. He was one of the great Torah scholars, who saw in Zionism and the return to Zion "the beginning of the Redemption." He was admired by all sectors of the Jewish community. He founded the yeshiva called *Mercaz HaRav*, and Kfar **HaRoe"h** (initials of **Ha**Rav **A**vraham **H**aCohen) was named after him. He was made an honorary citizen of the City of Tel-Aviv in 1935, and he also received Tel-Aviv's prize for Torah Literature (see the neighborhood of Mid-Town).

Ticho, Avraham, Dr. [Lane] (1883–1961)
HaRav Kook – Ticho House – dead end **H12**

Named after the pre-eminent ophthalmologist of his time in Jerusalem (see the neighborhood of Mid-Town).

Yafo Jaffa Gate – Weizmann Boulevard **F11-I12**

(See the neighborhoods of Batei Kollel Horodna/Damesek Eli'ezer, Batei Sa'idoff, Beit Ya'akov, Even Yisrael, 'Ezrat Yisrael, Mahane Yehuda, Mekor Baruch, Mid-Town, Nahlat Shiv'a, Ohel Shlomo, Romema, Russian Compound, Sha'arei Tzedek, Sha'arei Yerushalayim.)

Beit HaKerem

Name and establishment:

This neighborhood, located on the western side of the city, was founded in 1922, at the beginning of British civil rule. The name Beit HaKerem is mentioned in the Bible in the Book of Jeremiah 6:1: "...and sound a warning over Beit HaKerem, for evil has appeared from the north..." Some think the neighborhood is named for the Biblical city that was in nearby 'Ein Kerem, the path to which passed through this area.

The land here was acquired from the Greek Orthodox Church. The neighborhood's founders were teachers, clerks and writers, so at the beginning it was called by a name formed from the initials of these professions. Among the residents was the national poet Haim Nahman

Bialik. The construction of the buildings was done by the members of the Labor Legion (commune of workers) in Jerusalem.

In the early years, the neighborhood was a vacation area and, besides rental rooms, hotels and boarding houses were built there.

During the War of Independence, the neighborhood served as a base for the convoys reaching the city during the siege of Jerusalem in 1948, and during the Six Day War it was the point of departure for the paratroopers in the battles to liberate Jerusalem.

Beit HaKerem is one of the six garden neighborhoods built in the early twentieth century (see also the neighborhoods of Rehavia, Bayit VaGan, Talpiot, Kiryat Moshe and Mekor Haim).

Boundaries:
North – Kiryat Moshe
South – HaPo'alim, Giv'at Beit HaKerem, Ramat Beit HaKerem
East – Giv'at Ram
Northwest – Herzl Boulevard, Mount Herzl, Yefei Nof

Sites: within its boundaries or nearby are Denmark Square, the Hebrew Teachers Seminar today known as the David Yellin College of Education, the Garden of Twenty, the Old Committee House, the WIZO Day Center and the Na'amat Club.

Streets: the streets of the neighborhood are named after its founders and early residents (the teachers, clerks and writers) and for a heroic act from the Second World War and from the War of Independence. The central streets are Beit HaKerem Street, HeHalutz Street and Bialik Street.

The streets are:

Aharonov, Binyamin Cohen (1910 – 1979)
Brachyahu – Herzl Boulevard **D13**

A journalist, a highly respected member of the Persian community in Jerusalem and one of the Mashhad forced converts. During the period of the British Mandate, he was very active on behalf of the Jewish community in Jerusalem in his capacity as secretary at the French consulate.

Ariel, Thomas [Boulevard] (1920 – 1941)
Bialik – Beit HaKerem – dead end **D12**

He took part, together with twenty-three of his fellow Hagana members, in a daring sabotage mission on the coast of Lebanon during World War II. Their fate is unknown.

Avizohar, Yehoshu'a (1882 – 1966)
HeHalutz – Gafni, ends at Beyt **D13**

He was a teacher and a scientist in Jerusalem (see the neighborhoods of Giv'at Beit HaKerem, Ramat Beit HaKerem).

Beit HaKerem Herzl Boulevard – Herzl Boulevard **E12**

Named for the neighborhood, this is one of its central streets.

Bialik, Haim Nahman (1873 – 1934)
HaMeyasdim – Beit HaKerem **D12-13**

He was the greatest of the modern Hebrew poets. He was also a writer, did literary research, was a translator, editor and publisher. He was one of those who revived the Hebrew language. He was on the leading edge of Zionism even before it became a political movement, through the writing of his first poem, "To the Bird" (1891) in which he expressed longing for the Land of Israel. He was awarded honorary citizenship by the City of Tel-Aviv (1934). This is one of the central streets in the neighborhood.

Brachyahu, Aharon Michel (1870 – 1946)
HaMeyasdim – Aharonov **D13**

He was an educator and teacher in Jerusalem and chairman of the Hebrew Teachers Union in the Land of Israel. He was one of the founders of the neighborhood of Beit HaKerem.

Denya [Square] Beit HaKerem at Herzl Boulevard **D12**

Named for the country Denmark, in northern Europe, as a sign of appreciation to the Danish nation for helping in the rescue of its Jewish citizens during the time of the Nazi Holocaust. In the square stands a symbolic boat rowing toward a safe shore, alluding to the Danes who conveyed Jews in rowboats to safety in neighboring Sweden.

Gafni, Simha (1907 – 1997) Avizohar – Brachyahu **D13**

One of those who set up the customs taxation and revenue systems.

Givton, Hanoch [Square] (1917 – 1976) HaMeyasdim at Bialik **D13**

One of the founders of the government broadcasting service.

HaBroshim [Ascent] HeHalutz – Bialik **D12-13**

Cypress trees, ornamental trees that grow in Israel. Named for the cooperative agricultural village, Brosh, in the Negev.

Haft, Ya'akov [Square] (1884 – 1966) HeHalutz at Herzl Boulevard **E12**

He was an author and civic leader, and was one of the founders of the neighborhood.

HaGuy HeHalutz – dead end **D12-E13**

The valley, named for the valley that extends to the east of the neighborhood.

HaMehanech (1862 – 1943) HeHalutz – Karmon **E12**

Educator, named for the educator and linguist Yitzhak Epstein. He was one of the pioneers in Hebrew education and formulated the method of learning and teaching the language called "Hebrew in Hebrew". He wrote extensively on education and linguistics.

HaMeyasdim HeHalutz – Herzl Boulevard **D13**

The founders, named for the founders of the Beit HaKerem neighborhood.

HaMoreh Beit HaKerem – Ma'agal Beit Midrash **D-E12**

Teacher, named for Jewish teachers in general, in particular for Yitzhak Jaffe (1880–1929) and Bilha Jaffe (1891–1961), among the founders of the Beit HaKerem neighborhood.

Hanina Mizrachi [Steps] (1886 – 1974) Shahar – Karmon **E12**

Among the founders of the neighborhood and its synagogue, and one of the veterans of Hebrew education in Jerusalem.

Hazon Tzion Rabbi Binyamin – dead end **E12**

Vision of Zion, named for a book of remembrances by Rabbi Shlomo Zalman Rivlin (1884–1962). He did research into the history of the old Jewish community in Jerusalem, and established an institute of cantorial music at the *Shirat Yisrael* Synagogue in Jerusalem.

HeHalutz Herzl Boulevard – Avizohar, ends at HaSatat **D13-E12**

The pioneer, named for the early Hebrew pioneers in general, and in particular those who built the neighborhood of Beit HaKerem. This is one of the main streets of the neighborhood (see the neighborhoods of Giv'at Beit HaKerem, HaPoalim).

Herzl Boulevard Shazar Boulevard – HaPisga **F11-D13**

(See the neighborhoods of Bayit VaGan, Kiryat Moshe, Maimon, Yefei Nof.)

Kabak, Aharon Avraham (1880 – 1944)
Beit HaKerem – HeHalutz **D-E12**

A teacher, writer and literary critic, he developed the Hebrew novel.

Karmon, Moshe (1891 – 1954) HeHalutz – dead end **E12**

He was a teacher, writer and philosopher in Jerusalem.

Ma'agal Beit HaMidrash HaSofer – Herzl Boulevard – dead end **D-E12**

Seminar Circle. The street circles the building of the Hebrew Teachers Seminar/David Yellin College of Education.

Melavei HaShayarot [Square] Kaddish Silman at HeHalutz **E12**

Convoy escorts, named for the soldiers who protected the convoys of vehicles that supplied equipment to the battlefronts during the War of Independence.

Rabbi Binyamin HeHalutz – Shahar **E12**

Pen name of Yehoshu'a Redler-Feldman (1880–1957). He was a writer, journalist, and a promoter of the Second Aliya and of agricultural settlement. He was a founder of the Beit HaKerem neighborhood.

Schiller, Shlomo (1862 – 1925) HaMeyasdim – Brachyahu **D13**

He was a teacher, educator, writer and philosopher. He was one of the earliest teachers of Hebrew in Galicia and a spiritual leader for Zionist youth there. He was active in the labor movements in the Land of Israel. He was the principal of the first Hebrew high school in Jerusalem and one of the leaders of the teachers union in Israel.

Schlein, Shmuel (1889 – 1951) Bialik – HaMeyasdim **D13**

He was very involved in the public life of the neighborhood, and was one of its founders and leaders.

Shahar, Haim Dov (1891 – 1930) HaGuy – Rabbi Binyamin **E12**

He was a teacher, writer and leader in Hebrew education. He was also one of the founders of the Beit HaKerem neighborhood.

Shalem, Natan (1897 – 1959) Beit HaKerem – Bialik **D12**

He was an educator, researcher of the Land of Israel, the first researcher of the Judean Desert, and founder of the association of walking tour guides in Jerusalem.

Silman, Kaddish [Steps] (1881 – 1938)
Shahar – Beit HaKerem – dead end **E12**

He was a teacher, writer and popular poet, and was one of the founders of the neighborhood.

WIZO [Square] HeHalutz at HaMeyasdim **D13**

Named for the **W**omen's **I**nternational **Z**ionist **O**rganization, the world organization of Zionist women, founded in 1920. Its purpose was to prepare women for a creative life in the Land of Israel, and to enable them to care, physically and educationally, for a child.

Ya'akovi, Yitzhak and Rahel [Plaza] HeHalutz – Rabbi Binyamin **E12**

Among the founders of the neighborhood.

Zuta, Haim Leib (1865 – 1939) Beit HaKerem – Herzl Boulevard **D12**

He was a writer and educator and one of the founders of the Beit HaKerem neighborhood.

Beit Hanina

Name and establishment:

This neighborhood, located along the northern city limits of Jerusalem, is divided, so that the eastern part is within the municipality of Jerusalem and the western part is in the jurisdiction of the Palestinian Authority. The source of the name Hanina is unknown. One opinion is that this is the place which, in the Biblical book of Nehemiah, called Anania, to which the Babylonian exiles returned with Nehemiah in the year 455 BCE (Nehemiah 11:32).

Most of the residents of the neighborhood are Muslims, and a small number are Greek Catholic, belonging to the 'Abdaa clans, Abu Zahira, Abu Taha, Huri, Suman.

Boundaries:

North – 'Atarot-Industrial Zone
South – Shu'afat
East – Pisgat Zeev
West – western Beit Hanina

Sites: within its boundaries or nearby are ancient stone quarries, where orchids blossom during the winter. There are also churches and Christian monasteries.

Streets: the neighborhood streets are named for Arab poets and writers, famous Muslims and caliphs.

The streets are:

'Abd el-Hamid Suman (1895 – 1972)
Beit Hanina Road – dead end **H-I5**

One of the founders of the neighborhood, he was an economist. He founded the Arab Bank in Israel and in Arab countries in the Middle East.

'Abd el-Rahman Dajani Beit Hanina Road – Faidi el-Alami **I-J4**

He was a mayor of Jerusalem during the period of Turkish rule over the Land of Israel.

Abu Madi Taha Hussein – dead end **I3**

A well-known poet and writer, born in Lebanon.

Abu Tamam (9th cent. CE) Beit Hanina Road – Taha Hussein **I4**

A poet and one of the important Arab writers, both of prose and classical poetry.

Ahmed el-Sefadi (16th cent.) Derech Ramallah – El-Halsa **I2**

Born in Tzfat, he served as a judge.

Al-Ardashir Taha Hussein – dead end **I3**

A famous Arab poet.

Al-Barudi (b. 1838) Taha Hussein – dead end **I4**

A poet, born in Cairo.

Badr Hizma Road – Shejrat a-Dur **I5**

The name of a mosque in the area.

Beit Hanina Road Neve Ya'akov Boulevard – Adam **I4-5**

The main street in the neighborhood.

Bir Nballa Road E-Sakakini – dead end **I4**

The road leading to the village of Bir Nballa, north of the city.

Bisan Derech Ramallah – El-Banias **I2**

The name of this place from the time of the British Mandate.

Derech Ramallah **I3**

(See the neighborhoods of 'Atarot-Industrial Zone, Dahiyet el-Barid)
Neve Ya'akov Boulevard – city of Ramallah

El-'Abbas (7th cent. CE) Beit Hanina Road – dead end **I4**

An uncle of the Prophet Muhammed.

El-'Arbi Beit Hanina Road – dead end **I6**

The name means "western." The name of this place from the time of the British Mandate.

El-Banias Bisan – dead end **I2**

The name of this place from the time of the British Mandate.

El-Banji Khlat Mash'al – dead end **I2**

The name of this place from the time of the British Mandate.

El-Bukhturi (821 – 898 CE) Taha Hussein – dead end **I3**

A great poet of the period of the 'Abbasid caliphs.

El-Halsa Derech Ramallah – dead end **I2**

The name of this place from the time of the British Mandate.

El-Hilal Hizma Road – dead end **J5**

The sun, the name of this place from the time of the British Mandate.

El-Jozeh Taha Hussein – dead end **I3**

The name of the area around Beit Hanina.

El-Madars el-Jedida Suman – dead end **I5**

The street of the school.

El-Mamoun (786 – 833 CE) Suman – Khlat Sinad **I5-6**

A famous caliph of the 'Abbasid dynasty.

El-Munzar Muslim – Suman **I5**

The name of this place from the time of the British Mandate.

El-Mu'tasem Beit Hanina Road – dead end **I4**

A famous caliph of the 'Abbasid dynasty.

E-Nakhil Taha Hussein – Bir Nballa Road **I4**

The name of this place from the time of the British Mandate.

El-Qiandi (801 – 865 CE) Beit Hanina Road – Dajani **I4**

A famous Arab philosopher.

Faidi el-'Alami (1897 – 1984) Hizma Road – Dajani **I5**

He was mayor of Jerusalem during the period of Turkish rule over the Land of Israel, the representative of Jerusalem in the Turkish parliament, and a personal advisor to the British High Commissioner.

Hizma [Road] Beit Hanina Road – 'Uzi Narkiss **J5**

The Biblical Azmuth [*'Azmavet*].

Imam el-Bukhari Taha Hussein – dead end **I4**

One of the first authors of a book of the sayings and words of the Prophet Muhammed.

Imam Muslim El-Mamoun – Khlat Mash'al **I5**

A preacher and well-known scholar who transmitted the words of the Prophet Muhammed to the people.

Imam Shefai Khlat Mash'al – Khlat Mash'al **I5**

Muslim wise man and interpreter of the Koran.

Ishaq el-Mawsili (767 – 850 CE) Beit Hanina Road – El-Qiandi **I-J4**

He established Arabic song and melody during the 'Abbasid period.

Iskandar el-Khuri Taha Hussein – dead end **I3**

Born in Beit Jalla, he was a judge. He published a large number of collections of poetry, stories and articles.

Jisr e-Natf Derech Ramallah – Derech Ramallah **I3**

A bridge over a dry streambed near the village, the middle bridge, north of Beit Hanina.

Jubran Khalil Jubran (1883 – 1931) Jisr e-Natf – dead end **I2**

He was born in the village of Bishari in Lebanon. The literature he wrote is recognized on an international level, as, for example, "The Broken Wings."

Khalil e-Sakakini (1878 – 1953)
A-Tawil – Taha Hussein – dead end **I-J4**

Educator, writer, teacher and translator.

Khlat Mash'al El-Mamoun – dead end **I5**

The name of this place from the Mandate period.

Mai Ziyada (1886 – 1941) Derech Ramallah – dead end **I2**

Born in Nazareth, she moved to Egypt. She was an Arab writer and poet and was known for her literary salon.

Marj ibn 'Amer Derech Ramallah – dead end **I2**

During the Mameluke period, the Jezreel Valley was called by this name, the name of a Bedouin tribe that gained control over the valley at that time.

Maximus Chayeg, Patriarch Hizma Road – dead end **J5**

He bought the parcel of land and built the Christian neighborhood near Hizma Road, four buildings belonging to the local Greek Catholic Patriarchate.

Nurail Hoda Taha Hussein – Bir Nballa Road **I4**

The name of this place from the British Mandate period.

'Omar el-Khayam (12th cent.) Beit Ḥanina Road – Taha Hussein **I4**

He was a poet, mathematician and astrologer.

Qaeb bin-Zuhair (6th cent. CE) Beit Hanina Road – dead end **I4**

He was a poet during the time of the Prophet Muhammed.

Ras a-Tawil E-Sakakani – dead end **J4-5**

It means "the long head." It is the name of this place from the British Mandate period.

Shejrat a-Dur Beit Hanina Road – dead end **I5**

The queen of Egypt and Syria for eighty days. Originally Aramean, she was the commander of the Mameluke army and took part in expelling the Crusaders in the thirteenth century.

Sultan Kotoz Hizma Road – El-'Arbi **J5**

A Mameluke sultan who vanquished Mongol invaders at 'Ein Jalut (Harod) in 1259.

Taha Hussein (1889 – 1962) El-Khuri – Suman **I3-5**

One of the great Arab writers of the twentieth century.

'Ukba bin Nefa Taha Hussein – Bir Nballa Road **I4**

The name of this place from the British Mandate period.

Wadi Umm el-'Amid El-Mamoun – dead end **I6**

Named for the stream that passes near this street.

Beit Safafa

Name and establishment:

This neighborhood, located in the southern part of the city, south of the Pat and Gonenim/Katamonim neighborhoods, was divided from the end of the War of Independence until the Six Day War. In the cease-fire agreement at the end of the War of Independence, it was agreed with Jordan that the northern part of the village would be within Israel's borders, so that the railroad line between Jerusalem and Tel-Aviv, which passed through its center, could continue to function. The railroad track marked the border until the Six Day War, when the two parts of the village were reunited under Israeli rule.

There are those who think the name Safafa is a distorted form of the name HaTzobebah, which is mentioned in the Bible (First Chronicles 4:8) as the name of one of the descendants of the tribe of Judah, personal names that also became names of places. Others think that the name Beit Safafa, in an altered form, is first mentioned in a Crusader document from the twelfth century – Beit Hababa. The actual source of the name remains unknown.

From the beginning of the War of Independence, the neighborhood was an important base for Arab fighters against the Jews who were entrenched in nearby Mekor Haim (see the neighborhood of Mekor Haim).

The neighborhood's residents are Muslim.

Boundaries:

North – Pat, Gonenim/Katamonim

Southwest – Gilo

Northeast – Talpiot-Industrial Zone

East – Ramat Rahel

Sites: within its boundaries or nearby are burial caves, Christian remains from the Byzantine period, remains of a Crusader church.

Streets: the streets are named after sites connected with the neighborhood.

The streets are:

Al-Natar Ihud HaKfar – Pat **F17**

Named for the threshing floor that was in the village.

El-Butma Ihud HaKfar – E-Safa **F18**

Named for a tree that used to be in this place and that rarely brings forth fruit.

El-Dawar el-Awal E-Nahada – El-Jedid **F18**

Meaning: the first square.

El-Jabel el-Jedid E-Nahada – El-Awal **F18**

Meaning: the new mountain.

El-Kal'a E-Shifa – dead end **F18**

Named for a huge rock that was here.

El-Kasiel Al-Natar – dead end **F17**

Named for the parcels of land of the various clans in the village.

El-Madrasa el-Jedida El-Jedid – dead end **F18**

The street of the school.

El-Zeitoun E-Nahada – dead end **F18**

Named for the olive groves in the area.

E-Nahada El-Jedid – E-Safa **F18**

Meaning: knowledge, because of the schools on this street.

E-Rahma Sheikh Mahmud – El-Butma **F18**

Meaning: mercy, because of the cemetery here.

E-Safa Ihud HaKfar – HaRosmarin **F17-19**

The ancient name of the village.

E-Shifa El-Talj – dead end **G18**

Meaning: health, medicine.

HaMisgad HeHadash [Square] E-Nahada at E-Safa **F18**

Named for the mosque found nearby.

Ihud HaKfar Dov Yosef – Baram and ends at Harashei Barzel **F17-18**

Unification of the village. The village, divided by the Israel-Jordan armistice line from 1948 to 1967, was reunited after the Six Day War (see the neighborhood of Talpiot-Industrial Zone).

Ma'mal El-Talj El-Awal – dead end **F17-18**

Meaning: ice, because of the ice-making factory on this street.

Ras el-Tal'e Ihud HaKfar – dead end **F17-18**

Named for a slope in the village.

Sheikh Mahmud Ihud HaKfar – E-Rahma **F18**

Named after one of the village wise men. In his house was the first room in the village where men learned the Koran.

Beit Ya'akov

Name and establishment:

This neighborhood, located in the middle of the city, west of the Mahane Yehuda Market, was established in 1877 and is named for the founding association of seventy members and for the number of houses that were to be built, and thus is linked to the verse in Exodus 1:5 which states: "And all the offspring of Jacob [Ya'akov] were seventy..." At the top of the document establishing the neighborhood appears the verse: "O House of Ya'akov, let us go forward in God's light."

Beit Ya'akov was one of the first neighborhoods built outside of the Old City. In the year it was founded, the neighborhood was two kilometers distant from the Jaffa Gate and all around was desolate wasteland. It was entirely enclosed within its own walls, that is, it was enclosed by the back sides of the new buildings that were built in a square. Most of its residents were craftsmen. Some of the founders and builders of the neighborhood were men of the "Old Community", like Reb Zalman Baharan, one of the founders and builders of the Mea She'arim neighborhood, and likewise Rabbi Shmuel MiBarezhin Huminer, the first of the Huminer family in the Land of Israel – and who was also a founder of Mea She'arim. It is said of Rabbi Shmuel that he laid the cornerstone for this neighborhood and worked with great energy to expand the neighborhood in this desolate place.

On the plaza at the entrance to the neighborhood (today there is a Bank Discount on the site) was the station for the neighborhood carts of Jerusalem. The central station was located next to the Jaffa Gate, and there were two routes taken by the cart drivers – one to Mahane Yehuda, that is, to Beit Ya'akov, and the second to Mea She'arim. From Beit Ya'akov the carts left to go toward the city of Jaffa. The station functioned until the railroad from Jerusalem to Jaffa came into service.

Near the neighborhood, there was a market for fruit, vegetables and trade in livestock, which was called the Beit Ya'akov Market. Over time, the market's name changed to the Mahane Yehuda Market. The proximity to the Mahane Yehuda Market changed the character of the neighborhood from a residential area to a place of commerce and crafts.

Boundaries:
North – Yafo
South – Shmuel Baruch Street and Zichron Yosef
East – Mahane Yehuda Market
West – Sha'arei Tzedek

Sites: within its boundaries or nearby is the Mahane Yehuda Market

Streets: The street in this neighborhood is named for the neighborhood.

The streets are:

Baruch, Shmuel, Rabbi (1898 – 1994) Shazar – Agrippas **F-G11**

The spiritual leader of the Kurdish community, named an Honored Citizen of Jerusalem (see the neighborhoods of Mahane Yehuda, Mid-Town, Sha'arei Tzedek, Shevet Tzedek/Shchunat HaPahim, Zichron Yosef).

Beit Ya'akov Yafo – Shmuel Baruch **G11-12**

Named for the neighborhood (see the neighborhood of Mahane Yehuda).

Yafo Jaffa Gate – Weizmann Boulevard **F11-I12**

(See the neighborhoods of Batei Kollel Horodna/Damesek Eli'ezer, Beit David, Batei Sa'idoff, Even Yisrael, 'Ezrat Yisrael, Mahane Yehuda, Mekor Baruch, Mid-Town, Nahlat Shiv'a, Ohel Shlomo, Romema, Russian Compound, Sha'arei Tzedek, Sha'arei Yerushalayim.)

Beit Yisrael

Name and establishment:

This neighborhood, located in the center of town north of Mea She'arim, was founded in 1887 and attracted many Jews from various diasporas, Ashkenazim, Sepharadim and Jews from lands in the Middle East [Eidot HaMizrah]. The founders who purchased the land were also founders of nearby Mea She'arim, Reb

Eliyahu Goodal, the Baharan, Rav Yosef Haim Sonnenfeld, and Reb Aryeh Leib Hirshler the judge, and thus the neighborhood was at first called "New Mea She'arim." Only after a few years was the neighborhood called Beit Yisrael, according to the verse in Ezekiel 36:10: "And I will multiply the population on you, all the House of Israel, and the cities will be populated and the desolate places will be built up."

The speed with which the neighborhood was built was a result of the desire to support the poor who wanted to live outside the Old City walls and because of the great poverty in which the Jews of Jerusalem lived. The original plan was to build a hundred houses, but the plan changed, and they built two hundred houses because of the poverty and the great demand. The neighborhood was built on one long street from which a number of lanes branched off. In the middle is a synagogue and the *Beit Ya'akov* study hall, the central pillar of the neighborhood.

In later years, a new area called "New Beit Yisrael" was built in the northern section. Until the Six Day War, this neighborhood was near the front line, and in the battles of the War of Independence it suffered greatly from the shelling and shooting from nearby Arab positions.

The residents of the neighborhood are ultra-Orthodox.

Boundaries:

North – HaBucharim

South – borders Mea She'arim. Today's Mea She'arim Street separates the two neighborhoods.

Northeast – Shmuel HaNavi Street, an important traffic route in the city

West – Geula

Sites: within its boundaries or nearby are the yeshiva of the Karlin Hasidim; the Mir Yeshiva; the *Mahane Yisrael* Yeshiva, the famous yeshiva for Jews returning to a religious life; and the Beer Shev'a Synagogue named after Batsheva' Gnuzin of Vilna, who built it with her own money (corner of Sonnenfeld and Kfar HaShiloah Streets).

Streets: the streets are named after the neighborhood's founders and rabbis. The main street is named for Rabbi Yosef Haim Sonnenfeld.

The streets are:

'Aboud, Haim Shaul, Rabbi (1890 – 1977) Sonnenfeld – Karo **H-I11**

One of the great religious poets and wise men of Aram Tzova (Aleppo, Syria), author of religious songs, a teacher and educator.

'Adani, Shlomo, Rabbi (1567 – 1624) Dayan – Kapah **H11**

A rabbi and arbiter of religious law. One of the great commentators on the Mishna. One of the spiritual leaders of Yemenite Jewry (see the neighborhood of Sha'arei Pina).

Admor Rabbi Shlomo (1869 – 1945)
Sonnenfeld – Sha'arei Shamayim **H-I11**

Named for Rabbi Shlomo Goldmann of Zhvahil. The rabbi of the Hasidim of the Admor dynasty of the House of Zelechov, a miracle worker who loved his fellow man and helped the persecuted and the needy. He worked on behalf of the *'aliya* of Jews from Russia. There is a yeshiva and study hall of his Hasidim on this street.

Ashkenazi, Betzalel, Rabbi (b. 1520) Yoel – Polanski **H11**

The teacher of the Holy AR"I (Rabbi Yitzhak ben Shlomo Luria of Tzfat). The chief rabbi of Egypt and Jerusalem. He wrote a book called "Shita Mekubetzet" [the collected method] about the Talmud (see the neighborhood of HaBucharim).

Auerbuch, Efraim, Rabbi (d. 1948) Dayan – Ben Amram **H11**

One of the rabbis of Beit Yisrael and its environs, he was a civic leader and one of the founders of the neighborhood (see the neighborhood of Sha'arei Pina).

Beit Yisrael Sonnenfeld – Shmuel HaNavi **I11**

Named for the neighborhood.

Belzer, Yitzhak, Rabbi (1837 – 1907) Dayan – Ben Amram **H11**

One of the great rabbis of Russia, a leader of the Musar movement, and head of the Community Council of the old Jewish community in Jerusalem.

Dayan, Aryeh Leib, Rabbi (d. 1917) Mea She'arim – Rokeah **H11**

One of the prominent rabbis and civic leaders of Jerusalem. One of the founders of the Beit Ya'akov neighborhood and one of its leaders. He was a member of the municipal council during the period of Ottoman rule.

Edelman, Mordechai (1847 – 1922) Sonnenfeld – Dayan **H-I11**

A writer and civic leader. He toured the Jewish communities of the Middle East and published his journal.

Elkana Wiesenstar, Rabbi [Square] (1893 – 1976)
Sonnenfeld at Rapoport **I11**

The head of the office of the rabbinate in Jerusalem.

Eshlag, Yehuda Leib, Rabbi (1886 – 1955)
Dayan – Avino'am **H11**

A rabbi and kabbalist, the head of a yeshiva in Jerusalem. He translated the Zohar (the primary book of Kabbala mysticism) into Hebrew (from Aramaic).

Friedman, David, Rabbi (1828 – 1917) Yoel – Sonnenfeld **H11**

One of the great rabbis and arbiters of religious law. One of the heads of the Hibat Tzion (Lovers of Zion) movement.

Ha'Ameilim Sonnenfeld – Sha'arei Shamayim **I11**

(See the neighborhood of Batei Milner/Agudat Shlomo.)

HaBE'SH"T (1698 – 1760) Karo – Sonnenfeld **H-I11**

Acronym for **H**aRav Yisrael **Ba'al Sh**em **T**ov. The originator and father of the Hasidic movement.

Habshush, Haim, Rabbi (1833 – 1899) Mea She'arim – Belzer **H-11**

Traveler and sage of the Jews of Yemen. He wrote on the history of the Jews of Yemen in the years 1890 – 1893 (see the neighborhoods of Nahlat Zvi/Shchunat HaTeimanim, Sha'arei Pina).

HaNagar Sonnenfeld – Sha'arei Shamayim **I11**

The carpenter, named for the craft.

Hasidei Pinsk Karlin Sonnenfeld – Dayan **H-I11**

Named for the synagogue on this street.

Hochmei Lublin Karo – Sonnenfeld – dead end **H11**

"The Sages of Lublin", the famous yeshiva in Lublin, Poland, founded by Rabbi Meir Shapira (1887–1934). He was a rabbi and arbiter of Jewish law, the initiator of the practice of setting a daily time for learning a page of Talmud. The last rabbi of the Lublin community.

Karo, Yosef, Rabbi (1488 – 1575) Yoel – Shmuel HaNavi **H-I11**

One of the greatest masters and arbiters of Jewish law in any generation. His books *Beit Yosef* and the *Shulhan 'Aruch* (a compendium of all the laws and commandments) are well known, as is his Kabbalistic book *Magid Meisharim*.

Kfar HaShiloah Sonnenfeld – Eshlag **H11**

Named after the village of this name in eastern Jerusalem.

Kikar HaShabbat intersection of Straus-Yesha'yahu-Mea She'arim-Malchei Yisrael **H11**

(See the neighborhoods of Batei Kollel Warsaw/Nahlat Ya'akov, Geula.)

Lapidot, Gershom, Rabbi (1880–1956) Dayan – Kfar HaShiloah **H11**

One of the more important rabbis of Jerusalem. One of the heads of the *Hayei 'Olam* Yeshiva.

Leder, Zelig Sonnenfeld – Dayan **H11**

A civic leader in the neighborhoods through which this street passes.

Lendner, Moshe Dov (1895 – 1950) Sonnenfeld – Sha'arei Shamayim **I11**

One of the founders of the Beit Yisrael neighborhood.

Mea She'arim Straus – Shivtei Yisrael **H11**

(See the neighborhoods of Batei Kollel Ungarin/Nahlat Zvi, Batei Kollel Warsaw/Nahlat Ya'akov, Batei Naitin, Batei Perlman/'Ir Shalom, Geula, Mea She'arim, Nahlat Zvi/Shchunat HaTeimanim, Sha'arei Pina.)

Mizrahi, Yohanan Yosef (d. 1938) Sonnenfeld–Sha'arei Shamayim **H-I11**

A civic leader in Jerusalem. One of the first founders and the leader of the Beit Yisrael neighborhood. A man of many good works. He was murdered in the Old City of Jerusalem.

'Ozer (1863 – 1940) Shmuel HaNavi – Dayan **H-I11**

Rabbi Haim 'Ozer Grodzinski, the rabbi of Vilna. One of the great rabbis and arbiters of religious law in his generation, a leader of Polish and Lithuanian Jewry and a leader of the Council of Torah Sages of *Agudat Yisrael.*

Polanski, Shim'on Aharon (d. 1948) Beit Yisrael – dead end **H-I10**

One of the prominent Torah scholars in Jerusalem. He served as rabbi of the neighborhood and its environs for thirty years.

Rapoport, Baruch, Rabbi (d. 1946) Shmuel HaNavi – Dayan **H-I11**

One of the founders of the Beit Yisrael neighborhood and a civic leader in Jerusalem.

Ratzabi, Moshe Shlomo, Rabbi (1878 – 1936) Dayan – Habshush **H11**

One of the great Yemenite rabbis of Jerusalem. A man of ethics.

Reem, Eliyahu, Rabbi (d. 1960) Shmuel HaNavi – Beit Yisrael **I11**

One of the outstanding teachers of education in Jerusalem. A member of the superior court in Jerusalem. Head of the rabbinical office of the religious council.

Reichman, Yehoshu'a Meir, Rabbi (1862 – 1942)
Beit Yisrael – Sonnenfeld – dead end **H-I11**

A civic leader of the Ashkenazic community in Jerusalem. One of the organizers of the Jerusalem community and the religious council. A member of the municipal council for the Jews of Jerusalem.

Rokeah, Shim'on (1863 – 1922) Dayan – Shmuel HaNavi **H-I11**

A civic leader of the new Jewish community in the Land of Israel. He worked for the expansion of the Jewish community in the city of Jaffa. One of the founders of the neighborhoods of Neve Tzedek and Neve Shalom.

Sha'arei Shamayim Rapoport – dead end **I11**

(See the neighborhood of Batei Milner/Agudat Shlomo.)

Shmuel HaNavi Shivtei Yisrael – Bar-Ilan **H10-I11**

The prophet Samuel, one of the foremost prophets of Israel. He anointed Saul king of Israel. His grave is further north on this street (see the neighborhoods of HaBucharim, Ma'alot Dafna/Arzei HaBira, Mahanayim, Nahlat Shim'on, Sanhedria, Shikunei Shmuel HaNavi).

Sonnenfeld, Yosef Haim, Rabbi (1849 – 1932)
Mea She'arim – Yoel **H11**

(See the neighborhood of Batei Milner/Agudat Shlomo.)

Bnei Moshe/Neve Shalom

Name and establishment:

This neighborhood, located in the middle of town near Batei Wittenberg/Sha'arei Moshe, was established in 1891 and named for Sir Moses Montefiore. The neighborhood was also given a second name, Neve Shalom, for the peace that accrued to the Ashkenazic community with the acquisition of this parcel of land.

Its residents had been evicted from the area of "Kerem Moshe and Yehudit" on the land of Judah Touro. After the neighborhood of Mishkenot Shaananim was built, poor people from the Ashkenazic and Sephardic communities squatted there. After many efforts, these poor were forced to abandon the land on which the Yemin Moshe neighborhood was later built. With the help of the Ashkenazic community's committee, land was bought to the east of Batei Wittenberg/Sha'arei Moshe for the poor Ashkenazic Jews, and sixty apartments were built. (See the neighborhood of Shevet Tzedek/Shchunat HaPahim regarding the matter of the poor Sephardic Jews.)

Boundaries:

The neighborhood is located between the Histadrut buildings on Straus Street and the neighborhood of Mea She'arim.

North – Batei Werner/Ohalei Moshe

South – Bnei Brit [B'nai Brith] Street

East – Baharan Street and Mea She'arim

West – Hayei Adam Street and Batei Wittenberg/Sha'arei Moshe

Streets: the neighborhood is built as one large courtyard, like a box, which is bordered by central streets in the area.

The streets are:

Baharan, Shlomo Zalman, Rabbi (1838 – 1910)
Mea She'arim – Salant **H11**

(See the neighborhoods of Batei Werner/Ohalei Moshe, Mea She'arim.)

Bnei Brit Straus – HaNeviim **H12**

A worldwide Jewish organization whose purpose is the fostering of ethical principles and the support of charitable and benevolent institutions (see the neighborhood of Mid-Town).

Hayei Adam Straus – Mea She'arim **H11**

(See the neighborhoods of Batei Kollel Warsaw/Nahlat Ya'akov, Batei Werner/Ohalei Moshe, Batei Wittenberg/Sha'arei Moshe, Even Yehoshu'a).

Straus, Nathan (1848 – 1931)
Yafo – Kikar HaShabbat **H11-12**

(See the neighborhoods of Batei Kollel Warsaw/Nahlat Ya'akov, Batei Wittenberg/Sha'arei Moshe, Even Yehoshu'a, Mid-Town.)

Christian Quarter [HaRova' HaNotzri]

Name and establishment:

This neighborhood, located in the northwestern part of the Old City, from the Jaffa Gate to the New Gate to the Damascus Gate, extending along the western and northern walls, is named for the Christians who have lived here over many centuries. This area was part of the Upper City of the Second Temple period, and along its boundary stood a wall; in the wall was a fortress that became widely known for its role during the Roman siege of ancient Jerusalem. The Roman army broke through this wall and conquered Jewish Jerusalem in the year 70 CE.

During the Byzantine period, the number of Christians in the quarter increased due to the proximity of the burial place of Jesus, and Christians built houses and churches here. During the Middle Ages, especially during the time of the Crusaders and the Turks, the Christian population increased even more. In the nineteenth century, by request of the Christians, an additional gate was added in the northern wall, called the New Gate, and just outside it were built Christian institutions and monasteries that were closely linked to the Christian Quarter, the largest being Notre Dame, a convent for nuns and a French Christian hospital.

During the War of Independence, Jewish fighters tried and failed to break through to the Christian Quarter through the New Gate, and at the end of the war, the quarter, the gate and the entire Old City came under Jordanian rule, although the convent of Notre Dame and the hospital remained within the border of Israel, and the street between them turned into the front line.

In the Six Day War, the Old City was liberated by the IDF, and it came entirely under Israeli rule. Part of the dividing street was given a new name, Rehov HaTzanhanim, Paratroopers Road, instead of Suleiman Street, named for the Turkish sultan who built the wall.

In this quarter is a commercial center, rows of shops with a variety of displays geared for tourists. The Persian-Arabic name for this commercial area is Muristan.

Boundaries:
North – Morasha/Musrara and the Municipality
South – Armenian Quarter
East – Moslem Quarter
West – Arts & Crafts Lane, David's Village-Mamilla

Sites: within its boundaries or nearby are the Via Dolorosa (Path of Sorrows), the path by which Jesus was led, according to Christian tradition, to the hill of Golgotha for his crucifixion, and the Church of the Holy Sepulcher, which, according to Christian tradition, is the place of his burial. Around this church and in the entire quarter, various Christian groups built churches and monasteries, and a Christian hostel with the Latin name Casa Nova (new house), an inn for Christian pilgrims in ancient times. Also nearby are an abandoned, ancient water reservoir called Hezekiah's Pool, the Tower of David and the museum inside it.

Streets: most of the quarter's streets are named for the Christian churches and monasteries nearby and for people and events connected with the Christian religion. The quarter has two main streets, Christian Quarter Road and the Path of Sorrows, the Via Dolorosa.

The streets are:

Al-Jabsha cloth market – HaShlihim **I12**

"Stone". Named for the stones that were found in the street in earlier times.

Al-Khanaqa Christian Quarter – cloth market **I12**

Named for the Al-Khanaqa Mosque on this street built in the twelfth century.

Al-Sa'adiya Al-Khanaqa – HaShlihim **I12**

"Lady". Named for Jesus' mother. On this street is a church named for her.

Beit HaBad HaYehudim – HaGuy **I13**

"Cloth house", for the cloth workshops found on this street (see the Moslem Quarter).

Casa Nova Greek Patriarchate – St. Francis **I13**

Named for the hostel for Christian tourists on this street.

Christian Quarter Road [*HaNotzrim*] David – St. Francis **I13**

Named for the Christian shops on this street.

Damascus Gate [*Sha'ar Shchem*] the northern Old City wall **I12**

One of the eight gates in the wall surrounding the Old City, this gate is in the middle of the northern wall and serves as an important economic and commercial center and a kind of passageway between the Moslem Quarter of the Old City and the Arab neighborhoods of east Jerusalem. From this gate a road begins that leads northward all the way to the city of Damascus, in Syria. This gate is also known as the Nablus Gate, since the road leading from this gate goes through Nablus, in Samaria. The gate is considered the most beautiful of the gates in Jerusalem's walls (see the Moslem Quarter).

David Armenian Patriarchate – HaYehudim **I13**

(See the Armenian Quarter.)

Eptimus Muristan – Christian Quarter **I13**

Named for the builder of the commercial center in the Old City.

Greek Catholic Patriarchate El-Khatab – St. Dimitrios **I13**

Named for the Greek Catholic monastery on this street.

Greek Orthodox Patriarchate Christian Quarter – Casa Nova **I13**

Named for the Greek Orthodox monastery on this street.

HaAhim St. Francis – HaBurskaim **I13**

"Monks", *frères* (brothers) in French, named for the Christian teachers (monks) in this monastery.

HaBurskaim (al-Ghwalida) HaAhim – St. Peter **I13**

Tanners, named for the leatherwork shops that were on this street.

HaKneisiyot (Al-Knias) Al-Jabsha – HaShlihim **I12**

"Churches", named for the Christian churches on this street.

HaShlihim [Al-Rosul] HaKneisiyot – St. Francis **I12**

"Apostles", named for the twelve apostles of Jesus.

Hativat Yerushalayim Ma'ale HaShalom – HaTzanhanim –Yafo **I13-14**

(See the Armenian Quarter, David's Village-Mamilla, the Jewish Quarter, Yemin Moshe.)

HaTzanhanim TZaHa"L Square – Sultan Suleiman **I12**

The paratroopers, named for the paratroopers who fought to liberate Jerusalem in the Six Day War (1967) (see the neighborhoods of Mid-

Town, Morasha/Musrara, Russian Compound).

Jaffa Gate [*Sha'ar Yafo*] the western Old City wall **I13**

(See the Armenian Quarter.)

Kikar TZaHa"L [IDF Square] Yafo at HaTzanhanim at Shivtei Yisrael **I12-13**

Named for the Israel Defense Force (see Mid-Town, Russian Compound).

Latin Patriarchate El-Khatab – St. Peter **I13**

Named for the offices of the Latin Patriarchate located on this street.

Muristan David – St. Helena **I13**

Persian for "hospital". Nineteenth century German pilgrims built a hospital here and named it for St. John the Redeemer. Today the monastery of St. John the Redeemer stands here.

New Gate *[HaSha'ar HeHadash]* the northern Old City wall **I12-13**

One of the eight gates in the wall surrounding the Old City. This gate is called the *new gate* because it was built about three hundred fifty years after the other gates in the wall. The New Gate was opened in 1889 by the Turks. In the War of Independence the Jewish fighters tried to break through the New Gate, but without success. In the Six Day War the Old City was liberated and came under Israeli rule. The street passing before this gate, descending from TZaHa"L Square to east Jerusalem, which was the front line for nearly twenty years, was opened to traffic and renamed Rehov HaTzanhanim, Paratroopers Road.

'Omar ibn el-Khatab (592 – 644 CE)
Jaffa Gate – Armenian Patriarchate **I13**

(See the Armenian Quarter.)

St. Dimitrios El-Khatab – Greek Patriarchate – St. George **I13**

A Christian saint, he lived in the fourth century CE.

St. Francis Christian Quarter – Casa Nova **I13**

Monk who founded the order of Franciscan monks in the thirteenth century.

St. George St. Dimitrios – Coptic market **I11**

One of the Christian saints.

St. Helena Christian Quarter – cloth market **I13**

Mother of Constantine the Great (first Roman emperor to allow the

Christian religion), in the fourth century CE converted to Christianity. A pilgrim to Jerusalem. She built early churches here.

St. Peter HaBurskaim – Latin Patriarchate **I12-13**

One of the twelve apostles of Jesus.

Via Dolorosa Lions Gate Road – Church of the Holy Sepulcher **I-J12**

Path of Sorrows. According to Christian tradition, Jesus walked this street to the place of his crucifixion (see the Moslem Quarter).

City of David

Name and establishment:

The Biblical City of David [*'Ir David*] is the oldest part of Jerusalem. The city stretches across a mountain ridge from south of the Dung Gate, outside the existing Turkish wall, although it is within today's Jerusalem municipality. King David reigned from Hebron for seven years, and then conquered the city of Jebus (which was named for its residents in ancient times, the Jebusites) and the fortress in the city, in approximately 1000 BCE. He called the city 'Ir David, made it his capital and ruled there for thirty-three years, as is written: "And David captured the stronghold of Zion, that is the City of David...And David resided in the fortress and called it 'Ir David, the City of David..." (II Samuel 5:7, 9).

The city stretches between two streams, the Kidron Stream on the east and the Ben Hinom Valley Stream on the west, which served as natural defensive lines to either side of the ancient city. The city was also surrounded by a wall known as the "First Wall", which encircled the edges of the ridge. On the higher part of the ridge was a threshing-floor of the agricultural Jebusites, residents of the city, on which the Holy Temple was later built.

During the Second Temple period, when the city expanded to the heights of the nearby mountain to the west, Mount Zion, 'Ir David was called the Lower City because it was at a lower elevation. The part that was on the nearby mountain, which was higher, was called the Upper City and was surrounded by a wall, the Second Wall. Archeological excavations were begun in 'Ir David in the middle of the nineteenth century and they have continued until today. The remains that are being discovered reveal to us the Biblical City of David and its surroundings from the First and Second Temple periods.

Boundaries:
North – the Temple Mount
Northwest – the Jewish Quarter
Southeast – the Arab village Silwan and the Jewish Kfar HaShiloah
East – Mount of Olives

Sites: within its boundaries or nearby are the archeological excavations in the City of David, the Temple Mount, the Jewish Quarter, the Mount of Olives, the remains of the ancient Shiloah pool, the Kidron Stream, the Gihon spring – the most important water source for ancient Jerusalem – HaNikba (the tunnel) and the ‘Ofel.

Streets: the neighborhood streets bear names related to the City of David.

The streets are:

Derech Ha‘Ofel Derech Yeriho – Dung Gate **J13**

A neighborhood in Biblical Jerusalem (Nehemiah 3:26–28) between the City of David in the south and the Temple Mount to the north. It was called Ha‘Ofel [the citadel] because those who approached it from the direction of the City of David were climbing up, ascending the mountain. Today this is called the ‘Ofel Road, and it winds up the slope of the mountain along the southern wall up to the Dung Gate, and from the gate to the retaining wall of the Temple Mount. In the southern wall excavations, discoveries include the remains of buildings and stairs leading up from the ‘Ofel to the top of the Temple Mount (see the Moslem Quarter).

Derech HaShiloah Derech Yeriho – Ma‘alot ‘Ir David **J13-14**

Named for Kfar HaShiloah, a Jewish community on the western side of the Mount of Olives.

Derech Yeriho Suleiman – the city of Jericho **J12-K14**

Jericho Road, named for the first city west of the Jordan River to be conquered by Joshua bin-Nun (Joshua 6:2) (see the neighborhoods of E-Tur, the Moslem Quarter).

Gihon Square Derech HaShiloah at Ma‘ale Yoav **J13**

Named for the Gihon spring nearby.

Ma‘ale HaShalom Dung Gate – Hativat Yerushalayim **J13-14**

Ascent of peace, a symbolic name (see the Jewish Quarter).

Ma'ale Yoav Derech HaShiloah – dead end **J13**

Named for Yoav (Joab) ben Tzruya, the army commander of King David (see the Greek Colony).

Ma'alot 'Ir David Derech Ha'Ofel – Breichat HaShiloah **J13-14**

The name is taken from Nehemiah 12:37, "And by the fountain gate and straight ahead they went up the steps of the City of David on the way up to the wall above the House of David and on to the water gate in the east." The street continues along its Biblical path: from the Shiloah pool to the Kidron Spring, from there to the City of David, and from there to the city wall and the Dung Gate. The street also leads to the archeological excavations in the City of David.

Dahiyet el-Barid

Name and establishment:

This neighborhood, located at the northern edge of the city, northwest of the neighborhood of Neve Ya'akov and on the road to Ramallah, was founded in 1954 by postal employees and laborers. The Arabic name means "the postal neighborhood", hence the name. Daib Nashashibi, director of the post office in east Jerusalem, was the prime mover in the realization of this cooperative initiative. The area is far from the center of town, so the workers organized a connecting bus line to transport them into the middle of Jerusalem.

Following the Six Day War, the neighborhood remained outside the municipal boundaries, but the residents organized and succeeded in opposing the decision and, as a result of their suit, the neighborhood was added into the city boundaries.

Boundaries:

North – 'Atarot-Industrial Zone, the city of Ramallah
Southeast – Neve Ya'akov
Southwest – Beit Hanina

Sites: within its boundaries or nearby are 'Atarot-Industrial Zone and 'Atarot airport.

Streets: the neighborhood streets are named for famous Muslims.

The streets are:

Dahiyet el-Barid Derech Ramallah – dead end **I-J2**

Named for the neighborhood. It means: the postal neighborhood.

Derech Ramallah Neve Ya'akov Boulevard - the city of Ramallah **I3**

(See the neighborhoods of 'Atarot-Industrial Zone, Beit Hanina.)

El-Harami, Shukri Derech Ramallah – Derech Ramallah **I2**

An author, born in Haifa, he founded the El-Rima College and directed it for many years. Died in Jerusalem.

El-Karami Derech Ramallah – dead end **J3**

Born in Tul Karm, he worked in publishing and as a lawyer.

El-Kubatiye, Maryum El-Mutran – dead end **J3**

A Christian woman who converted to Islam and married the Prophet Muhammed.

Jafar el-Sadek Derech Ramallah – dead end **J3**

The Prophet Muhammed's aide.

Jibril el-Mutran (b.1907) Derech Ramallah – dead end **J2-3**

Born in Beit Sahur, he was an archbishop and wrote many books on various subjects.

David's Village-Mamilla

Name and establishment:

This neighborhood, *Kfar David*, located in the center of town in the Mamilla district, was established in 1990 and is named for King David and its proximity to the Old City, the city of King David. David's Village was built in a modern style with the inspiration of a Biblical village – a cluster of luxury apartment houses, the first stage of the development of the whole Mamilla district.

In 1890, with the development of commerce in the city, stores and warehouses, offices, workshops, coffeehouses and hotels were built here. In the area were also built the municipal building, the first post office outside the walls, the telegraph office and the first foreign bank in Jerusalem. During the British Mandate period, the Mamilla district was a prestigious commercial area. During the War of Independence, the commercial area was destroyed, and the area became a frontier. With the unification of the city in 1967, the Mamilla district, which was in a very rundown condition, became the geographic center of Jerusalem, and as a result it was decided to build the area anew.

Mamilla is surrounded: from the east by the Old City, from the south by hotels, parks and luxury neighborhoods, from the northwest by Safra Square with its new municipal complex.

Boundaries:
Northwest – the center of town and the Municipality
South – Yemin Moshe
East – the Old City

Sites: within its boundaries or nearby are the Old City, Safra Square and the new Municipality, Independence Park and Arts & Crafts Lane.

Streets: the streets of the neighborhood are called by names connected with King David.

The streets are:

David HaMelech (10th cent. BCE) Agron – 'Emek Refaim **H13-I14**

King David of Israel who ruled seven years in Hebron and later conquered Jerusalem and declared it the capital of Israel, where he ruled for thirty-three years (II Samuel 5:5). He was a military commander, statesman and poet. Before his death, he named his son Solomon (Shlomo) as his heir to rule after him. According to Jewish tradition, the Messiah will be a descendant of King David. Also according to tradition, David wrote the book of Psalms (see the neighborhoods of Komemiyut/Talbieh, Mahane Yisrael/Shchunat HaMa'aravim, Mid-Town, Yemin Moshe).

Eliel Dror (1905 – 1970) Shama'a – HaMigdal **I13**

A Jerusalem activist, he served as deputy mayor of Jerusalem (see the neighborhood of Yemin Moshe).

Hativat Yerushalayim Ma'ale HaShalom – HaTzanhanim – Yafo **I13-14**

(See the neighborhoods of the Armenian Quarter, the Christian Quarter, the Jewish Quarter, Yemin Moshe.)

Kariv, Yitzhak (1903 – 1999) David HaMelech – Hativat Yerushalayim **I13**

Mayor of Jerusalem 1952-1955 (see Mid-Town).

Meitiv Nagein Kariv – Shama'a **I13**

Plays well, a designation for King David (Psalms 33:3).

Ne'im Zmirot Kariv – Meitiv Nagein **I13**

Pleasant songs, one of the designations of King David (II Samuel 23:1).

Neot Deshe Yismah Melech – dead end **I13**

Grassy pastures, a phrase taken from the verse in Psalms 23:2, "He makes me lie down in green pastures, He leads me beside still waters."

Roeh Tzon Meitiv Nagein – dead end **I13**

Shepherd, another of the designations of King David (I Samuel 17:15).

Shama'a, Eliyahu Yosef (1881 – 1933) Eliel – David HaMelech **H-I13**

Founded the commercial center in Jerusalem in 1920 (see Mid-Town).

Yefei 'Einayim Meitiv Nagein – Neot Deshe **I13**

Beautiful eyes, a designation for King David (I Samuel 16:12).

Yismah Melech Meitiv Nagein – Kariv **I13**

The king will rejoice, another designation for King David (Psalms 21:2).

'Ein Kerem

Name and establishment:

This neighborhood, located in the southwestern part of the city, was established as a Jewish neighborhood in 1949 and named for the vineyards (*karmei hagefen*) and olive orchards growing in the area, and for the spring (*ma'ayan*) flowing between its buildings. Some think that 'Ein Kerem is the Biblical Beit HaKerem, "...and on Beit HaKerem set up a signal fire, for evil is appearing from the north and a great shattering (Jeremiah 6:1)."

According to Christian tradition, this village was the birthplace of John the Baptist, the herald of Jesus. During the Byzantine period, the village became a holy Christian site, and churches and monasteries connected to the events of John the Baptist's life were built there. Christian pilgrims who reached 'Ein Kerem over the generations were impressed by the sight of the olive orchards and vineyards and of the waters of the spring. Until the establishment of the State, the village residents were Arabs who did agricultural work. In the War of Independence, after harsh battles, the village was taken by the GaDN"A' company (an army unit of teenage fighters under age 18), the village residents fled, and in their place new immigrants and artists moved in. In those years, Rahel Yanait Ben-Zvi built an agricultural youth village there, above the spring, and today the former youth village is a youth hostel.

The typical tree of the 'Ein Kerem area is the olive tree. The stream beds and hills are dotted with olive trees six to seven hundred years old. The Arabs planted these olive trees in the area for the production of olive oil. If the olive tree is the symbol of Arab 'Ein Kerem, the grape vine is the symbol of Biblical-Jewish 'Ein Kerem. The grape is one of the earliest cultivated plants for which the Land of Israel was praised, and it is mentioned in the Biblical text, beginning with the story of the spies (Numbers 13:23), continuing in the time of King Solomon (I Kings 5:5) and finally in the period of the prophets (Zechariah 8:12).

Its residents are Jews and Christian minorities, monks and nuns who live in the monasteries and convents in the area.

Boundaries:

Northeast – Har HaZikaron and Mount Herzl

South – Kiryat Menahem

East – Kiryat HaYovel

West – campus of Hadassah Medical Center

Sites: within its boundaries or nearby are Hadassah Medical Center, Har HaZikaron (the site of Yad Vashem), Mount Herzl, the Church of the Visitation, the Church of John the Baptist, the Greek Orthodox Church of St. John, the Convent of the Rosary, the Convent of the Sisters of Zion, the Russian convent (called by its Arabic name Al Moskovia, from Moskow, the capital of Russia), art galleries, and the Targ Moskovia Music Center.

Streets: the neighborhood streets are named for trees, bushes, animals, names associated with vineyards, and names of Christian holy places.

The streets are:

Barkali, Shaul (1900 – 1970) 'Ein Kerem – Derech Binyamina **B14**

Educator, researcher of the Hebrew language and disseminator of the language through his writings, published poems, stories for children and articles on education, a public activist.

Derech Binyamina Barkali – dead end **B14**

Named for the Binyamina wine presses and vineyards found in the hilly surroundings here.

Derech HaAhayot HaOren – HaOren **A14**

Sisters, named for the Sisters of Zion Convent located on the summit of the opposite hill.

Derech HaIlanot ‘Ein Kerem – dead end **A14**

Named for a tree with a thick, tall trunk.

Derech HaSela‘ Shvil HaTzukim – dead end **A14**

Road of the rock, referring to the landscape.

Derech HaTatzpit ‘Ein Kerem – Shvil HaHoma **A14**

Referring to the look-out and watch tower, built on this rocky hill by the Egyptian pasha who conquered Jerusalem in his revolt against the Ottoman rulers in the 1830's. From this tower soldiers would signal to other observation towers in the Judean hills.

Derech Karmit ‘Ein Kerem – Hevroni **B15**

The road leading to the area of the vineyards.

Derech Sorek ‘Emek HaTeimanim – dead end **A14**

The road leading to *Nahal Sorek* (Sorek stream), an ancient stream in the Land of Israel, one of the longest and most winding in the country, forty-two kilometers (twenty-six miles) long. On the sides of the hills along the stream grows a choice grapevine, the Soreika, hence its name. This grapevine is mentioned in the patriarch Jacob's blessing to Judah, “Tying his young donkey to the vine, his ass's colt to the choice grapevine [*soreika*]” (Genesis 49:11).

‘Ein Kerem Herzl Boulevard – Kerem Junction **A-C14**

Named for the neighborhood.

‘Ein Kerem [Square] ‘Ein Kerem at HaSha‘ar **A14**

Named for the neighborhood.

‘Emek HaTeimanim ‘Ein Kerem – dead end **A14**

Named for the descendants of Shalom Butal the Elder, Yemenite immigrants, who still live in ‘Ein Kerem's northern valley and for whom the place is called the Valley of the Yemenites.

Giv'at HaYonim Ma'ale HaBustan – Madreigot HaRomaim **A15**

Named for the dovecotes in which, apparently, the Jews of the Second Temple period raised doves for use as sacrifices in the Holy Temple in Jerusalem.

HaDafna Derech Karmit – Madreigot HaKfar **A14-B15**

Laurel, a green ornamental bush. The leaves of the laurel are used for seasoning food. The Greeks and Romans crowned their poets and military victors with laurel wreaths.

HaHadasim 'Ein Kerem – dead end **A14**

The myrtle, an ornamental bush with shiny leaves and white-yellow flowers. It grows in the coastal area in northern Israel. The myrtle is one of the four species that are used in the Sukkot holiday rituals, and in the sources it is called *etz 'avot* (Leviticus 23:40).

HaMa'ayan 'Ein Kerem – Madreigot HaBikur **A14-15**

At the heart of the village is a *spring*, hence the name of the neighborhood, 'Ein Kerem, the spring of the vineyard. Christians see this spring as a holy site, and therefore gave the names: "Miriam's (Mary's) Spring", "Mother of Jesus", and "Spring of the Virgin". There are those who believe that Mary and her sister Elisabeth met by the spring. The spring is also holy to Muslims because, according to their sayings, Khalif 'Omar ibn el-Khatab prayed next to it when he set out to conquer Jerusalem in the seventh century CE.

HaOren HaMa'ayan – Derech HaAhayot **A14**

Pine, one of the most common coniferous trees. The wood is good for building and for making furniture.

HaSha'ar [Lane] 'Ein Kerem – the Church of St. John **A14**

Gate, named for the iron gate of the Church of St. John, that is in the hills.

HaYekev [Alley] 'Ein Kerem – dead end **A14**

Winepress, to indicate the vineyards found in the hilly surroundings of the neighborhood.

Homat HaTzlafim 'Ein Kerem – 'Ein Kerem **A14**

Caper, named for a wild bush of that family with simple leaves and large flowers. Grows on walls and rocks. This bush is mentioned in the Mishna as an edible plant (Ma'asrot 4:6).

Kikar HaKastel 'Ein Kerem at Madreigot Gan 'Eden at Derech HaIlanot **A14**

Named for the Kastel fortress, located on the summit of the hill.

Ma'agal HaNikba HaMa'ayan – HaMa'ayan **A15**

To indicate an archeological dig under the surface of the ground, related to the spring.

Ma'ale HaAchsaniya HaMa'ayan – dead end **A15**

Named for the youth hostel there.

Ma'ale HaBustan 'Ein Kerem – dead end **A15**

To indicate a *garden of fruit trees* in the area.

Ma'ale HaMoeitza 'Ein Kerem – Madreigot HaBatzir **A14**

The ascent of the council, a symbolic name.

Madreigot Gan 'Eden 'Ein Kerem – dead end **A14**

Steps of Paradise, a symbolic name.

Madreigot HaBatzir 'Ein Kerem – Derech Binyamina **A-B14**

Steps of the grape harvest. Referring to the vineyards on the hills around the neighborhood.

Madreigot HaBikur HaMa'ayan – dead end **A15**

Named for the steps that lead to the Church of the Visitation, the visit of Mary to Elisabeth.

Madreigot HaKfar HaDafna – Barkali – dead end **A-B14**

Refers to the steps ascending to the village nearby.

Madreigot HaRomaim 'Ein Kerem – dead end **A15**

Referring to the steps leading toward a site with archeological remains from the Roman period, the most outstanding of which were elegant mosaic floors and parts of statues.

Shvil HaHoma 'Ein Kerem – Homat HaTzlafim **A14**

Refers to the *path along the wall* that encircles the Monastery of John the Baptist.

Shvil HaShibolim HaOren – dead end **A14**

Named for ears of grain of the family of cereal grains, including wheat and barley.

Shvil HaTzofit Homat HaTzlafim – dead end **A14**

Named for a small songbird found in Israel and southern Syria.

Shvil HaTzukim Homat HaTzlafim – Derech HaSela‘ **A14**

Path of promontories.

Shvil Tzukei HaYeshu‘a Ma‘alot HaAchsaniya – dead end **A15**

Path of the precipice of redemption. Refers to an isolated path, very narrow and winding, leading upward to a secret cave at the top of one of the nearby hills.

Simtat Ha‘Atalef Madreigot Gan ‘Eden – dead end **A14**

Bat. Named for a nocturnal mammal that flies and spends the daytime hours in the dark.

Simtat HaBe-er HaOren – dead end **A14-15**

Named for the well nearby.

Simtat HaGiv‘a HaHadasim – Derech HaAhayot **A14**

Hill, named for the hill on which is built the Convent of the Sisters of Zion.

Simtat HaKashatot Homat HaTzlafim – Shvil HaHoma **A14**

Arches, named for the ancient arches in the area.

Simtat Ha‘Orev ‘Ein Kerem – Shvil HaHoma **A14**

Named for the family of ravens, birds of the order songbirds.

Simtat HaTzaftzafa ‘Ein Kerem – dead end **A14**

Poplar, named for an ornamental tree of the willow family.

Simtat HaYayin HaDafna – dead end **A-B14**

Alley of wine, named for the vineyards on the hills surrounding the neighborhood.

E-Tur (Mount of Olives)

Name and establishment:

The neighborhood occupies the heights of the Mount of Olives, and the meaning of the name is “the mountain”. Its residents are Muslim Arabs. In the mid-ninteenth century, Christian sects began to build churches there in honor of events connected with the life of Jesus. One of the important churches is the Church of the Ascension, identified in Christian tradition as the place where Jesus ascended to heaven. Today it is in Muslim hands. Next to it was built a Russian Orthodox church with a tall bell tower. It, too, was built to mark the ascension of Jesus to heaven. Another church, Pater Noster, was built, according to Christian tradition, above the cave where Jesus is said to have brought his disciples. This church belongs to the Carmelite nuns. Also in this neighborhood are the Intercontinental Hotel and two hospitals, Al-Muqased and the well-known hospital for the poor, Augusta Victoria.

Boundaries:
North – E-Suwana and Wadi el-Joz
South – Mount of Olives
West – the Old City
Southwest – the City of David and Silwan (Kfar HaShiloah)

Streets: the neighborhood streets are called by Christian and Muslim names.

The streets are:

Beit Fagi E-Sheikh – El-Farsi **K13**

Named for a Jewish site that existed on the Mount of Olives in the Second Temple period.

Derech Yeriho Suleiman – the city of Jericho **J12-K14**

(See the neighborhoods of the City of David and the Moslem Quarter.)

El-Hardob El-Koleh – dead end **L12**

A topographical area name.

El-Koleh El-Farsi – ‘Anbar **L13**

The name of a tree.

El-Mansuriya Rab‘a el-‘Adawiyeh – Yeriho [Jericho Road] **K12**

Named for a Christian monastery on this street.

E-Sheikh Yeriho – Derech Har HaZeitim [Mount of Olives Road] **L13**

Named for one of the Christian wise men.

E-Tur Mount of Olives – Yeriho **K13**

Named for the Mount of Olives and the neighborhood.

Rab‘a el-‘Adawiyeh (717 – 801 CE) ‘Anbar – E-Sheikh **K-L12**

The most renowned and traditional Arab woman in the Muslim world.

Salmi el-Farsi (d. 655 CE) El-Koleh – Rab'a el-'Adawiyeh **L12**

One of the Prophet Muhammed's prominent friends.

Sheikh 'Anbar Rab'a el-'Adawiyeh – dead end **L12**

One of the founders of the village.

The Mosque Rab'a el-'Adawiyeh – dead end **K13**

Named for the mosque on this street.

Wadi 'Abdullah E-Sheikh – Yeriho **L13**

Named for the dry streambed in this area.

'Etz Haim/Wolfson

Name and establishment:

This neighborhood (Tree of Life), located in the northern part of the city as one enters, facing Mosad HaRav Kook, was founded in 1929 and named for the *'Etz Haim* Yeshiva. Its name is also drawn from Proverbs 3:18, "It is a tree of life to those who hold onto it, and those who support it are happy." This was the first neighborhood to greet those who came from outside the city – to Rehov Yafo in Jerusalem. Its buildings were spread out near the central bus station, opposite Binyanei HaUma (the International Conference Center). The founders were ultra-Orthodox Ashkenazic Jews.

By 1934 the first two buildings were built, one bordering Rehov Yafo and the second to the south of the first. The neighborhood was also named after the philanthropist Shlomo Wolfson and his wife Sarah Necha, who loaned their own money for the construction of additional buildings. On the front of the lintel of the neighborhood's main gate (the gate itself has not survived), engraved in the stone, is the year the neighborhood was established and its name. In the courtyard, the water cistern that was dug by the residents still remains, as do the special, original flagstones paving the enclosure. On the eastern wall of the neighborhood is affixed a sign on which appear the names of Shlomo Wolfson and his wife.

Boundaries:

North – Romema
South – Giv'at Ram
East – Mekor Baruch

West – Kiryat Moshe

The neighborhood was located near main intersections in the city – the beginnings of Yafo and Yirmiyahu Streets to the east, the beginnings of Herzl and Shazar Boulevards to the west, and the starting point of the highway going down to Tel-Aviv.

Sites: within its boundaries or nearby are located the International Conference Center, Mosad HaRav Kook, the Central Bus Station.

Streets: the neighborhood has no internal streets. The buildings were put up within the four-sided area formed by the main streets: Yafo, Shazar, Herzl and Yirmiyahu. **F11**

Even Yehoshu'a

Name and establishment:

This neighborhood, in the center of town, just west of Mea She'arim and within the boundaries of the Batei Kollel Warsaw neighborhood, was founded in 1893. It is named for Yehoshu'a Helfman, who purchased the property from the Arabs and built twelve houses on the site. When his money ran out and he was unable to continue building, he sold the property to the neighboring Warsaw Kollel which then built houses for its Kollel students. Most of the neighborhood's residents belong to the ultra-Orthodox community.

Boundaries:

North – Batei Kollel Warsaw, Mea She'arim Street and Beit Yisrael

South – Mid-Town

East – Mea She'arim

West – Zichron Moshe

Northwest – Geula

Sites: within its boundaries or nearby is the chair of Rabbi Nahman of Breslav, situated in the large prayer hall of the Breslaver Hasidim.

Streets: the neighborhood streets are named for great Hasidic rabbis and books of religious law.

The streets are:

'Avodat Yisrael Hayei Adam – Straus **H11**

(See the neighborhood of Batei Kollel Warsaw/Nahlat Ya'akov.)

Even Yehoshu'a Hayei Adam – Straus **H11**

(See the neighborhood of Batei Wittenberg/Sha'arei Moshe.)

Hayei Adam Straus – Mea She'arim **H11**

(See the neighborhoods of Batei Kollel Warsaw/Nahlat Ya'akov, Batei Werner/Ohalei Moshe, Batei Wittenberg/Sha'arei Moshe, Bnei Moshe/Neve Shalom).

Levi Yitzhak of Berdichev, Rabbi (1740–1810)
Even Yehoshu'a – Nahman of Breslav **H11**

One of the leaders of the Hasidic movement, a rabbi and Hasidic master of his sect, and a great Torah scholar. The disciple of Rabbi Dov Ber, the Maggid of Mezeritch, known for his defense of Israel: Even in the Biblical verses which speak ill of Israel, he would always find in them words of praise. He is known by the name of his hometown.

Nahman of Breslav, Rabbi (1772 – 1810)
'Avodat Yisrael – 'Avodat Yisrael **H11**

A great-grandson of the Ba'al Shem Tov, founder and rabbinic leader of the Hasidic sect named for him. He visited Israel in 1798. He is known by the name of his hometown. Since his death, the Breslaver sect has had no official rabbinic leader. Many go to visit his grave, in Uman, Ukraine, and therefore, in recent years, he has been called Nahman from Uman.

Straus, Nathan (1848 – 1931) Yafo – Kikar HaShabbat **H11-12**

(See the neighborhoods of Batei Kollel Warsaw/Nahlat Ya'akov, Batei Wittenberg/Sha'arei Moshe, Bnei Moshe/Neve Shalom, Mid-Town.)

Even Yisrael

Name and establishment:

The neighborhood, located in the center of town, southeast of Mahane Yehuda and near the neighborhoods Sukkat Shalom and Mishkenot Yisrael, was founded in the year 1875 by a company of 53 (the numerical values of the Hebrew letters in the word "Even" add up to 53) Jews, and from this comes the name. It was the sixth Jewish neighborhood built outside the Old City walls. The land was acquired together with the land for the neighborhood of Mishkenot

Yisrael, and both were built in the same year. In the 1860s and 1870s, these neighborhoods were built by private initiative and funded by the residents of the Old City of Jerusalem themselves, members of the *Hurva* Synagogue (of Rabbi Yehuda HeHasid). The builders of these neighborhoods saw the building up and expansion of Jerusalem as a kind of "beginning of the Redemption".

As in the case of other neighborhoods like Mea She'arim and Mazkeret Moshe, Even Yisrael was built in the form of a closed, square box, for protection and safety. In the center was an internal courtyard, and the entrance to the houses was from this courtyard. The courtyard served as a public area in which there were cisterns for rainwater, synagogues, the ritual bath and more. The neighborhood was built for residential purposes only. In its early years, long-time city residents lived here, workers, merchants and craftsmen. Among the residents was Avraham Moshe Lunz, one of the researchers of Israel and Jerusalem, Yehiel Michal Pines, one of the important businessmen of the community, and others like them. As the years passed, the neighborhood changed, and today it is a commercial center, an area of craftsmen and shops, and its houses face onto the main commercial streets, Yafo and Agrippas Street.

Boundaries:
North – Yafo
South – Agrippas Street
East – King George Street and Mid-Town
West – Sukkat Shalom and Mishkenot Yisrael and the Mahane Yehuda Market

Sites: within its boundaries or nearby is the remnant of the glory of the neighborhood, the Mahane Yehuda Market.

Streets: the street is named for the neighborhood.

The streets are:

Agrippas (10 BCE – 44 CE) King George – Shmuel Baruch **G11-H12**

The last king of Judea, the grandson of Miriam the Hasmonean and Herod. He built the Third Wall of Jerusalem (see the neighborhoods of Mahane Yehuda, Mazkeret Moshe, Mid-Town, Mishkenot Yisrael, Nahlat Tzion, Ohel Moshe, Sukkat Shalom, Zichron Tuvia, Zichron Yosef).

Alboher, Haim, Rabbi [Passageway] (1880 – 1938)
Yafo – Agrippas **H12**

One of the founders of the Sephardic orphanage in Jerusalem that was built near this neighborhood through the generosity of the Borochov brothers, Avraham, Yitzhak, Ya'akov and Mashiah (see the neighborhood of Mahane Yehuda).

Even Yisrael Yafo – Agrippas **H12**

Named for the neighborhood. Formerly called Valero Street (see the neighborhood of Mahane Yehuda).

Yafo Jaffa Gate – Weizmann Boulevard **F11-I12**

(See the neighborhoods of Batei Kollel Horodna/Damesek Eli'ezer, Batei Sa'idoff, Beit David, Beit Ya'akov, 'Ezrat Yisrael, Mahane Yehuda, Mekor Baruch, Mid-Town, Nahlat Shiv'a, Ohel Shlomo, Romema, Russian Compound, Sha'arei Tzedek, Sha'arei Yerushalayim.)

'Ezrat Torah

Name and establishment:

This neighborhood, located in the northern part of the city, was founded about 1970 and called by the name of the religious Jewish organization *'Ezrat Torah* that offered help and support in the matter of housing for the residents, who belong to the ultra-Orthodox community.

Boundaries:

North – Sanhedria HaMurhevet

South – Shikun HaBa"D

East – Mahanayim and Sanhedria

West – Kiryat Zanz

Sites: within its boundaries or nearby are the Sanhedria Cemetery, tombs of the Sanhedrin.

Streets: this neighborhood has one street, which is named for the neighborhood.

The streets are:

Even HaEZe"L Ya'akovson – 'Ezrat Torah **G10**

A book on the RaMBa"M's *Mishne Torah* by Rabbi **I**sser **Z**a**l**man Meltzer (1870-1954), a rabbi and arbiter of religious law, one of the outstanding heads of yeshiva in the Land of Israel, director of the *'Etz Haim* Yeshiva in Jerusalem.

'Ezrat Torah Giv'at Moshe – Ya'akovson **G-H9**

Named for the neighborhood and for the religious Jewish organization that devoted great efforts in the Diaspora and in Israel to help poor Jewish scholars in Israel, especially to provide housing.

Giv'at Moshe [Boulevard] Golda Meir – 'Ezrat Torah **G9-H10**

Named for Rabbi Moshe Porush (1894-1983), deputy mayor of Jerusalem, one of the supporters of the religious education network (see the neighborhood of Mahanayim).

'Ezrat Yisrael

Name and establishment:

This neighborhood, located in the center of town, was founded during the period of Turkish rule, in 1892. At the top of the document establishing the neighborhood appear Biblical verses which include the root letters 'ayin, zayin, resh (the word "help"), the source of the neighborhood's name: "He will send forth help for you from the Sanctuary and from Zion your support" (Psalms 20:3), "My help comes from the Lord, Maker of heaven and earth" (Psalms 121:2), hence the name, the Help of Israel.

This is a neighborhood of one street, entered from Rehov Yafo and ending at HaNeviim. At the time of its founding, the neighborhood was built as two rows of buildings of one story each, facing each other, with a total of about thirty apartments. Over time, additional stories were built onto the buildings. At both ends of the street, iron gates were erected, and care was taken to lock them every evening for fear of thieves and robbers. Some think that the neighborhood was built as a connection between the southern and northern neighborhoods of the city, between Even Yisrael to the south and Mea She'arim to the north.

In its early years, the neighborhood was the center for the press in the country. At the entrance from Rehov Yafo was the printing business of the Israel researcher A.M. Lunz, who lived in nearby Even Yisrael. In his shop he printed his essays on Israel and Jerusalem. The newspaper

Herut was printed in his shop, called *'Azriel* Press after the name of the neighborhood. In another printing shop in a nearby neighborhood was printed the weekly *Ahdut* of *Po'alei Tzion* in the Land of Israel. Its editors were David Ben-Gurion, Yitzhak Ben-Zvi and his wife Rahel Yanait, who also lived in 'Ezrat Yisrael. In this neighborhood lived other important people: the chief rabbis of the Sephardic communities, the Rishon LeZion, Rabbi Haim Ya'akov Meir, one of the founders of the neighborhood, and Ben-Tzion Meir Hai 'Uziel. Because well-known people lived in this neighborhood, 'Ezrat Yisrael was then considered one of the prestigious neighborhoods in the city.

As the years passed, the number of neighborhoods in the city increased, the population around 'Ezrat Yisrael grew, and the neighborhood was swallowed up in the center of the city.

Boundaries:
North – Mea She'arim
South – Even Yisrael
East – Beit David/Beit HaRav Kook, Mid-Town
West – Mahane Yehuda Market

Sites: within its boundaries or nearby are Bikur Holim Hospital, Mahane Yehuda Market.

Streets: this is a one-street neighborhood, with the street named for the neighborhood.

The streets are:

'Ezrat Yisrael Yafo – Bikur Holim – dead end **H12**

Named for the neighborhood.

HaNeviim Yafo – Damascus Gate **H-I12**

(See the neighborhoods of Beit David/Beit HaRav Kook, Mid-Town, Morasha/Musrara, Zichron Moshe.)

Yafo Jaffa Gate – Weizmann Boulevard **F11-I12**

(See the neighborhoods of Batei Kollel Horodna/Damesek Eli'ezer, Batei Sa'idoff, Beit David/Beit HaRav Kook, Beit Ya'akov, Even Yisrael, Mahane Yehuda, Mekor Baruch, Mid-Town, Nahlat Shiv'a, Ohel Shlomo, Romema, Russian Compound, Sha'arei Tzedek, Sha'arei Yerushalayim.)

German Colony *[HaMoshava HaGermanit]*/ RaMBa"M

Name and establishment:

This neighborhood, located in the southern part of Jerusalem, was founded in 1873 and is the only neighborhood in Jerusalem established by European Christians, members of a congregation of Templers from Germany. Most of the group, which had already founded colonies in Haifa and Jaffa, were farmers, so the neighborhood was called a *moshava* [agricultural collective]. The name *Refaim* (of one of the streets) was linked to this colony because the houses were built in the valley called *'Emek Refaim.* This name appears in Joshua 15:8, where the borders of the tribe of Judah are described, and in II Samuel 5:18, 22, which describes the place where King David vanquished the Philistines.

The neighborhood continued to develop with the building of the railroad station in 1892 on its northern edge. The German Templers lived here from the neighborhood's founding until 1943, except for a brief period near the end of World War I, a period of about seventy-five years. Today, the neighborhood's residents are Jews.

The neighborhood was given a Hebrew name – RaMBa"M, but the name didn't catch on.

Boundaries:

North – the railroad station, Komemiyut/Talbieh
South – the Greek Colony
East – Derech Beit Lehem
West – Gonen/Katamon HaYeshana

Sites: within its boundaries or nearby are some of the first buildings of the Templers on 'Emek Refaim Street, the Templer cemetery, the nature museum, International Cultural Center for Youth, the German Catholic convent, the Israel Electric Company station, the railroad station, Liberty Bell Park.

Streets: the streets of the neighborhood are named for famous Jews and friends of Israel all over the world, and also for famous historians, periodicals, Biblical figures and Lovers of Zion. The main street is 'Emek Refaim.

The streets are:

Allon, Gedalia (1901 – 1950) Mohilewer – Marcus **H14**

A researcher of Jewish history of the Second Temple and Mishna and Talmud periods.

Ashberg, Eli Mordechai, Rabbi (1817 – 1889) Graetz – dead end **H14**

One of the pre-eminent rabbis of Lithuania and one of the Lovers of Zion.

Bacher, Binyamin Zeev, Dr. (1850 – 1913) Mohilewer – Klein **H15**

Linguist and researcher of Judaic studies, especially the Mishna and Talmud. He translated the Bible into Hungarian. In linguistics he was among those who laid the groundwork for researching Hebrew grammar from the time of the Talmud until the end of the Middle Ages.

Bajaio, Haim, Rabbi (1875 – 1962) Rahel Imeinu – Root **H15**

One of the leaders of the Jewish community in Hebron.

Cremieux, Yitzhak Adolphe (1796 – 1880)
Derech Beit Lehem – 'Emek Refaim **H-I15**

French statesman and leader of French Jewry. One of the founders of the association *Kol Yisrael Haverim* [Alliance Israelite] – KY"H, and president of the association.

Deedes, Wyndham (1883 – 1956) Smuts – 'Emek Refaim **H15**

A British military man and politician, he served as general secretary of the British government at the start of the British Mandate.

Derech Beit Lehem [Bethlehem Road] 'Emek Refaim – Bar'am, ends at the city of Bethlehem **H15-18**

A city south of Jerusalem. The foremother Rachel is buried there, and King David was born there. For Christians it is the birthplace of Jesus (see the neighborhoods of Geulim/Bak'a, Talpiot-Industrial Zone).

Dor Dor VeDorshav Graetz – Mohilewer **H14**

Named for the book by Rabbi Isaac Hirsch Weiss (1815-1905), which comprehends the development of the Oral Law from its inception until after the Expulsion from Spain. He was one of the spiritual leaders of the Jewish people during the Enlightenment period.

'Emanuel Noah, Mordechai (1785 – 1851)
HaMagid – dead end **H14-15**

Was an author, journalist, judge and statesman in the United States. Before the Zionist movement began, he initiated the establishment of a temporary shelter for persecuted Jews and called it "Ararat in the State of New York", but this effort failed in the end. Afterwards, he preached the goal of establishing a country for the Jews in the Land of Israel.

'Emek Refaim Remez – Rahel Imeinu, ends at El'azar HaModa'i **H15**

Named for the neighborhood and for the valley in which the first residents settled. According to the Bible, King David vanquished the Philistines in this place. 'Emek Refaim Street serves today as the central thoroughfare of the neighborhood (see the Greek Colony).

Freud, Sigmund [Square] (1865 – 1939)
Derech Beit Lehem at 'Emek Refaim **H14**

One of the greatest scientists in the modern period and the founder of psychoanalysis. Was a member of the Board of Trustees of the Hebrew University.

Gaster, Moshe, Rabbi [Alley] (1856 – 1939) Graetz – dead end **H14**

Historian and researcher of Israel and the Samaritans [*Shomronim*]. An early Lover of Zion.

Gedud Tuvia [Square] Rahel Imeinu at 'Uziyahu **H15**

Named for Tuvia Beer, commander of the battalion of yeshiva students in 1948.

Gottlieb, Maurycy (1856 - 1879) Cremieux – Patterson **H-I15**

A gifted Jewish artist, considered one of the great Jewish painters of the nineteenth century. Some of his paintings were dedicated to Jewish themes. Died of tuberculosis at a young age.

Graetz, Zvi Heinrich, Dr. (1817 – 1891) 'Emek Refaim – Pinsker **H14**

One of the prominent historians of Jewish history. Was the first who wrote on Jewish history from the Jewish point of view. His books were translated into Hebrew, Yiddish, English and other languages.

HaMagid Klein – 'Emek Refaim **H15**

Named for the first Hebrew weekly that appeared outside of Israel (1856-1890). This publication served as a clarion call for the Lovers of Zion.

HaMeilitz 'Emek Refaim – Hildesheimer **H15**

One of the earliest Hebrew newspapers printed in Russia in the years 1861-1904, it preached Love of Zion and later Zionism. Among the writers for the paper were: M.L. Lilienblum, Y.L. Gordon and Ahad Ha'Am.

Hanania 'Emek Refaim – HaRakevet **H15**

One of the three friends of the prophet Daniel: "And there were among them young men of Judah, Daniel, Hananiah, Mishael and 'Azariah" (Daniel 1:6). The four were thrown into a fiery furnace, yet they were not harmed by the fire.

HaRakevet [Road] Derech Beit Lehem – Pierre Koenig **H15-16**

Railroad, named for the rail line that runs along the length of this street (see the neighborhoods of Geulim/Bak'a, the Greek Colony, Mekor Haim).

HaTzfira 'Emek Refaim – Root – dead end **H15**

The first Hebrew newspaper published in Warsaw, Poland, not always regularly, between the years 1862-1931, it was dedicated to articles on science and technology. In its later years, the newspaper supported the idea of Zionism.

Hildesheimer, 'Azriel, Rabbi Dr. (1820 – 1899)
HaMagid – Rahel Imeinu **H15**

One of the leaders of Orthodox Jewry in Germany. One of the first Lovers of Zion, established a society for settlement of the Land of Israel. One of the founders of the association for building sheltered housing in the Old City.

King, Martin Luther (1929–1968)
'Emek Refaim – the Train Theater, Liberty Bell Park **H-I14**

An African-American leader and fighter for civil rights in the United States.

Klein, Shmuel, Rabbi (1886 – 1940) HaTzfira – Allon **H15**

Rabbi and spiritual leader of Hungarian Jewry. One of the outstanding researchers of the Land of Israel during the period of the Mishna and Talmud. Professor at the Hebrew University of Jerusalem.

Lloyd George (1863 – 1945) Derech Beit Lehem – 'Emek Refaim **H-I15**

David Lloyd George, British statesman and prime minister of Britain. During his term as prime minister, the Balfour Declaration was approved, and he expressed his full support of the Declaration.

MaLa"L (1843 – 1910) 'Emek Refaim – Hildesheimer **H15**

Moshe **L**eib **L**ilienblum, one of the earliest Lovers of Zion in Russia and Eastern Europe, who saw in Zionism the solution to the problem of the

Jews. He was an author in the Enlightenment period and was among the writers for the Hebrew newspaper *HaMeilitz*.

Masaryk, Thomas (1850 – 1937) ‘Emek Refaim – HaRakevet **H15**

A statesman and the first president of Czechoslovakia. He supported Zionism and the right of the Jewish people to the Land of Israel. He was the first head of state to visit the Land of Israel during the British Mandate. Was made an honorary citizen of the City of Tel-Aviv.

Mohilewer, Shmuel, Rabbi (1824 – 1898) Allon – HaMagid **H14-15**

One of the great rabbis of Russia. One of the heads of the early Lovers of Zion (see Pinsker Street in the neighborhood of Komemiyut/Talbieh). One of the fathers of Religious Zionism and a member of the Mizrahi movement (today part of the National Religious Party in Israel). He encouraged Baron Rothschild to support Jewish agricultural settlement in Israel.

Patterson, John Henry (1867–1947)
‘Emek Refaim – Derech Beit Lehem – dead end **I14-15**

British military commander. Was sent to the Land of Israel at the head of the Jewish Battalion during World War I. He supported Zionism and was a friend of Israel.

Rahel Imeinu ‘Emek Refaim – HaPortzim **G-H15**

Our mother Rachel, one of the four Biblical foremothers (Genesis 29:28). Her burial place is *Kever Rahel* (Rachel’s Tomb) on the outskirts of Bethlehem (see the neighborhoods of Gonen/Katamon HaYeshana, the Greek Colony).

Root Rahel Imeinu – HaTzfira **H15**

Ruth, the heroine of the Biblical scroll by this name. Wife of Boaz of Beit Lehem, great-grandmother of King David. The Scroll of Ruth is read on the holiday of Shavu‘ot.

Rosanes, Shlomo (1862 – 1938) Mohilewer – dead end **H14**

One of the pre-eminent historians of Turkish Jewry. Compiled research and wrote articles in Hebrew, Bulgarian, French and other languages. His most important books were six volumes on the history of the Jews in Turkey, *Divrei Yemei Yisrael BeTogarma*. He also wrote a book of research on the beginnings of human speech, *Safa Ahat uDevarim Ahadim*, according to which all languages derived originally from ancient Hebrew.

Sheskin, Ya'akov (1914-1999) Gedalia Allon – Dubnow **H14**

A professor, expert in skin diseases, medical director of the Hansen Hospital, located here.

Simtat Jimmy Masaryk – dead end **H15**

Jimmy's Lane, named for a dog named Jimmy that belonged to one of the street's residents and was allowed to roam the neighborhood freely. On the street sign is written: "Simtat Jimmy that wagged his tail and roamed happily here during the years 1988-1998."

Smuts, Jan [*Yohanan*] (1870 – 1950) Cremieux – Deedes **H15**

Statesman and prime minister of South Africa. Was a supporter of the World Zionist Movement and backed the Balfour Declaration. In 1948 as prime minister he gave *de facto* recognition to the newly-established State of Israel.

Wedgwood, Josiah Clement (1872 – 1943)
'Emek Refaim – Smuts **H15**

English statesman, supporter of Zionism, took part in the contacts that led to the Balfour Declaration in 1917, one of the supporters of the establishment of a Jewish state.

Zola, Emile (1840 – 1902) 'Emek Refaim – Smuts **H15**

French author who fought for human rights. He is remembered particularly as a defense attorney in the Dreyfus trial and for his penetrating front-page article: "I accuse."

Geula

Name and establishment:

This neighborhood located in the middle of town northwest of Mea She'arim and bordering the neighborhood of HaBucharim, was established in 1926, and the source of the name is from the verse: "And throughout the land in your possession, you shall provide for redemption of the land." (Leviticus 25:24) The name symbolizes the will and the desire of the Jews for their redemption in their land as the prophets of Israel had prophesied.

Part of the neighborhood was built on the site of a grove between Yona and Amos Streets known as Schneller's Grove. The remainder of the parcels, the "Chelouche Neighborhood", was purchased by the Chelouche brothers, who were active in the redemption of pieces of land. It was they who sold the land to the new residents. In 1930 in a sysnagogue in the Ahva neighborhood, there was a special meeting for property owners in Schneller's Grove and the Chelouche Neighborhood, with one item on the agenda: "naming the neighborhood." At this meeting it was decided to unite the two neighborhoods into one under the name "Geula." With the passing years, the other names were forgotten.

Jews from all communities lived in this neighborhood, religious, traditional, non-religious, scholars and simple laborers. Today, the residents belong to the ultra-Orthodox community.

Boundaries:

North – HaBucharim

South – Mea She'arim Street and neighborhood

East – Beit Yisrael

West – Kerem Avraham

Sites: within its boundaries or nearby are Talmudical academies: the *Knesset Yisrael* yeshiva, begun in Hebron and moved to Jerusalem after the 1929 anti-Jewish riots; the *Tiferet Zvi* Yeshiva and the Yavne Talmud Torah.

Streets: the streets are named after the later prophets of Israel, thus the neighborhood is also called HaNeviim. The main street is Malchei Yisrael, which in the past was called Geula Street.

The streets are:

Blumenthal, Avraham Yohanan, Rabbi [Square] (1887 – 1966)
Yehezkel at Hoshe'a **H11**

A rabbi and educator, one of the civic leaders of Jerusalem.

Hagai (6th cent. BCE) Yoel – Malachi **H11**

A prophet in Israel, the tenth in the book of the Twelve Minor Prophets in the Bible. He was a prophet at the time of the Return to Zion (approximately 520 BCE).

HaYeshiva Malchei Yisrael – Hoshe'a **H11**

Named for the famous Hebron Yeshiva that was on this street.

Hoshe'a (ben Beeri) (8th cent. BCE) Yona – Yoel **H11**

Hosea, a prophet in Israel, the first in the book of the Twelve Minor Prophets in the Bible. He prophesied "...in the days of 'Uziah, Jotham, Ahaz, Hezekiah, kings of Judah and in the days of Jeroboam ben Joash, king of Israel." (Hosea 1:1)

Kikar HaShabbat intersection of Straus-Yesha'yahu-Mea She'arim-Malchei Yisrael **H11**

(See the neighborhoods of Batei Kollel Warsaw/Nahlat Ya'akov, Beit Yisrael.)

Levush Mordechai (1866 – 1934) Malchei Yisrael – Hagai **H11**

Named for the book by Rabbi Moshe Mordechai Epstein, a rabbi and arbiter of religious law and the head of a yeshiva in Hebron and in Jerusalem. One of the activists in the Lovers of Zion, a member of the Council of Torah Sages of *Agudat Yisrael* in Jerusalem.

Malachi (5th cent. BCE) Malchei Yisrael – 'Ezra **H11**

A prophet in Israel, the last in the book of the Twelve Minor Prophets in the Bible. He was the last of the prophets, "...for with his death ended the period of prophecy in Israel (according to the commentary of the commentator Ibn 'Ezra)."

Malchei Yisrael Sarei Yisrael – Straus **G-H11**

(See the neighborhoods of Ahva, Kerem/Beit Avraham, Kerem Avraham, Mekor Baruch.)

Mea She'arim Straus – Shivtei Yisrael **H11**

(See the neighborhoods of Batei Kollel Ungarin/Nahlat Zvi, Batei Kollel Warsaw/Nahlat Ya'akov, Batei Naitin, Batei Perlman/'Ir Shalom, Beit Yisrael, Mea She'arim, Nahlat Zvi/Shchunat HaTeimanim, Sha'arei Pina).

Micha (8th cent. BCE) Malchei Yisrael – dead end **H11**

Micah, a prophet in Israel, the sixth in the book of the Twelve Minor Prophets in the Bible. He also prophesied "...in the days of Jotham, Ahaz, Hezekiah, kings of Judah." (Micah 1:1)

Nahum (HaElkoshi) Malchei Yisrael – dead end **H11**

A prophet in Israel, the seventh in the book of the Twelve Minor Prophets in the Bible. This book concerns a harsh prophecy about Nineveh.

Tzefania (ben Cushi ben Gedalia) (7th cent. BCE)
Yehezkel – Malachi and ends at Bar-Ilan **H10-11**

Zephaniah, a prophet in Israel, the ninth in the book of the Twelve Minor Prophets in the Bible. In the days of Josiah, he prophesied about Judea and called Jerusalem the "city like a dove (derogatory)." (See the neighborhood of Kerem Avraham.)

Yehezkel (ben Buzi HaCohen) (6th cent. BCE)
Malchei Yisrael – Shmuel HaNavi **H10-11**

Ezekiel, one of the three Major Prophets, along with Isaiah and Jeremiah. He went into exile with King Jehoiachin of Judah, and he prophesied in Exile. He is known as the prophet of the Babylonian Exile. His best-known prophecies are the "Vision of the Chariot" (Ch. 1), "Eating the Scroll" (Ch. 3) and the parable of the "Valley of the Dry Bones," a prophecy touching on the fate of the Jewish people in the final generations (Ch. 37).

Yellin, Avino'am (1900 – 1938) Yehezkel – Eshlag **H11**

A Jerusalem educator and Orientalist, the son of David Yellin. He was murdered in the 1938 pogroms.

Yona (ben Amitai) Tzefania – Malchei Yisrael **H11**

Jonah, a prophet in Israel, the fifth in the book of the Twelve Minor prophets in the Bible. His prophecy concerns another nation. The Book of Jonah is read on Yom Kippur at the afternoon service.

Geulim/Bak'a

Name and establishment:

This neighborhood, located in the southern part of Jerusalem between the German Colony and the neighborhood of Talpiot, was established as a Jewish neighborhood only after the War of Independence, in 1948. It is called by its Arabic name, Bak'a, a cognate of the Hebrew word meaning "valley", for the valley extending along its western side, thus indicating the topography of the area.

In 1892 when the railroad line from Jaffa to Jerusalem was inaugurated, the neighborhood began to develop. Its first residents were Muslims who had left the Old City and put up the first buildings there. In the 1920s, during the British Mandate period, Christians and Muslims of higher economic standing began to move in and built magnificent dwellings. It must be noted that until 1948 no Jews lived in the neighborhood at all. With the outbreak of war, the Arab residents abandoned their homes and fled the neighborhood, and in their places new immigrants from Morocco moved in and called the neighborhood Geulim, because they felt they had been redeemed from the bonds of the Diaspora. The Hebrew name did not take among the public.

Since the 1970s young middle-class couples have been streaming into the neighborhood, renovating the old houses and building houses similar to those built there originally.

Boundaries:
North – from the Khan Theater to the old railroad station
South – Rivka Street from Derech Hevron to Pierre Koenig
East – Derech Hevron
West – the railroad track

Sites: within its boundaries or nearby are the Khan Theater, the old railroad station, the Reform temple "Kol HaNeshama", the *Pelech* School, the "Rose Garden" buildings.

Streets: the streets in the neighborhood are named for the tribes of Israel (except for the tribe of Benjamin, which is missing; and the tribe of Joseph is represented by both Efraim [Ephraim] and Menashe [Manasseh] Streets) and famous judges from the Bible.

The streets are:

Asher Naftali – Pierre Koenig **H16**

Son of the Biblical Zilpah, the maid of the foremother Leah; one of the tribes of Israel (Genesis 30:12-13).

Avtalyon (1st cent. BCE)
Derech Beit Lehem – Derech Hevron **H15-I16**

The partner of Shema'ya, the president of the Sanhedrin. He was the head of the court called the Sanhedrin. Avtalyon and Shema'ya were the fourth pair of Sages of the Mishna in the time of the Second Holy Temple. One of the maxims attributed to Avtalyon is: "Scholars, be careful with your words." (Pirkei Avot 1: Mishna 11)

Barak (ben Avino'am) (11th cent. BCE) Yael – dead end **H15**

Military commander in the period of the Judges; he fought with Deborah the Judge and Prophetess against the Canaanites (Judges 4-5).

Ben 'Azai Naftali – dead end **H16**

Named for Shim'on ben 'Azai, a third generation Tanna (authority quoted in the Mishna), lived in Tiberias.

Ben Yefune, Calev Derech Beit Lehem – Gad **H16**

Caleb, from the tribe of Judah, one of the spies that Moses sent to survey the land of Canaan. Caleb and Yehoshu'a [Joshua] bin Nun reported that the land of Canaan was "a land flowing with milk and honey." The two men earned the right to a patrimony in the Land of Israel (Numbers 13-14).

Bo'az Derech Beit Lehem – dead end **H15**

One of the distinguished men of the city of Bethlehem in the period of the Judges. He redeemed and married Ruth; their descendant was King David (Scroll of Ruth 2-4).

Dan Yissachar – Tzidkiyahu **H16**

Son of the Biblical Bilhah, the maid of the foremother Rachel; one of the tribes of Israel (Genesis 30:6).

Derech Beit Lehem 'Emek Refaim – Bar'am, ends at the city of Bethlehem **H15-18**

(See the neighborhoods of the German Colony/RaMBa"M, Talpiot - Industrial Zone.)

Derech Hevron Hativat Yerushalayim – 'Ein Gedi, ends at the city of Hebron **I14-F20**

The route of Derech Hevron extends from the north from Hativat Yerushalayim, a street near Har Tzion, to the neighborhoods of Giv'at Hanania/Abu Tor, Geulim/Bak'a, North Talpiot, Talpiot, Arnona, Giv'at HaMatos, Homat Shmuel/Har Homa and comes to an end further south at Bethlehem and Hebron.

Ephraim Reuven – Shimshon **H15**

Son of Joseph in the Bible; one of the tribes of Israel (Genesis 41:52).

Ehud (ben Gera) (12th – 11th cents. BCE) Yael – Efraim **H15**

A judge, during the Biblical period of Judges, who saved Israel from the hands of the Moabites (Judges 3). It is written of him that he was "Ehud son of Gera son of HaYemini; he was left-handed." (Judges 3:15).

Ester HaMalca (5th cent. BCE) Derech Beit Lehem – Derech Hevron **H16**

Esther, the daughter of Abihayil of the tribe of Benjamin, Queen of Persia, heroine and central figure of the scroll named for her. The Scroll of Esther is read twice on the Purim holiday.

Gad Yehuda – Rivka **H16**

Son of the Biblical Zilpah, the maid of the foremother Leah; one of the tribes of Israel (Genesis 30:10-11).

Gedalyahu (ben Ahikam) (6th cent. BCE)
Derech Hevron – Derech Beit Lehem **I15**

The governor of Judah appointed by the Babylonian conqueror, he was the last Jew in authority after the destruction of the First Holy Temple, and he was murdered while carrying out his duties. In his memory the Fast of Gedalia is observed on the day after Roah Hashana.

Gid'on (ben Yoash) (11th cent. BCE) Derech Beit Lehem – Naftali **H15**

Gideon, a judge during the period of the Judges who led the nation prior to the period of Kings (Judges 8). The *moshav* (agricultural cooperative) Gid'on Village and the residential community Gid'ona, both in the Jezreel Valley, are named after him.

HaRakevet [Road] Derech Beit Lehem – Pierre Koenig **H15-16**

(See the neighborhoods of the German Colony/RaMBa"M, the Greek Colony, Mekor Haim.)

Heletz Pierre Koenig – dead end **H16**

A community in the northern Negev, where the search for oil was unsuccessful.

Kibutz Galuyot Tzipora – Ben Yefune **H16**

The Ingathering of the Exiles, a phrase denoting the return of the Jews from all over the Diaspora to the Land of Israel.

Levi Beit Lehem – Yissachar **H16**

Son of the foremother Leah; one of the tribes of Israel (Genesis 29:34).

Lifshitz, Nahum (1895 – 1974) Gad – dead end **H16**

One of the founders of and chairman of the association of manufacturers in Jerusalem.

Marton, Erno Yehezkel (1896 – 1960) Ester HaMalca – Avtalyon **H16**

A newspaper editor and one of the leaders of the Jewish communities of Hungary and Transylvania. He served on the executive committee of the World Zionist Organization.

Matityahu Derech Beit Lehem – dead end **H15**

Matityahu ben Yohanan [Mattathias], the high priest. Scion of the Hasmonean family who incited revolt against the Greek conquerors of Judea. With his death, his third son, Yehuda HaMacabi (Judah Maccabee), carried on with the revolt and succeeded in routing the Greeks and purifying the Holy Temple. In commemoration of the successful revolt and the miracle of the oil lamp in the sanctuary, the festival of Hanuka was established (Books of the Maccabees).

Menashe Naftali - Efraim – dead end **H15-16**

Manasseh, son of Joseph, one of the tribes of Israel (Genesis 41:51).

Miriam HaHashmonait (1st cent. BCE)
Derech Beit Lehem – Derech Hevron **H-I15**

Last descendant of the Hasmonean royalty and the wife of King Herod, who ruled the kingdom of Judea more than thirty years, and killed his wife Miriam and both of their sons.

Mordechai HaYehudi (5th cent. BCE) Ester HaMalca – Yehuda **H16**

Mordechai (the Jew) ben Yair ben Shim'i ben Kish the Benjamite (from the tribe of Benjamin), one of the leaders of the Jews of Persia and Medea in the time of King Ahasuerus (Artaxerxes). Queen Esther was Mordechai's cousin and, through her, he succeeded in saving the Jews in the kingdom from destruction (Scroll of Esther).

Naftali Yehuda – Gid'on **H15-16**

Naphtali, son of the Biblical Bilhah, the maid of the foremother Rachel; one of the tribes of Israel (Genesis 30:8).

'Otniel (ben Knaz) HaRakevet – Yiftah **H15**

From the tribe of Judah, he was the brother of Calev ben Yefune. He was the first judge during the period of the Judges. He subjugated the king of Aram (Judges 3:7-11).

Peretz Yehuda – Heletz **H16**

The son of Judah, one of the tribes of Israel (Genesis 38:29).

Reuven Derech Beit Lehem – Naftali **H16**

Reuben, son of the foremother Leah; one of the tribes of Israel (Genesis 29:32).

Rivka Derech Hevron – Pierre Koenig **H16**

Rebekah, one of the four foremothers (Genesis 24:67), wife of Isaac (see the neighborhood of Talpiot-Industrial Zone).

Shema'ya (1st cent. BCE) Derech Hevron – Derech Beit Lehem **H-I15**

President of the Sanhedrin and paired to Avtalyon as the fourth pair of sages of the Mishna. He was head of the court in the period of the Second Temple. One of the maxims attributed to him was: "Love work; hate the holding of public office; and do not be too close with the ruling authorities." (Pirkei Avot 1: Mishna 10)

Shim'on Derech Beit Lehem – Yissachar **H16**

Simeon, son of the foremother Leah; one of the tribes of Israel (Genesis 29:33).

Shimshon Derech Beit Lehem – HaRakevet **H15**

Samson, a judge in the period of the Judges who fought against the Philistines. Even blinded and bound in chains, he pulled down a large hall filled with Israel's enemies, saying: "Let me die with the Philistines." (Judges 15:30)

Tzidkiyahu Zvulun – Dan **H16**

Zedekiah, appointed by the king of Babylonia to rule over Judah after he exiled King Jehoiachin to Babylonia. Zedekiah rebelled against Babylonia but was defeated and exiled to Babylonia. In his place Nebuchadnezzar appointed Gedalyahu ben Ahikam as governor of Judah.

Tzipora Derech Beit Lehem – Gad **H16**

Zipporah, wife of Moses in the Bible, daughter of Jethro the priest of Midian (Exodus 2:21).

Ya'el (11th cent. BCE) Shim'on – Yiftah **H15**

Jael, the wife of Heber the Kenite, a heroine in the period of the Judges. She killed the commander of the army of King Jabin of Hatzor, against whom Deborah the Prophetess and Barak ben Avino'am fought, when he sought refuge in her tent. In the Song of Deborah it is written: "Blessed among women will be *Ya'el*, wife of *Hever* the Kenite, she will be blessed above women in their tents." (Judges 4-5)

Yair (HaGil'adi) HaRakevet – dead end **H15**

Jair, scion of one of the branches of the tribe of Manasseh and a judge during the period of the Judges (Judges 10:3-5).

Yehuda Derech Hevron – Pierre Koenig **H16**

Judah, son of the foremother Leah; one of the tribes of Israel (Genesis 29:35).

Yiftah (HaGil'adi) Beit Lehem – Yair **H15**

Jephthah, a judge during the period of the Judges who fought against and defeated the Ammonites. (Judges 11)

Yissachar Yehuda – Reuven **H16**

Issachar, son of the foremother Leah; one of the tribes of Israel (Genesis 30:18).

Yocheved Derech Beit Lehem – dead end **H16**

Jochebed the mother of Moses in the Bible; from the tribe of Levi (Exodus 2).

Zerubavel (ben Shealtiel) (6th cent. BCE)
Derech Beit Lehem – dead end **H16**

Zerubbabel, the grandson of King Jehoiachin, King of Judah, who was exiled to Babylonia. He was at the head of the Return to Zion, those who returned to the Land of Israel. He was appointed ruler of Jerusalem and was one of the builders of the Second Temple.

Zvulun Yehuda – Dan **H16**

Zebulun, son of the Biblical Zilpah, the maid of the foremother Leah; one of the tribes of Israel (Genesis 30:20).

Gilo

Name and establishment:

This neighborhood in the southwestern part of the city, founded in 1971, is the southernmost area of jurisdiction of the Jerusalem municipality, near the Arab Christian town of Beit Jalla on the lower slopes of Mount Gilo, and from this mountain comes its name. According to one opinion, this is the site of the city of the ancient Biblical Gilo, which name appears in the Bible in the Hebrew in condensed spelling, without the letter "yud" (Joshua 15:51), as one of the cities in the patrimony of the tribe of Judah. And in II Samuel 15:12 the name appears again: "And Absalom sent Ahitophel the Gilonite, David's advisor, from his city, from Gilo..."

In this neighborhood are many archeological remains from various historical periods: a fortress and agricultural structures from the First Temple period, the ruins of an agricultural farm, graves and structures from the Second Temple period, from the Roman-Byzantine period, and many other remains.

Control of this ridge passed to Israel following the Six Day War, and the neighborhood of Gilo was built on it. From the first, Gilo absorbed many new immigrants, in part because of the large absorption center in the heart of the neighborhood. Immigrants came from Iran, France, South America, Syria and the countries of the former Soviet Union.

Boundaries:
North – Pat, the Arab villages of Beit Safafa and Sharafat
East – Ramat Rahel
Northeast – Arnona and Talpiot
Northwest – Manhat/Malha

Sites: within its boundaries or nearby are two central parks, Gilo Park (at the edge of Gilo Hei) and Zeidenberg Park (next to HaGanenet Street).

Streets: neighborhood streets are named for plants used for perfumes and spices, fragrant plants, and ten (!) of the twelve stones on the breast-plate of the high priest's vestments.

The streets are:

Afarsemon HaMor – HaMor **F19-20**

Persimmon, a fragrant tree, used to make perfume; it bears a sweet, tasty orange fruit.

Agmon HaMargalit – Shoham **D20**

Bulrush, a water plant that grows in marshes and on the banks of streams.

Ahlama HaAhot Yehudit – Leshem **D-E20**

Amethyst, the name of a precious stone of a violet or purple color. The amethyst, the stone of the tribe of Gad, is one of the twelve stones on the breastplate of the vestments worn by the high priest (Exodus 28:19 "And the third row is a jacinth, an agate and an amethyst").

Almog Ahlama – HaGanenet – dead end **D-E20**

The name of a tree that grows near the sea in tropical areas, especially on the islands of Malaya and in India, and is also found near the Mediterranean Sea.

Aryeh ben Eli'ezer (1913 – 1970) Vardinon – Levona **E19**

One of the heads of ETZe"L, served as deputy speaker of the Knesset.

Ayala HaMargalit – HaMargalit **D20**

A female deer, a doe. One of the kosher animals, has split hooves and chews its cud.

Baruchi, Yehoshu'a (1910 – 1993) HaMehanechet – dead end **C19**

Director of the "National Orchards", a government company that held and operated the abandoned orchards in the Jerusalem Corridor and employed numerous new immigrants in agricultural work.

Berman, Ya'akov, Rabbi (1878 – 1974) HaRosmarin – dead end **E20**

An educator and one of the heads of religious education in Jerusalem, one of the leaders of the *Mizrahi* movement.

Bosem Yefe Rom – dead end **D19**

A good and pleasant aroma wafted from various plants as is written in the Song of Songs 4:16 "...blow upon my garden that the fragrances may flow out..." Also refers to a fragrant fluid made of the extract of plants or materials that give off a pleasant scent, as is written in the scroll of Esther 2:12 "...and six months with perfumes and women's cosmetics."

Bosmat [Lane] HaTzuf – dead end **E19**

A word for perfume.

Camon HaMargalit – dead end **C-D20**

Cumin, a garden plant whose seeds are used as seasoning for various foods.

Dagan Tzvia VeYitzhak – dead end **D19**

A general name given to field crops the grains of which serve as food for human beings, like wheat, barley, rice, corn and others.

della Pergola, Refael (1876 – 1923) HaMehanechet – dead end **C19**

An Italian rabbi, a Lover of Zion. In 1910 he was appointed head of the Jewish community in Alexandria, Egypt, and served in this position until near the time of his death. In 1918 he was invited to Jerusalem by Chaim

Weizmann to participate in the ceremony of laying the cornerstone of the Hebrew University.

Dov Yosef (1899 – 1979) HaGanenet – Pat **F17-E20**

A jurist, military governor of Jerusalem during the War of Independence, a leader of the Labor movement and a minister in the Israel government (see the neighborhood of Pat).

Duga, Shlomo (b. 1935) HaRosmarin – dead end **E20**

Was involved in many activities among the Jews from Kurdistan, was chairman of the association of immigrants from Kurdistan, was elected to the Jerusalem city council.

Dvash Ahlama – HaTzabar – dead end **D20**

Honey, a fluid produced in the body of a bee. Or, a sweet juice similar to honey made from various fruits (Judges 14:18 "...what is sweeter than honey?"). Honey is one of the seven species for which the Land of Israel is praised (Deuteronomy 8:8 "A land of wheat and barley and grapevine and fig and pomegranate, a land of olives for oil, and honey").

Giv'at Canada Yefe Rom – Yefe Rom **D19**

A section of the neighborhood built by Canadian donors.

HaAhot Yehudit (1905 – 1973) Ahlama – HaGanenet **E20**

Nurse. Yehudit Luria-Ginzburg, a nurse at Hadassah Hospital, one of the organizers of the Hagana in Jerusalem and a member of the city council.

HaAnafa HaMargalit – dead end **D20**

Heron, a bird with long legs and neck, that lives near marshes, streams and lakes. The heron is mentioned in the Torah as one of the birds that are unclean and therefore not allowed to be eaten: "And the stork, and the heron of every variety..." (Leviticus 11:19)

HaBareket HaGanenet – dead end **D20**

Emerald, a precious stone characterized by its lovely colors. The emerald, the stone of the tribe of Levi, is one of the twelve stones on the breastplate of the vestments worn by the high priest (Exodus 28:17 "...a carnelian, a topaz and an emerald are the first row.").

HaCarpas HaDolev – dead end **D20**

A garden green (parsley or celery); its leaves and stems are used for seasoning foods.

HaDmumit Yitzhar – dead end **D19**

A wild plant with cut leaves and small red flowers.

HaDolev HaCarpas – dead end **D19-20**

Plane tree, a deciduous tree that grows in groves on the banks of streams.

HaDudaim [Lane] Afarsemon – dead end **F19-20**

Mandrakes. A wild plant that grows in fields in almost all areas of the Land of Israel. The plant produces violet flowers and fruits that are juicy and golden when ripe (Genesis 30:14 "...and he found mandrakes in the field...").

HaEzov Yefe Rom – dead end **D19**

Marjoram, a fragrant plant common in the mountains, with bluish-white flowers.

HaGal'init Dov Yosef – HaNegbi **E19**

Fruit pit, a fruit seed having a hard shell.

HaGanenet (1889 – 1968) Dov Yosef – Yefe Rom **D-E20**

Nursery teacher. Hasia Sukenick (née Feinsod) was an educator and one of those who laid the groundwork for the first Jewish nursery school in Jerusalem and in all the Land of Israel.

HaGefen HaAhot Yehudit – dead end **E20**

Grapevine, a plant that produces clusters of grapes. The grapevine is one of the seven species for which the Land of Israel is praised (Deuteronomy 8:8 "A land of wheat and barley and grapevine and fig and pomegranate, a land of olives for oil, and honey").

HaGome Yefe Rom – dead end **D19**

Reed, a type of plant that grows mostly alongside streams or marshes. ("Can the reed grow without a marsh..." Job 8:11)

HaHasida HaMargalit – Tzvia VeYitzhak **C19**

Stork, a large marsh bird that flies over Israel twice a year on its migrations, in the fall on the way to Africa and in the spring on the return to its land of birth. The stork is mentioned in the Torah among the birds that are unclean and therefore not allowed to be eaten: "And the stork, and the heron of every variety..." (Leviticus 11:19)

HaKaneh Afarsemon – dead end **F19**

Cane, a wild plant growing on the banks of streams, lakes and marshes, with a tall stalk. Grows in sections: "...seven ears (of grain/corn) growing from one stalk..." (Exodus 41:5)

HaKinamon [Lane] Afarsemon – dead end **F20**

A plant whose bark is used as a spice called cinnamon. One of the types of cinnamon was used in the desert as an ingredient in the mixture for preparing the holy anointing oil for the Tabernacle – "...and half that of fragrant cinnamon, two hundred fifty..." (Exodus 30:23).

HaKore HaAnafa – dead end **D20**

Partridge, a wilderness bird of a species of poultry the size of a dove. Its basic color is light, the color of sand. Found in the Jordan River Valley and around the Dead Sea.

HaLot Afarsemon – dead end **F19**

A fragrant (resinous) sap mentioned in the Torah "...gum and balsam and *labdanum* ..." (Genesis 37:25).

HaMargalit Leshem – Tzvia VeYitzhak **C19-D20**

Pearl, a precious gem, yellowish white or black. Word used to denote a very precious thing.

HaMehanechet (1888 – 1956) HaMargalit – HaMargalit **C19**

Named for Hanna Miriam Spitzer, a teacher and outstanding educator; she published periodicals.

HaMor HaRosmarin – Afarsemon **F19-20**

Myrrh, a bush, the resins of which serve as perfumes and as medicinal ingredients (Esther 2:12 "...six months in oil of myrrh..."). In ancient times myrrh was used for incense.

HaNegbi, Shabtai (1914 – 1976) Dov Yosef – Vardinon **E-F19**

A commander of the underground ETZe"L group in Jerusalem. Deputy mayor of Jerusalem.

HaNesher HaMargalit – dead end **C-D20**

Eagle, a large bird of prey, king of birds. Builds its nest in rocky clefts high in the mountains.

Harduf HaMargalit – dead end **C19**

Oleander, a green plant with pink, sometimes white or yellow, flowers. In Israel it also grows as a wild plant on the banks of streams.

HaRosmarin Derech Hevron – Dov Yosef **F20**

Rosemary, an ornamental shrub whose leaves are fragrant and whose flowers are violet. An ether-like oil is produced from it that has many uses in making cosmetics and in medicine.

HaShayish Unterman – HaAhot Yehudit **E20**

Marble, a white or colored stone used for sculpture and building, as monuments or floors.

HaSigalit Dov Yosef – dead end **E18**

Violet, a kind of ornamental flower, some of whose varieties grow wild in Israel.

HaSitvanit Dov Yosef – dead end **E19**

Crocus, a perennial plant of the lily family, with large flowers of various colors, from violet to white. Some varieties of crocus bloom in the fall.

HaSlav Leshem – Leshem **D20**

Quail, a type of small bird of the poultry family. Its feathers are brownish-grey and it has a row of yellowish lines on its back. The majority are migratory birds crossing Israel twice a year, in the fall on the way to Africa and in the spring on the way home. The Children of Israel ate quail in the desert: "...quail appeared and covered the camp..." (Exodus 16:13).

HaTavlin HaMargalit – dead end **C19**

Spice or seasoning, parts of plants or ingredients produced from plants mixed with food to add taste or aroma.

HaTe-ayna Yefe Rom – dead end **D19**

Fig, a fruit tree. The fig's tiny flowers ripen into the fruit, which is eaten raw, dried or cooked. The fig is one of the seven species for which the Land of Israel is praised (Deuteronomy 8:8 "A land of wheat and barley and grapevine and fig and pomegranate, a land of olives for oil, and honey").

HaTzabar Leshem – Almog **D20**

Sabra cactus, a plant that has sharp prickles; hedges of these cacti are used as living fences for vineyards and orchards. Its fruits are sweet and juicy (a person born in Israel is known as a sabra – prickly and insolent on the outside but with a good heart inside).

HaTziporen Yefe Rom – Yefe Rom **E19-20**

Clove, an ornamental plant with colorful and pleasantly fragrant flowers, one of the perfume plants used in the Holy Temple for the incense, "Other ingredients for the incense were balsam and cloves..." (Kritot, *mishna* 6). The dried, fragrant and spicy flower buds are used in spices, and today are also used for the production of oil for medical use.

HaTzivoni Dov Yosef – HaNegbi **E19**

Tulip, a kind of wild or ornamental plant that grows from a bulb. Its flowers are large and usually dark red.

HaTzori [Lane] Afarsemon – dead end **F20**

A resinous sap from a tree, possibly balsam, that was used in ancient times in religious rites, in medicine, for embalming and other uses. Its origin is unknown; some think it was produced from aromatic trees or perhaps a mixture of several kinds of resin from different sources, "...some *balsam* and some honey, gum, labdanum, pistachios and almonds" (Genesis 43:11).

HaTzuf Levona – Saraf **E19-20**

Nectar, the sweet juice that is extracted from various flowers, as when bees gather nectar and produce honey from it (Proverbs 16:24 "Honey nectar...").

HaZehavit Dov Yosef – dead end **E19**

A wildflower of the lily family that blooms at the beginning of winter.

HeHavush Shayish – dead end **E20**

Quince, a tree with large, fleshy fruit, of the rose family; generally eaten cooked. A fruit for which the Land of Israel is praised.

Irit HaTziporen – dead end **E19**

Asphodel, a type of wild plant of the lily family, whose flowers are white and pink. In Rabbinic literature, the asphodel is mentioned as a plant used as feed for domestic animals.

Justman, Moshe (1887 – 1942) Ben Eli'ezer – HaRosmarin **E19-20**

One of the great newspapermen and authors of the Jewish community of Poland.

Ketura [Lane] Afarsemon – dead end **F19**

Incense, spices burned in fire to release their good aroma: "They will offer You incense to savor and whole offerings on Your altar" (Deuteronomy 33:10).

Ketzi'a [Lane] Afarsemon – dead end **F20**

The casing of one of the fragrant plants that was used in the Holy Temple for burning incense: "Myrrh and aloes and cassia bark..." (Psalms 45:9).

Kida [Lane] Giv'at Canada – dead end **D19**

A wild thornbush having yellow flowers. One of the fragrant plants mentioned in the Bible and used in the mixture for the preparation of the holy anointing oil.

Layish Snunit – dead end **D20**

Dough that has been kneaded: "the kneaded dough and oil and honey, like the kneaded dough that is prepared with oil and pricked with honey" (Sifrei, a homiletic work, on Parshat BeHa'alotcha, 24).

Leshem Ahlama – HaGanenet **D20**

Jacinth, resin which has hardened and petrified into stone. Its color ranges from pale yellow to red. The jacinth is the stone of the tribe of Dan, one of the twelve stones on the breastplate of the vestments worn by the high priest (Exodus 28:19 "And the third row is a jacinth, an agate and an amethyst.").

Levona Ben Eli'ezer – HaRosmarin **E19**

Frankincense, one of the kinds of resinous sap from fragrant trees that were used for incense on the altar of the Tabernacle in the desert and in the Holy Temple in Jerusalem ("And you shall place pure frankincense in each row..." Leviticus 24:7).

Marva HaMargalit – dead end **C20**

Sage, a plant with large flowers rich in nectar. Various types of sage are used for ornamentation, medicine, seasoning and more.

Nataf [Lane] Vardinon – dead end **E19**

Stacte, one of the kinds of resin used in the Tabernacle in the desert to prepare the anointing oil: "...Take the resins stacte, onycha and galbanum..." (Exodus 30:34).

Nofech HaShayish – dead end **E20**

There are those of the opinion that this is a greenish-blue stone called turquoise. This stone, that of the tribe of Judah, is one of the twelve stones on the breastplate of the vestments worn by the high priest (Exodus 28:18 "...and the second row is a turquoise, a sapphire and a diamond").

Odem HaMargalit – Tirosh **C19**

Carnelian, the name of a hard, red precious stone. It is the stone of the tribe of Reuben and is one of the twelve stones on the breastplate of the vestments worn by the high priest (Exodus 28:17 "...a carnelian, a topaz and an emerald are the first row.")

Polotzky, Ya'akov (1905 – 1991) Duga – dead end **E20**

One of the great researchers of Egyptology, of Semitic linguistics and general linguistics. He laid the groundwork for the method of structural/ syntactic analysis adopted by the Jerusalem school of thought.

Saraf [Lane] HaTzuf – dead end **E19-20**

Sap of plants, juice ("He who cuts olives that the juice may come out." Tractate Ma'asrot 4:1).

Shamir HaGanenet – Dov Yosef **E19-20**

Flint, a hard stone, the hardest after the diamond (Ezekiel 3:9 – "As a flint, harder than rock have I made your forehead...").

Shevo Snunit – Snunit **D20**

Agate, a stone whose color is layers of black and white. The agate, the stone of the tribe of Naftali, is one of the twelve stones on the breastplate of the vestments worn by the high priest (Exodus 28:19 "And the third row is a jacinth, an agate and an amethyst.")

Shoham HaMargalit – dead end **D20**

Thought to be a variety of black onyx. The onyx, the stone of the tribe of Joseph, is one of the twelve stones on the breastplate of the vestments worn by the high priest (Exodus 28:20 "...and the fourth row is a chrysolite, an onyx and a jasper...").

Snunit Tzvia VeYitzhak – HaMargalit **D20**

Swallow, a song bird distinguished for its light and rapid flight.

Tarshish HaMargalit – HaMargalit **D20**

According to the Septuagint, it is a gold-colored stone. Chrysolite is the stone of the tribe of Asher, one of the twelve stones on the breastplate of the vestments worn by the high priest (Exodus 28:20 "...and the fourth row is a chrysolite, an onyx and a jasper...").

Tirosh HaMargalit – HaHasida **C19**

New wine before it has fermented, grape juice – "...and you shall gather in your grain, new wine and fresh olive oil" (Deuteronomy 11:14).

Topaz HaMargalit – dead end **D20**

A semi-precious stone of a greenish hue. Some think this is the *piteda* stone symbolizing the tribe of Simeon, one of the twelve stones on the breastplate of the vestments worn by the high priest (Exodus 28:17 "...a carnelian, a topaz and an emerald are the first row.")

Tzeelim Yefe Rom – dead end **D20**

Acacia; it is thought to be one of the varieties of acacia tree that grows in the grasslands and the desert oases. Another opinion is that this is what is today called a jujube tree. It is one of the trees mentioned in the Bible: "Under the *tzeelim* tree he lies..." (Job 40:21).

Tzvia VeYitzhak (Yitzhak and Tzivia Lubetkin Cukierman)
Yefe Rom – HaMargalit **D19-20**

Yitzhak was one of the commanders of the fighters in the Warsaw Ghetto Uprising, one of the leaders of the Jewish partisans. A founder of Kibbutz Lohamei HaGhetaot in the Galilee.

Unterman, Isser Yehuda, Rabbi (1886 – 1976)
HaGanenet – HaShayish **E20**

Was active in supporting the yeshivot in Lithuania, was chief rabbi of Liverpool (England), Tel-Aviv, and finally, Ashkenazic chief rabbi of Israel.

Vardinon HaNegbi – Levona **E19**

Attar, an oil made from roses.

Ya'ari, Avraham (1899 - 1966) Justman – dead end **E19**

Bibliographer, historian, researcher of the history of Jewish colonization in the Land of Israel.

Yahalom HaAhot Yehudit – HaBareket **E20**

Diamond, a precious stone. The diamond is a brilliant mineral, the clearest and hardest known in nature. It has great value in industry. The diamond, the stone of the tribe of Zebulun, is one of the twelve stones on the breastplate of the vestments worn by the high priest (Exodus 28:18 "...and the second row is a turquoise, a sapphire and a diamond").

Yakinton Odem – HaMargalit **C19**

Hyacinth, a kind of wild plant from which clusters of blue flowers blossom. Various types of hyacinth are also used as ornamental flowers.

Yasmin [Lane] Vardinon – dead end **E19**

Jasmine, a kind of fragrant wild plant having yellow flowers.

Yefe Rom HaGanenet – Tzvia VeYitzhak **D20-D20**

Beautiful height, so named for the impressive view of the landscape visible from this street.

Yitzhar Giv'at Canada – HaDmumit – dead end **D19**

A name for pure oil, fresh oil pressed from olives. It is mentioned in the Torah in Deuteronomy 11:14, "...and you shall gather in your grain, new wine and fresh olive oil."

Giv'at Beit HaKerem

Name and establishment:

This neighborhood, on the western side of the city, south of the original neighborhood of Beit HaKerem, was established in 1960. The Housing Ministry at the time built apartment blocks in order to develop the area. New immigrants and young couples settled there, and many of them have remained until today.

Boundaries:

North – Beit HaKerem
South – Ramat Beit HaKerem and Bayit VaGan
East – Giv'at Ram
West – Mount Herzl

Sites: within its boundaries or nearby are the Sha'arei Tzedek Medical Center, Yad Sarah, Mount Herzl and Yad VaShem.

Streets: this is a neighborhood with only one street, named for the neighborhood.

The streets are:

Aluf Yohai bin Nun (1925 – 1995)
Kol – Giv'at Beit HaKerem, ends at Kol **D13-E14**

Admiral of the navy, a hero of Israel, a fighter and naval commander (see the neighborhood of Ramat Beit HaKerem.)

Avizohar, Yehoshu'a (1882 -1966)
HeHalutz – Mishkan Shilo, ends at Beyt **D13**

(See the neighborhoods of Beit HaKerem and Ramat Beit HaKerem.)

Giv'at Beit HaKerem Bin Nun – HeHalutz **D13**

Named for the neighborhood.

HeHalutz HaSatat – Avizohar, ends at Herzl Boulevard **D13-E12**

Some of the entrances to the buildings on Giv'at Beit HaKerem Street face HeHalutz Street (see the neighborhoods of Beit HaKerem, HaPo'alim).

Mishkan Shilo Avizohar – Bin Nun – dead end **D13**

Named for the book of Rabbi Shilo Refael (1941 – 1995), the rabbi of the Kiryat Moshe neighborhood. This street is parallel to Giv'at Beit HaKerem Street (see the neighborhood of Ramat Beit HaKerem).

Giv'at HaMatos

Name and establishment:

Airplane hill. This neighborhood, in the southern part of the city beside the road leading from Jerusalem to the neighborhoods of Har Homa and Gilo and to the city of Bethlehem, was founded in the early 1990s as a residential neighborhood for immigrants.

Until the Six Day War, on Giv'at HaArba'a (the hill of four), rising opposite, there was a Jordanian army position, overlooking Kibbutz Ramat Rahel, which was bombed by the Israeli air force in that war. At the time of the battles, an Israeli fighter jet was shot down over this hill and the pilot was killed. Hence the name of the hill.

As mentioned, in the early 1990s land was prepared on Giv'at HaMatos to absorb the large wave of immigration from the Former Soviet Union, and on this tract caravans were set up as dwellings for them. The municipality is now planning on building a new neighborhood here.

From the summit of the hill there is a superb view of Jerusalem and the surrounding hills.

Boundaries:
North – Talpiot-Industrial Zone
Southwest – Gilo
East – Homat Shmuel/Har Homa

Sites: within its boundaries or nearby are the Greek monastery Mar Elias, and opposite, Giv'at HaArba'a.

Streets: it is alongside Derech Hevron. The streets and lanes on the hill have no names.

The street is:

Derech Hevron Hativat Yerushalayim – the city of Hebron **I14-F20**

The route of Derech Hevron extends from the north from Hativat Yerushalayim, a street near Har Tzion, to the neighborhoods of Giv'at Hanania/Abu Tor, Geulim/Bak'a, North Talpiot, Talpiot, Arnona, Giv'at HaMatos, Homat Shmuel/Har Homa and comes to an end further south at Bethlehem and Hebron.

Giv'at HaMivtar [the Cut Hill]

Name and establishment:

This neighborhood, in the northern part of the city, on the upper elevations of Har HaTzofim [Mount Scopus] east of Ramat Eshkol, was founded in 1970 on the Jerusalem-Ramallah-Nablus road. The road forms an artificial center line to divide the hill, and thus the name.

Before the Six Day War there were Jordanian army positions in the area, and during the war fierce battles raged along the lane leading to Mount Scopus. In memory of the members of the Harel Brigade who fell in battle, a memorial panel was erected.

When the area was being prepared for the construction of the neighborhood and the paving of the streets, burial caves from the period of the Second Temple were uncovered.

Boundaries:
Northeast – Giv'at Shapira/French Hill
South – Ammunition Hill [*Giv'at HaTahmoshet*]

West – Ramat Eshkol

Sites: within its boundaries or nearby are Ammunition Hill and burial caves from the Second Temple period.

Streets: the streets are named for places and people connected to the Six Day War.

The streets are:

Aranne, Zalman [Square] (1899 – 1971) Paran at dead end street **I9**

A civic leader, one of the leaders of the Labor movement in the Land of Israel, and Minister of Education and Culture of the State of Israel (see the neighborhood of Ramat Eshkol).

Bar Lev, Haim [Boulevard] (1924 – 1994)
Yigael Yadin – Shmuel HaNavi **J9-I11**

An army chief of staff, a member of Knesset (parliament) and a minister in the government of Israel. He commanded the IDF during the War of Attrition, and the line of fortifications along the Suez Canal is named for him (the Bar Lev Line). (See the neighborhoods of Giv'at Shapira/French Hill, Kiryat Aryeh, Nahlat Shim'on, Sheikh Jarrah.)

Eshkol, Levi [Boulevard] (1895 – 1969)
Bar Lev – Eretz Hefetz – Hativat Harel **I-9**

The third prime minister of the State of Israel. He was drafted and fought in the Jewish Battalion in WWI, was one of the founders of the Histadrut Labor Federation and the agricultural commune Degania, was the head of the Settlement Department of the Jewish Agency for Israel, the Treasurer of the Jewish Agency and served many years as a minister in various Israeli governments. In the days before the outbreak of the Six Day War, he made Moshe Dayan the defense minister and continued to serve as prime minister until his death. In 1965 he gave instructions to bring the remains of Zeev Jabotinsky (see the neighborhood of Komemiyut/Talbieh) to Israel. (See the neighborhoods of Ma'alot Dafna/Arzei HaBira, Ramat Eshkol.)

Meitzarei Tiran Midbar Sinai – Midbar Sinai **J9**

Named for the Straits of Tiran near the southern end of the Sinai Peninsula, between the shore and the island of Tiran, that was blocked to Israeli shipping and set off the Six Day War.

Midbar Sinai Sheshet HaYamim – Sheshet HaYamim **J9**

Named for the Sinai Desert on the Sinai Peninsula, where the Bible tells that the Israelites wandered for forty years after leaving Egypt.

Mifratz Shlomo Meitzarei Tiran – dead end **J9**

The Hebrew name for the bay at the southern tip of the Sinai Peninsula. The Arabic name for the resort town there is Sharm-e-Sheikh and in Hebrew, Ophira. The Strait of Tiran is just to the north and is controlled from the shore. The strait was closed to Israeli shipping for a period before the Six Day War, preventing access to Eilat port through the Gulf of Eilat.

Nadav El'azar [Square] (1982 – 2001)
Sheshet HaYamim at Midbar Sinai **J9**

A fighter in the Engineering Corps, Jerusalem-born, killed in a military operation in Hebron.

'Omer [Square] Sheshet HaYamim at Midbar Sinai **J9**

Named for Staff Sergeant 'Omer Shalit, a resident of Giv'at HaMivtar and a soldier in the NaHa"L (an army unit combining military sevice with agricultural labor), who was killed in the tragic helicopter crash of 1997 while on his way to take part in a military operation in Lebanon.

Paran Sheshet HaYamim – Ma'avar HaMitla **I9**

A stream on the Negev plateau (see the neighborhood of Ramat Eshkol).

Sheshet HaYamim Bar Lev – Eshkol **I9-J8**

Named for the Six Day War (1967), a military victory won in six days against the armies of three countries, Egypt, Jordan and Syria, including the liberation of the Old City of Jerusalem, the Kotel HaMa'aravi (Western Wall) and Har HaBayit (the Temple Mount). A peace agreement with Egypt was achieved only in 1977, and with Jordan in 1994.

Tanne, David [Square] (1909 – 1973) Paran at dead end street **I9**

One of the civic leaders of Jerusalem, who promoted its development. One of the builders of Ramat Eshkol (see the neighborhood of Ramat Eshkol).

Giv'at Hanania/Abu Tor

Name and establishment:

This neighborhood, in the southern part of the city near the old railroad station, was founded in the middle of the nineteenth century. Until the War of Independence, it was an Arab neighborhood, and from the end of that war until the Six Day War, the neighborhood was divided by the municipality borderline, along 'Asael Street. In the upper part the residents were Jews and the area was called Giv'at Hanania after Hanania the High Priest in the Second Temple period. The Arabic name for the neighborhood, built lower on the hill, is Abu Tor, meaning father of the bull, taken from the name of a Muslim man who used to ride a bull in the army of Saladin, who captured Jerusalem from the Crusaders.

In 1887 on the site of today's Giv'at Hanania, a Jewish neighborhood was established and called Beit Yosef, named for Yosef Bey Navon, who was the initiator of the railway in Jerusalem and near whose neighborhood the railroad station stood. In the pogroms against Jews in 1929, the Jews left the neighborhood, and their houses were taken over by Arabs.Only after the War of Independence did the Jews return to their homes. Today, the residents include both Jews and Arabs.

Boundaries:

North – Ben Hinom Valley and Har Tzion

South – Sherover Promenade (Tayelet), North Talpiot

East – Kidron Valley

West – Derech Hevron, the old railroad station, the German Colony/ RaMBa"M

Sites: within its boundaries or nearby is an enclosed area near the highest elevation, belonging to the Greek Orthodox Church, and in it are remains of a Byzantine church. There is also a garden for the blind that was established with the help of the city of Vienna, Austria, and the Jewish community of Antwerp, Belgium.

Streets: the neighborhood streets are named for individuals from the tribe of Judah and names connected to the immediate area.

The streets are:

Abu Tor HaMefaked – Na'omi **I15**

Named for the neighborhood and for a Muslim soldier in the army of Saladin in the Middle Ages.

'Aminadav Derech Hevron – Yishai **I15**

Aminadab, from the tribe of Judah. Father-in-law of Aaron the High Priest (Exodus 6:23).

'Asael Gihon – 'Ein Rogel **I15**

Asahel, son of Tzruya and brother of Joab, who was commander of King David's army.

Avigayil Yishai – 'Asael **I15**

Abigail, the wife of Nabel of Carmel in Judah and, later, a wife of King David.

Bat Sheva' Yishai – Nahshon **I15**

Bathsheba, a wife of King David and the mother of King Solomon.

Derech Hevron Hativat Yerushalayim – Na'omi, ends at the city of Hebron **I14-F20**

The route of Derech Hevron extends from the north from Hativat Yerushalayim, a street near Har Tzion, to the neighborhoods of Giv'at Hanania/Abu Tor, Geulim/Bak'a, North Talpiot, Talpiot, Arnona, Giv'at HaMatos, Homat Shmuel/Har Homa and comes to an end further south at Bethlehem and Hebron.

'Ein Rogel Derech Hevron – 'Asael **I14**

Bir Ayub in Arabic. After the well in Jerusalem's Kidron Valley, mentioned in the Bible.

Gihon Derech Hevron – 'Asael **I15**

A spring at the foot of 'Ir David, an important source of water for the residents of Jerusalem in ancient times.

HaMefaked (1931 – 1967) Derech Hevron – Abu Tor **I14**

The Officer, named for Lt.-Gen. Michael Peeks, the commander of the Jerusalem Brigade in the Six Day War. He fell in battle in this neighborhood.

Nahshon 'Aminadav – Gihon **I15**

Nahshon, son of 'Aminadav, leader of the tribe of Judah. Also the name of a military operation during the War of Independence that enabled the Israelis to break through to the besieged city of Jerusalem.

Na'omi Derech Hevron – Abu Tor **I15**

Mother-in-law of the Biblical Ruth. Na'omi came from Bethlehem and moved with her husband and sons to Moab during a famine, later returning to Bethlehem.

Navon, Yosef [Square] (1858 – 1934)
HaMefaked at Derech Hevron **I14**

The initiator of the railway line from Jaffa to Jerusalem and the construction of the port at Jaffa. One of the civic leaders of the Sephardic community in Jerusalem. (See the neighborhood of Mahane Yehuda.)

'Oved Avigayil – Gihon **I15**

Obed, son of the Biblical Ruth and Boaz, grandfather of King David.

Tzruya Gihon – Na'omi **I15**

Zeruriah, sister of King David and mother of Joab, who was the commander of King David's army.

Yishai Gihon – 'Ein Rogel **I14-15**

Jesse was the son of Obed and the father of King David.

Giv'at HaVradim/Shikun Rassco

Name and establishment:

This neighborhood, in the southwestern part of the city, was founded in 1951 and named "Hill of Roses" for the Rose Stream that passes along the lower part of the hill and for the roses in the gardens there. It is also called Rassco Housing for the name of the company that built the first houses there, Rural and Suburban Settlement Company.

Boundaries:

North – Kiryat Shmuel
South – Gonen/Katamon
East – Giv'at Oranim
West – Giv'at Mordechai

Sites: within its boundaries or nearby is the Greek Catholic monastery San Simon.

Streets: the neighborhood streets are named for poets and writers.

The streets are:

'Abadi, Yitzhak (1898 – 1969) Tchernichovsky – Shim'oni **F15**

A writer, teacher, activist and a senior official in the British High Commission of the Mandate government.

'Agnon, Shmuel Yosef [Boulevard] (1888–1970) HaPaLMa"H – Yahil **F15-16**

A renowned Hebrew writer who merited international recognition and the Nobel Prize for Literature (1966). From his first story, "Agunot" (1909), he took his Hebrew name. He was twice awarded the Bialik Prize and twice received the Israel Prize for Literature (see the neighborhood of Giv'at Oranim). Known by his initials as **Sh**a**i** 'Agnon, from **Sh**muel **Y**osef.

Fichmann, Ya'akov (1881 – 1958) Tchernichovsky – 'Agnon **F15**

A poet, writer, educator, translator, editor and literary critic. He was one of the founders of the Writers Association, and he edited several periodicals.

Frischmann, David (1859 – 1922) 'Agnon – Katzenelson **F15**

A poet, writer, translator and editor of Hebrew literary periodicals.

HaTekufa Shim'oni – Nikanor **F15-16**

The name of a periodical edited by Ya'akov Cohen (1881 – 1960), one of the great poets and playwrights in modern Hebrew literature.

Herzog, Yitzhak Isaac HaLevi, Rabbi Dr. (1888 – 1959) 'Aza – Golomb **G14-E16**

Chief rabbi of the Land of Israel during the period of the British Mandate and the first decade of the State of Israel. After Rav Kook died, he was asked to serve as chief rabbi in Israel, so he immigrated from England to Jerusalem in 1937. During the years of World War II, he worked unceasingly to save the survivors of the Holocaust in Europe and to help them immigrate to Israel. He was made an honorary citizen of the city of Tel-Aviv in 1946, and received the Israel Prize for Religious Literature in 1958 (see the neighborhoods of Giv'at Mordechai, Gonenim/Katamonim,

Kiryat Shmuel, Nayot, Rehavia). His son, Chaim Herzog (1918–1997), was sixth president of the State of Israel (see the neighborhood of Giv'at Ram). His grandson Yitzhak [Isaac] Herzog is a member of Knesset and a government minister.

Katzenelson, Yitzhak (1886 – 1944) Tchernichovsky – 'Agnon **F15-16**

Poet, writer, educator and playwright who wrote in Hebrew and in Yiddish. He fought in the Warsaw Ghetto Uprising. He is considered to be the outstanding poet of the Holocaust and was killed in Auschwitz. Ghetto Fighters House at Kibbutz Lohamei Haghetaot is named for him.

Kimhi, Dov (1889 – 1961) HaTayasim – Tchernichovsky **F14-15**

A writer, educator and researcher of the Bible.

Sachs, Aryeh [Square] (1908 – 1986)
Tchernichovsky at Katzenelson **F15**

A musician and pianist, one of the first on *Kol Yisrael* Israel radio.

Schwartz, Armon [Square] (1915 – 1995)
Tchernichovsky at Fichmann **F15**

A pioneer of Roentgenology (X-ray technology), one of the prominent doctors in Jerusalem.

Selim Benin [Lane] (1868 – 1945) Fichmann – Frischmann **F15**

One of the main contractors in Jerusalem and one of its important civic leaders. He reclaimed many tracts of land in Jerusalem for construction. He was the owner of the second Jewish bank in the walled portion of the city.

Selma Lagerloff [Steps] Tchernichovsky – Shim'oni **F15**

A Swedish writer, one of the Righteous Gentiles, who acted to save Jewish victims of the Holocaust. She was awarded the Nobel Prize for Literature.

Shenhar, Yitzhak [Steps] (1902 – 1957)
Herzog – Tchernichovsky **F15**

Poet, writer, editor and translator.

Shim'oni, David (1886 – 1956) Herzog – Tchernichovsky **F14-15**

Poet, translator, editor, teacher. He was active in the Writers Association and is counted among the outstanding poets of modern Hebrew literature. In his poems he described the life of the pioneers and the vistas of the Land of Israel.

Tchernichovsky, Shaul (1875 – 1943) Herzog – Fichmann **F15-G14**

One of the great poets of modern Hebrew literature. A doctor, linguist and translator, he wrote ballads and poems, idylls, patriotic poems and a collection of thirty-three short stories. He was made an honorary citizen of the city of Tel-Aviv in 1935 (see the neighborhood of Kiryat Shmuel).

Yona, Jacques Carpas, Dr. [Square] (1909 – 1992)
Herzog at Shim'oni **F14**

He was the president of the Jewish community in Peru. He was appointed executive director of the Hadassah Medical Association in Jerusalem and was named an Honored Citizen of Jerusalem.

Giv'at Massua

Name and establishment:

This neighborhood, atop a ridge in the southwestern part of the city overlooking astonishingly beautiful views, was planned toward the end of the 1980s, and was built and settled in 1996. The population is mixed – secularists and religious Zionists.

Boundaries:

North and northwest – 'Ir Ganim, Kiryat Menahem
South – the new station for the railway to Tel-Aviv
East – the Biblical Zoo and Manhat/Malha

Sites: within its boundaries or nearby are Beit HaLohem Soldier's House, the Biblical Zoo, the new railroad station, Teddy Stadium, the Jerusalem Mall (Kenyon Yerushalayim) in the Manhat/Malha neighborhood.

Streets: the neighborhood streets are named for various professionals – communications specialists, an author, educators, a nurse, public figures.

The streets are:

Avidar, Yosef (1906 – 1995) El Salvador – dead end **B17**

In 1929 he was appointed commander of the Old City and deputy commander of the city of Jerusalem. He served in senior military positions in the Hagana. He was one of those who laid the groundwork for the military industries. In 1949 he was made a major general, in charge of the Northern Command. He served as the head of the army's operational branch and deputy chief of staff.

Ben Porat, Lea (1922 – 1980) Dultzin – Dultzin **B17**

A cultural activist, broadcaster, narrator and editor of programs for young people on Kol Yisrael radio. She served as director of culture and arts in the Ministry of Education and in this post initiated and set up numerous enterprises, such as the Khan Theater, the Beer Shev'a Theater, and the Hebrew Book Council.

Bitzur, Yehoshu'a (1926 – 1988) Tzur – dead end **A-B17**

A journalist and writer, winner of the Jerusalem Prize. He was one of the senior reporters for the newspaper Ma'ariv and served as writer, publisher and head of its editorial board in Jerusalem. He was also a member of Knesset.

Dultzin, Aryeh (1916 – 2000) Kolitz – Dultzin **B17**

He served as a chairman of the Jewish Agency and the Zionist Organization, as a government minister, was elected to the Zionist Executive, served as head of the Department of Education and Culture and head of the Immigration and Absorption Department of the Jewish Agency.

El Salvador Natan – Dultzin **B17**

Named for a country in Central America.

Hasidoff, Avraham (1898 – 1989) Miss Landau – El Salvador **B17-18**

Named a *Yakir Yerushalayim*, an Honored Citizen of Jerusalem.

Kolitz, Haim [Road] (1919 – 1993) Golomb - Tzur – dead end **B17**

A researcher and writer, learned in Torah, named *Yakir Yerushalayim*, an Honored Citizen of Jerusalem. The street is also called Massua Road after the name Giv'at Massua (see the neighborhoods of Kiryat HaYovel, Manhat/Malha).

Kraus, Gertrud, Prof. (1901 – 1977)
Dultzin – Nurse Zelma – dead end **B18**

A dancer and choreographer, creator of modern dance in the Land of Israel. She took up drawing and sculpture toward the end of her life. She won the Israel Prize in 1968.

Menashe Nehemia (1929 – 1999) Tzur – dead end **A17**

A community leader. Worked on behalf of the development of Jerusalem.

Miss Landau (Rina Yehudit) (1873 -1945)
El Salvador – El Salvador **B17**

A teacher and school principal. She was born in England and completed teachers college in London. In 1899 she immigrated to Israel and for many years was principal of the girls school named after Evelina de Rothschild. In 1924 the English government conferred a title on her.

Natan, Shmuel, Rabbi (1915 – 1977) Dultzin – dead end **B17**

A rabbi, a Jerusalemite, one of the pioneers in the development of tourism in Israel. For many years, he represented the Ministry of Tourism in international organizations. He served for a long period as president of the *Yeshurun* Synagogue in central Jerusalem.

Nuñez, Benjamin (1915 – 1994) El Salvador – dead end **B17**

A priest from Costa Rica, a Zionist and true friend of Israel.

Nurse Zelma (Meir) (19th-20th cent.) Dultzin – Kraus – dead end **B17**

The nurse who patterened and actualized, in the most praiseworthy fashion, the role of the compassionate nurse in Sha'arei Tzedek Hospital at the beginning of the 1920s and was mentor to the many nurses who were her students.

Ronen, Yoram (1933 – 1996) Dultzin – dead end **B18**

Narrator and broadcaster of programs for children. He was a news broadcaster on radio and started the weekly news review. While in the army, he was one of the initiators of Galei TZaHa"L, the army radio station. He narrated the first Israeli television broadcast when he described the "Victory Parade" after the Six Day War.

San Salvador [Square] Dultzin at El Salvador **B17**

The capital city of the Central American country of El Salvador.

Shalev, Yitzhak (1918 – 1992) Tzur – dead end **A17**

A poet, teacher and educator. He dedicated most of his life to teaching in the David Yellin Teachers College in the neighborhood of Beit HaKerem. He was one of the outstanding teachers of the Hebrew Bible and was the winner of the first National Bible Contest.

Tzur, Ya'akov (1907 – 1990) Dultzin – Kolitz **A17**

He served as the first ambassador of Israel to Argentina, as ambassador in France, as director-general of the Foreign Ministry, as head of the Information Department of the Jewish Agency, as chairman of Bialik Institute and for a long period as chairman of the directorate of *HaKeren HaKayemet LeYisrael* (the Jewish National Fund).

Giv'at Mordechai

Name and establishment:

This neighborhood, in the southwestern part of the city between Herzog and SHaHa"L Streets, was founded in 1955 and named after Mordechai (Maxwell) Abel, an American jurist, a Zionist activist who contributed a significant amount to the establishment of the neighborhood. A dry streambed named Hovevei Tzion passes by the lower part of Giv'at Mordechai. In the valley there are fruit orchards belonging to Kibbutz Ramat Rahel. Most of the residents of the neighborhood are observant Jews.

Boundaries:

North – Giv'at Ram
South – Gonenim/Katamonim
East – Giv'at HaVradim/Shikun Rassco
West – Ramat Sharett and Bayit VaGan

Sites: within its boundaries or nearby are the *Yeshivat Hevron* Campus, populated by rabbis and students of the yeshiva, and, at the entrance to the neighborhood from Herzog Street, a sculpture of *Sulam Ya'akov* [Jacob's Ladder].

Streets: the neighborhood streets are named after leaders of the religious Zionist movement, *Mizrahi*, and Lovers of Zion.

The streets are:

Avi'ad (1893 – 1957) Gold – SHaHa"L **E15**

The nickname of Yesha'yahu Wolfsberg, a doctor, writer, educator and Zionist activist. A leader of the religious Zionist *Mizrahi* movement; Israel's ambassador to Switzerland.

Bazak, Betzalel (1898 – 1975) Shneur – SHaHa"L **E14-15**

An educator, one of the religious Zionist leaders, and a delegate to Zionist Congresses (see the neighborhood of Nayot).

Beyt, Shmuel (Hans) (1902 – 1948) Herzl Boulevard – SHaHa"L **D13-14**

(See the neighborhoods of Bayit VaGan, Ramat Beit HaKerem.)

Gold, Zeev, Rabbi (1889 – 1956) Heller – SHaHa"L **E15**

A rabbi, civic leader and master of homiletics. A leader in the religious Zionist *Mizrahi* movement and head of the Jewish Agency's department for development of Jerusalem.

HaVa'ad HaLeumi SHaHa"L – dead end **E14-15**

(See the neighborhood of Bayit VaGan.)

Heller, Haim, Rabbi (1878 – 1960) Gold – SHaHa"L **E15**

Researcher of Talmudic literature, translations of the Bible and religious law. In 1947 he was awarded the prize named for HaRav Kook from the municipality of Tel-Aviv.

Herzog, Yitzhak Isaac HaLevi, Rabbi Dr. (1888–1959)
'Aza – Golomb **G14-E16**

(See the neighborhoods of Giv'at HaVradim/Shikun Rassco, Gonenim/Katamonim, Kiryat Shmuel, Nayot, Rehavia.)

Mann, Yitzhak David (1885 – 1963) Gold – dead end **E15**

One of the most respected men in Jerusalem and one of its civic leaders. One of the founders of the Bayit VaGan and Kiryat Moshe neighborhoods. He served as a member of the directorate of the Bikur Holim Hospital.

Masat Moshe Heller – Sarna – dead end **E15**

Moshe's Ideal, named for the book by Rabbi Avraham Moshe Hevroni (1904 – 1974), a head of the *Hevron* Yeshiva in Jerusalem.

Pinkas, David Zvi (1895 – 1952) SHaHa"L – dead end **E15**

A civic leader, one of the leaders of the Religious Zionist *Mizrahi* movement, and a minister of the State of Israel.

Sarna, Yehezkel, Rabbi (1889 – 1969) Avi'ad – dead end **E15**

A head of the *Hevron* Yeshiva in Jerusalem.

SHaHa"L (1892 – 1928) Herzog – Bazak **E15**

Acronym for **Sh**muel **H**aim **L**andau, a writer, educator, one of the founders of *HaPo'el HaMizrahi* (religious labor movement) and one of its leaders.

Giv'at Oranim

Name and establishment:

This neighborhood, Hill of Pines, in the southwestern part of the city, was established after the War of Independence (1948), and is named for the pine trees growing on this hill. From Giv'at Oranim, the soldiers in the War of Independence stormed the nearby Greek Catholic monastery of San Simon (Saint Simeon) and repulsed the Arab fighters who had taken up positions inside.

Boundaries:

North – Gonen/Katamon

South and east – Gonenim/Katamonim

West – Giv'at HaVradim/Shikun Rassco

Sites: within its boundaries or nearby is the Greek Catholic monastery of San Simon.

Streets: the streets in the neighborhood are named for a writer, a researcher, a poet and immigrants.

The streets are:

'Agnon, Shmuel Yosef [Boulevard] (1888 – 1970)
HaPaLMa"H – Yahil **F15-16**

(See the neighborhood of Giv'at HaVradim/Shikun Rassco.)

Aharoni, Yisrael (1876 – 1947) HaMa'apilim – Temkin **F15**

A naturalist, he did research into the world of nature in the Bible and the Talmud.

HaMa'apilim HaPaLMa"H – 'Agnon **F15**

Named for the illegal immigrants who sought to enter the Land of Israel without an immigration certificate, despite the prohibition of the British Mandate government. The illegal immigrant movement reached its peak in the 1940s, after the Holocaust, when huge numbers of Jewish survivors wanted to leave Europe and reach the Land of Israel (see the neighborhood of Gonen/Katamon).

Ha'Oleh [Lane] HaMa'apilim – dead end **F15**

The immigrant, named in honor of all the immigrants to the Land of Israel throughout the generations (see the neighborhood of Gonen/Katamon).

Temkin, Mordechai (1891 – 1960) HaPaLMa"H – Aharoni **F15**

A poet and teacher in Jerusalem.

Giv'at Ram

Name and establishment:

This neighborhood on the western side of the city was founded in 1949, when the government decided that Giv'at Ram would be the main official focal point of Jerusalem and would symbolize the national revival of the Jewish people after thousands of years of exile. The name of this hill, Ra"M, acronym for ***R****amat* ***M****efakdim* (commanders' height) or ***R****amat* ***M****eguyasim* (draftees' height), is for the commanders of the Hagana who, on this site, prepared the army draftees for the battles that raged during the War of Independence. Until the War of Independence, there was a small neighborhood of Arabs here who fled at the outbreak of the war. Afterwards the area became the National Campus.

Giv'at Ram is surrounded by gardens, and on its lower elevations are Sacher Park, the park of the Valley of the Cross and Monastery of the Cross, and the Botanical Garden.

Boundaries:

North – International Convention Center and Zalman Shazar Boulevard

Northwest – Kiryat Moshe

South – Israel Museum, Valley of the Cross and the Monastery

East – Haim Hazaz Boulevard and Ben-Zvi Boulevard

West – Beit HaKerem, Giv'at Beit HaKerem, HaPo'alim, Ramat Beit HaKerem

Sites: within its boundaries or nearby are the National Campus with its elements: the Hebrew University, the National Library, the Knesset building, the Menorah (official emblem of the State) opposite the Knesset, the Supreme Court, the offices of the government, *Yad LeVanim,* the Joint Distribution Committee, the Bank of Israel; the museums campus: the Israel Museum, the Science Museum, the Bible Lands Museum, the Shrine of the Book, the Billy Rose Sculpture Garden; the International Convention Center, the Zionist Archive, Sacher Park, the Botanical Garden, the Valley of the Cross.

Streets: the neighborhood streets are named for presidents of the State of Israel, a past prime minister, presidents and founders of the Hebrew University, statesmen, international Zionist leaders, authors and researchers and public figures of all kinds.

The streets are:

Agranat, Shim'on [Square] (1906 – 1992) Zusman at Rabin **F12**

One of those who laid the foundations of and strengthened the Israeli judiciary, he was a judge on the municipal court in 1940, became president of the district court in 1948, then acting president of the Supreme Court, served eleven years as the president of the Supreme Court (1965–1976), was chairman of the commission of inquiry into the Yom Kippur War (1974-1975), and was a recipient of the Israel Prize.

Balfour, Arthur James, Lord [Road] (1848 – 1930)
Elyashar – Magnes **E12-13**

A British prime minister and afterwards foreign minister, who became famous for his declaration for "...the establishment in Palestine of a national home for the Jewish people..." (November 2, 1917), he participated in the dedication of the Hebrew University on Mount Scopus in 1925. He was made an honorary citizen of the city of Tel-Aviv. The official residence of the prime minister is located on the street of this name in Rehavia (see the neighborhoods of Komemiyut/Talbieh, Rehavia).

Bank Yisrael Rabin – Bank Yisrael **F12**

In memory of David Horowitz, the first governor of the Bank of Israel (1954 – 1971).

Ben-Zvi, Yitzhak [Boulevard] (1884 – 1963)
Shmuel Baruch – Ruppin **G12**

Second president of the State of Israel. One of the leaders of the labor movement in Israel. He was one of the founders of the HaShomer organization (for self-defense), along with Rahel Yanait (who in time became his wife), and one of those who set up the first Hebrew high school in Jerusalem, where he was one of the first teachers. He was one of the organizers of the *HeHalutz* (pioneering) movement in the United States and in organizing the Jewish Legion that fought in the Land of Israel alongside the British army in World War I. He was president of the National Committee during the British Mandate period. He founded and headed the (Ben-Zvi) Institute for the Research of Jewish Communities in the Middle East. An institute for research on imparting knowledge of Israel was set up, also named for him, Yad Ben-Zvi (see the neighborhoods of Kiryat Wolfson, Nahlat Ahim/Nahlaot, Sha'arei Hesed, Sha'arei Rahamim, Shevet Tzedek/ Shchunat HaPahim, Zichron Ya'akov, Zichron Yosef).

Bourla, Yehuda (1888 – 1969) Shneur – Wise **F14**

A writer, one of the first authors who described the life experience of the Oriental Jewish community; he published articles on modern Hebrew literature. He received the Israel Prize for Hebrew Literature in 1961 (see the neighborhoods of Nayot, Neve Shaanan).

Brodetsky, Zelig Moshe [Road] (1888 – 1954)
HaMuseonim – Elyashar **-F13**

A mathematician. Head of the Political Department of the Jewish Agency, president of the Zionist Organization in England (1949), a source of significant assistance in the organization of the Second Aliya, president of the Hebrew University in Jerusalem.

Elyashar, Yitzhak [Road] (1873 – 1933) Brodetsky – Balfour **14**

One of the leaders of the Sephardic community in Jerusalem, a member of the Jerusalem municipality and president of the Jerusalem Jewish community during the British Mandate (see Mid-Town).

Gruenbaum, Yitzhak [Square] (1879–1970) Kaplan at Rothschild **F13**

A statesman, writer and journalist. A leader of Polish Jewry, one of the leaders of the Zionist Organization, first Minister of the Interior of the State of Israel.

Ha'Aliya Shazar – International Convention Center **F11-12**

Named for the immigration to the Land of Israel throughout the generations.

HaNasi HaShishi [Sixth President] **[Boulevard]**
Rabin – Shazar **F11-12**

Named for Chaim Herzog (1918–1997), Israel's sixth president. Born in Ireland, he immigrated to the Land of Israel in 1935 and was drafted into the Hagana. In WWII he served as an intelligence officer in the British army. In the War of Independence, he helped break through to besieged Jerusalem. During the Six Day War he gave daily news analyses on Kol Yisrael radio, bolstering Israeli spirits. After the war, he was appointed first military governor of united Jerusalem and of the West Bank. During the Yom Kippur War he again broadcast daily news analyses. Israel's ambassador to the UN, and president 1983–1993.

HaNitzan Shazar – dead end **F11**

Flower bud, a lane leading to the government campus.

Hazaz, Haim [Boulevard] (1898 – 1973) Ruppin – Herzog **G13-14**

One of the outstanding Hebrew writers of his generation. In his early books he described Jewish life in Eastern Europe during the Russian Revolution. He was a playwright and active in the Academy of the Hebrew Language. He was awarded the Israel Prize for Literature (see the neighborhood of Rehavia).

Herlitz, Yosef (Georg), Dr. (1885 – 1968)
Shazar – Central Zionist Archive **F11**

Founder of the Central Zionist Archive and its director.

Kaplan, Eli'ezer (1891 – 1952) Ruppin – Wolfson **F12-13**

An economist, one of the heads of the labor movement in the Land of Israel, a member of the administration of the Jewish Agency, first minister of the treasury of the State of Israel.

Kiryat David Ben-Gurion [Campus] (1886–1973)
Government Campus – Ruppin **F12**

Named for the first prime minister of Israel, who declared the establishment of the Jewish state in the Land of Israel on May 15, 1948. A thinker, one of the foremost leaders of the labor movement, one of the founders of the *Histadrut Ha'Ovdim* (Israel Labor Federation) and one of its leaders, an organizer of the *HeHalutz* movement in the United States. One of the heads of the Hagana, founder of the Jewish state, a creator of TZaHa"L (the Israel Defense Force) and one of those who formulated its image, and prime minister and defense minister for many years. He built his home in Kibbutz Sde Boker in the Negev. The University of the Negev, in Beer Shev'a, and Israel's international airport are named after him (see Giv'at Shaul).

Lilian, Ephraim Moshe (1874 – 1925)
descent from the Israel Museum to Hazaz/Valley of the Cross **F13-14**

Artist, one of the founders of the Betzalel Art School in Jerusalem and a teacher there.

Lorch, Netanel (1925 – 1997) Rabin – Wolfson **E-F12**

In 1941 he joined the Hagana and fought until the end of the War of Independence. He served as president of the Institute for Israeli Culture, head of the council of the Tolerance Movement, member of the board of directors of the Hebrew University and Honorary Friend of the University.

Lutan, Giora [Square] (1902 – 1974)
International Convention Center at Herlitz **F11**

A jurist, civic leader, first director-general of *Bituah Leumi* (Institute of National Insurance).

Magnes, Yehuda Leib, Dr. [Boulevard] (1877 – 1948)
Hebrew University Giv'at Ram Campus **E13-14**

Leader and spokesman for American Jewry and one of the initiators of Hebrew education there. One of the founders and first president of the Hebrew University of Jerusalem (see the neighborhood of Rehavia).

Rabin, Yitzhak [Boulevard] (1922 – 1995) Herzl – Ben-Zvi **F11-12**

Fifth and eighth prime minister of the State of Israel and also defense minister in the second term, and the seventh chief of staff of the IDF. He was one of the first to join the PaLMa"H, and in the War of Independence he commanded the Harel Brigade and served as chief of staff of the southern front, was the army chief of staff during the Six Day War, Israel's ambassador in the United States and minister of labor. He was awarded the Nobel Prize for Peace, signed a peace treaty with Jordan, and was assassinated in 1995 at the close of a demonstration of support that took place in the square in Tel-Aviv that today bears his name.

Rahel Yanait (Ben-Zvi) [Square] (1886 – 1979)
Hazaz at Ben-Zvi at Ruppin **G13**

One of the leadership of the labor movement and one of the heads of the Hagana in Jerusalem. An educator of youth and founder of the agricultural farms in Jerusalem and 'Ein Kerem. Wife of the second president of the State of Israel, Yitzhak Ben-Zvi, and partner in his endeavors.

Rakah, Yosef, Prof. (1909 – 1965) Elyashar – Elyashar **E-F14**

One of the foremost scientists in the Land of Israel, one of the leaders of Italian Jewry, a president and professor at the Hebrew University of Jerusalem.

Rothschild, Edmond de (1845 – 1934) the Knesset building **F13**

The greatest Jewish philanthropist of his generation, called "the father of the Yishuv (Jewish colony)" and "the well-known philanthropist", supported the Jewish agricultural communities in the Land of Israel.

Rothschild, James Armand de (1878 – 1957)
Kaplan to the Knesset **F13**

Son of the well-known philanthropist. One of the commanding officers of the Jewish Legion during World War I, he was a member of the British parliament, active on behalf of the agricultural community in the Land of Israel, and contributed the funds for construction of the Knesset building in Jerusalem.

Ruppin, Arthur Shim'on [Road] (1876 – 1943)
RaMBa"N – Wolfson **F-G13**

An agronomist, economist and sociologist. Initiated, planned and brought to fruition the plans of the Zionist Organization and its management in the matter of agricultural settlement of the Land of Israel. He founded the association for training people for settling the land and assisted in obtaining the funds for reclamation of the Land of Israel. He served as chairman of the Jewish Agency (see the neighborhood of Kiryat Wolfson).

Sacher, Harry [Park] (1881 – 1971)
Ben-Zvi, between Rabin and Ruppin **G12-13**

A jurist and one of the Zionist leaders in England. He was active in the development of the Hebrew University of Jerusalem.

Sderot HaMuseonim Ruppin – Wise **E12-F13**

The street on which are located the various museums on Giv'at Ram.

Sderot HaUma Shazar – Herzog **F11**

Boulevard of the Nation, a road alongside the International Convention Center.

Sha'arei Mishpat Zusman – Supreme Court **F12**

Gates of judgment, a symbolic name. The street leading to the Supreme Court.

Shazar, Shneur Zalman [Boulevard] (1889 – 1974)
Herzl Boulevard – Shmuel Baruch – Nordau **F11**

The third president of the State of Israel. A writer, researcher of Messianic movements in Israel's history, one of the leaders of the labor movement, editor of the newspaper *Davar*, head of the department of Diaspora education and chairman of the Zionist administration, and minister of education in the government of Israel (see the neighborhoods of Mahane Yehuda, Romema).

Shealtiel, Aluf [General] **David** (1903–1969)
Ben-Zvi – Beit HaHayal – dead end **G11-F12**

A Hagana member, commander of the Hagana in the Jordan Valley and the Galilee, commander of the Jerusalem front in the War of Independence, an activist in the rescue of European Jews at the end of World War II.

Sheetrit, Shalom Shmuel [Square] (1885 – 1965) Shazar at Herzl **F11**

One of the civic leaders and builders of Jerusalem. He is considered to be one of the greatest and most important initiators and developers of Jewish Jerusalem and its new neighborhoods at the beginning of the twentieth century and all through the British Mandate period, e.g.: Rehavia, Kiryat Shmuel, Geula and Kiryat Moshe. He was one of the developers of commerce on Rehov Yafo and is counted among the contributors to and founders of the Diskin Orphans Home.

Shilo, Yigael (1937 – 1988) Kaplan – Wolfson **G12**

An archeologist and researcher of the City of David. Was awarded the Israel Prize.

Simon, Leo Aryeh [Road] (1881 – 1965) Brodetsky – Brodetsky **E14**

A writer, philosopher, one of the leaders of the Zionist movement in England, acting president and chairman of the Executive Committee of the Hebrew University of Jerusalem, and a member of the Academy of the Hebrew Language.

Vilnay, Zeev (1900 – 1988) Wolfson – dead end **E12**

A researcher of the Land of Israel in general and Jerusalem in particular. Recipient of the Israel Prize and other prizes. Named *Yakir Yerushalayim*, an Honored Citizen of Jerusalem.

Wise, Stephen Shmuel (1874 – 1949) Ruppin – Bourla **F13**

A Zionist leader in the United States, a president of the American Jewish Congress, he participated as a member of the Jewish delegation to the Versailles Peace Conference in 1919 (see the neighborhood of Neve Shaanan).

Wolffsohn, David (1855 – 1914)
Herzl – Hebrew University Giv'at Ram Campus **E-F12**

The devoted assistant of Dr. Theodor Herzl and his escort on his travels and visits to the Land of Israel. The second president of the World Zionist Organization, one of the founders of the Jewish Colonial Trust and one of its directors.

Women's League [Road] Wise – dead end **F13**

A women's organization in the United States whose aim is to support cultural activities in the Land of Israel, preparation and rehabilitation of new immigrants who are women.

YiK"A [Square] Kaplan at Rothschild **F13**

The Jewish Colonization Association, founded in 1891 by Baron Maurice de Hirsch.

Zusman, Yoel (1910 – 1982) Rabin – Kaplan **F12**

A president of the Supreme Court. He published important books including: Order of Civil Law, Laws of Deeds. A recipient of the Israel Prize.

Giv'at Shapira / French Hill *[HaGiv'a HaTzarfatit]*

Name and establishment:

This neighborhood, in the northern part of the city on the heights of Mount Scopus, was established in 1971 and is named after Haim Moshe Shapira (1902-1970), one of the leaders of the religious Zionist *Mizrahi* movement and a former interior minister in Israel's government. Its other name is French Hill, named for Colonel French, who is buried in the British military cemetery on Mount Scopus.

This neighborhood, one of the highest in elevation in Jerusalem, is built on the east side of *HaMivtar* [the divide], the cut high up on Mount Scopus where the road passes from Jerusalem north to Ramallah and to Nablus. In this spot a battle of the Six Day War raged in 1967. Armored vehicles of the Harel Brigade broke through here to liberate east Jerusalem.

Boundaries:

North – Shu'afat
South – the Hebrew University Mount Scopus campus
East – Tzameret HaBira
West – Giv'at HaMivtar

Sites: within its boundaries or nearby are Ammunition Hill, Mount Scopus, Mount of Olives.

Streets: the streets of the neighborhood are called by names of the Jewish organizations for defense of the Land of Israel during the period of British rule, fighters and partisans in Europe during World War II.

The streets are:

Alkal'ai, David [Square] (1897 – 1982)
HaHagana at Lohamei HaGhetaot **K9**

A man of public affairs and a leader of the Sephardic Jewish community in Yugoslavia, a member of the executive of the union of Jewish communities, one of the Zionist leaders, one of the foremost activists on behalf of the Second Aliya, one of the civic leaders of Jerusalem.

Auerbach, Moshe [Square] (1904 – 1962) HaHagana at ETZe"L **J8-9**

A colonel, one of the commanders of the Hagana in Jerusalem, chairman of the IDF committee for commemoration, one of the civic leaders of Jerusalem.

Bar Kochva, Shim'on (2nd cent. CE)
Lohamei HaGhetaot – HaHagana **J8-K9**

He was the leader of the failed rebellion against Roman rule that lasted for three years, when coins were minted saying "Shim'on, president of Israel." His name was Bar Kosiva, and he may have been of the Hasmonean family, as Rabbi El'azar HaModa'i was his uncle. He fell in battle in the city of Beitar in the Judean hills (see the neighborhood of Tzameret HaBira).

Bar Lev, Haim [Boulevard] (1924 – 1994)
Yigael Yadin – Shmuel HaNavi **J9-I11**

(See the neighborhoods of Giv'at HaMivtar, Kiryat Aryeh, Nahlat Shim'on, Sheikh Jarrah.)

Dakar [Lane] Lohamei HaGhetaot – dead end **J9**

In memory of the sailors who died on the submarine that sank in the Mediterranean in 1968.

Derech Ma'ale Adumim Bar Lev – to the city of Ma'ale Adumim **J-K8**

Named for the Biblical place and for the modern city built east of Jerusalem (see the neighborhood of Tzameret HaBira).

ETZe"L HaHagana – Lohamei HaGhetaot – HaHagana **J9**

Acronym for: ***Irgun Tzvai Leumi***, an armed underground organization that worked against the rule of the British Mandate regime, against the decrees of the White Paper, and was active in the illegal immigration of Jews. Many members of ETZe"L fell in the confrontation with the British army and governing authority, and some of the members were sentenced to death and were hanged (see 'Olei HaGardom in the neighborhood of Talpiot Mizrah).

Golei Kenya Bar Kochva – dead end **J8**

Exiled to Kenya. The third place of imprisonment to which the ETZe"L and LeH"I fighters were transferred by the British Mandate regime after they had been kept in Eritrea and the Sudan. They were moved because of escapes from the previous camps. However, Yitzhak Shamir, one of the LeH"I commanders and later a prime minister of Israel, and Ya'akov Meridor, an ETZe"L commander and later an Israel government minister, succeeded in escaping from there, too.

Ha'Asara [Lane] Bar Kochva – dead end **J8**

The Ten. In memory of ten soldiers of the convoy that hurried to help the besieged Kfar 'Etzion in the Etzion Bloc and were killed in an ambush, on 28 Kislev 1947.

HaHagana Bar Lev – Lohamei HaGhetaot **J9**

The main military organization that defended the Jewish community in the Land of Israel during the British Mandate. The Hagana existed until the establishment of the State, and in it were laid the foundations for the creation of the IDF.

HaHaYi"L Bar Kochva – Lohamei HaGhetaot **K8-9**

Acronym for: ***Hail Lohem*** [fighting corps]. Named for the Jewish Brigade that fought in Europe in World War II (see the neighborhood of Tzameret HaBira).

HaHitnadvuyot [Lane] LeH"I – dead end **J9**

Named for the voluntarism of the residents of Israel in all the national missions, especially in the fighting force.

HaMaavak [Lane] HaHagana – dead end **J-K9**

Named for the struggle of the Jewish community in the Land of Israel against the regime of the British Mandate.

HaNaHa"L Bar Kochva – dead end **K9**

Acronym for: ***No'ar Halutzi Lohem.*** An army corps set up in 1948 as part of the GaDN"a' (youth battalions, for premilitary training). It served as a framework for agricultural pioneer groups.

HaPartizanim [Lane] Bar Kochva – dead end **J8**

Named for the Jewish partisans who fought behind the Nazi lines in World War II.

Katzir, Aharon (1914 – 1972) LeH"I – HaUniversita **J10**

A professor, president of the Academy of Sciences in the Land of Israel. Recipient of the Israel Prize (1961). He was killed in a terrorist attack at Ben-Gurion Airport in 1972 (see the neighborhood of Mount Scopus).

LeH"I ETZe"L – Katzir **J9**

Acronym for: ***Lohamei Herut Yisrael.*** An underground organization that operated against the British during the Mandate period.

Lohamei HaGhetaot HaHaYi"L – HaHagana **J-K9**

Named for the ghetto fighters in Poland and other Nazi-controlled lands in World War II (see the neighborhood of Tzameret HaBira).

Sderot HaUniversita Bar Lev – Katzir **J9-10**

The street leading to Mount Scopus and to the Hebrew University campus on Mount Scopus (see the neighborhoods of Mount Scopus, Sheikh Jarrah).

Smith, George Adam (1856 – 1942) LeH"I – Bar Lev **J9**

A British researcher of the Bible and of the geography of the Land of Israel.

Giv'at Shaul

Name and establishment:

This neighborhood, on the west side of the city, surrounded by hills, at the entrance to the city and at the beginning of the road south descending toward Motza, was founded in 1907. The founding association of Giv'at Shaul was set up the same year, but due to difficulties in acquiring land during the time of Turkish rule, the building up of the neighborhood was delayed until 1919, after the British conquest. It is named for Rabbi Ya'akov Shaul Elyashar, the chief rabbi, the "Rishon LeTzion" of the Sephardic Jews in the Land of Israel (see in the neighborhood of HaBucharim another street named for him, called **Yisa** Bracha, **Y**a'akov **S**haul **E**lyashar), whose son Rabbi Nissim Elyashar was a founder of the neighborhood.

The early residents were poor people who wanted to establish agricultural farmsteads to supply fresh produce, vegetables, to Jerusalem residents. Over the years the neighborhood turned into a manufacturing center which pushed out those very farm owners. Kanfei Nesharim Street leads to the industrial area in the neighborhood (see Giv'at Shaul-Industrial Zone).

Right next to Giv'at Shaul was the Arab village Dir Yasin that was a base for Arab attacks on Jews during the War of Independence. It was captured, after a difficult battle, by the forces of ETZe"L. Within the area of the village was built Kfar Shaul, which over the years has been swallowed up by the neighborhood of Giv'at Shaul. A hospital was built there for the mentally ill.

Many of the residents today are from the ultra-Orthodox community.

Boundaries:
North – Har (Mount) Tamir, Har (Mount) HaMenuhot
Northeast – Romema
Southeast – Kiryat Moshe
West – Har Nof

Sites: within its boundaries or nearby are various sites: the industrial zone, Har Tamir, Har HaMenuhot Cemetery, 'Ezrat Nashim Hospital, the Angel and Berman bakeries, Diskin Orphans Home, an airfield (on Kanfei Nesharim Street) put up during the War of Independence and not in use today.

Streets: the neighborhood streets are named for rabbis from the Gaonic period, Kabbalists, religious works, public figures.

The streets are:

Alfiye, Meir, Rabbi [Square] (d. 1941)
Kanfei Nesharim at HaMelamed **C11**

A Kabbalist, one of the Kurdish community's great rabbis (see the neighborhood of Har Nof).

Alkabetz, Shlomo, Rabbi (1505 – 1584)
Giv'at Shaul – HaReuveni – dead end **D11-E10**

A Kabbalist, a composer of liturgical poetry and head of a yeshiva in Tzfat, became famous for his poem "Lecha Dodi, Likrat Kalla" which is sung in the Friday evening Shabbat prayers.

'Amram Gaon (ben Sheshna) (9th cent. CE)
Giv'at Shaul – Shrira Gaon – dead end **E11**

The head (*Gaon*) of the Talmudical academy at Sura, and author of the first prayer book, which is named for him: *Seder Rav 'Amram*, which served as the basis for the prayer book according to the Sephardic custom. He was the disciple of Nitronai bar Hilai, and the title of *Gaon* was conferred on him already during the lifetime of his predecessor.

'Am Ve'Olamo Kanfei Nesharim – dead end **D11**

A People and Its World, named for the book by Prof. Aryeh Tratkover (1897-1983), researcher of Jewish society.

Angel, Shlomo [Square] (1893 – 1965)
Kanfei Nesharim at Farbstein **E11**

Son of an old Jerusalem family, educated in a teachers college, he built up the large bakery enterprise known in Jerusalem by his name. He was among the builders of the Bayit VaGan neighborhood, one of the biggest industrialists in the city.

'Azriel Hausdorf (1826 – 1905) Kehati – Giv'at Shaul **E10**

One of the civic leaders of Jerusalem and one of the builders of the city, one of the builders of the Batei Mahse quarter for the poor in the Old City.

Azulai, 'Akiva Giv'at Shaul – Kanfei Nesharim **D11**

Served in public positions in the Jerusalem Municipality, chairman of the workers committee, director of the sanitation department and deputy mayor of Jerusalem, responsible for the water supply to Jerusalem. After his retirement from the municipality, he served as the deputy chairman of the religious council and president of the Western community.

Ba'al HaSheiltot (8th cent. CE) Yemin Avot – 'Amram Gaon **E11**

Named for a book of religious law by Rabbi Ahai Gaon, one of the great religious legalists in Babylonia at the end of the first century of the Gaonic period.

Baronowicz [Lane] Alkabetz – dead end **D11**

Named for the martyrs of Baronowicz during the Holocaust (1940 – 1945).

Beit She'arim Reines – dead end **E11**

A city in the Jezreel Valley in the periods of the Second Temple, the Mishna and the Talmud. The place where Rabbi Yehuda HaNasi lived and was buried.

Ben-Gurion, David [Boulevard] (1886 – 1973)
Giv'at Shaul – Highway One **D-E10**

(See Kiryat David Ben-Gurion in the neighborhood of Giv'at Ram.)

Ben Tzion, Shim'on Shmuel (1894 – 1954)
Degel Reuven – 'Amram Gaon **E11**

A Zionist activist and active in the development of Jerusalem, one of the founders of the Ben Tzion neighborhood (see the neighborhoods of Kiryat Moshe, Maimon/Shchunat HaPo'el HaMizrahi).

Ben 'Uziel, Yonatan Kuenka – 'Amram Gaon **E11**

A disciple of Hillel the Elder during the Second Temple period; translated some of the books of the Bible into Aramaic *(Targum Yonatan).*

Cordovero, Moshe, Rabbi (1522 – 1570) HaReuveni – dead end D11

Known by the acronym, RaMa"C (**R**abbi **M**oshe **C**ordovero). A rabbi and arbiter of religious law, one of the greatest Kabbalists in Tzfat and a pre-eminent interpreter of the Zohar, he was a disciple of Rabbi Yosef Karo and of Rabbi Shlomo Alkabetz, as well as a head of yeshiva and initiator of a distinctive stream of Kabbala (mysticism) parallel to the approach of the AR"I.

Dvoretz, Yisrael Zissel, Rabbi [Square] (1886–1968)
Ba'al HaSheiltot at Ben Tzion **E11**

Founder and editor of the publication "Understanding Torah and Ethics" (see the neighborhood of Kiryat Moshe).

Eliav, Ya'akov Giv'at Shaul – dead end **D10**

In charge of the close supporters of David Raziel and afterwards of Yair Avraham Stern, commanders of ETZe"L and LeH"I. During the War of Independence he was put in command of the Golani Brigade in the north. Following his army discharge, he volunteered for Israel's intelligence service, and served also as police consultant in the war on terror.

'Ezrat Nashim [Square] Meginei Yerushalayim at Giv'at Shaul **D10**

The 'Ezrat Nashim Association was established originally in 1859 to help women who had just given birth, but it was quickly established that the main purpose of the organization was to care for the mentally ill. The organization was set up by Mrs. Haya Tzipora Pines and Mrs. Rosa Finestein.

'Ezrian, Nissim (1910 – 1984) 'Amram Gaon – Najara **E11**

Founder of the Beit Shmuel Yeshiva, and a *Yakir Yerushalayim*.

Giv'at Shaul Weizmann – Har HaMenuhot **C10-E11**

Named for the neighborhood and for **Ya**'akov **S**haul **E**lyashar (see the neighborhood of HaBucharim, **Yisa** Bracha Street).

Grajewski, Pinhas (1873 – 1941) Onkelos – HaReuveni **D11**

An Honored Citizen of Jerusalem and a researcher of the history of the city.

Haftzadi, Nahum (1895 – 1968) Azulai – HaMelamed **D11**

One of the early immigrants from Kurdistan and a builder of Jerusalem.

Hai Gaon (939 – 1038 CE) Ba'al HaSheiltot – dead end **E11**

Rabbi Hai ben Shrira Gaon, head of the Yeshiva of Pumbedita in Babylonia, one of the molders of the religious law and one of the great arbiters of the law.

HaMelamed (1887 – 1965) Kanfei Nesharim – Haftzadi **C-D11**

Named for Rabbi Gershon Cohen, rabbi of the neighborhood Nahlat Shim'on in Jerusalem.

HaReuveni, David (16th cent.) Ba'al HaSheiltot – Cordovero **D-E11**

He awakened a messianic movement in the first half of the sixteenth century, presented himself before kings, was imprisoned and died in Spain, was related to the tribe of Reuben and from thence his name.

Kanfei Nesharim Farbstein – HaMelamed **C-D11**

Named for a religious work by Rabbi Avraham Nesher (Adler), who died in 1969. He served as head of the rabbinate office in Jerusalem and as rabbi of Jerusalem for many years. The name ("wings of eagles") is also for the airfield that was in this area during the War of Independence (see the neighborhood of Giv'at Shaul Industrial Zone).

Kehati, Pinhas, Rabbi (1910 – 1977) Giv'at Shaul – Giv'at Shaul **E10**

Author of the commentary *Mishnayot Mevoarot* on the six orders of the Mishna. He was a member of the executive of the *Po'el Mizrahi* (religious labor) party representing the *Hazon VeHagshama* (vision and realization) faction and headed the youth department. He won the Rav Kook Prize for his major work in religious literature.

Kotler, Aharon, Rabbi (1892 – 1962)
Giv'at Shaul – Reines – Ba'al HaSheiltot **E11**

President of the Council of Torah Sages of *Agudat Yisrael*, head of the *'Etz Haim* Yeshiva, he worked hard to rescue European Jews during World War II.

Ktav Sofer Giv'at Shaul – Ben-Gurion Boulevard **E10**

Named for a book of religious law by Rabbi Avraham Shmuel Sofer (1815-1871), a rabbi and arbiter of religious law, one of the spiritual leaders of Hungarian Jewry, one of the founders of the Hungarian Kollel *Shomrei HaHomot* (guardians of the walls) in Jerusalem (see the neighborhood of Batei Kollel Ungarin/Nahlat Zvi).

Kuenka, Bentzion, Rabbi (1867 – 1937) Onkelos – 'Uziel **D11**

A rabbi and arbiter of religious law, he initiated a monthly religious publication in Jerusalem called *HaMeasef* and was its editor. He was chief judge of a Jerusalem court and the leading rabbi of Hebron.

Meginei Yerushalayim Giv'at Shaul – Ben-Gurion Boulevard **D10**

In memory of the defenders of the city during all the wars in history.

Najara, Yisrael, Rabbi (1555–1625)
Kanfei Nesharim – Giv'at Shaul **E11**

A rabbi, Kabbalist, considered one of the greatest Hebrew poets after the Expulsion from Spain, he wrote many books of poetry and a collection of his poems called *Zmirot Yisrael* (songs of Israel). A few of his religious poems were included in the prayer book. His best-known poem is *Ya Ribon 'Olam Ve'Olmaya*, which is sung for Shabbat on Friday evenings.

Nitronai bar Hilai (9th cent. CE) Shrira Gaon – Ben Tzion **E11**

The head of the Talmudical academy of Sura, Babylonia, one of the greatest arbiters of religious law during the period of the Geonim.

Onkelos (late 1st cent. and early 2nd cent. CE)
Ba'al HaSheiltot – Najara – dead end **E11**

Translated the Torah into Aramaic during the Second Temple period, was of the generation of Rabban Gamliel, Rabbi Eli'ezer ben Hyrcanus and Rabbi Yehoshu'a.

Plugat Yehonatan [Square] Kanfei Nesharim at Azulai **D11**

Named for the company of youth who fought in Jerusalem during the War of Independence.

Pu'a (Rakovsky) (1865 – 1955) Ba'al HaSheiltot – dead end **E11**

An educator and the founder of a school for girls in Warsaw, a Zionist activist.

Shrira Gaon, Rabbi (900 – 1006 CE)
Ba'al HaSheiltot – Alkabetz **D-E11**

One of the greatest of the heads of Talmudical academies in Babylonia, head of the yeshiva in Pumbedita, a well-known interpreter and arbiter of religious law. In his famous epistle, known as *Igeret Rav Shrira Gaon*, is found an exposition on the order of the writing and editing of the *Torah Sheb'al Peh* (Oral Law) – the Mishna, the Tosefta and the Talmud. His son was Rabbi Hai Gaon.

Tosefot Yom Tov Giv'at Shaul – 'Amram Gaon **E10**

Named after a book of commentary on the Mishna by Rabbi Yom Tov Lipman Heller (1579-1654), a rabbi and arbiter of religious law, one of the great commentators on the Mishna.

Vital, Haim, Rabbi (1543 – 1620) Kanfei Nesharim – Onkelos **E11**

One of the great Kabbalists, he set down in writing the teachings of the Holy AR"I. He was born in Tzfat and was the disciple of the Kabbalist Rabbi Moshe Cordovero. When the AR"I immigrated to Israel, he studied directly with him and set down the AR"I's teachings in his book *'Etz HaHaim*. In a later period he moved to Damascus, served as rabbi of the community there that was originally from Sicily, taught Kabbala according to the system of the AR"I and died there.

Weizmann, Chaim, Dr. [Boulevard] (1874–1952)
Herzl Boulevard – Giv'at Shaul **E10-F11**

First president of the State of Israel. Statesman, scientist, leader of the Zionist movement, initiated and drafted the Balfour Declaration (November 2, 1917), served as the fourth president of the Zionist Organization, and with the establishment of the enlarged Jewish Agency, he became head of it. He worked hard for the establishment of institutions of higher learning and for scientific research in the Land of Israel in the Hebrew University and the scientific institute in Rehovot that is named for him. When he turned sixty, he was made an honorary citizen of the city of Tel-Aviv. From 1949 until his death he was president of Israel.

Yemin Avot Ha'Ilui – Farbstein **D-E11**

Named for a religious work by Rabbi Yehoshu'a Betzalel Kantrowitz (1825–1885), one of Jerusalem's rabbis and one of the heads of *'Etz Haim Yeshiva* (see the neighborhood of Kiryat Moshe).

Giv'at Shaul-Industrial Zone

See the neighborhood of Giv'at Shaul, page 227.

Bachi, Roberto (1909 – 1996)
Kanfei Nesharim – Beit HaDfus **C11**

The first statistician in the State of Israel, he established the department of statistics and demographics at the Hebrew University of Jerusalem. He initiated the faculty of social sciences at the University and served as its first rector. After the Six Day War, he was responsible for the population census in the areas conquered by the IDF. Recipient of the Israel Prize and a *Yakir Yerushalayim*.

Beit HaDfus Farbstein – Katzenellenbogen **D11**

Named for the many printing businesses on this street, the center of the industrial area in the neighborhood.

Farbstein, Yehoshu'a, Rabbi (1870 – 1948)
Herzl Boulevard – Yemin Avot **E11**

One of the leaders of the religious Zionist *Mizrahi* movement, honorary president of the Jerusalem Jewish community (see the neighborhood of Kiryat Moshe).

Kanfei Nesharim Farbstein – HaMelamed **C-D11**

(See the neighborhood of Giv'at Shaul.)

Shatner, Mordechai Kanfei Nesharim – Beit HaDfus **D11**

One of the signers of Israel's Declaration of Independence.

Weitz, Yosef [Road] (1890 – 1972)
Beit HaDfus – Ya'ar Yerushalayim [Jerusalem Forest] **C-D12**

A writer, director of the Israel Lands Administration, an activist in the agricultural association, active in *HaKeren HaKayemet LeYisrael* (the Jewish National Fund) especially in the area of afforestation and settling of hilltop communities, director of the department of forests of the J.N.F.

Gonen/Katamon HaYeshana

Name and establishment:

Old Katamon. This neighorhood, located in the southwestern part of the city, was established as a Jewish neighborhood in 1948. The neighborhood was originally founded during the British Mandate period, in the 1920s, by well-to-do Arabs. The name Katamon is Greek, a mixture of two words, "kata" and "monis", meaning "near the monastery", referring to the San Simon Monastery located there.

In the War of Independence, the entire neighborhood came under Israeli rule following its capture by the PaLMa"H and Hagana fighters, the first victory in Jerusalem. The Arab residents abandoned their homes, and in their place came new immigrants from various lands. In 1952, housing blocks were built near Old Katamon to absorb the new immigrants, and these new sections were named Gonen Aleph, Gonen Bet and so on, according to the order in which they were built (see the neighborhood of Gonenim/Katamonim).

Until the Six Day War, Gonen was near the border with Jordan, on the defense line of the city, and from there is derived the name Gonen (protector), like a protective line for the Jewish side of the border in the capital. The Hebrew name given to the neighborhood was Gonen, but the name did not take with the public.

Boundaries:

North – Kiryat Shmuel
South – Gonenim/Katamonim
East – the Greek Colony and the German Colony
West – Giv'at HaVradim/Shikun Rassco

Sites: within its boundaries or nearby are the Denmark School, Horev School, the Museum for Islamic Art, the San Simon Monastery, Misgav LaDach Hospital.

Streets: the neighborhood streets are named for military units, Jewish fighting forces and battles that took place in Jerusalem during the War of Independence.

The streets are:

Alroi, David (12th cent.) Tel Hai – dead end **G15**

He was leader of a messianic movement in the Caucasus Mountains in Persia (Iran). He changed his name from Menahem to David and claimed to be king of Israel. He was murdered in Kurdistan. Legends about him provided material for a fictitious historical novel, called "David Alroy", written by Benjamin Disraeli, a British prime minister.

Asaf, Gavriel [Square] (1908 – 1982)
Kovshei Katamon at HaLamed Hei **G14**

A public activist and one of the builders of Jerusalem.

Bar Nisan (1890 – 1940)
Kaf-Tet BeNovember – HaGedud Ha'Ivri **G14-15**

Named for Yosef Katznelson (Bar Nisan), one of the activists in ETZe"L and an organizer of the illegal immigration from Poland before the Nazi Holocaust.

Bar Niv, Zvi [Square] (1916 – 1986) HaPaLMa"H at HaTayasim **F15**

The first president of the National Labor Court. A Jerusalemite from the day of his immigration, he took part in defending the city during the War of Independence.

Be-erot Yitzhak Rahel Imeinu – Yad Mordechai **G15**

The first kibbutz established in the Negev, it is today located north of Ben-Gurion Airport.

Beit Eshel Mishmar Ha'Am – Negba **G15**

One of three pioneering "watchtower" communities that were established in the Negev (the other two – Gvulot and Revivim). East of Beer Shev'a, it stood against the Egyptian army in the War of Independence and was destroyed. A memorial plaque was erected there.

Ben Zeev, Yehiel [Square] (1912 – 1985)
HaPaLMa"H at Fichmann **F15**

One of the first Hagana members in Jerusalem.

BIL"U Hizkiyahu – HaLamed Hei **G15**

Acronym for: ***Beit Ya'akov Lechu VeNelcha***, "House of Jacob, come let us go" (Isaiah 2:5). A group of young students in Russia, who organized in reaction to the pogroms of 1881, understood they must leave Europe, immigrate to the Land of Israel and settle there, in order to renew their lives and work the land. The nucleus of the First Aliya, they established the agricultural village Gedera.

Bustenai ben Hanina (7th cent. CE) Hizkiyahu – 'Eli Cohen **G15**

The first exilarch (head of the Jewish community in Exile) in Babylonia and Persia after the Muslim conquest. His descendants served as exilarchs after him.

Cohen, Eli (1924 – 1965) HaGedud Ha'Ivri – Bustenai **G14**

A member of Israeli intelligence who worked in Syria, was caught and executed in Damascus. Until today Israel has been trying to get back his remains, without success.

Freier, Recha [Square] (1892 – 1984) Bustenai at Rahel Imeinu **G15**

Founder of 'Aliyat HaNo'ar [Youth Aliya].

HaGaDN"A' HaShayarot – HaHI"SH **G15**

Acronym for: ***Gedudei No'ar***. A brigade for youth whose purpose was to give early training prior to army service. These units fought in battles in Jerusalem and other places.

HaGedud Ha'Ivri HaPaLMa"H – Kaf-Tet BeNovember **G-H14**

Named for the Jewish battalions, volunteers from America, England and the Land of Israel, who fought in World War I together with the British army to liberate the Land of Israel. In the Jewish battalions served such men as Jabotinsky, Ben-Gurion and Ben-Zvi.

HaHI"M Hizkiyahu – HaMa'apilim **F-G15**

Acronym for: ***Heil Mishmar***. Hagana members who served in Jerusalem in the War of Independence.

HaHI"SH Hizkiyahu – HaMa'apilim) **G15**

Acronym for: ***Heil Sadeh***. A field unit of the Hagana. In the War of Independence they were among those who captured Gonen/Katamon.

HaLamed Hei BIL"U – Bustenai **G14-15**

In memory of thirty-five (Lamed = 30, Hei = 5) PaLMa"H and HI"SH fighters who set out to reinforce the besieged residents of the 'Etzion Bloc in the War of Independence and fell to an ambush as they neared the Bloc. The Bloc fell on the day the State was declared, May 14, 1948. A kibbutz established near the 'Etzion Bloc was named Netiv (path) HaLamed Hei.

Halprin, Yisrael (1910 – 1971) HaPaLMa"H – HaPortzim **G14**

A historian and researcher of the history of the Jews of Eastern Europe.

HaMa'apilim HaPaLMa"H – Shai 'Agnon **F15**

(See the neighborhood of Giv'at Oranim).

HaMatzor HaMeshuryanim – HaHI"M **F-G15**

Siege, named for the siege of Jerusalem and its residents' bravery in the War of Independence.

HaMeshuryanim HaShayarot – HaPaLMa"H **G15**

Armored, named for the armored vehicles, metal-plated, that escorted the convoys bringing food and ammunition to the besieged Jerusalemites in the War of Independence.

Ha'Oleh [Lane] HaMa'apilim – dead end **F15**

(See the neighborhood of Giv'at Oranim).

HaPaLMa"H HaNasi – Fichmann **G14-15**

Acronym for: ***Plugot Mahatz***, the name of the Hagana's battle arm. Among the most daring fighters in the War of Independence (see the neighborhoods of Kiryat Shmuel, Merhavia).

HaPortzim HaLamed Hei – HaPaLMa"H **G14-15**

Named for a PaLMa"H battalion, the Harel Brigade, which broke through enemy lines in this neighborhood during the War of Independence.

HaShayarot HaHI"M – Mivtza Kadesh **G15**

Convoys, named for the convoys that brought food, medicine and ammunition to besieged Jerusalem in the War of Independence.

HaTayasim NIL"I – HaPaLMa"H **G14-15**

Named for the Jewish pilots who came to the assistance of the city of

Jerusalem in the War of Independence and in all of Israel's battles.

Heil Nashim [*He"N*] HaHI"SH – BIL"U **G15**

Named for the Jewish women in Israel who volunteered as soldiers in the British army in World War II and also the women drafted into the IDF.

Hizkiyahu HaMelech (746–693 BCE)
Rahel Imeinu – HaHI"M, ends at Ma'ale Zeev **G-H15**

Hezekiah, a king of the kingdom of Judah. It was said of him:"...after him there was none like him among all the kings of Judah, nor among those before him" (II Kings 18:5) (see the neighborhoods of Gonenim/ Katamonim Aleph, Vav, the Greek Colony).

Kaf-Tet BeNovember Kovshei Katamon – Dubnow **G15-H14**

The date (November 29, 1947) the United Nations General Assembly approved the partition plan providing for a Jewish state in the Land of Israel.

Kovshei Katamon Hizkiyahu – HaPaLMa"H **G14-15**

Named for Hagana members who captured Gonen/Katamon in the War of Independence.

Mehalkei HaMayim BIL"U – HaHI"M – dead end **F-G15**

For residents who distributed water in besieged Jerusalem in the War of Independence.

Mishmar Ha'Am BIL"U – Rahel Imeinu **G15**

Jerusalem civilians who volunteered to defend the city in the War of Independence.

Mivtza Kadesh HaLamed Hei – HaPaLMa"H **G15**

The 1956 IDF military action capturing the Sinai from Egypt, also called the Sinai Campaign.

Negba Mishmar Ha'Am – Bustenai **G15**

Named for a kibbutz on the southern coastal plain, established as part of the group of settlements built as defensive outposts that bravely withstood the Egyptian army in the War of Independence until the enemy was routed.

Netiv Zahara Levitov (1928 – 1948) HaPaLMa"H – HaTayasim **F-G15**

Path of Zahara Levitov, a female pilot, commander of a PaLMa"H squad.

She was killed in the line of duty in Jerusalem during the War of Independence.

NIL"I HaPaLMa"H – HaTayasim **G14**

Acronym for: ***Netzah Yisrael Lo Yeshaker***. Named for a Jewish underground organization active during World War I in gathering intelligence for the British army in its effort to conquer the Land of Israel.

Rahel Imeinu 'Emek Refaim – HaPortzim **G-H15**

(See the German Colony/RaMBa"M, the Greek Colony.)

Tel Hai Kaf-Tet BeNovember – Hizkiyahu **G15**

Named for a village in the Upper Galilee, where in 1920 a major battle was fought in which the hero Yosef Trumpeldor and his friends fell. Trumpeldor's name became a symbol for bravery. In his memory and that of the others, the monument of the "Roaring Lion" was put up in the cemetery near the village where he is buried.

Yad Mordechai Mishmar Ha'Am – Rahel Imeinu **G15**

A kibbutz in southern Israel named for Mordechai Anielewicz, one of the commanders of the Warsaw Ghetto. The kibbutz fought bravely against Egypt in the War of Independence.

Yoni [Square] (1946 – 1976) HaPortzim at HaLamed Hei **G15**

Named for lieutenant-colonel Yoni Netanyahu, commander of the rescue force in Entebbe in 1976, the sole Israeli casualty.

Yoram Katz [Lane] (1936 – 1955) HaGedud Ha'Ivri – dead end **G14**

A Jerusalemite, a scout, a youth counselor, a paratrooper, who was killed in a military action on the eastern shore of the Kineret during a battle with the Syrians.

Yordei HaSira BIL"U – BIL"U **G15**

Those who sank in a boat. In memory of twenty-three young Hagana members who set out on a mission for the British army during World War II against the oil installations at Tripoli in Lebanon and are believed to have died at sea when their boat sank without a trace.

Gonenim/Katamonim

Name and establishment:

This neighborhood, located in the southwestern part of the city, is subdivided into sections: Gonen Aleph, Bet, Gimel and so on, according to the order in which each section was built up. The neighborhood was founded in the 1920s, during the British Mandate period, by a wealthy Arab population that built homes there. The source of the name Katamon is Greek, a mixture of two words, "kata" and "monis", meaning "near the monastery", referring to the San Simon Monastery located there.

After the War of Independence, in the 1950s, the Arabs abandoned their houses in the neighborhood, and immigrants from many different countries moved in. Until the Six Day War the neighborhood was near the border with Jordan, on the city's defense perimeter. The residents defended the neighborhood from attacks by the Jordanians, and from that comes the name, Gonenim (protectors, defenders). Its central streets lead to other neighborhoods in the southern part of the city. Its residents are both religious and secular, but there are many synagogues in the neighborhood.

Boundaries:

North – Giv'at HaVradim/Shikun Rassco, Giv'at Mordechai, Giv'at Ram
South – Pat, Gilo
East – Gonen/Katamon HaYeshana, the Greek Colony, Mekor Haim
West – Manhat/Malha

Sites: within its boundaries or nearby are the San Simon Monastery, the Jerusalem Mall, Teddy Stadium

Streets: the streets of the neighborhood are named for Tannaim (authorities quoted in the Mishna) and Amoraim (scholars who explained the Talmud), well-known individuals, places and events from the time of the Second Temple. In Gonenim Het-Tet, most of the streets are called by the names of founders and commanders of the Hagana. The main streets are Yohanan ben Zakai and Yehuda HaNasi.

The streets are:

Gonenim/Katamonim Aleph, Vav

Antigonus (Ish Socho) (1st cent. CE) Ben Yo'ezer – Eli'ezer HaGadol **16**

Student of Shim'on HaTzadik in the Second Temple period and one of the last of the men of the Great Assembly. Socho was a town in Judah.

Ben Gamla, Yehoshu'a Ben Zakai – Bruria **G15-16**

The High Priest at the end of the Second Temple period, he established the regulation to permanently settle teachers throughout the city.

Ben Gamliel, Shim'on, Rabbi (RaSHBa"G) (1st cent. CE) Ben Yo'ezer – Ben Yo'ezer **F17-G16**

The president of the Sanhedrin at the time of the Great Rebellion and the destruction of the Second Temple (see the neighborhood of Gonenim/ Katamonim Bet, Gimel, Dalet).

Ben Hefetz, Tovia (1902 – 1959) Antigonus – dead end **G16**

One of the leading proponents of culture in Jerusalem, the director of the municipal community center.

Ben Yo'ezer, Yosi Ben Zakai – Eli'ezer HaGadol **G16**

A Cohen and president of the Sanhedrin, one of the Sages of the renowned "pairs" (*zugot*) of Sages (see HaArbeli Street in Gonenim/ Katamonim Bet, Gimel, Dalet and Yehuda ben Tabai Street in Gonenim/ Katamonim Hei) during the Second Temple period (see the neighborhoods of Gonenim/Katamonim Bet, Gimel, Dalet).

Ben Zakai, Yohanan, Rabban (1st cent. CE) HaModa'i – Eli'ezer HaGadol **F-G16**

One of the great Tannaim and sages of Israel in the days of the Second Temple and afterwards, he founded the spiritual center of Yavne after the destruction of the Temple and stood at its head. He turned Yavne into the religious center of the nation (see the neighborhoods of Gonenim/ Katamonim Hei and San Simon).

Bin Nun, Yehoshu'a Ben Gamla – El'azar HaModa'i, ends at Rahel Imeinu **G-H15**

Joshua, Moses' aide, the national leader after Moses' death, military commander in the conquest of Canaan. Joshua and Caleb ben Yefune were the only two of the twelve spies (Book of Joshua) who did not give a negative report on the Land (see the Greek Colony).

Bruria Ben Gamla – Hilkia **G15**

Wife of the Tanna Rabbi Meir and daughter of Rabbi Hanania ben Teradion, one of the Ten Martyrs (*'Aseret Harugei Malchut*, ten pre-eminent religious leaders tortured to death in the reign of the Roman emperor Hadrian). She became famous for her knowledge in matters of religious law and is mentioned in the Talmud and in homiletic interpretations.

Dostai (ben Rabbi Yehuda), Rabbi (2nd cent. CE)
Hizkiyahu – Ben Zakai **G15-16**

A fifth generation Tanna, in the generation of Rabbi Yehuda HaNasi.

Eli'ezer HaGadol (ben Hyrcanus), Rabbi (1st cent. CE)
Ben Zakai – Ben Yo'ezer **F16-17**

One of the great Tannaim in the period of the Mishna, he married the daughter of Shim'on ben Gamliel, president of the Sanhedrin (high court) in the days of the Great Rebellion and the destruction of the Second Temple. He was the disciple of Yohanan ben Zakai (see the neighborhood of Gonenim/Katamonim Bet, Gimel, Dalet).

HaAmoraim RaSHBa"G – dead end **G16**

Named after the sages of the Talmud who interpreted the words of the Tannaim (religious authorities quoted in the Mishna) and expanded on them.

Halafta, Rabbi (2nd cent. CE) Ma'ale Zeev – Dostai **G15-16**

A Tanna of the third generation, a communal leader in the city of Tzipori in the Lower Galilee.

HaModa'i, El'azar (1st-2nd cent. CE) 'Emek Refaim – Hizkiyahu **G-H15**

A Tanna from Modi'in and uncle of Shim'on bar Kochva. Known as the master of Aggada (anecdotes used to illustrate and interpret Biblical passages). In the Talmud Tractate *Shabbat*, Rabban Gamliel calls him "HaModa'i" (see the Greek Colony).

Hanina, Rabbi [Lane] (3rd cent. CE) Ben Zakai – Ma'aglei Yavne **G16**

An Amora of the first generation in the Land of Israel. One of the great masters of Aggada.

HeHacham Levi 'Amram [Square] RaSHBa"G at Ben Yo'ezer **G16**

One of the rabbis of the Kurdish community in Jerusalem.

Hermer, Yolanda [Square] Ben Gamla at Bruria **G15**

She worked on behalf of the establishment of the State from 1945 and served as a senior agent in the Arab Department of the Jewish Agency. She succeeded in gathering information vital for Israel from the inner circles of the Egyptian government.

Hilkia, Abba (2nd cent. CE) Ben Zakai – Dostai **G15**

A compassionate man and a miracle-worker in the days of the Second Temple; grandson of Honi HaMe'agel (the circle-maker) (see the neighborhood of Mea She'arim).

Hisda, Rabbi (217 – 309 CE) Ben Zakai – Bin Nun **G16**

One of the great Amoraim of Babylonia, in the second and third generation; head of the Sura Talmudical academy; an expert in matters of religious law and Aggada and a master of broad knowlege of agricultural matters.

Hiya, Rabbi (1st-2nd cent. CE) Hizkiyahu – Bruria **G15**

One of the last Tannaim in the generation of Rabbi Yehuda HaNasi. He was head of the study hall in Tiberias, the greatest of the sages of his generation.

Hizkiyahu HaMelech (746 - 693 BCE)
Ma'ale Zeev – El'azar HaModa'i, ends at Rahel Imeinu **G-H15**

(See the neighborhoods of Gonen/Katamon HaYeshana, the Greek Colony.)

Ma'aglei Yavne Ben Zakai – RaSHBa"G **G16**

An ancient city on the coastal plain, in the patrimony of the tribe of Judah; it became the spiritual center after the destruction of the Second Temple – "Kerem b'Yavne" and "Yavne and its sages" are familiar phrases. Rabban Yohanan ben Zakai came there with his disciples. This was the first seat of the Sanhedrin outside of Jerusalem, and the foundations of the Mishna were laid here.

Ma'ale Zeev (1916 – 1977) Halafta – Ben Bava **F16-G15**

Named for Zeev Schickler, an educator and one of the founders of the Zionist Youth Farm in Jerusalem that is nearby (see the neighborhood of Gonenim/Katamonim Hei and San Simon).

Nakdimon (ben Gurion) Dostai – Ben Zakai – dead end **G15-16**

One of the wealthy and philanthropic Jews of Jerusalem in the Second Temple period.

Nehorai (2nd cent. CE) RaSHBa"G – dead end **G16**

One of the great Tannaim in the fourth generation, known for his exceptional piety.

Rabbi Meir (2nd cent. CE) Hilkia – Ben Gamla **G16**

One of the great Tannaim in the fourth generation, one of the heads of the Sanhedrin, one of the compilers of the Mishna and Aggada. His name is mentioned in the Mishna more than three hundred times. Husband of Bruria and one of the disciples of Rabbi 'Akiva, he was ordained by Rabbi Yehuda ben Bava. He was the son-in-law of Hanania ben Teradion. These last three were among the Ten Martyrs.

Resh Lakish (2nd cent. CE) HaModa'i – Ben Gamla **G15**

One of the great second generation Amoraim of the Land of Israel, known as being particularly acute in his learning.

Tabi (1st and 2nd cent. CE) Hizkiyahu – Bruria **G15**

Faithful assistant of Rabban Gamliel, who resided in Yavne; known for his great knowledge of Torah learning.

Ze'ira, Rabbi Hizkiyahu – Bruria **G15**

One of the sages of religious law in the Land of Israel, of the third generation of Amoraim, known for his humility and piety.

Gonenim/Katamonim Bet, Gimel, Dalet

Alexandrion Yehuda HaNasi – Kanaei HaGalil **F16-17**

A fortress, from the time of the Hasmoneans, on Mount Sartaba in the hills of Samaria.

Ben Gamliel, Shim'on, Rabbi (RaSHBa"G) (1st cent. CE)
Ben Yo'ezer – Ben Yo'ezer **F17-G16**

(See the neighborhood of Gonenim/Katamonim Aleph, Vav.)

Ben Yair, El'azar Kanaei HaGalil – Kanaei HaGalil **F16-17**

One of the leaders of the Zealots in the war against the Romans, he was commander of the fortress of Masada in the rebellion of the Jews against the Romans. As the last survivor on Masada, he committed suicide in order not to fall captive to the Romans, in 73 CE.

Ben Yo'ezer, Yosi Ben Zakai – Eli'ezer HaGadol **G16**

(See the neighborhood of Gonenim/Katamonim Aleph, Vav).

Eli'ezer HaGadol (ben Hyrcanus), Rabbi (1st cent. CE)
Ben Zakai – Ben Yo'ezer **F16-17**

(See the neighborhood of Gonenim/Katamonim Aleph, Vav).

El-Walaje Ben Yo'ezer – dead end **F-G17**

Named for the village in this area.

HaArbeli, Nitai Kanaei HaGalil – Kanaei HaGalil **F16-17**

The Arbelite, one of the sages of the Pairs (see Ben Yo'ezer, Gonenim/Katamonim Aleph, Vav, and Ben Tabai, Gonenim/Katamonim Hei) in the days of the Second Temple; a Cohen and president of the Sanhedrin.

Kanaei HaGalil Yehuda HaNasi – Ben Yo'ezer **F17**

Named for the Zealots in the Galilee who fought against the Romans in the Great Rebellion at the end of the Second Temple period.

Pat, Ya'akov (1894 – 1956) Golomb – Bar'am **E16-F17**

A soldier in the Jewish Legion, one of the commanders of the Hagana in the Jerusalem District before the establishment of the State (1931-1940) (see the neighborhoods of Gonenim/Katamonim Hei and San Simon, Gonenim/Katamonim Het, Tet, Pat).

Rabbi Hanina (Ben Dosa) (1st cent. CE) Ben Yo'ezer – dead end **G16**

A first- generation Tanna.

Sa'adon, Baruch [Square] (1912 – 1972)
Yehuda HaNasi at Eli'ezer HaGadol **F16**

One of the leaders of the Zionist Movement in Kurdistan, he organized immigration from there (to Israel) and helped see to the absorption of the immigrants.

Tanhuma Ben Yo'ezer – Alexandrion – dead end **F17**

A fifth-generation Amora, one of the great commentators (Midrash Tanhuma) and a master of Aggada. He lived at the end of the creative period of Midrashic (homiletic) commentary.

Tovia ben Moshe HaCohen (1652 – 1729)
Yehuda HaNasi – dead end **F16**

He was the doctor of Sultan Ahmat III of Turkey, settled in Jerusalem in 1714 and occupied himself with communal needs, authored a book called *Ma'ase Tovia* (Tovia's occupation), whose contents included not just medicine but also astronomy, nature and philosophy.

Yehuda HaNasi, Rabbi (2nd-3rd cent. CE)
Eli'ezer HaGadol – Pat **F16**

One of the great Tannaim, he compiled the Mishna – the Oral Law – and set it down in writing. The son of Rabban Shim'on ben Gamliel, he led the Sanhedrin, revived the Jewish spiritual center of the Galilee that had been greatly damaged in the Bar Kochva Revolt, was an important authority in matters of religious law in his generation and afterwards. He is buried in Beit She'arim (see the neighborhood of Gonenim/Katamonim Hei and San Simon).

Gonenim/Katamonim Hei and San Simon

Ben Bava, Yehuda (2nd cent. CE) Ben Zakai – Ma'ale Zeev **F16**

A Tanna, and one of the Ten Martyrs killed by the Romans.

Ben Tabai, Yehuda, Rabbi Ben Bava – dead end **F16**

One of the sages of the Pairs (see Yosi ben Yo'ezer, Gonenim/Katamonim Aleph, Vav, and HaArbeli, Gonenim/Katamonim Bet, Gimel, Dalet) in the days of the Second Temple, a Cohen and president of the Sanhedrin.

Ben Zakai, Yohanan, Rabban HaModa'i – Eli'ezer HaGadol **F-G16**

(See the neighborhood of Gonenim/Katamonim Aleph, Vav.)

Bereniki (Berenice) Nikanor – Yehuda HaNasi **F16**

From Herod's family, she was the wife of Aristobulus, king of Judah at the end of the Second Temple period.

Bnei Beteira Ben Zakai – Yahil **F16**

A renowned family of scholars at the end of the Second Temple period and in the period of the Tannaim, which produced sages, a head of the Sanhedrin and national leaders. It is thought that they came from the city Beteira in northern Gilead and thus the name.

Hananel ben Hushiel, Rabbi (990 – 1053 CE)
Nikanor – dead end **E-F16**

A rabbi and arbiter of Jewish law in the large North African Jewish community, interpreter of the Bible and one of the earliest commentators on the Babylonian Talmud.

Herzog, Yitzhak Isaac HaLevi, Rabbi, Dr. (1888 – 1959)
'Aza – Golomb **G14-E16**

(See the neighborhoods of Giv'at HaVradim/Shikun Rassco, Giv'at Mordechai, Kiryat Shmuel, Nayot, Rehavia.)

Horkania Yehuda HaNasi – Nikanor **F16**

A famous fortress in the Judean wilderness, named after Yohanan Hyrcanus of the Hasmonean family.

Ma'ale Zeev (1916 – 1977) Ben Bava – Halafta **F16-G15**

(See Gonenim/Katamonim Aleph, Vav.)

Michvar Tarfon – Bnei Beteira – dead end **F16**

One of the three strongholds (the others are Herodion and Masada) from which the Zealots continued fighting after the destruction of the Second Temple by the Romans. Located east of the Jordan River on Mount Ha'Avarim.

Nikanor Yehuda HaNasi – Horkania **F16**

A Jewish philanthropist in Alexandria in the days of the Second Temple who donated golden doors for the gate of the Holy Temple that is named for him. His burial cave was uncovered on the Mount of Olives.

Pat, Ya'akov (1894 – 1956) Golomb – Bar'am **E16-F17**

(See the neighborhoods of Gonenim/Katamonim Bet, Gimel, Dalet, Gonenim/Katamonim Het, Tet, Pat.)

Rav Ashi (5th cent. CE) Yahil – dead end **F16**

An Amora, head of the Sura Talmudical academy for sixty years, together with his disciple Ravina compiled the Babylonian Talmud. He died approximately 472 CE.

Tarfon, Rabbi (1st cent. CE) Yahil – Horkania **F16**

One of the great Tannaim in the first generation after the destruction of the Second Temple. An expert in religious law. Apparently one of the disciples of Rabban Yohanan ben Zakai and the teacher of Rabbi 'Akiva.

Yahil, Haim (1905 – 1974) Horkania – dead end **F16**

A statesman, one of the organizers of the immigration from Czechoslovakia to Israel. Ambassador of Israel in the Scandinavian countries, chairman of the executive of Israel's Broadcasting Authority.

Yehuda HaNasi, Rabbi (2nd-3rd cent. CE) Eli'ezer HaGadol – Pat **G-H14**

(See the neighborhood of Gonenim/Katamonim Bet, Gimel, Dalet.)

Gonenim/Katamonim Het, Tet

Almaliah, Avraham (1885 – 1967) San Martin – Bar Yohai **E16-17**

An author, journalist, researcher of Jewish history in the eastern countries, president of the Western community (Jews from North Africa) and one of the leaders of the Sephardic community in Israel, a member of the Jerusalem municipal council.

Bar Yohai, Shim'on (2nd cent. CE) Pat – San Martin **E-F16**

A great Tanna of the fourth generation, disciple of Rabbi 'Akiva, with whom his name is connected in many Aggadic texts. A member of the Sanhedrin in Usha, an ancient city from Mishna times, he participated in deliberations to fix the Hebrew calendar leap years to keep the lunar months in their proper seasons. Rabbi Yehuda HaNasi was his disciple. According to tradition, he and his son are buried in Meiron (Galilee). In the sixteenth century Lag Ba'Omer was set as the day of his death, and many make the pilgrimage to his grave on that date. Kabbalists credit him with writing the Zohar, the central book of Kabbala mysticism.

Berger, Ya'akov (1907 – 1938) Yitzhak Sade – HaShomer **E16**

One of the heads of the Hagana in Jerusalem and one of its commanders. He fell at Hanita in the Upper Galilee on the eve of Jewish settlement of the Galilee.

Golomb, Eliyahu (1893 – 1945) Pat – Tahon **C15-E16**

A soldier in the Jewish Legion in World War I, one of the heads of the Labor movement in the Land, one of the founders of the Labor Federation. A founder of the Hagana and its top commander for many years. One of those who set up the PaLMa"H, and one of the heads of the movement to settle the Land of Israel (see the neighborhoods of Holyland

Park, Kiryat HaYovel, Manhat/Malha, Ramat Denya, Ramat Sharett).

HaNotrim Hoz – Margolin **E16**

Named after the civilian guards [*notrim]* who served as reinforcements for the police in the Jewish villages during the British Mandate period.

HaShomer Pat – Margolin **E16**

A self-defense organization established before the existence of the Hagana, whose purpose it was to protect the Jewish population in the Land of Israel from attack.

Hoz, Dov (1894 – 1940) HaNotrim – San Martin **E16**

A statesman and activist, one of the heads of the workers movement and one of the pioneers of flying in the Land of Israel. One of the heads of the Hagana, and one of its commanders, a soldier in the Jewish Legion, a member of the municipal government in Tel-Aviv from 1925 to 1935 and deputy mayor after that. The Sde Dov airport north of the Yarkon River in Tel-Aviv is named after him.

Margolin, Eli'ezer (1874 – 1944) HaShomer – HaNotrim **E16**

Commander of the Jewish Legion during World War I, along with Zeev Jabotinsky and Yosef Trumpeldor.

Pat, Ya'akov (1904 – 1956) Golomb – Bar'am **E16-F17**

(See the neighborhoods of Gonenim/Katamonim Bet, Gimel, Dalet, Hei and San Simon, Pat.)

Rabbi Tzadok Yitzhak Sade – dead end **E16**

One of the great Tannaim during the Second Temple period.

San Martin, Jose de (1778 – 1850) Golomb – Rabbi Tzadok **E16-17**

Argentine statesman and military commander. The national hero of Argentina.

Yitzhak Sade, HaAluf (1890 – 1952) Berger – Rabbi Tzadok **E16**

A commander in the Hagana, one of the founders of the PaLMa"H and one of its commanders, commander of the tank corps during the War of Independence, a general, one of the first members of the Third Aliya to come to Jerusalem.

Greek Colony *[HaMoshava HaYevanit]*

Name and establishment:

This neighborhood, located in the southwestern part of Jerusalem, was founded at the beginning of the twentieth century by Greek-Orthodox Christians in Jerusalem, hence its name. They were descendants of long-time residents of the city, and their language was Arabic.

Until World War I, this community was the largest and wealthiest of Christian groups in the city. Their wealth came from Czarist Russia, but after the Communist Revolution the situation changed, and the community came to the verge of bankruptcy. It was forced to sell the majority of the properties that were in its hands. In response, Jews bought many valuable properties in the middle of Jerusalem from them, on Hillel, Shamai, Ben Yehuda and King George Streets, as well as in Mamilla, Rehavia and Komemiyut/Talbieh.

Until the War of Independence, there were no Jews living in this neighborhood. During the war the neighborhood was captured by the IDF, and then Jews, mostly immigrants, moved into the neighborhood and turned it into a Jewish area. Since then additional buildings have been built and institutions opened.

Boundaries:
North – the German Colony/RaMBa"M
South – Gonenim/Katamonim
East – 'Emek Refaim
West – Gonen/Katamon HaYeshana

Sites: within its boundaries or nearby is 'Emek Refaim Street.

Streets: the neighborhood streets are named for kings of Judah, well-known personalities in the Bible, especially from the Books of Samuel and Kings. The central streets are Rahel Imeinu, 'Emek Refaim and El'azar HaModa'i.

The streets are:

Amatzia (8th-7th cents. BCE) Yehoshafat – HaModa'i **G-H15**

Amaziah, a great king of the monarchy of Judah (II Kings 14).

Asa (10th-9th cents. BCE) ‘Emek Refaim – Yehoshafat **H15**

A king of the monarchy of Judah (I Kings 15:9).

Avishai ben Tzruya ‘Emek Refaim – Yehoshu‘a bin Nun **H15**

Abishai, one of King David’s warriors, the brother of Asael and of Joab, the commander of David’s army. Born in Bethlehem (I Samuel 26).

Avner ben Ner Yehoshu‘a bin Nun – Yehoshafat **H15**

Abner, a commander in King Saul’s army and the army of King David. He killed Asael, the brother of Joab and Abishai, David’s warriors, and was himself killed by Joab ben Tzruya (I and II Samuel).

‘Azaria ‘Emek Refaim – Derech HaRakevet **H15**

One of the three friends of the prophet Daniel: “And there were among them young men of Judah, Daniel, Hananiah, Mishael and Azariah” (Daniel 1:6). The three friends and Daniel were thrown into a fiery furnace, but the fire did not burn them at all.

Bin Nun, Yehoshu‘a Rahel Imeinu – HaModa‘i, ends at Ben Gamla **G-H15**

(See the neighborhood of Gonenim/Katamonim Aleph, Vav.)

Bnayahu ben Yehoyada‘ (10th cent. BCE) Yehoash – ‘Uzia **H15**

Benaiah, military commander in the time of King David and King Solomon (II Samuel – I Kings).

‘Emek Refaim HaModa‘i – Rahel Imeinu, ends at Remez **I14-H15**

(See the German Colony.)

HaModa‘i, El‘azar (1st-2nd cents. CE) ‘Emek Refaim – Hizkiyahu **G-H15**

(See the neighborhood of Gonenim/Katamonim Aleph, Vav.)

HaRakevet [Road] Derech Beit Lehem – Pierre Koenig **H15-16**

(See the neighborhoods of the German Colony/RaMBa”M, Geulim/Bak‘a, Mekor Haim.)

Hizkiyahu HaMelech (7th-6th cents. BCE)
Rahel Imeinu – HaModa‘i, ends at Ma‘ale Zeev **G-H15**

(See the neighborhoods of Gonen/Katamon HaYeshana, Gonenim/Katamonim Aleph, Vav.)

Maccabee Salzburger [Square] (1924–1983)
HaModa‘i at Hizkiyahu **G15**

Doctor and researcher.

Mishael 'Emek Refaim – Yehoshu'a bin Nun **H15**

One of the three friends of the prophet Daniel: "And there were among them young men of Judah, Daniel, Hananiah, Mishael and Azariah" (Daniel 1:6). The three friends and Daniel were thrown into a fiery furnace, but the fire did not burn them at all.

Rahel Imeinu 'Emek Refaim – HaPortzim **G-H15**

(See the neighborhoods of the German Colony, Gonen/Katamon HaYeshana.)

'Uzia (7th cent. BCE) 'Emek Refaim – Rahel Imeinu **H15**

A king of the kingdom of Judah (II Kings 15).

Yehoash (8th-7th cents. BCE) Yehoshafat – Rahel Imeinu **H15**

Jehoash, a king of the kingdom of Judah (II Kings 12).

Yehoshafat (8th cent. BCE) Yonatan – Amatzia **H15**

Jehoshaphat, a king of the kingdom of Judah (I Kings, 22:41-52).

Yoav Yehoshu'a bin Nun – Yehoshafat **H15**

Military commander of King David. Brother of Abishai and Asael, the three were warriors of King David. He killed Abner ben Ner when he assumed command for King David, because Abner had supported Adonijah, and he killed Benaiah ben Jehoiada of Bethlehem on the order of King Solomon (II Samuel – I Kings).

Yonatan (Yehonatan) 'Emek Refaim – Rahel Imeinu **H15**

Jonathan, King Saul's son, dear friend of David, killed in battle on Mount Gilboa (I Samuel – II Samuel 1).

Yotam (7th cent. BCE) Hizkiyahu – Amatzia **G15**

Jotham, a king of the kingdom of Judah (II Kings 15:32-38).

HaBucharim/Batei HaBucharim

Name and establishment:

This neighborhood, in the center of town, northwest of the neighborhood of Mea She'arim, was founded in 1891 by immigrants from Buchara, a state in the former Soviet Union, hence its name. Its original name, which didn't come into general use, was Rehovot, a name drawn from the Biblical passage connected with the forefather Isaac: "...and he called it Rehovot because he said that now the Lord has given us more space and made us fruitful in the Land" (Genesis 26:22).

As opposed to other neighborhoods built in Jerusalem, this neighborhood was built of wealth and honor rather than of poverty and hardship. The residents of the neighborhood were given the opportunity to plan their houses as they wished, with the only condition being that they be built of stone. The houses were large and pleasant, surrounded by paved courtyards. The streets were wide, something unusual in the Jerusalem of those days. The neighborhood was considered to be the grandest of those built at the end of the nineteenth century. With the outbreak of World War I, these Jews were cut off from their country of origin. Many of the residents were dependent on funds from their families in Buchara, and the connection to their money was lost. In addition, the Russian Revolution in 1917 had a damaging effect on the wealthy Jews of Buchara, and many of them lost their sources of income and their assets, and as a result were no longer able to help their brothers in the Land of Israel.

At the start of British rule, this neighborhood turned into one of the main focal points of Zionist activity and the center of the top leadership of the Jewish community in the Holy Land.

With the passing years, the number of Bucharan residents decreased, and in their place came Jews of various ethnic backgrounds, many of them from Persia-Iran. Today the neighborhood's residents are members of the ultra-Orthodox community who have overflowed from the nearby ultra-Orthodox neighborhoods.

Boundaries:
Northwest – Bar-Ilan Street
South – Kerem Avraham and Geula
East – Beit Yisrael

Sites: within its boundaries or nearby are the Bucharan Market, the Great Eucalyptus (the boulevard of trees that were planted in the neighborhood was felled by the Turks during World War I for heating fuel, and only one eucalyptus was left to survive, on the sidewalk at 37 Yehezkel Street) and Beit Davidoff.

Streets: the streets here are named for the founders of the neighborhood, prominent rabbis, personages and prophets in the Bible, statesmen and a Bible commentator.

The streets are:

Adoniyahu HaCohen, Rabbi Bar-Ilan – Yoel **H10-11**

He immigrated to Jerusalem in the year 1900 and built a synagogue on this street. He was the rabbi and head of the community in Jerusalem of Jews from Mashhad, Persia, who decades earlier had been forcibly converted to Islam.

Amdursky, Yerahmiel (1876 – 1956) Yoel – Mosayoff – dead end **H10**

One of the communal leaders of Jerusalem, who bought pieces of land here and helped build it up.

Ashkenazi, Betzalel, Rabbi (b. 1520) Yoel – Polanski **H11**

(See the neighborhood of Beit Yisrael.)

Avinadav Bar-Ilan – Yehezkel **H10**

Abinadab, a son of King Saul. He fell with his father on Mount Gilboa, during the war against the Philistines.

Bakshi, Aharon [Square] (1890 – 1955) Yoel at Sonnenfeld **H11**

One of the heads of the Afghan Jewish community.

Bar-Ilan (Berlin), Meir, Rabbi (1880 – 1949)
Shmuel HaNavi – Yirmiyahu **G-H10**

Author, journalist and statesman, he was one of the leaders of the *Mizrahi* movement (today's National Religious Party). He was an ardent Zionist who opposed the Uganda Plan and coined the saying: "The Land of Israel for the Jewish People, according to the Torah of Israel." He was one of the founders of the Joint (the Joint Distribution Committee), a member of the board of directors of *HaKeren HaKayemet LeYisrael* (the Jewish National Fund) and an editor of the newspaper *HaTzofeh*. Bar-Ilan University was named after him. He was made an honorary citizen of the city of Tel-Aviv in the year 1946 (see the neighborhoods of Mahanayim and Tel-Arza).

David Hafetz [Square] Rehovot HaBucharim at Talmudi **H10**

One of the founders of the Bucharan Streets. He was among those who paved the way for Bucharan Jews to immigrate to Israel.

David HeHazan, Rabbi (1790 – 1869) 'Ezra – Rabbeinu Gershom **H10**

The Sephardic chief rabbi, the leader of the rabbis in Israel. One of the great Jewish legal arbiters of his generation.

Evyatar HaCohen [the Priest] Bar-Ilan – Rabbeinu Gershom **H10**

Abiathar, a priest from the family of Eli, in the time of King David.

'Ezra (6th - 5th cents. BCE) Yoel – HeHazan **H11**

Ezra the Scribe immigrated to Jerusalem from Babylonia as one of the leaders of those who returned to Israel from the Exile. He served as head of the Great Assembly. He strengthened the renascent Jewish community and, together with Nehemiah, established a legal system. It is said of him "When the Torah was totally forgotten in Israel, Ezra came up from Babylonia and re-established it" (Tractate Sukka, 20).

Farhi, Haim, Minister (1760 – 1820)
Nehemiah – Adoniyahu HaCohen **H10**

Counselor and minister of the treasury of Pasha Ghazar, the governor of Akko. He was a defender of Akko during the invasion by Napoleon. He was executed by order of Pasha 'Abdullah.

Fishel, Yisrael Aharon (1865 – 1948) Shmuel HaNavi – 'Ezra **H10-11**

American Jewish philanthropist who contributed to the upkeep of educational, charitable and benevolent institutions in America and Israel. He founded an institute in Jerusalem, named for him, for research in Talmud and Jewish studies.

Gol, Bentzion (1898 – 1947) Rabbeinu Gershom – Shmuel HaNavi**H10**

One of the communal leaders of the community of Afghan Jews in Jerusalem. He was killed while fulfilling his military duties.

Knesset Mordechai [Lane] Avinadav – Talmudi **H10**

Named after the second Hasidic master and rabbi of the Sadgora sect.

Mosayoff, Shlomo (1852 – 1922) 'Ezra – Amdursky **H11**

One of the founders of this neighborhood, president of the community of Bucharan Jews in Jerusalem.

Rabbeinu Gershom (960 – 1040 CE) Bar-Ilan – Yoel **H10**

The designation for Rabbeinu Gershom ben Yehuda, the Light of the Exile. He is known as one of the earliest Bible commentators (RaSH"I was born the year Rabbeinu Gershom died). He set down many regulations, especially the one called "the Excommunication of Rabbeinu Gershom," which forbids a man to have more than one wife (at a time).

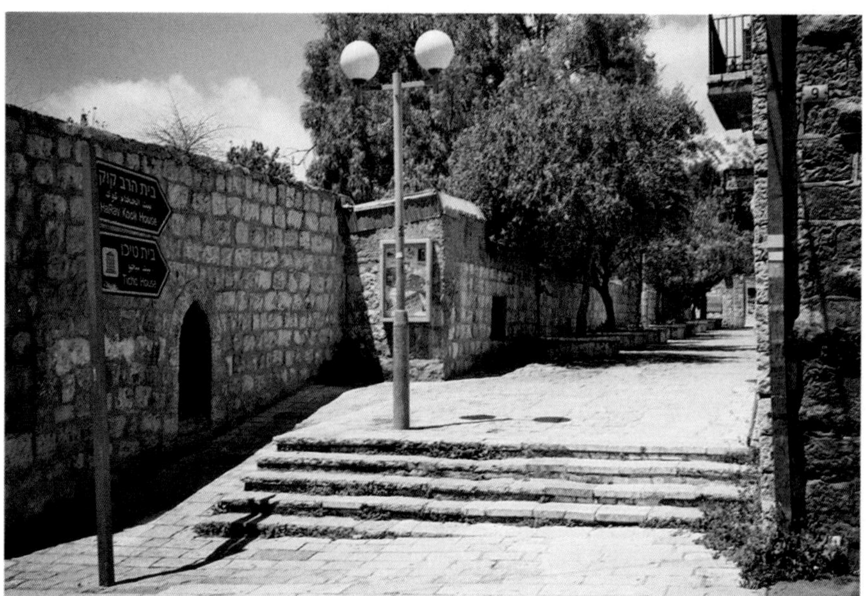

The neighborhood of Beit David/Beit HaRav Kook (est. 1872)

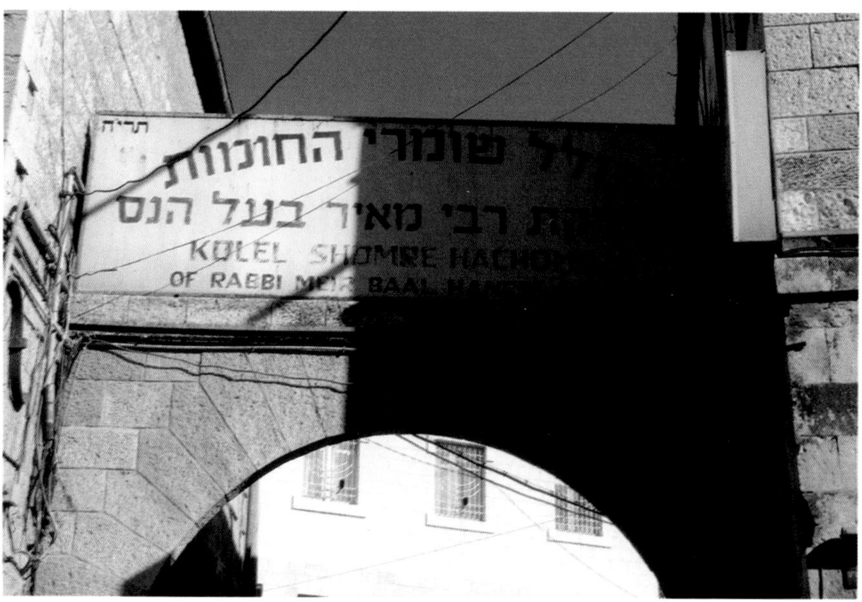

The gateway into the neighborhood of Batei Kollel Ungarin (est. 1891)

The neighborhood of Beit Ya'akov (est. 1877)

The Bell Building, in Mid-Town

Ben Yehuda Street (Pedestrian Mall), in Mid-Town

Huminer family house, in Mea She'arim (est. 1874)

David's Village – Mamilla (est. 1990)

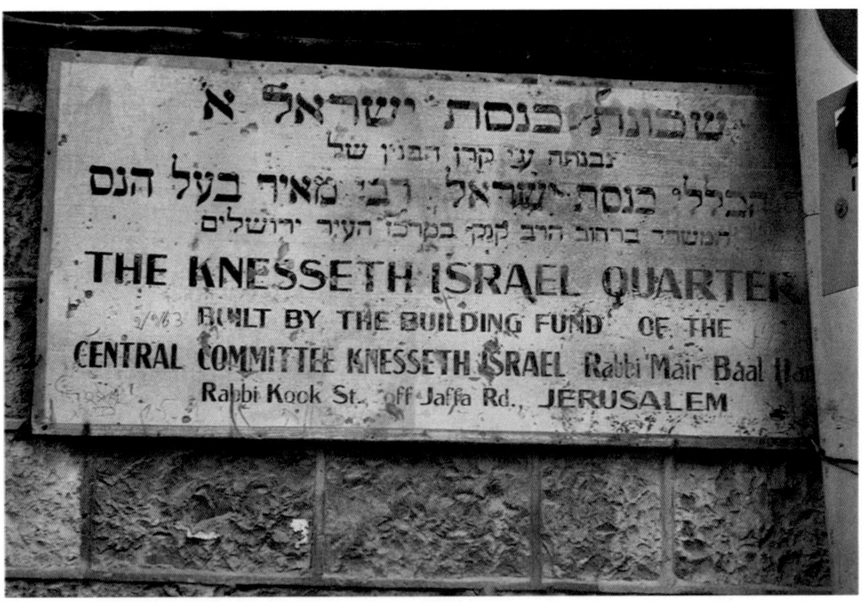

The neighborhood of Knesset Yisrael (est. 1891)

HaKotel HaMa'aravi, the Western Wall

The Lamel School in the neighborhood of Zichron Moshe (est. 1906)

The Mahane Yehuda Market (est. 1929)

Gateway into the neighborhood of Batei Wittenberg/Sha'arei Moshe (est. 1886)

Intersection of Yafo Road and King George Street

Arched gateway into the neighborhood of Mazkeret Moshe (est. 1883)

The Great Synagogue in the neighborhood of Ohel Moshe (est. 1883)

Gateway into the neighborhood of Ohel Moshe (est. 1883)

The neighborhood of Nahlat Shiv'a (est. 1869)

The Supreme Court building

The Tower of David (Migdal David) and the Old City walls

The "Zoharei Hama" Synagogue in the neighborhood of Mahane Yehuda (est. 1887)

The windmill in the neighborhood of Yemin Moshe (est. 1892)

Mea She'arim Street (neighborhood established in 1874)

The Billy Rose Sculpture Garden in the neighborhood of Giv'at Ram (est. 1949)

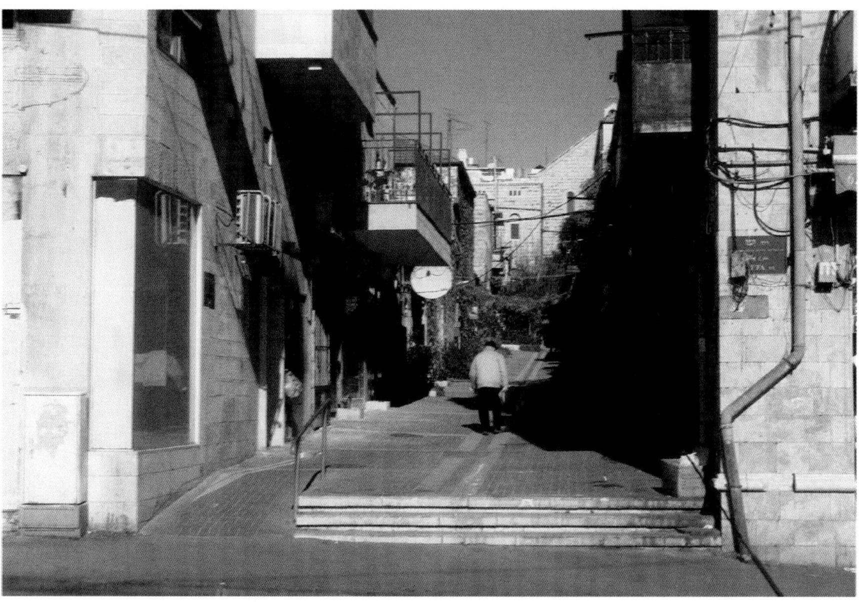

The neighborhood of 'Ezrat Yisrael (est. 1892)

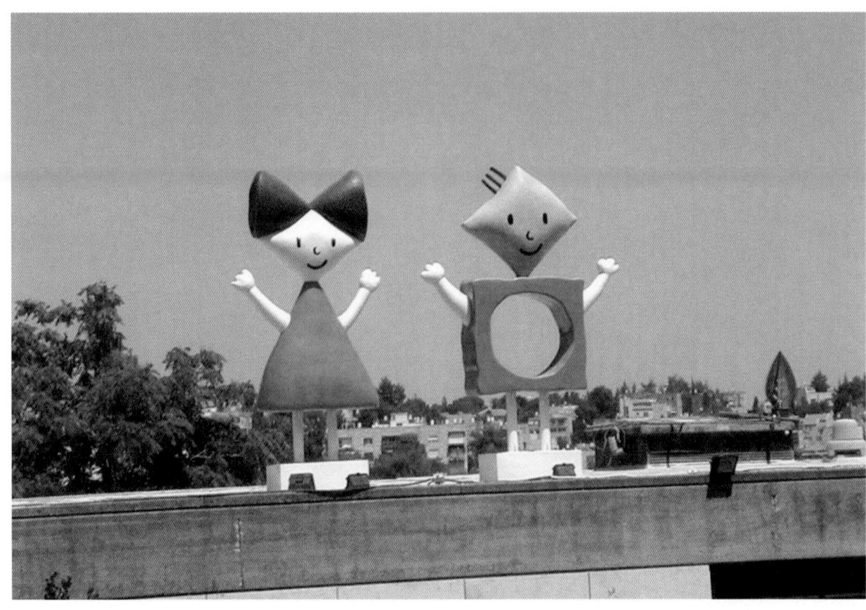

The logo of the Israel Museum, in the neighborhood of Giv'at Ram (est. 1949)

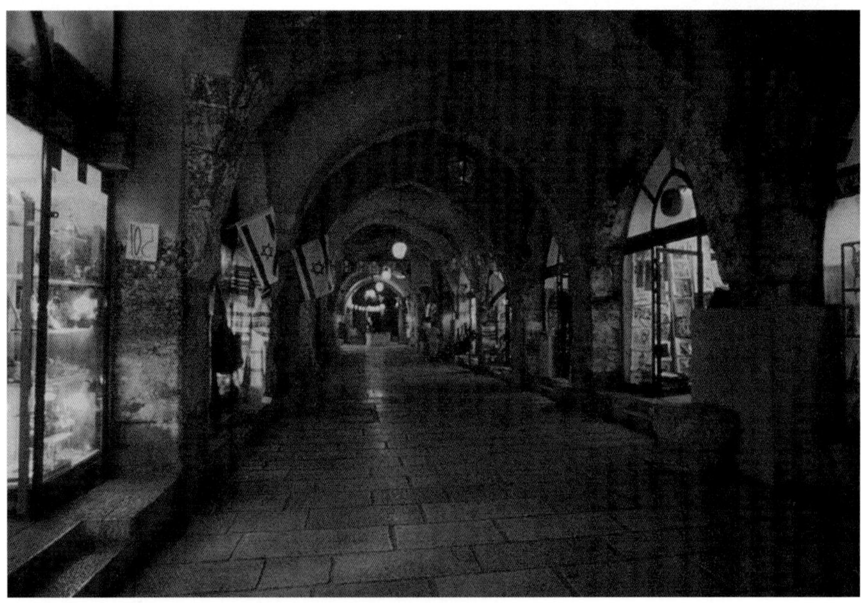

The Cardo, in the Jewish Quarter of the Old City

A mural on a building in Mid-Town

Teddy Stadium in the neighborhood of Manhat/Malha

Rehovot HaBucharim Bar-Ilan – Yoel **H10-11**

The Bucharan Streets. Called by the original name of this neighborhood.

Shmuel HaNavi Shivtei Yisrael – Bar-Ilan **H10-I11**

(See the neighborhoods of Beit Yisrael, Ma'alot Dafna/Arzei HaBira, Mahanayim, Nahlat Shim'on, Sanhedria, Shikunei Shmuel HaNavi.)

Talmudi, Avraham 'Ezra – Knesset Mordechai **H10**

Rabbi Avraham Aminoff (Talmudi) – was born in the year 1854. He was the spiritual leader of the Bucharan community in Jerusalem and one of the founders of the neighborhood.

Yisa Bracha (1817 – 1906) Yoel – Bar-Ilan **H10-11**

Acronym for **Y**a'akov **Sh**aul **E**lyashar, the Sephardic chief rabbi, the leader of the rabbis in Israel; he was one of the great Jewish legal arbiters of his generation and the spiritual leader of the Sephardic Jewish community in Jerusalem (the neighborhood of Givat Shaul in the western part of the city is named after him).

Yoel Mea She'arim – Shmuel HaNavi **H10-11**

Joel, a prophet in Israel, the second of the Twelve Minor Prophets in the Bible that are grouped together and known as the "Trei 'Asar."

HaPo'alim

Name and establishment:

This neighborhood, located next to Beit HaKerem, was founded in 1928 and named for the founders of the neighborhood and its residents, who were pioneering laborers who worked on the construction of the new neighborhoods of Jerusalem.

Boundaries:

North and west – Beit HaKerem

South – Bayit VaGan

East – Menahem Begin Boulevard and Giv'at Ram

Sites: within its boundaries or nearby is the Hebrew University – Giv'at Ram campus.

Streets: the neighborhood streets are called by the names of the types of laborers who were its founders and residents.

The streets are:

HaBanai HaGuy – HeHalutz **E13**

Named for the Jewish construction workers who worked on new construction in Jerusalem.

HaHotzev HaBanai – dead end **E13**

Named for the Jewish quarrymen who worked to provide building material for the new parts of Jerusalem.

HaSatat HaBanai – dead end **E13**

Named for the stonemasons who dressed the stones for buildings in the new neighborhoods.

HaSolelim HeHalutz – HaBanai **D-E13**

Named for the laborers who built the roads and streets in the new parts of Jerusalem.

HeHalutz HaSatat – Avizohar, ends at Herzl Boulevard **D13-E12**

(See the neighborhoods of Beit HaKerem, Giv'at Beit HaKerem.)

Har Nof

Name and establishment:

This neighborhood in the northwest part of the city, surrounded on three sides by the Jerusalem Forest, was begun in 1981 and at the end of 1984 the first tenants moved into their homes. Its founders were Jerusalem contractors, mostly from Oriental Jewish communities. Its name means mountain view.

The mountain ridge on which the neighborhood was built is very steep, causing great differences in elevation between the parallel streets. The buildings overlook the landscape of the Judean hills, hence the name of the neighborhood. In the Talmudic period, Har Nof was an agricultural area that supplied the needs of the city of Jerusalem. The neighborhood buildings are crowded together and most are of multiple stories. The residents are ultra-Orthodox or national religious.

From Har Nof a street heads eastward through the neighborhood of Giv'at Shaul and the industrial area, continuing to Kiryat Moshe and reaching the middle of the city. From Har Nof another street goes southward down into the Jerusalem Forest, and at the Revida streambed it splits into three directions: northeast to the industrial area, west to Beit Zayit, and to the neighborhoods along the western municipal boundary, Motza, and Mevasseret Tzion.

Boundaries:
North, south and west – the Jerusalem Forest
East – Giv'at Shaul and the Industrial Zone

Sites: within its boundaries or nearby are the Giv'at Shaul-Industrial Zone, Har Tamir, Har HaMenuhot Cemetery, 'Ezrat Nashim (Herzog) Hospital, Kfar Shaul Hospital.

Streets: the streets are named according to the religious range of residents: Hasidic religious leaders, rabbis, civic leaders and contractors who founded the neighborhood. The main streets are Hai Tayyib, Schaulsohn, Katzenellenbogen.

The streets are:

Agasi, Hacham Shim'on (1852 – 1914)
Katzenellenbogen – Katzenellenbogen **B12-C11**

A rabbi, a great Kabbalist of the Babylonian Exile (Iraq), wrote many books on Kabbala mysticism, an outstanding sage of Iraqi Jewry, wrote religious hymns and liturgical poetry.

Ahavat Yisrael [Square] Katzenellenbogen at Agasi **C12**

The major work of and the name used for the Vizhnitz Hasidic master, Israel Hager.

Alfiye, Meir, Rabbi [Square] (d. 1941)
Kanfei Nesharim at HaMelamed **C11**

(See the neighborhood of Giv'at Shaul.)

Barnett, Zerah, Rabbi (1883 – 1935)
Schaulsohn – Parnes – dead end **B12**

One of the activists of the Jewish community in Jerusalem, a founder of Petah Tikva who also helped build up the Jewish community in Jaffa.

Beit Yitzhak (1891 – 1973) HaKablan – dead end **C11**

Named for Rabbi Shalom Yitzhak HaLevi, a member of the council of the chief rabbinate in Israel. He organized the aliya of the Jews of Yemen, helped facilitate their absorption and served as chief rabbi of the Yemenite Jews in Israel.

Brand, Aharon, Dr. (1910 – 1977) Hai Tayyib – Hai Tayyib **B11-12**

A veteran doctor of children and of public health, who was active in the underground movements of Hagana and ETZe"L and a defender of Jerusalem. He founded the medical society in Jerusalem.

HaAdmor MiBoston [Steps] (1876 – 1942) Schaulsohn – Mishkelov **B12**

Named for Rabbi Pinhas David HaLevi Horowitz, one of the great Hasidic masters, a leader of the Jewish community of Boston, and a builder of Jerusalem.

HaAdmor MiBoyan (1850 – 1917) Hai Tayyib – Hai Tayyib **B11**

Named for Rabbi Ya'akov Friedman, one of the outstanding personalities of the Hasidic movement in the Ruzhin dynasty. His followers were among the pioneers of the Jewish community in the Land of Israel and among the builders of Jerusalem.

HaAdmor MiRuzhin (1798 – 1843) Schaulsohn – dead end **B11**

Named for the founder of this Hasidic dynasty, Rabbi Yisrael Friedman, the greatest Hasidic master of his generation. The *Tiferet Yisrael* Synagogue in the Old City of Jerusalem was named for him, and for Rabbi Mordechai Shalom Friedman of Sadgora, another of the outstanding Hasidic masters of the Ruzhin dynasty. He built magnificent educational institutions and a synagogue in Jerusalem.

Haflaa (1721 – 1805) Katzenellenbogen – dead end **C11**

Named after the *Sefer Haflaa* (book of wonder) by the Gaon Rabbi Pinhas HaLevi Horowitz, one of the sages of Ashkenazic Jewry and one of its great arbiters of religious law. He served in the rabbinate in Frankfurt. One of his outstanding pupils was the Hatam Sofer (Rav Moshe Sofer).

Hai Tayyib, Yitzhak, Rabbi (1743 – 1839) Schaulsohn – Katzenellenbogen **B12-C11**

One of the outstanding Kabbalists and exceptional rabbis of Tunisian Jewry, one of the heads of the activists on behalf of Jerusalem in his country.

HaKablan (1906 – 1981) Katzenellenbogen – Katzenellenbogen **B-C11**

The contractor. Named for Yitzhak 'Abud Levi, one of Jerusalem's major contractors and builders.

Ibn Danan, Shaul, Rabbi (b. 1882) Hai Tayyib – dead end **B12**

A descendant of a family of rabbis and sages from the fifteenth century, chief rabbi of Moroccan Jewry, a *Yakir Yerushalayim*.

Imrei Shefer [Square] (1815 – 1882)
Schaulsohn at Katzenellenbogen **B11**

Shefer's sayings. Named for Rabbi **Sh**muel **Fr**ankel, chosen to serve the community of Darag as chief judge of the religious court.

Katzenellenbogen, Refael HaLevi, Rabbi (1894 – 1975)
HaKablan – Schaulsohn **B11-C11**

Author, philosopher, head of the *'Etz Haim* Yeshiva in Jerusalem, a member of the Jerusalem city council.

Levi, Yosef, Rabbi [Square] (b. 1875) Ibn Danan **B12**

One of the foremost rabbis of Jerusalem, president of the Sephardic Jewish community, one of those who laid the groundwork for the chief rabbinate of the Land of Israel, one of the leaders of the *Mizrah*i labor federation.

Mishkelov, Menahem Mendel, Rabbi (d. 1827)
Schaulsohn – Schaulsohn **B11**

One of the foremost Kabbalists and rabbis, revived the Ashkenazic Jewish community in Jerusalem and led it.

Parnes Schaulsohn – Barnett – dead end **B11-12**

Named for the Parnes family that did much to protect the Jewish community in Jerusalem, especially in the period of Turkish rule. A family that was involved for generations in matters concerning Jerusalem, they were guardians of the property of the Mount of Olives cemetery.

Rabin, Hizkiyahu, Rabbi (1872 – 1945) Schaulsohn – Weitz **B-C12**

One of the outstanding rabbis of Bucharan Jewry and one of its most important arbiters of religious law in his generation. He sat in a Russian jail as a Prisoner of Zion. He appointed many of his disciples in Jerusalem to be rabbis.

Schaulsohn, Shmuel A., Rabbi (1922 – 1980)
Hai Tayyib – Hai Tayyib **B12-C11**

One of the heads of *Agudat Yisrael*, a member of the leadership of the Jerusalem municipality, one of the builders of Jerusalem and one of the city's activists.

Slonim, Yehuda Leib, Rabbi [Square] (1895 – 1980)
Schaulsohn at Hai Tayyib **C11**

Grandson of the *Ba'al HaTanya* (Shneur Zalman of Lyady), a founder and leader of the HaBa"D movement in Jerusalem, he worked for many years on behalf of public causes.

Holyland Park

Name and establishment:

This new neighborhood, located on the western side of the city near the Holyland Hotel, began construction in 2003, and the first tenants entered their apartments in 2005. The neighborhood is built on the top of a hill overlooking the entire surroundings, and from the hill there is an amazing, magical panoramic view of the city of Jerusalem and the hills around it .

Boundaries:

<u>North</u> – Bayit VaGan
<u>South</u> – Manhat/Malha
<u>Northeast</u> – Giv'at Mordechai
<u>West</u> – Ramat Sharett

Sites: within its boundaries or nearby are the high-tech center, the Technological Park in Manhat/Malha, the Biblical Zoo, the Manhat/Malha Mall, the municipal sports facilities.

Streets: the single street in the neighborhood is named for the singer Ferrera.

The streets are:

Avi Yona, Michael (1904 – 1974) Begin Boulevard – Hausner **D16**

An author and archeologist, he directed and arranged archeological digs in Israel.

Begin, Menachem [Boulevard] (1913 – 1992)
Golomb – Golda Meir **E13-14**

Sixth prime minister of the State of Israel. Commander of ETZe"L in its struggle against the British government until the declaration of the State. He started a political party and headed it in its various reincarnations –

Herut, Gahal, Likud. In 1977 he put together a government with himself at its head and served as prime minister until 1983. He conducted negotiations with President Sadat of Egypt and signed a peace agreement with him. In 1978 he received the Nobel Prize for Peace along with Sadat.

Ferrera, Avraham (1934 – 1985)
from the main entrance up to the buildings **D16**

Graduate of the Academy of Music, a vocalist and originator, he performed, composed and wrote songs. He was connected to Jerusalem in every fiber of his being, which came through in his songs and in the way he lived his life.

Golomb, Eliyahu (1893 – 1945) Pat – Tahon **C15-E16**

(See the neighborhoods of Gonenim/Katamonim Het, Tet, Kiryat HaYovel, Manhat/Malha, Ramat Denya, Ramat Sharett).

Hausner, Gideon (1916 – 1991) Avi Yona – Avi Yona **D-E16**

(See the neighborhood of Bayit VaGan.)

Homat Shmuel/Har Homa

Name and establishment:

This neighborhood is located in the southeastern corner of the city, southeast of Kibbutz Ramat Rahel. The decision to build a new neighborhood in this area was made in 1997, and two years later the first bids were put out for construction. Over the years, the hill on which the neighborhood was built was called *Har Homa* (the hill of the wall) because of ruins that are standing at the top of the hill, below which are remains of a Byzantine church, and they appeared to the PaLMa"H fighters of the 1940s like a wall. With the new construction, the name was changed to *Homat Shmuel* (Shmuel's wall) after a member of the Jerusalem city council, Shmuel Shamir, who fought in favor of erecting the neighborhood. Unfortunately, he died in a traffic accident before he could see his vision realized.

Historically, the neighborhood was built on lands that, for the most part, belonged to Jews even before the establishment of the State. The Jewish National Fund had planted hundreds of trees in the area before it fell into the hands of the Jordanians in 1948. This neighborhood now constitutes a buffer between east Jerusalem and the Bethlehem-Hebron area, and is part of a belt of Jewish neighborhoods around nearly all of the center of Jerusalem.

In order not to disturb the hill's topography, the construction was designed on the model of high density on a small scale. That is, the buildings on top of the hill are multi-story with few apartments per floor. In addition, a large public garden surrounds each building.

The population of the neighborhood is varied, with a slight tendency toward religious/traditional, but with consideration for other types of residents.

Boundaries:
North – Kibbutz Ramat Rahel and Arnona
South – Bethlehem
East – the Judean wilderness
West – Derech Hevron and Gilo

Sites: From the top of the hill on which the neighborhood is built, one can see the magical scenery of Jerusalem.

Streets: the neighborhood streets are named for people who fought to defend Jerusalem and for educators, authors and lecturers.

The streets are:

Avigur, Shaul (1899 – 1978) Lichtenstein – Picard **K-L20**

One of the first residents of Kibbutz Kineret, he worked on behalf of the Land of Israel and was one of the leaders of the illegal immigration and of the rescue of Jews outside of Israel. He established Israel's Defense Ministry.

Baum, Shlomo (1928 – 1999) Nissim – dead end **K20**

A member of the Hagana, he took part in all of Israel's wars, including the raid on Nabi Samuil (an important strategic position, as it is the highest hill in the area around Jerusalem). He founded Unit 101 of the IDF, and while in it, he served as Ariel Sharon's deputy. One of the first to reach the Suez Canal in the Sinai Campaign of 1956.

Ben Hamu, Shim'on (1945 – 1999) Lichtenstein – dead end **L20**

Member of the city council, chairman of the Labor Federation for the Jerusalem area.

Derech Hevron Hativat Yerushalayim – the city of Hebron **I14-F20**

The route of Derech Hevron extends from the north from Hativat Yerushalayim, a street near Har Tzion, to the neighborhoods of Giv'at Hanania/Abu Tor, Geulim/Bak'a, North Talpiot, Talpiot, Arnona, Giv'at HaMatos, Homat Shmuel/Har Homa and comes to an end further south at Bethlehem and Hebron.

Falk, Zeev (1933 – 1998) Nissim – dead end **L20**

Attorney and law professor, he served as judicial advisor in the Ministry of the Interior, and on the board of directors of the College for Jewish Studies. He published books on Jewish studies and Jewish philosophy and a collection of poems called "Jerusalem from Generation to Generation" and was a *Yakir Yerushalayim*.

HaMamtzi (1903 – 1989) Picard – dead end **L19**

Inventor, named for Brig.-General David Laskov, who developed special battle plans designed to break the siege around Jerusalem in 1948. He founded and developed the unit for inventing new battle equipment for the IDF and commanded the unit for many years, won prizes among which were three Israel Defense prizes and a citation of praise from the Prize Committee for Israel Defense.

Lichtenstein Nehama – Nissim **L19-20**

Three brothers who served in the PaLMa"H and fought for Jerusalem in 1948. ***Ya'akov*** also served in the PaLYa"M (PaLMa"H - naval branch) was killed on Nisan 24, 1948, in a battle over the village near Mount Scopus. ***Avner***, a sapper, fought in many battles in and around Jerusalem, was killed in the 1948 attempt to capture Armon HaNatziv (British Mandate headquarters turned over to Arab forces when the Mandate ended). ***Elimelech*** escorted convoys going up to Jerusalem in 1948, fought as an officer in battles in the Sinai Campaign and Six Day War. After the Six Day War he was appointed military governor of Hebron.

Lipzin, Sol (1901 – 1995) Avigur – Avigur **K-L20**

Active in many areas, a researcher and author of many books on comparative literature and Yiddish, one of the founders of Bar-Ilan University and the American College in Jerusalem, a lecturer in the Popular University, a writer and critic for The Jerusalem Post, winner of the Shalom Aleichem Prize.

Meir, Shmuel [Boulevard] (1954 – 1996)
Derech Hevron – Nehama **K-L19**

Deputy mayor of Jerusalem, an educator, a man of vision and deed and a fighter for Jerusalem. As chairman of the city's education committee, he worked for the advancement of special education and of youth movements.

Nehama Leibowitz, Prof. (1905 – 1997) Meir – dead end **L19**

A teacher and lecturer of Bible, she was a recipient of the Israel Prize for education for the weekly Torah portion sheets she prepared and published herself. She held home study sessions on Torah for researchers, lecturers and students. She fulfilled the verse: "If you have studied Torah a lot, don't think well of yourself, it is for that you were created."

Nissim, Yitzhak, Rabbi (1896 – 1981) Meir – Lichtenstein **L19-L20**

The Rishon LeTzion, chief Sephardic rabbi of Israel.

Picard, Yehuda Leo, Prof. (1900 – 1997) Nissim – Avigur **K20-L19**

One of Israel's senior geologists, world-renowned in hydrogeologic research (study of the occurrence and distribution of underground water), founded the geology department and first geological collection of the Hebrew University. Recipient of the Israel Prize, a *Yakir Yerushalayim.*

'Ir Ganim

Name and establishment:

This neighborhood, located in the southwestern part of the city on the edge of Kiryat HaYovel, is divided into sub-neighborhoods: 'Ir Ganim Aleph, Bet and Gimel, according to the order in which they were built. 'Ir Ganim Aleph was founded in 1953 and given this name, *city of gardens*, because of the manner of construction: buildings surrounded by gardens. Over time the buildings became villas with private gardens. In addition the neighborhood also has public parks. 'Ir Ganim Bet and Gimel were founded afterwards.

The earliest residents were immigrants.

Boundaries:

Northeast – Kiryat HaYovel
South – Giv'at Massua
West – Kiryat Menahem

Sites: within its boundaries or nearby are the Hadassah Medical Center campus, the Biblical Zoo, the Jerusalem Mall (Malha), Teddy Stadium, the Kennedy Memorial – a monument in memory of an American president.

Streets: the streets of the neighborhood are named for wild plants.

The streets are:

'Ir Ganim Aleph

Costa Rica HaHelmit – HaAvivit **B16-17**

Named for a Central American country that is a friend of Israel (see 'Ir Ganim Gimel).

Grossman, Meir (1888 – 1964) HaCarcom – Korczak **B16**

Journalist, civic activist, one of the founders of the Jewish brigades, one of the heads of the Revisionist Movement, director of the Department of Education and Culture of the Jewish Agency in Jerusalem (see the neighborhood of Kiryat HaYovel).

HaCalanit Grossman – dead end **B15-16**

Anemone, a common wildflower in Israel, with large flowers of red, white, purple or blue.

HaCarcom HaNeird – Grossman **B16**

Crocus, a fragrant Israeli wild plant, blossoming while it is yet winter, from whose flowers is produced saffron, an orange powder used for seasoning foods, for medicinal uses and more.

HaHelmit Mexico – HaNurit **B16**

Mallow, a common wild plant with pink or lavender flowers, of the same family as okra, whose fruit is edible.

HaLilach HaCarcom – dead end **B16**

Lilac, an ornamental shrub having fragrant lavender flowers arranged in large clusters.

HaNeird HaCarcom – HaCarcom **B16**

One of the fragrant perfume plants mentioned in the Bible: "*Spikenard* and saffron, sweet flag and cinnamon..." (Song of Songs 4:14).

HaSahlav HaShalechet – HaNeird **B16**

Wild orchid. The flowers are lavender or purple. Cultivated orchids are highly valued.

HaShalechet HaCarcom – HaNeird **B16**

Refers to the annual fall of leaves from deciduous trees that characterizes the autumn.

HaTzalaf HaCarcom – dead end **B16**

Caper, a wild shrub, with simple green leaves and large blossoms from red to lavender, that grows on rocks and walls. The buds of the caper are used as seasoning.

Ringelblum, Emanuel, Dr. (1900 – 1944) Korczak – dead end **B16**

Author and historian, one of the ghetto fighters during the Holocaust, was the historian of the Warsaw Ghetto and perished in the Holocaust (see the neighborhood of Kiryat HaYovel).

'Ir Ganim Bet

Dahomey Mexico – Panama **A16**

An African country, a friend of the State of Israel (see the neighborhood of Kiryat Menahem).

Dominican Republic Dahomey – HaHelmit **B16**

Central American country, on an island in the Caribbean.

HaAvivit Costa Rica – HaNurit **A-B17**

An annual wild plant, with small white flowers.

HaRakefet HaSeifan – Dominican Republic **A17-B16**

Cyclamen, a perennial wild plant that grows in the crevices of rocks, with pinkish-lavender flowers.

HaSavyon HaSeifan – Dominican Republic **A-B16**

Ragwort, a very common wild plant, producing fruit and having yellow flowers with white fringe. Appears in fields and beside roadways from the beginning of winter until the summer.

HaSeifan Dahomey – Costa Rica **A16-17**

Gladiolus, an ornamental flower.

'Ir Ganim Gimel

Costa Rica HaHelmit – HaAvivit **B16-17**

(See 'Ir Ganim Aleph.)

HaNurit HaAvivit – HaAvivit **B16-17**

Buttercup, a wild plant having red or yellow flowers, common in Israel.

Jewish Quarter *[HaRova' HaYehudi]*

Name and establishment:

This neighborhood, located in the southeastern part of the Old City and extending along the southern wall between the Zion Gate and the Dung Gate, looks out on the Western Wall and the Temple Mount, and beyond that to the Mount of Olives, and is named for the Jews who lived in the neighborhood from generations ago until today. The Jewish Quarter is located in the area of the "Upper City" of Second Temple times.

This quarter was settled earliest during the First Temple period, and during Second Temple times the residents were well-to-do Jews. During the period of Roman rule, Jews lived here, close to the Temple Mount, and after the Crusader period the Jewish population in Jerusalem was renewed around Mount Zion. It was there that the RaMBa"N (Nahmanides) established his home in 1267 and apparently built a synagogue for the Jews of the city. In the fifteenth century, the Jewish neighborhood moved to the area of today's Jewish Quarter, which is also close to the Western Wall (of the Temple Mount), separated from the Wall by the Mughrabi neighborhood, a poor neighborhood. In the nineteenth century a wave of European Jewish immigrants settled in this quarter, and by the middle of the century, the Jewish Quarter was the largest of the city's quarters. From 1860 the distress and crowding in the residential areas and the lack of available apartments in this quarter caused many Jews to leave the quarter and move to the new neighborhoods (Mishkenot Shaananim, Nahlat Shiv'a, Mea She'arim and others) being built outside the walls. From that period until the War of Independence, the population of this neighborhood decreased.

During the War of Independence (1948) the Old City fell into the hands of the Jordanians, and the quarter was destroyed, including the glorious synagogues like the *Hurva* (Synagogue of Rabbi Yehuda HeHasid) and *Tiferet Yisrael* [the splendor of Yisrael (Friedman)]. In the

Six Day War (1967), the IDF broke through into the Old City and reclaimed the whole walled city, the Jewish Quarter in particular. After the war it was decided to rehabilitate the Jewish Quarter, where a combination of old and new buildings maintains the traditional building style of a courtyard surrounded by apartment buildings (*khush* in Arabic). Parallel to the rehabilitation, archeological digs were conducted at the Southern Wall (of the Temple Mount) and in the City of David (the "Lower City" in Second Temple times), where important remnants of the area's past have been discovered, from the period of the First Temple onward.

Boundaries:
North – the Moslem Quarter and the market area
South -- Mount Zion and the Ben-Hinom Valley
East – the Western Wall and the Temple Mount
West – the Christian Quarter and the Armenian Quarter

Sites: within its boundaries or nearby are the Western Wall, the Temple Mount, the Mount of Olives, the Zion Gate, the Dung Gate, the Museum of the Old Yishuv Courtyard, the Museum of the Burnt House, the Cardo, the City of David, the Western Wall Tunnels, the Southern Wall Archeological Excavations, the *Hurva* Synagogue, the *HaKotel* and *Porat Yosef* yeshivot, the cluster of four Sephardic synagogues, the Tower of David and its museum, new public institutions.

Streets: the neighborhood streets are named for musical instruments (played by the Levites in the Holy Temple), functions and procedures connected with the Holy Temple, and fighting units that took part in the defense of the Jewish Quarter in the War of Independence.

The central streets are Rehov HaYehudim (Jews Street) and HaBa"D Street, from which narrow alleyways branch off toward the apartment houses in the open and closed courtyards, where the courtyard is enclosed on all sides by apartment buildings.

The streets are:

Aravna HaYevusi Hativat 'Etzioni – Zion Gate **I14**

Arauna the Jebusite, a resident of the city Jebus before it was conquered by King David, from whom David bought the threshing-floor on which the Holy Temple was built.

Barkai HaYehudim – HaBa"D **I-J13**

Morning star, a phrase heard in the Holy Temple when the High Priest asked whether the morning light was yet visible, the time for offering the daily morning *Tamid* sacrifice.

Batei Mahse Kikar Tiferet Yerushalayim – Dung Gate **J13**

Shelters for the poor. The main street of this quarter, a remembrance of the sheltered housing built by German and Dutch Jews.

Batei Mahse [Square] Beit HaShoeiva at Gal'ed **J13**

In remembrance of the shelters for the poor of the city. At the entrance from Gal'ed Street, there remains an archway showing that in this area there were shelters for the poor.

Beit El HaYehudim – Gal'ed **J13**

House of God, named for the yeshiva of the Kabbalists on this street, founded in 1755 by the Kabbalist rabbi, Rabbi Shalom Shar'abi.

Beit HaShoeiva Batei Mahse Square – dead end **J13**

A place where water is drawn, a symbolic name.

Bikur Holim Ararat – dead end **I13**

(See the Armenian Quarter.)

Bonei HaHoma Tiferet Yisrael – Shonei Halachot **J13**

Builders of the wall. Named for the builders of the wall of Jerusalem in the time of Nehemiah, as is written: "Those who built the wall and those who carried burdens, at the same time did the work with one hand and carried a weapon in the other" (to defend themselves from attack while they were working) (Nehemiah 4:11).

Dung Gate [*Sha'ar HaAshpot*] the southern wall of the Old City **J13**

One of the eight gates in the wall surrounding the Old City. This gate, in the southern part of the wall, is the gate closest to the Western Wall (of the Temple Mount) and is one of the two gates closest to the Jewish Quarter. It is named for a gate that was part of the ancient first wall around Jerusalem that was further south than today's gate. The original was the smallest of the Jerusalem gates, and so called because the city's refuse was taken outside the walls for disposal through this gate. Today's gate was built in 1540, at the beginning of Turkish rule in the Land of Israel.

Gal'ed Beit El – HaHatzotzrot – dead end **J13**

A marker, in memory of the slain of the Old City who fell while defending the Jewish Quarter in the War of Independence (1948) and were temporarily buried along this street.

Goetz, Meir Yehuda, Rabbi [Steps] (1924 – 1995)
Western Wall Plaza – the market **J13**

An immigration activist and a man of deeds. An IDF officer, rabbi of the Western Wall and Israel's holy sites. Head of the Kabbalist yeshiva in the Old City, a *Yakir Yerushalayim*.

Goren, Shlomo, Rabbi [Steps] (1917 – 1994)
Batei Mahse – entrance to Western Wall Plaza **J13**

He joined the Hagana and fought in its service in the Jerusalem area during the War of Independence; founded the army rabbinate, and during the Six Day War was the chief rabbi of the IDF. In 1968 he was elected chief rabbi of Tel-Aviv–Jaffa, and in 1973 he was elected fourth Ashkenazic chief rabbi of Israel and served in that position for ten years. In 1961 he was the recipient of the Israel Prize for Judaism.

HaBa"D Zion Gate – Kikar Tiferet Yerushalayim – David **I13**

Acronym for: **H**ochma, **B**ina and **D**a'at (wisdom, understanding, knowledge) – a Hasidic movement founded by Rabbi Shneur Zalman of Lyady, called the *Ba'al HaTanya* for his book *Tanya* of interpretations of the Kabbala. The spiritual center of the movement is in Brooklyn, New York.

HaBikurim Shonei Halachot – Plugat HaKotel **J13**

The first fruits of the harvest of the Land of Israel that were brought to the Holy Temple.

HaCardo HaBa"D – HaYehudim – HaShalshelet **J13**

A main commercial street of Jerusalem in the Roman-Byzantine period. At that time the Cardo extended the length of the city, from the north (Damascus Gate) to the south (Zion Gate) of Jerusalem, and the important churches of the period were built there at the same time. During Crusader times, some of the stalls of the Cardo became an area of markets and shops. Today, this place is an archeological site and passes the shells of the ancient shops.

HaGitit Batei Mahse – dead end **J13**

A musical instrument.

HaHatzotzrot Gal'ed – Mishmerot HaKehuna **J13**

Trumpets. A musical instrument having a strong, loud sound, as is written: "With trumpets and the sound of the shofar..." (Psalms 98:6).

HaKaraim HaMekubalim – dead end **J13**

Named for the members of the Karaite sect who lived on this street.

HaKhush HaBa"D **I13**

An Arabic word meaning a courtyard of residential buildings. At the beginning of the nineteenth century, in the northern part of what is HaBa"D Street today, courtyards were built completely surrounded by apartment houses. Most of them were not destroyed in the War of Independence, and they were rehabilitated in the years 1997-1998.

HaKinor HaMalach – Ararat **I13**

A musical instrument, harp.

HaKotel HaShalshelet to Western Wall Plaza **J13**

The wall, named for the Western Wall of the Temple Mount in the Old City of Jerusalem.

HaLevi, Yehuda, Rabbi [Steps] (1080 – 1140)
Misgav LaDach – Western Wall Plaza **J13**

One of the greatest poets, composers of religious poetry and philosophers of Spanish Jewry. His poems and religious poetry, especially songs of Zion, are known throughout all the Jewish communities of the world. His philosophy is written in the book "The Kuzari". According to tradition, he immigrated to Jerusalem and was fatally run over next to the Western Wall while he was kissing the ground.

HaMalach HaBa"D – Ararat – HaBa"D **I13**

(See the Armenian Quarter.)

HaMekubalim Tiferet Yisrael – Gal'ed **J13**

The Kabbalists, named for scholars of Kabbala mysticism.

HaMeshorerim Tiferet Yisrael – Ha'Ugav **J13**

Singers, named for the Levites who were singers in the First and Second Holy Temples.

HaMetziltayim Ha'Omer – Bonei HaHoma **J13**

Cymbals, a musical instrument.

HaNevel HaBa"D – HaMalach **I13**

The lyre, a musical instrument.

Ha'Omer Shonei Halachot – Ha'Ugav **J13**

Meaning: the measure. The first fruits of the harvest, brought to the Holy Temple.

HaShminit Beit HaShoeiva – dead end **J13**

A musical instrument.

HaSho'arim Tiferet Yisrael – Ha'Ugav **J13**

The gatekeepers, named for the Levites who were gatekeepers of the Holy Temple.

HaShofar HaBa"D – HaMalach **I13**

The ram's horn, blown in ancient times to alert the army and to announce festival days. In modern times, the shofar is blown throughout the month of Elul (the month preceding the Jewish New Year), on Rosh Hashana (New Year's Days) and after the end of Yom Kippur.

HaTamid Misgav LaDach – Yehuda HaLevi **J13**

The name for the "perpetual" (daily) animal sacrifice that was brought in the Holy Temple every morning and evening.

Hativat 'Etzioni Zion Gate – Jaffa Gate **I14**

(See the Armenian Quarter.)

Hativat Yerushalayim Ma'ale HaShalom – HaTzanhanim – Yafo **I14**

(See the neighborhoods of the Armenian Quarter, the Christian Quarter, David's Village-Mamilla, Yemin Moshe.)

HaTupim Mishmerot HaKehuna – HaYehudim **J13**

A percussion instrument used in ancient times.

Ha'Ugav HaSho'arim – Bonei HaHoma **J13**

The organ, a musical instrument.

HaYa"D [Square] Gal'ed at Batei Mahse Square **J13**

The fourteen. Here were buried the remains of the fourteen (*Yud* = ten + *Dalet* = four) slain of the Jewish Quarter, who fell in heroic battle during the War of Independence after suffering through half a year of siege. In 1967 the remains of the fourteen were transferred to their eternal rest in the cemetery on the Mount of Olives.

HaYehudim Batei Mahse parking lot – HaShalshelet **J13**

Named for the Jewish residents of the area from earliest times. A central street in the quarter.

Hayei 'Olam [Lane] Misgav LaDach – Gal'ed **J13**

Named for the *Hayei 'Olam* yeshiva high school that used to be on this street and was destroyed during the War of Independence (1948).

Lohamei HaRova' BeTashah HaMekubalim – HaYehudim **J13**

Fighters of the Quarter in 1948, named for the defenders and fighters who fought to the death to protect the Jewish Quarter in the Old City in the War of Independence.

Ma'ale HaShalom Dung Gate – Hativat Yerushalayim **J13-14**

(See the neighborhood of the City of David.)

Ma'ale SHaZa"CH (1905 – 1998) Mount Zion **I14**

Acronym for **Sh**lomo **Z**alman **K**ahana, called SHaZa"CH, the last rabbi of the city of Warsaw and later, the last rabbi of the Old City (1948), he worked to develop the religious experience and the leaders connected with Mount Zion. Published dozens of books about Jerusalem.

Ma'alot Benny (1917 – 1975) Hativat Yerushalayim – Mount Zion **I14**

Steps named for Benny Marshak, who took an active part in the fighting for the liberation of Jerusalem in 1948, especially around Mount Zion; one of those who captured Mount Zion.

Ma'amadot Yisrael Misgav LaDach – Batei Mahse Square **J13**

Named for the heads of the groups that came up to Jerusalem in the time of the First and Second Temples; they were sent by the people in the various regions of Israel to represent the nation in the presence of the priests during their work in the Temple.

Malki Tzedek Dung Gate – Hativat Yerushalayim **J13-14**

Melchizedek, the king of Jerusalem in the days of the Biblical Abraham: "And Malki Tzedek, king of Shalem, put out bread and wine..." (Genesis 14:18).

Misgav LaDach Beit HaShoeiva – HaShalshelet **J13**

Refuge for the suffering, the name of one of the first hospitals in Jerusalem, in the Old City. It was funded by the Rothschild family and opened in 1854 in the Jewish Quarter and later bought by the association of "Bikur Holim Misgav LaDach", founded in 1879 by religious leaders of the Sephardic Jews of Jerusalem. The hospital was destroyed almost to its foundations by the

Arab Legion during the War of Independence, and the medical departments were moved to the neighborhood of Gonen/Katamon HaYeshana.

Mishmerot HaKehuna Batei Mahse – Beit El **J13**

Divisions of priests, named for those whose work was in the Holy Temple. There were twenty-four divisions of priests carrying out various tasks connected with the Temple, on a rotating basis.

Nahamu Misgav LaDach – dead end **J13**

After the phrase *Nahamu, nahamu, 'ami* (Be comforted, be comforted, my people) of Isaiah's prophecy (Isaiah 40:1), read on the Shabbat after Tish'a BeAv.

Or HaHaim HaBa"D – Ararat **I13**

Named for a book (by that name) of homiletic commentary on the Torah by Rabbi Haim son of Moshe Ben-'Attar (1696-1743), a Kabbalist and arbiter of religious law. He was head of a yeshiva in the Old City of Jerusalem, among those who paved the way for immigration to the Land of Israel from North Africa.

Plugat HaKotel HaYehudim – HaShalshelet **J13**

Western Wall company, named for the members of Beitar who took up residence in the Old City and strengthened the Jewish population within the walls at the time of the pogroms of 1936-1939, and escorted and protected people who wished to pray at the Western Wall.

Segal, Moshe, Rabbi (1904 – 1986) **I14**
Hativat Yerushalayim – Mount Zion

The first to blow a shofar (forbidden) at the Western Wall in the period of the British Mandate.

Shonei Halachot Misgav LaDach – Plugat HaKotel **J13**

Named for the associations of "those who learn religious law."

Shvut Ma'amadot Yisrael – dead end **J13**

Return, drawn from the Biblical verse "...Now will I bring back the returnees of Jacob..." (Ezekiel 39:25), the return of the Jewish people to their land.

Tiferet Yerushalayim [Square] HaBa"D at Batei Mahse **J13**

Named for the *metivta gedola* (high-level religious academy) of the Sephardic community in the Old City.

Tiferet Yisrael HaYehudim – Batei Mahse **J13**

Named for the magnificent *Tiferet Yisrael* Synagogue built by Rabbi Nissan Bek (1815–1889), an activist and builder of Jerusalem neighborhoods.

Zion Gate [*Sha'ar Tzion*] the southern wall of the Old City **I13**

Through this gate, during the War of Independence, PaLMa"H units came to the assistance of the Jewish Quarter. After the Six Day War, PaLMa"H soldiers fixed a memorial plaque inside the gate, which was refurbished and repaired in memory of those same daring soldiers of 1948 (see the Armenian Quarter).

Zion Gate [Square] the plaza inside the Zion Gate **I13**

Was restored in memory of Alexander Haim Solomon, a philanthropist, a community and Zionist activist, who – by devotion and action – helped establish the State of Israel.

Kerem/Beit Avraham

Name and establishment:

This neighborhood [Vineyard], located in the middle of town east of Mekor Baruch, was founded in 1885 and named for the vineyard that was there before the neighborhood was built. The name of the association that built the neighborhood is Beit Avraham, and it is also the official name of the neighborhood. Despite this, the neighborhood is known by its short name, Kerem.

The vineyard that was on this site served the Jews of the Old City as a kind of resort area or summer retreat to which they would go for enjoyment and a change of atmosphere. The residents today are members of the ultra-Orthodox community.

Boundaries:

North – Kerem Avraham

South – Mahane Yehuda and the Mahane Yehuda Market

East – Yegiy'a Kapayim

West – Mekor Baruch

Sites: within its boundaries or nearby is the Mahane Yehuda Market.

Streets: the neighborhood streets are named for ancient cities.

The streets are:

Arbel Malchei Yisrael – Tahkemoni – dead end **G11**

A fortified city in the Lower Galilee in the time of the great rebellion against the Romans at the end of the Second Temple period.

Ben Matityahu, Yosef (Josephus Flavius) (1st cent. BCE and CE)
Malchei Yisrael – Yafo **G11**

(See the neighborhoods of Ahva, Mahane Yehuda, Ruhama, Yegiy'a Kapayim, Zichron Moshe.)

Ilan, Mordechai Zvi (1882 – 1957) Modi'in – Menahem **G11**

Educator, principal of the *Tahkemoni* School in Jerusalem.

Kfar Nahum [Capernaum] Ben Matityahu – Tahkemoni **G11**

A city from the Second Temple, Mishnaic and Talmudic periods, north of Lake Kineret. Remains were found there of a large ancient synagogue.

Kineret Ben Matityahu – Ilan **G11**

Sea of Galilee, the lake into which the Jordan River flows from the north and from which it exits on its way south to the Dead Sea. It serves as the main reservoir from which the National Water Carrier draws its water.

Malchei Yisrael Sarei Yisrael – Straus **G-H11**

(See the neighborhoods of Ahva, Geula, Kerem Avraham, Mekor Baruch.)

Meiron RaSH"I – Menahem **G11**

An ancient city where Rabbi Shim'on bar Yohai lived, who was one of the Mishnaic sages of the second century CE. He and his son El'azar are buried there. On Lag Ba'Omer (between Passover and Shavuot), a celebration takes place in memory of Rabbi bar Yohai.

Menahem Natan Auerbach, Rabbi (1858 – 1930)
Ben Matityahu – Tahkemoni **G11**

Head of a yeshiva, one of the leaders of the *Mizrahi* movement in Jerusalem, one of the first members of the chief rabbinate at the beginning of the British Mandate period.

Modi'in Ben Matityahu – Tahkemoni **G11**

An ancient city in the Judean hills, the birthplace of Mattathias the Hasmonean and his five sons (among whom was Judah Maccabee), where the Hasmonean rebellion began. In recent years, communities with names connected to that historical period have been built – Modi'in itself, Hashmonaim and Macabim.

Peki'in RaSH"I – Menahem **G11**

A village in the Upper Galilee, near Tzfat, where Jews have lived continuously from the Second Temple period until today. According to tradition, Rabbi Shim'on bar Yohai and his son lived there in hiding in a cave near the village.

RaSH"I (1040 – 1105)
Pines – Tahkemoni, ends at Hashmonaim **G11**

Acronym for **R**abbi **Sh**lomo **Y**itzhaki, the foremost commentator on the Bible and Talmud, the spiritual leader of French Jewry, one of the greatest sages of all generations (see the neighborhoods of Mahane Yehuda, Mekor Baruch, Ruhama, Sha'arei Yerushalayim, Zichron Moshe).

Tahkemoni Malchei Yisrael – Yellin **G11**

Named for an elementary school that was on this street (see the neighborhood of Mekor Baruch).

Kerem Avraham

Name and establishment:

This neighborhood, located in the center of town west of Geula, was founded in 1933 and named for the Biblical forefather Abraham. The Arabic name for the area is "Karm al Halili". "Halili" means friend, which is a designation for the forefather Abraham.

In 1852 the wife of the British Consul James Finn, a Christian woman, purchased the land in this area and built an agricultural farmstead for the purpose of providing a means of support for the Jewish poor of the city. The name "Kerem Avraham" was given to the neighborhood by her husband, the British Consul. After she left Israel, at the end of her husband's term of service, the agricultural farmstead she built became neglected and the enterprise failed. Years later, the land was bought by London's "Society for the Community of Oppressed Jews", and the Jewish neighborhood Kerem Avraham was built on it.

Within the neighborhood is the Schneller campus built in 1855 as an orphanage. During World War II the campus became an army camp, known as the "Schneller Camp", which was included in the "British Security Zone". Stationed there were the Mandate's permanent force in Jerusalem and key platoons of the British army in the Middle East. In 1947, months before the declaration of the State, ETZe"L fighters broke into the compound in a daring and difficult battle, overcame its defenders and blew up the structures inside it.

Today its residents are members of the ultra-Orthodox community.

Boundaries:
North – HaBucharim
South – Ahva and Zichron Moshe
East – Geula
West – Romema

Sites: within its boundaries or nearby are Finn House, that served as a GaDN"A' (**Ged**udei **N**o'**a**r – youth battalions) base, the Schneller Camp and the Mahane Yehuda Market.

Streets: the streets of the neighborhood are named for Biblical prophets of Israel.

The streets are:

'Amos (8th cent. BCE) Malchei Yisrael – Tzefania **H11**

A prophet of Israel, the third in the Book of Minor Prophets in the Bible. His prophecies are concerned with foreign nations, Judah and Israel. At the end of his book appears a prophecy of consolation.

Feldman, Moshe Zeev, Rabbi (1931 – 1997)
Malchei Yisrael – dead end **G11**

Head of the *Imrei Emet* Yeshiva and chairman of the *Agudat Yisrael* movement.

Malchei Yisrael Sarei Yisrael – Straus **G-H11**

(See the neighborhoods of Ahva, Geula, Kerem/Beit Avraham, Mekor Baruch.)

Nehemia (ben Hachalia) (5th cent. BCE) Yirmiyahu – Hazan **H10**

Nehemiah, builder of the walls of Jerusalem following the Return to Zion from the Babylonian Exile. He served as governor of Judah during the period of Persian rule. Jointly with Ezra, the religious authority, he initiated the writing and sealing of a new constitution with the nation, in the spirit of the Torah.

'Ovadia 'Amos – 'Amos **H11**

Obadiah, a prophet of Israel, the fourth and shortest of the books of Minor Prophets in the Bible. It consists of only one chapter with twenty-one verses.

Tzefania (ben Cushi ben Gedalia) (7th cent. BCE) Yehezkel – 'Amos, ends at Bar-Ilan **H10-11**

(See the neighborhood of Geula.)

Zecharia (6th cent. BCE) Malachi – 'Amos **H11**

Zechariah, a prophet of Israel, the eleventh in the books of Minor Prophets in the Bible. He prophesied during the Return to Zion. The first part of the book includes eight visions of redemption and the rebuilding of Jerusalem. The second part is prophecies of Messianic times.

Kiryat Aryeh

Name and establishment:

This neighborhood, located in the northern part of town near Ma'alot Dafna, was established in 1982 and named after Aryeh Polluk, the father of the contractor who built the neighborhood. In addition, the residents wanted to express the words of the Biblical Jacob's blessing in the name of their neighborhood (*aryeh* means lion), "Judah is a lion's cub..." (Genesis 49:9). The lion is also used as a symbol for Israel and for Jerusalem.

Until the Six Day War, this area was under the jurisdiction of Jordan, and in 1967 a hard battle was waged here to liberate east Jerusalem. Today, the neighborhood stretches between two main roads going up from the city to Mount Scopus: on the western side is Hativat Harel Street-Levi Eshkol Boulevard, while on the east is Bar Lev Boulevard going up from east Jerusalem to the heights of Mount Scopus.

Boundaries:

North – Ammunition Hill and Ramat Eshkol
South – Nahlat Shim'on and Beit Yisrael
East – Sheikh Jarrah
West – Ma'alot Dafna/Arzei HaBira

Sites: within its boundaries or nearby are the police academy, Ammunition Hill.

Streets: the neighborhood streets are named after archeologists.

The streets are:

Albright, William (1891 – 1971) Shim'on HaTzadik – dead end **I10**

One of the outstanding non-Jewish archeologists who researched the Land of Israel.

Ba'al Or Sameiah (1843 – 1926) Shim'on HaTzadik – dead end **I10**

Named for Rabbi Meir Simha Medvinsky, a prominent Torah scholar and outstanding Torah commentator (see the neighborhood of Ma'alot Dafna/Arzei HaBira).

Bar Lev, Haim [Boulevard] (1924 – 1994)
Yigael Yadin – Shmuel HaNavi **9-I11**

(See the neighborhoods of Giv'at HaMivtar, Giv'at Shapira/French Hill, Nahlat Shim'on, Sheikh Jarrah.)

MaHa"L Netter – Bar Lev and ends at Nablus Road **I10**

Named for the volunteers from abroad who, immediately after their *'aliya* to the Land of Israel, took part in the War of Independence (1948). (See the neighborhood of Sheikh Jarrah.)

Netter, Ya'akov (Charles) (1826 – 1882)
Shim'on HaTzadik – Eshkol **I10**

Educator and public activist in France, one of the founders of the Alliance Israelite society (Kol Yisrael Haverim, KY"H) in Paris, founder and director of the agricultural school *Mikve Yisrael* in the Land of Israel (see the neighborhood of Ma'alot Dafna/Arzei HaBira).

Shim'on HaTzadik Eretz Hefetz – Nablus Road **I10**

High Priest and leader of the nation in the period of the Second Temple, one of the men of the Great Assembly (see the neighborhoods of Ma'alot Dafna/Arzei HaBira, Nahlat Shim'on).

Sukenik, Eli'ezer Lipa (1889 – 1953)
Shim'on HaTzadik – dead end **I10**

Teacher, archeologist, carried out and directed excavations throughout the Land of Israel and Jerusalem, deciphered the Dead Sea Scrolls that were found in the Judean wilderness, uncovered synagogues in Beit Alpha and Hamat Gader, as well as burial caves around Jerusalem and the Third Wall (of Jerusalem) built in the period of Agrippas I.

Kiryat Belz

Name and establishment:

This neighborhood, located in the northwest part of the city near the neighborhood of Kiryat Zanz, was founded in the 1960s and named for a city in the Diaspora, in eastern Galicia. The Hasidim who made *'aliya* from there founded this neighborhood.

The city of Belz was a spiritual center for tens of thousands of Hasidim and their supporters in Europe. Their rabbinic masters belong to a well-known and important Hasidic dynasty.

Boundaries:

North – Kiryat Ta'asiyot 'Atirot Mada'/Har Hotzvim
South – Romema Industrial Zone
East – Kiryat Zanz
West – Kiryat Mattersdorf/Kiryat Sheva'

Sites: within its boundaries or nearby are Romema-Industrial Zone, Kiryat Ta'asiyot 'Atirot Mada'/Har Hotzvim.

Streets: the neighborhood streets are named for writings of the rabbinic masters of Belz.

The streets are:

Belza [Square] Ohel Yehoshu'a at Shamgar **G10**

Named for the neighborhood.

Binat Yissachar Ohel Yehoshu'a – dead end **G10**

Named for the rabbinic master Rabbi Yissachar Rokeah (1854–1927), director of the *Mahzikei HaDat* movement, opponent of the *Agudat Yisrael* movement and the Zionist movement.

Divrei Haim Ohel Yehoshu'a – Dover Shalom **G10**

Named for the book by Rabbi Haim Halberstam, the rabbinic master of Zanz-Klausenberg (1793-1876).

Dover Shalom Ohel Yehoshu'a – Divrei Haim **F-G10**

A book containing a collection of stories about the works of the Hasidic master Rabbi Shalom Rokeah (1779-1885), father of the dynasty, an expert in Talmud, who emphasized the great importance of Talmud study and the importance of learning in general among his followers.

Kedushat Aharon Ohel Yehoshu'a – dead end **G10**

Named for the Hasidic master Rabbi Aharon Rokeah (1880-1957), who succeeded in reaching the Land of Israel in 1944 after years of imprisonment in European ghettos, supported the *Agudat Yisrael* movement, founded yeshivot and study halls throughout all of Israel. His home in Tel-Aviv became a center for Belz Hasidim.

Ohel Yehoshu'a Zayit Ra'anan – Petah Tikva **G10**

A book dealing with the principles of faith of the rabbinic master Rabbi Yehoshu'a Rokeah (1825–1894) who founded the movement of *Mahzikei HaDat,* opponents of the Haskalah movement.

Schnirer, Sarah (1883 – 1935) Sorotzkin – dead end **F9-10**

Educator, initiator of the Beit Ya'akov educational movement and director of its institutions in the Land of Israel and abroad.

Shamgar (ben 'Anat) Malchei Yisrael – Ohel Yehoshu'a **G10-11**

A judge in the period of the Judges (Judges 3:31). (See the neighborhood of Romema-Industrial Zone.)

Sorotzkin, Zalman, Rabbi (1881 – 1966)
Torat Hesed – Panim Meirot **F10-G9**

Rabbi of the city of Lutsk, later chairman of the Council of Torah Sages in the *Agudat Yisrael* movement, one of the founders of the *Hinuch 'Atzmai* independent network of religious schools in Jerusalem (see the neighborhoods of Kiryat Mattersdorf/Kiryat Sheva', Kiryat Zanz).

Torat Hesed Zayit Ra'anan – Divrei Haim **G9-10**

Named for the book by Rabbi Shneur Zalman of Lublin (1830–1902), one of the pre-eminent arbiters of religious law in the world. He made *'aliya* to the Land of Israel and settled in Jerusalem, served as chief rabbi of the Hasidic communities in Jerusalem and built their institutions.

Kiryat HaYovel

Name and establishment:

This neighborhood, located in the southwestern part of the city, south of Mount Herzl and Yad VaShem, was founded in 1951 and named *yovel* [jubilee] for the fiftieth anniversary of the founding of HaKeren HaKayemet LeYisrael (JNF) that began in that year. The neighborhood was built in an abandoned area, on the ruins of the Arab village Beit Mazmil, and over the years it grew and spread out and additional neighborhoods were built nearby.

During the War of Independence (1948), a hard battle was fought on the land where Kiryat HaYovel stands today, between Jews who were in a fortified position in the nearby neighborhood of Bayit VaGan and Arabs who had fortified themselves in Har Ora, which overlooks this area. In the end, the hill was overpowered with great effort by Jewish forces.

Over time many social and health services have been developed in the neighborhood, like the Hadassah community health center, a Ministry of Health mental health center, student dormitories, sheltered housing for the elderly, senior residences and more.

Boundaries:
North – Mount Herzl and Yad VaShem
South – 'Ir Ganim and Kiryat Menahem
East – Ramat Denya, Ramat Sharett, Manhat/Malha, Bayit VaGan
West – 'Ein Kerem

Sites: within its boundaries or nearby are Mount Herzl, Yad VaShem, the "monster" slide (an iron structure in the shape of a monster) that was put up as a gift to the children of Jerusalem, the Jerusalem Mall (Malha), the Biblical Zoo.

Streets: the neighborhood streets are named for countries in Latin America and for people in the Zionist movement and the labor movement.

The streets are:

Akiva Kos-Bina (b. 1891) Hevroni – dead end **B15**

Was chairman of the association of pharmacists in Israel, was among the founders of the School of Pharmacy and was its first secretary general, a public activist.

Anielewicz, Mordechai (1919 – 1943)
Tahon – Borochov – dead end **B14-15**

One of the founders of *Irgun Yehudi Lohem* [the Jewish Fighting Organization] and its commander, commander and leader of the Warsaw Ghetto Uprising until he was killed in the fighting. Kibbutz Yad Mordechai, founded in the year of his death, is named for him.

Armoza, Eliyahu [Square] (1910 – 1978)
Tahon at Borochov **B15**

Activist in the Sephardic community, one of the commanders of the Hagana in Jerusalem.

Ashbel, Sara and 'Aminadav [Square] Korczak at Grossman **B16**

Among the activists and builders of Jerusalem.

Baruch, Marco (1872 – 1899) Uruguay – Sereni **C15-16**

One of the early leaders of Zionism.

Blumenfeld, Yehuda (Kurt) (1884 – 1963)
Olsvanger – Olsvanger **B14**

One of the leaders of the Zionist movement in Germany, a member of the directorate of *Keren HaYesod* in Jerusalem.

Bodenheimer, Max Isidor (Yitzhak) (1865 – 1940)
Rabinovich – dead end **B-C15**

Jurist, one of the early Lovers of Zion in Germany, a founder of the Zionist Organization.

Bolivia Golomb – HaTzionut **C16**

A country in South America.

Borochov, Dov Ber (1881 – 1917) Tahon – Gordon **B15-C14**

Thinker, founder of the Zionist-socialist movement *Po'alei Tzion* and one of its leaders.

Brazil Levin – Olsvanger **B14**

A country in South America.

Chile Tahon – Korczak **B15**

A country in South America.

Ebner, Meir (1872 – 1955) Sharon – Levin **B14-15**

Attorney, journalist and Zionist activist in Jerusalem.

Epstein, Ya'akov Nahum, Rabbi (1878 – 1952)
Levin – dead end **C14**

A researcher of the Mishna and Talmud, he formulated a new system of investigation for researching the Talmud, a professor at the Hebrew University in Jerusalem.

Ettinger, 'Akiva (1872 – 1945) Rabinovich – dead end **C15**

Agronomist, director of the department for agricultural settlement of the Zionist Organization.

Florentin, David (1874 – 1941) Nissan – Chile **B15**

A journalist, one of the leaders of Zionism in Greece, was involved in the *'aliya* of Jews from Greece to the Land of Israel, a delegate at Zionist Congresses.

Geoni, Ya'akov (1913 – 1996) Stern – dead end **C16**

An activist of the Herut and Beitar movements, a veteran of The Jerusalem Post.

Golomb, Eliyahu (1893 -1945) Pat – Tahon **C15-E16**

(See the neighborhoods of Gonenim/Katamonim Het, Tet, Holyland Park, Manhat/Malha, Ramat Denya, Ramat Sharett.)

Gordon, Aharon David (1856 – 1922) Borochov – Borochov **C14**

One of the thinkers of the labor movement in the Land of Israel. Zionist youth movements adopted his doctrine of labor, which they preached for the purpose of physical labor in the Jewish homeland, and in 1925 the Gordonia movement was founded and named for him.

Greenwald, Meir (1871 – 1953) Nissan – dead end **C16**

Researched Jewish folklore and the history of synagogues in Poland.

Grossman, Meir (1888 – 1964) Korczak – HaCarcom **B16**

(See the neighborhood of 'Ir Ganim Aleph.)

Guatemala Uruguay – Uruguay **C15-16**

A country in Central America.

Hantke, Arthur (Menahem) (1874 – 1955) Tahon – Levin **B14-15**

One of the leaders of the Zionist Organization in Germany, director of the main office of *Keren HaYesod* in Jerusalem.

HaTzionut Bolivia – Uruguay **C17**

Named for the Zionist movement in Jewish history.

Haviv, Haim, Rabbi (1882 – 1941) Hantke – Levin **B14**

Rabbi and spiritual leader of the Saloniki Jewish community, one of the early Lovers of Zion among Greek Jewry, died along with his community in the European Holocaust.

Hellman, Ya'akov, Dr. [Square] (1880 – 1950)
Rubinstein at Borochov **C14**

Author, one of the pioneers of Zionist journalism in Latvia, one of the heads of the Zionist-socialist movement.

Hevroni, Pesah (1884 – 1952) Szold – Olsvanger **B15**

A teacher and mathematician in Jerusalem.

Kann, Jacobus [Square] (1872 -1944) Hantke at Zangwill **C14**

One of the early Zionist leaders in Holland, member of the Zionist executive, co-founder of the Colonial Trust Bank, killed in the Holocaust.

Kellner, Aryeh (1859 – 1928) Brazil – dead end **B14**

A Zionist leader, one of Herzl's assistants.

Kiryat HaYovel Zangwill – HaPisga **C13-14**

Named for the neighborhood.

Kleinman, Moshe (1870 – 1948) Borochov – Rabinovich **B-C15**

Author, literary critic, journalist and activist, he edited the newspaper of the World Zionist Organization.

Kolitz, Haim [Road] (1919 – 1993) Golomb – Tzur – dead end **A-C17**

(See the neighborhoods of Giv'at Massua, Manhat/Malha.)

Korczak, Janusz (1878 – 1942) Chile – Uruguay **B16**

The pen name by which Dr. Henrik Goldschmidt was known. Doctor, educator and author, he dedicated his life to the education of orphans and to writing children's books and books on educational theory. He and his charges were killed together in the Holocaust.

Kremenetzky, Johann-Yona (1850 – 1936)
Borochov – dead end **C14**

Engineer and industrialist, first director of *HaKeren HaKayemet LeYisrael* (JNF), one of Herzl's assistants, elected to the Zionist executive at the first Zionist Congress in Basel in 1897. He thought up the familiar Blue Box of the JNF for collecting funds and the Golden Book in which were listed the names of the donors. He founded industries and agricultural works in the Land of Israel, was named an Honorary Citizen of Tel-Aviv (1934).

Levin, Shmaryahu, Dr. (1867 – 1935) Hantke – Olsvanger **B-C14**

One of the leaders of the Lovers of Zion in Germany and the United States, one of the promoters of the Technion in Haifa, a delegate to World Zionist Congresses and an opponent of the Uganda Plan, a founder of Dvir Publications. Kfar Shmaryahu near Herzliya, named for him, was established by immigrants from Germany about a year after his death.

Lipov, Dov [Square] Kleinman at dead end **B15**

General secretary of the council of Jerusalem workers, made a significant contribution to the development of Jerusalem and to the transfer of government offices to the city.

Mottke (Sofer) (1931 – 1995) Chile – Nissan **B15**

Known for his activities on behalf of Jerusalem, a *Yakir Yerushalayim.*

Motzkin, Yehuda Leo-Leib (1867 – 1933) Rabinovich – dead end **C15**

President of the Zionist workers committee, one of the first Lovers of Zion in the Ukraine, he preached the Return to Zion and the national renaissance of the Jewish people in its own land, one of the first to join Herzl, one of the framers of the Basel Program, active in reviving the Hebrew language and its literature, a president of the Zionist Congress. Kiryat Motzkin, north of Haifa, is named for him.

Naiditsch, Yitzhak (1868 – 1949) Borochov – Ebner **B14**

A Zionist activist, one of the first Lovers of Zion in Russia, a founder of *Keren HaYesod* in Jerusalem.

Nissan, Avraham, Dr. (Katznelson) (1888 – 1956)
Sereni – Uruguay **C15-16**

A doctor, statesman, member of the executive of the National Committee, Israeli representative in Scandinavia.

Olsvanger, 'Immanuel (1888 – 1961) Levin – Brazil **B14-15**

Author, researcher of folklore and Zionist activist in Jerusalem.

Rabinovich, Aharon (1901 – 1945) Warburg – Borochov **C15**

One of the leaders of the labor movement and secretary of the Jerusalem workers council.

Ringelblum, Emanuel, Dr. (1900 – 1944) Korczak – dead end **B16**

(See the neighborhood of 'Ir Ganim Aleph.)

Rubinstein, Yitzhak, Rabbi (1880 – 1945)
Borochov – Borochov **C14**

Chief rabbi of the Vilna Jewish community, one of the heads of the *Mizrahi* movement in Lithuania and Poland, a member of the Polish Senate (legislature) during World War I.

Schmorak, Ephraim, Dr. (1886 – 1953) Borochov – dead end **C15**

One of the Zionist leaders in Galicia, a member of the Zionist workers committee, a director of the Jewish Agency in Jerusalem.

Sereni, Enzo Haim (1905 – 1944) Uruguay – Chile **B15**

Educator, pioneer, youth guide for culture and self-defense, one of the founders of Kibbutz Giv'at Brenner, he parachuted behind the Nazi enemy lines in World War II and was caught and executed.

Shapira, Zvi Herman (1840 – 1898) Borochov – dead end **C14**

Originator of the idea of *HaKeren HaKayemet LeYisrael*, lecturer in mathematics at the universities of Berlin and Heidelberg, one of the founders of the Lovers of Zion movement, a representative at the first world Jewish congress, one of the formulators of the Basel Program, a supporter of Jewish colonization in the Land of Israel. The street in Tel-Aviv where the headquarters of the JNF is located is named for him.

Sharon, Avraham (1878 – 1957) Hantke – Ebner **B15**

Journalist, he established the collection of signatures and portraits of the great men of the Jewish people at the Hebrew University of Jerusalem.

Stern, Avraham (Yair) (1907 – 1942) Uruguay – Bolivia **C16-17**

A poet. His underground name was "Yair", he invested his energy in the underground movement ETZe"L, but when during World War II that organization announced a cease-fire in the battle against the British in the Land of Israel, he resigned and founded the LeH"I organization, was caught and executed by the British.

Szenes, Hannah (1921 – 1944) Tahon – Ringelblum **B15-16**

Poetess, among the parachutists who volunteered for the British army and were flown behind enemy lines, fell into the hands of the Nazis and were killed. Poems that she wrote were set to music after her death, the most well-known being "Halicha LeKeisaria" (Walking to Caesarea) and "Ashrei HaGafrur" (Happy is the Match). Kibbutz Yad Hannah, built in 1950 when her remains were brought to Israel for burial, is named for her.

Szold, Henrietta (1860 – 1945) Hantke – Hadassah Hospital **B15-16**

Educator, Zionist leader, founder of the women's organization Hadassah that greatly helped the Jewish community in the Land of Israel after World War I, one of the heads of the health and welfare structure in the Land of Israel, elected to the executive of the world Zionist movement, member of the National Committee. She stood at the head of *'Aliyat HaNo'ar* [Youth Aliya], an organization that saved thousands of children and youth in the Holocaust period and brought them to Israel, named an Honorary Citizen of Tel-Aviv (1935). Kfar Szold is named for her, as is the Szold Institute for research in the behavioral sciences (see the neighborhood of Kiryat Menahem).

Tahon, Ya'akov (1880 – 1950) Golomb – Szold **B15**

Chairman of the Jewish community in Jerusalem and head of the National Committee, director of the Land of Israel office of the Zionist Organization, one of the founders of a society to prepare the Jewish community in the Land of Israel for agricultural work.

Torah Va'Avoda Gordon – HaPisga **C14**

(See the neighborhood of Bayit VaGan.)

Tschlenow, Yehiel, Dr. (1863 – 1918) Borochov – dead end **C14**

Doctor, Zionist leader in Russia, one of the first Lovers of Zion to oppose the Uganda Plan, was vice-president of the Zionist executive, laid the cornerstone for the Technion in Haifa.

Tur-Sinai, Naphtali Herz (Torczyner) (1886 – 1973)
Hevroni – dead end **C15**

Scholar of Bible and linguistics, president of the Academy of the Hebrew Language, professor at the Hebrew University of Jerusalem.

Upper Volta Guatemala – Uruguay **C16**

Former name of the country Burkina Faso in western Africa.

Uruguay Tahon – HaTzionut **C15-16**

A country in South America.

Warburg, Otto, Prof. (1859 – 1938) Zangwill – Borochov **C15**

Third president of the Zionist Organization, researcher in natural sciences, was an activist in the Zionist movement, head of the research station for agriculture in Rehovot, and head of the Botany Department at the Hebrew University of Jerusalem, an initiator of the establishment of the Betzalel Art School in Jerusalem.

Zangwill, Israel (1864 – 1926) Hantke – Tahon **C14-15**

Jewish author who wrote in English, an early Lover of Zion in England, one of Herzl's devoted followers, among those who laid the groundwork for the Jewish Territorial Organization, a worldwide organization aiming to secure a large territory somewhere in the world where Jews would be the majority and have autonomy, in order to resolve the problem of continual Jewish migrations. After the Balfour Declaration, the idea was abandoned.

Kiryat Mattersdorf / Kiryat Sheva'

Name and establishment:

This neighborhood, located in the northwestern part of the city near the neighborhood of Romema, was founded in 1963 and named for the city in Austria from which came the founders of the neighborhood and its residents. Rabbi Shmuel Aaronfeld, the last rabbi of the Mattersdorf Jewish community, initiated the building of this neighborhood. The neighborhood was also named for the seven communities near the city of Mattersdorf, Austria, which were destroyed in the Holocaust.

The neighborhood is built along the edges of a hill on whose lower slopes was the Arab village of Lifta.

The residents of the neighborhood belong to the ultra-Orthodox community.

Boundaries:

North – Kiryat Ta'asiyot 'Atirot Mada'/Har Hotzvim

South – Romema

East – Kiryat Belz

West – Mei Neftoah (Lifta)

Sites: within its boundaries or nearby are the Romema-Industrial Zone, Kiryat Ta'asiyot 'Atirot Mada'/Har Hotzvim.

Streets: the streets of the neighborhood are named for religious books.

The streets are:

Gabai, Yosef, Rabbi Panim Meirot – dead end **F10**

The Hasidic master of Buzhed.

Ma'ane Simha HaMem-Gimel – HaMem-Gimel **E-F10**

Named for a religious text by Rabbi Simha Bunim Ehrenfeld (1842-1907), head of a yeshiva, one of the spiritual leaders of Hungarian Jewry (see the neighborhood of Romema 'Ilit).

Panim Meirot Ma'ane Simha – Sorotzkin **F10**

Named for a book of innovative commentaries on the Mishna, by Rabbi Meir Eisenstadt (1670-1744), a rabbi and arbiter of religious law, one of the leaders of Austrian Jewry, an authority in his generation (see the neighborhood of Romema 'Ilit).

Sha'arei Yerushalayim Ben Gurion Boulevard – Golda Meir **E10-F9**

Gates of Jerusalem. Named for the western entrance to the city of Jerusalem, near this neighborhood (see the neighborhoods of Romema, Romema 'Ilit).

Sorotzkin, Zalman, Rabbi (1881 – 1966)
Panim Meirot – Torat Hesed **F10-G9**

(See the neighborhoods of Kiryat Belz, Kiryat Zanz.)

Kiryat Menahem

Name and establishment:

This neighborhood, located in the southwestern part of town near Kiryat HaYovel, was founded in 1958 and named for the Zionist activist and president of the JNF in the United States, Menahem Bresler. Bresler helped build the neighborhood to aid in the absorption of new immigrants and also promoted the building of *Yad Kennedy* [the Kennedy Memorial] in the nearby Jerusalem hills in memory of assassinated U.S. President John F. Kennedy.

Boundaries:
Northeast – Kiryat HaYovel
Southeast – 'Ir Ganim
Northwest – the campus of Hadassah Hospital

Sites: within its boundaries or nearby are the Hadassah campus – Hadassah Medical Center, Yad Kennedy (a memorial to the murdered American president), the communal settlements Ora and 'Aminadav.

Streets: the neighborhood streets are named for countries in Central and South America and other countries throughout the world.

The streets are:

Colombia Mexico – Iceland **A-B16**

A country in South America.

Dahomey Mexico – Panama **A16**

(See the neighborhood of 'Ir Ganim Bet.)

HaHartzit Nicaragua – dead end **A16**

Chrysanthemum, a wild plant that grows in the Land of Israel.

Iceland Dahomey – Nicaragua **B16**

A European island country in the northernmost part of the North Atlantic Ocean.

Mexico Szold – Dahomey **B16**

A country in the southern part of North America.

Nicaragua Iceland – Dahomey **A16**

A country in Central America.

Panama Nicaragua – Szold **A16**

A country in Central America.

Szold, Henrietta (1860 – 1945)
Hadassah Hospital – Hantke **B15-16**

(See the neighborhood of Kiryat HaYovel.)

Kiryat Moshe

Name and establishment:

This neighborhood, located on the west side of the city near the entrance to the capital, was founded in 1923 and named for Sir Moses Montefiore. It is the sixth neighborhood in Jerusalem that bears his name. It was built with the help of the Mazkeret Moshe Foundation established in Montefiore's honor, and it was the last to be built with money from this fund. The neighborhood was called "New Montefiore" because it was built last and in order to distinguish it from the neighborhood of Yemin Moshe, called "Old Montefiore", founded in 1892. The parcel of land for this neighborhood was bought with the help of Professor David Yellin, who held the power-of-attorney for the foundation.

In spite of the rules of the foundation, no gate was put up in the neighborhood in memory of Sir Moses as was done in the other neighborhoods, and the heads of the foundation apparently found it sufficient to name the neighborhood after him.

The founders of the neighborhood were national-religious, people of the *Mizrahi* organization in Jerusalem, who were active in the national project of building up the Land. Kiryat Moshe was one of two neighborhoods in the city which were closed off by a chain on the Sabbath (the second was Sha'arei Hesed).

Herzl Boulevard, the central thoroughfare for traffic and public transportation, runs along the eastern side of the neighborhood. The street begins at Rehov Yafo and leads to the nearby neighborhoods of Beit HaKerem, Yefei Nof and Bayit VaGan, as well as to the sites of Mount Herzl and Yad VaShem.

Kiryat Moshe is one of six garden neighborhoods built in the beginning of the twentieth century (see the neighborhoods of Bayit VaGan, Beit HaKerem, Mekor Haim, Rehavia, Talpiot).

Boundaries:

North – Giv'at Shaul
South – Beit HaKerem and Yefei Nof
East – Herzl Boulevard
West – the industrial and commercial area of Giv'at Shaul

Sites: within its boundaries or nearby are Herzl Boulevard, the former HaMekasher neighborhood and the large *Egged* bus terminal, the *Mercaz HaRav* Yeshiva (the central yeshiva founded by Rabbi Avraham Yitzhak HaCohen Kook), Machon Meir, the School for the Blind, and the Weingarten Orphanage.

Streets: the neighborhood streets are named for founders and leaders of the religious Zionist *Mizrahi* movement and rabbis.

The streets are:

Abula'fia, David [Square] (1894 – 1953)
Rav Tza'ir at HaBaron Hirsch **E12**

An honored member of Jerusalem's Sephardic community, civic activist and builder of Jerusalem.

'Amiel, Moshe Avigdor, Rabbi (1883 – 1946)
Kosovsky – HaLevi **E11-12**

One of the foremost rabbis in Poland to join the *Mizrahi* movement, one of the leaders of the religious Zionist *Mizrahi* movement. Served as chief rabbi of Tel-Aviv – Jaffa from 1936 until his death.

Angel, Vidal, Rabbi [Steps] (d. 1907) Pick – Kosovsky **E12**

One of the important rabbis in Jerusalem.

Basel Herzl Boulevard – HaLevi **E11-12**

A city in Switzerland where the first Zionist Congress took place in 1897. At that same Congress, Herzl declared that in five years, or at most fifty years, after that Congress, a Jewish state would arise! His prophecy came true.

Ben Tzion, Shim'on Shmuel (1894 – 1954)
Degel Reuven – Ba'al HaSheiltot **E11**

(See the neighborhoods of Giv'at Shaul, Maimon/ Shchunat HaPo'el HaMizrahi.)

Degel Reuven HaRav Zvi Yehuda – Ben Tzion **E11**

Named for the book by Reuven Katz (1880-1963), who served as chief rabbi of the city of Petah Tikva (see the neighborhood of Maimon/ Shchunat HaPo'el HaMizrahi).

Dvoretz, Yisrael Zissel, Rabbi [Square] (1886 – 1968)
Ben Tzion at Ba'al HaSheiltot **E11**

(See the neighborhood of Giv'at Shaul.)

Farbstein, Yehoshu'a, Rabbi (1870 – 1948)
Herzl Boulevard – Yemin Avot **E11**

(See the neighborhood of Giv'at Shaul-Industrial Zone.)

Gat, Ben Tzion (1909 – 1956) Kiryat Moshe – Kiryat Moshe **E11**

A teacher and researcher of the history of the old Jewish community in the Land of Israel, one of the commanders of the Hagana in Jerusalem.

HaBaron Hirsch, Maurice de (1831 – 1896)
Herzl Boulevard – HaLevi **E12**

A Jewish philanthropist, known as the father of Jewish agricultural settlement in Argentina, he supported the Alliance Israelite (KY"H). Herzl did not succeed in convincing Baron de Hirsch to invest his efforts and his money in the Land of Israel.

Ha'Ilui (1877 – 1928) HaRav Zvi Yehuda – Ben Tzion **E11**

The nickname for Rabbi Shlomo Poliacheck, known as a genius thanks to his studiousness and his broad knowledge of Torah and religious law. He was head of a yeshiva in New York.

HaLevi, Eli'ezer (1809 – 1888) Yemin Avot – Rav Tza'ir **E11-12**

A scholar of Oriental studies, he was secretary to Moses and Judith Montefiore in their travels in the Land of Israel.

HaMeiri, Moshe, Rabbi [Boulevard] (1886 – 1947)
Kosovsky – HaRav Zvi Yehuda **E11**

A teacher, activist and one of the leaders of the *Mizrahi* movement, a member of the directorate of the National Committee, one of the founders of the neighborhood.

HaRav Zvi Yehuda HaCohen Kook (1891 – 1982)
Herzl Boulevard – Ha'Ilui **E11**

A rabbi and leader, head of the *Mercaz HaRav* Yeshiva in Jerusalem.

Herzl Boulevard Shazar Boulevard – HaPisga **F11-D13**

(See the neighborhoods of Bayit VaGan, Beit HaKerem, Maimon/ Shchunat HaPo'el HaMizrahi, Yefei Nof.)

Kiryat Moshe Herzl Boulevard – Farbstein **E11**

Named for the neighborhood and for the memory of Moses Montefiore. A central street in the neighborhood.

Korot Ha'Itim Sirkis – dead end **E11**

Named for a book by Rabbi Menahem Mendel of Kaminitz (1800-1873), that presents impressions of his *'aliya* to the Land of Israel, and of the life story of the author, including the Druze rebellion in Tzfat. He was a rabbi and activist. His family built the first hostel in Jerusalem, in 1842.

Kosovsky, Haim Yehoshu'a, Rabbi (1873 – 1960)
HaMeiri – HaMeiri **E11-12**

A rabbi and researcher of the literature of the Mishna and Talmud, he authored concordances for the Mishna, Tosefta, Targum Onkelos and part of the Babylonian Talmud.

Maimon, Yehuda Leib HaCohen [Fishman], Rabbi (1875 – 1962)
Degel Reuven – Herzl Boulevard **E-F11**

A rabbi, author and one of the founders of the *Mizrahi* movement. He worked for the establishment of the chief rabbinate in the Land of Israel and the appointment of Rav Kook as the chief rabbi, built the Rav Kook Institute in 1936, supported the struggle against the British Mandate and was one of the formulators of the Declaration of Independence. He served as minister of religions in Ben-Gurion's government, and won the Israel Prize for Torah Literature in 1958 (see the neighborhood of Maimon/Shchunat HaPo'el HaMizrachi).

Meltzer, Feivel (1897 – 1973) Herzl Boulevard – Maimon **E11**

Educator, author and Biblical commentator, he worked for the spread of Torah study.

Meshulam, Yitzhak [Square] (1914 – 1987)
Kiryat Moshe at HaMeiri **E11**

Active in civic matters, one of the builders of Jerusalem.

Mevo Yitzhak Herzl Boulevard – the School for the Blind **E12**

Named for Yitzhak Ya'akov Yellin (1885 -1962), a journalist, author and activist.

Nissenbaum, Yitzhak, Rabbi (1868 – 1942)
Beit She'arim to Mosad HaRav Kook **E11**

A rabbi and author, one of the heads of religious Zionism, active in the *Mizrahi* movement and a president of the *Mizrahi* Organization, one of the Lovers of Zion, wrote books of homilies in the Zionist spirit, died in the Warsaw Ghetto.

Nurok, Mordechai, Rabbi (1879 – 1962) HaLevi – Farbstein **E11**

One of the honored leaders of Latvian Jewry, a leader of religious Zionism, a minister in the government of Israel.

Pick, Haim Herman (1878 – 1952)
Kiryat Moshe – Herzl Boulevard **E11-12**

Linguist, researcher and one of the heads of the religious Zionist *Mizrahi* movement, he served as director of the 'Aliya Department of the Zionist Organization. The street is also named after his son, Pinhas Herman, an army historian.

Polyakov, Shoshana (d. 1917) Kiryat Moshe – HaBaron Hirsch **E11-12**

A philanthropist, she established a fund for the religious institutions of Jerusalem.

Rav Tza'ir (1870 – 1950) HaBaron Hirsch – Basel **E12**

Young rabbi, the nickname of Rabbi Haim Tchernowitz, an author and scholar of the Talmud and religious law. He founded the "modern yeshiva" in Odessa, which functioned on the system of traditional learning together with modern research, a system that within two years became the accepted basis for the rabbinical seminary he directed.

Reines, Yitzhak Ya'akov, Rabbi (1839 – 1915)
Ben Tzion – Ba'al HaSheiltot **E11**

Rabbi, author, head of a yeshiva and one of the leaders of religious Zionism, he founded the *Mizrahi* movement and was its first president, was one of the first rabbis who joined Herzl and supported the Uganda Plan, was a delegate to Zionist Congresses.

Sar Shalom [Steps] Polyakov – Kosovsky **E12**

Named for Rahamim Sar-Shalom, one of the leaders of Persian Jewry (Iran), who made *'aliya* to Jerusalem with his family in 1906, one of the builders of this neighborhood and a civic leader in Jerusalem.

Shifra HaMeiri – Yemin Avot **E12**

Shiphrah, named for one of the two Hebrew midwives (the second was Puah), during the period of slavery of the Israelites in Egypt, who disobeyed Pharaoh's decree by keeping the newborn Hebrew babies alive (Exodus 1:15-17).

Sirkis, Daniel, Rabbi (1881 – 1965)
Ben Tzion – HaRav Zvi Yehuda **E11**

One of the founders of the religious Zionist movement in Poland, a member of the National Committee, a member of the provisional council of the State of Israel, and a member of the directorate of *HaKeren HaKayemet LeYisrael.*

Weingarten, David [Square] (1873 – 1941) Ben Tzion at Ha'Ilui **E11**

Founder, educator and director of the general orphanage named for him.

Yemin Avot Ha'Ilui – Farbstein **D-E11**

(See the neighborhood of Giv'at Shaul.)

Kiryat Shmuel

Name and establishment:

This neighborhood, located in the middle of town near the neighborhood of Rehavia, was established in 1928 and named after Rabbi Shmuel Salant (see the neighborhood of Mea She'arim). The neighborhood was built, on rocky terrain, by ultra-Orthodox Jews from veteran families in the city. From the by-laws of the neighborhood, one learns that the founders planned it as a Jewish neighborhood run on the principles of the written Torah and tradition. A wagon service was established for the transportation of passengers and goods.

During the riots of 1928 and 1936-1939, the neighborhood stood up to the rioters, thanks to the help of members of the Hagana in Jerusalem. Until the War of Independence (1948), the neighborhoods of Kiryat Shmuel and Merhavia were the southernmost neighborhoods in the New City. The edge of the neighborhood became the front line opposite the fortified Christian neighborhood of Katamon. From the two neighborhoods, Israeli forces pushed south and overcame nearby Katamon and its surroundings.

Boundaries:

North – Rehavia
South – Gonenim/Katamonim
East – Komemiyut/Talbieh
West – Neve Granot

Sites: within its boundaries or nearby are the President's Residence, Jerusalem Theater and the Yad Meir Museum for Islamic Art.

Streets: the neighborhood streets are named for founders of the neighborhood, rabbis, authors, scholars, musicians and a parachutist.

The streets are:

Aluf Simhoni, Asaf (1922 – 1956) Berlin – dead end **G14**

An IDF commander in the Sinai Campaign (1956), killed in the war.

Ben AV"I, Itamar (1882-1943) Harlap – HaNasi **G14**

Itamar ben Yehuda, the son of the reviver of the Hebrew language, **E**li'ezer **b**en **Y**ehuda. Author, journalist and activist in Jerusalem. He was the first child born in the Land of Israel whose mother-tongue was Hebrew (see the neighborhood of Merhavia).

Berlin, Haim, Rabbi (1832 - 1913) 'Aza at Herzog – HaTayasim **G14**

Son of HaNeTZI"V (**Ha**Rav **N**aftali **Z**vi **Y**ehuda **B**erlin) of Volozhin, a rabbi and arbiter of religious law, head of the *'Etz Haim* Yeshiva in Jerusalem.

Boehm, Yohanan [Square] (1914 – 1986) Berlin at NIL"I **G14**

A musician, a member of the Hagana who took part in the defense of Jerusalem during the War of Independence, founder of the youth orchestra of Jerusalem.

Brodi, Haim, Rabbi (1868 – 1942) Berlin – Herzog **G14**

Author, one of the scholars of medieval poetry, head of the Institute for the Study of Hebrew Poetry, rabbi of Prague, the capital of Czechoslovakia.

Chopin, Frederic (1810 – 1849)
HaNasi at HaPaLMa"H – Marcus **G-H14**

One of the great composers and pianists of the Romantic Period in Europe.

Ettinger, Yitzhak Zvi [Steps] (1906 – 1985) Berlin – Ben AV"I **G14**

One of the founders of the neighborhood, a *Yakir Yerushalayim*.

Galaktion, Gala [Square] (20th cent.) Brodi at Herzog **G14**

Romanian author, humanist, theologian, translated the Bible into Romanian.

HaADeRe"T (1843 – 1905) HaNasi – Harlap **G14**

Acronym for **Ha**Rav **E**liyahu **D**avid **R**abinowitz-**T**eomim, one of the most prominent rabbis of the early modern period, the rabbi of important communities in Lithuania, chief rabbi of Jerusalem, authored books of innovative commentaries on Torah, religious law and Aggada.

HaAR"I (1534 – 1572) HaNasi – Harlap, ends at ‘Aza **G14**

Acronym for **HaE**lohi **R**abbi **Y**itzhak, Rabbi Yitzhak ben Shlomo Luria, the greatest Kabbalist of his generation, who lived in Tzfat. He was one of the formulators of Kabbalist teachings and had a strong influence on future generations of Kabbalists. He also wrote verses and religious poetry (see the neighborhood of Merhavia).

HaNasi Jabotinsky – HaPaLMa"H at Chopin **G-H14**

Named for the President's Residence, located on this street (see the neighborhood of Merhavia).

HaPaLMa"H HaNasi – Fichmann **G14-15**

(See the neighborhoods of Gonen/ Katamon HaYeshana, Merhavia.)

HaRav Hen, Avraham (1880 – 1957) Berlin – Tchernichovsky **G14**

Author, one of the activists of Russian Jewry, a religious Zionist activist, head of the culture department of the National Committee.

Harkavi, Avraham Eliyahu, Rabbi [Lane] (1835–1919)
HaNasi – dead end **G14**

A scholar of Jewish history of the period of the Geonim and the Karaites, he published articles on the Geonim and on the great sages of Spain.

Harlap, Ya‘akov Asher, Rabbi (1883 – 1951)
HaAR"I – HaPaLMa"H **G14**

One of Jerusalem's important rabbinical figures, one of the heads of the *Merkaz HaRav* Yeshiva, he supported the Zionist enterprise and the building up of Israel (see the neighborhood of Merhavia).

Herzog, Yitzhak Isaac HaLevi, Rabbi Dr. (1888 – 1959)
‘Aza – Golomb **G14-E16**

(See the neighborhoods of Giv‘at HaVradim/Shikun Rassco, Giv‘at Mordechai, Gonenim/ Katamonim, Nayot, Rehavia.)

Jabotinsky, Zeev (1880 – 1940) HaNasi – David HaMelech **G-H14**

Author, journalist, one of the leaders of world Zionism. He founded the Jewish Legion within the British Army in World War I, was a founder of the Revisionist movement in 1909 and was its president. He died in the

United States while on a lecture tour. In his will he wrote that his remains might be brought to Israel for burial only if this was at the direction of a prime minister of the Jewish state that would be established in the Land of Israel. In 1964 Prime Minister Levi Eshkol fulfilled this condition of Jabotinsky's will, and his remains were brought to Israel and buried on Mount Herzl in Jerusalem (see the neighborhood of Komemiyut/Talbieh).

Raik, Haviva [Lane] (1914 – 1944) HaPaLMa"H – dead end **G14**

A paratrooper who was flown behind the Nazi enemy lines in World War II, caught and executed.

Rivlin, Moshe [Steps] (1895 – 1978) Harlap – Berlin **G14**

One of the outstanding founders of the neighborhood.

Rotenberg, Shmuel Aryeh (1855 – 1937) HaAR"I – Jabotinsky **G14**

One of the founders of this Jerusalem neighborhood.

Shimron, Erwin Shaul [Square] (1919 – 1978) Chopin at Marcus **H14**

The second State Attorney of Israel, one of the leading attorneys and a public figure.

Shneurson, Menahem [Square] (1885 – 1960)
Ben AV"I at HaNasi **G14**

A Jerusalem activist, one of the organizers of Jewish education in Russia and active in *'Aliyat HaNo'ar* (bringing youth to settle in Israel), one of the heads of the Hebrew University in Jerusalem (see the neighborhood of Merhavia.)

Siton, David [Square] (1909 – 1989) HaAR"I at 'Aza **G14**

Author, journalist, educator, member of LeH"I, chairman of the governing committee of the Sephardic community and the Oriental communities of Jerusalem, one of the founders of the World Sephardic Federation, a *Yakir Yerushalayim* (see the neighborhood of Rehavia).

Stern, Menahem [Square] (1925 – 1989)
Tchernichovsky at HaRav Hen **G14**

One of the outstanding historians and scholars of the Second Temple period.

Tchernichovsky, Shaul (1875 – 1943) Herzog – Fichmann **F15-G14**

(See the neighborhood of Giv'at HaVradim/Shikun Rassco.)

Kiryat Ta'asiyot 'Atirot Mada'/Har Hotzvim

Name and establishment:

This campus, located in the northern part of the city alongside the highway leading to Ramot Allon, was established in 1972. The name reflects the fact that the industries here specialize in various sciences, with electronics and computers being the dominant branches. This is also the area where stone was quarried for building the houses in Jerusalem, thus giving rise to the neighborhood's second name, which means "quarrymen's hill".

Until the Six Day War (1967), the Israel-Jordan border crossed the nearby valley. Today this industrial area is the site of the starting points of the highway to mid-town Jerusalem, the highway to nearby Ramot Allon and the road connecting to the highway to Tel-Aviv.

Boundaries:

Northwest – Ramot Allon

South – Kiryat Zanz and Kiryat Belz

East – Sanhedria, Sanhedria HaMurhevet, Ramat Eshkol

Sites: within its boundaries or nearby are such science-based companies as Intel, Teva, Sigma Yisrael, DigiTel.

Streets: the streets of the campus are named for institutions of science-based industry located in the area.

The streets are:

Artom, Elia Samuele (1887 – 1965)
Golda Meir – HaMarpe – dead end **G9**

A rabbi, professor and commentator on the Bible.

Golda Meir [Boulevard] (1898 – 1979) Bar-Ilan – Mirski **D5-H9**

Fourth prime minister of the State of Israel. She made *'aliya* in 1921 and became a member of Kibbutz Merhavya, was active in the Histradrut Labor Federation and the National Committee, served as a delegate to the Zionist Congress and was the senior female representative there, made a campaign trip to raise funds in America just before the War of Independence, was one of the signers of the Declaration of Independence, served as Israel's first representative to the Soviet Union, was a member of

Knesset from the establishment of the State until 1974 and through those years held a number of ministerial portfolios. After the sudden death of Levi Eshkol, she was elected prime minister in his place in 1969, in which position she served until after the Yom Kippur War. She was made an Honorary Citizen of the city of Tel-Aviv. The Theater for the Performing Arts in Tel-Aviv is named after her (see the neighborhoods of Kiryat Zanz, Ramot Allon).

HaLevi, Shlomo (Momo) (1942 – 2001) Golda Meir – dead end **G9**

Economist, initiator, one of the promoters of Jerusalem development, member of the city council.

HaMarpe Kiryat Mada' – Artom **G9**

Named for the Marpe plant located on this street.

Kiryat Mada' Golda Meir – dead end **G9**

Science campus, named for the hi-tech industrial campus.

Kiryat Wolfson

Name and establishment:

This neighborhood, located in the western part of the city near the neighborhoods of Sha'arei Hesed and Rehavia, was founded in 1970 and named for the British Jewish philanthropist Sir Isaac Wolfson, who initiated construction of the neighborhood.

Within the area of the neighborhood, during World War I, a railroad ran which served the British army in its war against the Turks in the northern part of the city.

In this neighborhood, five residential towers were built, faced with stone, and well-to-do Jews moved into these buildings from Israel and the United States.

Boundaries:

Northeast – Sha'arei Hesed

South – Rehavia

West – Yitzhak Ben-Zvi Boulevard

Sites: within its boundaries or nearby are the Knesset building, the Israel Museum, Sacher Park, the Monastery of the Cross.

Streets: the streets in the neighborhood are named for rabbis.

The streets are:

Ben-Zvi, Yitzhak [Boulevard] (1884 – 1963)
Ruppin – Shmuel Baruch/Agrippas **G12**

(See the neighborhoods of Giv'at Ram, Nahlat Ahim/Nahlaot, Sha'arei Hesed, Sha'arei Rahamim, Shevet Tzedek/Shchunat HaPahim, Zichron Ya'akov, Zichron Yosef.)

Diskin, Yehuda Leib, Rabbi (1816 – 1898) HaGR"A – RaMBa"N **G13**

"The Rabbi from Brisk", an arbiter of religious law, leader of the old Ashkenazic Jewish community in Jerusalem, was active in public institutions (see the neighborhood of Sha'arei Hesed).

HaGR"A (1720 - 1797) Diskin – Ussishkin **G13**

Acronym for **HaG**aon **R**av **E**liyahu (ben Shlomo), called the Gaon of Vilna, one of the great rabbis and arbiters of religious law, the spiritual leader of Lithuanian Jewry, an authority on religious law. During his lifetime, the Hasidic movement arose, and he stood at the head of the *Mitnagdim*, those who opposed it (see the neighborhood of Sha'arei Hesed).

Rahvat HaSha'an Diskin – HaKeren HaKayemet LeYisrael **G13**

A plaza named for Rabbi Abraham Nahman Rudnitzky (1896-1947), artist, a man of spirit and creativity (see the neighborhood of Sha'arei Hesed).

Ruppin, Arthur Shim'on [Road] (1876 – 1943)
RaMBa"N – Wolfson **F-G13**

(See the neighborhood of Giv'at Ram.)

Kiryat Zanz

Name and establishment:

This neighborhood, located in the northwestern part of the city near Kiryat Belz, was founded in 1965 and named for a town in northern Galicia, in Poland, whose citizens founded this neighborhood in Jerusalem. The city of Zanz was a spiritual center for tens of thousands of Hasidim and supporters of the Hasidic movement in Europe.

Boundaries:

North – Kiryat Ta'asiyot 'Atirot Mada'/Har Hotzvim

South – Shikun HaBa"D

East – 'Ezrat Torah, Tel-Arza

West – Kiryat Belz

Sites: within its boundaries or nearby are the industrial area of Romema and Kiryat Ta'asiyot 'Atirot Mada'/Har Hotzvim.

Streets: the neighborhood streets are mostly named for various Hasidic masters of Zanz and religious works.

The streets are:

Doreish Tov 'Ezrat Torah – dead end **G10**

Named for the Hasidic master Rabbi Nahum Mordechai of Chortkov (d. 1946).

Golda Meir [Boulevard] (1898 – 1979) Bar-Ilan – Mirski **D5-H9**

(See the neighborhoods of Kiryat Ta'asiyot 'Atirot Mada'/Har Hotzvim, Ramot Allon.)

Imrei Bina Zayit Ra'anan – dead end **G10**

Named for the book of responsa of Rabbi Meir Auerbach (1815-1878), a rabbi of important communities in Poland, the rabbi of Jerusalem and a founder of Petah Tikva.

Menahem Meishiv Sorotzkin – dead end **G11**

Named for the book by Rabbi Menahem Sofer (1880-1944), who was killed in the Holocaust after serving in the rabbinate for over forty years. He was head of the office of the rabbinate in Romania, one of the grandsons of the Hatam Sofer.

Shefa' Haim Golda Meir – Doresh Tov **G9-10**

Named for the Hasidic master of Klausenberg (b. 1905), named rabbi of the Sephardic community in Klausenberg, transported to Auschwitz during World War II and liberated from the death camp by the American army. He later expended great effort toward rebuilding the ruins and rehabilitation of Jewish survivors of the Holocaust. He built schools for children and youth and built Kiryat Zanz into a very large network of educational institutions and schools for all age groups, a Talmudical academy, community service organizations like Laniado Hospital, and Mif'al Shas, that includes thousands of students of religious studies.

Sorotzkin, Zalman, Rabbi (1881 – 1966)
Torat Hesed – Panim Meirot **F10-G9**

(See the neighborhoods of Kiryat Belz, Kiryat Mattersdorf/Kiryat Sheva'.)

Ya'akovson, Binyamin Zeev, Rabbi (1894–1973)
Ohel Yehoshu'a – 'Ezrat Torah **G10**

A rabbi and educator, he rescued Jewish children during the Holocaust, was the rabbi of the Sanhedria neighborhood in Jerusalem.

Zayit Ra'anan Ohel Yehoshu'a – Torat Hesed **G9-10**

Named for a book of commentary on the Mishna by Rabbi Moshe Yehuda Leib of Kutno, one of the great rabbis of Jerusalem.

Knesset Yisrael

Name and establishment:

The bloc of neighborhoods called Knesset Yisrael, or just "Knesset", is located in the center of town near Mahane Yehuda north of Nahlat Ahim/Nahlaot. The decision to establish these neighborhoods was made in 1891 by the "General Committee of Knesset (the assembly of) Yisrael" of the Ashkenazic community, hence its name. The neighborhoods were built from the money of donations of American Jews and from donations by people of means among the residents of Jerusalem, as housing set aside for the poor of the city. The name is also drawn from the verse: "God is the builder of Jerusalem, He shall gather in the dispersed of Israel" (Psalms 147:2).

In 1892 the cornerstone was laid for Knesset Yisrael Aleph, in which were built thirteen apartments and the *Beit Rahel* Synagogue, the central building of the neighborhood. It was built in the shape of the letter Het (three sides of a rectangle), with the eastern side open, the buildings of one story, attached on both sides. The entrance to the neighborhood is from Tavor Street, behind the Ohel Moshe neighborhood.

In 1902 the committee decided to purchase additional land southeast of Knesset Aleph, for the construction of Knesset Yisrael Bet and Batei Broyde. This time two-story buildings were built in order to utilize the space better, again in the shape of a letter Het. Above the entrances to the apartments were fixed plaques in tribute to the donors. Some of the housing blocks were also named after the donors. The entrance to this neighborhood is from HaNeTZI"V Street.

In 1908 a further piece of land was acquired on Betzalel Street, southeast of Knesset Bet, for the purpose of building Knesset Yisrael Gimel. The cornerstone was laid in 1925 by Rabbi Avraham Yitzhak HaCohen Kook, who was then the chief rabbi of the Land of Israel.

Today the residents of this bloc of neighborhoods are ultra-Orthodox Ashkenazic Jews, descendants of the Old Yishuv in Jerusalem from generations ago.

Boundaries:
North – Mahane Yehuda and the Mahane Yehuda Market
South – Nahlat Ahim/Nahlaot
East – Mid-Town
West – Zichron Yosef

Sites: within its boundaries or nearby are the Gerard Behar community center and the Mahane Yehuda Market.

Streets: the neighborhood streets are named for places in northern Israel and for one of the prominent arbiters of religious law. The main street is HaNeTZI"V Street.

The streets are:

Betzalel ben Uri Ben-Zvi – Mesilat Yesharim **G12**

(See the neighborhoods of Batei Kollel Minsk/Beit HaLevi, Batei Kollel Munkacs, Mid-Town, Nahlat Ahim/Nahlaot, Nahlat Tzion, Sha'arei Rahamim, Zichron Ahim, Zichron Ya'akov, Zichron Yosef.)

HaLevanon HaNeTZI"V – Rama **G12**

(See the neighborhoods of Batei Kollel Munkacs, Mazkeret Moshe.)

HaNeTZI"V (1817 – 1893) Betzalel – Tavor **G12**

(See the neighborhoods of Batei Broyde/Ohalei Ya'akov, Batei Kollel Minsk/Beit HaLevi, Batei Kollel Munkacs, Batei Rand, Mazkeret Moshe.)

Tavor Shomron – 'Ezra Refael **G12**

(See the neighborhoods of Batei Broyde/Ohalei Ya'akov, Batei Rand, Mazkeret Moshe, Ohel Moshe).

Yizra'el Betzalel – HaNeTZI"V **G12**

(See the neighborhoods of Batei Kollel Minsk/Beit HaLevi, Batei Kollel Munkacs.)

Komemiyut/Talbieh

Name and establishment:

This neighborhood, alongside the neighborhood of Rehavia to the north and the German Colony to the south, was established in 1923. The source of the name is unknown, and, as a result, there are many conjectures about it. Some think the neighborhood is named for Khalif 'Ali abu-Taleb, whose relatives lived in the area; others think the name came from the Muslim prayer that pilgrims to Mecca customarily recite: "El-Talbieh"; yet others think the name Talbieh existed here before the neighborhood was built. The riddle remains unsolved.

The land for the neighborhood was bought from the Greek Orthodox Church after World War I by an Arab Christian contractor. The plots were sold to Arab Christian families, and they built residential housing on the properties in various styles, for their personal use or to rent out. At that same time, a small number of Jewish families lived here. After the War of Independence, the Arabs abandoned their houses, which were then taken over by Jewish families. Since then many more houses have been built in the neighborhood, and today it is considered one of the most beautiful and prestigious neighborhoods in the city.

The neighborhood has a Hebrew name, Komemiyut – marking the Jewish aspiration for independence and strength – but the name did not gain general acceptance.

Boundaries:

North – Rehavia

South – the German Colony/RaMBa"M

East – David HaMelech Street and Yemin Moshe

West – Kiryat Shmuel

Sites: within its boundaries or nearby are the President's Residence, the official residence of the prime minister, the national academy for science, the Van Leer Institute, Jerusalem Theater, Liberty Bell Park, the Rose Garden.

Streets: the neighborhood streets are named for Lovers of Zion, great authors of modern Hebrew literature and pro-Zionist British politicians. There are three main streets, Jabotinsky, Balfour and Marcus, which intersect at Wingate Square.

The streets are:

Ahad Ha'Am (1856 – 1927) Keren HaYesod – Jabotinsky **H13-14**

The literary pen name of the well-known author Asher Zvi Ginsberg. He was one of the prominent thinkers of modern Hebrew literature and is thought of as the father of "spiritual Zionism". He thought it was not possible to eliminate the Diaspora and that it was better to focus on building a spiritual center for the Jewish people in the Land of Israel and thereby unite the Jews of the Diaspora. He became an Honorary Citizen of the city of Tel-Aviv.

Aktzin, Binyamin [Square] (1904 – 1985)
'Ovadia MiBartenura at Arlosoroff **H13**

Diplomat, Zionist and jurist.

Alkala'i, Yehuda, Rabbi (1798 – 1878) Jabotinsky – Pinsker **H14**

Rabbi and author. Heralded the return to Zion even before the establishment of the Zionist movement. In his writings he claimed that the Redemption would come "naturally".

Arlosoroff, Haim, Dr. (1899 – 1933)
Jabotinsky – 'Aza and ends at RaMBa"N **H13-14**

Statesman, Zionist, one of the leaders of the Labor movement in the Land of Israel. Director of the political department of the Jewish Agency. In the last year of his life, he was active in bringing Jews from Nazi Germany on *'aliya* (see the neighborhood of Rehavia).

Asaf, Simha, Rabbi [Square] (1889 – 1953)
Molcho at RaDa"K at 'Ovadia MiBartenura **H14**

Author and researcher of the period of the Geonim, professor at the Hebrew University. In spite of not being an attorney, he was appointed a justice of the Supreme Court in Jerusalem.

Bakshi-Doron, Ben-Zion, Rabbi [Square] (1909 – 1993)
Jabotinsky at Ahad Ha'Am **H14**

A Jerusalemite, a respected lay leader of his congregation and community activist, faithfully dealt with community needs.

Balfour, Arthur James, Lord (1848 – 1930)
Jabotinsky – 'Aza at Ben Maimon **H14**

(See the neighborhoods of Giv'at Ram, Rehavia.)

Brenner, Yosef Haim (1881 – 1921) Balfour – Sokolow **H13-14**

Author and literary critic of Hebrew literature, one of the leaders of the Labor movement in the Land of Israel. Kibbutz Giv'at Brenner near Rehovot, founded in 1928, is named after him.

Chile [Square] Sokolow **H14**

A country in South America.

David HaMelech (10th cent. BCE) Agron – 'Emek Refaim **H13-I14**

(See the neighborhoods of David's Village-Mamilla, Mahane Yisrael/ Shchunat HaMa'aravim, Mid-Town, Yemin Moshe.)

Disraeli, Benjamin (1804 – 1881) Marcus – Elhanan **H14**

Born Jewish, one of the great statesmen of the British Empire, he served a number of times as prime minister there. In his well-known book, *David Alroy*, he expanded on the subject of the Return to Zion and the redemption of the Jewish people.

Dubnow, Simon (1860 – 1941) Marcus – Graetz **H14**

Renowned as a historian of the Jewish people. Researcher of the Hasidic movement. He believed that it was possible to resolve the Jewish question by giving national autonomy to the Jews in each and every country in which they lived. His greatest written work was a world history of the Jewish people, in ten volumes and published in several languages.

Einstein, Albert, Prof. [Square] (1879 – 1955)
Arlosoroff at Jabotinsky **H14**

One of the world's greatest scientists, he expounded the Theory of Relativity. A supporter of Zionism and one of the founders of the Hebrew University of Jerusalem. The first Honorary Citizen of Tel-Aviv (1923).

Elhanan, Yitzhak, Rabbi (12th cent.) Jabotinsky – Pinsker **H14**

Composer of religious poetry, one of the *Ba'alei HaTosafot* in France.

Was martyred in 1184.

Goldberg, Ariela Deem [Plaza] (1935 – 1988)
Jabotinsky at RaDa"K **G14**

Authoress and researcher.

Hovevei Tzion Marcus – Elhanan **H14**

In memory of various associations founded during the years 1881-1896 in Russia and central Europe, whose goal was the Jewish colonization of the Land of Israel. These associations pre-dated the Zionist movement founded by Herzl. The outstanding personages in these associations were Yehuda Leib Pinsker (see Rehov Pinsker in this neighborhood) and Rabbi Shmuel Mohilewer (see Rehov Mohilewer in the German Colony).

Jabotinsky, Zeev (1880 – 1940) HaNasi – David HaMelech **G-H14**

(See the neighborhood of Kiryat Shmuel.)

Keren HaYesod King George – David HaMelech **H13**

The foundation that funds the activities of the Jewish Agency for Israel and the Zionist directorate. Founded in 1920 for the purpose of soliciting donations to fund immigration and settlement, but not land purchases, it was within the charge of the Jewish National Fund (see Mid-Town).

Lev Ha'Ivri Jabotinsky – Disraeli **H14**

Named after the book by Rabbi 'Akiva Yosef Shlezinger (1837-1922). He was one of the first to preach the Return to Zion, the speaking of the Hebrew language and defense of the Land.

Manne, Mordechai Zvi (1859 – 1886) Disraeli – dead end **H14**

Hebrew poet and painter.

Marcus, David (1902 – 1948) Jabotinsky – Kaf-Tet BeNovember **H14**

An American Jew who, as a volunteer, helped the Jewish community in Israel during the War of Independence and was appointed commander of the Jerusalem front. He was the first general in the IDF. He was killed while his unit was in Abu Ghosh as a result of his not understanding an order given in Hebrew by a soldier on guard duty.

Mendele Mocher Sforim (1835 – 1917)
Keren HaYesod – Jabotinsky **H14**

The pen name of the well-known author Shalom Ya'akov Abramowitsch.

One of the great Hebrew authors of the Haskala (Jewish Enlightenment), one of those who laid the foundations of modern Hebrew literature and who revived the Hebrew language. In his books he described the life of poverty of the Jews of the villages of Eastern Europe.

Molcho, Shlomo, Rabbi (1500 – 1532) RaDa"K – Jabotinsky **H14**

Born in Portugal to a family of Marranos (Jews forced to convert to Christianity). A Kabbalist, he believed that he was the Messiah and preached the renaissance of the Jewish people in its own land. He was burned at the stake.

Oliphant (1829 – 1888) Alkala'i – Pinsker **H14**

Named for Sir Laurence Oliphant, who was a British statesman and diplomat, a Lover of Zion, and very active in the widespread Jewish colonization in the Land of Israel.

'Ovadia MiBartenura (1450 – 1516) Balfour – RaDa"K **H13-14**

A Jewish sage, known by the name of his birthplace in Italy, one of the outstanding sages of Italian Jewry and author of the most popular commentary on the Mishna. He revived the Jewish community in Jerusalem.

Pinsker, Yehuda Leib (Leon), Dr. (1821 – 1891)
Marcus – Elhanan **H14**

Physician and thinker. One of the founders of the Lovers of Zion (see above, Hovevei Tzion Street in this neighborhood) and one of its leaders. At first he advocated the establishment of a national Jewish center in one country, not necessarily in Israel, in the framework of the doctrine of "Auto-Emancipation" which he expounded (1882). In this doctrine, he recommended freeing the Jews, who had suffered harsh pogroms, and giving them self-rule within a specific territory. After coming into contact with the Lovers of Zion movement, he was convinced that this could be realized only in the Land of Israel. His remains were brought to Jerusalem for burial.

RaDa"K (1160 – 1235)
Jabotinsky – 'Aza and ends at Ben Maimon **G13-14**

Acronym for **R**abbi **D**avid **K**imhi, one of the outstanding commentators on the Bible and one of the great linguists of Spanish Jewry during the Middle Ages (see the neighborhood of Rehavia).

Rotenstreich, Nathan [Square] (1914–1994)
Marcus at Pinsker **H14**

Philosopher, one of those who promoted higher education in Israel.

Shalom 'Aleichem (1859 – 1916) Keren HaYesod – Jabotinsky **H14**

The pen name of the well-known author Shalom Ya'akov Rabinovitz. One of the great authors of modern Hebrew literature in the Haskala period. He is recognized as an artist in his description of Jewish life in Eastern Europe. The outstanding characters he created in his stories are Tevya the Milkman, Menahem Mendel, and the boy Mottel ben Peissy the cantor. One of the first in the Lovers of Zion movement.

Shmueli (Reisenberg), Yitzhak [Square] (1913 – 1988)
Pinsker at Graetz **H14**

Journalist, demonstrated continuously on behalf of Zion and Jerusalem.

Smolenskin, Peretz (1840 – 1885)
Balfour – Keren HaYesod **H13**

One of the outstanding Hebrew authors of the Haskala and one of those who heralded Zionism as a national Jewish movement. An author, he was founder and editor of the literary journal *HaShahar*. His remains were brought to Jerusalem for burial.

Sokolow, Nahum (1859 – 1936)
Keren HaYesod – Jabotinsky **H13-14**

Author, one of the pioneers of Jewish journalism, a Zionist leader, chairman of all the Zionist Congresses from 1921 until his death (1936), president of the World Zionist Organization and its spokesman. He was the person who suggested the name "Tel-Aviv" for the new city (1903) and was made an Honorary Citizen of Tel-Aviv.

Wingate, Charles Orde [Square] (1903 – 1944)
Balfour at Marcus at Jabotinsky **H14**

British army officer who sympathized with Israel and fought on her behalf. He initiated the Special Night Squads of the Hagana in 1938 following the great Arab rebellion, and was called *HaYedid*, "the Friend". Various educational institutions named after him were established in Israel.

Ma'alot Dafna/Arzei HaBira

Name and establishment:

Laurel steps. This neighborhood, located in the northern part of the city, south of Sanhedria and Ramat Eshkol, was founded in 1972 and named for the laurel plant common in the area and for the topography of the area and the steps to climb to reach it. The Greeks and Romans used to crown the heads of their rulers and sports champions with laurel leaves.

The architects of the neighborhood were strict about the outer design of archways, angles and slanted lines. The neighborhood was built to include allotments of private areas for the residents and internal courtyards for pedestrians and children.

Boundaries:

North – Sanhedria and Ramat Eshkol
South – Beit Yisrael
East – Kiryat Aryeh and Sheikh Jarrah
West – HaBucharim

Sites: within its boundaries or nearby are the police academy, Ammunition Hill

Streets: the neighborhood streets are named for rabbis, builders of the Jewish community in the Land of Israel and for fighters who defended it in various periods.

The streets are:

Arzei HaBira Shim'on HaTzadik – Yehoyariv **I10**

Cedars of the capital, a designation for the rabbis of Jerusalem throughout history.

Ba'al Or Sameiah (1843 – 1926) Shim'on HaTzadik – dead end **I10**

(See the neighborhood of Kiryat Aryeh.)

Eretz Hefetz Hativat Harel – Shim'on HaTzadik **H-I10**

Desired land, named for the book by Rabbi Moshe Nehemia Kahanov (1817-1888), rabbi and arbiter of religious law, head of the *'Etz Haim* Yeshiva, builder of Jerusalem neighborhoods, promoter of general development in Jerusalem (see the neighborhood of Shikunei Shmuel HaNavi).

Eshkol, Levi [Boulevard] (1895 – 1969)
Bar Lev – Eretz Hefetz – Hativat Harel **I-J9**

(See the neighborhoods of Giv'at HaMivtar, Ramat Eshkol.)

Gargi, Matityahu, Rabbi [Square] (1845 – 1918)
Shim'on HaTzadik at Shmuel HaNavi **H10**

One of the great rabbis of the Afghan Jewish community and a leader of this community in Jerusalem, master of homiletics and a Kabbalist.

Hativat Harel Shmuel HaNavi – Ma'avar HaMitla – Eshkol **H10**

One of the PaLMa"H brigades that took part in the War of Independence (1948) in the Judean hills and Jerusalem (see the neighorhoods of Sanhedria, Shikunei Shmuel HaNavi).

Ma'alot Dafna Mikve Yisrael – Netter **I10**

Named for the neighborhood.

Mikve Yisrael Netter – Netter **I9-10**

Named for the first modern Jewish agricultural school in the Land of Israel, set up at the initiative of Ya'akov (Charles) Netter in 1869.

Netter, Ya'akov (Charles) (1826 – 1882)
Shim'on HaTzadik - Eshkol **I10**

(See the neighborhood of Kiryat Aryeh.)

Pituhei Hotam (1789 – 1886)
Shmuel HaNavi – Eretz Hefetz – dead end **H-I10**

Seals for engraving, named for Rabbi Yitzhak P.H. (Pituhei Hotam) Rosenthal, a founder of the Ashkenazic community in the Land of Israel and its representative to the government, one of the first printers in Jerusalem (see the neighborhood of Shikunei Shmuel HaNavi).

Shim'on HaTzadik Eretz Hefetz – Nablus Road **I10**

(See the neighborhoods of Kiryat Aryeh, Nahlat Shim'on.)

Shmuel HaNavi Shivtei Yisrael – Bar-Ilan **H10-I11**

(See the neighborhoods of Beit Yisrael, HaBucharim, Mahanayim, Nahlat Shim'on, Sanhedria, Shikunei Shmuel HaNavi.)

Tidhar, David (1897 – 1970)
Shmuel HaNavi – Shim'on HaTzadik **H-I10**

One of the first Jewish officers in the Jerusalem police force in the British

Mandate period, defended the Jews of the Old City in the War of Independence, wrote the encyclopedia of personalities of the Land of Israel: authors, rabbis and civic leaders.

Mahanayim

Name and establishment:

Two camps. This neighborhood, located in the northern part of the city south of Sanhedria HaMurhevet and north of Tel-Arza, was founded in 1926. Its name was taken from Genesis 32:3, "And Jacob said, 'This is God's encampment', and he called that place *Mahanayim*."

Some of the buildings in the neighborhood are built on the site of ancient graves from the Second Temple period. Among the residents are Jews from Yemen.

Boundaries:

North – Sanhedria HaMurhevet, Ramat Eshkol
South – Tel-Arza, HaBucharim
East – Sanhedria
West – 'Ezrat Torah

Sites: within its boundaries or nearby are the Sanhedria Cemetery, tombs of the Sanhedrin.

Streets: the streets of the neighborhood are named for rabbis.

The streets are:

Bar-Ilan (Berlin), Meir, Rabbi (1880 – 1949)
Shmuel HaNavi – Yirmiyahu **G-H10**

(See the neighborhoods of HaBucharim and Tel-Arza.)

Bek, Nissan, Rabbi (1815 – 1889) Shmuel HaNavi - Ohalei Yosef **H10**

A Jerusalem activist, one of the founders of the first Hasidic Kollel in Jerusalem, built the large *Tiferet Yisrael* Synagogue in the Old City, also named for him. One of the initiators of construction of Jewish neighborhoods outside the walls, one of the pioneers of Jewish agriculture in the Galilee.

Eli'ezrov, Shlomo Yehuda Leib, Rabbi (19th-20th cents.)
Ohalei Yosef – Bek **H10**

An Ashkenazic rabbi who worked hard on behalf of the Bucharan Jews in Jerusalem and traveled to Buchara to help the Jews there. An educator, rabbi of the Bucharan Jewish community in Jerusalem, founded educational institutions and ritual baths and took care of religious needs. Chief rabbi of Hebron.

Elifaz (HaTeimani) Shmuel HaNavi – Eli'ezrov **H10**

One of Job's friends in the Bible (Job 2:11).

Giv'at Moshe [Boulevard] Golda Meir – 'Ezrat Torah **G9-H10**

(See the neighborhood of 'Ezrat Torah.)

Hacham Shim'on, Rabbi (1843 – 1910) Bar-Ilan – Bar-Ilan **H10**

The spiritual leader of the Bucharan Jews, translated the Bible, prayers and religious poetry from Hebrew into Persian, a founder of the neighborhood of HaBucharim in Jerusalem.

Mahanayim Shmuel HaNavi – Eli'ezrov **H10**

Named for the neighborhood.

Ohalei Yosef Bar-Ilan – Giv'at Moshe **H10**

Named for the book by Elia Yosef, who founded a yeshiva at the direction of the leader of HaBa"D, Rabbi Menahem Mendel Shneerson (see the neighborhood of Tel-Arza).

Shmuel HaNavi Shivtei Yisrael – Golda Meir **H10-I11**

(See the neighborhoods of Beit Yisrael, HaBucharim, Ma'alot Dafna/ Arzei HaBira, Nahlat Shim'on, Sanhedria, Shikunei Shmuel HaNavi.)

Mahane Yehuda

Name and establishment:

Yehuda's Camp. This neighborhood, located in the northwestern part of the city north of Yafo Road, was founded in 1887 during the period of Turkish rule. Yosef Navon, the initiator of the Jerusalem-Jaffa railroad, purchased the land from its Arab owners and named the new neighborhood after his brother, Yehuda Navon, who had died in his youth.

The name "Mahane Yehuda" is connected today to the largest central open-air market in Jewish Jerusalem, but this name for the market actually comes from the neighborhood. The shops were built only in 1929, at the initiative of the committee for the Jerusalem community and its secretary, Shmuel Mosayoff, using loans from the *Halvaa veHisachon* (loan and savings) Bank. At first the market was called the "Savings and Loan Market".

The building of the neighborhood was the result of the great awakening that had begun among the Jews of the Old City, who wished to increase the growth of the city and the movement into neighborhoods outside the city walls, a process that had started in 1860.

Mahane Yehuda is primarily populated by Sephardic and Oriental Jews.

Boundaries:
North – Zichron Moshe, Mekor Baruch
South – Agrippas Street
East – King George Street and Mid-Town
West – Shazar Boulevard

Sites: within its boundaries or nearby are the Mahane Yehuda Market; the sundial synagogue, *Zoharei Hama* on Yafo Road, which has two clocks and a large sundial on its façade, the synagogue inside holding prayer services twenty-four hours a day; the *'Etz Haim* Yeshiva originally established in the Old City's Jewish Quarter; the Ministry of Health; police headquarters; the Alliance School; the Gur Hasidim *Sfat Emet* Yeshiva; *Binyan Klal* (the General Building); *Kikar HaHeirut* [Freedom Square], with the "Davidka".

Streets: the neighborhood streets are named for various fruits sold in the market. Other streets are named after dignitaries and civic leaders of Jerusalem's Sephardic community.

The streets are:

Agrippas (10 BCE – 44 CE) King George – Shmuel Baruch **G11-H12**

(See the neighborhoods of Even Yisrael, Mazkeret Moshe, Mid-Town, Mishkenot Yisrael, Nahlat Tzion, Ohel Moshe, Sukkat Shalom, Zichron Tuvia, Zichron Yosef.)

Alboher, Haim, Rabbi [Passageway] (1880 – 1938)
Yafo – Agrippas **H12**

(See the neighborhood of Even Yisrael.)

Alfandari, Shlomo El'azar, Rabbi (1826 – 1930)
Ben Matityahu – HaTurim **G11**

A Kabbalist and one of the great arbiters of religious law in the early years. He served as a rabbi in Tzfat, Jerusalem and other Middle Eastern communities (see the neighborhoods of Mekor Baruch, Ohel Shlomo, Ruhama).

'Alwan, Shabtai, Rabbi (1873 – 1941) Dinowitz – HaTurim **G11**

One of the rabbis of Jerusalem (see the neighborhood of Ohel Shlomo).

Avisar, David (1888 – 1963) Beit Ya'akov – Eliyahu Mani **G11**

Educator, principal of the Sephardic religious elementary school in the Old City, one of the activists in the labor movement and in the Oriental communities of Jerusalem.

Banai, Eliyahu Ya'akov (1874–1944) 'Etz Haim - Mahane Yehuda **G11**

As his name indicates, one of the builders of Jerusalem. Many of his descendants are actors and singers (the original name of the street was *Rehov HaAgas*, Pear Street).

Baruch, Shmuel, Rabbi (1898 – 1994) Ben-Zvi – Agrippas **F-G11**

(See the neighborhoods of Beit Ya'akov, Mid-Town, Sha'arei Tzedek, Shevet Tzedek/Shchunat HaPahim, Zichron Yosef.)

Baruch, Ya'akov, Rabbi [Square] (1900 – 1956)
Agrippas at 'Eliash **H12**

A writer and teacher. Secretary in the chief rabbinate.

Baruchof, Mashiah (1872 – 1946) Yafo – Agrippas H12

A founder of the Sephardic orphanage, dignitary of the Sephardic community (see Mid-Town).

Beit Ya'akov Yafo – Shmuel Baruch **G11-12**

(See the neighborhood of Beit Ya'akov.)

Ben Matityahu, Yosef (Josephus Flavius) (1st cent. BCE and CE)
Malchei Yisrael – Yafo **G11**

(See the neighborhoods of Ahva, Kerem/Beit Avraham, Ruhama, Yegiy'a Kapayim, Zichron Moshe.)

Cohen, Ya'akov [Square] (1908 – 1977) Agrippas at KY"H **G12**

One of the first members of Beitar and ETZe"L, one of the defenders of Jerusalem.

Dinowitz, Gittel (1879 – 1939) Yafo – Alfandari **G11**

A woman of valor. One of the protectors of the city within the walls of Jerusalem, she aided Jews who were imprisoned and especially the Hagana forces who fought to protect Jerusalem. She organized the provision of supplies for them (see the neighborhood of Ohel Shlomo).

'Etz Haim Yafo – Agrippas **G11-12**

Named for the *'Etz Haim* Yeshiva on this street.

Even Yisrael Yafo – Agrippas **H11**

(See the neighborhood of Even Yisrael.)

Gaon, Moshe David (1889 – 1958) Yehosef Schwartz – Meyuhas **G11**

(See the neighborhoods of Batei Kollel Horodna/Damesek Eli'ezer, Sha'arei Shalom.)

HaAfarsek 'Etz Haim – Mahane Yehuda **G12**

Peach, named for a sweet and juicy fruit sold in the market. First mentioned in the Talmud.

HaAgas 'Etz Haim – Mahane Yehuda **G11**

Pear, named for a sweet fruit sold in the market. First mentioned in the Talmud (the name of the street was changed to Banai Street).

Ha'Armonim Agrippas – HaEshkol **G12**

Chestnuts, named for a fruit tree whose fruits are sold in the market.

HaDekel Beit Ya'akov – Eliyahu Mani **G11-12**

Named for a palm tree, many of whose varieties are planted as fruit trees or ornamentals. Its fruit is sold in the market. *Dekel* is another name for *tamar*, date palm.

HaEgoz Agrippas – HaShaked **G11**

Nut, named for this fruit which has a hard shell and is sold in the market. Mentioned in the Song of Songs 6:11, "I went down into the nut garden..."

HaEshkol Mahane Yehuda – HaShikma **G12**

Cluster, named for the clusters of grapes sold in the market. Mentioned in the Biblical story of the spies, Numbers 13:23, "...they cut down a branch with one cluster of grapes..."

HaShaked 'Etz Haim – Mahane Yehuda **G12**

Almond, named for a tree whose fruits are sold in the market. Mentioned in

Genesis 43:11, "...take of the choice fruits of the land...nuts and almonds."

HaShazif 'Etz Haim – Mahane Yehuda **G12**

Plum, named for a fruit tree whose fruits are sold in the market.

HaShikma Beit Ya'akov – HaEshkol **G11-12**

Sycamore, named for a fruit tree (the Middle Eastern sycamore, related to the fig), whose fruits are sold in the market.

HaTapuah 'Etz Haim – Mahane Yehuda **G11**

Apple, named for a fruit tree whose fruits are sold in the market.

HaTut Mahane Yehuda – HaEgoz **G12**

Mulberry, named for a fruit tree whose fruits are sold in the market. The mulberry is mentioned in the Mishna among the fruit-bearing trees (Ma'asrot 1:2).

HeHaruv HaTut – HaShaked **G12**

Carob, named for a fruit tree that produces fruit all year round. Its fruits are sold in the market and are rich in sugars and protein.

King George (V) (1865 – 1935)
Yafo – Agrippas, ends at Keren HaYesod **H12-13**

British monarch. The Balfour Declaration was made during his reign (see the neighborhoods of Mid-Town, Rehavia).

Kol Yisrael Haverim (KY"H) Agrippas – Yafo **G12**

After the Alliance Israelite society founded in Paris in 1860 to protect the rights of Jews in the Middle East, Eastern Europe and North Africa. The name is from the Jerusalem Talmud and is in the Shabbat morning prayer following the Torah reading, "... may He redeem us speedily and gather in our dispersed brothers from the four corners of the earth; *all Israel are colleagues*, and let us say Amen." One of the founders was Yitzhak Adolphe Cremieux (see the German Colony). They set up schools throughout Israel, including in the Mahane Yehuda market.

Levi, Yitzhak 'Azaria [Square] (d. 1963) SHaDa"L at Valero **G11**

The leader of the neighborhood.

Mahane Yehuda Yafo – Agrippas **G11-12**

Named for the neighborhood.

Mani, Eliyahu, Rabbi (1818 – 1898) Yafo – Shmuel Baruch **G11**

A rabbi and Kabbalist. Chief rabbi of Hebron and builder of the Jewish community there. Also named for his son Malchiel Mani (1861-1933), a jurist.

Meyuhas, Yosef Baran (1868 – 1942) Yafo – David Yellin **G11**

(See the neighborhoods of Batei Kollel Horodna/Damesek Eli'ezer, Sha'arei Shalom.)

Navon, Yosef (1858 – 1934) Yafo – RaSH"I **G11**

He bought the land for Mahane Yehuda from its Arab owners and initiated the Jerusalem-Jaffa railroad line and the construction of the port of Jaffa. One of the activists of the Sephardic community in Jerusalem (see the neighborhood of Giv'at Hanania/Abu Tor).

Netiv Yitzhak Navon – dead end **G11**

Yitzhak's path. Rabbi Yitzhak Nahum Levi, a civic leader and one of the builders of Jerusalem (see the neighborhood of Ohel Shlomo).

RaSH"I (1040 – 1105)
Pines – HaTurim, ends at Hashmonaim **G11**

(See the neighborhoods of Kerem/Beit Avraham, Mekor Baruch, Ruhama, Sha'arei Yerushalayim, Zichron Moshe.)

Schwartz, Yehosef, Rabbi (1805 – 1866) Yafo – David Yellin **G11**

(See the neighborhoods of Batei Kollel Horodna/Damesek Eli'ezer, Sha'arei Shalom.)

Sfat Emet Ben Matityahu – Meyuhas **G11**

(See the neighborhoods of Batei Kollel Horodna/Damesek Eli'ezer, Ruhama, Sha'arei Shalom.)

Sha'arei Tzedek Yafo – Shmuel Baruch **G11**

Named for the neighborhood founded in 1890 and for the hospital of the same name, formerly located here (see the neighborhood of Sha'arei Tzedek).

SHaDa"L (Shmuel David Luzzato) (1800 – 1865)
Meyuhas – Valero **G11**

Historian, researcher of literature, poet, Biblical commentator. His books on Hebrew grammar and Aramaic grammar serve as the basis for research in these areas. He wrote hundreds of books and articles, including on the Jewish composer de Rossi.

Shazar, Shneur Zalman [Boulevard] (1889 – 1974)
Shmuel Baruch – Nordau, ends at Herzl Boulevard **F11**

(See the neighborhoods of Giv'at Ram, Romema.)

Valero, Haim (1845 – 1923) Yafo – Ben Matityahu **G11**

(See the neighborhoods of Batei Kollel Horodna/Damesek Eli'ezer, Ruhama, Sha'arei Shalom.)

Yafo Jaffa Gate – Weizmann Boulevard **F11-I12**

The street passes between the neighborhood and the market (see the neighborhoods of Batei Kollel Horodna/Damesek Eli'ezer, Batei Sa'idoff, Beit David/Beit HaRav Kook, Beit Ya'akov, Even Yisrael, 'Ezrat Yisrael, Mekor Baruch, Mid-Town, Nahlat Shiv'a, Ohel Shlomo, Romema, Russian Compound, Sha'arei Tzedek, Sha'arei Yerushalayim).

Yellin, David (1854 – 1942)
Meyuhas – Ben Matityahu, ends at Yesha'yahu **G-H11**

(See the neighborhoods of Batei Kollel Horodna/Damesek Eli'ezer, Ruhama, Sha'arei Shalom, Zichron Moshe.)

Mahane Yisrael/ Shchunat HaMa'aravim

Name and establishment:

This neighborhood, located in the middle of town on lower Agron Street opposite the Muslim cemetery in Mamilla, was founded in 1868 by members of the "Western community", Jews from countries west of the Land of Israel, in North Africa: Tunisia, Morocco and Algeria, and called "Yisrael's Camp". An additional name given to the neighborhood was the "Mamilla neighborhood", due to its proximity to the Mamilla Pool. This was the second neighborhood built outside the walls of the Old City.

With the *'aliya* of the Western community's rabbi, Rabbi **D**avid **b**en **Sh**im'on, called DVa"SH, the Western community withdrew from the committee for the Sephardic community. Among the important steps taken by David ben Shim'on and the leaders of the Western community was resolving the urgent need for housing by building this neighborhood.

The format of construction was characteristic of the period – the façades of the houses faced toward a single central courtyard, and the backs of the buildings formed a kind of wall surrounding the neighborhood and protecting it. The internal alleyways were short and narrow, and some were paved with small stones. Inside the neighborhood was a synagogue that was lit up even at night, as it was used as a study hall in shifts. Today, the area has completely changed, due to the addition of businesses, offices, workshops and institutions.

Boundaries:
North – the Mamilla cemetery and Russian Compound
South – Yemin Moshe
East – David's Village-Mamilla and the Old City
West – Mid-Town

Sites: within its boundaries or nearby are the Palace Hotel, completed in 1929 and today housing the Ministry of Industry and Trade, although recently a decision was made to turn the building back into a hotel and apartments; the Old City; the Jerusalem Municipality at Safra Square; David's Village-Mamilla; the Muslim cemetery in Mamilla.

Streets: the streets of the neighborhood are named for its Western residents, Lovers of Zion, and the founder of the neighborhood.

The streets are:

Agron, Gershon (1894 – 1959)
David HaMelech – Keren HaYesod **H13**

Journalist, founder of the first English-language newspaper in the Land of Israel, the "Palestine Post" (now The Jerusalem Post), Jerusalem's mayor 1955-1959 (see Mid-Town).

Ben Shim'on, David, Rabbi (1824 – 1880)
Agron – David HaMelech **H13**

Leader and rabbi of the Western community (Jews from North Africa) in Jerusalem, founder of the neighborhood (see Mid-Town).

David HaMelech Agron – 'Emek Refaim **H13-I14**

(See the neighborhoods of David's Village-Mamilla, Komemiyut/Talbieh, Mid-Town, Yemin Moshe.)

HaMa'aravim Agron – dead end **H13**

Westerners, named for the Jews who made *'aliya* from North Africa (west of Israel), settled in Jerusalem and built this neighborhood (see Mid-Town).

HaMechess [Square] David HaMelech at Agron **H13**

Customs, named for the customs offices nearby (see Mid-Town).

Hess, Moshe (1812 – 1875) David HaMelech – Lincoln **H13**

One of the first advocates of the Return to Zion in the nineteenth century and an advocate for revival of a Jewish state in the Land of Israel (see Mid-Town).

Zamenhof, Eli'ezer (1859 – 1917) Agron – Hess **H13**

A doctor, one of the early Lovers of Zion in Russia (see Mid-Town).

Maimon (Shchunat HaPo'el HaMizrahi)

Name and establishment:

This neighborhood, located in the western part of the city near Kiryat Moshe, was founded in 1937 and named for Rabbi Yehuda Leib HaCohen Maimon (Fishman). The land was purchased by *HaKeren HaKayemet LeYisrael* and turned over to a nucleus (*gar'in*) of pioneers from the *Po'el Mizrahi*, the religious labor movement, who wanted to build an urban neighborhood in Jerusalem. In the beginning, the neighborhood was called *HaPo'el HaMizrahi*, but after the establishment of the State, it was changed to *Maimon*, the name of the man who was then serving as the first minister of religions of the State of Israel. He was the first resident to build his house in the neighborhood.

Today the neighborhood has been combined with the adjoining Kiryat Moshe neighborhood.

Boundaries: see the neighborhood of Kiryat Moshe.

Sites: see the neighborhood of Kiryat Moshe.

Streets: see the neighborhood of Kiryat Moshe.

The streets are:

Ben Tzion, Shim'on Shmuel (1894 - 1954)
Degel Reuven – Ba'al HaSheiltot **E11**

(See the neighborhoods of Giv'at Shaul, Kiryat Moshe.)

Degel Reuven Ben Dor – Maimon – Ben Tzion **E11**

(See the neighborhood of Kiryat Moshe.)

Herzl Boulevard Shazar Boulevard – HaPisga **F11-D13**

(See the neighborhoods of Bayit VaGan, Beit HaKerem, Kiryat Moshe, Yefei Nof.)

Maimon, Yehuda Leib HaCohen [Fishman], Rabbi (1875 – 1962)
Degel Reuven – Herzl Boulevard **E-F11**

(See the neighborhood of Kiryat Moshe.)

Manhat/Malha

Name and establishment:

This neighborhood, located in the southwestern part of the city between the neighborhoods of Kiryat HaYovel and Gonenim/Katamonim, was established as a Jewish neighborhood in 1949 in an area where there was an Arab village. It is positioned on a ridge continuing past the Arab village of Malha that was defeated by forces of ETZe"L. In the grueling battle, eighteen fighters fell, and in their memory a monument was set up on nearby Golomb Street with the names of the eighteen fighters.

In those same early days after the War of Independence, Bayit VaGan was the nearest neighborhood, and a path led from it to Manhat/Malha. Years later, other new neighborhoods rose around it ('Ir Ganim, Giv'at Massua, Ramat Sharett, Ramat Denya), and Golomb Street was paved from the Rehavia Valley to the Kiryat HaYovel neighborhood, thus relieving Manhat/Malha of its isolation.

Its first residents were immigrants from Kurdistan, Tunisia and Morocco. In Manhat/Malha and the surrounding area were discovered burial caves from the periods of the First and Second Holy Temples, cisterns, mosaic floors, and many pottery fragments.

Today the area serves as a center of commerce, leisure activities and sports.

Boundaries:

North – Ramat Sharett, Ramat Denya

South – the new railroad station for the Tel-Aviv line and Gilo
East – Gonenim/Katamonim
West – Kiryat HaYovel

Sites: within its boundaries or nearby are the Jerusalem (Malha) Mall, the Biblical Zoo, Teddy Stadium, the railroad station for the Tel-Aviv line, the technological park for hi-tech industries, Soldier's House.

Streets: the streets of the neighborhood are named for animals, sports teams, rabbis and immigrant ships.

The streets are:

Agudat Sport Beitar [Road] Golomb – Moda'i **D16-17**

Named for the Beitar sports association.

Agudat Sport HaPo'el [Road] Agudat Sport Beitar – Moda'i **D17**

Named for the HaPo'el sports association.

Agudat Sport Maccabi [Road] Agudat Sport Beitar – Agudat Sport HaPo'el **D17**

Named for the Maccabi sports association.

'Amasa Golomb – Patria **C-D16**

One of King David's warriors killed by Joab ben Tzruya, the commander of King David's army.

'Arad HaAyal – dead end **C-D17**

A Jewish town in the northern Negev.

Ayalon, David (1917 – 1983) Agudat Sport Beitar – dead end **D-E17**

One of those who laid the groundwork for popular and competitive sports in Jerusalem.

Benvenisti, David [Road] (1897 – 1993) Moda'i – Dov Yosef **D-E17**

Author, guide, teacher, member of the committee to name the Jerusalem streets, he was a fighter in the Jewish Battalion during World War I, published books and articles on knowledge of the Land of Israel, among them guidebooks to Jerusalem. *Yakir Yerushalayim*.

Derech Gan HaHayot Golomb – Kolitz **C16-17**

Zoo, named for the nearby Biblical Zoo.

Golomb, Eliyahu (1893 – 1945) Pat – Tahon **C15-E16**

(See the neighborhoods of Gonenim/Katamonim Het, Tet, Holyland

Park, Kiryat HaYovel, Ramat Denya, Ramat Sharett.)

HaAyal Agudat Sport HaPo'el – HaDishon **C-D17**

Buck, an animal mentioned in the Torah in a list of kosher animals (Deuteronomy 14:5).

Hacham Avraham (1900 – 1991) Kolitz – Kedoshei Struma **C-D16**

Rabbi Avraham ben Menahem, one of the sages of Kurdistan Jewry and one of the organizers of the *'aliya* of Kurdish Jews to Israel, a founder of the Manhat/Malha neighborhood in Jerusalem.

HaDishon HaNamer – Kala'i **C17**

Antelope, an animal mentioned in the Torah in a list of kosher animals (Deuteronomy 14:5).

HaDov HaKfir – dead end **D17**

Bear, a large predatory animal.

HaHa"I [Square] Golomb at Moshe Sharett **D16**

Eighteen, named for the eighteen ETZe"L fighters who fell in battle in the area of Malha (Manhat) village in the War of Independence (see the neighborhood of Ramat Sharett).

HaKfir HaAyal – HaAyal **D17**

Lion cub, a word meaning the same as young lion.

HaNamer HaShu'al – HaDishon **C17**

Leopard or tiger, a predatory animal of the cat family.

HaShu'al Kolitz – HaDishon **C16**

Fox, a nocturnal animal, it goes out at night to hunt its prey.

HaYa'en HaAyal – dead end **C17**

Ostrich, the largest bird in existence on earth in modern times.

Kala'i, Hanoch (1900 – 1979) Patria – dead end **C17**

A member of the command of ETZe"L before the establishment of the State. A lecturer in Hebrew language at the Hebrew University, he was an editor of Mosad Bialik publications, and a member of the Academy of the Hebrew Language, responsible for the proper use of Hebrew on radio and television.

Kedoshei Struma Yetziat Eropa – Patria – dead end **C16-17**

In memory of the Holocaust refugees who set sail in 1942 on the ship "Struma" but failed to reach Israel. When the ship foundered off the coast of Turkey, the passengers were not allowed to disembark nor were they allowed to make repairs, and the ship was blown up with all passengers on board. There was only one survivor.

Kolitz, Haim [Road] (1919 – 1993) Golomb – Tzur – dead end **A-B17**

(See the neighborhoods of Giv'at Massua, Kiryat HaYovel.)

Moda'i, Yitzhak [Road] (1926 – 1998)
Agudat Sport Beitar – Derech Shulov **C18-D17**

An Israeli government minister. He served in many public posts and in particular as the treasury minister who brought stability to Israel's economy.

Nuriel, Z., HaRav [Steps] (1889 – 1967) Golomb – Yetziat Eropa **D16**

One of the rabbis of Kurdistan Jewry and one of its civic leaders.

Patria 'Amasa – Kedoshei Struma **C-D16**

Named for a boat of Jewish refugees that reached Israel's coast during World War II, was seized by the British and brought to Haifa harbor. The refugees were to be sent to Mauritius, an island off the southeast coast of Africa where Holocaust survivors were interned, but the ship blew up and sank, and 260 of the refugees on board were killed.

Rekem HaAyal – dead end **D16-17**

One of the tribe of Benjamin in the Bible.

Shlomo Nehemia [Square] (1937 – 1994)
HaAyal at HaNamer at HaDishon **C17**

One of the builders of Jerusalem, was a partner in the building of many projects in the city, such as the Mormon University and Mount Zion Hotel.

Shulov, Aharon [Road] (1907 – 1997) Kolitz – Moda'i **C17-18**

The founder and director of the Biblical Zoo. He was one of the first zoologists of the Hebrew University and continued in his research and academic work throughout his years at the zoo.

Yetziat Eropa Kedoshei Struma – dead end **D16**

After the name of a ship of immigrants, Holocaust survivors, that was stopped in 1947 by the British when it reached the coast of Israel and, following a battle, was turned back to the coast of France and from there to Germany. The ship is known by its name in other languages, "Exodus".

Yovav HaAyal – dead end **D16-17**

A descendant of Benjamin in the Bible.

Mazkeret Moshe

Name and establishment:

This neighborhood, located in the center of town south of Mahane Yehuda and east of Ohel Moshe, was founded in 1883 and named after Sir Moses Montefiore, one of the leaders of the Jewish community in England and one of the pre-eminent philanthropists of the nineteenth century. Mazkeret Moshe, a neighborhood for Ashkenazic Jews, Lithuanians and people from the Old City, and Ohel Moshe for the Sephardic community, were the first two of the six neighborhoods eventually named after Sir Moses Montefiore. (The other four are Bnei Moshe/Neve Shalom, Yemin Moshe, Zichron Moshe, Kiryat Moshe.) At the time of their founding, these two neighborhoods were considered luxury areas, in which people from the highest economic levels lived.

The construction of these two neighborhoods was made possible thanks to the support of the "Mazkeret Moshe" Fund, named in honor of Sir Moses, for the purpose of expanding the Jerusalem neighborhoods. Each of the two neighborhoods is built in the shape of a square – the houses arranged in adjoining rows around one central courtyard, toward which the facades of the houses face. The back side of each house faces outward, and together the houses form a kind of protective wall for the neighborhood. The central courtyard serves public purposes: cisterns, a bakery, a mikve, synagogues and a religious school.

Above the entrance gate of each neighborhood, on Agrippas Street, is fixed a plaque on which are inscribed the name of the neighborhood and words of gratitude to Sir Moses.

Boundaries:

North – Agrippas Street and the Mahane Yehuda Market

South – Knesset Yisrael

East – Mishkenot Yisrael

West – Ohel Moshe

Sites: within its boundaries or nearby are the Mahane Yehuda Market, the *Yismah Moshe* Synagogue on 'Einayim LaMishpat Street, two giant eucalyptus trees planted when the neighborhood was founded.

Streets: the neighborhood streets are named after rabbis and famous mountains in Israel.

The streets are:

Agrippas (10 BCE – 44 CE) King George – Shmuel Baruch **G11-H12**

(See the neighborhoods of Even Yisrael, Mahane Yehuda, Mid-Town, Mishkenot Yisrael, Nahlat Tzion, Ohel Moshe, Sukkat Shalom, Zichron Tuvia, Zichron Yosef.)

'Einayim LaMishpat HaCarmel – Rabbi Aryeh **G12**

A book of citations on the RaMBa"M's works, by Rabbi Yitzhak Arieli (1896-1974). He was one of the heads of the *Mercaz HaRav* (Kook) Yeshiva. Recipient of the Israel Prize.

HaCarmel Shomron – Zichron Tuvia **G12**

A well-known mountain in the city of Haifa and to its south, along the Mediterranean shore (see the neighborhood of Ohel Moshe).

HaLevanon HaNeTZI"V – Rama **G12**

(See the neighborhoods of Batei Kollel Munkacs, Knesset Yisrael.)

HaNeTZI"V (1817 – 1893) Betzalel – Tavor **G12**

(See the neighborhoods of Batei Broyde/Ohalei Ya'akov, Batei Kollel Minsk/Beit HaLevi, Batei Kollel Munkacs, Batei Rand, Knesset Yisrael.)

Mazkeret Moshe Agrippas – Tavor **G12**

Named for the neighborhood.

Rabbi Aryeh (Levin) (1885 – 1969) Shomron – Ohel Moshe **G12**

The prisoners' rabbi, who supported the families of the prisoners and encouraged them during the period of the British Mandate (see the neighborhood of Mishkenot Yisrael).

Shirizli, Shlomo Yisrael, Rabbi (1878 – 1938)
HaCarmel – Rabbi Aryeh **G12**

Author, editor, and the indispensable assistant of Eli'ezer Ben Yehuda, he published a calendar called "**Shayish**" (from the initials of his name). He lived in this neighborhood, on this street. One of the most respected of the Sephardic Jews (see the neighborhood of Ohel Moshe).

Tavor Shomron – ‘Ezra Refael **G12**

(See the neighborhoods of Batei Broyde/Ohalei Ya‘akov, Batei Rand, Knesset Yisrael, Ohel Moshe.)

Mea She‘arim

Name and establishment:

The Mea She‘arim Society was founded on Rosh Hodesh Kislev 5635 (1874). Mea She‘arim was the fifth Jewish neighborhood built outside the walls of the Old City and the first in the area in which it is located. The current name of the neighborhood (the original name was Rehovot, but over the years has been forgotten) was taken from the Torah portion *Toldot*, which was read during the week that the society was founded: “And Isaac sowed in that land and the return in that year was a hundredfold (*mea she‘arim*)” (Genesis 26:12). The founders saw in Isaac’s success, described in this verse, a good omen for their own success. Second, the neighborhood’s founders, residents of the Old City, saw in the building of this neighborhood a kind of symbol of their aspiration to gradually build a large amount of new housing outside the walls for the members of the Old Yishuv. Third, the name Mea She‘arim was an allusion to the number of units the founders wished to put up, one hundred, yet the number actually grew in the end to one hundred forty. And fourth, the name was also an indication of the number of gates that were eventually to be built around the neighborhood, although the number of gates built in reality totals only six.

The land for the building of the neighborhood was purchased from the Arabs of the village of Lifta, who were the owners. Six months after the establishment of the society, in the month of Iyar 5635 (1875), the cornerstone for the neighborhood’s first house was laid, and on Hanuka of 5636 (1875), the construction of the first ten houses was completed. The construction of the neighborhood according to the original plan was completed in 1881.

The guiding principle in the planning of the construction for this neighborhood was to build the houses in the shape of a closed square, which could be defended at the six gates, and that one could identify his house and his street to others only by the gate closest to it. This was because streets were not named in those days. In the center of the enclosed area, space was allocated for cisterns, a synagogue, a study hall and a public garden. The gates, locked every night, were:

On the west – the "Lifta Gate", the main gate on Baharan Street, faced toward the village of that name (today the Geula neighborhood is on that side), also called the "Shlomo Schuster Gate", named for the shoemaker ("schuster") of that name who lived in the neighborhood. It was also called "Raitza's Gate", after a woman manager of a synagogue, named Raitza, who lived there.

On the south – the "Millstone Gate", in the southwest corner at the corner of Honi HaMe'agel Street. In the distant past, a flour mill operated in the area and later a baker named Berman from Odessa built his bakery there, and so the gate was also called the "Odessa Gate."

"The Intermediate Gate" – the middle gate on the south side, at the corner of Bleicher Street, facing the Ethiopian neighborhood.

"Beit David Gate" – gate at the southeastern corner, where it meets Oneg Shabbat Street. The gate faces toward the Beit David neighborhood. The gate's archway was destroyed.

On the east – the "Jerusalem Gate", on Salant Street, facing toward the Old City.

On the north – the "Middle Gate", on Mea She'arim Street, facing toward Batei Kollel Ungarin/Nahlat Zvi. It was also called "Muhammed's Gate" after the Arab watchman who guarded the neighborhood in the early years, whose room was built into the wall of the gate.

Boundaries:

North – Batei Kollel Ungarin/Nahlat Zvi, Batei Naitin, Mea She'arim Street

South – Salant Street

East – Shivtei Yisrael Street

West – Hayei Adam and Bnei Brit Streets

Sites: within its boundaries or nearby are the Mea She'arim market, the *Mea She'arim* Yeshiva, yeshiva elementary schools, study halls and synagogues. Each group and each community has its own synagogue and study hall. The neighborhood today is characterized by its mix of ultra-Orthodox populations.

Streets: the neighborhood streets have names that reflect the life experience of its residents: names of Torah scholars and of well-known books of rabbinic literature.

The streets are:

Avraham MiSlonim (1884 – 1933) Salant – Baharan **H-I11**

Rabbi Avraham Weinberg, a Hasidic master, the rabbi of the Lithuanian Hasidim in Poland and the Land of Israel. Founded the *Beit Avraham* Yeshiva in Jerusalem.

Ba'al HaTanya (1745 – 1813) 'Ein Ya'akov – Hevrat Shas **I11**

Named for Rabbi Shneur Zalman of Lyady, founder of the Hasidic movement of HaBa"D (**H**ochma, **B**ina and **D**a'at – wisdom, understanding and knowledge). The book *Tanya* (1796) serves as the basic book of religious law for the HaBa"D Hasidic movement.

Baharan, Shlomo Zalman, Rabbi (1838 – 1910)
Mea She'arim – Salant **H11**

(See the neighborhoods of Batei Werner/Ohalei Moshe, Bnei Moshe/Neve Shalom.)

Bleicher Hevrat Shas – Yeshu'at Ya'akov **H-I11**

A designation for Rabbi Nahum Auerbach (1876-1942), who was a tinsmith ("bleicher") by trade. He lived during the period of the British Mandate. He was energetic in his endeavors on behalf of the community and the poor, and encouraged others to do the same.

Chasanowich, Joseph (1844 – 1919) Bnei Brit – Ethiopia **H11**

One of the early of the Lovers of Zion, a doctor and founder of the National and University Library in Jerusalem.

Dvora HaNevia (11th cent. BCE) HaNeviim – Salant **I12**

(See the neighborhood of Batei Perlman/'Ir Shalom.)

'Ein Ya'akov (16th cent.) Baharan – Salant **H-I11**

Named for a book containing selections from Talmud, RaSH"I's commentaries and innovations of contemporary sages concerning religious law, by Rabbi Ya'akov ibn Haviv (16th cent.).

Hachnasat Orhim 'Ein Ya'akov – Hevrat Shas **I11**

Hospitality, named for the guest hospice that was on this street.

HaMasger Baharan – dead end **H11**

Locksmith, in honor of the locksmith and metal workshops on this street.

HaMelacha Baharan – dead end **H11**

Named in honor of the various crafts workshops for metalwork and woodwork on this street.

HaRakah (15th cent.) Baharan – Salant **H11**

Named for Rabbi Eli'ezer bar Yehuda HaRakah, one of the great teachers of ethics. Aside from that, on this street there are shops selling spices and pharmaceutical items (*rokeah* is Hebrew for pharmacist).

HeHarash Baharan – dead end **H11**

The artisan, in honor of the artisans, craftsmen in iron and wood, who worked on this street.

Hevrat Mishnayot Hevrat Shas – 'Ein Ya'akov **I11**

In honor of those who regularly learn Mishna.

Hevrat Shas 'Oneg Shabbat – Honi HaMe'agel **H-I11**

In honor of those who learn Talmud/Shas (the six orders of the Mishna).

Hevrat Tehillim 'Ein Ya'akov – Hevrat Shas **H11**

In honor of those who regularly repeat Psalms.

Honi HaMe'agel (1st cent. BCE)
'Ein Ya'akov – Avraham MiSlonim **H11**

Named for a miracle-worker in the Second Temple period, who was outstanding for his ability to bring on rain. In years of drought, he would draw a circle around himself on the ground and declare that he would not step out of the circle until the rains came down, and rain did come down, as he had stipulated.

Horowitz, Yosef Gershon, Rabbi (1869 – 1951)
Admon – Dvora HaNevia **I11**

He was head of the first religious council in Jerusalem. A rabbi and religious judge in Jerusalem, head of the *Mea She'arim* Yeshiva. One of the founders of the religious Zionist *Mizrahi* movement.

Huminer, Shmuel MiBarezhin, Rabbi (1843 – 1907)
'Ein Ya'akov – Yeshu'at Ya'akov **I11**

One of the founders of the neighborhood, one of the important civic leaders of Jerusalem, one of the founders of the Beit Ya'akov neighborhood and of the Diskin Orphans Home in Giv'at Shaul, one of the founders of the community of Petah Tikva.

Joffen, Avraham, Rabbi (1886 – 1970)
Avraham MiSlonim – HeHarash **H11**

One of the great rabbis of Russia and of the *Musar* (ethics) movement.

Mea She'arim Straus – Shivtei Yisrael **H11**

(See the neighborhoods of Batei Kollel Ungarin/Nahlat Zvi, Batei Kollel Warsaw/Nahlat Ya'akov, Batei Naitin, Batei Perlman/'Ir Shalom, Beit Yisrael, Geula, Nahlat Zvi/Shchunat HaTeimanim, Sha'arei Pina.)

Nahum Ish Gamzu (beginning of 2nd cent. CE)
'Ein Ya'akov – Hevrat Shas **H11**

A native of the town of Gamzu. Also, he used to see everything in a positive light and say about whatever happened: "*Gam zu* letova - This, too, is for good", hence the name.

'Oneg Shabbat 'Ein Ya'akov – Hevrat Shas **I11**

A mark of the festive observance customarily held on Friday evening, the start of Shabbat.

Rosenthal, Avraham (1875 – 1938) Baharan – dead end **H11**

One of the founders of modern medicine in the Land of Israel, he was a doctor in Jerusalem and was killed on the way to the capital while carrying out his medical duties.

Salant, Shmuel, Rabbi (1816 – 1909)
Mea She'arim – Baharan **H11-I11**

One of those who laid the groundwork for the Ashkenazic community in Jerusalem, one of the great rabbis and arbiters of religious law in the city, a founder and head of the *'Etz Haim* Yeshiva.

Shivtei Yisrael Heil HaHandasa – HaTzanhanim **I12**

(See the neighborhoods of Batei Kollel Ungarin/Nahlat Zvi, Morasha/Musrara, Russian Compound.)

Yeshu'at Ya'akov Hevrat Tehillim – Hevrat Mishnayot **H-I11**

Named for the first synagogue built after the construction of the first twenty houses in the neighborhood, in 1875. The name is also that of the first study hall in the neighborhood.

Mekor Baruch

Name and establishment:

This neighborhood, located in the center of town opposite the former site of Sha'arei Tzedek Hospital and north of Mahane Yehuda and the Mahane Yehuda Market, was founded in 1924, and named for Rabbi Baruch Hirschenoff (also called Aharonoff), an activist from the United States. The named is also taken from Proverbs 5:18, "May your fountain [*mekor*] be blessed [*baruch*]..." The builders of the neighborhood and those who joined them later were of the educated middle class: teachers, merchants, clerks and artisans.

When founded, the neighborhood was considered to be modern and progressive both in its physical appearance and in the level of education and culture of its residents. Today, one of the largest centers of industry is located in this neighborhood, and many printing businesses.

The earliest residents were Ashkenazim, Sephardim and Oriental Jews, a mixed population. Today, the majority of the residents are members of the ultra-Orthodox community.

Boundaries:

Northwest – Romema, the Schneller Camp

South – Mahane Yehuda and the Mahane Yehuda Market, Sha'arei Tzedek

East – Kerem/Beit Avraham, Zichron Moshe

Sites: within its boundaries or nearby are the Tahkemoni School, Katznelson School, Policeman's House, Schneller Camp, Mahane Yehuda Market.

Streets: the streets of the neighborhood are named for the Maccabees and commentators on religious texts.

The streets are:

Alfandari, Shlomo El'azar, Rabbi (1826 – 1930)
Ben Matityahu – HaTurim **G11**

(See the neighborhoods of Mahane Yehuda, Ohel Shlomo, Ruhama.)

Bar Giora Tahkemoni – Yehuda HaMacabi **G11**

One of the leaders of the Zealots and an initiator of the great rebellion against the Romans at the end of the Second Temple period.

della Rosa, Haim, Rabbi [Square] (d. 1786) Yafo at Gesher HaHaim **G11**

Kabbalist, author of the book *Torat Hacham* (Torah of the wise).

El'azar HaMacabi HaHashmonaim – Malchei Yisrael **G11**

One of the sons of Mattathias the Hasmonean. He fought against the Greeks at Beit Zecharia in the Hebron hills.

Gesher HaHaim Yafo – HaHashmonaim **G11**

Named for the book by Rabbi Yehiel Michel Tikochinsky (1872-1955), rabbi and activist, who supported the establishment of new neighborhoods in Jerusalem, wrote the guide of religious laws and customs in effect in Israel, one of the heads of the *'Etz Haim* Yeshiva (see the neighborhood of Sha'arei Yerushalayim).

HaHashmonaim HaTurim – Sarei Yisrael **G11**

Hasmoneans, a family of heroes, kings and priests in the Second Temple period, who liberated the Land of Israel from Greek rule, and went on to rule over Israel for a century and a half during the Second Temple period.

HaTurim Malchei Yisrael – Yafo **G11**

Named for a book containing all the religious laws, judgments and customs of the Jewish people, by Rabbi Ya'akov ben Asher (1270-1340). One of the great arbiters of religious law in the Middle Ages (see the neighborhood of Sha'arei Yerushalayim).

HaZayit Tahkemoni – HaTurim **G11**

Olive, a long-lived, green fruit tree. One of the seven species for which the Land of Israel is praised. Oil is produced from olives.

Kav VeNaki Sarei Yisrael – HaHashmonaim **G11**

Named for Rabbi Eli'ezer ben Ya'akov, a Tanna who lived in the Second Temple period. Of his Torah teaching it was said, "Kav veNaki", brief and to the point.

Malchei Yisrael Sarei Yisrael – Straus **G-H11**

(See the neighborhoods of Ahva, Geula, Kerem/Beit Avraham, Kerem Avraham.)

Ohel Shlomo Dinowitz – HaTurim **G11**

Named for the nearby neighborhood.

RaSHBa"M (12th cent.) RaSH"I – Bar Giora **G11**

Acronym for **R**abbi **Sh**lomo **b**en **M**eir, grandson of RaSH"I, one of the great rabbis of his generation, one of the great Torah and Talmud commentators in France, one of the masters of the Tosafot.

RaSH"I (1040 – 1105)
HaHashmonaim – Tahkemoni, ends at Pines **G11**

(See the neighborhoods of Kerem/Beit Avraham, Mahane Yehuda, Ruhama, Sha'arei Yerushalayim, Zichron Moshe.)

Sarei Yisrael Yafo – Malchei Yisrael **F-G11**

Named for the princes and ministers of Israel throughout history (see the neighborhood of Romema).

Shim'on HaMacabi HaHashmonaim – dead end **G11**

One of the sons of Mattathias the Hasmonean, president and high priest, who expanded the borders of Israel in the war against the Greeks. He established the groundwork for the fleet of ships off the coast of Jaffa.

Tahkemoni Malchei Yisrael – David Yellin **G11**

(See the neighborhood of Kerem/Beit Avraham.)

TaSHBe"TZ Yafo – RaSH"I **G11**

Acronym for **T**eshuvot **Sh**im'on **b**en **Tz**emah. Named for the book of questions and responsa by Rabbi Shim'on ben Tzemah Duran (1361-1444), one of the great arbiters of Jewish law of North African Jewry, philosopher, doctor, Kabbalist (see the neighborhood of Sha'arei Yerushalayim).

Yafo Jaffa Gate – Weizmann Boulevard **F11-I12**

(See the neighborhoods of Batei Kollel Horodna/Damesek Eli'ezer, Batei Sa'idoff, Beit David/Beit HaRav Kook, Beit Ya'akov, Even Yisrael, 'Ezrat Yisrael, Mahane Yehuda, Mid-Town, Nahlat Shiv'a, Ohel Shlomo, Romema, Russian Compound, Sha'arei Tzedek, Sha'arei Yerushalayim).

Yehuda HaMacabi RaSH"I – HaHashmonaim **G11**

Judah Maccabee, one of the sons of Mattathias the Hasmonean. Commander and fighter against the Syrian-Greeks, re-dedicated the Second Holy Temple in Jerusalem in 165 BCE and established the festival of Hanuka for future generations.

Yosef Nasi, Don (1524 – 1579) Bar Giora – RaSH"I **G12**

Statesman, of a Marrano (Jews forced to convert to Christianity by the Spanish Inquisition) family that returned to Judaism. He and his mother-in-law, Doña Gracia de Mendes, together initiated the building up of Tiberias and the villages around it. He built the walls of Tiberias in 1564/5.

Mekor Haim

This neighborhood, located in the southern part of the city west of Geulim/Bak'a, was founded in 1925 and named for the philanthropist Haim Cohen. A few years before World War I, he donated money to the Lovers of Zion society to buy land near Jerusalem on which to build a neighborhood for Jews who kept the laws of Torah and Jewish tradition. The Lovers of Zion society disbanded after the war and the properties it owned were transferred to *HaKeren HaKayemet LeYisrael* (the Jewish National Fund), and this property was also turned over to the JNF, which laid the foundations for the first houses in the neighborhood. Its first residents were middle class: merchants, clerks and a building contractor.

During the War of Independence, this neighborhood stood on the battle front. Only the young stayed in the area, and their participation alongside the Hagana fighters sent to defend the neighborhood bravely repulsed the enemy, but the neighborhood was besieged and cut off. Mekor Haim became a symbol for the steadfastness and bravery of the Jewish community. Its liberation accompanied the Israeli conquest of the surrounding neighborhoods: Bak'a, Beit Safafa, Katamon and the German and Greek Colonies. After the Six Day War, the Talpiot Industrial Zone developed in the southern part of Mekor Haim. Alongside the neighborhood runs the Jerusalem-Tel-Aviv railroad line from that period.

Mekor Haim is one of six garden neighborhoods built in the early twentieth century (see the neighborhoods of Bayit VaGan, Beit HaKerem, Kiryat Moshe, Rehavia, Talpiot).

Boundaries:
North – the Greek Colony
South – Talpiot-Industrial Zone
East – Geulim/Bak'a
West – the railroad line and Gonenim/Katamonim

Sites: within its boundaries or nearby are the old railroad line, the industrial area of Talpiot, the Reform temple/community center *Kol HaNeshama*.

Streets: the neighborhood streets are named for builders of the State.

The streets are:

Avital Tzeret – dead end **G17**

One of King David's wives (II Samuel 3:4).

Ben Dov, Ya'akov (1882 – 1968) Pierre Koenig – dead end **G16**

Photographic artist, activist in the labor movement in Jerusalem and a founder of Talpiot.

Betesh, Shim'on, Dr. (1906 – 1975) Pierre Koenig – dead end **G16**

Doctor, director-general of Israel's Ministry of Health.

HaMusachim HaParsa – Tzeret **G17**

Auto body shops. Named for the automobile repair shops on this street.

HaRakevet [Road] Derech Beit Lehem – Pierre Koenig **H15-16**

(See the neighborhoods of the German Colony/RaMBa"M, Geulim/Bak'a, the Greek Colony.)

Harchavim Betesh – Tzeret **G16-17**

Members of a family who lived during the First Temple period.

Mekor Haim Pierre Koenig – Tzeret – dead end **G16**

Named for the neighborhood.

Pierre Koenig, General (b.1898) 'Emek Refaim – HaTenufa **G16-17**

French military commander, chairman of the "Israel-France Friendship" association (see the neighborhood of Talpiot-Industrial Zone).

Tzeret Pierre Koenig – Mekor Haim – dead end **G17**

Named for hot springs on the eastern shore of the Dead Sea.

Merhavia

Name and establishment:

This neighborhood, located in the middle of town near Kiryat Shmuel, was founded in 1938. The name of the neighborhood symbolizes the state of the Jewish community in that period, in spite of difficult circumstances. During that time there were murderous attacks on the Jewish communities in Israel, and despite that the Jews were able to overcome the difficulties posed and move out of the old crowded cities and establish new neighborhoods in more open areas, as is written in Psalms 118:5, "From the straits I cried out to God, and he answered me with His broad spaces," hence the name. Land was bought for this neighborhood from the Greek Orthodox Church. Today it is part of Kiryat Shmuel.

Boundaries:
North – Rehavia
South – Kiryat Shmuel
East – Komemiyut/Talbieh
West – Neve Granot

Sites: within its boundaries or nearby are the President's Residence, Jerusalem Theater, the Yad Meir Museum for Islamic Art.

Streets: the neighborhood streets are named for rabbis and for an author-journalist.

The streets are:

Ben AV"I, Itamar (1882-1943) Harlap – HaNasi **G14**

(See the neighborhood of Kiryat Shmuel.)

HaAR"I (1534 – 1572) HaNasi – Harlap, ends at 'Aza **G14**

(See the neighborhood of Kiryat Shmuel.)

HaNasi Jabotinsky – HaPaLMa"H at Chopin **G-H14**

(See the neighborhood of Kiryat Shmuel.)

HaPaLMa"H HaNasi – Fichmann **G14-15**

(See the neighborhoods of Gonen/Katamon HaYeshana, Kiryat Shmuel.)

Harlap, Ya'akov Asher, Rabbi (1883 – 1951)
HaAR"I – HaPaLMa"H **G14**

(See the neighborhood of Kiryat Shmuel.)

Shneurson, Menahem [Square] (1885 – 1960)
Ben AV"I at HaNasi **G14**

(See the neighborhood of Kiryat Shmuel.)

Mid-Town

This area stretches from the heart of the city, surrounded in all directions by smaller neighborhoods more than a hundred years old, with the Mahane Yehuda Market at the center (see the boundaries of this area). The Mid-Town area includes the following neighborhoods: Batei Broyde/Ohalei Ya'akov, Batei Goral/ Mishkenot HaTeimanim, Batei Kollel Horodna/Damesek Eli'ezer, Batei Kollel Minsk/Beit HaLevi, Batei Kollel Munkacs, Batei Rand, Batei Sa'idoff, Beit Ya'akov, Even Yisrael, 'Ezrat Yisrael, Knesset Yisrael Aleph, Bet, Gimel, Mahane Yehuda – the neighborhood and the Market, Mahane Yisrael, Mazkeret Moshe, Mekor Baruch, Mishkenot Yisrael, Nahlat Tzion, Ohel Moshe, the Russian Compound, Sha'arei Tzedek, Shevet Tzedek, Sukkat Shalom, Zichron Tuvia, Zichron Ya'akov, Zichron Yosef.

In 1985 physical renovation and development of the Mahane Yehuda Market was begun. At the same time the process of establishing the community administration "Heart of the City" was begun in order to save those hundred-year-old neighborhoods which are both historic and cultural assets to the city and are slowly crumbling. The physical rehabilitation began in 1987-1988, together with laying modern infrastructure in the old neighborhoods and doing renovation of the public areas in them. However, there is still a great deal of work remaining!

Most of the neighborhoods in the middle of the city were built in the 1880s. The characteristic form of building in that period was courtyard neighborhoods, in the center of which were a synagogue and a cistern. In many neighborhoods the lifestyle remains the same.

Boundaries:
North – Zichron Moshe and Mekor Baruch
South – Nahlat Ahim/Nahlaot, Rehavia, Komemiyut/Talbieh
East – the Russian Compound, Yemin Moshe
West – Ben-Zvi Boulevard, Sacher Park

Sites: within its boundaries or nearby are the Mahane Yehuda Market, the sundial of the *Zoharei Hama* Synagogue, the Mahane Yehuda police station which is a Turkish structure from the mid-nineteenth century, the

Ministry of Health building which is Ottoman, the Pargod Theater, Freedom Square, Zion Square, the Ben Yehuda Pedestrian Mall, the Jerusalem Time Elevator, Independence Park, Safra Square with the new Municipality Building, the King David Hotel, the YMCA, Gozlan Garden (formerly called *HaBustan*, the Orchard, because of the herbal plants growing there), France Square.

Streets: There are streets named for kings of the Hasmonean dynasty from the Second Temple period. Other streets are named for Tannaim, doctors, judges, linguists and artists.

The streets are:

Adler, Shaul, Dr. (1895 – 1966) HaNeviim – dead end **H12**

One of the most important doctors in Israel, an international researcher in medicine, particularly of tropical diseases. Received the Israel Prize in medical sciences.

AGa"N, Rabbi (1787 – 1848) Yafo – Straus **H12**

(See the neighborhood of Beit David/Beit HaRav Kook.)

Agrippas (10 BCE – 44 CE) King George – Shmuel Baruch **G11-H12**

(See the neighborhoods of Even Yisrael, Mahane Yehuda, Mazkeret Moshe, Mishkenot Yisrael, Nahlat Tzion, Ohel Moshe, Sukkat Shalom, Zichron Tuvia, Zichron Yosef.)

Agron, Gershon (1894 – 1959)
David HaMelech – Keren HaYesod **H13**

(See the neighborhood of Mahane Yisrael.)

Aristobulus, Yehuda (2nd cent. BCE)
Heleni HaMalka – Elyashar **H12**

Sixth in the Hasmonean dynasty to rule over Judea in the Land of Israel, the first to call himself king. Eldest son of Yohanan Hyrcanus.

Avida', Yehuda Leib Zlotnick, Rabbi (1887 – 1962)
King George – Independence Park **H13**

Author, a researcher of Jewish folklore.

Avigdori, Shneur, Dr. (1891 – 1960) Straus – Bnei Brit **H11**

A Jerusalem doctor. One of the founders and directors of the medical society.

Baruch, Natan [Square] (1874 – 1945)
HaHavatzelet at Hyrcanus **H12**

One of the activists of the Sephardic community and a judge in Jerusalem.

Baruch, Shmuel, Rabbi (1898 – 1994) Ben-Zvi – Agrippas **F-G11**

(See the neighborhoods of Beit Ya'akov, Mahane Yehuda, Sha'arei Tzedek, Shevet Tzedek/Shchunat HaPahim, Zichron Yosef.)

Baruchof, Mashiah (1872 – 1946) Yafo – Agrippas **H12**

(See the neighborhood of Mahane Yehuda.)

Be-eri (1887 – 1944) King George – HaNagid **H12**

Designation for Berl Katznelson, leader of the Labor Zionist movement, founder of HaMashbir consumer cooperatives and of Kupat Holim, the sick fund. A strong advocate of "illegal" immigration of European Jews to the Land of Israel starting in the late 1930s.

Ben Baruch, Shalom (1887 – 1965) HaHistadrut – dead end **H12**

Journalist and activist in Jerusalem, a founder of the General Zionists Party in Israel.

Ben Shetah, Shim'on, Rabbi (1st cent. BCE)
Shlomtzion – Rivlin **H12**

President of the Sanhedrin in the days of Alexander Yannai and Queen Shlomtzion (Salome). He was the sage paired to Rabbi Yehuda ben Tabai, the chief judge of the court. From Ben Shetah's sayings, the following advice is preserved: "Examine witnesses extensively and be heedful of your words, lest they learn from them to lie (Pirkei Avot 1:9)."

Ben Shim'on, David, Rabbi (1824 – 1880)
Agron – David HaMelech **H13**

(See the neighborhood of Mahane Yisrael.)

Ben Sira, Shim'on (3rd cent. BCE) Shlomtzion – Ben Shetah **H12-13**

Composed aphorisms (wise sayings) in Hebrew in his book "Wisdom of Ben Sira." Wrote his book in Jerusalem around the time of Shim'on HaTzadik, approximately a generation before the Hasmonean rebellion.

Ben Yehuda, Eli'ezer [Pedestrian Mall] (1858 – 1922)
Yafo – King George **G-H12**

Revived the spoken Hebrew language, renewed and invented many words for fluency in spoken Hebrew and for science and literature, promoted the Lovers of Zion movement, founded the Committee on the Hebrew Language and served as its president until his death, compiled the "Dictionary of the Old and New Hebrew Language." Was the first to teach in Hebrew, in a school in Jerusalem, and published newspapers in Hebrew.

Betzalel ben Uri Ben-Zvi – Mesilat Yesharim **G12**

(See the neighborhoods of Batei Kollel Minsk/Beit HaLevi, Batei Kollel Munkacs, Knesset Yisrael, Nahlat Ahim/Nahlaot, Nahlat Tzion, Sha'arei Rahamim, Zichron Ahim, Zichron Ya'akov, Zichron Yosef.)

Bianchini, Angelo Levi (1897 – 1920) Hillel – Shamai **H12**

Zionist activist, member of the delegates committee, died while on a mission from Jerusalem to Damascus for the Zionist institutions.

Bnei Brit Straus – HaNeviim **H12**

(See the neighborhood of Bnei Moshe/Neve Shalom.)

Botta, Paul Emile (1802 – 1870) David HaMelech – Eliel **H-I13**

French archeologist who researched the Assyrian period. He served as the French consul in Jerusalem (see the neighborhood of Yemin Moshe).

Darom Shamai – Hillel **H12**

Named for the bookstore of author and collector Rabbi Michel Rabinowitz (1872–1949). The store served as a meeting place for authors and intellectuals of the time.

David HaMelech (10th cent. BCE) Agron – Emek Refaim **H13-I14**

(See the neighborhoods of David's Village-Mamilla, Komemiyut/Talbieh, Mahane Yisrael/ Shchunat HaMa'aravim, Yemin Moshe.)

Di Zahav [Goldstein], **Efraim [Square]** (1903 – 1958)
HaNeviim at HaHavatzelet at Monobaz **H12**

A gifted singer, narrator for Israel's broadcasting service, he organized cantorial concerts, was cantor of the Yeshurun Synagogue in Jerusalem and in the *Torah veDa'at* Yeshiva.

Dorot Rishonim Ben Yehuda – Lunz **H12**

Early Generations, named for the book by rabbi and historian Yitzhak Isaac HaLevi Horowitz (1847-1914), rabbi, activist and researcher of the Talmud. A founder of *Agudat Yisrael.*

Du-Nuwas, Yosef (d. 526 CE) Yafo – Aristobulus **H12**

King of Khimir in Arabia (on the eastern shore of the Red Sea), converted to Judaism and established a Jewish country there. He died in his war against the Abyssinians (Ethiopians).

'Eliash, Mordechai (1892 – 1950) Ben Yehuda – Agrippas **H12**

(See the neighborhood of Batei Goral/Mishkenot HaTeimanim.)

Eliot, George (1819 – 1880) Lincoln – Agron **H13**

English authoress. One of the Righteous Gentiles, she preached the Return to Zion.

Elyashar, Menashe [Square] (1902 – 1994) Hillel **H12**

President of the Chamber of Commerce in Jerusalem, *Yakir Yerushalayim*.

Elyashar, Yitzhak (1873 – 1933) Yafo – Hyrcanus – dead end **H12**

(See the neighborhood of Giv'at Ram.)

Ethiopia HaNeviim – Chasanowich **H11-12**

A country in east Africa. Most of the houses and properties on this street belong to the institutions for the poor established by the Ethiopian Church. In the middle of this street is the main Ethiopian church.

Even Shoshan, Avraham [Square] (1906 – 1984)
HaNeviim at Straus **H12**

Educator, lexicographer (compiler of a Hebrew dictionary), a man of many talents.

Frumkin, Gad (1881 – 1960) Elyashar – HaHavatzelet **H12**

A Supreme Court judge in Jerusalem during the British Mandate period.

Gan Daniel (also *Gan Ha'Ir* – City Park)
Safra Square – the new Municipality **I12**

Named for Daniel Auster, 1893-1963 (see the neighborhood of Rehavia). The land was set aside in 1891 by the Turkish government as a public park and was redesigned during the British Mandate period as a continuation of the entrance area to the adjacent Municipality building.

Ha'Atzmaut [Park] Agron – Hillel – King George **H13**

Named for the independence of the Jewish people in its land.

HaBonim HaHofshiim [Square] Wallenberg at Yafo **H12**

Freemasons, a worldwide brotherhood organization.

Hachsharat HaYishuv [Plaza] King George – Ben Yehuda **H12**

The name, "preparation of the Jewish community in the Land of Israel", is that of an organization that focused on reclamation of land and Jewish settlement in the Land of Israel.

HaHavatzelet Yafo – Monobaz **H12**

Hebrew weekly published in Jerusalem with some interruptions from 1863 until 1911, under the management and editorship of Yisrael Dov Frumkin (1851 – 1914), journalist, author, one of the heads of Kollel HaBa"D. The weekly was named "The Sand Lily" after a plant bearing a large, white flower shaped like a goblet.

HaHistadrut Hillel – King George **H12**

Named for the Jewish Labor Federation in the Land of Israel, founded in 1920, whose institutions in Jerusalem were located on this street.

HaMa'alot King George – HaNagid **G-H12**

To mark a residential building on this street (see Beit HaMa'alot – Neighborhoods That Were Built and No Longer Exist).

HaMa'aravim Agron – dead end **H13**

(See the neighborhood of Mahane Yisrael/Shchunat HaMa'aravim.)

HaMatmid [Lane] Hillel – dead end **H12**

Named for the poem of that name ("The Diligent One") by Haim Nahman Bialik.

HaMechess [Square] David HaMelech at Agron **H13**

(See the neighborhood of Mahane Yisrael/Shchunat HaMa'aravim.)

HaNagid, Shmuel ben Yosef HaLevi (993 – 1056 CE)
King George – Ben Yehuda **G12-13**

One of the great poets of Spanish Jewry, a grammatician and very knowledgeable in religious law, minister and statesman in the court of the Muslim ruler.

HaNeviim Yafo – Damascus Gate **H-I12**

(See the neighborhoods of Beit David/Beit HaRav Kook, 'Ezrat Yisrael, Morasha/Musrara, Zichron Moshe.)

HaSoreg Shlomtzion – Ben Shetah **H12**

Bars, named for the barbed-wire fences the British authorities put up in this area in 1948.

Hasson, 'Uzi (Yehezkel) (1944 – 1994) Shlomtzion – Yafo **H12**

A Jerusalem district attorney.

HaTnu'a HaTzionit [Square]
HaKeren HaKayemet LeYisrael at King George **H13**

The Zionist Movement. The plaza in front of the national institutions – the Jewish Agency, the Jewish National Fund and Keren HaYesod, the Palestine Foundation Fund (financial arm of the World Zionist Organization). (See the neighborhood of Rehavia.)

HaTzanhanim Kikar TZaHa"L – Sultan Suleiman **I12**

(See the neighborhoods of the Christian Quarter, Morasha/Musrara, Russian Compound.)

Hefetz, Shma'aya Baruch [Square] (1894 – 1932)
Lunz at Dorot Rishonim **H12**

Founded the public transportation system in Jerusalem.

Heleni HaMalca (1st cent. CE) Yafo – HaNeviim **H-I12**

Queen Helena of Adiabene in northern Syria. She converted to Judaism and settled in Jerusalem, helped the Jews of the city during a famine at the end of the Second Temple period (see the neighborhoods of Morasha/Musrara, Russian Compound).

Hess, Moshe (1812 – 1875) David HaMelech – Lincoln **H13**

(See the neighborhood of Mahane Yisrael/Shchunat HaMa'aravim.)

Hillel (HaZaken) [the Elder] (1st cent. BCE – 1st cent. CE)
King George – Ben Sira **H12**

One of the greatest of the Tannaim, president of the Sanhedrin in the time of Herod. Known for moderation and patience and for his ability to bring people closer to Judaism. The continuing differences (scholarly) between himself and his paired sage Shamai, the chief judge of the court, continued among their disciples, Beit Hillel and Beit Shamai, and was eventually decided in favor of Hillel: "The decision in religious law is according to Hillel." He laid down the following maxims: "Judge not your fellowman until you stand in his place," "The shy person cannot learn, nor can the impatient teach" (Pirkei Avot 2:4-5). (See the neighborhood of Nahlat Shiv'a.)

Hyrcanus, Yohanan [John] (2nd cent. BCE)
Heleni HaMalka – HaRav Kook **H12**

Hasmonean dynasty ruler of Judah during the Second Temple period.

Kariv, Yitzhak (1903 – 1999)
David HaMelech – Hativat Yerushalayim **I13**

(See the neighborhood of David's Village-Mamilla.)

Keren HaYesod King George – David HaMelech **H13**

(See the neighborhood of Komemiyut/Talbieh.)

Kikar HaHatulot Hillel at Ben Israel **H12**

Cat Square, to mark the large number of cats wandering around in this area.

Kikar HaHerut – HaDavidka HaNeviim at Yafo **G12**

Freedom Square, to mark the liberty of Jerusalem. The "Davidka" is a home-made mortar, one of the few in the Jewish arsenal in 1948, nick-named for David Ben-Gurion.

Kikar TZaHa"L [IDF Square]
Yafo at HaTzanhanim at Shivtei Yisrael **I12-13**

(See the neighborhoods of the Christian Quarter, the Russian Compound.)

Kikar Tzarfat [France Square]
King George at Keren HaYesod at RaMBa"N at 'Aza **H13**

The square was named in appreciation of the good relations obtaining then between Israel and France, to thank France for helping Israel (see the neighborhood of Rehavia).

Kikar Tzion [Zion Square] Yafo at Salomon at Ben Yehuda **H12**

Named for the Biblical Zion, another name for Jerusalem.

King George (V) (1865 – 1935) Yafo – Keren HaYesod **H12-13**

(See the neighborhoods of Mahane Yehuda, Rehavia.)

Kook, Avraham Yitzhak HaCohen, Rabbi (1865 – 1935)
Haneviim – Yafo **H12**

(See the neighborhood of Beit David/Beit HaRav Kook.)

Koresh (6th cent. BCE) Shlomo HaMelech – Shlomtzion **I12**

Cyrus, King of Persia, known for having encouraged the Babylonian exiles to return to the Land of Israel and build the Second Holy Temple in Jerusalem. He defeated the Babylonians and made Persia into a mighty empire.

Lincoln, Abraham (1809 – 1865)
Keren HaYesod – David HaMelech **H13**

President of the United States. In 1863 he abolished slavery, fought for human liberty. In 1864 he was elected to a second term and was assassinated at a theatrical performance.

Lunz, Moshe (1854 – 1918) Yafo – Shamai **H12**

A researcher of the history of the Land of Israel, counted among the founders of the Jewish society for research of the Land of Israel, a member of the Committee on the Hebrew Language. In 1902 he founded the school for the blind in Jerusalem.

Macabi, Mutzerai [Square] (1914 – 1948) Hillel at Salomon **H12**

Named for Mutzerai Macabi Mani, who fell during the War of Independence while defending a convoy bringing food and weapons through Sha'ar HaGuy (in the Jerusalem Corridor) up to besieged Jerusalem.

Mamilla Shlomtzion – Agron **H13**

Named for the Muslim cemetery on this street.

Mapu, Avraham (1808 – 1868)
David HaMelech – Keren HaYesod **H13-14**

One of the first authors in the Enlightenment period and one who was considered the father of Hebrew literature in that period. He created the Hebrew novel, his writing influenced the Lovers of Zion, Zionist philosophers and authors in the following generations.

Mazia, Aharon Haim, Dr. (1858 – 1930)
Mesilat Yesharim – 'Eliash **G-H12**

(See the neighborhood of Batei Goral/Mishkenot HaTeimanim.)

Menashe ben Israel, Rabbi (1604 – 1657) Hillel – Agron **H12-13**

Philosopher, one of the outstanding rabbis of Amsterdam, he secured permission for Jews to once again live in England.

Menora Betzalel – Ussishkin **G12**

Named for the discharged soldiers club that was on this street.

Mesilat Yesharim Ben Yehuda – Agrippas **G-H12**

(See the neighborhoods of Batei Goral/Mishkenot HaTeimanim, Sukkat Shalom.)

Monobaz II Heleni – HaNeviim **H12**

King of Adiabene (a country in northern Aram Naharayim – Syria), converted to Judaism and supported the Jews of Jerusalem during the Second Temple period. He had graves dug in Jerusalem for Helena his mother, and family members, known as the "graves of the kings".

Mordechai ben Hillel HaCohen (1846 – 1937)
Shamai – King George **H12**

A Hebrew writer, journalist, economist, one of the founders of the Lovers of Zion in Russia, one of the founders of Tel-Aviv, a member of the first governing council of Tel-Aviv and author of the city regulations, one of the founders of the Writers Association. He was made an honorary citizen of Tel-Aviv in 1936.

Na'amat [Square] Straus at Bnei Brit **H11**

Acronym for **N**ashim **'O**vdot **Mit**nadvot, an organization of Jewish women working as volunteers in the Land of Israel to care for children and their education.

Narkiss, Mordechai (1897 – 1957) HaNagid – Lod **G12**

Author, researcher of Jewish art, directed the Betzalel Art School in Jerusalem (see the neighborhood of Nahlat Ahim/Nahlaot, Neve Betzalel).

Netiv HaRakevel Ben Yehuda – Shamai **H12**

Cable car path, a memorial to Uriel Hefetz, who built the secret cable car to Mount Zion during the War of Independence.

Ornstein, Yitzhak, Rabbi (1893 – 1948) Pines – Pines **G11**

A founder of the Jewish village of Neve Ya'akov in northern Jerusalem, a Hagana fighter in the Old City, chief supervisor of the Western Wall, fell while on guard duty in 1948.

Rabbi 'Akiva ben Yosef (2nd cent. CE)
Hillel – Independence Park – Shaham **H12-13**

One of the greatest of the Tannaim, he joined the rebellion of Bar Kochva and was the most famous of the Ten Martyrs. It is said he taught tens of thousands of students, who were struck by a plague that killed many of them beginning one Passover and stopping suddenly on the thirty-third day (Lag Ba'Omer) between the second night of Passover and Shavu'ot.

Refael Haim HaCohen [Square] (1884 – 1955)
Ben Yehuda at HaNagid **H12**

President of the Persian Jews in Jerusalem, one of the first publishers in the city, one of the builders of the city.

Refaeli, Shmuel (1857 – 1924) Menora – Ussishkin **G12**

A researcher of Jewish coins of the Land of Israel (see the neighborhood of Nahlat Ahim/Nahlaot).

Rejwan, 'Ovadia Shaul [Plaza]
Agrippas at Even Yisrael at King George **H12**

Served for many years as president of the council of the Babylonian (Iraqi) Jewish community in Jerusalem, one of the builders of Jerusalem.

Remez, David (1886 – 1951) David HaMelech – Derech Hevron **I14**

One of the leaders of the labor movement in the Land of Israel, chairman of the executive of the National Committee, was among the signers of Israel's Declaration of Independence, served as first minister of transportation in Israel's government, and was appointed minister of education and culture, but died in his first months in that position.

Rivlin, Eli'ezer (1889 – 1942) HaMa'alot – HaNagid **H12-13**

A civic leader, author, researcher of the history of the sages of Jerusalem.

Samuel, Herbert (1870 – 1963) Shamai – Ben Yehuda **H12**

British Jewish statesman, the first high commissioner during the British Mandate in the Land of Israel.

Shaham, Meir (1914 – 1988) Rabbi 'Akiva – King George **H12**

An active member of the national-religious movement, was active in the management of the Red Magen David (*Magen David Adom*) and of Ot Va'ed for perpetuation of the memory of the Holocaust, and also of the Great Synagogue, and of the Bnai Brith organization.

Shama'a, Eliyahu Yosef (1881 – 1933) Eliel – David HaMelech **H-I15**

(See the neighborhood David's Village-Mamilla.)

Shamai (1st cent. BCE – 1st cent. CE) Salomon – HaHistadrut **H12**

One of the great Torah sages and one of the spiritual leaders of the Jews during the Second Temple period. He taught many pupils (Beit Shamai), was in continual disagreement with his paired sage, Hillel the Elder, but the decisions eventually went according to Hillel: "the ruling is according to Beit Hillel" (see the neighborhood of Nahlat Shiv'a).

Shatz, Boris [Baruch] (1866 – 1932) HaNagid – King George **G-H12**

Painter and sculptor, he founded the Betzalel Art School and was its director.

Shlomo HaMelech (10th cent. BCE)
Kikar TZaHa"L – Shlomtzion **I12-H13**

King Solomon, king of Israel, son of King David. Built the First Holy Temple (see the neighborhood of the Russian Compound).

Shlomtzion HaMalca (139 – 67 BCE)
Yafo – Shlomo HaMelech **H12-13**

The only queen ever to rule the kingdom of Judah in the Second Temple period. She was the wife of Aristobulus, the first king of the Hasmonean dynasty, and after he died she married his brother Alexander Yannai. When he died, the crown passed to her.

Shushan Hasson – Yafo – dead end **I12**

The capital city of the ancient kingdom of Persia (see the Book of Esther in the Bible).

Stoyanovsky, Rivka (1905 – 1995)
Shaham – Independence Park – 'Akiva **H12**

A teacher, directed the Alliance School for Girls, worked as a volunteer in communal activities at Yad LaKashish (a sheltered workshop for the elderly). At her initiative, a fund was started in the oncology department at Hadassah Hospital 'Ein Kerem.

Straus, Nathan (1848 – 1931) Yafo – Kikar HaShabbat **H11-12**

(See the neighborhoods of Batei Kollel Warsaw/Nahlat Ya'akov, Batei Wittenberg/Sha'arei Moshe, Bnei Moshe/Neve Shalom, Even Yehoshu'a.)

Ticho, Avraham, Dr. [Lane] (1883 – 1961)
HaRav Kook – Beit Ticho – dead end **H12**

(See the neighborhood of Beit David/Beit HaRav Kook.)

Trumpeldor, Yosef (1880 – 1920) Narkiss – Betzalel **G12**

Founded the *HeHalutz* (Pioneer) Movement in Russia and the Jewish Brigade group called the Zion Mule Corps that fought on the front against Turkey in World War I, founded the Jewish Battalion in the British Army fighting in World War I, was named the hero of Tel Hai in the

Galilee and on his grave and those of the seven defenders of Tel Hai was erected a memorial monument of a roaring lion. The **Beitar** Movement is named for him (acronym for **B**rit **Y**osef **Tr**umpeldor).

Tzimuki, Aryeh [Square] (1919 - 1985)
Hillel at Menashe ben Israel **H12**

Journalist, chairman of the Zionist Council and one of its founders.

Wallenberg, Raoul (b. 1912) HaNeviim – Yafo **H12**

Swedish diplomat, a Righteous Gentile who saved tens of thousands of Hungarian Jews during the Holocaust.

Washington, George (1732 – 1799) Lincoln – David HaMelech **H13**

First president of the United States, military commander, one of the planners and builders of America in his time.

Ya'betz, Zeev, Rabbi (1847 – 1924)
Yafo – Mordechai ben Hillel **H12**

Historian, educator, one of the first Lovers of Zion. One of those who laid the foundation of Jewish education in the Land of Israel, he authored textbooks and wrote Aggadic material in Biblical Hebrew. He was first to observe Tu B'Shvat as a holiday of planting trees.

Yafo Jaffa Gate – Weizmann Boulevard **F11-I12**

(See the neighborhoods of Batei Kollel Horodna/Damesek Eli'ezer, Batei Sa'idoff, Beit David/Beit HaRav Kook, Beit Ya'akov, Even Yisrael, 'Ezrat Yisrael, Mahane Yehuda, Mekor Baruch, Nahlat Shiv'a, Ohel Shlomo, Romema, Russian Compound, Sha'arei Tzedek, Sha'arei Yerushalayim).

Yallon, Hanoch (1886 – 1970) Narkiss – dead end **G12-13**

Teacher, researcher of Hebrew linguistics and the linguistic traditions preserved by Jerusalem's various Jewish communities in their speech.

Yannai, Alexander Shlomtzion – Shlomo HaMelech **H-I13**

Second king in the Hasmonean dynasty, in the period of the Second Temple.

Yehudit (Montefiore) (1784 – 1862) Yafo – David Yellin **G11**

Judith, the wife of Sir Moses Montefiore. She accompanied her husband on his travels and wrote down all that befell him on the way (see the neighborhood of Ruhama).

Zamenhof, Eli'ezer (1858 – 1917) Agron – Hess **H13**

(See the neighborhood of Mahane Yisrael/Shchunat HaMa'aravim.)

Mishkenot Yisrael

Name and establishment:

This neighborhood, located in the middle of town southeast of Mahane Yehuda and near the neighborhoods of Sukkat Shalom, Mazkeret Moshe and Ohel Moshe, was founded in 1875, and its name, Israel's dwellings, was taken from the verse in Numbers 24:5, "How fair are your tents, O Jacob, your dwellings, O Israel." This is the seventh Jewish neighborhood that was built outside the walls of the Old City.

The property was bought along with property for the neighborhood of Even Yisrael, and both were built the same year. The area of Mishkenot Yisrael was much larger than that of Even Yisrael. Only a portion of the houses planned were built, and construction stopped due to a financial crisis. On the land that was still empty, the neighborhood of Mazkeret Moshe was built years later. The neighborhood was built as two parallel rows of houses.

The residents of the neighborhood prepared part of the land for planting wheat, in order to be able to fulfill commandments specific to the Land of Israel. Mishkenot Yisrael was intended to be a spacious and magnificent residential neighborhood. The founders tried to convince well-to-do Jews in the Diaspora to buy homes in the neighborhood not only in order to build up the city, but also in order to infuse money into the economy.

For many years, Rabbi Aryeh Levin, the "prisoners' rabbi", lived in the neighborhood. He was the rabbi of members of the underground imprisoned by the Mandate authorities, and he gave encouragement to the families of the prisoners. He lived in a modest apartment in the southern part of the neighborhood, and there is a street there today that bears his name (see the neighborhood of Mazkeret Moshe), a street near the apartment he occupied. In the courtyard of his building a yeshiva was established that is named for him.

Boundaries:
North – Agrippas Street
South – Knesset Yisrael
East – Sukkat Shalom
West – Mazkeret Moshe, Ohel Moshe

Sites: within its boundaries or nearby are the home of Rabbi Aryeh Levin and the Mahane Yehuda Market.

Streets: the streets of the neighborhood are named for the neighborhood and the founders of the Jewish community in Tiberias.

The streets are:

Abula'fia, Haim, Rabbi (1775 – 1861) Beirav – Mesilat Yesharim **G12**

The Rishon LeTzion (Sephardic Chief Rabbi), chief rabbi of Jerusalem, worked energetically for the development of the Jewish community in Jerusalem and renewed the Jewish community in Tiberias.

Agrippas (10 BCE – 44 CE) King George – Shmuel Baruch **G11-H12**

(See the neighborhoods of Even Yisrael, Mahane Yehuda, Mazkeret Moshe, Mid-Town, Nahlat Tzion, Ohel Moshe, Sukkat Shalom, Zichron Tuvia, Zichron Yosef).

Beirav, Ya'akov ben Haim, Rabbi (end 17th – early 18th cent.)
Mishkanot – Shomron **G12**

One of those who renewed the Jewish community in Tiberias, a poet.

Mishkanot Agrippas – Mesilat Yesharim **G12**

(See the neighborhood of Batei Goral/Mishkenot HaTeimanim.)

Rabbi Aryeh (Levin) (1885 – 1969)
Shomron – Ohel Moshe **G12**

(See the neighborhood of Mazkeret Moshe.)

Shomron Agrippas – Mesilat Yesharim **G12**

(See the neighborhoods of Batei Goral/Mishkenot HaTeimanim, Batei Rand.)

Morasha/Musrara

Name and establishment:

This neighborhood, located on the east side of the New City nearest the Old City walls, the Damascus Gate and east Jerusalem, was built by a group of well-to-do Christian Arabs at the beginning of the twentieth century, and in 1949 it became a Jewish neighborhood. It is called Musrara in Arabic because it was built on an area covered with small stones, called "srar" in Arabic, meaning batches or quantities. The Hebrew name Morasha ("inheritance") is taken from Ezekiel 11:15, "...unto us this land is given for an inheritance."

Until the War of Independence, this was a luxury neighborhood in the center of the city. During the war it became a fighting base for the Arab fighters against the nearby Jewish neighborhoods of Mea She'arim and Batei Kollel Ungarin/Nahlat Zvi, on the edges of which many battles took place. When the British left, Jews took over the abandoned buildings of Musrara and moved into them, primarily new immigrants. The name of the neighborhood was changed to Morasha, and the main street was renamed Ha'A"H (the seventy-eight) in memory of the victims in the convoy of doctors and nurses who were ambushed and killed on their way up to Hadassah Hospital on Mount Scopus in 1948. During the following nineteen years, until the Six Day War, Morasha was a frontier neighborhood on the border between Israel and Jordan. It suffered from frequent attacks. In 1967 when Jerusalem was reunited, the neighborhood became a contact point between the two parts of the city, east and west. In 1979 a project of renewal was begun in the neighborhood, which continued for twelve years. The neighborhood has been adopted by the Jewish community of Los Angeles, California.

Boundaries:

North – Mea She'arim
South – the Old City
East – Arab neighborhoods in east Jerusalem
West – the Russian Compound

A number of central traffic routes pass the neighborhood: in the south, HaTzanhanim (Paratroopers Road); in the west, Shivtei Yisrael; in the north, HaNeviim, which crosses the neighborhood; in the east, Heil HaHandasa.

Sites: within its boundaries or nearby are the municipality complex at Safra Square, the Ministry of Education, Yad LaKashish (help for the elderly), Pikud HaMercaz Square – the former Mandelbaum Gate (border crossing point into Jordan), the museum of the imprisoned members of the Jewish underground, the Turjeman House Museum, Notre Dame Hostel, the French Hospital.

Streets: the neighborhood streets are named for prophets and IDF forces. The main street is Ha'A"H Street, named in memory of Jewish medical personnel who were victims of an ambush on the mountain nearby.

The streets are:

Adahan, Yihye (d. 1989) HaNeviim – 'Ido HaNavi **I12**

Rabbi, author and civic activist in the Morasha neighborhood.

Ben Shadad, 'Antara (5th-6th cent. CE)
Heil HaHandasa – Nablus Road **I12**

Arab poet.

Daniel Elisha' – Heleni HaMalka **I12**

Central figure in the Biblical book of Daniel. One of the exiles of Judah in the court of King Nebuchadnezzar of Babylonia, known as an interpreter of dreams and seer of the future.

Elisha' H'aA"H – Shivtei Yisrael **I12**

A prophet during the period of the kingship in Israel.

Ha'A"H HaNeviim – HaTzanhanim **I12**

The seventy-eight. Named in memory of the Jews who were ambushed and killed in a convoy going up to Hadassah Hospital on Mount Scopus in Jerusalem, in 1948, which included doctors, nurses, college professors, drivers and others.

HaHoma HaShlishit Shivtei Yisrael – Heil HaHandasa **I11-12**

The third wall, built in the time of Agrippas I in northern Jerusalem, remains of which were also found on this street.

HaKaldiim Heil HaHandasa – Nablus Road **I12**

Chaldeans, a Christian sect whose prayers are written in Aramaic.

HaNeviim Yafo – Damascus Gate **H-I12**

(See the neighborhoods of Beit David/Beit HaRav Kook, 'Ezrat Yisrael, Mid-Town, Zichron Moshe.)

HaTzanhanim Kikar TZaHa"L – Sultan Suleiman **I12**

(See the neighborhoods of the Christian Quarter, Mid-Town, Russian Compound.)

Heil HaHandasa HaTzanhanim – Shivtei Yisrael **J11-12**

Named for the soldiers of the IDF engineering corps, who participated in the liberation of Jerusalem in the Six Day War.

Heleni HaMalca (1st cent. CE) Yafo – HaNeviim **H-I12**

(See the neighborhoods of Mid-Town, Russian Compound.)

Hulda HaNevia Heleni HaMalca – Natan HaNavi **I12**

Hulda, the prophetess, in the period of the kingdom of Judah.

'Ido HaNavi Shivtei Yisrael – dead end **I12**

A prophet in the period of the kingdom of Judah.

Katz, Michel Leib (1846 – 1923)
Shivtei Yisrael – Heil HaHandasa **I11**

A civic leader, helped in the reclamation of land and building neighborhoods in Jerusalem. Built the first steam-powered flour mill in Jerusalem.

Kiss, Naomi (1941 – 1985) Heil HaHandasa – Nablus Road **I11-12**

She fought for equal rights for all human beings.

Mishmarot Ha'A"H – dead end **I12**

Guard shifts, named for the citizens who defended Jerusalem.

Natan HaNavi Ha'A"H – Shivtei Yisrael **I12**

Nathan, a prophet during the reigns of King David and King Solomon, who voiced this prophecy to David: "...your throne shall be established forever" (II Samuel 7:16). According to tradition, Nathan the prophet is buried in Bethlehem.

Pierrotti, Ermat (1804 – 1866) Ben Shadad – dead end **I12**

A researcher of Jerusalem, city engineer during the period of Turkish rule.

Pikud HaMercaz [Square] Shivtei Yisrael at Nablus Road **I11**

Central Command: One of the three commands of the Jerusalem Brigade, it was assigned the task of liberating Jerusalem in the Six Day War.

Shivtei Yisrael Heil HaHandasa – HaTzanhanim **I12**

(See the neighborhoods of Batei Kollel Ungarin/Nahlat Zvi, Mea She'arim, Russian Compound.)

Straus, Shmuel [Square] Shivtei Yisrael at HaNeviim **I12**

One of the activists and builders of Jerusalem.

Moslem Quarter *[HaRova' HaMuslemi]*

Name and establishment:

This neighborhood, located in the northeastern part of the Old City from the Damascus Gate east to the Flower or Herod's Gate and then south to the Lions Gate, on the northern and eastern walls, is the largest in area of the Old City's quarters, and is named for the Muslims who have lived there for several generations.

It began as a Muslim area at the beginning of the eleventh century when the Christian residents were expelled from the section near the Temple Mount, and it was settled by Muslims. The quarter is split into three subdivisions: the northeastern part is mainly residential, the area extending north from the Temple Mount, from the eastern wall to HaGuy Street. There are only a few religious institutions and historic sites here. The second part is the area from the Temple Mount west to the markets, one of the central places in which are located most of the public buildings, many religious institutions and the markets which impart the special Eastern flavor. The residents of the third section, the Mughrabi neighborhood, were relocated to another area and the apartment buildings razed following the Six Day War in order to create a wide plaza in front of the Western Wall. Large portions of the Moslem Quarter are the property of the Islamic religious authority, al-Wakf in Arabic.

Jews lived in what is today the Moslem Quarter at the beginning of the British Mandate period, but were forced to leave that quarter by the pogroms of 1929. The Jewish community renewed itself in this quarter after the Six Day War in buildings that belonged to Jews from the earlier period.

Boundaries:

North – Bab e-Zahara

South – the Jewish Quarter and the Temple Mount

East – Mount of Olives

West – the Christian Quarter

Sites: within its boundaries or nearby are the Muslim market, the Dome of the Rock and the Al Aksa Mosque on the Temple Mount, the Western Wall

Streets: the neighborhood streets are named for Muslim holy men, sages and rulers.

The streets are:

'Ala e-Din Temple Mount – El-Wad **J12**

Muslim emir who lived in the thirteenth century.

Al-Hakari Khalidiye – HaShalshelet **J13**

Bader e-Din Hakari, an Arab emir who fought against the Crusaders in the thirteenth century.

Al-Kirami Khalidiye – A-Saraye **J13**

Muslim holy man of the tenth century CE.

Al-'Omari Antonia – HaHasidut **J12**

A Muslim holy man.

Antonia Lions Gate Road – el-Mu'azmiye **J12**

Fortress in the Second Temple period, protected the Temple Mount on the north side.

A-Saraye HaBad – Khalidiye **J13**

Named for the Turkish government building that was on this street.

Barkuk Temple Mount – El-Wad **J12**

A Mameluke caliph who ruled Jerusalem at the end of the fourteenth century.

Beit HaBad HaYehudim – El-Wad **I12-13**

(See the Christian Quarter.)

Borj Laqlaq Road /Shvil HaHasidut
Lions Gate Road – el-Mu'azmiye **J12**

The northeast corner of the wall of the Old City.

Derech Ha'Ofel Yeriho – Dung Gate **J13**

(See the neighborhood of the City of David.)

Derech Yeriho Suleiman – the city of Jericho **J12-K14**

(See the neighborhoods of City of David, E-Tur.)

El-Bustami HaTzariah HaAdom – Flower Gate Road **J12**

Founded the order of dervishes (Muslim monks) in the ninth century CE.

El-Khalidiye [Steps] El-Wad – al-Kirami **J12**

Muslim sage, lived at the end of the nineteenth century. The Hebrew name is Hevron Street.

El-Mu'azmiye HaHasidut – Flower Gate Road **J12**

An Arab girls high school named for Sultan Mu'azam 'Isa, nephew of Saladin, who lived in the thirteenth century.

El-Salakhiya Laqlaq – Antonia **J12**

An Arab girls high school named for Saladin [Salakh a-Din], who conquered Jerusalem from the Crusaders in 1187.

El-Wad [*HaGuy*] Damascus Gate – HaShalshelet **I12-J13**

The valley, named for the Tyropean Valley which is the route of this street.

E-Toota [Steps] El-Wad – HaBad **I-J12**

Mulberry, a fruit tree.

Flower Gate [Sha'ar HaPrahim] the northern wall of the Old City **J12**

One of the eight gates in the wall surrounding the Old City. Another name for this gate is Herod's Gate, after King Herod who lived in Jerusalem and ruled in the years 37 – 4 BCE. In front of the Flower Gate passes the street that begins at the nearby Damascus Gate and continues east, along the Kidron streambed and past the Mount of Olives to Jericho and the Dead Sea. Flower Gate Road, that begins at the gate, runs southward into the Moslem Quarter of the Old City to the northern gates of the Temple Mount.

Flower Gate Road Flower Gate – Via Dolorosa **J12**

The road leads south from the gate into the Old City and to the northern gates of the Temple Mount.

HaKimronim El-Wad – Via Dolorosa **J12**

Named for the arches, the semicircular protrusions above the street.

HaMadrasa [Steps] El-Wad – HaBad **I13-J12**

Residence of the dervishes (Muslim monks).

HaMelech Faisal Temple Mount – Lions Gate Road **J12**

Named for Faisal, king of Iraq and then of Syria, of the Hashemite family. After World War I, he met with Dr. Chaim Weizmann regarding the future of the Land of Israel.

HaRemachim El-Wad – HaSohar **J12**

Translation from the Arabic name: *Al-Asile*, meaning 'noble mare' ("...riding on swift royal steeds, bred of the stud," Esther 8:10).

HaShalshelet Temple Mount – HaBad **J13**

Chain, named for one of the gates on the west side of the Temple Mount.

HaTzariah HaAdom Via Dolorosa – Flower Gate **J12**

Red fortress. In Arabic – El-Madna el-Hamra.

Ibn Jarrah Mawlawiya – Sa'adiya **J12**

A Muslim military commander of the sixth century CE.

Lions Gate [*Sha'ar HaArayot*] eastern wall of the Old City **J12**

One of the eight gates in the wall surrounding the Old City. This gate, also called St. Stephen's Gate, in the eastern part of the wall, is called the Lions Gate because of the two pairs of lions carved into the stone on the outer sides of the gate. In the Six Day War (1967), soldiers of the paratrooper brigade broke through the Lions Gate into the Old City and liberated it. Opposite the gate a monument was erected in memory of the fighters who fell in that hard campaign. The gate is opposite the Mount of Olives, and to the left is Mount Scopus. From this gate, the road leads into the Old City, and from there begins the Via Dolorosa, the Path of Sorrows. Christians call this gate St. Stephen's Gate for the early Christian saint who, according to their tradition, was taken out of the city by this gate and stoned to death nearby.

Lions Gate Road Lions Gate – Via Dolorosa **J12**

The road leads from the gate into the Old City, and from there continues as the Path of Sorrows, the Via Dolorosa that is sacred to Christians.

Mawlawiya HaTzariah HaAdom – Ibn Jarrah **J12**

The name of the dervish order (Muslim monks).

Sa'adiya HaTzariah HaAdom – Ibn Jarrah **J12**

Named for a respected Arab family that lived on this street.

Sha'ar HaBarzel Temple Mount – El-Wad **J13**

Iron gate, named for one of the gates on the west side of the Temple Mount.

Sha'ar Shchem [Damascus Gate]
the northern wall of the Old City **I12**

(See the Christian Quarter.)

Sha'ar Shchem [Square]
the plaza from Damascus Gate to HaBad at El-Wad **I12**

Named for the gate in the middle of the northern wall.

Shadad (bin Awis) Flower Gate Road – HaTzariah HaAdom **J12**

The escort of 'Omar ibn el-Khatab.

Sheikh Hasan Antonia – Flower Gate Road **J12**

A Muslim holy man.

Sheikh Lulu Damascus Gate – Ibn Jarrah **I12**

A Muslim holy man who lived at the end of the fifteenth century.

Sheikh Rihan El-Wad – HaTzariah HaAdom **J12**

A Muslim holy man buried on this street.

Shuq el-Qatanin [*Shuk HaCutna*]
Temple Mount – El-Wad **J13**

The cotton market. Named for one of the gates on the west side of the Temple Mount, the most beautiful, open to the courtyard of the Holy Temple; it is also the name of the area of the former shops of the cotton workers that were near the Temple.

Sultan Suleiman (1495 – 1566) Nablus Road – Yeriho **J12**

(See the neighborhood of Bab e-Zahara.)

Via Dolorosa Lions Gate Road – Church of the Holy Sepulcher **I-J12**

(See the Christian Quarter.)

Mount Scopus *[Har HaTzofim]*

Name and establishment:

Mount Scopus is located in the northeastern part of the city. The name alludes to the marvelous scenery of old and new Jerusalem, the mountains surrounding it, the expanse of the Judean desert, the wilderness around Jericho, the Dead Sea and the mountains of Gilead and Moab across the Jordan River – all of which can be seen from this vantage point, and thus its name. The name Mount Scopus is the Greek translation of the Hebrew name Har HaTzofim (the mount of observers/lookouts). The Arabs called this mountain "Ras el-Masaraf" – the highest observation place. After the destruction of the Second Temple, the sages established the following rule regarding this lookout point: "Whoever looks upon Jerusalem from [Har] HaTzofim is obligated to tear his garment (in mourning)" (Jerusalem Talmud, Mo'ed Katan, 3:7). The sages included Mount Scopus within the boundaries of Jerusalem.

On the heights of Mount Scopus were built the first buildings of the Hebrew University, Hadassah Hospital, and also the School of Nursing and the British military cemetery. In 1916 the Mount Scopus home of Sir John Grey Hill, an English Christian, was purchased and became the first building of the Hebrew University. The dedication ceremony for the university took place in 1925 in the presence of the heads of world Jewry and of the British government. Likewise, Hadassah Hospital was built. All the institutions functioned until the War of Independence, when Mount Scopus and its institutions were cut off from the western (Jewish) part of the city. With no safe access, these institutions remained abandoned by all but a skeleton guard until the Six Day War (1967), when the IDF forces broke through the blockaded street of the "cut" of Giv'at HaMivtar, captured Mount Scopus and re-connected the mountain to the western city. After this victory, the buildings of Hadassah Hospital and the University were renovated and a new structure was built, the center for peace named for the American president Harry Truman. In addition, student dormitories were built, and in the battle areas, Giv'at HaTahmoshet and Giv'at HaMivtar, whole new neighborhoods were built: Giv'at Shapira/French Hill, Giv'at HaMivtar, Ramat Eshkol and Tzameret HaBira.

Mount Scopus is the northern continuation of the Mount of Olives. Jews in earlier times used to bury their dead on Mount Scopus as well as on the Mount of Olives. Jewish tombstones and memorial monuments have been found dating back to the Second Temple period – the Cave of Nikanor, a Jewish philanthropist who donated doors for one of the gates to the Second Temple courtyard — and at the foot of the mountain is the cave of Shim'on HaTzadik, the tombs of the Sanhedrin and the tomb called Absalom's Pillar.

Boundaries:
North – Tzameret HaBira, Giv'at Shapira/French Hill
South – Mount of Olives
East – the Judean wilderness
West – Giv'at HaTahmoshet, Giv'at HaMivtar, Ramat Eshkol

At the foot of Mount Scopus, on the western side toward the city, is the neighborhood of Sheikh Jarrah; on the lower eastern slope of Mount Scopus is the Arab village of 'Issawiya; and nearby is the village of 'Anata – ancient 'Anatot, the birthplace of the prophet Jeremiah.

Sites: within its boundaries or nearby are the Hebrew University, Hadassah Hospital, the Truman Institute, the Mount of Olives, the British military cemetery, Augusta Victoria Hospital and the Center for Near Eastern Studies, Brigham Young University (Mormon).

Streets: most of the neighborhood's streets are named for the initiators, activists and founders of the Hebrew University on Mount Scopus, and those who defended Mount Scopus during the War of Independence.

The streets are:

Buber, Martin (Mordechai) (1878 – 1965)
Rab'a el-'Adawiyeh – HaUniversita – Churchill **L11-12**

Author, philosopher and researcher of the Bible and of Hasidism. One of the initiators of the establishment of the Hebrew University of Jerusalem and a professor there.

Churchill, Winston [Boulevard] (1874 – 1965)
Shayeret Har HaTzofim – Katzir **K10**

Prime minister of England, one of the great British statesmen and authors, a political hero of World War II.

HaMeiri, Avigdor [Square] (1890 – 1970) Mount Scopus **K10**

Poet and author of the song, *Mei-'al Pisgat Har HaTzofim* (from the peak of Mount Scopus), he wrote more than one hundred works of literature of all types, translated many works of world literature into Hebrew, and won many prizes for his works, including the Israel Prize.

Katzir, Aharon (1914 – 1972) LeH"I – HaUniversita **J10**

(See the neighborhood of Giv'at Shapira/French Hill.)

Lempel, Hadassa (Helena) (1929 – 1948) Buber – dead end **K11**

Signalman, served in Battalion 73 of Israel's army that succeeded in breaking through to the police station at Latrun. She was attached to the penetrating force, which was heavily bombarded, and she was killed.

Mazar, Binyamin (1906 – 1994)
Shayeret Har HaTzofim – Buber **K10-11**

President and rector of the Hebrew University. He initiated and saw to the building of the university campus. He received recognition as the senior archeologist and historian of the Biblical period in Israel. He was president of the Israel Exploration Society, one of the initiators and founders of the Ben-Zvi Institute, helped establish the Hadassah Hospital in 'Ein Kerem, was active in the Mosad Bialik publishing house and was a *Yakir Yerushalayim.*

Schocken, Salman Shlomo (1877 – 1959)
Churchill – Shayeret Har HaTzofim **K10**

A businessman, philanthropist and publisher, founded the Research Institute for Medieval Hebrew Poetry. Founded the Schocken publishing house which published all of Agnon's works, was chairman of the executive of the Hebrew University of Jerusalem. He was a member of Knesset and wrote poems that were published under his pen name, Robert Posen.

Sderot HaUniversita Bar Lev – Shayeret Har HaTzofim **J9-10**

(See the neighborhoods of Giv'at Shapira/French Hill, Sheikh Jarrah.)

Shayeret Har HaTzofim Boulevard
HaUniversita – Churchill **J-K10**

Mount Scopus convoy. Named for the Jewish convoys that, once every two weeks following the War of Independence, took supplies to the top of Mount Scopus under United Nations escort and returned the same day. A convoy started out from the Mandelbaum Gate (border post between Israel and

Jordan), passed through the Jordanian-held Sheikh Jarrah neighborhood in east Jerusalem, and ascended to the Israeli enclave on Mount Scopus.

Shomrei HaHar the street running through the bus tunnel on Mount Scopus **K10**

Guardians of the mountain, named for the guards on Mount Scopus during the period that it was an Israeli enclave in Jordanian-held east Jerusalem after the War of Independence.

Yassky, Haim, Dr. (1896 – 1948)
Hadassah Campus, Mount Scopus K10

A doctor, director of medical institutions of the Hadassah Medical Organization in Jerusalem. Killed during the War of Independence while accompanying a convoy up to Mount Scopus.

Yitzhak HaNadiv (1860 – 1935)
Buber – Shayeret Har HaTzofim **J10-K11**

Generous, named for Yitzhak Leib Goldberg, whose donation made possible the purchase of the site on Mount Scopus on which the Hebrew University of Jerusalem was built. A founder of the Carmel Mizrahi (wine) Company, and a delegate to the first Zionist Congress in Basel, Switzerland.

Nahlat Ahim/Nahlaot

Name and establishment:

This neighborhood, located in the western area of the city north of Sha'arei Hesed, was founded in 1924 and given this name in order to mark the aspiration of the Yemenite community, its first residents, to unite and build themselves a heritage in Jerusalem on which to live in brotherhood and fellowship. The founder of the neighborhood, Rabbi Shlomo Haim 'Iraqi Katz (indicating he was a Cohen, of the priestly line) remarked that the main purpose of founding this neighborhood "was for the sake of purchasing a parcel of land, for a public building, on which would be built a large synagogue and an absorption center for immigrants from Yemen" (from a booklet he wrote named "A Financial and Actual Accounting").

The neighborhood of Nahlat Ahim was built around the *Mekor*

Haim Synagogue, famous for its special architectural style, while inside its dome are drawn the symbols of the tribes. The stone houses of the neighborhood are beautiful and spacious, and the streets are broad and open.

In 1927 the neighborhood of Nahlat Ya'akov was built adjacent to it, and in 1934 the neighborhood of Zichron Ahim was built next to Nahlat Ya'akov. Nahlat Ahim impressed its name on the entire area, which adopted the name of Nahlaot, and passed it along as a general name for all the neighborhoods around.

Boundaries:
North – Zichron Ahim, Zichron Yosef
South – Neve Betzalel, Sha'arei Hesed
East – Mid-Town
West – Yitzhak Ben-Zvi Boulevard

Sites: within its boundaries or nearby are the *Mekor Haim* Synagogue, the central site in the neighborhood which is named for Rabbi Haim 'Iraqi, Pargod Theater, Sacher Park, the Valley of the Cross, the Government Campus.

Streets: the streets of the neighborhood are named for ancient Jewish cities. The main street in the neighborhood is Even Sapir Street.

The streets are:

'Alma Betzalel – Shabazi – dead end **G12**

Named for a community in the Upper Galilee (see the neighborhood of Sha'arei Rahamim-Sha'arei Yeshu'a).

Ben-Zvi, Yitzhak [Boulevard] (1884 – 1963)
Shmuel Baruch – Ruppin **G12**

(See the neighborhoods of Giv'at Ram, Kiryat Wolfson, Sha'arei Hesed, Sha'arei Rahamim, Shevet Tzedek/Shchunat HaPahim, Zichron Ya'akov, Zichron Yosef.)

Betzalel ben Uri Ben-Zvi – Mesilat Yesharim **G12**

(See the neighborhoods of Batei Kollel Minsk/Beit HaLevi, Batei Kollel Munkacs, Knesset Yisrael, Mid-Town, Nahlat Tzion, Sha'arei Rahamim, Zichron Ahim, Zichron Ya'akov, Zichron Yosef.)

Corazin Betzalel – Shabazi – dead end **G12**

An ancient city in the Upper Galilee from the Second Temple period and later. Today there is a small community by that name near Lake Kineret (see the neighborhood of Sha'arei Rahamim).

Even Sapir Narkiss – Betzalel **G12**

Named for the book of travels written by Rabbi Ya'akov HaLevi Sapir (1822-1885), a researcher and traveler in the countries of the Middle East, especially Yemen, and the Far East (see the neighborhood of Zichron Ahim).

HaGalil Betzalel – Shabazi **G12**

An area of northern Israel.

HaMadreigot Even Sapir – Nibarta **G12**

Named for the steps on this street (see the neighborhood of Zichron Ahim).

Hatzor Betzalel – dead end **G12**

An ancient city in the Upper Galilee, conquered by Joshua bin Nun in his war against the Canaanites (Joshua 15:23). Today the town Hatzor HaGlilit and Kibbutz Hatzor are there.

'Iraqi, Haim, Rabbi [Steps] (1887 – 1967)
Even Sapir – dead end **G12**

One of the first builders of the Nahlat Ahim neighborhood, one of the great rabbis of the Yemenite and Sephardic communities and of the Oriental community in general. Served as president of the spiritual committee of the community.

Kfar Bar'am Betzalel – Shabazi **G12**

A place in the Upper Galilee, it was settled by Jews in the period of the Mishna and the Talmud. Remnants of a synagogue of that period have been found there.

Lifshitz, Aryeh [Square] (1902 – 1986) Ussishkin at Narkiss **G12**

Author, one of the first contractors in Jerusalem.

Lod Shabazi – Narkiss **G12**

A city in the Judean plain, an important Jewish center after the destruction of the Second Temple, the location of the Sanhedrin and schools of advanced Jewish learning.

Matityahu, Moshe [Square] (1874 – 1981) Narkiss at Tzfat **G12**

One of the most loyal citizens of Jerusalem, a *Yakir Yerushalayim*.

Narkiss, Mordechai (1897 – 1957) HaNagid – Lod **G12**

(See the neighborhoods of Mid-Town, Neve Betzalel.)

Nibarta HaMadreigot – Shabazi **G12**

Named for a place in the Upper Galilee where remains were found of a synagogue from the period of the Mishna and Talmud (see the neighborhood of Zichron Ahim).

Refaeli, Shmuel (1867 – 1923) Ussishkin – Menora **G12**

(See Mid-Town.)

Shabazi, Shalom ben Yosef, Rabbi (1686 – 1719)
Even Sapir – Ben-Zvi – dead end **G12**

Greatest poet of Yemenite Jewry. A spiritual leader of the Jewish community in all the cities and villages of Yemen. He wrote many religious poems for the penitential days preceding Rosh Hashana and for the High Holy Days (see the neighborhood of Zichron Ahim).

Shfar'am Ussishkin – Narkiss **G12**

An ancient city of the Lower Galilee in the time of the Mishna and the Talmud, it served as a religious center after the Bar Kochva revolt.

Tamuz, Yitzhak HaCohen, Rabbi [Square] (1888 – 1975)
Betzalel at Ussishkin **G12**

One of the first builders and residents of the Nahlaot neighborhood.

Tiberias [*Tveria*] Ussishkin – Lod **G12**

An ancient city in the Lower Galilee on the shore of Lake Kineret, the capital of the Galilee during the Second Temple period. After the destruction of the Second Temple, it became a center of Torah study, the Sanhedrin moved to Tiberias from Tzipori, and the Jerusalem Talmud was completed. Tiberias is counted as one of the four holy cities in Israel; the other three are Jerusalem, Hebron and Tzfat. According to tradition, Rabbi Yohanan ben Zakai, the RaMBa"M, Rabbi Meir Ba'al HaNess and others are buried there.

Tzfat Ussishkin – Lod **G12**

An ancient city in the Upper Galilee, built in the Second Temple period. In the time of the Mishna and Talmud it was a center of learning and Torah, and torches were lit there to announce the beginning of each new month. In the sixteenth century it became an important center of the sages of religious law and Kabbala. In the eighteenth century, Hasidic followers of the Ba'al Shem Tov immigrated to and settled in Tzfat, as did disciples of HaGR"A in the nineteenth century. It is one of the four holy cities of Israel; the three others are Jerusalem, Tiberias and Hebron. Today it is a city of artists and Kabbalists.

Tzipori Lod – dead end **G12**

A town in the Lower Galilee, a Torah center in the period of the Mishna and the Talmud, the city of Yehuda HaNasi. Archeological remains have been found there from that period, as well as a mosaic floor called the "Mona Lisa of the Galilee".

Usha Tiberias – dead end **G12**

An ancient city in the Galilee in the time of the Mishna, the location of the seat of the Sanhedrin after the Bar Kochva rebellion. Today there is a kibbutz of that name in the Zebulun Valley that was built not far from the remains of the ancient city.

Ussishkin, Menahem Mendel (1863 – 1941)
Betzalel – Ben Maimon Boulevard **G12-13**

One of the leaders of the Lovers of Zion movement, a Zionist leader and opponent of Herzl's Uganda Plan (to create the Jewish state in Uganda), he worked to organize the Jewish population in the Land of Israel. He was president of *HaKeren HaKayemet LeYisrael* (JNF), was one of the founders and organizers of the Israeli parliament and of the Jewish Teachers Federation, and was one of the founders of the Hebrew University. He was made an Honorary Citizen of Tel-Aviv in 1933 (see the neighborhoods of Rehavia, Sha'arei Hesed, Zichron Ahim).

Yir-on Kfar Bar'am – Shabazi – dead end **G12**

A kibbutz in the Upper Galilee, named for the Biblical Yiron (Joshua 19:38).

Yizhar, 'Armoni [Lane] (1929 – 1948) Narkiss – Israels **G13**

Bearer of the title "Hero of Israel", he lived in the neighborhood and fell during the War of Independence in the battle for the police station at Nebi-Yusha' (*Metzudat Koach*), while serving as a soldier in the PaLMa"H's *Yiftah* Brigade (see the neighborhood of Nahlat Tzadok).

Nahlat Shim'on

Name and establishment:

This neighborhood, located in the northern part of the city near the grave of Shim'on HaTzadik [the Righteous], was founded in 1891. The grave of Shim'on HaTzadik is in nearby Wadi el-Joz, hence the name. With the establishment of the neighborhood, members of the Sephardic community began building houses there, and later, Ashkenazim came as well. During the War of Independence, fierce battles took place here against the Jordanian Arab Legion, the neighborhood was destroyed and most of the houses were left in ruins. The neighborhood remained in Jordanian hands until the Six Day War (1967), when the IDF liberated the area.

Boundaries:

North – Ma'alot Dafna/Arzei HaBira and Kiryat Aryeh

South and west – Beit Yisrael

East – Derech Bar Lev

Sites: within its boundaries or nearby are the grave of Shim'on HaTzadik and Ammunition Hill.

Streets: the streets of the neighborhood are named for priests and a warrior from the time of King David.

The streets are:

Bar Lev, Haim [Boulevard] (1924 – 1994)
Yadin – Shmuel HaNavi **J9-I11**

(See the neighborhoods of Giv'at HaMivtar, Giv'at Shapira/French Hill, Kiryat Aryeh, Sheikh Jarrah.)

Elyashiv Shmuel HaNavi – Yakim **I11**

A priest during the time of King David.

Gemul Shmuel HaNavi – Shmarya **I11**

Meaning reward. Named for two paratroopers who fell in battle on this street during the Six Day War.

Petahia (12th cent.) Yakim – Gemul **I10-11**

Named for Rabbi Petahia ben Ya'akov HaLavan from Regensburg, who traveled among the Jewish communities in many countries and in

Jerusalem. His journal *Sibuv Petahia* contains important information, especially on the Jewish community in the Land of Israel of that period.

Sachs, Moshe, Rabbi (1800 – 1870) Shmuel HaNavi – Bar Lev **I11**

Rabbi and civic leader, helped pave the way for agricultural settlement and for Jewish labor in the Land of Israel, one of the founders of the shelters for the poor in the Old City.

Shim'on HaTzadik Eretz Hefetz – Nablus Road **I10**

(See the neighborhoods of Kiryat Aryeh, Ma'alot Dafna/Arzei HaBira.)

Shmarya Gemul – Elyashiv **I11**

An outstanding warrior in King Davids army.

Shmuel HaNavi Shivtei Yisrael – Bar-Ilan **H10-I11**

(See the neighborhoods of Beit Yisrael, HaBucharim, Ma'alot Dafna/ Arzei HaBira, Mahanayim, Sanhedria, Shikunei Shmuel HaNavi.)

Yakim Shmuel HaNavi – Petahia **I11**

A priest in the time of King David.

Yehoyariv Yakim – dead end **I10**

The head of a priestly family in the time of King Saul and King David.

Nahlat Shiv'a

Name and establishment:

The neighborhood, located in the center of town near Yafo, north of Independence Park, was established in 1869, named for its seven founders and nicknamed "the mother of neighborhoods". This was the third neighborhood to be established outside the walls of the Old City.

The seven founders were young men from the veteran families of the Old City and were thought of as the young Ashkenazic leadership of the time. The seven were Yosef Rivlin, Yehoshu'a Yellin, Michal HaCohen, Yoel Moshe Salomon, Aryeh Leib Horowitz, Beinush Salant and Haim HaLevi Kovner. Yosef Rivlin was the first to settle in the neighborhood, and his house was on the easternmost piece of property, on the site where Beit Yoel stands today. However, of the seven, Yoel Moshe

Salomon was the only one who settled there and continued to live in the neighborhood for the rest of his life. The neighborhood's first houses were torn down during the 1950's, and Beit Yoel (named for Yoel Moshe Salomon) was built at the entrance to the neighborhood, a multiple-story building for shops and offices (at the corner of Yafo and Rivlin Streets).

The first purpose of the neighborhood's builders was to establish an agricultural neighborhood near the city, but as the years passed the neighborhood became urbanized and reached its peak of development during World War I. Its further development was cut short after the war, when the area within the triangle of Yafo, King George and Ben Yehuda Streets became the center of town. In 1989 the neighborhood underwent significant renovation and renewal. Today the whole Nahlat Shiv'a neighborhood has become a pedestrian mall and the entertainment and commercial center of the city – with popular eateries, coffee shops and nightclubs. Most of the residences have become prestigious restaurants and shops for various types of handicrafts.

Boundaries:

North – Beit David/Beit HaRav Kook
South – Hillel Street and Independence Park
East – the Russian Compound
West – Ben Yehuda Street, Kikar Tzion, Mid-Town

Sites: within its boundaries or nearby are the Nahlat Ya'akov Synagogue, on Nahlat Shiv'a Stairs, on which is written "Nahlat Ya'akov Synagogue was the first built outside the Wall of Jerusalem, 5633/1873"; Zion Square, Independence Park and *T'mol Shilshom* Restaurant.

Streets: the streets of this neighborhood are named for its seven founders. The two main streets Yosef Rivlin and Yoel Moshe Salomon, are named for two of the founders.

The streets are:

Beit David [Lane] Salomon – Nahlat Shiv'a Stairs **H12**

Named for Beit David, the first spin-off neighborhood from Nahlat Shiv'a, on the opposite side of Yafo Road.

Beit Knesset [Lane] Salomon – Hillel **H12**

The passageway to the Italian Synagogue and museum of Italian Jewry.

Bichacho, Avraham, Rabbi [Lane] (1858-1923)
Nahlat Shiv'a Stairs – inner courtyard **H12**

One of Jerusalem's rabbis and builders.

Geneo, David and Sons inner courtyard and water cistern **H12**

The Geneo family, descendants of the expellees from Spain and of the Saloniki community, were among the pioneers of the wine industry in Jerusalem. Their vineyard was established in the Jewish Quarter of the Old City, within the walls, in 1840. Family members resided in the Nahlat Shiv'a neighborhood until 1957.

Havillo [Square] Rivlin at Nahlat Shiv'a Stairs **H12**

Named for the Havillo family, among those who renewed the Jewish community in Jerusalem.

Hillel (HaZaken) (1st cent. BCE - 1st cent. CE) King George – Ben Sira **H12**

(See Mid-Town.)

Horowitz, Aryeh Leib Lomzer [Lane]
Salomon – Nahlat Shiv'a Stairs **H12**

One of the seven founders of the Nahlat Shiv'a neighborhood.

Kovner, Haim HaLevi [Lane] Salomon – Nahlat Shiv'a Stairs **H12**

One of the seven founders of the neighborhood.

Michal HaCohen [Square] (1834 – 1914)
Horowitz at Nahlat Shiv'a Stairs **H12**

One of the seven founders of the Nahlat Shiv'a neighborhood.

Nahlat Shiv'a [Stairs] Yafo – Kovner – Rivlin **H12**

Named for the neighborhood.

Rivlin, Yosef (1837 – 1896) Yafo – Hillel **H12**

One of the seven founders of the Nahlat Shiv'a neighborhood. Author, businessman, one of the founders of a number of the early neighborhoods in Jerusalem, among them Mea She'arim. He was the first who settled outside the Old City walls in the Nahlat Shiv'a neighborhood, and was secretary of the Community Council of the Ashkenazic community in Jerusalem.

Salant, Binyamin Beinush [Lane]
Salomon – Nahlat Shiv'a Stairs **H12**

One of the seven founders of the Nahlat Shiv'a neighborhood.

Salomon, Yoel Moshe (1838-1912) Yafo – Hillel **H12**

One of the seven founders of the Nahlat Shiv'a neighborhood. Born in Jerusalem, he opened a printing house in the city and published the first Hebrew periodical in the Land of Israel, "HaLevanon", in 1863. One of the first who worked to get out and build neighborhoods outside the walls of the Old City. He participated as well in the establishment of the Mea She'arim neighborhood and was one of the founders of the city of Petah Tikva.

Shamai (1st cent. BCE - 1st cent. CE) Salomon – HaHistadrut **H12**

(See Mid-Town.)

Yafo Jaffa Gate – Weizmann Boulevard **F11-I12**

(See the neighborhoods of Batei Kollel Horodna/Damesek Eli'ezer, Batei Sa'idoff, Beit David/Beit HaRav Kook, Beit Ya'akov, Even Yisrael, 'Ezrat Yisrael, Mahane Yehuda, Mekor Baruch, Mid-Town, Ohel Shlomo, Romema, Russian Compound, Sha'arei Tzedek, Sha'arei Yerushalayim).

Yahadut Tzarfat Salomon – dead end **H12**

French Jewry, in honor of the initiative of the United Jewish Appeal in France to mark the 40th anniversary of the United Jewish Socialist Foundation.

Yellin, Yehoshu'a [Lane] Salomon – Nahlat Shiv'a Stairs **H12**

One of the seven founders of the Nahlat Shiv'a neighborhood.

Nahlat Tzadok

Name and establishment:

This neighborhood, located in the western part of the city near Neve Betzalel and north of Sha'arei Hesed, was founded in 1908 and named for Rabbi Tzadok HaCohen, the chief rabbi of French Jewry at the time the neighborhood was built. The neighborhood was built by the Jewish Colonization Association (ICA) for poor laborers and craftsmen, who earned their living from work in the institutions of the Alliance society, work made possible thanks to the help of the Jews of France. In the year it was founded, seventeen houses were built, with a garden beside each house, and the remainder of the parcels of land were sold by ICA to the nearby Neve Betzalel association.

For many years, Nahlat Tzadok and Sha'arei Hesed were the westernmost neighborhoods in the area. In the violent attacks on Jews during the British Mandate period, this neighborhood was on the front line facing the Arabs who lived on the opposite hill, today's Giv'at Ram. In the last house at the end of the neighborhood, the defenders set up a fortified position from which to protect the neighborhood.

Today the neighborhood has been swallowed up into the larger neighborhoods on either side, Nahlat Ahim/Nahlaot and Sha'arei Hesed.

Boundaries:

Northeast – Nahlat Ahim/Nahlaot

Southwest – Sha'arei Hesed

West – Neve Betzalel

Sites: within its boundaries or nearby are Sacher Park, the Knesset, the Israel Museum.

Streets: the streets of the neighborhood are named for people connected to the neighborhood.

The streets are:

'Antebbe, Avraham (Albert) (1869 – 1919)
HaGR"A – Israels **G12-13**

Director and representative of Alliance Israelite (KY"H) in Jerusalem, one of the leaders of the Sephardic community in the city, served as a member of the Jerusalem municipality under Turkish rule, worked for the reclamation of Jewish land in general and in the neighborhood of Nahlat Tzadok in particular (see the neighborhood of Sha'arei Hesed).

Antokolsky, Mordechai (Mark) (1843 – 1902)
HaGR"A – Israels **G13**

One of the great sculptors, an artist/author. The motifs in his works were connected to Jerusalem (see the neighborhoods of Neve Betzalel, Sha'arei Hesed).

Israels, Jozef (1824 – 1911) 'Antebbe – dead end **G13**

A famous Dutch Jewish painter, a religious man. Among his works were paintings with themes from Jewish life (see the neighborhoods of Neve Betzalel, Sha'arei Hesed).

Nahlat Tzadok 'Antebbe – dead end **G13**

Named for Rabbi Tzadok HaCohen (1839-1905), who served as the chief rabbi of the Jews of France and worked for the benefit of the Jewish community in the Land of Israel.

Yizhar, 'Armoni [Lane] (1929 – 1948) Narkiss – Israels **G13**

(See the neighborhood of Nahlat Ahim/Nahlaot.)

Nahlat Tzion

Name and establishment:

This neighborhood, located in the center of town southeast of Zichron Yosef, was founded in 1893 and is named for Biblical Zion. Already in 1891 civic leader and director of the Alliance Israelite institutions Avraham (Albert) 'Antebbe began to purchase lands from the Arabs of Lifta to build a residential neighborhood for the poor of the Aleppo (Syrian) Jewish community in Jerusalem. Two years later the Aleppo community, called the "Aram Tzova" community, began to build houses in the neighborhood with the help of loans from Alliance.

The neighborhood populace is mixed – there are residents from Turkey, Iraq and Yemen.

Boundaries:

North – Agrippas Street and the Mahane Yehuda Market

South – Betzalel Street and Nahlat Ahim/Nahlaot

East – Zichron Tuvia and Ohel Moshe

West – Zichron Yosef

Sites: within its boundaries or nearby is the Mahane Yehuda Market.

Streets: the streets of the neighborhood are named for historic cities in the ancient Land of Israel and names of spiritual leaders in Babylonia.

The streets are:

Agrippas (10 BCE – 44 CE) King George – Shmuel Baruch **G11-H12**

(See the neighborhoods of Even Yisrael, Mahane Yehuda, Mazkeret

Moshe, Mid-Town, Mishkenot Yisrael, Ohel Moshe, Sukkat Shalom, Zichron Tuvia, Zichron Yosef).

'Anatot Dalton – Nov **G12**

A Biblical city near Jerusalem. Birthplace of the prophet Jeremiah.

Bachar, Nissim (1848 – 1931)
Agrippas/Shmuel Baruch – Betzalel **G12**

A teacher, born in Jerusalem, and important civic leader. He was a founder of the Alliance school *Kol Yisrael Haverim* and incorporated into the curriculum the study of the Hebrew language. One of the respected members of the Sephardic community in Jerusalem (see the neighborhood of Zichron Yosef).

Beer Sheva' Shilo – Bachar **G12**

Beersheba, one of the ancient cities in the Land of Israel and the capital of the Negev. The name of the city comes from the recurring oath (*shvu'a*) taken by Abraham the Patriarch (Genesis 21:22-34) and afterwards by Isaac (Genesis 26:18-33) on the one side and Abimelech, the king of Gerar, on the other side, regarding seven wells of water.

Beit Tzur Yosef Haim – Bachar **G12**

A historic city near the city of Hebron.

Ben Neria, Baruch Nov – Rama **G12**

A disciple of the prophet Jeremiah.

Betzalel ben Uri Ben-Zvi – Mesilat Yesharim **G12**

(See the neighborhoods of Batei Kollel Minsk/Beit HaLevi, Batei Kollel Munkacs, Knesset Yisrael, Mid-Town, Nahlat Ahim/Nahlaot, Sha'arei Rahamim, Zichron Ahim, Zichron Ya'akov, Zichron Yosef).

Dalton Ben Neria – Shilo **G12**

A Jewish agricultural community in the hills of the Upper Galilee, in the environs of Tzfat.

Dvir Teko'a – Bachar **G12**

A city of the Biblical period, in the Judean hills, near the city of Hebron.

Eilat Gezer – Tzo'ar **G12**

The southernmost city in the Land of Israel, on the shore of the Red Sea. An important port city during the monarchy of King Solomon.

'Ezra Refael Agrippas – Rama **G12**

One of the leaders of the Jews of Aleppo (Syria) in Jerusalem (see the neighborhoods of Ohel Moshe, Zichron Tuvia).

Geva' Rama – Betzalel **G12**

A Biblical city in the tribal inheritance of Benjamin, the birthplace of King Saul and his capital.

Gezer Agrippas – Bachar **G12**

A centrally-located city between Jerusalem and Jaffa in the Biblical period and in the days of the Hasmoneans.

Giv'on Shilo – Teko'a **G12**

A city in the tribal inheritance of Benjamin.

Halhul Agrippas – Yosef Haim **G12**

A Biblical city that was near Hebron.

Lachish Geva' – Tzo'ar **G12**

A fortified city in the time of the monarchy in Judah.

Ma'on Teko'a – Bachar **G12**

A place near Tiberias in the period of the Mishna and Talmud. Today, a suburb of Tiberias.

Mitzpe Geva' – Bachar **G12**

A city in the Judean hills. There Gedalia ben Ahikam established the capital city after the destruction of the First Temple, and it was also the meeting place of the forces which took part in the Maccabean revolt against the Greeks.

Nov Betzalel – Ben Neria **G12**

A city during the Biblical period, a priestly city on the border between the tribes of Benjamin and Judah.

Rama Ohel Moshe – Yosef Haim **G12**

A Biblical city, the city of the prophet Samuel (see the neighborhood of Zichron Tuvia).

Shilo Agrippas – Betzalel **G12**

A city in the hills of Shomron that served as a religious center for Israel in the time of Joshua bin Nun (Joshua 18:1-10) and in the time of the Judges (I Samuel 1).

Somech, ʻOvadia, Rabbi (1812 – 1889) Halhul – Rama **G12**

One of the great rabbis and religious judges of Babylonian Jewry, and its spiritual leader.

Tekoʻa Bachar – Beer Shevaʻ **G12**

A city in the Bible, in the Hebron hills. Birthplace of the prophet Amos (Amos 1:1).

Tzoʻar Eilat – Yosef Haim **G12**

A Biblical city at the southeastern end of the Dead Sea.

Yosef Haim, Rabbi (1832 – 1909) Rama – Gezer **G12**

Named for Rabbi Yosef Haim ben Eliyahu el Hacham, a rabbi and arbiter of religious law and the spiritual leader of Babylonian Jewry in his generation.

Nahlat Zvi/Shchunat HaTeimanim

Name and establishment:

This neighborhood, located in the middle of town near Batei Kollel Ungarin/Nahlat Zvi, and extending between Mea Sheʻarim and Shaʻarei Pina, was founded in 1894 and is named for the philanthropist Baron Maurice (Moshe) de Hirsch ("Hirsch" in German is *Zvi* in Hebrew). Most of its earliest residents were Yemenites and thus the neighborhood is also called *Shchunat HaTeimanim* [the Yemenites' neighborhood].

The building of the neighborhood was made possible thanks to money the founders received from the philanthropist Baron Hirsch's foundation. The money was solicited by the teacher and principal Nissim Bachar, director of the Alliance (KY"H) schools. The architectural style of the houses was Yemenite: narrow streets and corridors, with attics and cellars. There were two synagogues, one of them named for the Yemenite poet Rabbi Shalom Shabazi. Those who came to pray in the synagogue took off their shoes at the entrance, as is the custom in Yemen, and sat Eastern style on pillows and rugs. The second synagogue, Beer Yaʻakov, was built in the center of the neighborhood, near the cistern, and is named for Rabbi Ya'akov Aryeh.

Today's residents are Yemenites, members of other communities and a minority of Ashkenazim.

Boundaries:

Northeast – Beit Yisrael

Southeast – Mea She'arim

West – Sha'arei Pina and Geula

Sites: within its boundaries or nearby is the synagogue named for Rabbi Shalom Shabazi.

Streets: the main street of the neighborhood is called "TaRMa"V" (the year 1882), the year of the organized Yemenite *'aliya* to the Land of Israel.

The streets are:

Habshush, Haim, Rabbi (1833 – 1899) Mea She'arim – Belzer **H11**

(See the neighborhoods of Beit Yisrael, Sha'arei Pina.)

Mea She'arim Straus – Shivtei Yisrael **H11**

(See the neighborhoods of Batei Kollel Ungarin/Nahlat Zvi, Batei Kollel Warsaw/Nahlat Ya'akov, Batei Naitin, Batei Perlman/'Ir Shalom, Beit Yisrael, Geula, Mea She'arim, Sha'arei Pina.)

TaRMa"V (1882) Zecharia HaRofe – Habshush **H11**

To indicate the year of the start of the Second Aliya in general, and to mark the *'aliya* of the Jews of Yemen to the Land of Israel in particular, especially those who settled in Jerusalem (see the neighborhood of Sha'arei Pina).

Zecharia HaRofe (first half of the 15th cent.)
Habshush – Havakuk **H11**

Rabbi Zecharia ben Shlomo HaRofe [the doctor], one of the outstanding sages of Yemen in knowledge of homiletics and religious law (see the neighborhood of Sha'arei Pina).

Nayot (HaShikun HaAnglo-Saxi)

Name and establishment:

This neighborhood, located in the southwestern part of the city next to 'Aza and Herzog Streets, was founded in 1962. At first it was called the "Anglo-Saxon neighborhood" because the resi dents were mostly English-speaking immigrants from America and England.

The name *Nayot* was mentioned in the Bible in the recounting of David's flight from King Saul, I Samuel 19:18-19, "He and Samuel went and took up residence in *Nayot*. And it was told to Saul saying, 'Here is David in *Nayot* in the *Rama*,'" *Nayot* from *noy*, meaning beauty. The Aramaic translation (of the Bible) explains the name *Nayot* as *beit ulpana*, a house of study where Samuel the prophet and David the shepherd learned Torah.

The neighborhood is built on rocky land where there were quarries in years past.

Boundaries:
North – Neve Granot, the Israel Museum, the Shrine of the Book
South – Rabbi Herzog Boulevard
East – the Valley of the Cross
West – the Botanical Garden of the Hebrew University

Sites: within its boundaries or nearby are the Israel Museum, the Bible Lands Museum, the Shrine of the Book, the Valley of the Cross, the Botanical Garden of the Hebrew University.

Streets: the neighborhood streets are named for authors and poets.

The streets are:

Bazak, Betzalel (1898 – 1975) Shneur – Shahal **E14-F14**

(See the neighborhood of Giv'at Mordechai.)

Bourla, Yehuda (1888 – 1969) Shneur – Wise **F14**

(See the neighborhoods of Giv'at Ram, Neve Shaanan.)

Davidson, Yisrael (1870 – 1939) Bourla – Nayot **F14**

Researcher of medieval Jewish poetry, collector of general and religious poetry until the beginning of the Enlightenment (*Haskala*) (see the neighborhood of Neve Granot).

Davidson, Yosef [Square] (1898 – 1947) Shneur at Yeivin **F14**

One of the leaders of Polish Jewry.

Else Lasker Schüler (1869 – 1945) Davidson – dead end **F14**

Poetess. Her poems contain Jewish motifs.

Herzog, Yitzhak Isaac HaLevi, Rabbi (1888 – 1959)
'Aza – Golomb **G14-E16**

(See the neighborhoods of Giv'at HaVradim/Shikun Rassco, Giv'at

Mordechai, Gonenim/Katamonim, Kiryat Shmuel, Rehavia.)

Nayot Davidson – Davidson **F14**

Named for the neighborhood (see the neighborhood of Neve Granot).

Shami, Yitzhak (1888 – 1949) Davidson – dead end **F14**

Teacher, author, first author to describe the Sephardic Jewish experience in Israel.

Shneur, Zalman (1887 – 1959) Herzog – Bazak **F14**

Poet, author, playwright, editor. Was one of the outstanding Hebrew poets in modern Hebrew literature. Winner of the Israel Prize in 1955.

Yeivin, Yehoshua H. (1891 – 1970) Shneur – dead end **F14**

Author, editor, an activist in the Revisionist Movement and a member of the underground in the struggle against the British Mandate rule in the Land of Israel. 1960 winner of a prize in Bible.

Neve Betzalel (Shchunat HaOmanim)

Name and establishment:

This neighborhood, located in the center of town to the south of Nahlat Ahim/Nahlaot, was founded in 1927 by Professor Boris Shatz, founder of the Betzalel Art School, and it is named for the school and for Betzalel ben Uri, the artist/builder of the Mishkan (portable Sanctuary) in the days of the Israelites' wanderings in the desert (Exodus 31:2). This artists' neighborhood was built to provide housing for the workers at the art school. Professor Shatz bought from ICA (the Jewish Colonization Association) the large property that remained after the building of the Nahlat Tzadok neighborhood. With the construction of the Israel Museum, the Betzalel Museum was transferred to one of the Israel Museum's wings. In 1989 the school itself, now called "Academy", moved to Mount Scopus.

Today, this neighborhood has been swallowed up in the larger neighborhoods around it, Nahlat Ahim/Nahlaot and Sha'arei Hesed.

Boundaries:

Northeast – Nahlat Ahim/Nahlaot

Southwest – Sha'arei Hesed and Nahlat Tzadok

Sites: within its boundaries or nearby are the Artists' House, Sacher Park, the Knesset, the Israel Museum.

Streets: the neighborhood streets are named for well-known Jewish artists who were teachers in the Betzalel School.

The streets are:

Antokolsky, Mordechai (Mark) (1843 – 1902)
HaGR"A – Israels **G13**

(See the neighborhoods of Nahlat Tzadok, Sha'arei Hesed.)

Hirschenberg, Shmuel (Rabbi Zvi) (1865 – 1908)
HaGR"A – Narkiss **G12-13**

A famous Jewish painter, born in Lodz (Poland), known primarily for his work of art entitled "*HaGalut* [Exile]" (see the neighborhood of Sha'arei Hesed).

Israels, Jozef (1824 – 1911) 'Antebbe – dead end **G13**

(See the neighborhoods of Nahlat Tzadok, Sha'arei Hesed.)

Narkiss, Mordechai (1897 – 1957) HaNagid – Lod **G12**

(See the neighborhoods of Mid-Town, Nahlat Ahim/Nahlaot.)

Neve Granot

Name and establishment:

This neighborhood, located in the southwestern part of the city, near the Israel Museum and north of the neighborhood of Nayot, was founded in 1963 and named after Dr. Avraham Granot, an expert on agrarian (land) policy, active in and president of *HaKeren HaKayemet LeYisrael*. He devoted the better part of his life to working on behalf of the Jewish National Fund, and he wrote books on the problems of the soil in the Land of Israel.

Boundaries:

North – Israel Museum
South - Nayot
East – Haim Hazaz Boulevard
West – Neve Shaanan

Sites: within its boundaries or nearby are the Israel Museum, the Bible Lands Museum, the Shrine of the Book, the Valley of the Cross, the botanical garden of the Hebrew University.

Streets: the streets of this neighborhood are named for an author and a researcher.

The streets are:

Davidson, Yisrael (1870 – 1939) Bourla – Nayot **F14**

(See the neighborhood of Nayot.)

Granot, Avraham, Dr. (1890 – 1962) Avigad – Davidson – Nayot **F14**

Author and publicist, president of the Jewish National Fund, one of those who was active on behalf of the Hebrew University of Jerusalem (see the neighborhood of Neve Shaanan).

Nayot Davidson – Davidson **F14**

(See the neighborhood of Nayot.)

Neve Shaanan

Name and establishment:

This neighborhood, located in the southwestern part of the city near the Israel Museum and the Bible Lands Museum, was founded in 1925. Its name is taken from the words of the prophet Isaiah 33:20, in his prophecy on Jerusalem at the end of days, "Look at Zion, the city of our solemn gatherings; your eyes shall see Jerusalem a peaceful dwelling place..." Its founders were ultra-Orthodox Jews, residents of the city, who wished to fulfill the commandment "You shall bring redemption to the land."

During the War of Independence, this neighborhood served as the base for the Harel Brigade fighters, the PaLMa"H battalion that broke through to capture the Old Katamon neighborhood. In 1960 the neighborhood houses were condemned and torn down by the State, and in their place was built the Israel Museum and the Shrine of the Book. At first the neighborhood was located on the ridge where the museum now stands, and today Neve Shaanan is comprised of a row of residential buildings along the western slope of that same ridge.

Boundaries:

North – Israel Museum, Bible Lands Museum, Shrine of the Book

South - Nayot

East – Neve Granot

West – Giv'at Ram – Hebrew University

Sites: within its boundaries or nearby are the Israel Museum, Bible Lands Museum, Shrine of the Book, Giv'at Ram – Hebrew University, Botanical Garden.

Streets: the neighborhood streets are named for authors and a researcher and professor.

The streets are:

Avigad, Nahman (1905 – 1992) Bourla – Granot **F13-14**

Researcher, *Yakir Yerushalayim*.

Bourla, Yehuda (1888 – 1969) Shneur – Avigad **F13-14**

(See the neighborhoods of Giv'at Ram, Nayot.)

Granot, Avraham, Dr. (1890 – 1962) Avigad – Davidson – Nayot **F13-14**

(See the neighborhood of Neve Granot.)

Michaelson, Y. Z., Prof. (1903 – 1982) Avigad – dead end **F13-14**

Professor, father of modern ophthalmic medicine in Israel.

Neve Shaanan Bourla – dead end **F13-14**

Named for the neighborhood.

Wise, Shmuel (Stephen) (1874 – 1949) Ruppin – Bourla **F13**

(See the neighborhood of Giv'at Ram.)

Neve Ya'akov

Name and establishment:

This neighborhood, in the northern part of the city, north of Pisgat Zeev, was established first in 1924, was destroyed in the War of Independence and was rebuilt in 1972. It is named for Rabbi Yitzhak Ya'akov Reines (see the neighborhood of Kiryat

Moshe), one of the spiritual leaders of the religious Zionist movement.

In the beginning the neighborhood was called Kfar 'Ivri ("Jewish village"), a village built by residents of Jerusalem who wished to establish a national-religious agricultural settlement where Torah learning and work could be combined. Because they were youth of the Young Mizrahi movement, they called the village by the name Neve Ya'akov, after the name of the founder of the *Mizrahi* movement, Rabbi Yitzhak Ya'akov Reines.

Boundaries:
Northwest – 'Atarot-Industrial Zone
South – Pisgat Zeev
Southeast – the Arab village Hizma
West – the Jerusalem – Ramallah – Nablus Road

Sites: within its boundaries or nearby are the mound [*tel*] of the ancient city of Giv'at Shaul, known from the Biblical period as the first capital of Israel.

Streets: the neighborhood streets are named for rabbis, statesmen, members of the Hagana and the IDF, newspapermen, authors and researchers, public activists.

The streets are:

Abir Ya'akov (1807 – 1880) Eliach – dead end **L3**

Named for Rabbi Ya'akov Abuhatzera, a central and outstanding Torah figure, father of the Abuhatzera dynasty, spiritual leader of Moroccan Jewry and an expert in all Torah subjects. Rabbi Ya'akov wanted very much to make *'aliya* to Israel, but when he finally succeeded in leaving Morocco, he got only as far as Egypt and died there.

Ahimeir, Abba, Dr. (1896 – 1962)
Neve Ya'akov Boulevard – dead end **J3-4**

Journalist, author and thinker, one of the opponents of British rule in the Land of Israel, a member of the underground during the British Mandate period, he was tried for the murder of Arlosoroff but was acquitted. He was a member of the editorial board of the Hebrew encyclopedia.

Astora Meir Ma'aglot HaRav Pardes – Zevin **L3**

Honorary consul of Israel in Milan, Italy, one of the leaders of Italian Jewry, contributed greatly to various institutions and enterprises in the State of Israel.

Balaban, Meir (1877 – 1942) Ma'aglot HaRav Pardes – dead end **K2-3**

A renowned historian of Polish Jewry, founded the Institute for Jewish Thought in Warsaw. Perished in the Holocaust.

Bar-Yakar, Dov [Lane] (1893 – 1951)
Ma'aglot HaRav Pardes – dead end **K3**

Author, journalist, one of the founders of the Jewish village of Neve Ya'akov, and editor of *Luah Yerushalayim*, Jerusalem Calendar.

El'azar, David (1925 – 1976) Metzudat Kfir – Derech Ramallah **J3**

General, army chief of staff, hero of the Yom Kippur War.

Eliach, Shlomo Yosef (1860 – 1941)
Zevin – Abir Ya'akov – dead end **L3**

Founded a kitchen and boarding house intended to help in absorbing new immigrants, saw to supplying food and upkeep for immigrants, founded the association *Knesset Tzion*, the first organization of Orthodox rabbis in America in support of the Jewish community in the Land of Israel, and especially that in Jerusalem. One of the builders of the neighborhood of Knesset Yisrael.

Fleg, Edmond [Lane] (1874 – 1963)
Ma'aglot HaRav Pardes – dead end **K3**

Jewish author in France, poet, playwright and philosopher, one of the spiritual leaders of Jewish youth in France, Zionist leader and chairman of the Jewish National Fund in France.

Funt, Yisrael (1923 – 1978) Ma'aglot HaRav Pardes – dead end **K3**

One of the heads of the Hagana in Jerusalem and one of its commanders in the Old City, Neve Ya'akov and 'Atarot.

Gamzon, Reuven (Robert) [Lane] (1905 – 1961)
Neve Ya'akov Boulevard – dead end **K2**

Scientist, one of the leaders of French Jewry, was a member of the Jewish underground in France, worked as a scientist at the Weizmann Institute.

Goldberg, Leah [Lane] (1911 – 1970)
Neve Ya'akov Boulevard – dead end **K3**

Poetess, authoress and literary critic, she crafted tales and literary works, was one of the editors of the publishing house *Sifriyat HaPo'alim*, and lecturer in general literature at the Hebrew University of Jerusalem.

Gulak, Asher (1881 – 1940) Ma'aglot HaRav Pardes – dead end **K2-3**

Jurist, researcher of Jewish law in the period of the Talmud, professor at the Hebrew University of Jerusalem.

Hayot, Zvi Peretz, Rabbi (1877 – 1928)
Neve Ya'akov Boulevard – dead end **K2-3**

A researcher of the Bible and Jewish history, head of the rabbinical court in Vienna, chairman of the Zionist Executive, served as a member of the Jewish delegation at the San Remo Peace Conference (of April 1920), where the Balfour Declaration was formally included in the treaty establishing the British Mandate for Palestine.

Katznelson, Reuven [Square] (1890 – 1977)
Ma'aglot HaRav Pardes at Neve Ya'akov Boulevard **K3**

A founder of Hadassah Hospital in Jerusalem, a pioneer in medicine in the Land of Israel, a member of the British Army Jewish Brigade Zion Mule Corps in WWI, a *Yakir Yerushalayim*.

Kfar 'Ivri Astora – dead end **L3**

First name of the Jewish agricultural village of Neve Ya'akov in northern Jerusalem.

Livneh, Eli'ezer (1903 – 1975) Ma'aglot HaRav Pardes – dead end **K3**

Philosopher, a leader of the Labor movement in the Land of Israel, a member of Knesset.

Lutz, Charles (1895 – 1975) Ma'aglot HaRav Pardes – dead end **K3**

Swiss statesman, a Righteous Gentile who saved many Jews during the Holocaust.

Ma'aglot HaRav Pardes (1893 – 1972)
from Neve Ya'akov Boulevard, circles the neighborhood **K2-K3**

Named for Rabbi Eliyahu Pardes, a rabbi and educator, the chief rabbi of Jerusalem.

Naiman, Shmuel Gedalia, Rabbi (1888 – 1959) Zevin – Zevin **L2-3**

A rabbi and teacher in the *'Etz Haim* Yeshiva, he wrote the book *Gedolei Shmuel.*

Neve Ya'akov [Boulevard]
Ma'aglot HaRav Pardes – Derech Ramallah **I3-K2**

The main street in the neighborhood, named for the neighborhood (see the neighborhood of Pisgat Zeev Tzafon).

Otzar HaGeonim Eliach – dead end **L3**

Named for the book by Dr. Binyamin Menashe Levin (1879-1944), in which he collected the Torah thoughts of the Babylonian Geonim which had been hidden in archival collections, among manuscripts in various libraries around the world and old and new periodicals. Dr. Levin collected and organized the material according to the tractates of the Talmud.

Panigel, Refael Meir, Rabbi (1804 – 1893)
Ma'aglot HaRav Pardes – dead end **K2-3**

Chief rabbi of the Land of Israel, the *Rishon LeTzion*, one of the foremost arbiters of religious law in his generation, a founder of *Tiferet Yerushalayim* Yeshiva.

Shadiker, Nahum, Rabbi Eliach – dead end **L3**

He was one of the earliest and most central figures among the founders of the old Jewish community of Jerusalem, one of the initiators and founders of neighborhoods in the city, a community activist and builder of Jerusalem.

Shauli, Moshe Cohen, Rabbi (1920 – 1994) Astora – dead end **L3**

Rabbi, author, philosopher, educator and man of deeds, a member of religious councils, a member of the management of *Hevra Kadisha* organizations (burial societies) in Jerusalem, chief rabbi of Iranian Jewish communities in Israel and the Diaspora, was active in the "Magic Carpet" operation to bring Yemenite and Bulgarian Jews to Israel.

Sneh, Moshe, Dr. (1909 – 1972)
Neve Ya'akov Boulevard – dead end **J3**

Statesman, author, head of the central committee of the Zionist Federation in Poland, one of the leaders of the Jewish Agency and of the Hagana, a member of Knesset.

Tabenkin, Yitzhak (1887 - 1971)
Neve Ya'akov Boulevard – dead end **K3**

One of the heads of the Labor movement in the Land of Israel, one of the founders of the *Po'alei Tzion* labor party, one of the founders of the United Kibbutz movement and the Labor Federation, a delegate to Zionist Congresses, a member of Knesset.

Victor veYulius Ma'aglot HaRav Pardes – dead end **K3**

Named for Victor Levy (1893-1946), one of the commanders of the Jewish Battalion in World War I, and for Julius (Yehuda) Jacobs, a senior official in the days of the British Mandate. The two acted as representatives of the national institutions and were killed in an explosion in the King David Hotel in Jerusalem in 1946.

Wasserman, Pinhas, Rabbi (1917 – 1977)
Neve Ya'akov Boulevard – dead end **K3**

Spiritual leader of the remnants of the Romanian Jewish community, teacher and founder of the *Torah VaDat* institutions, was a ritual slaughterer, *mohel* and cantor. All matters of religion were given over to him during the days of horror of the Shoah and of the Communist regime in Romania.

Winograd, Yitzhak, Rabbi (1851 – 1913) Zevin – Zevin **L3**

One of the outstanding rabbis of Jerusalem.

Zevin, Shai, Rabbi (1885 – 1978) Winograd – Winograd **L2-3**

Editor of the Talmudical Encyclopedia.

Zuckerman, Baruch (1887 – 1971)
Ma'aglot HaRav Pardes – dead end **K2**

Journalist, teacher in the United States, Zionist leader active on behalf of Israel even before its founding.

Ohel Moshe

Name and establishment:

The neighborhood, in the center of town, south of Mahane Yehuda and west of Mazkeret Moshe, was founded in 1883, and named after Sir Moses Montefiore, one of the leaders of Jewry in England and one of the great Jewish philanthropists of the nineteenth century, who built the first neighborhoods outside the walls of the Old City. The Ohel Moshe neighborhood was built for Sephardic Jews and was actually the first Sephardic neighborhood established outside the walls of the Old City. Along with Mazkeret Moshe, which was built for Ashkenazic Jews, it was the first of the six neighborhoods named for Sir Moses Montefiore (the other four are Bnei Moshe/Neve Shalom, Yemin Moshe, Zichron Moshe and Kiryat Moshe).

The building of these two neighborhoods was made possible thanks to the support of the Mazkeret Moshe Fund, named after and in honor of Sir Moses, for the purpose of increasing the number of Jerusalem neighborhoods. This neighborhood, like others of that period, was built on the "courtyard model", although the need for security which dictated this construction no longer existed. Therefore, the neighborhood's gates, except for the main one on Agrippas Street, remained open all hours of the day and night. At the entrance to the neighborhood hangs a marble plaque in commemoration of Montefiore's name.

In this neighborhood lived the printer and publisher "Shayish" – **Sh**lomo **Y**israel **Sh**irizli, whose home and business served as a center of culture, literature and language.

Boundaries:
North – Agrippas Street and the Mahane Yehuda Market
South – Knesset Yisrael
East – Mazkeret Moshe
West – Zichron Tuvia

Sites: within its boundaries or nearby are the Mahane Yehuda Market, the *Ohel Moshe* Synagogue and the Sephardic garden in memory of the neighborhood's founders and early residents.

Streets: the neighborhood streets are named for well-known mountains in Israel.

The streets are:

Agrippas (10 BCE – 44 CE) King George – Shmuel Baruch **G11-H12**

(See the neighborhoods of Even Yisrael, Mahane Yehuda, Mazkeret Moshe, Mid-Town, Mishkenot Yisrael, Nahlat Tzion, Sukkat Shalom, Zichron Tuvia, Zichron Yosef).

'Ezra Refael Agrippas – Rama **G12**

(See the neighborhoods of Nahlat Tzion, Zichron Tuvia.)

HaCarmel Shomron – Zichron Tuvia **G12**

(See the neighborhood of Mazkeret Moshe.)

HaERe"Z (1870 – 1954) Ohel Moshe – 'Ezra Refael **G12**

Acronym of Rabbi **I**sse**r** **Z**alman Meltzer, one of the foremost heads of yeshiva, the head of the *'Etz Haim* Yeshiva in Jerusalem.

HaGilbo'a HaCarmel – HaERe"Z – Ohel Moshe **G12**

A mountain in the Jezreel Valley. King Saul died there during battle.

HaHermon Agrippas – HaGilbo'a **G12**

The highest mountain in Israel, on the northeast border.

Har Nevo Mazkeret Moshe – HaGilbo'a **G12**

One of the mountains east of the Jordan River, which, according to the Bible, Moses climbed before his death in order to see the land of Canaan from its heights.

Ohel Moshe Nevo – Tavor **G12**

Named for the neighborhood.

Shirizli, Shlomo Yisrael, Rabbi (1878 – 1938)
HaCarmel – Rabbi Aryeh **G12**

(See the neighborhood of Mazkeret Moshe.)

Tavor Shomron – 'Ezra Refael **G12**

(See the neighborhoods of Batei Broyde/Ohalei Ya'akov, Batei Rand, Knesset Yisrael, Mazkeret Moshe.)

Ohel Shlomo

Name and establishment:

This neighborhood, in the center of town, northwest of the Mahane Yehuda Market and at the border of the Mekor Baruch neighborhood beside Yafo, was established in 1891 by Rahamim Mizrachi. He named it in memory of his father Shlomo Mizrachi, one of the two Jewish members of the Jerusalem City Council in the period of Turkish rule. It was he who convinced the Turkish government to allow the Jews to pave the plaza in front of the Western Wall.

One street in the neighborhood is named for an exceptional woman, Gittel Dinowitz, whose life was closely connected with the houses of the Jewish Quarter in the Old City. She was known as a pillar of community life there, for her warm relationship with everyone and her kind and charitable acts.

Most of the residents of the neighborhood belong to the ultra-Orthodox community.

Boundaries:
North – Mekor Baruch
South/southeast – Yafo and the Mahane Yehuda Market
West – Sha'arei Yerushalayim, Romema

Sites: within its boundaries or nearby is the Mahane Yehuda Market

Streets: the streets of the neighborhood are named after rabbis.

The streets are:

Alfandari, Shlomo El'azar, Rabbi (1826 – 1930)
Ben Matityahu – HaTurim **G11**

(See the neighborhoods of Mahane Yehuda, Mekor Baruch, Ruhama.)

'Alwan, Shabtai, Rabbi (1873 – 1941) Dinowitz – HaTurim **G11**

(See the neighborhood of Mahane Yehuda.)

Dinowitz, Gittel (1879 – 1939) Yafo – Alfandari **G11**

(See the neighborhood of Mahane Yehuda.)

Netiv Yitzhak Navon – dead end **G11**

(See the neighborhood of Mahane Yehuda.)

Yafo Jaffa Gate – Weizmann Boulevard **F11-I12**

(See the neighborhoods of Batei Kollel Horodna/Damesek Eli'ezer, Batei Sa'idoff, Beit David/Beit HaRav Kook, Beit Ya'akov, Even Yisrael, 'Ezrat Yisrael, Mahane Yehuda, Mekor Baruch, Mid-Town, Nahlat Shiv'a, Romema, Russian Compound, Sha'arei Tzedek, Sha'arei Yerushalayim).

Pat

Name and establishment:

This neighborhood, located in the southwestern part of the city near the neighborhoods of Gonenim/Katamonim and Beit Safafa, was established in 1971 and named for Ya'akov Pat (1894-1956), a member of the guard organization *HaShomer* in the period of Turkish rule, a soldier in the Jewish Brigade of the British army in World War I and a Hagana commander in the Jerusalem district during the British Mandate period.

The neighborhood is located at the edge of ʻEmek Refaim, the locale of King David's victory over the Philistines.

Boundaries:

North and Northwest – Gonenim/Katamonim

South – Beit Safafa

East – Talpiot-Industrial Zone

Sites: within its boundaries or nearby are the Jerusalem Mall (Malha), Teddy Stadium.

Streets: the streets are named for Labor movement leaders and Lovers of Zion.

The streets are:

Arest, Avraham (1905 – 1967) Locker – Pat **F17**

One of the leaders of the Labor movement in Jerusalem, a Hagana commander, a member of the Jerusalem municipality.

Barʻam, Moshe [Road] (1911 – 1987) Pat – HaUman **G17-18**

A commander in the Hagana, one of the civic leaders in Jerusalem, general secretary of *Poʻalei Yerushalayim*, a member of the city council, a member of Knesset, a coalition chairman in the Knesset, a labor minister in the government of Israel, one of the builders of Jerusalem (see the neighborhood of Talpiot-Industrial Zone).

Boehm, Aryeh (1887 – 1941) Pat – Locker **F17**

A doctor in Jerusalem, he established and directed the Pasteur Institute in the city, one of the initiators of the Medical Association of the Land of Israel, founded the health committee.

Dov Yosef (1899 – 1979) Pat – HaGanenet **F17-E20**

(See the neighborhood of Gilo.)

Fischer, Maurice (1903 – 1965) Locker – dead end **F17**

A diplomat, a member of the underground, ambassador of Israel in France and in Italy.

Locker, Berl (1887 – 1972) Pat – Pat **F17**

One of the leaders of the Zionist movement and of the Labor movement in the Land of Israel, chairman of the Jewish Agency executive, a member of Knesset, a *Yakir Yerushalayim*.

Pat, Ya'akov (1894 – 1956) Golomb – Bar'am **E16-F17**

(See the neighborhood of Gonenim/Katamonim Hei and San Simon, Gonenim/Katamonim Het, Tet.)

Pineles, Shmuel (1843 – 1928) Locker – dead end **F17**

One of the early Lovers of Zion in Romania, one of the founders of the Association for the (Jewish) Colonization of the Land of Israel in Romania, deputy chairman of the First Zionist Congress in Basel.

Rosenstein, Dov [Lane] (1889 – 1948) Pat – Locker **F17**

Zionist activist in Warsaw, one of the first builders of the Beit HaKerem neighborhood, economic initiator, assisted in the purchase of properties for Jewish neighborhoods and was active in the defense of the Jewish community in the Land of Israel.

Pisgat Zeev

Name and establishment:

This neighborhood, located in the northern part of the city between Giv'at Shapira/French Hill to the south and Neve Ya'akov to the north, was founded in 1984 and named in memory of Zeev Jabotinsky, the founder and leader of the Revisionist movement. The neighborhood's original name was "Pisgat Tel", a short form of the Arabic name for this hill, "Ras e-Tawil", the high hill, on which the neighborhood was built.

The neighborhood is divided into five sections: Pisgat Zeev Mercaz [central] which is the oldest part, Pisgat Zeev Ma'arav [west] bordering the Arab community of Beit Hanina, Pisgat Zeev Tzafon [north], Pisgat Zeev Mizrah [east] and Pisgat Zeev Darom [south].

The neighborhood is an additional link in the belt of neighborhoods built around the capital after the Six Day War.

Boundaries:

North – Neve Ya'akov

South – Giv'at Shapira/French Hill

East – Hizma

West – Beit Hanina

Sites: within its boundaries or nearby are the mound [*tel*] of the Biblical Giv'at Shaul - the first capital of Israel, the monument to the soldiers of the Duchifat reconnaissance patrol, and the Meir promenade.

Streets: many of the streets in the neighborhood are named for youth who fought and survived or fought and fell in the military campaigns of Israel in the hills of Jerusalem, and also named for the commanders of the underground fighting organizations ETZe"L and LeH"I. Other streets are named for army men, educators, authors, historians, public figures, government ministers and signs of the zodiac.

The streets are:

Pisgat Zeev Mercaz

Aaronfeld, Nahum (1912 – 1992) Bar On – Bar On **K-L5**

One of the senior doctors in Israel in the field of internal medicine and cardiology, he was the physician of Israel's presidents and the personal physician of David Ben-Gurion.

Altman, Aryeh (1902 – 1982)
HaSayeret HaYerushalmit – Heil HaAvir **K-L5**

One of the heads of the Revisionist organization, a member of the Provisional Government, a member of Knesset, a *Yakir Yerushalayim*.

Bar-On, Uri (1925 – 1985) Gal – Sayeret Duchifat **K-L5**

A fighter in the Jerusalem Brigade and its commander, took part in all of Israel's wars, established the reconnaissance unit, was involved in settlement of the Land.

Basravi, Betzalel Ya'akov Yehoshu'a – dead end **K-L4**

Educator, founder of the youth movement in Damascus and a counselor in the movement, one of the leaders of the movement in Jerusalem, a community activist, especially in the council of teachers in support of *HaKeren HaKayemet LeYisrael.*

Gal Sayeret Duchifat – Rahmilewitz **K5**

Named after Yehoshu'a Goldschmidt (1925–1948), a fighting officer of ETZe"L, he stood out from the beginning as a superior organization person and an outstanding commander, a brave fighter and very resourceful. He was appointed to the position of commander of the fighting force of ETZe"L.

Gedud Hermesh HaArba'a – Heil HaAvir **K4-5**

A battalion of the first armored infantry established in the IDF during the time of the War of Independence. Later it became an organic part of the armored regiment and took part in all of Israel's wars.

Gedud Michmash HaSayeret HaYerushalmit – HaArba'a **K5**

Brigades or reconnaissance units that operated and fought in the Jerusalem area during the War of Independence (1948).

Gedud Moriah [Square]
Moshe Dayan Boulevard at HaShisha 'Asar **K5**

A battalion of field troops of the 'Etzioni Brigade (Jerusalem Brigade). The battalion fought in the framework of the Harel Brigade in battles in and around Jerusalem, especially in the Jerusalem Corridor between Neve Ya'akov and 'Atarot, in the War of Independence (1948).

HaArba'a Sayeret Duchifat – Heil HaAvir **K4-5**

Four. Named for fighters who fell in the battle for Neve Ya'akov in the Six Day War (1967). They were members of an armored battalion that supported the fighters of the Harel Brigade.

HaGedud HaHamishi Hativat Giv'ati – HaArba'a **K5**

The fifth battalion. The first PaLMa"H battalion to reach Sha'ar HaGuy, operated to secure the road to Jerusalem and helped in escorting the convoys to the city. In the Nahshon Campaign in 1948, the battalion was attached to the Harel Brigade and also fought in the Jerusalem Corridor.

HaGedud HaShishi [Square]
HaSayeret HaYerushalmit at Heil HaAvir **K4**

The sixth battalion. Named for the Jerusalem battalion of the PaLMa"H.

HaGesher HaHai [Square]
Moshe Dayan Boulevard at Sayeret Duchifat **K5**

Living bridge. Marks the historic meeting of the Jewish Brigade and volunteers of the Old Jewish Community in Israel with the Jewish survivors of the Holocaust at the end of World War II, as well as the rescue operations and bringing the survivors to a safe haven in the Land of Israel.

HaNayadot HaArba'a – HaArba'a **K5**

Mobile guard units that operated on the eve of the establishment of the State and the War of Independence, in order, among other things, to maintain contact with settlements under siege and to distribute food and arms to the besieged residents.

HaSayar Heil HaAvir – dead end **K4**

An army scout, a symbolic name.

HaSayeret HaYerushalmit Sayeret Duchifat – Heil HaAvir **K4-5**

The reconnaissance unit of the Jerusalem Brigade that helped capture Armon HaNatziv, in Talpiot Mizrah, during the Six Day War, and the enemy posts to the south as far as Ramat Rahel. In the remaining days of the war, the unit joined with other units of the Brigade and advanced with them past the Hebron hills.

HaShiryonai Heil HaAvir – dead end **K4-5**

Soldier of the armored corps, a symbolic name.

HaShisha ʻAsar Heil HaAvir – Moshe Dayan Boulevard **K5**

Sixteen, in memory of the sixteen Hagana fighters of Gedud Moriah – the ʻEtzioni Brigade – who fell in battle near ʻAtarot during the War of Independence (1948).

Hativat Givʻati Mishteret HaYishuvim – Gedud Hermesh **K5**

One of the brigades of HaHI"SH (field companies), established at the beginning of the War of Independence, that fought in the area of Tel-Aviv and on the way to Jerusalem, conducted battles to stop the Egyptian army in the south and break through to the Negev. In the Six Day War it fought in Shomron, and in the Yom Kippur War it fought on the Egyptian front.

HaTotehan HaArbaʻa – HaArbaʻa – dead end **K4**

The gunner, a symbolic name.

Heil HaAvir Moshe Dayan Boulevard – Sayeret Duchifat **K4-5**

The air corps, one of the important forces of the IDF. In Israel's battles it carried out important missions: bombing, transporting arms and soldiers, executing advance reconnaissance flights and aerial battles. In the Six Day War, the air force supported ground battles and contributed to subduing the enemy and achieving victory in the war.

Heil HaKesher Gedud Michmash – dead end **K5**

The signal corps. The roots of this force lie in the communications service of the PaLMa"H, which afterwards became the signal and electronics corps of the IDF. Its goals: providing communications services to the ground forces, purchasing, development and maintenance of communications and electronic equipment for the needs of the army, and more.

Heil Himush Sayeret Golani – dead end **K5**

Ordnance corps. Its beginnings lie in the Hagana, and afterwards, during the War of Independence, it became the engineering and ordnance corps of the IDF. Its areas of responsibility are: supply and maintenance of armaments, ammunition, and armored battle vehicles.

Imre Kalman (1896 – 1956) Plugat HaTankim – dead end **L4-5**

One of the leaders of Hungarian Jewry, an activist in *'aliya*, worked energetically in the years 1939–1944 to promote the illegal *'aliya*, through Hungary to the Land of Israel, of Jews from the countries conquered by the Nazis.

Laskov, Haim (1919 – 1982) HaArba'a – Heil HaAvir **K4**

A general, commander of the Hagana, commander of the Jewish Brigade in the British army. He laid the foundations of the IDF training setup, wrote books on the subject, was army chief of staff.

Mishteret HaYishuvim Heil HaAvir – HaGedud HaHamishi **K5**

A police unit not of the regular force, with about fourteen thousand officers, that was established by the British at the time of the Arab rebellion in 1936-1939. These policemen were deployed throughout all the Jewish communities for the purpose of protection. Nearly all members of the force were Hagana men.

Moshe Dayan Boulevard (1915 – 1981)
Ma'ale Adumim Road – Neve Ya'akov Boulevard **J3-K8**

A military commander and politician, a PaLMa"H commander and a military leader in Israel's wars, an IDF chief of staff. One of the leaders of the Labor movement, a minister in Israel's government. In 1967 he was appointed Defense Minister and was one of the prominent partners in the victory of the Six Day War (see the sub-neighborhoods: Pisgat Zeev Mizrah, Pisgat Zeev Ma'arav, Pisgat Zeev Tzafon, Pisgat Zeev Darom).

Pazner, Haim (1899 – 1981)
HaSayeret HaYerushalmit – Heil HaAvir **K4-5**

A Zionist leader, active in the Second Aliya. A purchaser of military equipment for the protection of the Land, he worked in Switzerland during the Holocaust to save Jews.

Plugat HaTankim HaYerushalmit
Heil HaAvir – Ya'akov Yehoshu'a **L4-5**

The IDF's Jerusalem Tank Company, whose soldiers were from Jerusalem. It protected the convoys going up to Mount Scopus and helped capture Armon HaNatziv during the Six Day War.

Sayeret Duchifat [Boulevard] Moshe Dayan Boulevard – Heil HaAvir – Bar On **K-L5**

A reconnaissance unit operating during the Six Day War (1967) under the command of Captain Ehud Shani. The unit's members took part in various battles and fell in the Neve Ya'akov campaign, in the place where the new neighborhood was built – Pisgat Zeev.

Sayeret Egoz [Square]
HaShisha 'Asar at HaSayeret HaYerushalmit **K5**

A unit of the IDF Northern Command responsible for ongoing security, that was established in 1966 and took part in operations of ongoing security in the Northern Command sector and beyond the border.

Sayeret Golani HaSayeret HaYerushalmit – HaArba'a **K5**

A company of IDF regulars doing reconnaissance. Its first action was in the War of Independence, and afterwards it was integrated into the regular operations of the IDF in all of Israel's wars. It led the campaign to take the buffer zone in the first Lebanon war, "Shlom Hagalil" (Peace for Galilee), and in the Six Day War (1967) also fought in this part of Jerusalem, later to be called Pisgat Zeev.

Sayeret Haruv [Square] HaArba'a at HaShisha 'Asar **K5**

A unit of the IDF Central Command responsible for ongoing security. In the Six Day War the unit fought in the Latrun sector.

Sayeret Shaked [Square] Heil HaAvir at HaShisha 'Asar **K4**

A unit of the IDF Southern Command responsible for ongoing security, the oldest of the reconnaissance units. It operated in the Southern Command sector and over the border.

Schwarzbard, Shalom (1886 – 1938) Aaronfeld – dead end **K-L5**

A Jewish watchmaker, in 1926 he killed Ataman ("Commander") Petlyura who was responsible for his armed bands killing tens of thousands of Jews (among them, relatives of Schwarzbard) in the Ukraine in 1919. In his trial, Schwarzbard was charged with carrying out the killing as revenge for the murders of those Jews. He was acquitted.

Yehoshu'a, Ya'akov (1905 – 1983)
Heil HaAvir – HaTankim HaYerushalmit **K-L4**

An author who described in his books the life experience of Oriental Jews in Jerusalem. He directed the Department for Muslims and Druse in the Land of Israel, a *Yakir Yerushalayim.*

Zilberstein Ya'akov Yehoshu'a – dead end **K4**

Named for the Zilberstein family, builders of Jerusalem.

Pisgat Zeev Mizrah

Arazi, Reuven (1906 – 1983) Gershon – Gershon **K6**

One of the founders and leaders of the *HaShomer HaTza'ir* movement in Poland, he was a delegate to Zionist Congresses until the outbreak of World War II, served as political secretary of the MaPa"M party, was elected to the Knesset in 1965 and served there on the constitution, law and justice committee, and as deputy speaker of the Knesset.

Bavli, Hana (1901 – 1993) Raful – Garami **L6**

A violinist in the Israel Philharmonic Orchestra, wrote a column in the daily newspapers (*Ma'ariv, HaAretz*), was on many radio programs, lectured to air force officers, gave courses for El Al stewardesses, and courses for junior personnel in the Foreign Ministry.

Brandwin, Yosef Shmuel, Rabbi Rahmilewitz – dead end **L7**

A *Yakir Yerushalayim.*

Bruchiali, Aryeh [Square] (1929 – 1988) Rahmilewitz at Yaffe **L6**

Respected lay leader in his synagogue, served as secretary of *HaPo'el* (workers' sports league) in the Jerusalem area, in 1978 began to work as secretary of the professional association of the department of metals, electricity and electronics.

Bruskina, Masha Bavli – Raful **L6**

A Jewish heroine who fought against the Nazis, was caught by the enemy and executed at age 17.

Elitzur, Yehuda (1911 – 1998) Livni – dead end **L6-7**

A researcher of the Bible and the Land of Israel, a *Yakir Yerushalayim.*

Federman, David (1909 – 1990) Tunik – dead end **L6**

One of the commanders of the Beitar movement, an ETZe"L fighter, a *Yakir Yerushalayim.*

Fridler, Yoel (1928 – 1948) Meridor – dead end **L7**

The first ETZe"L commander in the Old City of Jerusalem, fell in the courtyard of the Misgav LaDach Hospital during a joint military action with the Hagana.

Garami, Tzion (1934 – 2000) Shochat – Bavli **L6**

A man of good deeds, deputy director of the Ministry of Religious Affairs and an activist in the National Religious movement in Jerusalem.

Gedud Beit Horon [Square] Gershon at Aluf Yekutiel Adam **K6**

A field battalion in the War of Independence.

Gershon, Meir (1903 -1988)
Rahmilewitz – Moshe Dayan Boulevard **K6**

At the time of the establishment of the State, he headed the organizers of the mass *'aliya* of Kurdish Jews from Iraq, Persia and the other areas of Kurdistan, was active in their absorption in Israel, founded the association of the Kurdish community in Jerusalem and their burial society, was a *Yakir Yerushalayim.*

Goitein, Yehezkel David Nedava – dead end **L6**

A justice of the Supreme Court.

Grininger, Paul (1891 – 1972) Meridor – dead end **L6**

A Swiss police officer who saved thousands of Jews during the Holocaust.

Gvaryahu, Haim (1918 – 2000) Josephthal – dead end **K6**

Founded the Society for Biblical Research in Israel and the society for distribution of the Bible in the Diaspora, was director of the world Jewish agency for the Bible, was a founder of Kibbutz Tirat Zvi, one of the initiators of Bible study groups and international Bible quizzes.

Gvirtzman, Moshe Yaffe – Gershon **L6**

A member of the municipal council and deputy mayor, served as the appointee over the city's education portfolio. His last task before retirement was the rehabilitation of the Jewish cemetery on the Mount of Olives. A *Yakir Yerushalayim.*

Harari, Shlomo (d. 1986) Sadan – dead end **K6**

One of the senior commanders in ETZe"L and LeH"I, was active in civic matters after the establishment of the State, served as secretary of the association of merchants and craftsmen in the city, was an activist in the National Labor Federation in Jerusalem, a builder of Jerusalem.

Hativat HaNaHa"L Gal – dead end **K6**

Named for the brigade whose best fighters (forty-four of them) fell in Israel's wars, and among them four Jerusalemites.

Josephthal, Giora (1912 – 1962) Yosha' – Gershon **K-L6**

General secretary of the MaPA"I party, member of Knesset and government minister.

Kahan, Haim, Rabbi Livni – dead end **L6**

Attorney, public figure, a member of the council of the office of attorneys, a member of the plenum of the Broadcasting Authority. He founded and served as an advocate in the first government committee to investigate the matter of the Children of Yemen (a large number of Yemenite immigrant children are said to have disappeared during the early years of the State.) He also established the Institute for Medicine, Ethics and Religious Law.

Kisei Rahamim Rahmilewitz – Rahmilewitz **L5**

Named for a book on the Torah by Rabbi Rahamim Melamed HaCohen (1865-1932), rabbi of the Persian Jewish community, who taught education, was a Bible commentator and author.

Leon, Ben Tzion (1843 – 1883) Garami – dead end **L6**

One of the first initiators of the building of Mea She'arim, paid for some of the properties there. One of the founders of Petah Tikva, was a judge in the commerce court in Jerusalem, was the first person to impor wood furniture and kerosene lamps and donated them to the synagogue.

Livni, Eitan (1920 – 1992) Rahmilewitz – dead end **L6**

An officer who took part in the military campaigns of ETZe"L, member of Knesset, chairman of a Knesset committee.

Maunoury, Maurice Bourges (1914–1993) Grininger – dead end **L7**

A French minister of defense, helped Israel build a strong base for the IDF.

Meridor, Eliyahu (1914 – 1967) Natanson – Yosha‘ **L7**

A member of ETZe"L and its commander in Jerusalem, he joined *Plugat HaKotel* [the Western Wall Company] of Beitar in the Old City of Jerusalem to fight in its defense, a member of Knesset.

Moshe Dayan Boulevard (1915 – 1981) Derech Ma‘ale Adumim – Neve Ya‘akov Boulevard **J3-K8**

(See the sub-neighborhoods: Pisgat Zeev Darom, Pisgat Zeev Mercaz, Pisgat Zeev Ma‘arav, Pisgat Zeev Tzafon.)

Natanson, Isser (1916 – 1977) Meridor – dead end **L7**

An ETZe"L commander and fighter in the Old City, he dedicated his life to defending the Jewish nation in its homeland.

Nedava, Yosef (1916 – 1988) Meridor – Gershon **L6-7**

An author, historian, one of the senior disciples of Zeev Jabotinsky.

Nikova, Rina (1895 – 1974) Nedava – dead end **L7**

Founder of the School of Dance in Jerusalem, a dancer and choreographer, she danced and created choreography for the Israel Opera, founded the first studio for dance in Israel.

Pagis, Dan (1931 – 1986) Tunik – dead end **L6**

Poet and researcher of Italian poetry, professor of Hebrew literature.

Perl, William (1906 – 1995) Natanson – dead end **L7**

Active in the rescue of Jews during the Holocaust and active in the Jabotinsky movement, which rescued many during World War II.

Raful, Avraham Harari, Rabbi (1935 – 1994) Rahmilewitz – Bruskina **L6**

A rabbi of the *Porat Yosef* Yeshiva, worked hard on behalf of education for children in Israel.

Rahmilewitz, Moshe, Dr. (1899 – 1985) Moshe Dayan Boulevard – Natanson **K-L6**

One of the senior doctors in Israel, served as dean of the School of Medicine of the Hebrew University, served as the personal physician of many of the nation's leaders, was awarded the Israel Prize in 1964, a *Yakir Yerushalayim.*

Sadan, Dov (1902 – 1990) Rahmilewitz – Gershon **K6**

Professor of language and literature, author and essayist.

Segulat Yisrael Natanson – dead end **L7**

Named for a book by Dr. Yehuda Menahem Pacifici, one of the leaders of the Zionist movement in Italy.

Shalom, Binyamin [Lane] (1924 – 1951) Livni – dead end **L6**

Fell while defending Jerusalem, was in the LeH"I underground and took part in the bombing of the British armored vehicle that defended the Arab village of Lifta, in the conquest of 'Ein Kerem and Katamon, and in the penetration of the Old City during the War of Independence.

Sharef, Zeev (1906 – 1984) Rahmilewitz – Gvirtzman **K-L6**

The first secretary of the government and a government minister of Israel.

Shochat, Mania (1879 – 1961) Garami – dead end **L6**

Was active in the revolutionary movement in Russia and was jailed for this activity, was among the leaders of the Second Aliya and, in Israel, among the founders of the Bar Giora group and *HaShomer* (defense groups that guarded Jewish areas).

Tajer, Shlomo uMoshe Rahmilewitz – Rahmilewitz **L5**

Moshe Tajer was the president of the Jerusalem religious court, served eighteen years as the chief rabbi of Turkistan, was head of the rabbis in Beirut and later in Damascus. Shlomo Tajer was a courageous leader of the Jewish communities in Buchara and Damascus and defended the rights of the Jews there.

Toren, Haim (1916 – 1988) Moshe Dayan Boulevard – Gershon **K6**

Author and researcher.

Tunik, Yitzhak (1911 – 1989) Gvirtzman – Shochat **L6**

The third state comptroller of the State of Israel.

Ventura, Moshe (1893 – 1973) Tunik – dead end **L6**

Chief rabbi of Alexandria, Egypt, a researcher and educator, a leader of Sephardic Jewry.

Yaffe, Shmuel (1900 – 1965) Rahmilewitz – Gvirtzman **L6**

One of the first defenders of Jerusalem.

Yosha', Meir Meridor – Gershon **L6**

Member of the municipal council, activist on behalf of the city as a member of the council and also as an outside factor, built the Young Jewish Club that worked to educate for Jewish and Zionist values.

Zer, Mordechai (1901 – 1977) Yosha' – dead end **L6-7**

Deputy speaker and speaker of the Knesset, one of the builders of Jerusalem.

Pisgat Zeev Ma'arav

Adam, Yekutiel, Aluf (d. 1982) Moshe Dayan Boulevard – Uzi Narkiss, ends at Derech Shu'afat **J-K6**

Major general, served in the IDF as deputy chief of staff, was killed in the first Lebanon war 'Operation Peace for Galilee' (see the neighborhood of Shu'afat).

Baradnov, Yirmiyahu (1934 – 1957) Tamir – dead end **J6**

A paratrooper, a hero of reprisal actions, fell in Kalkilya.

'Eden, Shmuel (1885 – 1967) Moshe Dayan Boulevard – dead end **J5**

A member of the municipal council of Jerusalem, director of the Diskin Orphanage, close aide of Rabbi Moshe Blau, an educator and man of good deeds.

Levanon, Zvi (1889 – 1972) Moshe Dayan Boulevard – Niv **J6**

General secretary of the merchants association, a *Yakir Yerushalayim*.

Lichtman, Avraham David (1897 – 1984) Niv – dead end **J6**

Established the basis of the Jewish public transportation system in the Land of Israel, a *Yakir Yerushalayim*.

Moshe Dayan Boulevard (1915 -1981) Derech Ma'ale Adumim – Neve Ya'akov Boulevard **J3-K8**

(See the sub-neighborhoods: Pisgat Zeev Darom, Pisgat Zeev Mercaz, Pisgat Zeev Mizrah, Pisgat Zeev Tzafon.)

Narkiss, 'Uzi, HaAluf [Road] (1925 – 1998) Derech Ma'ale Adumim – Neve Ya'akov Boulevard **I3-J8**

Major general, a PaLMa"H commander in battles for Jerusalem and in the Negev, commander of the Central Command in the Six Day War (see the neighborhoods of Pisgat Zeev Tzafon, Shu'afat).

Niv, David (1916 – 1989) Aluf Yekutiel Adam – Levanon **J6**

Historian, engaged to a great extent in documenting the history of

ETZe"L, served as the director of the radio and newspaper department of the head office of the Jewish National Fund (KKL) for Israel and edited its journal, edited the minutes of Knesset sessions. His main contribution was his research "Battles of *HaIrgun HaTzvai HaLeumi*" about the Jewish underground and its war to liberate the Land of Israel and establish an independent Jewish state.

Shalom VeTzedek 'Eden – dead end **J5**

"Peace and Justice". Named for a book by Rabbi Shalom Hadaya (1862-1945), head of the Kabbalist *Beit El* Yeshiva in Jerusalem.

Tamir, Shmuel (Katznelson) (1923 – 1987)
Aluf Yekutiel Adam – Aluf Yekutiel Adam **J6**

One of the commanders of ETZe"L in Jerusalem, was one of the senior attorneys in Israel, a legislator, member of Knesset and Minister of Justice.

Pisgat Zeev Tzafon

Heil HaRefua Netiv HaMazalot – dead end **J4**

The IDF medical corps, which began as a medical service at the end of 1947, based on the medical service of the Hagana, which acted jointly with the civilian medical institutions. After the War of Independence, the IDF began to organize internally and in doing so, organized the medical corps as well.

Holtzberg, Simha (1924 – 1994)
Neve Ya'akov Boulevard – Moshe Dayan Boulevard **J4**

Called the "father of the wounded", he gave assistance and encouragement to wounded IDF soldiers.

Mazal Aryeh Netiv HaMazalot – dead end **J4**

The zodiac sign associated with the constellation Leo, the lion. It reaches mid-sky in the month of Av (July–August), between Ursa Major and the Sextant (Sextans). Its characteristic element is fire, and from July 23 to August 22 its ruling star is the sun.

Mazal Dli Holtzberg – Holtzberg **J4**

The zodiac sign associated with the constellation Aquarius, the water-bearer. It reaches mid-sky in the month of Shevat (January– February), beyond Pegasus. Its characteristic element is air, and from January 20 – February 18 it is ruled by Saturn and Uranus.

Mazal Gdi Holtzberg – Holtzberg **J4**

The zodiac sign associated with the constellation Capricorn, the goat. It reaches mid-sky in the month of Tevet (December–January), beyond Cygnus and Delphinus. Its characteristic element is earth, and from December 22 – January 19 it is ruled by Saturn.

Mazal Keshet Moshe Dayan Boulevard – dead end **J3**

The zodiac sign associated with the constellation Sagittarius, the archer. It reaches mid-sky in the month of Kislev (November–December), beyond Aquila. Its characteristic element is fire, and from November 22 – December 21 it is ruled by Jupiter.

Mazal Moznayim Moshe Dayan Boulevard – dead end **J4**

The zodiac sign associated with the constellation Libra, the scales. It reaches mid-sky in the month of Tishrei (September–October), just beyond Scorpius and near Taurus. Its characteristic element is air, and from September 23 – October 23 it is ruled by Venus.

Mazal Shor Moshe Dayan Boulevard – dead end **J4**

The zodiac sign associated with the constellation Taurus, the bull. It reaches mid-sky in the month of Iyar (April–May), beyond Perseus. Its characteristic element is earth, and from April 20 – May 20 it is ruled by Venus.

Mazal Taleh Moshe Dayan Boulevard – dead end **J4**

The zodiac sign associated with the constellation Aries, the ram. It reaches mid-sky in the month of Nisan (March – April), beyond the area between Perseus and Andromeda. Its characteristic element is fire, and from March 21 – April 19 it is ruled by Mars.

Mazal Teomim Holtzberg – dead end **J3**

The zodiac sign associated with the constellation Gemini, the twins. It reaches mid-sky in the month of Sivan (May–June), is recognizable by its two brightest stars, Castor and Pollux, seen as twin hunters whose sister was Helen of Troy. Its characteristic element is air.

Moshe Dayan Boulevard (1915 -1981)
Derech Ma'ale Adumim – Neve Ya'akov Boulevard **J3-K8**

(See the sub-neighborhoods: Pisgat Zeev Darom, Pisgat Zeev Mercaz, Pisgat Zeev Mizrah, Pisgat Zeev Ma'arav.)

Narkiss, 'Uzi, HaAluf [Road] (1925 – 1998)
Derech Ma'ale Adumim - Neve Ya'akov Boulevard **I3-J8**

(See the neighborhoods of Pisgat Zeev Ma'arav, Shu'afat.)

Netiv HaMazalot Moshe Dayan Boulevard – Mazal Taleh **J4-5**

Constellations, drawn by ancient peoples as various figures, among which are animals and useful objects.In the Bible these star clusters and their changing patterns are mentioned together with the sun and moon. The earth's orbit around the sun causes a different constellation of stars to appear mid-sky each month, and that is regarded as the constellation for that month.

Neve Ya'akov [Boulevard]
Ma'aglot HaRav Pardes – Derech Ramallah **I3-K2**

(See the neighborhood of Neve Ya'akov.)

Pisgat Zeev Darom

Moshe Dayan Boulevard (1915 -1981)
Derech Ma'ale Adumim – Neve Ya'akov Boulevard **J3-K8**

(See the sub-neighborhoods: Pisgat Zeev Mercaz, Pisgat Zeev Mizrah, Pisgat Zeev Ma'arav, Pisgat Zeev Tzafon.)

Tavin, Eli (1919 – 1994) Gershon – dead end **K6-7**

A member of the ETZe"L command, a fighter, headed the Department for Education and Culture in the Diaspora of the World Zionist Organization, was chairman of The Jabotinsky Institute, one of the founders of the Herut movement. His public activities focused on government bodies and included Yad VaShem, the Society for Biblical Research, the Shazar Center and the Broadcasting Authority.

Ramat Beit HaKerem

Name and establishment:

The neighborhood, located on the west side of the city between the original neighborhoods of Beit HaKerem and Giv'at Mordechai, was founded at the beginning of the 1990s. The neighborhood is built on a topographical ridge, hence its name, "height of Beit HaKerem". It is one of the new neighborhoods that developed in the city toward the end of the century.

Boundaries:
North – Giv'at Beit HaKerem and Beit HaKerem
South and west – Bayit VaGan
East – Giv'at Ram

Sites: within its boundaries or nearby are Sha'arei Tzedek Medical Center, Yad Sarah, Mount Herzl, Yad VaShem.

Streets: the neighborhood streets are named for musicologists, educators and public figures. The central street is Moshe Kol Street, a ring road inside the neighborhood.

The streets are:

Aluf Yohai bin Nun (1925 – 1995) Kol – Kol **D13-E14**

(See the neighborhood of Giv'at Beit HaKerem.)

Arnon, Ya'akov (1913 – 1955) Kol – dead end **D14**

One of the central figures in the economic and industrial life of Jerusalem. One of the builders of the general economy and promoters of peace.

Avizohar, Yehoshu'a (1882 – 1966)
Beyt – Gafni, ends at HeHalutz **D13**

(See the neighborhoods of Beit HaKerem and Giv'at Beit HaKerem.)

Beyt, Shmuel (Hans) (1902 – 1948)
Herzl Boulevard – SHaHa"L **D13-14**

(See the neighborhoods of Bayit VaGan and Giv'at Mordechai.)

De Rossi (17th cent.) Kol – dead end **D13**

Named for Rabbi 'Azaria and Rabbi Shlomo de Rossi, whose last name in Italian means "of the reds". 'Azaria was the outstanding Jewish philosopher and scholar of the Italian Renaissance. Shlomo is well-known for his musical compositions, was the most prominent composer of Jewish music of the period, published important musical compositions for prayers.

Dinur, Ben Tzion, Prof. (1884 – 1973) Kol – Kol **E14**

One of the early professors of Jewish history at the Hebrew University of Jerusalem. One of the founders of *Tzion*, a periodical of research on Jewish history. He served as Minister of Education and Culture in four governments of Israel, from the start of the Third Knesset until the formation of the seventh government.

Goldblum, Natan [Square] (1920 – 2001)
Avizohar at Mishkan Shilo **D13**

He developed in Israel the vaccine against polio and saved thousands of children from becoming paralyzed. Vice-president of the authority for research and development of the Hebrew University of Jerusalem, and its chairman. Received the Israel Prize.

Hovav, Moshe (1930 – 1987) Kol – dead end **D13**

Director of the *Kol Yisrael* radio station, known mainly as a news broadcaster for many years.

Kol, Moshe (1911 - 1989) Avizohar – Bin Nun **D-E14**

Head of *'Aliyat HaNo'ar*, a minister in the government of Israel.

Mara Kol – Kol **E14**

Underground name given to the Jewish partisan Estriya 'Ovadia (1922-1944), a national heroine of the Yugoslav peoples, who fell in battle.

Mishkan Shilo Avizohar – Bin Nun – dead end **D13-14**

(See the neighborhood of Giv'at Beit HaKerem.)

Palombo, David (1920 – 1966) Kol – dead end **D14**

A Jerusalem sculptor, the creator of the Knesset gates and the gates at Yad VaShem.

Rimon, Yosef Zvi (1889 – 1958) Kol – dead end **D-E14**

A poet and educator.

Shreibaum, Ya'akov (1913 – 1991) Kol – dead end **E14**

First city comptroller of Jerusalem.

Siman Tov, Ya'akov (1846 – 1928) Kol – dead end **D14**

Educator, spiritual leader, chief rabbi of the Jews of Afghanistan. He helped the Jews of the community and raised funds through special campaigns for needy families.

Tchorz, Catriel (1906 – 1993) Kol – dead end **D13**

One of the pioneers of industry in Jerusalem, a *Yakir Yerushalayim*.

Thelma (1895 – 1959) Kol – dead end **D-E14**

Named for Thelma Yellin, one of the pioneers in music in Jerusalem and Israel.

Tov, Moshe Aharon (1911 – 1989) Bin Nun – dead end **D-E14**

Ambassador of Israel to countries in Latin America.

Tusiya Cohen, Shlomo (1917 – 1994) Beyt – Kol **D13-14**

Among those who laid the foundation for the legal profession in Israel.

Ramat Denya

Name and establishment:

This neighborhood, located in the southwestern part of the city between the neighborhoods of Ramat Sharett and Kiryat HaYovel, was founded in 1970 and named for the construction company that built its houses. From Ramat Denya a street begins that connects to the main road from nearby Kiryat HaYovel, then passes through all of Gonenim/Katamonim and reaches the middle of the city.

Boundaries:

North and west – Kiryat HaYovel
South – Manhat/Malha
East – Ramat Sharett and Bayit VaGan

Sites: within its boundaries or nearby are Mount Herzl, Yad VaShem, the Jerusalem Mall (Malha), the Biblical Zoo.

Streets: the streets of the neighborhood are named for jurists, painters, authors, poets and public figures.

The streets are:

Daskal Kubovy – Luz **C15**

Named for Hanna Daskal (1907-1995), active on behalf of communities and *Yekirat Yerushalayim*, and Avraham Daskal (1905-1997), one of the founders of the electric company and *Yakir Yerushalayim.*

Gelber, Edward (1904 – 1971) Pann – dead end **C15**

Jurist, a Hagana activist, active also in the institutes of education and art named after his wife Hanna Rofa, a painter and member of the leadership of the WIZO Organization in the Holy Land. He was a member of the Zionist Workers Committee.

Golomb, Eliyahu (1893 – 1945) Pat – Tahon **C15-E16**

(See the neighborhoods of Gonenim/Katamonim Het, Tet, Holyland Park, Kiryat HaYovel, Manhat/Malha, Ramat Sharett.)

Granados, Jorge Garcia (1900 – 1961)
Kubovy – HaTzayar Yossi – dead end **C15**

A friend of Israel, ambassador of Guatemala to the United Nations and in Israel, one of the initiators of the decision concerning the establishment of a Jewish state in the Land of Israel.

HaShofet Binyamin (1900 – 1996) Luz – dead end **C-D15**

Named for Dr. Binyamin HaLevi, a judge of the district court and justice of the Supreme Court, member of Knesset.

HaTzayar Yossi (1923 – 1992) Kubovy – dead end **C15**

Named for Yossi Stern, a Jerusalem artist.

Kubovy, Aryeh (Louis), Dr. (1896 – 1966) Pann – Pann **C15**

One of the leaders of the Zionist labor movement in Belgium, ambassador of the State of Israel to Poland and Czechoslovakia.

Leibowitz, Zvi (1897 – 1980) Pann – dead end **C16**

Served for many years as the city engineer of Jerusalem, saw to the supply of water for the city's residents during the period of siege in the War of Independence.

Luz, Kadish (1895 – 1973) Silberg – Daskal – dead end **D15-16**

One of the leaders of the kibbutz movement in the Land of Israel, speaker of the Knesset, a minister in the government of Israel (see the neighborhood of Ramat Sharett).

Pann, Abel (1887 – 1963) Kubovy – Golomb **C15-16**

An artist, one of the teachers at the Betzalel School of Art in Jerusalem.

Sharett, Moshe [Boulevard] (1894 – 1965) Golomb – Bernstein **D16**

Second prime minister of the State of Israel, author, statesman, a leader of the labor movement in the Land of Israel and one of those who shaped its image, a Knesset member, first foreign minister of the government of Israel (see the neighborhood of Ramat Sharett).

Shir LiShlomo (1925 – 1995) Daskal – dead end **C15**

Named for Rabbi Shlomo Carlebach, the "Singing Rabbi", whose melodies and prayers are sung in every synagogue, in various choirs and among a great many Jews.

Shrem, Yosef Haim, Rabbi (1851 – 1949) Pann – dead end **C-D16**

A rabbi, a civic activist, was sent as a representative to Jewish communities in the Middle East, was active in promoting increased settlement in Jerusalem. One of the honored members of the Aleppo (Syrian) Jewish community in the city.

Silberg, Moshe, Prof. (1900 – 1975) Bernstein – Frank **D15**

A justice of the Supreme Court, head of the institute for the study of the Jewish tribunal, a professor at the Hebrew University of Jerusalem (see the neighborhood of Ramat Sharett).

Yemima (1909 – 1998) Daskal – dead end **C15**

Named for the children's author Yemima Avidar Tchernowitz, whose works were popularized through the media, from youth broadcasts on *Kol Yisrael* radio during the British Mandate period until the era of television. Translated stories from other languages into Hebrew and served as a member of the directorate of the Theater for Children and Youth. She received the Israel Prize and the Zeev Prize for children's literature and was a *Yekirat Yerushalayim*.

Zeitlin Kubovy – dead end **C15**

Named in memory of the Zeitlins, Hillel Zeitlin (1872–1942), a thinker and scholar of the history of Hasidism, who was killed in the Holocaust, and his son, Aharon Zeitlin (1895-1973), Hebrew and Yiddish author, poet and thinker.

Ramat Eshkol

Name and establishment:

This neighborhood, located in northern Jerusalem west and northwest of Giv'at HaMivtar and Ammunition Hill, was founded in 1969 and named after Levi Eshkol, the prime minister of Israel. Until the Six Day War (1967), this area was a wasteland between a fortified position of the IDF and nearby Ammunition

Hill, where there were Jordanian army positions. From this area Jewish paratroopers stormed the nearby hill and conquered it, thereby opening the way for the liberation of the Old City and all of east Jerusalem.

After the war it was decided to build a Jewish neighborhood here that would connect Mount Scopus with the western side of the city. The neighborhood developed very quickly.

Boundaries:
Northwest – Sanhedria HaMurhevet
South – Sanhedria
Southeast – Ammunition Hill
East – Giv'at HaMivtar

Sites: within its boundaries or nearby are Ammunition Hill and burial caves of the Second Temple period.

Streets: the neighborhood streets are named for places that were liberated by the IDF in the Six Day War. Levi Eshkol Boulevard, the central thoroughfare passing through the neighborhood, leads to nearby Mount Scopus and to Hadassah Hopital and the Hebrew University that are on Mount Scopus.

The streets are:

Aranne, Zalman [Square] (1899 -1971) Paran at dead end **I9**

(See the neighborhood of Giv'at HaMivtar.)

Bassan, Yitzhak (1873 – 1961) Paran – dead end **I9**

Teacher, educator, contributed greatly to the field of education, one of the supporting pillars of the Alliance Israelite in Israel and abroad.

Di Zahav Ramat HaGolan – dead end **H9**

Dahab, a place on the shore of the Gulf of Eilat.

Elyashar, Eliyahu [Square] (1900 – 1981) Eshkol at Netter **I-9**

One of the leaders of Sephardic Jewry in the Holy Land, he served in the British Mandate government in the department of commerce and customs duty. One of the founders and leaders of the organization of pioneers from the Oriental lands, he published a comprehensive book on the Sephardic community in Jerusalem. A member of Knesset.

Eshkol, Levi [Boulevard] (1895 – 1969)
Bar Lev – Eretz Hefetz – Hativat Harel **I-J9**

(See the neighborhoods of Giv'at HaMivtar, Ma'alot Dafna/Arzei HaBira.)

'Etzion Gever Ramat HaGolan – Ma'avar HaMitla – dead end **I9**

One of the encampments of the Israelites in the Sinai Wilderness after the Exodus from Egypt (Numbers 33:35), a port city on the Gulf of Eilat in the time of King Solomon (I Kings 9:26) and in the days of the kings of Judah (I Kings 22:49).

'Evrona Mishmar HaGvul – dead end **H9**

One of the encampments of the Israelites in the Sinai Wilderness after the Exodus from Egypt (Numbers 33:34).

Har Shefer Mishmar HaGvul – dead end **H9**

One of the encampments of the Israelites in the Sinai Wilderness after the Exodus from Egypt (Numbers 33:24).

Hatzerot Yam Suf – dead end **H-I9**

One of the camping sites of the Israelites in the Sinai Wilderness after the Exodus from Egypt (Numbers 33:17).

Livne Shaul HaMelech – dead end **H9**

One of the encampments of the Israelites in the Sinai Wilderness after the Exodus from Egypt (Numbers 33:20).

Ma'avar HaMitla Eshkol – Yam Suf **I9**

The mountain pass in the Sinai Peninsula where a fierce battle was fought against the Egyptian army in the Sinai Campaign (1956).

Mishmar HaGvul Eshkol – Yam Suf **H9**

Named for the army brigade that guards Israel's borders.

Nahal Tzin Ma'avar HaMitla – dead end **I9**

Named for one of the streams in the Negev.

Nahaliel Yam Suf – dead end **I9**

Named for a stream in the mountains along the eastern shore of the Dead Sea, where the Israelites encamped before entering Canaan (Numbers 21:19).

Paran Sheshet HaYamim – Ma'avar HaMitla **I9**

(See the neighborhood of Giv'at HaMivtar.)

Ramat HaGolan Yam Suf – Ma'avar HaMitla **H-I9**

Golan Heights, a region in northern Israel, east of the Jordan River.

Refidim [Lane] Mishmar HaGvul – dead end **H-I9**

One of the encampments of the Israelites in the Sinai Wilderness after the Exodus from Egypt (Numbers 33:14). In modern times the place served as a central army camp for the IDF in the Sinai (1967–1975).

Tanne, David [Square] (1909 – 1973) Paran at dead end **I9**

(See the neighborhood of Giv'at HaMivtar.)

Timna' Mishmar HaGvul – dead end **H9**

An ancient site of mines in the southern Land of Israel. The State of Israel renewed the mining of copper at the site, which is north of Eilat. Timna' is also the name of the sister of one of the chiefs of Edom (Genesis 36:22).

Tzalmona Yam Suf – Ramat HaGolan **H-I9**

One of the encampments of the Israelites in the Sinai Wilderness after the Exodus from Egypt (Numbers 33:41).

Wiener, Shim'on Dov, Dr. [Ascent] Paran – dead end **I9**

A doctor, a man of great kindness, liked and beloved, especially by his patients.

Yam Suf Ma'avar HaMitla – Golda Meir – dead end **H9**

The sea that lies to the east of the Sinai Peninsula, the Red Sea (see the neighborhoods of Sanhedria, Sanhedria HaMurhevet).

Yotvata Mishmar HaGvul – dead end **H9**

One of the encampments of the Israelites in the Jordan rift valley (Numbers 33:33). Today there is a kibbutz with this name.

Ramat Sharett

Name and establishment:

This neighborhood, located in the southwestern part of the city between the neighborhoods of Bayit VaGan and Ramat Denya, was founded in 1974 and named after Moshe Sharett, the first foreign minister of the State of Israel and its prime minister. The name of the neighborhood also expresses the topographical location of the area, on a high elevation.

Near this site in the past there was an Arab village named Malha that was overcome by the IDF forces after they had attacked it from the hill on which the neighborhood is built. From the southern part of the neighborhood, a main road starts that connects to the highway leading down from nearby Kiryat HaYovel and reaching Mid-Town.

Boundaries:
North and east – Bayit VaGan
South – Manhat/Malha
West – Ramat Denya

Sites: within its boundaries or nearby are Mount Herzl, Yad VaShem, the Jerusalem Mall (Malha), the Biblical Zoo.

Streets: the neighborhood's streets are named for Lovers of Zion, educators and professionals.

The streets are:

Abohav, Yitzhak, Rabbi (14th cent.) Minzberg – Cassuto **D15**

(See the neighborhood of Bayit VaGan.)

Argov, Eli'ezer (1920 – 1972) Meretz – dead end **D15**

An educator and public figure involved in many activities, he served as president of the Jerusalem office of the Bnai Brith organization, a member of the Israel Committee of the World Organization of Bnai Brith, one of the founders of *Kol Tzion LaGola* radio station (The Voice of Zion to the Diaspora), and a member of the directorate of the *Brit 'Ivrit 'Olamit* (World Association for Hebrews).

Bernstein, Peretz (1890 – 1971) Silberg – Nezer **D16**

Author and editor, a Zionist activist in Holland, one of the founders of the liberal movement, a member of the directorate of the Jewish Agency, a minister in the Israel government.

Bracha Tzefira (1920 – 1990) Sharett – dead end **D16**

A singer, she presented Yemenite songs which eventually formed the basis of Israeli music and the earliest Israeli songs. She succeeded in creating a bridge between her own musical heritage and the Israeli artistic work that had already developed.

Gani, Meir [Square] (1848 – 1931)
Sharett at Bernstein at Silberg **D16**

One of the activists of the Jewish community in the Old City of Jerusalem, one of the honored Sephardic Jews of the community, a builder of the synagogue in the Christian Quarter, the construction of which led to the expansion of the Jewish Quarter.

Golomb, Eliyahu (1893 – 1945) Pat – Tahon **C15-E16**

(See the neighborhoods of Gonenim/Katamonim Het, Tet, Holyland Park, Kiryat HaYovel, Manhat/Malha, Ramat Denya.)

HaHa"I [Square] Sharett at Golomb **D16**

(See the neighborhood of Manhat/Malha.)

HaTzalam Rahamim [Lane] (1943 – 1993)
Sharett – dead end **D16**

Rahamim Israeli, one of the veteran photographers of Jerusalem, he emphasized the beauty and singularity of the city in his photographs, and he mounted large exhibits at the Israel Museum and abroad.

Luz, Kadish (1895 – 1973) Silberg – Daskal – dead end **D15-16**

(See the neighborhood of Ramat Denya.)

Meretz, David, Dr. (1894 – 1981) Nezer – Silberg **D-15-16**

He served as the last chairman of the Zionist movement in Czechoslovakia, was deputy chief judge of the tribunal of the Zionist Congress, a civic activist.

Mu'alem, Shim'on Nissim (1873 – 1953) Meretz – Meretz **D15-16**

Educator, one of the spiritual leaders of Babylonian (Iraqi) Jewry, one of those who assisted the absorption of immigrants from Iraq and their settlement in Jerusalem.

Novomeysky, Moshe (1873 – 1961) Meretz – Silberg **D16**

Engineer and chemist, initiator and founder of the Dead Sea potash works, a civic activist.

Rejwan, Goga (Giora) (1930 – 1987) Aboab – Aboab **D15**

She was a civic activist in Jerusalem.

Rosen, Pinhas (1887 – 1978) Sharett – dead end **D16**

Jurist, politician, one of the leaders of Zionism in Germany, a member of the World Zionist directorate, a minister in the government of Israel.

Shaki, Ino, Prof. (1912 – 1982) Sharett – dead end **D16**

One of the important physicians in Jerusalem.

Sharett, Moshe [Boulevard] (1894 – 1965) Golomb – Bernstein **D16**

(See the neighborhood of Ramat Denya.)

Silberg, Moshe, Prof. (1900 – 1975) Bernstein – Frank **D15**

(See the neighborhood of Ramat Denya.)

Tiltan Argov – dead end **D15**

Clover, named after a plant of the legume family which serves as an important part of the fodder for animals.

Ramat Shlomo/Rechess Shu'afat

Name and establishment:

This neighborhood, located in the northern part of the city east of Ramot Allon, was founded in 1996 and named after Rabbi Shlomo Zalman Auerbach. Originally, the neighborhood was called Rechess Shu'afat because of its proximity to the village of that name and as an indication of its topography (*rechess* is a ridge).

At the beginning of the 1980s, the authorities planned to put up a municipal stadium in this area. However, as a result of pressure from the ultra-Orthodox community in favor of building residential neighborhoods on the northern side of the city, and due to its opposition to desecration of the Sabbath in the area, the plans were changed. The stadium was built, in the end, in the Manhat/Malha neighborhood, and Rechess Shu'afat became a residential neighborhood for the ultra-Orthodox population.

In 1995 the Jerusalem municipal council decided to name the neighborhood after Rabbi Shlomo Zalman Auerbach (1910-1995), who had died just months earlier. Rabbi Auerbach served as the director of the *Kol Torah* Yeshiva for sixty years and was one of the important arbiters of religious law of the twentieth century. He was known for his innovative legal decisions, demonstrated great expertise in all the latest technologies, and his rulings were acceptable to all segments of Orthodox religious Jewry.

The residents of the neighborhood belong to the ultra-Orthodox community.

Boundaries:

North – ‘Atarot-Industrial Zone

South – Kiryat Ta‘asiyot ‘Atirot Mada‘/Har Hotzvim, Sanhedria HaMurhevet

East – Giv‘at Shapira/French Hill

West – Ramot Allon

Sites: within its boundaries or nearby are the grave of the prophet Samuel and high-tech companies.

Streets: most of the neighborhood streets are named for rabbis and religious books.

The streets are:

Almushnino, Moshe, Rabbi (16th cent.) Druk – dead end **H7**

One of the great rabbis and arbiters of religious law in Saloniki, Greece, a thinker, historian and philosopher. In the days of Don Yosef Nasi, he traveled to Turkey in order to persuade Sultan Suleiman to grant rights to the Jews of Saloniki.

Birkat Avraham Kehilot Ya‘akov – HaAdmor MiSadgora **H7**

Named for the book by the Hasidic master Rabbi Avraham Weinberg of Slonim (1889-1981), one of those who laid the foundation for ultra-Orthodox education, one of the founders of the *Beit Ya‘akov* movement. He served as Admor for over twenty-seven years.

Brim, Yehoshu‘a, Rabbi (1913 – 1986) Zholti – dead end **H7**

He stood out as an exceptional student already as a child, as a pupil at the *‘Etz Haim* Yeshiva in Jerusalem. Later, he was considered to be one of the select students of this yeshiva, and similarly was counted among the young prodigies from Jerusalem who learned in the *Beit HaHoraa* of the Teplich Gaon.

Buxbaum, Mordechai (20th cent.) Druk – Igrot Moshe **H-I8**

A prominent attorney, one of the heads of *Agudat Yisrael*, a member of the pre-State Jerusalem municipal council at the time that it announced the establishment of a Jewish city council, deputy mayor of Jerusalem.

Druk, Shlomo Zalman, Rabbi (d. 1987)
Yadin – Kehilot Ya‘akov **G-H7-8**

One of the veteran members of the municipal council, he served for many years as a member of the directorate and as the appointee in charge of the department of water supply. One of the heads of *Po'alei Agudat Yisrael* in Jerusalem.

Elnekave, Yisrael, HaRav HaGaon (14th cent.)
Zholti – Lafian – dead end **H7-8**

An important rabbi from a rabbinic dynasty in North Africa, he was born in the first half of the fourteenth century. An author and religious poet in Spain, he was martyred in 1391, along with many members of the Jewish community.

Faatal, Hacham Avraham (1862 -1981) Druk – dead end **H7**

A rabbi, Kabbalist and educator, one of the honored members of Urfa Jewry, in Turkey.

Goldknopf, Aryeh, Rabbi (d. 1989)
Birkat Avraham – Buxbaum – dead end **H7**

A member of the Jerusalem municipal council, he served as deputy mayor of the city, was one of the founders of the ultra-Orthodox education network Beit Ya'akov.

HaAdmor MiLubavitch (1902 – 1994) Druk – Hazon Ish **H8**

Named for Rabbi Menahem Mendel Schneersohn, who stood at the head of the HaBa"D Hasidic movement and under whose leadership the activity of HaBa"D spread throughout the world and in Israel. This increase in activity was made possible thanks to the *shlichim* (envoys) who were sent to distant places to work and are still working to strengthen Jewish identity, to reach out to other Jews and to bring non-religious Jews closer to Torah and Judaism.

HaAdmor MiSadgora (b. 1897) Birkat Avraham – dead end **H7**

Named for Rabbi Mordechai Shalom Yosef Friedman, who headed the Sadgora institutions in Jerusalem and was active in promoting the building and founding of Hasidic institutions in the city.

HaBracha [Alley] Goldknopf – Kehilot Ya'akov **H7**

Blessing, a symbolic name.

Hadash, Meir, Rabbi (20th cent.) Igrot Moshe – Hazon Ish **H8**

The spiritual director of *Yeshivat Hevron*, he trained tens of thousands of students, founded the *Or Elhanan* Yeshiva.

HaHosen [Alley] Buxbaum – Druk **H7**

Strength, a symbolic name.

Hazon Ish (1878 – 1953) Igrot Moshe – Kehilot Ya'akov **H-I8**

Named for Rabbi Avraham Yesha'yahu Karlitz, one of the outstanding Torah scholars and one of the prominent arbiters of religious law in his generation, one of the leaders of ultra-Orthodox Jewry at the time of the establishment of the State.

Hershler, Moshe, Rabbi (1922 – 1991)
Kahaneman – dead end **H-I8**

One of the founders of the Mir Yeshiva, a member of the editorial board of the Institute of the Complete Israeli Talmud, chief editor of the Heritage of the Complete Mishna, and served as head of the *Marom Tzion* Yeshiva.

Igrot Moshe Hazon Ish – Hadash **I8**

Named after the book by Rabbi Moshe Feinstein (1895–1986), who immigrated to the United States from his home town of Luban in 1936, was named head of the *Tiferet Yerushalayim* Yeshiva, and over time became a leading authority on religious law in his generation.

Kahaneman, Yosef, Rabbi (1886 – 1969) Igrot Moshe – Hadash **H-I8**

He founded the Ponevitz Yeshiva and served as its rabbi, was active in public life. During the Holocaust he lost all his students and most of his family. In Israel he founded senior residences and institutions for boys and girls who survived the Holocaust.

Kalcheim, 'Uzi, Rabbi (1935 – 1994)
Igrot Moshe – Igrot Moshe **H7-I8**

A rabbi, educator and thinker in the field of Land of Israel studies, in all periods.

Kalonymos, Rabbeinu (16th cent.)
HaAdmor MiLubavitch – dead end **H8**

One of the outstanding rabbis of Jerusalem.

Kehilot Ya'akov Druk – Buxbaum **H7**

Named for the book by Rabbi Ya'akov Kanevsky – the Steipler Rav (1899–1985). In 1925 he published his first book, *Sha'arei Tvuna*. He was appointed director of the *Beit Yosef* Yeshiva in Pinsk, with seven hundred pupils, and made *'aliya* in 1934 and headed the *Beit Yosef* Yeshiva in Bnei Brak.

Lapian, Eliyahu, Rabbi (1876 – 1970)
HaAdmor MiLubavitch – dead end **H8**

He bravely led his students in World War I during the time that the Lithuanian region was conquered by the Germans. After the war he went around to the towns in the area to strengthen and encourage the Jews who remained, then he made *'aliya* and served as spiritual director of the *Knesset Hizkiyahu* Yeshiva in Zichron Ya'akov, and afterwards served in a similar position in Kfar Hasidim.

Mahlouf, 'Adan, Rabbi (1880 – 1947) Druk – Goldknopf **H7**

One of the prominent Kabbalists in Jerusalem.

Sharabani, Yehoshu'a, Rabbi (1879 – 1973)
Birkat Avraham – Druk **H7**

One of the prominent Kabbalists, a student of the Ben Ish Hai, he served as rabbi of the Geulim/Bak'a neighborhood. One of the founders and sustainers of *Beit Midrash Shoshanim LeDavid* in the neighborhood of HaBucharim.

Toledano, Refael Baruch, Rabbi (1890 – 1971) Druk – dead end **H8**

He served as chief judge of the religious court in the city of Meknes, Morocco, saw to the education of thousands of Jewish children, and made *'aliya* with his children and established yeshivot and educational institutions in Israel.

Vamshe, David, Rabbi [Square]
HaAdmor MiLubavitch at Hazon Ish **H8**

Jerusalem-born, he was sent to Morocco by the rabbis of the Holy Land to collect money for the Land of Israel, and while there he decided to make the ultimate atonement for a Jewish village struck by plague. While his grave was being dug, two miracles occurred. He is considered a Tzadik (righteous), and on Rosh Hodesh Heshvan every year, the community holds a *hilula* (celebration) in his honor. In addition, a synagogue was built in Jerusalem and named after him.

Yadin, Yigael (1917 – 1981) Bar Lev – Golda Meir **F-J8**

One of the top commanders of the Hagana, an IDF chief of staff, one of the prominent archeologists of Israel, a minister of the State of Israel, recipient of the Israel Prize (see the neighborhood of Shu'afat).

Zholti, Betzalel, Rabbi (d. 1984) Hazon Ish – Druk **H7-8**

A chief rabbi of Jerusalem.

Ramot Allon

Name and establishment:

This large neighborhood, located in the northern part of the city south of the grave of Samuel the Prophet, was founded in 1971 and is located on an elevation [*rama*], from which comes the name. According to the Bible, the prophet Samuel is buried in Ramah, referring to this, one of the higher elevations in the Jerusalem area, as is written: "Now Samuel was dead, and all of Israel had eulogized him, and they buried him in Ramah, his city..." (I Samuel 28:3). In recent years the name "Allon" was added to the name of this neighborhood, after Yigal Allon.

This area is located on a major traffic artery leading from northern Jerusalem to Tel-Aviv. It closes the gap between the city of Jerusalem and the residential communities spread along this artery and in its immediate surroundings. In the years since its founding, the neighborhood has grown until it is as large as a "mid-sized city", with a population of about sixty thousand residents. Accordingly, it is referred to as the "neighborhood city".

This entire area was under Jordanian rule until the Six Day War, during which it was captured and came under the jurisdiction of Israel. The first shelling of Jerusalem in the War of Independence (1948) came from Jordanian artillery positions on these heights.

The highest area of Ramot is called Ramat Polin, for its religious residents who came from Poland. Their houses are built in a particular style, similar to beehives.

The neighborhood is divided into several sections: Ramot Allon, Ramot Bet, Ramot Gimel, Ramot Dalet and Ramat Polin.

The residents are a mix of secular, religious and ultra-Orthodox, native-born Israelis and immigrants, young and old – a very diverse population.

Boundaries:

North – Beit Hanina

South – Kiryat Ta'asiyot 'Atirot Mada'/ Har Hotzvim

East – Ramat Shlomo/Rechess Shu'afat

West – Ramot Forest

Sites: within its boundaries or nearby are the grave of Samuel the Prophet, remains of a Roman fortress, *Hirbet Halilia* in Arabic, meaning "small mound". This fortress guarded the road leaving Jerusalem which passed this area and ended at the Mediterranean coast.

Streets: the neighborhood streets are named for Zionist leaders and institutions, wild plants, rabbis, religious and professional books, educators, jurists, philosophers, authors, poets, linguists, doctors and architects.

The streets are:

Albo, Yosef (1360 – 1444) Zarhi – dead end **D-E7**

One of the outstanding philosophers of Spanish Jewry in the Middle Ages, he is known by his book *Sefer Ha'Ikarim*, in which he sets out the principles of the Jewish faith.

'Aliyat HaNo'ar Zondek – dead end **E7-E8**

Named for the enterprise of bringing youth on *'aliya* from Diaspora lands, which began in 1932 at the initiative of Recha Freier, headed by Henrietta Szold.

Ari BeMistarim (1960 -1988) Wallenstein – dead end **E6**

Named for the book by Rabbi Yehuda Aryeh Alter, who was the neighborhood rabbi of Romema for several years and served as head of the Gur Talmudical academies in Jerusalem.

Asirei Tzion Zondek – Golda Meir **E7**

Prisoners of Zion, named for those who struggled for the freedom to make *'aliya* and were persecuted by the governments of countries in the Diaspora for their Zionist activism.

Avi'ezer Yellin (1890 – 1972)
Recanati – HaTzadik MiTchechanov **E7**

An educator, one of the founders of the Maccabiah Games, director-general of the teachers federation, one of the first fighters in the language controversy whether to use Hebrew or not in the Land of Israel in the early twentieth century.

Bazov, David, Rabbi Zarhi – dead end **D6**

One of the Zionist leaders in Russia and Georgia (southern Russia).

Beilis, Mendel (1874 – 1934) HaTzadik MiTchechanov – Zarhi **E7**

A Jew, the victim of a blood libel accusation in Russia in 1911. His trial drew the attention of many countries throughout the world. He was eventually acquitted.

Ben 'Attar, Haim (1886 – 1919) Sivan – dead end **E6-7**

One of the important Sephardic authors in Jerusalem, he published a newspaper named *HaHerut*, that played an important role within the Jerusalem community. He translated poems and stories from Hebrew to Ladino (a language comprised of Spanish and Hebrew, spoken by Spanish Jews).

Ben Yehezkel, Mordechai (1883 – 1971) Even Shmuel – Mass **E8**

A teacher and author, he published essays on language, literature and Hasidism and books of folk-tales.

Ben Zeev, Yisrael (1899 – 1980) Zarhi – Recanati **D7**

A teacher and educator, outstanding author, one of the builders of Jerusalem, he founded the association for sincere converts, researched the history of the Jews in Muslim countries and advanced the teaching of the Arabic language in Israeli schools.

Brown, Eliyahu (1910 – 1996) Zarhi – dead end **D6**

He initiated technical education in Israel, preparing students to take up technical occupations and published vocational study texts on the theory of electricity. He was sent as an expert by the United Nations to assist developing countries.

Bublik, Gedalia (1875 – 1948) Morgenthau – dead end **F7**

Journalist, Zionist leader in the United States, one of the founders of the American Jewish Congress and the *Mizrahi* movement in America, a member of the Zionist directorate.

Cohen, Binyamin [Square] (1894 – 1983) Golda Meir at Yigal **F7**

Benjamin Cohen, a Zionist and long-time political advisor in the United States.

De-Haas, Ya'akov (1872 – 1933) Morgenthau – dead end **F7**

Author, journalist, Zionist leader in the United States, one of the first to assist Dr. Herzl, a delegate at the First Zionist Congress.

De Lima, Nehemia (1882 – 1948) Eig – Even Shmuel **E8**

Economist, founded the Bank for Insuring the Workers of Holland, general secretary and chairman of the Zionist Alliance in Holland, a member of the executive and chairman of the JNF, a member of the Zionist directorate.

Derech HaHoresh Yigal – Recanati **E-F7-8**

Named for the subdivision "Horesh Ramot" built in the "Build your own house" area.

Eig, Alexander (1895 – 1938) Zondek – HaAhim Lehren **E7-8**

One of the prominent botanists in Israel and the Middle East, he published the first guide in Hebrew to plants of the Land of Israel.

El'azar, Yehuda, Rabbi [Square] (1888 – 1950)
Golda Meir at Recanati **D6**

A Jerusalem rabbi and activist, one of the organizers of the *'aliya* from the Balkans, a redeemer of lands in this area, the prophet Samuel's home.

Em HaBanim HaTzadik MiTchechanov – Zarhi **E7**

Mother of the sons, named for Rivka Guber (*Em HaBanim*) and her husband Mordechai, pioneer settlers of the Lachish region in the Land of Israel, whose sons fell in battles for Israel's independence.

Eshkoli, Aharon Zeev (1901 – 1948) Zondek – Zondek **E7-8**

Researcher and educator, he founded the college of horticulture during the British Mandate period. During World War I, he published historic works of research, was a chaplain in Jewish units in the British army.

Even Shmuel (Kaufmann), Yehuda, Dr. (1886 – 1976)
Zondek – Derech HaHoresh **E7**

An educator, author, scholar, he published a scientific edition of *Moreh Nevuchim* [Guide to the Perplexed] by the RaMBa"M and of *HaKuzari* by Rabbi Yehuda HaLevi. He was an editor of Dvir Publications' English-Hebrew dictionary and was a recipient of the Israel Prize.

Frankfurter, Felix (1882 – 1965) Morgenthau – dead end **F7**

A jurist, one of the Zionist leaders in the United States, a member of the delegation headed by Dr. Chaim Weizmann that entered into discussions with King Faisal regarding the political status of the Holy Land. A civic activist.

Giza (Fleischman) (1896 – 1944) Mass – Even Shmuel **E8**

She was involved with saving Jews in Slovakia during the Holocaust, a

Zionist leader who saved Jewish children and youth from the Nazis and brought them to a safe shore.

Glueck, Nelson, Dr. (1900 – 1971) Zondek – dead end **E7**

Researcher and archeologist, conducted archeological research projects, wrote articles and books on the Negev, Transjordan and the Jordan River, conducted digs at ‘Etzion Gever during the 1950s, conducted a broad survey of the Negev.

Golda Meir [Boulevard] (1898 – 1979) Bar Ilan – Mirski **D5-H9**

(See the neighborhoods of Kiryat Ta‘asiyot ‘Atirot Mada‘/Har Hotzvim, Kiryat Zanz.)

Greenberg, Haim (1889 – 1953) Ben Zeev – dead end **D-E7**

Author, socialist Zionist leader, a member of the Zionist directorate (head of the Department of Education and Culture) in the United States starting in 1946, actively promoted the establishment of the State of Israel.

Gross, (William) Zeev (1857 – 1928)
HaTzadik MiTchechanov – Zarhi **D-E7**

Delegate to the First Zionist Congress from the Jewish community in the Land of Israel.

HaAhim Lehren Even Shmuel – Mass **E8**

Named for brothers from the Lehren family, Zvi Hirsch (1784-1853), Ya‘akov Meir (1793-1861) and ‘Akiva (1795-1876) who headed the association Clerks and Administrators of the Holy Land, worked extensively on behalf of the Land of Israel and raised money for Jewish colonization there. Their name is linked to many charitable organizations in Israel.

HaAhim Roth [Square] Zondek at Even Shmuel at Yigal **E8**

Named for the philosopher Haim Yehuda Roth (1896-1963) and for his brother, the historian and educator Betzalel Cecil Roth (1899-1970).

HaCongress HaTzioni Golda Meir – Recanati **E6-7**

Named for the First Zionist Congress, which took place in Basel (1897), as a conference of representatives of the Zionist movement, set up by Theodor (Binyamin Zeev) Herzl.

HaDaf HaYomi Hertz – Lipsky **F7**

The daily page. Refers to the daily custom of study of a page of the Babylonian Talmud, which was set by Rabbi Meir Shapira, head of the

Hochmei Lublin Yeshiva, in 1923.

HaHa'avara Kutscher – dead end **D6**

The transfer. Named for Solly Hirsch (1895-1951), a member of the directorate of the Ha'avara Company, owned jointly by the Ango-Palestine Bank and the Jewish Agency, which was involved with saving Jewish property in Germany and transferring it to Israel.

HaHavtaha Even Shmuel – Eshkoli **E7-8**

The promise, a symbolic name.

HaMalhin [Square] Golda Meir at HaCongress HaTzioni **E6**

The composer. Named for the Russian composer Dmitri Shostakovich.

HaMeshorer ATZa"G (1886 – 1981) Recanati – dead end **D5-6**

Acrronym for the poet **U**ri **Z**vi **G**reenberg, one of the prominent poets of our time, a member of the first Knesset, a central figure in the Revisionist movement, recipient of the Israel Prize.

HaMeshoreret Zelda (Mishkovsky) (1914 – 1984) Zarhi – ATZa"G **D6**

A prominent Hebrew poetess, she had an impressive command of the Hebrew language.

HaRoeh Golda Meir – Ramot **E-F6**

For the prophet Samuel, who earned the designation *HaRoeh*, the Seer: "'Come let us go to the Seer,' for he who is now called a prophet was formerly called a seer" (I Samuel 9:9).

HaTzadik MiTchechanov (1789 – 1875) Zarhi – Avi'ezer **D-E7**

Rabbi Avraham Landau of Ciechanov, one of the prominent Hasidic masters, an outstanding educator in Hasidism and religious law and an important arbiter of religious law in his time.

Hedva [Steps] HaDaf HaYomi – Nerot Shabbat **F7**

Joy, a symbolic name.

Hertz, Yosef Zvi, Rabbi (1892 – 1946) HaDaf HaYomi – Lipsky **F7**

The chief rabbi of British Jewry and one of its Zionist leaders.

Hoofien, Eli'ezer (1881 – 1957) Even Shmuel – Eig **E8**

He made *'aliya* in 1904 as deputy director of the bank of the Anglo-Palestine Company, was elected chairman of the directorate of the bank, worked extensively on behalf of Israel and especially for the establishment of the State.

Idelsohn, Avraham Zvi (1882 – 1938) Recanati – Recanati **D6**

Laid the groundwork for research into Jewish music, did research and recordings of Jewish song and the cantillations (musical markings for chanting Torah readings) of all Jewish ethnic groups, the first music educator in Jerusalem.

Jacobson, Edward [Square] (1891 – 1955)
Ramot at Shivat Tzion **F6**

Named for Eddie Jacobson, an American businessman who influenced President Truman to recognize Israel immediately after the state was declared.

Jineo, Meir (1894 – 1968) Zarhi – dead end **D6**

An attorney, member of the first Elected Assembly, member of the committee of the Sephardic and Oriental Jewish communities. He fought in favor of the Hebrew language in the language disputes, a public activist.

Kadima Morgenthau – dead end **E-F7**

Forward. The first national organization of Jewish students in Western Europe, founded in 1882 in Vienna in the Lovers of Zion period.

Kagan, Helena, Dr. [Ascent] Zarhi – HaTzadik MiTchechanov **E7**

One of the prominent physicians in Jerusalem.

Kamson, Ya'akov David (1907 – 1981) Eshkoli – dead end **E7**

A poet known primarily for his poetry on Jerusalem. His works are studied in schools.

Karni, Yehuda (1884 – 1949) Mass – dead end **E8**

A poet and journalist, known for his collection of poetry called *Shirei Yerushalayim*.

Karnibad, Refael (1912 – 1974) HaHa'avara – dead end **D6**

A commander of the Hagana in Jerusalem, one of the first to call up veteran Hagana fighters to guard and security duties even before the civil guard was founded. He coordinated activities involved in organizing Hagana members and labored on behalf of building a home for the organization of Hagana members.

Kaufmann, Yehezkel (1889 – 1963) Recanati – Ben-Zeev **E7**

Served as the first president of the World Jewish Society for Biblical Research, a historian, one of the outstanding Bible scholars of his generation. Among the books he wrote are *Toldot HaEmuna HaYisreelit* (The History of the Religion of Israel), *Gola VeNeichar* (Exile and Foreign Land), *BeHevlei HaZman* (In the Cords of Time).

Kehilat Ungvar Wallenstein – dead end **E6**

Named in memory of the martyrs of the Ungvar (southwestern Ukraine) community who were killed in the Holocaust.

Kehilot SHU"M Recanati – dead end **D-E6-7**

In memory of the sages of Ashkenaz (Germany and eastern France) who lived during the eleventh to fourteenth centuries (when they were expelled) in the cities of **S**peyer, **W**orms and **M**ainz, the initials of which form the Hebrew acronym SHU"M. This is the way these communities are known in Jewish history, referring to the Jews who lived in Germany during the Middle Ages.

Kisufim [Steps] Shivat Tzion – HaRoeh **E7**

Yearnings, a symbolic name.

Kushnir, Nisan (1927 – 1981) Zarhi – dead end **D6**

A founder of the association of contractors and builders in Jerusalem, he served as the first chairman of that organization.

Kutscher, Yehezkel (1909 – 1971) ATZa"G – ATZa"G **D5-6**

The world's top scholar of the language of the Dead Sea Scrolls, he served as head of the Hebrew Language Department at the Hebrew University. He was one of the heads of the Academy of the Hebrew Language and a recipient of the Israel Prize.

Lavi, Theodor (1900 – 1983) Idelsohn – dead end **D6-7**

One of the Zionist leaders in Romania and the country's leading author, he directed the *Pinkesei HaKehillot* (Books of the Communities) project at Yad VaShem. He was one of the organizers of the *'aliya* from Romania in the early 1950s.

Lipsky, Louis (1876 – 1963) Shivat Tzion – HaDaf HaYomi **F7**

Chairman of the Zionist Organization in the United States, he worked energetically on behalf of the establishment of the State of Israel, a civic activist.

Ma'ale HaOranim Even Shmuel – Derech HaHoresh **E8**

Ascent of the pines. Named for the most common conifer, the pine tree, whose wood is good for building and making furniture.

Ma'oz Ramot – dead end **F6**

Stronghold, a symbolic name.

Maslianski, Zvi (1856 – 1943) Zarhi – dead end **D7**

Vice-president of the Zionist Organization in the United States, spoke out in support of Zionism in the US after he was exiled from Russia, continued to work on behalf of Zionism in Western Europe and England.

Mass, Reuven (1894 – 1979) Zondek – Even Shmuel **E7-8**

One of the prominent publishers in Jerusalem, chairman of *Yad LeVanim* for soldiers, one of the civic activists and builders of Jerusalem, a *Yakir Yerushalayim*.

Mendelsohn, Eric (1887 – 1953) Zarhi – dead end **D7**

One of the outstanding architects in Israel, he designed important public buildings in Israel and abroad, including Hadassah Hospital on Mount Scopus.

MiLyzhansk, Elimelech, Rabbi (1717 – 1784) Mirski – dead end **E6**

The founder of Hasidism in Galicia, an early Hasidic master and one of the supporting pillars of Hasidism. His son Eli'ezer edited his book, *No'am Elimelech*, which deals with commentaries on the Torah. He served as a rabbi for most of his life, ending in Lyzhansk.

Minz, Benjamin (1903 – 1961) Golda Meir – Mirski **D5-E6**

One of the leaders of *Po'alei Agudat Yisrael* and a member of the movement's directorate, one of the heads of the committee to rescue Holocaust survivors, a Knesset member and minister of the State of Israel.

Mirski, Yitzhak (1870 – 1942) Golda Meir – HaRoeh **E6**

An educator, author, one of the Zionist leaders in White Russia. Before World War I, he founded a yeshiva for combined Talmud study and general education, was one of the few Hebrew speakers in the Diaspora.

Mish'ol HaDekalim Yigal – dead end **F8**

Named for a type of palm tree, many of which either bear fruit, like the date palm and the coconut palm, or are ornamental trees.

Mish'ol HaHadas Derech HaHoresh – dead end **E7-D8**

Named for an ornamental bush, the myrtle, which grows along the northern coast of Israel, and whose branches are one of the four species taken on the Sukkot festival. In the Torah it is called "...a branch of a thick tree..." (Leviticus 23:40).

Mish'ol HaKitron Derech HaHoresh – dead end **E8**

Named for an annual plant of the legume family which bears small, butterfly-shaped flowers.

Mish'ol HaKoranit Even Shmuel – dead end **E7-8**

Named for a perennial plant, thyme, whose leaves are fragrant, and from which an ether-like oil is produced.

Mish'ol HaKurtam Derech HaHoresh – Mish'ol HaDekalim **F8**

Named for a thorny, wild plant, an annual, a type of safflower called painters' safflower. As a cultivated plant, its flowers are used for food coloring, and oil is produced from the seeds.

Mish'ol HaMagalit Derech HaHoresh – dead end **E8**

Named for plants and trees.

Mish'ol HaRotem Derech HaHoresh – dead end **E8**

Named for a wild shrub, the broom, that grows in the sands of Israel and in its wilderness areas. Most of the year it has no leaves. Mentioned in the Bible as a plant that gives shade "...and he sat down under a broom bush..." (I Kings 19:4).

Mish'ol HaYa'ra Derech HaHoresh – dead end **E-F8**

Named for an upright bush or creeper, the honeysuckle, that bears fragrant, nectar-filled flowers and small, juicy fruit.

Mish'ol Moran Derech HaHoresh – dead end **D-E8**

Named for a perennial wild bush, the viburnum, of the honeysuckle family, that bears white flowers and grows on Mount Carmel and Mount Tavor.

Mish'ol 'Uzrad Derech HaHoresh – Derech HaHoresh **F8**

Named for a wild shrub, the hawthorn, that grows in groves in hilly parts of Israel. Its flowers are white, and its fruits resemble small apples.

Mishpat Dreyfus Zarhi – dead end **D7**

The trial of Alfred Dreyfus, a Jewish army officer, in 1894 for treason. He was accused of spying against France; the trial set off protests among many people around the world. Due to the efforts of Emile Zola, a French author, the truth was revealed, and Dreyfus was found innocent and returned to service in the French army.

Mo'adim [Steps] HaDaf HaYomi – Nerot Shabbat **F7**

Festivals. Named for the Jewish holidays and festivals.

Morgenthau, Henry (1856 – 1946) Shivat Tzion – Silver **F7**

Ambassador of the United States to Turkey, he aided the Jews of the Holy Land during World War I, between 1914–1918.

Nerot Shabbat HaDaf HaYomi – Truman **F-G7**

Named for the book by Rabbi Mordechai HaCohen (1905 – 1974), one of the prominent rabbis of Jerusalem, one of its builders and a scholar of the history of Jerusalem.

Netivei 'Am Zarhi – dead end **D7**

Named for the book by Rabbi 'Amram Avorbia', chief rabbi of the city of Petah Tikva, in which he assembled and studied the particular customs of Jerusalem in all areas of life and religious law, from all generations. He wrote many sermons on religious law and Aggada.

Peduyim [Steps] Nerot Shabbat – HaDaf HaYomi **F7**

The ransomed, a symbolic name.

Porath, Yisrael, Rabbi (1886 – 1974) Zarhi – dead end **D7**

Educator, author, homileticist, a founder of Bayit VaGan, represented the Jewish community in Jerusalem before the Turkish authorities, one of the leaders of American Jewry.

Prawer, Yehoshua' (1918 – 1990) Zarhi – dead end **D6**

A member of the directorate of the Jewish Agency, a *Yakir Yerushalayim*.

Propes, Aharon Zvi (1905 – 1978) Kadima – dead end **E7**

One of the leaders of the Revisionist Movement, one of the heads of the cultural centers in Jerusalem, a founder of the song festival.

Ramot Truman – HaRoeh **E-F6**

Heights, refers to the area of northern Jerusalem, the same Rama mentioned in the time of the prophet Samuel.

Recanati, Avraham (1888 – 1980) Zondek – Golda Meir **D6-E7**

One of the earliest Zionists in the city of his birth, Saloniki, a leader and teacher, he urged many people, in writing and verbally, to work on behalf of the Jewish colony in the Holy Land. He made *'aliya* and served as a member of Knesset from the Herut party.

Renanim [Steps] Nerot Shabbat – HaDaf HaYomi **F7**

A symbolic name meaning joy, song.

Revivim Shivat Tzion – Sulam Ya'akov **F7**

A symbolic name meaning rain or showers.

Rosenblatt, Yosele (1882 – 1933) Recanati – dead end **E6-7**

One of the outstanding cantors of his generation, the recordings of whose songs made him famous throughout the world.

Rubin, Mordechai Leib, Rabbi (1841 – 1929) Minz – Minz **D5-E6**

Head of the high religious court in Jerusalem, he became widely known primarily for his exceptional knowledge of the commandments dependent on being in the Holy Land. Head of the *Torat Haim* Yeshiva.

Schechtman, Yosef (1891 – 1968) Lipsky – dead end **F7**

A scholar of the history of Zionism, president of the Revisionist movement in the United States, a member of the directorate of the *Keren HaYesod.*

Schiff, Avraham, Rabbi (1898 – 1986) Rubin – dead end **E6**

A great and important rabbi before the Holocaust, people turned to him from all over the world for decisions of religious law. Upon making *'aliya* he did much to organize the life of the ultra-Orthodox community in the Holy Land, and after the Holocaust he was involved in many fundraising drives on behalf of Israel and to help Holocaust survivors.

Schoenberger, Yosef (1913 – 1982) Mirski – dead end **E6**

Architect, one of the builders of Jerusalem, he built neighborhoods and senior residences, planned and initiated the construction of yeshivot in various places in the city, a member of the committee of the Biblical Zoo, a member of the regional committee for building cities.

Schorr, Moshe (1874 – 1941) 'Aliyat HaNo'ar – dead end **E-F8**

A scientist, Zionist, honorary president of the Institute for Jewish Studies in Poland. He was unable to make *'aliya* because he was imprisoned by the Soviets and died in jail.

Schreiber, Yisrael, Rabbi (1927 – 1993) Idelsohn – dead end **D6**

One of the heads of the kashrut-certifying system in Jerusalem, one of the prominent activists in the *Po'alei Agudat Yisrael* party, and, as a member of the party, he was involved in many ways with the building up and development of Israel.

Segal, Moshe Zvi, Prof. (1876 – 1968) Zarhi – dead end **D6**

Father of modern Israeli Biblical scholarship in Jerusalem, linguist and author of *Grammar of the Language of the Mishna*, recipient of the Israel Prize.

Sfinat Mefkure [Square] Golda Meir at Asirei Tzion **E7**

Named for a small boat with 380 children and youth aboard, mostly orphans, that set sail for Israel in 1944 from the port of Constanza in Romania. The boat was sunk by the Germans as it neared the coast of Turkey, and until today there is neither remnant nor grave of its passengers.

Shabtai, Hizkiyahu, Rabbi (1892 – 1950)
Va'ad Arba' HaAratzot – Wallenstein **E6**

Served as rabbi in congregations in Aleppo (Syria), Tripoli (Libya) and Saloniki (Greece), was an envoy from the Holy Land to Sephardic Jewish communities in many lands.

Shahor, Binyamin [Square] (1916 – 1979) Mirski at Minz **E6**

One of the leaders of the national religious youth movement, a member of Knesset.

SHa"I (1903 – 1978) Yigal – dead end **E-F8**

Acronym for **Sh**muel Bechar **Y**esha'yahu, educator, native Jerusalemite, who was appointed supervisor of Jewish schools by the British Mandate authority.

Shari, Reuven (1903 – 1989) Zarhi – dead end **D6**

He served in many positions, as general secretary of the Haifa workers council, as a representative in the service of the country, founder of the umbrella organization of retirees of Jerusalem and chairman of the organization, a public figure involved in many activities.

Shear Yashuv De Lima – Even Shmuel **E8**

A symbolic name meaning “a remnant will return”.

Shem MiShim‘on [Square] Silver at Nerot Shabbat **F7**

Named for the book by Rabbi Shim‘on Yehiel Abersterk (1895–1981).

Shirat HaYam Shivat Tzion – Tzafririm **E6-F7**

Named for the song of praise sung by the Israelites in the wilderness after the parting of the Red Sea (Exodus 15:1-18).

Shivat Tzion Ramot – Golda Meir **F7**

A name symbolizing the return of Jewish exiles to the Holy Land, first from Babylonia, as is written in Psalms 126:1, “When the Lord returned the exiles to Zion, we were like dreamers.”

Shraga, Or, Rabbi (d. 27 Heshvan) Rubin – dead end **E5**

A Tzadik and Kabbalist, he was among the prominent rabbis and spiritual leaders of the Jews of Iran, a well-known worker of miracles among the Jews of Iran.

Silver, Abba Hillel (1893 – 1963) Shivat Tzion – Truman **F7**

A Zionist leader in the United States and a director of the Jewish Agency.

Sivan, Shalom (1904 – 1979) Idelsohn – Recanati **D6**

Active in Zionist youth groups in Russia, he was caught and tried for his Zionist activity and put in jail, was freed and made *‘aliya* in 1962, and started a publishing house and printing business in Jerusalem that printed books only in the Hebrew language.

Struck, Hermann (1876 – 1944) Zarhi – HaTzadik MiTchechanov **E7**

An artist, etcher, graphic artist, one of the outstanding artists in the Land of Israel, one of the founders and leaders of the *Mizrahi* organization.

Sulam Ya‘akov Ramot – Tlalim **F6-E7**

Jacob’s ladder, a symbolic name related to the dream of Biblical Jacob (Genesis 28:12).

Tlalim Shivat Tzion – Sulam Ya‘akov **E7**

Dew drops, formed in the night-time hours from the condensation of moisture in the air.

Truman, Harry (1884 – 1972) Golda Meir – Ramot **F7-F7**

The thirty-third president of the United States, he supported the establishment of the State of Israel and was the first statesman to recognize the State. He helped Jewish refugees from the Holocaust after World War II.

Tzafririm Sulam Ya'akov – Shirat HaYam **E-F6**

A symbolic name meaning light, pleasant morning breezes.

Ulshan, Yitzhak (1895 – 1985) Zarhi – dead end **D6**

President of the Supreme Court, he served in Jewish battalions in World War I.

Va'ad Arba' HaAratzot Shabtai – Wallenstein **E6**

Council of the Four Lands. Named for the central institutions of the Jewish autonomous administration in Poland from the mid-sixteenth century until 1764.

Vitkon, Alfred (1910 – 1984) Zarhi – dead end **D7**

A jurist, a justice of the Supreme Court and lecturer at the Hebrew University of Jerusalem, he conducted important research into tax law, legal matters and social issues.

Wallenstein, Moshe Nahum, Rabbi (1841 – 1921)
Shabtai – Ari BeMistarim **E6**

One of the prominent Jerusalem rabbis, he served for decades as president of the religious court, one of those who laid the foundations of the Jerusalem rabbinate.

Yigal (1915 – 1980) Golda Meir – Zondek **E-F8**

Named for Yigal Allon, a politician and one of the commanders of the PaLMa"H, an IDF commander during the War of Independence, one of the labor movement leaders in Israel, a deputy prime minister and a minister of the State of Israel.

Zarhi, Yisrael (1909 – 1947) Recanati – ATZa"G **D6-E7**

He published more than a dozen books and novels, wrote extensively about Jerusalem. He wrote about the city, lived in it and worked there.

Zaritsky, David, Rabbi (1914 – 1978)
Schoenberger – Rubin – dead end **E6**

An author and thinker, he wrote scores of books and thousands of articles. He eventually became the most prominent author in the ultra-Orthodox community and the leading figure in all areas of ultra-Orthodox literature – philosophy, poetry, short stories, and as a publicist.

Zondek Recanati – 'Aliyat HaNo'ar **E7-E8**

Named for the brothers Hermann Zondek (1887-1979) and Bernhard Zondek (1891–1966). Professor Hermann Zondek was president of the Academy of Medicine in Jerusalem, a world-renowned medical scientist and *Yakir Yerushalayim*. Bernhard was an outstanding physician of world renown.

Rehavia

Name and establishment:

This neighborhood, located in the center of the New City, was one of the first neighborhoods built in the period of the Brit ish Mandate. The name Rehavia is mentioned in the Bible as a given name, that of one of the descendants of Moses: "And Eli'ezer's (a son of Moses) children were Rehavia, the chief, and Eli'ezer had no other children, but the sons of Rehavia were many" (Chronicles I 23:17).

The land for this neighborhood was purchased in 1921, and the neighborhood was built in two stages:

Rehavia Aleph was built in the first stage, between the years 1923 – 1928, in the area between HaKeren HaKayemet LeYisrael Street on the north and RaMBa"N Street on the south. Rehavia Bet went up in the second stage, between the years 1928 – 1936, in the area south of RaMBa"N Street up to Derech 'Aza. The first residents were workers and men of the Labor Battalion and some of the leaders of the old Jewish community, like Yitzhak Ben-Zvi and his wife Rahel, Dr. Arthur Ruppin, Menahem Ussishkin and Prof. Gershom Scholem. In the view of the neighborhood's founders, the name *Rehavia* symbolized their goal of expanding (*rahav* means broad) and developing Jewish Jerusalem.

Rehavia is one of the six garden neighborhoods built in the early twentieth century (see also the neighborhoods Bayit VaGan, Beit HaKerem, Kiryat Moshe, Mekor Haim and Talpiot).

Boundaries:

North – Kiryat Wolfson, Sha'arei Hesed
South – Kiryat Shmuel

East – Mid-Town

West – Haim Hazaz Boulevard, the Israel Museum

Sites: within its boundaries or nearby are important public institutions, among them the national institutions of the State – the Jewish Agency, *HaKeren HaKayemet LeYisrael* and *Keren HaYesod*; the Hebrew High School, Beit Yad Ben-Zvi, Hechal Shlomo, the Great Synagogue, Yeshurun Synagogue, Kuzari Park, the "Windmill", Terra Sancta College, Beit Yad HaNadiv and the Rehavia stream at the edge of the neighborhood.

Streets: the neighborhood streets are named for sages of medieval Spain (except for the poet Judah HaLevi), rabbis and poets, and a few streets are named for Zionist leaders. Two internal streets have become main thoroughfares that cross the neighborhood: RaMBa"N and 'Aza.

The streets are:

Abrabanel, Don Yitzhak (1437 – 1508) Alharizi – Ibn Shaprut **G13**

Statesman, philosopher, and a scholar and commentator on the Bible, an intellectual of Spanish Jewry. He tried to intercede to prevent the expulsion of the Jews from Spain in 1492, but was unsuccessful. In the end, he also was expelled from Spain.

Afodi (late 14th cent. – early 15th cent.) Alfasi – MiTudela **G13-14**

Named for the book of philosophy, *Ba'al HaEfod*, by Rabbi Yitzhak ben Moshe HaLevi, who was one of the prominent philosophers of Spanish Jewry.

Alfasi, Yitzhak, Rabbi (1013 – 1103)
Ben Maimon – Sa'adia Gaon **G13-14**

One of the prominent early arbiters ("Rishonim") of religious law, he lived in Fez, Morocco, and was called by the name of his city (Alfasi, "the man from Fez"). Known by the acronym RI"F.

Alharizi, Yehuda (1170 – 1235) RaMBa"N – Ussishkin **G-H13**

A Hebrew poet and translator, one of the prominent intellectuals among Spanish Jewry. His main work, *Tahkemoni*, was written in the form of rhymed stories, thought to be the first work of its kind in Hebrew literature.

Arlosoroff, Haim, Dr. (1899 – 1933)
RaMBa"N – 'Aza and ends at Jabotinsky **H13-14**

(See the neighborhood of Komemiyut/Talbieh.)

Auster, Daniel [Square] (1893 – 1963)
Balfour at Ben Maimon at 'Aza **H13**

One of the founders of the neighborhood and the first Jewish mayor of Jerusalem (1948-1951). Auster Square is located at the edge of the neighborhood, near the house in which he lived (see Gan Daniel in Mid-Town).

Balfour, Arthur James, Lord (1848 – 1930)
Jabotinsky – 'Aza at Ben Maimon **H14**

(See the neighborhoods of Giv'at Ram, Komemiyut/Talbieh.)

Ben Labrat, Dunash HaLevi (mid-10th cent. CE)
MiTudela – dead end **G14**

Composer of religious poetry, poet, linguist and Hebrew grammarian of medieval Spanish Jewry. He established, in opposition to his fellow linguist Ben Saruk, that Hebrew nouns are for the most part based on root words of three letters.

Ben Maimon, Moshe, Rabbi [Boulevard] (1138 – 1204)
King George – RaSHB"A **G13**

Known by the acronym HaRaMBa"M. The greatest Jewish sage of the Middle Ages, the authority on religious law among the early arbiters ("Rishonim") of religious law. A doctor of the royal court in Egypt. He is buried, according to tradition, in Tiberias.

Ben Saruk, Menahem (10th cent. CE) Ben Labrat – 'Aza **G14**

A linguist, he compiled a dictionary of the Bible, one of the earliest among medieval Spanish Jewry to study Hebrew grammar. He theorized, in opposition to his fellow linguist, Ben Labrat, that there are roots in Hebrew of two letters and even of one letter.

Derech 'Aza Kikar Auster – Herzog **G13-14**

Named for an ancient coastal city in the southern part of the Land of Israel, the capital of the Gaza Strip, located on the shore of the Mediterranean Sea. In the past this road ran from Jerusalem to the city of Gaza.

Duchan, Moshe [Square] (1884 – 1958) Alharizi **H13**

A judge in Jerusalem and president of the organization of attorneys in Israel.

Eli'ezer [Park] (1888 – 1945) RaMBa"N – Abravanel **G13**

Named after Eli'ezer ben David Yellin, a Jerusalemite, one of the first builders of Rehavia. The garden is also named (Gan) HaKuzari.

Eliyahu Sasson [Promenade] (1902 – 1979)
Ben Maimon from Arlosoroff to Ibn 'Ezra **G-H13**

A minister of the State of Israel, statesman, head of the Arabic department in the Zionist directorate.

HaKeren HaKayemet LeYisrael (HaKK"L)
King George – Diskin **G-H13**

The Jewish National Fund, founded in 1901, assigned by the Zionist Organization to fulfill the mission of redeeming the territories of the Land of Israel and developing them. The properties that the JNF purchased were turned over by law to the Israel Lands Administration after the establishment of the State. The world headquarters of the JNF is located at the beginning of this street (see the neighborhood of Sha'arei Hesed).

HaKuzari [Park] (12th cent.) RaMBa"N – Abravanel **G13**

Named for a philosophic work of the poet Yehuda HaLevi (there is no street named for him in the neighborhood of Rehavia).

HaRa"N (1315 – 1375)
Ussishkin – HaKeren HaKayemet LeYisrael **G13**

Acronym for the name **HaR**av **N**issim ben Reuven Gironde, one of the prominent rabbis and arbiters of religious law of Spanish Jewry in the fourteenth century.

HaRAVe"D [Alley] (12th cent.) Ben Maimon – 'Aza **G-H13**

Named for **R**abbi **A**vraham **b**en **D**avid, the outstanding arbiter of religious law of the twelfth century.

HaSalah (1055 – 1135) Alfasi – Ben Maimon **G13**

A designation of the poet Moshe ibn 'Ezra, who lived in medieval Spain and wrote very intricate, secular poetry, as well as sacred poetry, especially penitential poems which earned him the title *HaSalah*, "the one who forgives".

HaTibonim (12th-13th cents.) 'Aza – dead end **G14**

Named for several generations of a family of medieval Spanish Jewry, who translated the works of the great Jewish authors in Spain from Arabic into Hebrew.

HaTnu'a HaTzionit [Square]
HaKeren HaKayemet LeYisrael at King George **H13**

(See Mid-Town.)

Hazaz, Haim [Boulevard] (1898 – 1973)
Ruppin – Herzog **G13-14**

(See the neighborhood of Giv'at Ram.)

Hel-Or, Avraham Yitzhak [Square] (1903 – 1991)
RaMBa"N at Ibn 'Ezra **G13**

Deputy chairman of the religious council, a *Yakir Yerushalayim.*

Herzog, Yitzhak Isaac HaLevi, Rabbi (1888 – 1959)
'Aza – Golomb **G14-E16**

(See the neighborhoods of Giv'at HaVradim/Shikun Rassco, Giv'at Mordechai, Gonenim/ Katamonim, Kiryat Shmuel, Nayot.)

Ibn 'Ezra, Avraham (1089 – 1164)
HaKeren HaKayemet LeYisrael – Ben Maimon **G13**

A Bible commentator, poet, doctor, scientist, linguist specializing in Hebrew grammar, and one of the most prominent sages in medieval Spain. The first one who set down the rules of Hebrew grammar in Hebrew. Known by the acronym for his name, RAV"'Eh.

Ibn Gvirol, Shlomo (1022 – 1058)
HaKeren HaKayemet LeYisrael – RaMBa"N **H13**

One of the outstanding Hebrew poets and philosophers of Spanish Jewry in the Middle Ages. He is known by the acronym for his name: RaSHBa"G (**R**abbi **Sh**lomo **b**en **G**virol).

Ibn Shaprut, Hasdai (915 – 970 CE)
HaKeren HaKayemet LeYisrael – RaMBa"N **G13**

A doctor, government minister and statesman at the court of the Muslim king of Spain, he translated scientific writings and supported Jewish poets and philosophers (see the neighborhood of Sha'arei Hesed).

Kikar Tzarfat King George at Keren HaYesod at RaMBa"N at 'Aza **H13**

(See Mid-Town.)

King George (V) (1865 – 1935) Keren HaYesod – HaKeren HaKayemet LeYisrael and ends at Yafo **H12-13**

(See the neighborhoods of Mahane Yehuda, Mid-Town.)

Ma'ale Yitzhak Shiryon (1871 – 1941) MiTudela – Kikar Magnes **G13**

A Jerusalemite.

Magnes, Yehuda Leib, Dr. [Square] (1877 – 1948)
Alfasi at RaSHB"A at Sa'adia Gaon **G14**

(See Magnes Boulevard in the neighborhood of Giv'at Ram.)

Melamed [Square] (1910 – 1992) RaMBa"N at Arlosoroff **H13**

Named for Rabbi Ya'akov Melamed-Cohen, a *Yakir Yerushalayim.*

MiTudela, Binyamin (12th cent.) Derech 'Aza – Sa'adia Gaon **G14**

Rabbi Binyamin ben Yona of Toledo, Spain, called *MiTudela,* the first European Jew to visit the Holy Land in the Middle Ages, during a period of Crusader rule. The journal he wrote of his travels serves as an important source for the study of his time. On the wall of a building at the beginning of this street, at the intersection with Derech 'Aza, is fixed a tile bearing the symbol of the city of Toledo, a gift from the mayor of that city.

Mohilewer, Yosef [Square] (1872 – 1943)
HaKeren HaKayemet LeYisrael at Ussishkin **G13**

One of the earliest Zionists and Hebrew educators in the Diaspora and one of the educators of the Jewish renaissance generation. A delegate to many of the early Zionist Congresses. He worked hard to advance education in Jerusalem.

Molcho, Yitzhak Refael [Square] (1894 – 1976)
Ben Maimon at Ussishkin **H14**

An author, journalist and activist in Jerusalem. A *Yakir Yerushalayim.* One of the founders of the neighborhood.

Mordechai Levanon [Square] (1888 – 1986)
Abravanel at Ibn 'Ezra **G13**

A jurist and teacher. A *Yakir Yerushalayim.*

Moreno Meyuhas [Square] (1901 – 1985)
HaKeren HaKayemet LeYisrael at Ibn Gvirol **G11**

An engineer and resident of Jerusalem and one of its builders.

RaDa"K (1160 – 1235)
Ben Maimon Boulevard – 'Aza, ends at Jabotinsky **G13-14**

(See the neighborhood of Komemiyut/Talbieh.)

RaMBa"N (1194 – 1270) King George – Ruppin **G13**

Acronym for **R**abbi **M**oshe **b**en **N**ahman, one of the outstanding rabbis of the Jewish people in the Middle Ages. He was a Kabbalist, a commentator on the Bible and Talmud, a poet and physician. He made *'aliya* in his later years, settling in Jerusalem, where he reorganized and revived the Jewish community.

RaSHB"A (1235 – 1310) Sa'adia Gaon – RaMBa"N – dead end **G13**

Acronym for **R**abbi **Sh**muel **b**en **A**vraham Aderet, one of the prominent commentators on the Talmud and an outstanding rabbi of Spanish Jewry.

Refael (Rafi) Weiss [Square] (1940 – 1975) 'Aza at RaDa"K **G13**

Researched the Bible and the Hebrew language.

Rivlin, Ya'akov Moshe [Square] (1954 – 1976)
Sa'adia Gaon at Ruppin **H12-13**

A researcher of Jerusalem, a youth movement leader.

Sa'adia Gaon (882 – 942 CE) RaMBa"N – MiTudela **G13-14**

One of the outstanding Torah scholars in the period of the Geonim, a scholar of the Hebrew language, a composer of sacred poetry and a philosopher. He translated the Bible into Arabic. He compiled a Hebrew dictionary and set the order of the prayers in the prayerbook.

Shoshana HaLevi [Square] (1901 – 1985) 'Aza at Arlosoroff **H13**

A scholar of the history of the Old Jewish community in the Land of Israel and in Jerusalem.

Siton, David [Square] (1909 – 1989) MiTudela at 'Aza **G14**

(See the neighborhood of Kiryat Shmuel.)

Ussishkin, Menahem Mendel (1863 – 1941)
Betzalel – Ben Maimon Boulevard **G12-13**

(See the neighborhoods of Nahlat Ahim/Nahlaot, Sha'arei Hesed, Zichron Ahim.)

Romema

Name and establishment:

This neighborhood, located in the northwestern part of the city at the entrance to Jerusalem, was founded in 1921 and named for the fact that it is located at the point of highest elevation on the west side of town. The name was given at the suggestion of Rabbi Yehuda Leib Maimon, one of the early residents of the city, one of the signers of the Scroll of Independence and a minister of religious affairs in the government of Israel. Rabbi Maimon suggested taking the name for the neighborhood from the verse, "The right hand of the Lord is *raised*, the right hand of the Lord does mighty deeds" (Psalms 118:16). Romema was the first neighborhood established after the British conquest, at the private initiative of one man, the neighborhood's founder, attorney Yom Tov Hamon. The municipality's committee for names called one of the streets by his name. The house he built stands on that same street, and his descendants are living in it (number 3 Hamon Street, at the corner of HaAdrichal).

Romema today includes the village of Lifta, as well as the lands belonging to it on the eve of the War of Independence. Most of the original houses of the neighborhood were private houses, built in the Arab style – with high ceilings, pillars with capitals and large courtyards. The purchasers of the properties were of the long-time, wealthy Jewish society and the intellectuals of the city of Jerusalem.

On the edge of Romema is an industrial area with various manufacturing plants.

Today's residents belong to the ultra-Orthodox community.

Boundaries:
North – Romema-Industrial Zone
South – 'Etz Haim, Giv'at Ram
East – Kerem Avraham, Geula
West – Kiryat Moshe

Sites: within its boundaries or nearby are the Broadcasting Authority for Israel television, the Central Bus Station, Binyanei HaUma, Allenby Square in which stands the monument honoring the British soldiers who vanquished the Turks and conquered Jerusalem on Hanuka 1917. The monument is built of Jerusalem stone.

Streets: the streets of this neighborhood are named for Jerusalem periodicals and newspapers. The streets surround the square named for General Allenby, who conquered Jerusalem.

The streets are:

Allenby, Edmund [Square] (1861 – 1936)
HaOr at Romema at HaTzvi **F11**

A British commander, conqueror of the Land of Israel and Jerusalem in World War I.

Ariel HaMeasef – HaOr **F11**

One of the earliest periodicals in Jerusalem, founded in 1874 and edited by Rabbi Michal HaCohen (1834-1911).

Brandeis, Louis (1856 – 1941) Malchei Yisrael – dead end **G10-11**

One of the great jurists of the United States, a justice of the US Supreme Court, one of the leaders of the Zionist movement, honorary president of the Zionist Organization of America.

Broshi, Zalman [Steps] (1906 – 1993)
Sarei Yisrael – Torah MiTzion **G11**

One of the builders of the Land of Israel and paver of its roads, a *Yakir Yerushalayim.*

HaAdrichal Hamon – dead end **F11**

The architect, named for architect Yitzhak Kaufmann (1887-1958), one of the first modern architects in the Land of Israel.

HaMeasef HaTzvi – dead end **F11**

A religious periodical in Jerusalem during the years 1896-1915, edited by Bentzion Kuenka (see the street named for him in Giv'at Shaul).

HaMem-Gimel Yirmiyahu – Panim Meirot **F10-11**

Named for the forty-three (Mem=forty, Gimel=three) Moroccan immigrants who drowned in the Mediterranean Sea while sailing to the Land of Israel (see the neighborhood of Romema 'Ilit).

Hamon, Yom Tov (1882 – 1952) HaOr – dead end **F11**

A jurist, appointed by the Turkish government to the bench of the district court in Jerusalem. During the British Mandate period, he worked as a private attorney specializing in real estate matters. He was one of the honored members of the Sephardic community in Jerusalem, an activist, a founder of this neighborhood.

HaOr Allenby Square – Hamon **F11**

A Jerusalem periodical which appeared in 1890, edited by Eli'ezer Ben Yehuda, the reviver of the Hebrew language, and by his son, Itamar Ben AV"I.

HaTzvi Yirmiyahu – Allenby Square **F11**

Named for a Hebrew periodical in Jerusalem, published during the years 1881 – 1899, edited by Eli'ezer Ben-Yehuda. The name alludes to *Eretz*

HaTzvi ["land of the gazelle" or "lovely land"], a designation for the Land of Israel.

Lampronti, Yitzhak, Rabbi (1679 – 1756) Yafo – Shazar **F11**

A doctor and educator in Italy, author of the Biblical encyclopedia *Pahad Yitzhak*, historian of matters of Jewish religious law.

Moria Yafo – dead end – Allenby Square **F11**

Named for a Jerusalem periodical founded in 1910.

Nordau, Max, Dr. (1849 – 1923) Shazar – Yafo **F11**

Doctor, statesman, author, thinker, one of the founders of the World Zionist Organization, a president of Zionist Congresses. He formulated the Basel Program and used the term "Jewish state" to replace "national homeland".

Rokah, Y. L. [Square] (1890 – 1951)
Sarei Yisrael at Malchei Yisrael **G11**

One of the pioneers of medicine in Jerusalem, chairman of the League to Combat Tuberculosis, editor of the periodical *HaRefua* [Medicine].

Romema Allenby Square – Yafo **F11**

Named for the neighborhood.

Sarei Yisrael Yafo – Malchei Yisrael **F-G11**

(See the neighborhood of Mekor Baruch.)

Sha'arei Yerushalayim Ben Gurion Boulevard – Golda Meir **E10-F9**

(See the neighborhoods of Kiryat Mattersdorf/Kiryat Sheva', Romema 'Ilit.)

Shazar, Shneur Zalman (1889 – 1974)
Herzl Boulevard – Shmuel Baruch – Nordau **F11**

(See the neighborhoods of Giv'at Ram, Mahane Yehuda.)

Torah MiTzion Allenby Square – Sarei Yisrael **F-G11**

A religious periodical that appeared in Jerusalem in 1887.

Tuval Yirmiyahu – Yirmiyahu **F10-G10**

From the verse, "...Tuval Kayin (Tubal Cain), who forged all implements of copper and iron" (Genesis 4:22). The word *tuval* is related to the word *tavlin* [seasoning].

Wallach, Moshe, Dr. (1866 – 1957) Yafo – Shazar **F11**

One of the medical pioneers of Jerusalem, he founded Sha'arei Tzedek

Hospital and was its director for many years.

Yafo Jaffa Gate – Weizmann Boulevard **F11-I12**

(See the neighborhoods of Batei Kollel Horodna/Damesek Eli'ezer, Batei Sa'idoff, Beit David/Beit HaRav Kook, Beit Ya'akov, Even Yisrael, 'Ezrat Yisrael, Mahane Yehuda, Mekor Baruch, Mid-Town, Nahlat Shiv'a, Ohel Shlomo, Russian Compound, Sha'arei Tzedek, Sha'arei Yerushalayim).

Yirmiyahu (ben Hilkiyahu HaCohen) (7th cent. BCE) Weizmann – Bar-Ilan **F11-G10**

Jeremiah, a prophet of the kingdom of Judah, one of the three Major Prophets (the other two are Isaiah and Ezekiel). In his prophecies he envisioned the destruction, but he also promised the realization of the Return to Zion (see the neighborhoods of Romema-Industrial Zone, Shikun HaBa"D).

Romema 'Ilit

Name and establishment:

See the neighborhood of Romema, page 452.

The streets of the neighborhood are named for towns and villages in the Land of Israel.

The streets are:

Gedera HaMem-Gimel – dead end **E-F10**

A town in the Judean plain whose founders were members of the BIL"U movement (acronym for ***B****eit* ***Y****a'akov* ***L****echu* ***V****eNelcha*).

HaMem-Gimel Yirmiyahu – Panim Meirot **F10-11**

(See the neighborhood of Romema.)

Ma'ane Simha Panim Meirot – Gedera **E-F10**

(See the neighborhood of Kiryat Mattersdorf/Kiryat Sheva'.)

Neftoah Sha'arei Yerushalayim to the village of Lifta **E10**

Named for the village of Neftoah, the Hebrew name for Lifta (village).

Panim Meirot Ma'ane Simha – Sorotzkin **F10**

(See the neighborhood of Kiryat Mattersdorf/Kiryat Sheva'.)

Petah Tikva Zichron Ya'akov – Shamgar **F10**

A city on the caostal plain, the "mother of settlements" in the Land of Israel, founded by Jerusalemites in 1878 (see the neighborhood of Romema-Industrial Zone).

Rishon LeTzion Zichron Ya'akov – HaMem-Gimel **F10**

The first pioneering settlement in the Land of Israel, located on the Judean plain.

Rosh Pina Rishon LeTzion – HaMem-Gimel **F10**

One of the earliest modern villages, located in the Upper Galilee.

Sha'arei Yerushalayim Ben-Gurion Boulevard – Golda Meir **E10-F9**

(See the neighborhoods of Kiryat Mattersdorf/Kiryat Sheva', Romema.)

Zichron Ya'akov Oholiav – HaMem-Gimel **F10**

A village in the southern foothills of the Carmel range.

Romema-Industrial Zone

Name and establishment:

See the neighborhood of Romema, page 452.

The streets bear names connected with the Tabernacle built by the Israelites when they went up out of Egypt.

The streets are:

Elashvili, Shabtai [Square] (1918 – 1971)
Petah Tikva at Zichron Ya'akov **F10**

One of the organizers of the *'aliya* of the first eighteen families from Soviet Georgia to the Land of Israel.

HaArgaman Yirmiyahu – Oholiav **F10**

The name of a color (red-violet) used in the work of the Tabernacle (Exodus 26:1).

HaRikma Yirmiyahu – dead end **F10-11**

Woven fabric. "Zion wears a colorful, woven fabric" (Ezekiel 16:10).

HaTecheilet Yirmiyahu – Yirmiyahu **F10**

The name of a color (blue) that was used for the fabrics of the Tabernacle

(Exodus 26:1).

Hiram Yirmiyahu – Shamgar **G10**

King of Tyre in the Lebanon. He was an ally of King David and of King Solomon.

Oholiav (ben Ahisamach) Yirmiyahu – Techeilet Mordechai **F10-11**

Of the tribe of Dan, he was involved in the work of building the Tabernacle in the wilderness (Exodus 31:6).

Petah Tikva Zichron Ya'akov – Shamgar **F-G10**

(See the neighborhood of Romema 'Ilit.)

Shamgar (ben 'Anat) Malchei Yisrael – Ohel Yehoshu'a **G10**

(See the neighborhood of Kiryat Belz.)

Techeilet Mordechai Shamgar – HaArgaman **F-G10**

Named for Rabbi Mordechai from Bulgaria, who built a campus and a network of institutions involved with education, with charitable acts and the provision of community services to all circles and communities. He stood at the head of the rehabilitation and absorption of refugees from the Holocaust.

Yirmiyahu (ben Hilkiyahu HaCohen) (7th cent. BCE)
Weizmann – Bar-Ilan **F11-G10**

(See the neighborhoods of Romema, Shikun HaBa"D.)

Ruhama

Name and establishment:

This neighborhood, located in the middle of town between Zichron Moshe and Mahane Yehuda and between Mekor Baruch and Kerem/Beit Avraham, was founded in 1921, at the beginning of British rule in the Land of Israel. Its name, compassion, is taken from the verse, "...And I will have compassion upon her that had not obtained compassion, and I will say to them that were not My people, 'You are My people'..." (Hosea 2:25).

The story of the Ruhama neighborhood begins as early as 1908, when Ephraim Cohen-Reis, director of the Ezra association in Berlin, bought a piece of land in Jerusalem for the purpose of building a rabbinical seminary and institutions of the Ezra association in the city.World War I cut off all his plans, and in 1921 Yesha'yahu Press, the holder of the power of attorney for the association in Israel, was requested to sell the parcel and use the proceeds to pay off the association's expenses from the war period and pay severance to its teachers who had been fired when the association's schools were closed. The parcel of land was finally sold to private individuals, thanks to the devoted efforts of Rabbi Menahem Auerbach. The neighborhood of Ruhama was built on the land, and the houses there were beautiful and magnificent.The first house built was Beit Vangofli, in which the girls school *HaMizrahi Ruhama* was located. The *Sfat Emet* Yeshiva is also in this neighborhood, founded by the Gur Hasidim in 1925. The Hasidic master of Gur was buried in the courtyard of the yeshiva, and a special burial monument was built over the grave.

The founders of the neighborhood were of the middle and upper class, and well-to-do merchants lived there, among them the well-known cloth merchant Rabbi Yitzhak Nissim, who was elected Rishon LeTzion (Sephardic chief rabbi). The residents today are religious Ashkenazic and Sephardic Jews.

Boundaries:
Northeast – Zichron Moshe
South – Mahane Yehuda and the Mahane Yehuda Market
West – Mekor Baruch, Kerem/Beit Avraham

Sites: within its boundaries or nearby are the *Sfat Emet* Yeshiva, Mahane Yehuda Market.

Streets: the neighborhood streets are named for rabbis, educators and a religious text.

The streets are:

Alfandari, Shlomo El'azar, Rabbi (1826 – 1930)
Ben Matityahu – HaTurim **G11**

(See the neighborhoods of Mahane Yehuda, Mekor Baruch, Ohel Shlomo.)

Ben Matityahu, Yosef (Josephus Flavius) (1st cent. BCE and CE)
Malchei Yisrael – Yafo **G11**

(See the neighborhoods of Ahva, Kerem/Beit Avraham, Mahane Yehuda,

Yegiy'a Kapayim, Zichron Moshe.)

RaSH"I (1040 – 1105)
Pines – Gesher HaHaim, ends at HaHashmonaim **G11**

(See the neighborhoods of Kerem/Beit Avraham, Mahane Yehuda, Mekor Baruch, Sha'arei Yerushalayim, Zichron Moshe.)

Sfat Emet Ben Matityahu – Meyuhas **G11**

(See the neighborhoods of Batei Kollel Horodna/Damesek Eli'ezer, Mahane Yehuda, Sha'arei Shalom.)

Valero, Haim (1845 – 1923) Yafo – Ben Matityahu **G11**

(See the neighborhoods of Batei Kollel Horodna/Damesek Eli'ezer, Mahane Yehuda, Sha'arei Shalom.)

Yehudit (Montefiore) (1784 – 1862) Yafo – David Yellin **G11**

(See Mid-Town.)

Yellin, David (1854 – 1942)
Meyuhas – Ben Matityahu, ends at Yesha'yahu **G-H11**

(See the neighborhoods of Batei Kollel Horodna/Damesek Eli'ezer, Mahane Yehuda, Sha'arei Shalom, Zichron Moshe.)

Russian Compound *[Migrash HaRussim]*

Name and establishment:

This neighborhood, located in the middle of town northwest of the Old City, was acquired by Russian Christians during the period of Turkish rule, in 1858, and is named for the Russians and for the structures they built there.

During the same period, the residences served as an inn for the multitudes of Christian Orthodox pilgrims who came from Russia to the Holy Land. This pilgrimage continued until World War I.

During the British Mandate period, the compound – known then as "Bevingrad" after British Foreign Minister Ernest Bevin – served as British government offices and army installations, and was protected by barbed wire fences against attack by Jewish underground forces like ETZe"L. From 1948 most of the buildings in the compound have served as Israeli administrative offices. The British jail was converted into

Israel's national "Hall of Heroism" in honor of the members of the various underground organizations that opposed the restrictive British Mandate government.

Boundaries:

North – Mea She'arim

South – Kikar TZaHa"L

Southeast – the Old City

Southwest – Yafo Road

East – Morasha/Musrara

West – Mid-Town

Sites: within its boundaries or nearby are the historic municipality building, the new municipality complex at Safra Square, the main post office, police district headquarters, the courts, the "Hall of Heroism", Notre Dame Hostel, the French Hospital, the Holy Trinity Cathedral in the midst of the Russian Compound.

Streets: the streets of the neighborhood are named for jurists.

The streets are:

Goldman, Ya'akov, Rabbi [Square] (1906 – 1986)
Grusenberg at Zemora **H12**

The rabbi for the members of the Jewish undergrounds in Israel imprisoned by the British.

Grusenberg, Oscar (Yisrael) (1866 – 1940)
Shivtei Yisrael – Zemora **H-I12**

One of the prominent Jewish attorneys in Russia who fought for the rights of Jews, was a defense attorney for Mendel Beilis (the blood libel trial) in Russia in 1913.

HaTzanhanim Kikar TzaHa"L – Sultan Suleiman **I12**

(See the neighborhoods of the Christian Quarter, Mid-Town, Morasha/Musrara.)

Heleni HaMalca (1st cent. CE) Yafo – HaNeviim **H-I12**

(See the neighborhoods of Mid-Town, Morasha/Musrara.)

Heshin, Shneur Zalman (1903 – 1959)
Yafo – Zemora – Safra Square **H12**

Supreme Court justice of the State of Israel, wrote a book on the Jewish experience in court.

Kikar TZaHa"L Yafo at HaTzanhanim **I12**

(See the neighborhoods of the Christian Quarter, Mid-Town.)

Shivtei Yisrael Heil HaHandasa – HaTzanhanim **I12**

(See the neighborhoods of Batei Kollel Ungarin/Nahlat Zvi, Mea She'arim, Morasha/Musrara.)

Shlomo HaMelech (10th cent. BCE) Yafo – Shlomtzion **H13-I12**

(See Mid-Town.)

Yafo Jaffa Gate – Weizmann Boulevard **F11-I12**

(See the neighborhoods of Batei Kollel Horodna/Damesek Eli'ezer, Batei Sa'idoff, Beit David/Beit HaRav Kook, Beit Ya'akov, Even Yisrael, 'Ezrat Yisrael, Mahane Yehuda, Mekor Baruch, Mid-Town, Nahlat Shiv'a, Ohel Shlomo, Romema, Sha'arei Tzedek, Sha'arei Yerushalayim.)

Yohanan MiGush Halav (1st cent. CE)
Kikar TZaHa"L – Safra Square **I12**

A leader of the Zealots, one of the leaders of the rebellion against Rome at the end of the Second Temple period.

Zemora, Moshe (1888 – 1961) Heleni HaMalca – Heshin **H12**

A jurist, the first president of the Supreme Court of the State of Israel.

Sanhedria

Name and establishment:

This neighborhood, located in the northern part of the city south of Sanhedria HaMurhevet and Ramat Eshkol, was founded in 1926 by members of *HaMizrahi HaTza'ir* (Young Mizrahi) in the Land of Israel who organized the company *Nahlat Bayit* and named the neighborhood for the tombs of the Sanhedrin found nearby. During the attacks of 1929, the neighborhood was abandoned, and the residents returned when the attacks ended.

In 1947 a block of buildings was constructed at the northern end of the neighborhood by ***Po'alei Agudat Yisrael*** (the ultra-Orthodox labor party), and they called them Batei PAG"I. These buildings served in the War of Independence as a forward position for the Hagana facing the enemy. In the Six Day War, near Batei PAG"I, there was an IDF position called the PAG"I post, from which the IDF stormed and captured Ammunition Hill and the police academy. Today, on the site of this position stands the René Cassin School, founded by the Alliance Israelite.

Near this neighborhood, during the War of Independence, the Sanhedria Cemetery was established, after the Mount of Olives fell into the hands of the Jordanians and Jews could no longer bury the dead in the cemetery there.

After the Six Day War, the neighborhood of Ramat Eshkol was established on the eastern edge of Sanhedria, and on its northern edge, the neighborhood of Sanhedria HaMurhevet.

Today its residents are of the ultra-Orthodox community.

Boundaries:

Northeast – Ramat Eshkol

Northwest – Sanhedria HaMurhevet

South – HaBucharim

East – Ma'alot Dafna/Arzei HaBira

West – Mahanayim

Sites: within its boundaries or nearby are the Sanhedria Cemetery, Ammunition Hill, the police academy.

Streets: the neighborhood's streets are named for people connected with King Saul, rabbis of the ultra-Orthodox community and communities in northern Israel and in the Sinai Desert.

The streets are:

Ahino'am HaRav Blau – HaRav Blau **H9-10**

Daughter of Ahimaaz from Jezreel, wife of King Saul and mother of Jonathan son of Saul; later, a wife of King David.

Beit HaHaim [Square] Shmuel HaNavi at Hativat Harel **H10**

"House of life", to indicate the cemetery nearby.

Blau, Moshe, Rabbi (1886 – 1946)
Shmuel HaNavi – Shaul HaMelech **H9-10**

Rabbi, author and politician, one of the leaders of the *Agudat Yisrael* movement and the ultra-Orthodox community in Jerusalem.

El'asa Ahino'am – dead end **H9**

A city north of Jerusalem during the Second Temple period, where Judah Maccabee was killed in the war against the Greeks.

HaAdmorim MiLeiner Shmuel HaNavi – Yam Suf **H9**

Named for the Hasidic rabbis of Radzin, starting with Rabbi Leiner, who advocated the renewal of the commandment of including a blue string in the fringe on the *tallit* (prayer shawl).

HaReE"M (1879 – 1946) HaRav Blau – Shaul HaMelech **H9**

Named for **R**abbi **E**li'ezer **M**eir Lipshitz, educator and author, who founded and directed the religious teachers college in Jerusalem, was a researcher of Jewish history.

HaSanhedrin Shmuel HaNavi – HaAdmorim **H10**

The Jewish judicial institution during the Second Temple period and under Roman rule, up to the fifth century CE. The word is Greek in origin and means "council of elders". After the destruction of the Second Temple, the Sanhedrin moved from place to place, at first to Livne, then Usha, Shfar'am, Beit She'arim, Tzipori and Tiberias. Until the destruction of the Temple in the year 70 CE, the Sanhedrin decided questions of religious law and public matters and had the authority to decide cases of capital crimes. The president of the Sanhedrin represented the nation before the Roman authorities.

Hativat Harel Shmuel HaNavi – Ma'avar HaMitla – Eshkol **H10**

(See the neighborhoods of Ma'alot Dafna/Arzei HaBira, Shikunei Shmuel HaNavi.)

Michal Ahino'am – El'asa **H10**

Daughter of King Saul and a wife of King David.

Ofira Shaul HaMelech – dead end **H9**

Named for the community of Ofira (Sharm-e-Sheikh) on the Red Sea in Sinai.

Shaul HaMelech HaRav Blau – Yam Suf **H9-10**

First king of Israel, conquered Amalek, withstood the Philistines until he fell during a battle on Mount Gilbo'a.

Shmuel HaNavi Shivtei Yisrael – Bar-Ilan **H10-I11**

(See the neighborhoods of Beit Yisrael, HaBucharim, Ma'alot Dafna/Arzei HaBira, Mahanayim, Nahlat Shim'on, Shikunei Shmuel HaNavi.)

Uriel Tzimmer (d. 1962) HaRav Blau – dead end **H10**

Journalist, author and philosopher, one of the founders of Shikun Ariel in Sanhedria, one of the builders of the neighborhood.

Yam Suf Ma'avar HaMitla – Golda Meir – dead end **H9**

(See the neighborhoods of Ramat Eshkol, Sanhedria HaMurhevet.)

Sanhedria HaMurhevet

Name and establishment:

This neighborhood, located northwest of Sanhedria, was founded in 1971 as a continuation and enlargement of the Sanhedria neighborhood. When it was first established, the neighborhood was named "Lower Ramat Eshkol", but the name did not catch on and it was called, as it is today, Sanhedria HaMurhevet, due to its proximity to the tombs connected with the men of the Sanhedrin during the Second Temple period.

Today, the residents of this neighborhood are of the ultra-Orthodox community.

Boundaries:

North – Ramat Shlomo/Rechess Shu'afat

South - Sanhedria

East – Ramat Eshkol

West – Kiryat Ta'asiyot 'Atirot Mada'/Har Hotzvim

Sites: within its boundaries or nearby are the tombs of the Sanhedrin, Sanhedrin Park, Ammunition Hill, the police academy.

Streets: the streets of the neighborhood are named after the rabbinic masters of the ultra-Orthodox community in recent generations, belonging to *Agudat Yisrael.* The neighborhood is encircled by a ring road named for a past president of World *Agudat Yisrael.*

The streets are:

Atun, Ben Tzion, Rabbi (1878 – 1975) Golda Meir – Artom **G-H9**

One of the prominent Sephardic rabbis in Jerusalem, a homileticist and cantor, one of the civic leaders of the Jewish community in the Old City during the seige in 1948.

Dushinsky, Yosef Zvi, Rabbi (1868 – 1948)
Ma'aglei HaRI"M – Yam Suf – dead end **H9**

Rabbi and arbiter of religious law, rabbi of the ultra-Orthodox community in Jerusalem, member of the Council of Torah Sages of *Agudat Yisrael.*

Founded the *Beit Yosef Zvi* Yeshiva in Jerusalem and was its director.

HaAdmor MiBelz (1880 – 1957) Ma'aglei HaRI"M – dead end **H9**

Named for Rabbi Aharon Rokeah, one of the spiritual leaders of Galician Jewry. The majority of his family perished during the Holocaust, he escaped from Europe, made *'aliya* in 1944 and set up his Hasidic "court", which served as a center for all of Belz Hasidim in Israel.

HaAdmor MiGur (1864 – 1948) Ma'aglei HaRI"M – dead end **H9**

Named for Rabbi Avraham Mordechai of Gur and Rabbi Yisrael Alter of Gur, who stood at the head of their Hasidim, were among the founders of *Agudat Yisrael* and heads of the Council of Torah Sages, and encouraged the *'aliya* of their followers to the Land of Israel.

HaAdmor MiVizhnitz (1888 – 1972)
Ma'aglei HaRI"M – dead end **H9**

Rabbinic leader of Vizhnitz Hasidim, continued the dynasty of the rabbinic masters of Vizhnitz, built a campus in Bnei Brak for his followers.

HaShalom VeHaAhdut [Lane] Ma'aglei HaRI"M – dead end **H9**

Named for Rabbi Haim Meir Yehiel Shapira (1862-1925), Hasidic rabbinic leader and congregational leader, philosopher of Hasidism, encouraged *'aliya* of Hasidim to Israel.

Ma'aglei HaRI"M Levin (1894 – 1971)
Yam Suf – Yam Suf **H9**

Acronym for: **HaR**av **Y**itzhak **M**eir Levin, past president of World *Agudat Yisrael*, a minister in the Israel government.

Petayya, Yehuda, Rabbi [Lane] (1859 – 1942)
Ma'aglei HaRI"M – dead end **H9**

Rabbi of the Babylonian (Iraqi) Jewish community in Jerusalem, head of a yeshiva.

Rosen, Moshe, Rabbi [Square] (1912 – 1994)
Ma'aglei HaRI"M at Yam Suf **H9**

The chief rabbi of Romanian Jewry for forty-six years, also took part in the effort to bring the Jews of Romania on *'aliya* to Israel.

Yadler, Ben Tzion, Rabbi [Lane] Ma'aglei HaRI"M – dead end **H9**

Rabbi and preacher, one of the leaders of the ultra-Orthodox community in Jerusalem.

Yam Suf Ma'avar HaMitla – Golda Meir – dead end **H9**
(See the neighborhoods of Ramat Eshkol, Sanhedria.)

Sha'arei Hesed

Name and establishment:

This neighborhood, located on the west side of the city northwest of Rehavia, was founded in 1909. Its name was meant to indicate the benevolence of the founders, *Hevrat Hesed Gmilut Hasadim HaKlali* (GeMa"H), the association for benevolence/general benevolent fund, whose purpose was to help needy religious Jews to build their own homes, "...in order that they may not have to move each and every year, from house to house and from place to place," as was written in the introduction to the book of regulations of the neighborhood.

The benevolent association was founded in 1870 by Rabbi Moshe Nehemia Kahanov, the head of the *'Etz Haim* Yeshiva, and by Rabbi Shlomo Zalman Porush. Naftali Zvi Porush, the son of Rabbi Shlomo Zalman Porush, came up with the idea of building a neighborhood as a means of solving the shortage of housing for the city's poor.

Until the neighborhood of Sha'arei Hesed was built, most of the existing neighborhoods were concentrated in the center and northern areas of the city. With the establishment of Sha'arei Hesed in southwestern Jerusalem, there was a geographic breakthrough in the development of the city, and in its spread toward the south, which was then wasteland surrounded by empty fields. From its construction until today, the neighborhood has kept its religious character. It was originally intended for ultra-Orthodox families only, people of the old Jerusalem Jewish community, and today it is still populated by religious residents of mostly Ashkenazic origin.

Boundaries:
North – Neve Betzalel, Nahlat Ahim/Nahlaot
Southeast – Rehavia
West – Kiryat Wolfson and Ben-Zvi Boulevard

Sites: within its boundaries or nearby are Sacher Park, the Valley of the Cross, the Knesset, the Israel Museum, the Shrine of the Book.

Streets: the neighborhood streets are named for Ashkenazic rabbis.

The streets are:

'Antebbe, Avraham (Albert) (1869 – 1919) HaGR"A – Israels **G12-13**

(See the neighborhood of Nahlat Tzadok.)

Antokolsky, Mordechai (Mark) (1843 – 1902)
HaGR"A – Israels **G13**

(See the neighborhoods of Nahlat Tzadok, Neve Betzalel.)

Bar Zakai, Yeshay'ahu, Rabbi (Bardaki) (1790 – 1863)
HaGR"A – HaKeren HaKayemet LeYisrael **G13**

One of the organizers and leaders of the Ashkenazic community in Jerusalem.

Ben-Zvi, Yitzhak [Boulevard] (1884 – 1963)
Agrippas – Ruppin **G12**

(See the neighborhoods of Giv'at Ram, Kiryat Wolfson, Nahlat Ahim/Nahlaot, Sha'arei Rahamim, Shevet Tzedek/Shchunat HaPahim, Zichron Ya'akov, Zichron Yosef.)

Diskin, Yehoshu'a Leib, Rabbi (1816 – 1898)
RaMBa"N – HaGR"A **G13**

(See the neighborhood of Kiryat Wolfson.)

HaGeonim HaKallir – Ibn Shaprut **G13**

A general name given to the heads of the Talmudical academies at Sura and Pumbedita in Babylonia after the period of the Talmud. This title was also given to the heads of the Talmudical academies in the Holy Land in the tenth and eleventh centuries CE.

HaGR"A (1720 – 1797) Diskin – Ussishkin **G13**

(See the neighborhood of Kiryat Wolfson.)

HaKallir, El'azar (7th cent. CE)
HaKeren HaKayemet LeYisrael – dead end **G13**

One of the great Jewish religious poets of the Land of Israel, composed religious poetry for all the festivals, and had a strong influence on the prayerbook.

HaKeren HaKayemet LeYisrael (HaKK"L)
King George – Diskin **G-H13**

(See the neighborhood of Rehavia.)

HaTa"M Sofer Ibn Shaprut – HaKallir **G13**

Named for a book of commentaries on religious law, called HaTa"M (acronym for **H**idushei **T**orat **M**oshe, innovative interpretations on the Torah of Moshe) by Rabbi Moshe Sofer (1762–1839), the spiritual leader of ultra-Orthodox Jewry in Hungary, head of a yeshiva, one of those who encouraged *'aliya* and supported Jewish colonization of the Holy Land.

Hirschenberg, Shmuel (Rabbi Zvi) (1865 – 1908)
HaGR"A – Narkiss **G12-13**

(See the neighborhood of Neve Betzalel.)

Ibn Shaprut, Hasdai (915 – 970 CE)

HaKeren HaKayemet LeYisrael – RaMBa"N **G13**

(See the neighborhood of Rehavia.)

Israels, Jozef (1824 – 1911) 'Antebbe – dead end **G13**

(See the neighborhoods of Nahlat Tzadok, Neve Betzalel.)

Kahanov, Moshe Nehemia, Rabbi (1817 – 1887)
HaKeren HaKayemet LeYisrael – HaGR"A **G13**

A rabbi and arbiter of Jewish law, one of the founders of the association for benevolence/general benevolent fund, a founder of the Sha'arei Hesed neighborhood, head of the *'Etz Haim* Yeshiva.

Porush, Shlomo Zalman, Rabbi (d. 1898)
HaGR"A – HaKeren HaKayemet LeYisrael **G13**

One of the founders of the association for benevolence/general benevolent fund and a founder of the Sha'arei Hesed neighborhood.

Rahvat HaSha'an Diskin at HaKeren HaKayemet LeYisrael **G13**

(See the neighborhood of Kiryat Wolfson.)

Sha'arei Hesed Porush – Kahanov **G13**

Named for the neighborhood.

SHLa"H Porush – Kahanov **G13**

Acronym for the book ***Sh****nei* ***L****uhot* ***H****aBrit*, which deals with religious law and Kabbala, by Rabbi Yesha'yahu HaLevi Horowitz (1565-1630), one of the outstanding Ashkenazic rabbis and Kabbalists in Jerusalem.

Ussishkin, Menahem Mendel (1863 – 1941)
Betzalel – Ben Maimon Boulevard **G12-13**

(See the neighborhoods of Nahlat Ahim/Nahlaot, Rehavia, Zichron Ahim.)

Sha'arei Pina

Name and establishment:

This neighborhood, located in the middle of town west of Mea She'arim and near the neighborhoods of Beit Yisrael and Geula, was founded in 1889 as a kind of corner entry gate to Mea She'arim and Beit Yisrael, and thus its name, corner gates. Unlike other neighborhoods, this one was not built by patrons and known philanthropists, but by a handful of Jews from Yemen who decided to build homes for themselves.

The founders established a private building association and offered apartments for sale on easy terms. Most of the residents are of Yemenite origin.

Boundaries:

Northeast – Beit Yisrael
Southeast – Mea She'arim
West - Geula

Sites: within its boundaries or nearby are the *Mea She'arim* Yeshiva, religious elementary schools, study halls and a variety of synagogues.

Streets: the neighborhood streets are named after Yemenites or places on the Arabian Peninsula that are known in Jewish history. Kafah Street is an important street here.

The streets are:

'Adani, Shlomo, Rabbi (1567 – 1624) Dayan – Kafah **H11**

(See the neighborhood of Beit Yisrael.)

Auerbuch, Efraim, Rabbi (d. 1948) Dayan – Ben 'Amram **H11**

(See the neighborhood of Beit Yisrael.)

Ben 'Amram, David (14th cent.) Eshlag – 'Adani **H11**

One of the rabbis of Yemenite Jewry, author of *HaMidrash HaGadol*,

"The Great Midrash."

Habshush, Haim, Rabbi (1833 – 1899) Mea She'arim – Belzer **H11**

(See the neighborhoods of Beit Yisrael, Nahlat Zvi/Shchunat HaTeimanim.)

Havakuk Mea She'arim – Yoel **H11**

Habakkuk, a prophet in Israel, the eighth in the books of the twelve Minor Prophets in the Bible. Some of his words have become familiar phrases: "You won't believe it when I tell you", "The time will come", "The righteous shall live by his faith."

Heivar Tzahari – Kafah **H11**

City north of Najd on the Arabian Peninsula, where there was an ancient Jewish village.

Kafah, Yihya, Rabbi (1850 – 1932) 'Adani – Havakuk **H11**

One of the prominent rabbis of Yemenite Jewry, he began the Haskala (Enlightenment) movement among the Jews of Yemen, wrote books on religious law and Jewish thought.

Mea She'arim Straus – Shivtei Yisrael **H11**

(See the neighborhoods of Batei Kollel Ungarin/Nahlat Zvi, Batei Kollel Warsaw/Nahlat Ya'akov, Batei Naitin, Batei Perlman/'Ir Shalom, Beit Yisrael, Geula, Mea She'arim, Nahlat Zvi/Shchunat HaTeimanim.)

Sha'arei Pina Havakuk – Eshlag **H11**

Named for the neighborhood.

TaRMa"V (1882) Zecharia HaRofe – Habshush **H11**

(See the neighborhood of Nahlat Zvi/Shchunat HaTeimanim.)

Teima Tzahari – Kafah **H11**

A place in Yemen where there was a Jewish village in the seventh century CE.

Yatriv Tzahari – Kafah **H11**

A place on the Arabian Peninsula where Jews live.

Yitzhari, Yihya, Rabbi (circa 1516 – 1585)
Ben 'Amram – Havakuk **H11**

One of the prominent rabbis of Yemen, a master of ethics.

Zecharia HaRofe (first half of the 15th cent.)
Habshush – Havakuk **H11**

(See the neighborhood of Nahlat Zvi/Shchunat HaTeimanim.)

Sha'arei Rahamim (Sha'arei Yeshu'a)

Name and establishment:

This neighborhood, located in the middle of town south of the neighborhood of Zichron Yosef, was founded in 1891 by the committee for the Kurdish community, who sought mercy from the God of Israel and help to become adjusted in the land of their fathers, and thus the name, Gates of mercy. The Kurdish Jews reached Israel from Kurdistan, Babylonia of old, which today is north of Iraq. They came to Israel with nothing, out of their longing for the Holy Land and for Jerusalem, the Holy City. Sha'arei Rahamim was one of the poorest neighborhoods in the city. Some of its houses were built like the houses of Shevet Tzedek, whose roofs were covered with tin. The first houses were built on Corazin Street (numbers 2 to 14) and on 'Alma Street (numbers 6 and 8). The Kurdish Jews were manual laborers, working in construction and as porters.

Until World War I, the neighborhood was populated only partially. Only in the period of the British Mandate did the neighborhood begin to be rehabilitated, and the population grew.

With the passing years, the neighborhood was swallowed up in the neighborhood of Nahlat Ahim/Nahlaot.

Boundaries:

North – Zichron Ahim and Zichron Yosef
South – Nahlat Ahim/Nahlaot
East – the Mahane Yehuda Market
West – Ben-Zvi Boulevard

Sites: within its boundaries or nearby are the Mahane Yehuda Market, Sacher Park, the government campus.

Streets: the neighborhood streets are mostly named for historic cities in Jewish history.

The streets are:

'Alma Betzalel – Shabazi – dead end **G12**

(See the neighborhood of Nahlat Ahim/Nahlaot.)

Ben-Zvi, Yitzhak [Boulevard] (1884 – 1963)
Shmuel Baruch – Ruppin **G12**

(See the neighborhoods of Giv'at Ram, Kiryat Wolfson, Nahlat Ahim/Nahlaot, Sha'arei Hesed, Shevet Tzedek/Shchunat HaPahim, Zichron Ya'akov, Zichron Yosef.)

Betzalel ben Uri Ben-Zvi – Mesilat Yesharim **G12**

(See the neighborhoods of Batei Kollel Minsk/Beit HaLevi, Batei Kollel Munkacs, Knesset Yisrael, Mid-Town, Nahlat Ahim/Nahlaot, Nahlat Tzion, Zichron Ahim, Zichron Ya'akov, Zichron Yosef.)

Corazin Betzalel – Shabazi – dead end **G12**

(See the neighborhood of Nahlat Ahim/Nahlaot.)

Sha'arei Shalom

Name and establishment:

This neighborhood, Gates of Peace, located in the center of town bordering the neighborhood of Mahane Yehuda, was established in 1892. Some say the neighborhood was never built and only the building plans remain. But according to the grandson of the neighborhood's initiator, Moshe Friedman, the neighborhood was indeed built north of Mahane Yehuda. The promoters planned to build twenty-six houses there, but in fact even more were built – thirty houses. Moshe Friedman, who owned a shop for cloth and woven materials in the new market in the Old City, lived in the neighborhood of Sha'arei Hesed, but after the construction of Sha'arei Shalom, he moved into and lived in the new neighborhood until his death.

The ancient cistern still exists in the neighborhood, although the opening has been sealed (Meyuhas Street, between Valero and Gaon Streets).

Boundaries:

North – Batei Kollel Horodna/Damesek Eli'ezer

South – Mahane Yehuda Market

East – Ruhama, Mea She'arim
West – Ohel Shlomo, Sha'arei Tzedek

Sites: within its boundaries or nearby is the Mahane Yehuda Market.

Streets: the neighborhood streets are named for honored members and activists of the Sephardic community in Jerusalem.

The streets are:

Gaon, Moshe David (1889 – 1958) Yehosef Schwartz – Meyuhas **G11**

(See the neighborhoods of Batei Kollel Horodna/Damesek Eli'ezer, Mahane Yehuda.)

Meyuhas, Yosef Baran (1868 – 1942) Yafo – Yellin **G11**

(See the neighborhoods of Batei Kollel Horodna/Damesek Eli'ezer, Mahane Yehuda.)

Schwartz, Yehosef, Rabbi (1805 – 1866) Yafo – Yellin **G11**

(See the neighborhoods of Batei Kollel Horodna/Damesek Eli'ezer, Mahane Yehuda.)

Sfat Emet Ben Matityahu – Meyuhas **G11**

(See the neighborhoods of Batei Kollel Horodna/Damesek Eli'ezer, Ruhama.)

Valero, Haim (1845 – 1923) Yafo – Ben Matityahu **G11**

(See the neighborhoods of Batei Kollel Horodna/Damesek Eli'ezer, Mahane Yehuda, Ruhama.)

Yellin, David (1854 – 1942) Meyuhas – Yesha'yahu **G-H11**

(See the neighborhoods of Batei Kollel Horodna/Damesek Eli'ezer, Mahane Yehuda, Ruhama, Zichron Moshe.)

Sha'arei Tzedek

Name and establishment:

This neighborhood, Gates of Righteousness, located in the center of town west of the Mahane Yehuda Market and the neighborhoods of Beit Ya'akov and Mahane Yehuda, was founded in 1890, and its name is taken from the Book of Psalms 118:19: "Open to me the gates of righteousness..." This verse appears at the top of the document establishing the neighborhood. When it was founded, it was the neighborhood furthest west of the Old City.

The neighborhood was built as a large courtyard, surrounded by houses of one story, in the style of the houses of the Old City. Over many years, until 1982, Sha'arei Tzedek Hospital operated in the neighborhood, until it was moved to a new location near Mount Herzl between the neighborhoods of Beit HaKerem and Bayit VaGan. The hospital was built at the initiative of Dr. Moshe Wallach and was also called "Wallach Hospital" because of him. Later, the hospital fulfilled an important role in the War of Independence and afterwards, up to and during the Six Day War, while access was blocked to the hospital on Mount Scopus.

The neighborhood was founded as part of the plan to expand the Jewish settlement outside the walls of the Old City.

Boundaries:

North – Yafo Road

South – Shmuel Baruch Street and Shevet Tzedek/Shchunat HaPahim

East – Beit Ya'akov and the Mahane Yehuda Market

West – Ben Zvi Boulevard – Shazar

Sites: within its boundaries or nearby are the former building of Sha'arei Tzedek Hospital, the Mahane Yehuda Market.

Streets: one street of the neighborhood is named for the neighborhood and the other is called by another word for medication.

The streets are:

Baruch, Shmuel, Rabbi (1898 – 1994) Shazar – Agrippas **F-G11**

(See the neighborhoods of Beit Ya'akov, Mahane Yehuda, Mid-Town, Shevet Tzedek/ Shchunat HaPahim, Zichron Yosef.)

Mazor Sha'arei Tzedek – dead end **G11**

Another name for medicine or medication. It was given this name because it was the street near Sha'arei Tzedek Hospital.

Sha'arei Tzedek Yafo – Shmuel Baruch **G11**

(See the neighborhood of Mahane Yehuda.)

Yafo Jaffa Gate – Weizmann Boulevard **F11-I12**

(See the neighborhoods of Batei Kollel Horodna/Damesek Eli'ezer, Batei Sa'idoff, Beit David/Beit HaRav Kook, Beit Ya'akov, Even Yisrael, 'Ezrat

Yisrael, Mahane Yehuda, Mekor Baruch, Mid-Town, Nahlat Shiv'a, Ohel Shlomo, Romema, Russian Compound, Sha'arei Yerushalayim.)

Sha'arei Yerushalayim

Name and establishment:

This neighborhood, Gates of Jerusalem, located in the middle of town opposite the former site of Sha'arei Tzedek Hospital, north of Mahane Yehuda and the Mahane Yehuda Market, was founded in 1894. This name was given to the neighborhood because, at the time of its establishment, it was the northernmost neighborhood on the west side and stood at the entrance to Jerusalem. The public called the neighborhood "Abu-Basal" in Arabic, *Avi HaBatzal* in Hebrew, meaning "father of the onion", because the founder, Rabbi Yitzhak Lipkin, was one of the pioneer merchants and builders of Jerusalem and was engaged in the produce business, especially the sale of onions.

Rabbi Yitzhak Lipkin built the neighborhood with his own money and sold the houses on easy installment terms. He was opposed to the *haluka*, the dole, and supported people who earned their living by their own labor. At first forty houses were built near Yafo Road, and later additional houses were built, within the neighborhood, at some distance from the main street. The appearance of the neighborhood was characteristic for that period, one-story buildings built around a large courtyard in which a cistern was dug for the whole neighborhood. In later years the cistern was sealed and additional stories were added onto a few of the buildings.

Two important institutions were built near the neighborhood, a residence for elderly men and women of the Sephardic community and the hospital of Dr. Wallach, Sha'arei Tzedek Hospital, that stood facing the neighborhood across Yafo Road.

As the years passed, the neighborhood was swallowed up in the neighborhood of Mekor Baruch.

Boundaries:

North – Mekor Baruch

South and southeast – Yafo Road and the Mahane Yehuda Market

East – Ohel Shlomo
West – Romema

Sites: within its boundaries or nearby is the Mahane Yehuda Market.

Streets: the neighborhood streets are named for religious works.

The streets are:

Gesher HaHaim Yafo – HaHashmonaim **G11**

(See the neighborhood of Mekor Baruch.)

HaTurim Malchei Yisrael – Yafo **G11**

(See the neighborhood of Mekor Baruch.)

RaSH"I (1040 – 1105) HaHashmonaim – Pines **G11**

(See the neighborhoods of Kerem/Beit Avraham, Mahane Yehuda, Mekor Baruch, Ruhama, Zichron Moshe.)

TaSHBe"TZ Yafo – RaSH"I **G11**

(See the neighborhood of Mekor Baruch.)

Yafo Jaffa Gate – Weizmann Boulevard **F11-I12**

(See the neighborhoods of Batei Kollel Horodna/Damesek Eli'ezer, Batei Sa'idoff, Beit David/Beit HaRav Kook, Beit Ya'akov, Even Yisrael, 'Ezrat Yisrael, Mahane Yehuda, Mekor Baruch, Mid-Town, Nahlat Shiv'a, Ohel Shlomo, Romema, Russian Compound, Sha'arei Tzedek.)

Sheikh Jarrah

Name and establishment:

This neighborhood, located in the northern part of the city on the road to the Hebrew University on Mount Scopus and on the highway to Nablus, was founded about 1925 and named after Sheikh Jarrah, a physician, who is buried in the mosque at the entrance to the neighborhood. Sheikh Jarrah was one of the first Muslim neighborhoods built outside the Old City walls in the twentieth century.

Next to the mosque, the Husseini family built its summer palace, as did other well-to-do Muslim families like the Nashashibi and Jarrala families. These were summer palaces, surrounded by large areas of grounds and fruit gardens.

According to existing maps, at the end of World War I, two Jewish neighborhoods went up nearby, Shim'on HaTzadik and Nahlat Shim'on.

During the War of Independence, bands of Arab fighters attacked the northern part of the city and vehicles traveling up to Mount Scopus, and among these was the convoy to Hadassah Hospital of physicians and medical personnel, all seventy-eight of whom were killed. In the Six Day War, the neighborhood was captured by a battalion of the IDF Paratroopers brigade.

At the edge of the neighborhood, on the upper slope of the hill, is the area of Kiryat Menahem Begin (the government campus), with the national police headquarters and various government offices.

Most of the neighborhood's residents are Muslims.

Boundaries:
North – Giv'at Shapira/French Hill, Giv'at HaMivtar
South – Bab e-Zahara
East – Mount Scopus
West – Kiryat Aryeh

Sites: within its boundaries or nearby are the mosque where Sheikh Jarrah is buried, numerous consular residences and a number of hotels.

Streets: the neighborhood streets are named after famous Muslims.

The streets are:

Bar Lev, Haim [Boulevard] (1924 – 1994)
Yadin – Shmuel HaNavi **J9-I11**

(See the neighborhoods of Giv'at HaMivtar, Giv'at Shapira/French Hill, Kiryat Aryeh, Nahlat Shim'on.)

Baybars (1223 – 1277) Derech Har HaZeitim – dead end **I-J10**

A Mameluke sultan, he fought against the Crusaders in the Land of Israel and in Syria, gave orders to repair and renovate the Dome of the Rock on the Temple Mount and budgeted money for the maintenance of holy sites in Jerusalem.

Clermont-Ganneau, Charles (b. 1846)
Derech Har HaZeitim – Bar Lev **J10**

French archeologist and historian, he discovered Biblical Gezer and the Mesha' Stone, served as deputy consul for France in Jerusalem.

Derech Har HaZeitim Nablus Road – Wadi el-Joz **J10**

(See the neighborhood of Bab e-Zahara.)

El-Adib As'ef Derech Har HaZeitim – dead end **J10**

An author and famous physician, he contributed much to the development of medicine in the Arab world. Jerusalem-born, known for his many literary publications, one of the important linguists of the twentieth century.

MaHa"L Nablus Road – Bar Lev and ends at Netter **I10**

(See the neighborhood of Kiryat Aryeh.)

Meinertzhagen, Colonel Richard [Square] (1878 – 1967) Bar Lev at HaUniversita **J9**

A British officer and political adviser, one of the Righteous Gentiles.

Mujr e-Din (1456 – 1522) Nablus Road – dead end **I-J10**

Arab historian and judge in Jerusalem.

Nablus Road Suleiman – the city of Nablus **I10-12**

(See the neighborhood of Bab e-Zahara.)

Rajib Nashashibi Derech Har HaZeitim – Nablus Road **J10**

Jerusalem mayor from the beginning of British rule over the Land of Israel, from when Sir Herbert Samuel was stationed in the land as British High Commissioner.

Sderot HaUniversita Bar Lev – Katzir **J9-10**

(See the neighborhoods of Giv'at Shapira/French Hill, Mount Scopus.)

Sheikh Jarrah Nablus Road – Sayiq **J10**

Named for the neighborhood.

Shevet Tzedek/Shchunat HaPahim

Name and establishment:

This neighborhood, located in the center of town northwest of Zichron Yosef, was established during the years 1890-1892. During those years the poor of the city, the most poverty-stricken, were removed from the area of "Kerem Moshe ViYehudit" (see the neighborhood of Yemin Moshe–Mishkenot

Shaananim), and, with the help of the committee of the Ashkenazic community, land was bought for Ashkenazim near Batei Wittenberg. For the Oriental community, land was purchased with the assistance of the committee for the Sephardic community, near Beit Ya'akov, and on this parcel was built Shevet Tzedek, a neighborhood for the poor – Yemenites, Persians and others.

The residents of Shevet Tzedek built wooden shacks, and they covered the roofs with roofing tiles and sheets of tin. For protection against the wind and rain, the residents bought empty kerosene cans and used them also to cover the walls of the shacks, and this is the basis for the alternate names of the neighborhood, *Shchunat Batei HaPah* or *Shchunat HaPahim* – the neighborhood of tin houses.

Boundaries:
North – Shmuel Baruch Street and Sha'arei Tzedek
Southeast – Zichron Yosef
West – Ben-Zvi Boulevard

Sites: within its boundaries or nearby are the yeshiva of the Gur Hasidim and the Mahane Yehuda Market.
Streets: the streets of the neighborhood are named for Sephardic rabbis.

The streets are:

Baruch, Shmuel, Rabbi (1898 – 1994) Shazar – Agrippas **F-G11**

(See the neighborhoods of Beit Ya'akov, Mahane Yehuda, Mid-Town, Sha'arei Tzedek, Zichron Yosef.)

Ben-Zvi, Yitzhak [Boulevard] (1884 – 1963)
Shmuel Baruch – Ruppin **G12**

(See the neighborhoods of Giv'at Ram, Kiryat Wolfson, Nahlat Ahim/ Nahlaot, Sha'arei Hesed, Sha'arei Rahamim, Zichron Ya'akov, Zichron Yosef.)

Bibas, Yehuda, Rabbi (1780 – 1852)
Shmuel Baruch – Arnon – dead end **G12**

The spiritual leader of the Jews of the island of Corfu, who were among the first to dream of the Return to Zion. He believed that in order to gain control over the Holy Land, it was necessary first to impart to Jews knowledge in the areas of science and military know-how. He lived his last years in Hebron.

Chelouche, Yosef, Rabbi (1891 – 1960) Shevet Tzedek – Bibas **G11-12**

A member of the chief rabbinate of Israel, one of the leaders and rabbis of the Western (North African) community in Jerusalem.

Shevet Tzedek Shmuel Baruch – Chelouche **G11**

Named for the neighborhood.

Shikun HaBa"D

Name and establishment:

This neighborhood, located in the northwestern part of the city between the neighborhoods of Tel-Arza and the Romema Industrial Zone, is named for the Hasidic movement HaBa"D (**H**ochma, **B**ina, **D**a'at), whose members built housing there and took up residence. The HaBa"D movement has a synagogue and a study hall in the Old City. One of the central streets in the Old City is named HaBa"D Street (see the Jewish Quarter).

Boundaries:

North – 'Ezrat Torah and Kiryat Zanz

South – Mekor Baruch

East – Tel-Arza

West – Romema-Industrial Zone

Sites: within its boundaries or nearby are the industrial zone of Romema, the Central Bus Station.

Streets: the neighborhood streets are named mostly for Biblical figures from the period of the Judges.

The streets are:

Abramsky, Ya'akov David [Square] (1879 – 1914)
'Eli HaCohen at Yirmiyahu **H11**

A Zionist from his youth, an author, literary critic, translator and bibliographer, he contributed greatly of his skills and his knowledge, especially to the students at the Hebrew University of Jerusalem. Called a master of the Hebrew language.

'Eli (HaCohen) Yirmiyahu – Giv'at Moshe **G-H10**

He was the priest at the temple in Shilo in the time of the Judges (I Samuel 1:9). (See the neighborhood of Tel-Arza.)

Elkana (ben Yeruham ben Elihu)
'Eli HaCohen – Yirmiyahu – dead end **G10**

From the tribe of Ephraim, the father of the prophet Samuel (I Samuel 1:1).

Hanna 'Eli HaCohen – Ya'akovson **G10**

Of the tribe of Ephraim, the wife of Elkana and mother of the prophet Samuel (I Samuel 1:20).

Levin [Square] (1900 – 1980)
Brandeis at Yirmiyahu at Minhat Yitzhak **G10**

Named for Rabbi Pinhas Ya'akov HaCohen Levin, a rabbi, educator, one of the leaders of World Agudat Yisrael, director of the *Beit Ya'akov* teachers seminary here for women, editor of the newspaper *HaModi'a* in Jerusalem.

Minhat Yitzhak Yirmiyahu – Ohel Yehoshu'a **G10**

Named for the book by Rabbi Yitzhak Ya'akov Weiss (1902 – 1989).

Slonim, 'Azriel Zelig, Rabbi [Square] (b. 1896)
Elkana at Yirmiyahu **G10**

He initiated and built the HaBa"D neighborhood in Jerusalem, a pioneer of ultra-Orthodox settlement in the northern areas of the city. He built educational institutions and religious elementary schools for boys and *Beit Hanna* for girls, and rehabilitated the *Tzemah Tzedek* synagogue in the Old City immediately after it was liberated by the IDF in 1967.

Yirmiyahu (ben Hilkiyahu HaCohen) (7th cent. BCE)
Weizmann – 'Eli HaCohen – Bar-Ilan **F11-G10**

(See the neighborhoods of Romema, Romema-Industrial Zone.)

Shikunei Shmuel HaNavi

Name and establishment:

This neighborhood, located in the northern part of town south of Sanhedria, includes buildings built originally in the 1960s and is named for the prophet Samuel [*Shmuel HaNavi*]. From this neighborhood begins a road that leads northward to the grave of the prophet. The residential buildings in the neighborhood were built in the "railroad" style that was common in those years, and thanks to this design it was possible to add further construction to the neighborhood from 1984 on, as a part of the project of rehabilitation of older neighborhoods.

The residents of this neighborhood belong to the ultra-Orthodox community.

Boundaries:

North – Sanhedria
South – Beit Yisrael
East – Ma'alot Dafna/Arzei HaBira
West – HaBucharim

Sites: within its boundaries or nearby are the Sanhedria funeral hall, Ammunition Hill, the police academy.

Streets: the neighborhood streets are named mostly for religious works.

The streets are:

Emuna [Square] Magein HaElef at Pituhei Hotam **H10**

Named for the international religious women's movement that has focused on education for children and youth, and their care.

Eretz Hefetz Hativat Harel – Shim'on HaTzadik **H-I10**

(See the neighborhood of Ma'alot Dafna/Arzei HaBira.)

'Etz Hadar (1825 – 1890) Shmuel HaNavi – Hativat Harel **H10**

Named for Rabbi Meir Shenbaum (*'Etz Hadar* means "beautiful tree" from the Yiddish "shein boim", his family name), a civic activist who founded the Jewish postal service in Jerusalem and directed it and was one of the founders of various institutions for sheltered housing in the Old City of Jerusalem.

Hativat Harel Shmuel HaNavi – Ma'avar HaMitla – Eshkol **H10**

(See the neighborhoods of Ma'alot Dafna/Arzei HaBira, Sanhedria.)

Magein HaElef Eretz Hefetz – Pituhei Hotam **H-I10**

Named for the religious work by Rabbi Aryeh Leib Frumkin (1845–1916), rabbi, author, a founder and settler of the city of Petah Tikva, who wrote a book on the history of Jerusalem.

Pituhei Hotam (1789 – 1886)
Shmuel HaNavi – Eretz Hefetz – dead end **H-I10**

(See the neighborhood of Ma'alot Dafna/Arzei HaBira.)

Shmuel HaNavi Shivtei Yisrael – Bar-Ilan **H10-I11**

(See the neighborhoods of Beit Yisrael, HaBucharim, Ma'alot Dafna/Arzei HaBira, Mahanayim, Nahlat Shim'on, Sanhedria.)

Shu'afat

Name and establishment:

This neighborhood, located in the northern part of the city between the neighborhoods of Giv'at Shapira/French Hill and Beit Hanina on the road to Ramallah, was founded, according to the traditions of the villagers, hundreds of years ago by immigrants from Hijaz. The meaning of the name *Shu'afat* is (mountain) "peaks", and the neighborhood was named for its location on a high peak.

Shu'afat is considered a prestigious rural neighborhood. There are many commercial businesses and magnificent shops, and likewise, there are still fields being worked by residents who do agricultural work.

During the Six Day War, the Harel Brigade captured the neighborhood on their way to Jerusalem. At the highest point of the neighborhood, an unfinished building still stands, a palace for King Hussein of Jordan, the construction of which began just before that war.

The neighborhood residents are mostly Muslims, with a minority of Christians and Jews who moved in after the 1967 war.

Boundaries:

North – Beit Hanina
South – Giv'at Shapira/French Hill
East – Pisgat Zeev
West – Ramat Shlomo/Rechess Shu'afat

Sites: within its boundaries or nearby is Tel el-Ful, which is identified with the Biblical Giv'at Shaul, King Saul's capital.

Streets: the neighborhood's streets are mostly named for Muslim poets and scholars.

The streets are:

Adam, Yekutiel, Aluf (d. 1982)
Derech Shu'afat – 'Uzi Narkiss, ends at Moshe Dayan Boulevard **J-K6**

(See the neighborhood of Pisgat Zeev Ma'arav.)

Ahmad Shawqi (1868 – 1932) Derech Shu'afat – Bir e-Sabil **I7**

The most prominent of Muslim poets.

Ben Rabah, Bilal (7th cent. CE) Derech Shu'afat – Derech Shu'afat **I7**

The first of the Muslim sages who taught believers to pray in public.

Bir e-Sabil E-Dahr – dead end **I7**

A word meaning the well of E-Sabil, the name of this place since the British Mandate period.

Dar e-Salam Marj el-Muhur – dead end **J7**

The name of this place since the British Mandate period.

Derech 'Anatot Derech Shu'afat – to 'Anatot **J-L8**

Named for the nearby neighborhood of 'Anatot.

Derech Shu'afat Adam – Yadin **I-J7**

Named for the neighborhood. This is the main street of the neighborhood.

E-Dahr Bir E-Sabil – dead end **I7**

A word meaning the back, called this since the British Mandate period.

E-Darj Hafez Ibrahim – dead end **J7**

The name of this place since the British Mandate period.

El-Asma'i (740 – 831 CE) Derech Shu'afat – 'Uzi Narkiss **J7**

A famous Muslim poet.

El-Farabi (870 – 950 CE) Derech Shu'afat – Khlat Sinad **I6**

A Muslim philosopher.

El-Hajaj ibn Yusef (8th cent. CE) Abu Hurayra – E-Shabi **I6**

An Arab leader of the famous 'Abbasid dynasty.

El-Khansa (7th cent. CE) Derech Shu'afat – E-Shabi **I6-J7**

A famous Muslim poetess.

El-Ma'ari (973 – 1057 CE) Derech Shu'afat – Shawqi **I7**

A great poet and author.

El-Masani' E-Dahr – dead end **I7**

A word meaning enterprises, the name of the place since the British Mandate period.

El-Maslah El-Samad – dead end **I-J8**

The name of the place since the British Mandate period.

El-Wa'ir Shawqi – dead end **I7-8**

A word meaning not straightened. The place name since the British Mandate period.

E-Sahl E-Dahr – E-Shabi **I7**

A word meaning the plain, the name of this place since the British Mandate period.

E-Shabi (1906 – 1943) Derech Shu'afat – dead end **I6-J7**

A famous Arab poet.

Hafez Ibrahim (20th cent.) Derech Shu'afat – dead end **J7**

A famous Muslim poet of modern Arabic literature.

Hasan bin Tabet Ansari (563 – 614 CE)
Derech Shu'afat – Ibn Rushd **J8**

The personal poet of the prophet Muhammed.

Ibn Rushd (1126 – 1198) Ansari – dead end **J8**

Physician, philosopher, expert in the Islamic religion.

Imam abu Hurayra El-Farabi – dead end **I6**

A scholar who preached the words of the prophet Muhammed to the masses.

Khlat Sinad El-Farabi – dead end **I6**

The name of this place since the British Mandate period.

Marj el-Muhur El-Asma'i – El-Asma'i **J7**

A phrase meaning: the valley of horses, the name of the place from the

British Mandate period.

Masharif El-Samad – El-Wa'ir **I-J8**

A word meaning the peak, the name of the place since the British Mandate period.

Mu'adi bin Jubail (7th cent. CE) Derech Shu'afat - Derech 'Anatot **J8**

A Muslim judge from the period of the founding of the Muslim religion.

Narkiss, 'Uzi, HaAluf [Road] (1925 – 1998)
Derech Ma'ale Adumim – Neve Ya'akov Boulevard **I3-J8**

(See the sub-neighborhoods of Pisgat Zeev Ma'arav, Pisgat Zeev Tzafon.)

Um el-Samad Masharif – El-Wa'ir **J7**

The name of the place since the British Mandate period.

Yadin, Yigael (1917 – 1981) Bar Lev – Golda Meir **F-J8**

(See the neighborhood of Ramat Shlomo/Rechess Shu'afat.)

Zayid ibn Tabet Ansari – dead end **J8**

A Muslim scholar, the first to set down all the chapters of the Koran in one unit.

Sukkat Shalom

Name and establishment:

This neighborhood, located in the center of town southeast of Mahane Yehuda and close to Mishkenot Yisrael, Mazkeret Moshe and Ohel Moshe, was established in 1888. It was named for the man who bought the land, Shalom Kunstrom, a Russian Jewish immigrant who dealt in banking and the acquisition of properties. The source of the neighborhood name is Psalms 76:3, "In Shalem is His tabernacle (*sukka*), His dwelling place in Zion." Shalem is an ancient name for the city of Jerusalem (Genesis 14:18).

Sukkat Shalom is one of the business districts built in that same period by businessmen or companies. They built four neighborhoods: Sukkat Shalom, Mahane Yehuda, Beit Yosef, Batei Perlman/'Ir Shalom.

Its first residents were Oriental Jews, mostly Yemenites.

Boundaries:
North – Agrippas Street
South – Knesset Yisrael
East – King George Street and Mid-Town
West – Mishkenot Yisrael, Mazkeret Moshe, Ohel Moshe

Sites: within its boundaries or nearby is the Mahane Yehuda Market.

Streets: the single street in this neighborhood is named for the neighborhood.

The streets are:

Agrippas (10 BCE – 44 CE) King George – Shmuel Baruch **G11-H12**

(See the neighborhoods of Even Yisrael, Mahane Yehuda, Mazkeret Moshe, Mid-Town, Mishkenot Yisrael, Nahlat Tzion, Ohel Moshe, Zichron Tuvia, Zichron Yosef.)

Mesilat Yesharim Betzalel – Agrippas **G12**

(See the neighborhoods of Batei Goral/Mishkenot HaTeimanim, Mid-Town.)

Sukkat Shalom Agrippas – dead end – Mesilat Yesharim **G12**

Named for the neighborhood and for the purchaser of the land, Shalom Kunstrom.

Talpiot

Name and establishment:

This neighborhood, located in the southern part of the city, was founded in 1922 at the beginning of the British Mandate rule. The name of the neighborhood is taken from the Bible, from Song of Songs 4:4: "Like the Tower of David is your neck, built to draw all eyes *[letalpiot]*."

At first, thirty houses were built by the first thirty residents. The houses spread out over a wide area, and the residents maintained contact among themselves by blowing a shofar. During the War of Independence, the neighborhood was cut off from the center of the New City of Jerusalem, and it was possible to travel there only in armed convoys. From the

War of Independence until the Six Day War, the no-man's land between Israel and Jordan passed along the edge of the neighborhood. After the Six Day War, the neighborhood developed further. The large private houses slowly began to disappear, and in their places were built apartment buildings of three and four stories, in order to accomodate more residents.

Among the first residents of the neighborhood were author and recipient of the Nobel Prize for Literature, Shai 'Agnon (16 Klausner Street), the historian, Professor Yosef Klausner (7 Klausner Street), and the reviver of the Hebrew language, Eli'ezer Ben Yehuda ('Ein Gedi Street), who laid the cornerstone for his own house but died before he had a chance to live in it (the house has been recently renovated).

At the edge of Talpiot is an industrial area with many workshops. During the British Mandate period, a large British army camp was located in this industrial area, and it was known as "El 'Alamein", the site of a decisive British victory in North Africa during World War II.

Talpiot was one of six garden neighborhoods built in the early twentieth century (see also the neighborhoods of Rehavia, Bayit VaGan, Beit HaKerem, Kiryat Moshe and Mekor Haim). In addition one should not forget the view visible from the neighborhood: to the east, the hills of Moab, the Dead Sea and the Judean wilderness; to the north, Armon HaNatziv and, beyond it, the spread of the Old City, full of beauty and grandeur.

Boundaries:
North – Daniel Yanovsky Street and Talpiot Tzafon (North Talpiot)
South – Siegfried Moses Street and Arnona
East – Talpiot Mizrah
West – Derech Hevron and the Talpiot-Industrial Zone

Sites: within its boundaries or nearby are the home of Shai 'Agnon which today serves as a center of commemoration and literary activity in his memory, the renovated Eli'ezer Ben Yehuda house, the Diplomat Hotel, the Indian cemetery where Indian soldiers from the British army were buried who died in the successful British effort to capture Jerusalem from the Turks during World War I. At the edge of the neighborhood there were British army camps in both world wars, Camp Allenby and Camp El 'Alamein.

Streets: the neighborhood streets are named for Biblical cities, historical places near Jerusalem, historians, leaders of Zionist movements, fighters who fought for Israel's freedom in the War of Independence, civic activists of the Jewish community in Jerusalem, and places in the area of the Dead Sea and the Jordan River.

The streets are:

Abeles, Walter, Dr. (20th cent.) 'Ein Gedi – Nahum Shadmi **H16**

Worked as a district doctor of the Kupat Holim Clalit health fund in Jerusalem, served as an ambassador of Israel to Latin American countries. He was a member of the Jerusalem municipal council and of the executive committee of the Histadrut (Labor Federation), a *Yakir Yerushalayim.*

Bar'am, Ruti [Boulevard] (1938 – 1996) Lankin – Ben Dor **I16-17**

She battled on behalf of the status of the working woman and for women's increased awareness of breast cancer (see the neighborhood of Talpiot Mizrah).

Barzilai, Yehoshu'a (1855 – 1918) Korei HaDorot – Efrata **H-I17**

Hebrew author, journalist, general secretary of the committee of Lovers of Zion and one of the activists of the Jewish colony in Jerusalem.

Beit Ha'Arava Korei HaDorot – Revadim **H17**

(See the neighborhood of Arnona.)

Beit Hogla Beitar – Korei HaDorot **I17**

A historical place in the wilderness of Jericho in the area between the tribes of Judah and Benjamin.

Beitar Daniel Yanovsky – Klausner **I16-17**

An old city near Jerusalem, the center of the Bar Kochva rebellion against the Romans.

Ben Gavriel, Moshe (1891 – 1961) Beit Ha'Arava – 'Ein Tzurim **H17**

A journalist and author in Jerusalem.

Carlebach, Yosef, Rabbi (1882 – 1942) Beitar – dead end **I17**

A rabbi, educator and one of the leaders of German Jewry.

Derech Hevron Hativat Yerushalayim – the city of Hebron **I14-F20**

The route of Derech Hevron extends from the north from Hativat

Yerushalayim, a street near Har Tzion, to the neighborhoods of Giv'at Hanania/Abu Tor, Geulim/Bak'a, North Talpiot, Talpiot, Arnona, Giv'at HaMatos, Homat Shmuel/Har Homa and comes to an end further south at Bethlehem and Hebron.

Dostrovsky, Aryeh, Dr. (1887 – 1975) Efrata – Derech Hevron **H17**

A physician, he laid the groundwork for research in skin diseases. He served as dean of the medical school in Jerusalem.

Efrata Gil'adi – Dostrovsky – dead end **H17**

An ancient Biblical city south of Jerusalem, known today as Bethlehem (Genesis 35:19, "Rachel died and was buried on the road toward Efrat which is Beit Lehem.") Beit Lehem is also known as the place where King David was born.

'Ein Gedi Derech Hevron – Beitar **H16-17**

An ancient Biblical city in the Judean wilderness, on the western shore of the Dead Sea. Known especially for the palm trees and other fruit trees growing there. A NaHa"L (pioneer) settlement was built there in 1953 which became a permanent kibbutz in 1959.

'Ein Tzurim [Boulevard] Korei HaDorot – Derech Hevron **H17**

One of the four kibbutzim of the 'Etzion Bloc south of Jerusalem, in the Hebron Hills, that was captured by the enemy in the War of Independence. The Bloc was retaken by the Israel Defense Force in the Six Day War, and today the community has been rebuilt and named Rosh Tzurim, as 'Ein Tzurim was rebuilt earlier in another location.

Eldad, Yisrael (Sheib) (1911 – 1996) Beitar – Beitar **I17**

A fighter for Israel's freedom, Zionist educator, defender of Jerusalem, a *Yakir Yerushalayim.*

Gil'adi, Yisrael (1886 – 1918) Efrata – Beitar **I16**

One of the founders and leaders of the *HaShomer* and Bar Giora movements, which believed in the idea of Jewish self-defense. He was also a founder of Kfar Gil'adi.

HaKatzin Silver (1894 – 1945)
Derech Hevron – Derech Beit Lehem **H17**

Named for Aubrey Harris Silver, a British Jew, a soldier in the Jewish Battalion, an officer serving in the Old City of Jerusalem, one of the organizers of the Jews there. He conducted the orchestra of the Jerusalem Police.

HaMizrehan (1863 – 1941) Derech Hevron – Derech Beit Lehem **H17**

The Orientalist, a designation for author Yitzhak Yehezkel Yehuda, an Orientalist, one of the scholars of Jewish folklore, Arab folklore and the history of Jewish settlement in the Land of Israel. He conducted comprehensive research on the Western Wall (of the Holy Temple).

HaYarden Beitar – Efrata **I17**

The Jordan River, the largest river in Israel. Its length is 168 km. (105 miles), and it marks the border between Israel and Jordan. Its waters derive from three streams: the Dan, the Banias and the Hatzbani at the foot of Mount Hermon in the north, and it empties into the Dead Sea in the south and is swallowed by it.

Kfar 'Etzion Yam HaMelah – Siegfried Moses and ends at Leib Yaffe **I17-18**

(See the neighborhood of Arnona.)

Klausner, Yosef Gedalia, Dr. (1874 – 1958) Kfar 'Etzion – Korei HaDorot **I17**

A well-known historian, he lived on the street that bears his name. He was chief editor of the Hebrew Encyclopedia. A scholar of Hebrew literature, a founder of the Hebrew University of Jerusalem, and holder of the chair in History of the Second Temple Period, the chair for which is in his name. Recipient of the Israel Prize in Jewish Studies in 1958.

Korei HaDorot 'Ein Gedi – Siegfried Moses and ends at Revadim **H-I17**

(See the neighborhood of Arnona.)

Lankin, Eliyahu (1914 – 1994) Beitar – Ha'Askan **I17**

A member of the ETZe"L command and member of the First Knesset, commander of the arms boat *Altalena*. A *Yakir Yerushalayim* (see the neighborhood of Talpiot Mizrah).

Leib Yaffe (1875 – 1948) Klausner – Siegfried Moses and ends at Gedud Ha'Avoda **H18**

(See the neighborhood of Arnona.)

Levi, Yitzhak [Square] (1919 – 1977) 'Ein Gedi at Abeles **H16-17**

He collected and publicized the cantorial music and lyrical songs of the Jews of Spain.

Moses, Siegfried (1887 – 1974) Korei HaDorot – Kfar 'Etzion **H-I18**

(See the neighborhood of Arnona.)

Peleg, Shneur (1923 – 1996) Eldad – Beitar **I17**

One of Jerusalem's defenders and builders.

Rabbeinu Politi (b. 1891) Beit Ha'Arava – 'Ein Tzurim **H17-18**

(See the neighborhood of Arnona.)

Revadim 'Ein Tzurim – Kfar 'Etzion **H17-18**

(See the neighborhood of Arnona.)

Shadmi, Nahum (1898 – 1985) Abeles – Efrata **H-I16**

One of the Hagana commanders in Jerusalem.

Shalom Yehuda, Avraham (1877 – 1951) 'Ein Gedi – 'Ein Tzurim **H17**

Author, Orientalist, linguist and Bible commentator.

Ulitzur, Avraham (1894 – 1947) Korei HaDorot – Leib Yaffe **I17**

One of the neighborhood's founders.

Yam HaMelah Lankin – Klausner **I17**

The Dead Sea, an inland sea, 398 meters below sea level, known as the lowest place on the surface of the earth. It forms part of the border between Israel and Jordan.

Yanovsky, Daniel (1918 – 1978)
Derech Hevron – Beitar and ends at Raziel **I16**

One of the ETZe"L commanders and an activist in Jerusalem (see the neighborhoods of Talpiot Mizrah and Talpiot Tzafon).

Talpiot-Industrial Zone

Name and establishment:

See the neighborhood of Talpiot, page 488.

Boundaries:

North – Rivka Street and Mekor Haim

South – Bar'am

East – Derech Hevron

West – the track of the old railroad to Tel Aviv

Sites: within its boundaries or nearby are the Lev Talpiot, Beit Hadar and Ahim Yisrael Malls, the Jerusalem Diamond Center.

Streets: the streets of the neighborhood are called by names connected with the occupations of the people working in the area.

The streets are:

Ba'alei Melacha HaRechev – HaRechev **G17**

Craftsmen, named for the tradesmen in this industrial area.

Bar'am, Moshe [Road] (1911 – 1987) HaUman – Pat **G17-18**

(See the neighborhood of Pat.)

Beit HaYotzer HaRechev – HaRechev – dead end **G17-18**

Workshop, a symbolic name.

Buzaglo, Ashriel (1922–1995) Rivka – dead end H16

A member of the city council and the city administration, a public leader, a founder of this neighborhood, a *Yakir Yerushalayim*, and an honored member of the Labor Federation.

Derech Beit Lehem 'Emek Refaim – Bar'am, ends at the city of Bethlehem **H15-18**

(See the neighborhoods of the German Colony/RaMBa"M, Geulim/Bak'a.)

HaGalgal Harashei Barzel – HaRechev **G17**

Wheel, a symbolic name. Named for those who work in auto shops in the area.

HaHaroshet HaUman – HaTa'asiya **G17-18**

Industry, named for the industrial workmen in the area.

HaMahteret HaYehudit BeTzarfat [Square] HaSadna at Pierre Koenig **G17**

The Jewish underground in France. Named for the Jewish underground that fought against the Nazis in World War II (1940-1945).

HaParsa HaUman – dead end **G17**

Horseshoe, a symbolic name. Named for the forge workers in the area.

Harashei Barzel HaRechev – HaUman **G17**

Named for the metalworkers in this industrial area.

HaRechev HaUman – Harashei Barzel **G17**

Vehicle. To mark the motor vehicle licensing bureau located in the area.

HaSadna HaUman – Derech Beit Lehem **G-H17**

Workshop, named for the workers in small industries in the area.

HaTa'asiya HaSadna – HaUman **G17**

Industry. Named for the industrial centers in the area.

HaTenufa Derech Beit Lehem – Pierre Koenig **F15-16**

Momentum. To mark the power that pushes and motivates living things and even activates the thought process of human beings.

HaUman Bar'am – HaParsa – Derech Hevron **F17-H18**

Named for Jerusalem's craftsmen.

Ihud HaKfar Harashei Barzel – Bar'am and ends at Dov Yosef **F17-18**

(See the neighborhood of Beit Safafa.)

Ma'ase Hoshev Yad Harutzim – Derech Beit Lehem **H17**

A craftsman's work, named for the craftsmen working in this area.

Pierre Koenig, General (b. 1898)
'Emek Refaim – HaTenufa **G16-17**

(See the neighborhood of Mekor Haim.)

Po'alei Tzedek Yad Harutzim – Pierre Koenig **G16-H17**

Named after the first workers organization, founded in Jerusalem in 1875 to provide mutual help among its members.

Rivka Derech Hevron – Pierre Koenig **H16**

(See the neighborhood of Geulim/Bak'a.)

Spiegel, Sam [Alley] (1901 – 1985)
Yad Harutzim – dead end **H16**

An American Jew, a pioneering motion-picture producer, winner of Oscars for his films, a Lover of Zion.

Yad Harutzim HaSadna – Rivka **H16-17**

The hand of the industrious, a symbolic name.

Talpiot Mizrah [East Talpiot]

Name and establishment:

This neighborhood, located in the southeast part of Jerusalem, east of Talpiot and Arnona, was founded in 1972. The neighborhood is situated near Armon HaNatziv (the original name for the neighborhood), the residence of the British high commissioner during the Mandate period. Today it is the seat of the UN inspectors.

Talpiot Mizrah is one of the neighborhoods built after the Six Day War with a political purpose, to form part of the belt of Jewish neighborhoods encircling the city.

The neighborhood looks out over the Judean wilderness from the north, and on its southeastern edges are the Arab villages of Jebel Mukabir, E-Sawahira and Sur Bahir.

Boundaries:

North – the Armon HaNatziv promenade, the Haas and Sherover Promenades

South and East – the above-mentioned Arab villages

West – Talpiot and Arnona

Sites: within its boundaries or nearby are Armon HaNatziv, the Armon HaNatziv promenade, the Haas Promenade, the Sherover Promenade, the Moriah Educational Complex of the Jewish Agency, and next to that the educational farm established by Rahel Yanait Ben-Zvi before the War of Independence and which now serves as the center for agricultural experiments of the Hebrew University. Through this neighborhood a channel (aqueduct) passed that brought water from Solomon's Pools to Jerusalem; today the tunnel still exists which held the ancient water-carrier.

Streets: the neighborhood streets are named for the fighters of the Jewish underground who were executed by the British. The main street is called *'Olei HaGardom*, those who went up on the scaffold, and from it lead streets bearing the names of those fighters who sacrificed their lives in Israel's battles.

The streets are:

Abu Rabay'a, Muhamad Hamdan Barazani – dead end **K17-18**

One of the sheikhs of the city.

Adam (1914 – 1976) Raziel – Rav HaHovel **I17**

An underground alias for 'Immanuel HaNegbi, one of the commanders of LeH"I.

'ALa"R (1922 – 1978) Raziel – Armon HaNatziv **K16-17**

Named for **R**ahamim **'A**boud **L**evi, one of the builders of Jerusalem.

Alkahi, Mordechai (1925 – 1947) Raziel – Raziel **J17**

He joined ETZe"L, fought against British rule in the Land of Israel, and was arrested with two friends, Yehiel Drezner and Eli'ezer Kashani, who were executed on the scaffold of the Akko prison in 1947. They are modern martyrs.

Anusei Mashhad Raziel – Eliyahu Hakim **J18**

Named for the Jews of Mashhad, Persia, who were forced to convert to Islam (1838) against their will. Early in the twentieth century many made *'aliya* and returned openly to Judaism.

Archie Sherman [Square] (1911 – 1986)
Raziel at 'Olei HaGardom **J17**

A generous British donor, a lover of Israel, who did much for the residents of Jerusalem. Among other things, he built public institutions and a large park in this neighborhood.

'Azaar, Shmuel (1929 – 1955) Feinstein – dead end **J17**

An Israeli intelligence agent in Cairo. He and Dr. Moshe Marzouk were caught by the Egyptian authorities and put to death.

Bar'am, Ruti [Boulevard] (1938 – 1996) Ben-Dor – Lankin **I16-17**

(See the neighborhood of Talpiot.)

Barazani, Moshe (1926 – 1947) Ben Yosef – 'Olei HaGardom **J-K18**

He joined LeH"I, fought against the British regime in the Land of Israel, and died a martyr's death along with Meir Feinstein, one of those hanged on the scaffold at the Akko prison in 1947, a martyr of our time.

Beit Tzuri, Eliyahu (1922 – 1945) Hakim – dead end **J18**

He joined ETZe"L and later, together with Avraham Stern, founded the

LeH"I organization and fought against the British regime in the Land of Israel. He was caught along with Eliyahu Hakim, the two were imprisoned in the Akko prison in 1945, and they were executed on the scaffold, modern martyrs.

Ben Dor, Yitzhak (1893 – 1948) Ha'Askan – Beitar **I16**

A journalist and activist in the labor movement in Jerusalem.

Ben Yosef, Shlomo (1913 – 1938) Barazani – dead end – Raziel **J17-18**

He joined ETZe"L, fought against the British regime in the Land of Israel, and was the first Jewish fighter hanged in the Akko prison, in 1938, a modern-day martyr.

Bonaventura, Enzo Yosef, Prof. (1892 – 1948)
Ha'Askan – dead end **I16**

An educator, a leader of Italian Zionism, chairman of the department of education, founded the department of psychology at the Hebrew University and joined its faculty, chaired the committee on psychological terminology of the Hebrew Language Committee. He fell in the War of Independence.

Drezner, Yehiel (1922 – 1947) Raziel – dead end **J17-18**

He joined ETZe"L, fought against the British regime in the Land of Israel, was arrested along with two of his friends, Mordechai Alkahi and Eli'ezer Kashani, and all three were executed on the scaffold at Akko prison in 1947, modern-day martyrs.

Feinstein, Meir (1927 – 1947) Hakim – Kashani **J17-18**

He joined ETZe"L, fought against the British regime in the Land of Israel, and he and Moshe Barazani died on the scaffold at Akko prison in 1947, a martyr of our time.

Greenspan, Hershel (Zvi) (1921 – 1945) Kashani – dead end **J18**

He killed a Nazi diplomat in Paris in order to draw the attention of the world to the Nazi persecutions of Jews.

Gruner, Dov (1912 – 1947)
'Olei HaGardom – dead end – 'Olei HaGardom **J17**

He joined ETZe"L, fought against the British regime in the Land of Israel, was one of those hanged on the scaffold at Akko prison in 1947, a modern-day martyr.

Ha'Askan (1903 – 1977) Yanovsky – Lankin **I16-17**

The activist, named for 'Ezra Shapira, one of the activists among American Jewry and one of the directors of *Keren HaYesod.*

Hakim, Eliyahu (1925 – 1945) Anusei Mashhad – Feinstein **J18**

A member of LeH"I, he fought against the British regime in the Land of Israel, was caught along with Eliyahu Beit Tzuri, and both were executed on the scaffold at Akko prison in 1945, modern-day martyrs.

Halperin, Michael [Square] (1860 – 1919)
Raziel at Rav HaHovel **I-J17**

One of the builders of agricultural villages in the Land of Israel. He was very involved in research of the Bible and worked energetically for the absorption of immigrants from Russia.

HaMahtarot 'Olei HaGardom – dead end **J-K18**

Named for the underground groups that formed in the Land of Israel during the years of struggle against British rule, and for the Jewish partisan groups that battled the enemies of the Jewish people during the Holocaust.

Havat HaLimud Ha'Askan – Remba **I16**

A farm that was built by Rahel Yanait Ben-Zvi before the War of Independence and today serves as a center for agricultural experimentation for the Hebrew University.

Haviv, Avshalom (1926 – 1947) 'Olei HaGardom – Nakar **K17**

He joined ETZe"L, fought against the British regime in the Land of Israel, and was one of those executed on the scaffold at Akko prison in 1947. He, Meir Nakar and Ya'akov Weiss were the last three Jewish fighters to be hanged by the British, modern-day martyrs.

Kashani, Eli'ezer (1923 – 1947) Raziel – Hakim **J17-18**

He joined ETZe"L and fought against the British regime in the Land of Israel. He, Mordechai Alkahi and Yehiel Drezner were arrested and hanged at Akko prison in 1947, martyrs of our time.

Kedoshei Bavel 'Olei HaGardom – dead end **K17**

Named for Iraqi Jews who were hanged by the local authorities in Iraq from 1968 to 1970.

Kurz, Moshe Aryeh, Rabbi Dr. (1909 – 1995) Lankin – Diplomat Hotel **I17**

One of the founders of the "religious HaShomer" youth movement. He established the department for religious youth and pioneering of the Zionist Organization.

Lankin, Eliyahu (1914 – 1994) Ha'Askan – Beitar **I17**

(See the neighborhood of Talpiot.)

Levi, Primo (1919 – 1987) Ha'Askan – dead end **I17**

One of the survivor-authors of the Holocaust, an Italian Jew.

Marzouk, Moshe (Gil), Dr. (1926 – 1955) Feinstein – dead end **J17**

A physician, an intelligence agent for Israel in Cairo. He and Shmuel 'Azaar were caught by the Egyptian authorities and put to death.

Nakar, Meir (1926 – 1947) Haviv – dead end **K17**

He joined ETZe"L, fought against the British regime in the Land of Israel, and was one of those executed on the scaffold at Akko prison in 1947. He, Ya'akov Weiss and Avshalom Haviv were the last three Jewish fighters to be hanged by the British, modern-day martyrs.

'Olei HaGardom Raziel – Barazani **J17-K18**

"Those who went up on the scaffold," the heroes of ETZe"L and LeH"I who were hanged by the British in the struggle to liberate the Land of Israel. Most of the streets in Talpiot Mizrah are named for underground fighters who were sentenced to death by the British for their part in trying to liberate the Land of Israel from British rule. They are considered modern-day martyrs.

Rav HaHovel (1901 – 1962) Lankin – Raziel **I17**

Sea captain, named for Yirmiyahu Halperin, one of the defenders of Jerusalem and one of the leaders of the Zionist Revisionist movement.

Raz, Ya'akov (d. 1938) Raziel – dead end **J18**

A fearless fighter for Jerusalem, first of the ETZe"L fighters to fall in battle (1938 – the Hebrew letters for this year spell *tirtzah*, coincidentally from the root word meaning "kill").

Raziel, David (1910 – 1941) Adam – Feinstein **J17-18**

Appointed commander of ETZe"L by Zeev Jabotinsky, he fought the British authorities in the Land of Israel and was arrested by them. After he was freed, he stopped his activities for ETZe"L and devoted his life to the war against the Nazis. He traveled to Iraq on a mission for the British army during World War II, and there he was killed.

Remba, Isaac (1907 – 1969) Adam – Adam **I17**

A journalist, he edited several periodicals of the Revisionist movement. In Zeev Jabotinsky's later years, Remba was his personal secretary.

Rubovitz, Alexander (1929 – 1947) Barazani – dead end **J-K18**

A member of LeH"I who fought against the British regime in the Land of Israel and was hanged at Akko prison in 1947, a modern-day martyr.

Tadesky, Gad (Guido) (1908 – 1993) Ha'Askan – dead end **I17**

One of those who laid the foundations for judicial doctrine in Israel.

Weiss, Ya'akov (1924 – 1947) 'Olei HaGardom – dead end **K17**

He joined ETZe"L, fought against the British regime in the Land of Israel, and was one of those executed on the scaffold at Akko prison in 1947. He, Meir Nakar and Avshalom Haviv were the last three Jewish fighters to be hanged by the British, modern-day martyrs.

Wiener, Asher (1936 – 2000) Derech Hevron – Barazani **H-J18**

Director-general of the Ministry of Housing during the years 1978-1985, a builder of the city.

Yanovsky, Daniel (1918 – 1978)
Raziel – Beitar and ends at Derech Hevron **I16**

(See the neighborhood of Talpiot and Talpiot Tzafon.)

Talpiot Tzafon [North Talpiot]

Name and establishment:

This neighborhood, located in southeastern Jerusalem north of Talpiot, was founded in 1935. On its southern side, the neighorhood borders on the Haas Promenade, and on the eastern side – the Sherover Promenade.

Boundaries:

North – Giv'at Hanania/Abu Tor
South – Talpiot and the Haas Promenade
East – the Sherover Promenade
West – Derech Hevron and Geulim/Bak'a

Sites: within its boundaries or nearby are the Haas and Sherover Promenades.

Streets: the neighborhood streets are named for educators, an ETZe"L commander and heroes of the Holocaust period.

The streets are:

Albeck, Hanoch (1890 – 1972) Yanovsky – Derech Hevron **I15-16**

A scholar of the Mishna and Talmud, a professor at the Hebrew University.

Bulgaria [Square] Albeck at Derech Hevron **I15**

A country in Eastern Europe that maintains friendly relations with Israel. During the Holocaust its citizens saved many members of the Jewish community.

Caspi, Mordechai (1885 – 1947) Albeck – dead end **I16**

An activist in Jerusalem, one of the founders of the nearby Talpiot neighborhood.

Derech Hevron Hativat Yerushalayim – the city of Hebron **I14-F20**

The route of Derech Hevron extends from the north from Hativat Yerushalayim, a street near Har Tzion, to the neighborhoods of Giv'at Hanania/Abu Tor, Geulim/Bak'a, North Talpiot, Talpiot, Arnona, Giv'at HaMatos, Homat Shmuel/Har Homa and comes to an end further south at Bethlehem and Hebron.

Kedoshei Saloniki Albeck – dead end **I16**

In memory of the Jews of Saloniki, Greece, who perished in the Holocaust during World War II.

Lupo, Shmuel (1867 – 1941) Albeck – Caspi **I16**

One of the framers of Hebrew education in Bulgaria, director of the educational institutions of the Alliance Israelite in Jerusalem and president of the Sephardic community in the city.

Yanovsky, Daniel (1918 – 1978)
Derech Hevron – Beitar and ends at Raziel **I16**

(See the neighborhoods of Talpiot and Talpiot Mizrah.)

Tel-Arza

Name and establishment:

This neighborhood, located in the northern part of the city south of Mahanayim and north of HaBucharim, was founded in 1931 and named for the cedars from the forests of the Lebanon that were used by King Solomon for the construction of the Holy Temple. In Tel-Arza there are various factories and workshops. In the southern part of the neighborhood a main road passes through leading to the neighborhoods of Ramat Eshkol and Giv'at Shapira/French Hill. The residents of the neighborhood belong to the ultra-Orthodox community.

Boundaries:

North – Mahanayim, 'Ezrat Torah
South – HaBucharim
East – Sanhedria, Ma'alot Dafna/Arzei HaBira
West – Shikunei HaBa"D

Sites: within its boundaries or nearby are the Sanhedria cemetery and tombs of the men of the Sanhedrin.

Streets: the neighborhood streets are named mostly after rabbis.

The streets are:

Bar-Ilan (Berlin), Meir, Rabbi (1880 – 1949)
Shmuel HaNavi – 'Eli HaCohen – Yirmiyahu **G-H10**

(See the neighborhoods of HaBucharim and Mahanayim.)

Dovev Meisharim Pnina – Giv'at Moshe **G10**

Named for the book by Rabbi Dov Barish Wiedenfeld from Tshebin (1881-1965), one of the prominent arbiters of religious law in the last generation, one of the heads of the *Hochmei Lublin* Yeshiva, a founder of the *Dovev Meisharim* Yeshiva in Jerusalem.

'Eli HaCohen Yirmiyahu – Giv'at Moshe **G-H10**

(See the neighborhood of Shikun HaBa"D.)

Grossberg, Hanoch, Rabbi (d. 1977)
'Eli HaCohen – Ohalei Yosef **H10**

A Torah scholar renowned for his learning, wrote books on the commandments to be performed only in the Land of Israel.

Hacham Shmuel Bruchim (1890 – 1971) Bar-Ilan – Grossberg **H10**

Spiritual leader, composer of religious poetry, author, poet and educator, was one of the honored members of Kurdistan Jewry, wrote Torah scrolls and megilot (he was a "sofer STa"M", an expert Torah scribe), served as an arbiter of religious law.

HaGaon MiTurda (1885 – 1977) Bar-Ilan – Ki Tov **H10**

Named for Rabbi Yosef Adler of Turda, Transylvania, who became one of the heads of the Council of Torah Sages in the Holy Land.

Ki Tov (d. 1761) Bar-Ilan – Grossberg **H10**

Named for Rabbi Avraham Gershon from the city of Kutow, Ukraine. He Hebraicized the name of the city and took it as his family name. He was the brother-in-law of the Ba'al Shem Tov (the BE'SH"T), was an early member of the Hasidic movement, made *'aliya* and settled permanently in Israel, one of the sages of the Kabbalist yeshiva in Jerusalem.

Ohalei Yosef Bar-Ilan – Giv'at Moshe **H10**

(See the neighborhood of Mahanayim.)

Pnina 'Eli HaCohen – Even HaEZe"L **G10**

Peninnah, a woman of the tribe of Ephraim, wife of Elkana ben Yeruham (I Samuel 1:2).

Ziv, Yosef (1868 – 1924) Bar-Ilan – Grossberg **H10**

Director of the *Bikur Holim* Hospital, one of the founders of the Zichron Moshe neighborhood in Jerusalem, supported the Jewish population in Jerusalem during World War I and worked extensively on its behalf.

Tzameret HaBira

Name and establishment:

This neighborhood, located in the northern part of the city on the northeast ridge of Mount Scopus near the neighborhood of Giv'at Shapira/French Hill, was founded in 1972 and named "the top of the capital" because of its high elevation. This is one of the highest neighborhoods in the city of Jerusalem. Near the neighborhood was a large artillery position of the Jordanian army; it was blown up by the Israel air force during the Six Day War (1967).

The buildings of the neighborhood were constructed on a slope overlooking the Jordan Valley, and toward the surface of the Dead Sea.

Boundaries:
Northwest – Giv'at Shapira/French Hill
Southeast – the Hebrew University Campus – Mount Scopus

Sites: within its boundaries or nearby are Mount Scopus, Har HaZeitim [Mount of Olives].

Streets: the neighborhood streets are named for Jewish paratroopers and battalions of Jewish soldiers.

The streets are:

Abba Berdiczew (1918 – 1945) HaHaYi"L – dead end **K8**

A paratrooper who was flown from Israel behind the enemy lines of the Nazis, was captured and executed in 1945. He was a doctor in World War II.

Bar Kochva, Shim'on (2nd cent CE)
Lohamei HaGhetaot – HaHagana **J8-K9**

(See the neighborhood of Giv'at Shapira/French Hill.)

Derech Ma'ale Adumim Bar Lev – to the city of Ma'ale Adumim **J-K8**

(See the neighborhood of Giv'at Shapira/French Hill.)

HaHaYi"L Bar Kochva – Lohamei HaGhetaot **K8-9**

(See the neighborhood of Giv'at Shapira/French Hill.)

Harari, Yehuda (1919 – 1954) HaHaYi"L – dead end **K8**

A PaLMa"H paratrooper who was flown behind the enemy lines of the Nazis in World War II, returned safely, fought in the War of Independence and died when his jet crashed in Kibbutz Ma'agan in 1954.

Lohamei HaGhetaot HaHaYi"L – HaHagana **J-K9**

(See the neighborhood of Giv'at Shapira/French Hill.)

Nehagei HaPradot [Lane] HaHaYi"L – dead end **K8-9**

Mule drivers, named for a battalion of Jewish volunteers from the Land of Israel and abroad who fought in Gallipoli (Turkey) alongside the British forces against the Turks in World War I.

PaLYa"M [Lane] HaHaYi"L – dead end **K8-9**

Named for the soldiers of the naval company of the PaLMa"H, the sea arm of the PaLMa"H in the 1940s, established in 1945 and disbanded in 1948. It was re-established as an interim naval service until the Israeli navy was set up, operating as part of the IDF. Units of the PaLYa"M sabotaged ships of the British fleet and prevented them from foiling the efforts to bring illegal Jewish immigrants into the Land of Israel.

Wadi el-Joz

Name and establishment:

This neighborhood, located in east Jerusalem near the Flower or Herod's Gate, was founded in the 1890s. This Arabic name is *Nahal Egoz* in Hebrew, meaning Nut Stream. At the beginning of the twentieth century a gasoline storage tank was built in the neighborhood and a distribution station called Casa Hana. The neighborhood has a large concentration of automobile body repair shops.

After the War of Independence, the neighborhood came under Jordanian rule. In the Six Day War, Israeli paratroopers took the area, advanced on and took control of the nearby Rockefeller Museum, then continued on to the Old City and broke through by way of the Lions Gate.

Boundaries:

Northeast – Mount Scopus

South – the Old City, Mount of Olives

West – Bab e-Zahara

Sites: within its boundaries or nearby are the Rockefeller Museum for Archeology and the Cave of Shim'on HaTzadik.

Streets: the streets of the neighborhood are named for well-known individuals in the history and literature of Islam. The main street is Muhammed el-Muqadasi.

The streets are:

Abu Firem el-Hamdani (10th cent. CE) Tabari – Ibn Tulun **J11**

Muslim geographer.

Bani Omaya Wadi el-Joz - El-Muqadasi **J10**

The Muslim Umayyad dynasty that ruled from Damascus during the years 661-750 CE.

Ben 'Adaya, Shmuel (6th cent. CE) Suleiman – Rab'a el-'Adawiyeh **K11**

Jewish poet, wrote in Arabic and lived on the Arabian peninsula prior to the rise of Islam.

El-Muqadasi, Muhammed (10th cent. CE) Suleiman – El-Hanbali **K10-J12**

(See the neighborhood of Bab e-Zahara.)

El-Mutanabi (915 – 965 CE) Bani Omaya – El-Muqadasi **J10-11**

A Muslim poet.

E-Tabari (839 – 923 CE) El-Mutanabi – El-Mutanabi **J11**

Muslim historian, one of the great interpreters of the Koran.

Ibn Tulun (835 – 884 CE) Wadi el-Joz – El-Muqadasi **J11**

Senior commander of the Arab army.

Imam abu Hanifa (7th cent. CE) El-Muqadasi – dead end **J11**

The greatest Muslim *imam* (cleric), a researcher of Islamic religion and law.

Imam el-Hanbali El-Muqadasi – dead end **J-K10**

A Muslim sage, head of the school for interpretation of the Koran.

Imam el-Malaki El-Muqadasi – dead end **J-K11**

A Muslim sage, one of the interpreters of the Koran.

Khalif el-Baldi El-Muqadasi – dead end **K11**

One of the sages of the Islamic religion, president of the Muslim religious court in the period of the British Mandate.

Shams e-Din Asyuti (15th cent.) El-Muqadasi – dead end **J-K11**

A Muslim scholar, he wrote a book about the mosques on the Temple Mount.

Umru el-Qeis (6th cent. CE) Ben 'Adaya – El-Muqadasi **J11**

One of the great Arab poets of the pre-Muslim period.

Wadi el-Joz El-Muqadasi – Yitzhak HaNadiv **J10-11**

Meaning: Nut stream, named for the stream that flows near this street.

Yaqut el-Hamawi Ben 'Adaya – Abu Hanifa **J11**

Arab geographer and traveler, he wrote a geographical dictionary.

Yefei Nof

Name and establishment:

This neighborhood, located at the edge of Beit HaKerem, alongside Herzl Boulevard and bordering Mount Herzl, was founded in 1929. The name Yefei Nof, beautiful view, is drawn from the Book of Psalms 48:3, referring to Jerusalem: "Beautiful landscape, the joy of all the earth, Mount Zion, the northernmost part (in Biblical times, the Temple Mount was furthest north), city of the great King." The name reflects the magical scenery visible from this neighborhood toward the Jerusalem Forest to the west.

Boundaries:

North – Giv'at Shaul
Northeast – Kiryat Moshe
Northwest – Nahal Revida, branches of Nahal Sorek descending to the Mediterranean
South – Bayit VaGan
East – Beit HaKerem
West – the Jerusalem Forest
Southwest – Mount Herzl and the military cemetery

Sites: within its boundaries or nearby are Mount Herzl, the military cemetery, the Jerusalem Forest, the Yad Sarah headquarters.

Streets: neighborhood street names are drawn from nature and the surrounding scenery. The main street of the neighborhood is Yefei Nof Street.

The streets are:

Amir Yefei Nof – dead end **D13**

Synonym for treetop: "Two or three berries at the top of the highest bough..." (Isaiah 17:6).

Degania Farbstein – dead end **D12**

A kibbutz at the southern end of Lake Kineret, called the "mother of communal settlements." The first agricultural commune in the Land of Israel.

HaArazim Herzl Boulevard – Yefei Nof **D12**

Cedars, a type of forest tree. Cedars from the Lebanon were used to build the First Holy Temple, "...that they may cut for me cedars from the Lebanon..." (I Kings 5:20).

HaMeshoreret (Rahel) (1890 – 1931) HaArazim – dead end **D12**

The poetess, named for the poet and author Rahel Sela' (Bluwstein).

HaTomer HaArazim – Herzl Boulevard **D12**

The date palm tree: "She was sitting under the palm tree..." (Judges 4:5).

Herzl Boulevard Shazar Boulevard – HaPisga **F11-D13**

(See the neighborhoods of Bayit VaGan, Beit HaKerem, Kiryat Moshe, Maimon.)

Marat, Zalman [Square] (1914 – 1985) Yefei Nof at HaArazim **C-D12**

Commander of the Moriah Battalion in the War of Independence.

Megadim Yefei Nof – dead end **C-D13**

Meaning a good and tasty fruit. "...an orchard of pomegranates with sweet, tasty fruits..." (Song of Songs 4:13).

Mordechai Ish Shalom [Road] (1901 – 1991)
Farbstein – HaArazim **D-E12**

A pioneer in the Gedud Ha'Avoda, "Labor Battalion". Fifth mayor of Jerusalem.

Nof Harim Pirhei Hen – dead end **C12-D13**

Landscape of hills, to indicate the superb panoramic view that can be seen from this street.

Pirhei Hen Yefei Nof – dead end **C13**

Charming flowers, to indicate the bounty of wildflowers found in this area.

Semadar Megadim – dead end **D12-13**

A fruit in its early development: "...whether the vine has blossomed, the nascent fruit has begun to develop..." (Song of Songs 7:13).

Tirtza Herzl Boulevard – Semadar **D13**

Named for the capital city of the kingdom of Israel, in Samaria (I Kings 14:17).

Tzemah, Shlomo (1886 – 1975) Pirhei Hen – dead end **C12-13**

Author, literary critic, philosopher and agronomist. Founded the Kadourie School. Was a recipient of the Israel Prize in 1965.

Yefei Nof Herzl Boulevard – HaArazim **D12-13**

Named for the neighborhood, it is the main street.

Yegiy'a Kapayim

Name and establishment:

This neighborhood, located in the center of town west of the Ahva neighborhood and near Zichron Moshe, was founded in the year 1908 by an association of craftsmen called "Yegiy'a Kapayim in Jerusalem", who aspired to live from the fruit of their labors, hence the name. Its name is drawn from the verse: "When you eat of the labor of your hands, you shall be happy and it will be well with you." (Psalms 128:2)

Most of the neighborhood's founders were from Oriental Jewish communities who wanted to support themselves by their own work and did handicrafts as craftsmen, artisans, and the like (see the similar neighborhood – Ahva).

The residents today belong to the ultra-Orthodox community.

Boundaries:

North – Geula and Kerem Avraham

South – Zichron Moshe

East – Ahva

West – Mekor Baruch

Sites: within its boundaries or nearby are the *Yegiy'a Kapayim* Synagogue, founded in 1914, the Mahane Yehuda Market, the Schneller Orphanage.

Streets: the neighborhood streets are named after rabbis.

The streets are:

Algazi, Yom Tov, Rabbi (1727 – 1802) Pines – Ben Matityahu **G-H11**

The Rishon LeTzion, chief of the rabbis of the Land of Israel. He served as head of the Kabbalist *Beit El* Yeshiva in the Old City of Jerusalem.

Ben Matityahu, Yosef (Josephus Flavius) (1st cent. BCE and CE)
Malchei Yisrael – Yafo **G11**

(See the neighborhoods of Ahva, Kerem/Beit Avraham, Mahane Yehuda,

Ruhama, Zichron Moshe.)

Meir, Ya'akov, Rabbi (1856 – 1937) Malchei Yisrael – Sholal **H11**

(See the neighborhood of Ahva.)

Pines, Yehiel Michel (1843 – 1913) Yafo – Rabbeinu Tam **H11**

Author, linguist, one of the heads of the Committee on the Hebrew Language, the first director of the Montefiore Foundation appointed in Israel, one of the builders of new Jerusalem neighborhoods. Haya Tzipora Pines (1844–1918), a public leader, founded the organization "'Ezrat Nashim (help for women)" that provided help for widows, needy new mothers and orphans. Through her initiative the hospital 'Ezrat Nashim was founded (see the neighborhood of Zichron Moshe).

Rabbeinu Tam (1100 – 1171) Meir – RaSH"I **G-H11**

Rabbi Ya'akov ben Meir Tam, grandson of RaSH"I, chief of the sages of France in the twelfth century. One of the Masters of the Tosafot, he composed many religious poems and formulated and established important regulations in the Jewish communal life of his generation and for future generations.

Yemin Moshe

Name and establishment:

This neighborhood, located opposite Mount Zion and the walls of the Old City, was founded in 1892 and named "Moshe's right hand". It is one of the six neighborhoods in Jerusalem that are named for Sir Moses Montefiore, thus its name "the old Montefiore", to distinguish it from Kiryat Moshe, founded in 1923, "the new Montefiore". The founders chose a verse from the Book of Isaiah (63:12), in which the name Moshe (Moses) appears: "who led with His glorious arm at Moshe's right hand...to make Himself an everlasting name."

Before the founding of the neighborhood, its residents were the poor of the Old City who had made their way into this area and claimed plots of land. With pressure on the part of Montefiore's heirs and with the intercession of the head of the Jewish community in Jerusalem, the Sephardim were removed and relocated to the area of Nahlaot, and there the neighborhood of Shevet Tzedek/Shchunat HaPahim was established. At the same time, the Ashkenazic Jews were moved to an area near Mea She'arim, facing Batei Wittenberg, and there the neighborhood of Bnei Moshe/Neve Shalom was built for them.

After its founding, Yemin Moshe was divided into two parts: the Sephardic neighborhood in the southern portion, between today's Yemin Moshe Street north to Migdal Street; and the Ashkenazic neighborhood that extended from Migdal Street northward.

During the War of Independence, the neighborhood suffered greatly because of its position on the seamline between Israel and Jordan. At the time, the area was almost completely abandoned except for the fighters. After the Six Day War the neighborhood went through a process of rehabilitation and gentrification and became a luxury neighborhood. Residents who had lived there previously moved to other neighborhoods and new, more well-established residents took their places, artists and people with means. Its alleyways are paved with cobbles like the alleyways of the Old City, and are meant for pedestrians only.

At the southern edge of the neighborhood is the long building *Mishkenot Shaananim* ("serene dwelling places"), belonging to the neighborhood of the same name, which was the first neighborhood built outside the walls of the Old City, in 1860. With the passing of time, the two neighborhoods became one.

Boundaries:
North – David's Village-Mamilla
South – the German Colony
East – Mount Zion and the walls of the Old City
West – Komemiyut/Talbieh and Liberty Bell Park

Sites: within its boundaries or nearby are the windmill that Montefiore built for the poor residents of Jerusalem, the long building *Mishkenot Shaananim*, the Bloomfield Garden, the Sephardic synagogue on Malki Street, the Ashkenazic synagogue on Pele Yo'etz Street, the Menachem Begin Heritage Center, Arts & Crafts Lane.

Streets: the neighborhood streets are named for historical sites connected with the neighborhood, for leaders of the Sephardic community and for national symbols.

The streets are:

Admoni, Elimelech (1900 – 1964) David HaMelech – dead end **H-I13**

Pioneer in developing the Jerusalem landscape.

Badhav, Yitzhak, Rabbi [Steps] (1859 – 1947)
HaMevaser – Malki **I14**

Researcher of the history of Jerusalem's sages, one of the highly respected members of the Sephardic community and one of the veteran residents of the neighborhood. He was known as a collector and researcher of old manuscripts from the thirteenth century.

Botta, Paul Emile (1802 – 1870) David HaMelech – Eliel **H-I13**

(See Mid-Town.)

David HaMelech (10th cent. BCE) Agron – 'Emek Refaim **H13-I14**

(See the neighborhoods of David's Village-Mamilla, Komemiyut/ Talbieh, Mahane Yisrael/Shchunat HaMa'aravim, Mid-Town.)

Eliel Dror (1905 – 1970) Shama'a – HaMigdal **I13**

(See the neighborhood of David's Village-Mamilla.)

Even Sikra HaTzayar – David HaMelech **I14**

Was the head of a group of fighters called Sikrim (Sicarii) who fought the Romans at the end of the Second Temple period.

Felt, James [Lane] Eliel – Hativat Yerushalayim **I13**

Contributed to the building and renovating of *Hutzot HaYotzer*, Arts & Crafts Lane, an area that includes, among others, art galleries and drawing workshops.

HaBreicha HaTahana – Nachon **I14**

Pool, named for the pool in the eastern part of the neighborhood, in the Ben Hinom Valley, known by the name Birkhet e-Sultan (in Hebrew, *Breichat HaSultan*), or Sultan's Pool.

HaMetzuda Eliel – Touro **I-13**

Citadel, named for Metzudat David [David's Citadel], which can be seen at the Old City wall.

HaMevaser Yemin Moshe – HaMigdal **I14**

Messenger, named for the messenger of Israel's redemption, Elijah the Prophet.

HaMigdal Nachon – Heine **I13**

Tower, named for Migdal David [Tower of David], which can be seen at the Old City wall.

HaMishlat HaMigdal – HaBreicha **I13-14**

Commanding position, so named because the neighborhood was a point of strategic dominance over the hills of Jerusalem during the War of Independence.

HaTahana Yemin Moshe – HaBreicha **I14**

Mill, named for the windmill built by Moses Montefiore in the *Mishkenot Shaananim* section.

HaTikva HaMigdal – dead end **I13**

Hope, named for the national anthem of the State of Israel, composed by the poet Naftali Herz Imber (1856 -1909).

Hativat Yerushalayim Ma'ale HaShalom – Yafo **I13-14**

(See the neighborhoods of Armenian Quarter, the Christian Quarter, David's Village-Mamilla and the Jewish Quarter.)

HaTzayar Ya'akov Steinhardt (1887 – 1968)
Bloomfield Boulevard – Mishkenot Shaananim **I13**

The artist, named for the Jewish artist and teacher Ya'akov Steinhardt.

Heine, Heinrich (1797 – 1856)
Bloomfield Boulevard – dead end **I13-14**

One of the great poets of Germany, a lover of Jerusalem.

Malki, Refael Mordechai, Rabbi (d. 1705)
Yemin Moshe – HaMigdal **I13-14**

A doctor in Jerusalem. He was one of Jerusalem's rabbis and an activist.

Mishkenot Shaananim Yemin Moshe – Derech Hevron **I14**

Named for the first neighborhood established outside the walls of the Old City.

Nachon, Shlomo Omerti (1906 – 1974)
Mishkenot Shaananim – Derech Hevron **I13-14**

One of the highly respected members of Italian Jewry and one of the directors of the Keren HaYesod in Jerusalem.

Pele Yo'etz HaMigdal – dead end **I13**

Named for the book of that name by Rabbi Eli'ezer Papu (1785 -1828). A rabbi and arbiter of Jewish law, one of the spiritual leaders of the Sephardic Jewish community in Serbia.

Pierre Mendes-France [Square] (1907 – 1982)
David HaMelech at Mishkenot Shaananim **I14**

A Jewish statesman, prime minister of France.

Plumer, Herbert Charles [Square] (1857 – 1932)
Keren HaYesod at David HaMelech **H14**

British statesman and military commander, served as the second High Commissioner during the period of the British Mandate in the Land of Israel.

Sderot Bloomfield David HaMelech – HaTzayar **I14**

Boulevard named for the Bloomfield Garden located here next to the national park. Bloomfield Garden was built with a contribution from the Bloomfield family.

Touro, Yehuda (Judah) (1775 – 1854) Yemin Moshe – HaMetzuda **I13**

A Jewish philanthropist from the United States whose generous bequest to help the Jews of the Holy Land was used towards building Mishkenot Shaananim, the first neighborhood outside the walls of the Old City.

Yemin Moshe Heine – Nachon **I14**

Named for the neighborhood.

Zichron Ahim

Name and establishment:

Memory of brothers. This neighborhood, located in the center of town north of the neighborhood of Nahlat Ahim/Nahlaot, was founded in 1934 as part of Nahlaot, which is the general name for a cluster of neighborhoods in the New City, each of whose names starts with the word Nahala. Its residents, from a variety of places of origin, came together as brothers in this neighborhood, hence its name.

Its earliest residents were immigrants from Oriental Jewish communities, many of them from Urfa in Turkey, near the border with Syria and Iraq. They built a distinctive synagogue in the neighborhood, in the Urfa style.

Boundaries:
North – Betzalel Street and Zichron Yosef
South – Nahlat Ahim/Nahlaot
East – Mahane Yehuda Market
West – Ben-Zvi Boulevard and Sacher Park

Sites: within its boundaries or nearby are the neighborhood of Mahane Yehuda and the Mahane Yehuda Market, Sacher Park, the Government Campus.

Streets: the neighborhood is now part of the Nahlat Ahim/Nahlaot neighborhood, and most of its streets are named for ancient cities in the Galilee.

The streets are:

Betzalel ben Uri Ben-Zvi – Mesilat Yesharim **G12**

(See the neighborhoods of Batei Kollel Minsk/Beit HaLevi, Batei Kollel Munkacs, Knesset Yisrael, Mid-Town, Nahlat Ahim/Nahlaot, Nahlat Tzion, Sha'arei Rahamim, Zichron Ya'akov, Zichron Yosef.)

Even Sapir Betzalel – Narkiss **G12**

(See the neighborhood of Nahlat Ahim/Nahlaot.)

HaMadreigot Even Sapir – Kfar Bar'am **G12**

(See the neighborhood of Nahlat Ahim/Nahlaot.)

Nibarta HaMadreigot – Shabazi **G12**

(See the neighborhood of Nahlat Ahim/Nahlaot.)

Shabazi, Shalem ben Yosef, Rabbi (1686 – 1719)
Even Sapir – Ben-Zvi – dead end **G12**

(See the neighborhood of Nahlat Ahim/Nahlaot.)

Ussishkin, Menahem Mendel (1863 – 1941)
Betzalel – Ben Maimon Boulevard **G12-13**

(See the neighborhoods of Nahlat Ahim/Nahlaot, Rehavia, Sha'arei Hesed.)

Zichron Moshe

Name and establishment:

This neighborhood, located in the middle of town west of the neighborhood of Mea She'arim, was founded in 1906 and named for Sir Moses Montefiore. The neighborhood is one of six in Jerusalem that are named after Montefiore. Before the neighborhood was even built, two institutions were opened there: the Laemel School, the first modern educational institution in the Land of Israel, and a kindergarten and school established by the *'Ezra BaAretz* (help in the land) organization. The building of these two educational institutions, among other causes, stimulated the development of this area as a residential neighborhood.

The neighborhood was built according to a modern plan, with lovely, spacious houses, wide streets, front-yard gardens and space between the houses. When built, this neighborhood was considered the most modern, where public, cultural and Zionistic life were concentrated. Most of the intellectuals and civic leaders of Jerusalem established their homes in this neighborhood: Yesha'yahu Press, a teacher, researcher and Jerusalemite; Efraim Cohen, the principal of the Lamel School; David Yellin, one of the founders of the neighborhood and principal of the teachers seminary; Yehiel Michel Pines, the first director of the Montefiore Foundation in the Land of Israel; Eli'ezer ben Yehuda, who revived the Hebrew language and wrote his important dictionary while living here; the author Yosef Haim Brenner; Reb Yisrael Dov Fromkin, editor of the newspaper *Havatzelet*, and others.

A number of important institutions were founded in the neighborhood and nearby, and after some years were moved to more permanent locations: the Hebrew High School, the teachers seminary, the national library, the Israel Exploration Society.

Today the neighborhood's residents are members of the ultra-Orthodox community.

Boundaries:

North – Ahva and Kerem Avraham

South – the Mahane Yehuda Market and Mahane Yehuda

East – Mea She'arim

West – Mekor Baruch

Sites: within its boundaries or nearby are the Lamel School, Bikur Holim Hospital that was moved to here from the Old City, the Ziv Hospital, the Mahane Yehuda Market, and the old Edison cinema, one of the earliest movie theaters in Jerusalem, which no longer exists.

Streets: the neighborhood streets are named after educators, rabbis and books of religious law.

The streets are:

Ben Matityahu, Yosef [Josephus Flavius] (1st cent. BCE and CE) Malchei Yisrael – Yafo **G11**

(See the neighborhoods of Ahva, Kerem/Beit Avraham, Mahane Yehuda, Ruhama, Yegiy'a Kapayim.)

Birnbaum, Natan (1864 -1937) Cohen – Soloveitchik – dead end **H11**

Author and philosopher, one of the first in the Zionist movement, an *Agudat Yisrael* leader.

Blilius, Simcha (Sima) (d. 1927) Straus – Yesha'yahu **H11**

A philanthropist from Hong Kong, she donated large sums of money to support the Sephardic community in Jerusalem.

Cohen, Ephraim (1863 – 1943) David Yellin – Pri Hadash **H11**

One of those who laid the groundwork for modern education in the Land of Israel, director of educational institutions for the "'Ezra Society".

Hafetz Haim Cohen – Pri Hadash **H11**

Named for a book concerning matters of ethics according to the sources of Jewish law, written by Rabbi Yisrael Meir HaCohen of Radun (1838–1933). Considered one of the great arbiters of Jewish law.

Hagiz, Moshe, Rabbi (1672 – 1751) Cohen – Pines **H11**

A Kabbalist, a prominent rabbi, known for his battle against Sabbetaianism. Born in Jerusalem.

HaNeviim Yafo – Damascus Gate **H-I12**

(See the neighborhoods of Beit David/Beit HaRav Kook, 'Ezrat Yisrael, Mid-Town, Morasha/Musrara.)

HaRiDBa"Z (1478 – 1573) Cohen – Pines **G-H13**

Acronym for **HaR**av **D**avid (ben Shlomo) **b**en **Z**imra, a rabbi, arbiter of Jewish law, Kabbalist, spiritual leader of Egyptian Jewry, and one of the great rabbis of Tzfat.

Pines, Yehiel Michel (1843 – 1913) Yafo – Rabbeinu Tam **H11**

(See the neighborhood of Yegiy'a Kapayim.)

Prag, Yitzhak, Rabbi (1819 – 1900) Yesha'yahu – Straus **H12**

Rabbi, teacher and civic leader. He worked to integrate Jews from the various diasporas in education and society, founded the *Doreish Tzion* school in Jerusalem and was its principal.

Press, Yesha'yahu (1874 – 1955) Yesha'yahu – Blilius **H11**

Educator, Land of Israel researcher, member of the Committee on the Hebrew Language.

Pri Hadash Yesha'yahu – Ben Matityahu **H11**

(See the neighborhood of Batei Hornstein/Kollel Volyn.)

RaSH"I (1040 – 1105) Pines – Ben Matityahu, ends at HaHashmonaim **G11**

(See the neighborhoods of Kerem/Beit Avraham, Mahane Yehuda, Mekor Baruch, Ruhama, Sha'arei Yerushalayim.)

Soloveitchik, Yitzhak Zeev HaLevi, Rabbi (1886 – 1959)
David Yellin – Hafetz Haim **H11**

One of the outstanding rabbis of Poland and one of the leaders of ultra-Orthodox Jewry in Jerusalem.

Yellin, David (1854 – 1942)
Yesha'yahu – Pines, ends at Meyuhas **G-H11**

(See the neighborhoods of Batei Kollel Horodna/Damesek Eli'ezer, Mahane Yehuda, Ruhama, Sha'arei Shalom.)

Yesha'yahu Malchei Yisrael – HaNeviim **H11**

(See the neighborhood of Batei Hornstein/Kollel Volyn.)

Zichron Tuvia

Name and establishment:

This neighborhood, located in the middle of town south of Mahane Yehuda, between the neighborhoods of Ohel Moshe and Nahlat Tzion, was founded in the year 1890 as a neighborhood of one street. The name Memory of God's Goodness was taken from a verse in Psalms 145:8, "They shall utter the memory of Your great goodness, and shall sing of Your righteousness." From this neighborhood, one street goes in the direction of Agrippas Street, a central artery for traffic in the area. The earliest residents of this neighborhood were Persian, Babylonian (Iraqi) and Ashkenazi Jews.

Boundaries:
North – Agrippas Street and the Mahane Yehuda Market
South – Betzalel Street and Nahlat Ahim/Nahlaot
East – Ohel Moshe
West – Nahlat Tzion
Sites: within its boundaries or nearby is the Mahane Yehuda Market
Streets: the sole street is named for the neighborhood.

The streets are:

Agrippas (10 BCE – 44 CE) King George – Shmuel Baruch **G11-H12**

(See the neighborhoods of Even Yisrael, Mahane Yehuda, Mazkeret Moshe, Mid-Town, Mishkenot Yisrael, Nahlat Tzion, Ohel Moshe, Sukkat Shalom, Zichron Yosef.)

'Ezra Refael Agrippas – Rama **G12**

(See the neighborhoods of Nahlat Tzion, Ohel Moshe.)

Rama Ohel Moshe – Yosef Haim **G12**

(See the neighborhood of Nahlat Tzion).

Zichron Tuvia Agrippas – Rama **G12**

Named for the neighborhood.

Zichron Ya'akov

Name and establishment:

This neighborhood, located in the middle of town west of Mahane Yehuda, was founded in 1937 and named in memory of the father of Nahum Mizrachi, the builder of the neighborhood. The parcels of land for building the neighborhood were purchased from the Arabs of Lifta. The first residents of the neighborhood were Jews from Kurdistan who had been living in the Old City. Today the area is part of the neighborhood of Zichron Yosef.

Boundaries:
North – Agrippas/Shmuel Baruch Street
South – Betzalel Street and Nahlat Ahim/Nahlaot
East – Nahlat Tzion
West – Ben-Zvi Boulevard

Sites: within its boundaries or nearby are the Mahane Yehuda Market and Sacher Park.

Streets: the neighborhood streets are named for a river and for Sephardic rabbis.

The streets are:

Ben-Zvi, Yitzhak [Boulevard] (1884 – 1963)
Shmuel Baruch – Ruppin **G12**

(See the neighborhoods of Giv'at Ram, Kiryat Wolfson, Nahlat Ahim/Nahlaot, Sha'arei Hesed, Sha'arei Rahamim, Shevet Tzedek/Shchunat HaPahim, Zichron Yosef.)

Betzalel ben Uri Ben-Zvi – Mesilat Yesharim **G12**

(See the neighborhoods of Batei Kollel Minsk/Beit HaLevi, Batei Kollel Munkacs, Knesset Yisrael, Mid-Town, Nahlat Ahim/Nahlaot, Nahlat Tzion, Sha'arei Rahamim, Zichron Ahim, Zichron Yosef.)

Hacham Shalom (1884 – 1977) HaYarkon – Betzalel – dead end **G12**

Named for Rabbi Haim Shalom Shim'oni, one of the important rabbis of the Kurdish community and a leader of those who immigrated to Jerusalem (see the neighborhood of Zichron Yosef).

Nehar Prat HaYarkon – Betzalel **G12**

Euphrates River, a river in Aram Naharayim, present-day Iraq. It is mentioned in the Bible as a boundary of the Land of Israel (see the neighborhood of Zichron Yosef).

Salman, Eliyahu, Rabbi (1882 – 1966)
Bachar – Hacham Shalom **G12**

One of the rabbis of Jerusalem and a leader of the Kurdish community in the city, one of the builders of Jerusalem (see the neighborhood of Zichron Yosef).

Zichron Yosef (Shchunat HaKurdim)

Name and establishment:

This neighborhood, located in the center of town, west of Mahane Yehuda, founded in 1931, was named for Yosef Levi, whose son sold the land to new residents on the condition that the neighborhood would be named for his father. The first residents were Jews from the Iraqi part of Kurdistan who had lived previously in the Old City.

Boundaries:

North – Agrippas/Shmuel Baruch Street
South – Betzalel Street and Nahlat Ahim/Nahlaot
East – Nahlat Tzion
West – Ben-Zvi Boulevard

Sites: within its boundaries or nearby are the Mahane Yehuda Market and Sacher Park.

Streets: the neighborhood streets are named for rivers east of the Jordan River and for leaders of the Kurdish community.

The streets are:

Agrippas (10 BCE – 44 CE) King George – Shmuel Baruch **G11-H12**

(See the neighborhoods of Even Yisrael, Mahane Yehuda, Mazkeret Moshe, Mid-Town, Mishkenot Yisrael, Nahlat Tzion, Ohel Moshe, Sukkat Shalom, Zichron Tuvia.)

Arnon Shmuel Baruch – HaYarkon **G12**

A stream, east of the Jordan River, that flows into the Dead Sea.

Avidani, Hacham Eluan [Square] (1885 – 1981)
Shmuel Baruch at Arnon **G12**

An outstanding rabbi and a man of kind deeds, he served as a superior spiritual authority for the members of his community, the Jews from Kurdistan. A *Yakir Yerushalayim*.

Bachar, Nissim (1848 – 1931) Agrippas/Shmuel Baruch – Betzalel **G12**

(See the neighborhood of Nahlat Tzion.)

Baruch, Shmuel, Rabbi (1898 – 1994) Ben-Zvi – Agrippas **F-G11**

(See the neighborhoods of Beit Ya'akov, Mahane Yehuda, Mid-Town,

Sha'arei Tzedek, Shevet Tzedek/Shchunat HaPahim.)

Ben-Zvi, Yitzhak [Boulevard] (1884 – 1963)
Shmuel Baruch – Ruppin **G12**

(See the neighborhoods of Giv'at Ram, Kiryat Wolfson, Nahlat Ahim/Nahlaot, Sha'arei Hesed, Sha'arei Rahamim, Shevet Tzedek/Shchunat HaPahim, Zichron Ya'akov.)

Betzalel ben Uri Ben-Zvi – Mesilat Yesharim **G12**

(See the neighborhoods of Batei Kollel Minsk/Beit HaLevi, Batei Kollel Munkacs, Knesset Yisrael, Mid-Town, Nahlat Ahim/Nahlaot, Nahlat Tzion, Sha'arei Rahamim, Zichron Ahim, Zichron Ya'akov.)

Hacham Shalom (1884 – 1977) HaYarkon – Betzalel – dead end **G12**

(See the neighborhood of Zichron Ya'akov.)

Haftzadi, Salah [Square] (1922 – 1995) Salman at Nehar Prat **G12**

One of the activists of the Kurdish community and chairman of the Hevra Kadisha (burial) society of the community, a member of ETZe"L before the establishment of the State and one of its fighters. He worked actively for the welfare of residents and elderly people in need.

HaYabok Bachar – Arnon **G12**

A stream, east of the Jordan River, on whose banks the Biblical Jacob fought with an angel (Genesis 32:24).

HaYarkon Bachar – Arnon **G12**

The largest river in the coastal plain, in the area of Tel-Aviv and Ramat Gan.

HaYarmuch Bachar – Arnon **G12**

A river east of the Jordan River that flows from the Bashan (Syria) into the Jordan River.

Kehilat Yehudei 'Amadiya [Square] Arnon at HaYarkon **G12**

Jews of 'Amadiya. The city of 'Amadiya (today in northwestern Iraq) a spiritual center, was founded in 791 CE.

Nehar Prat HaYarkon – Betzalel **G12**

(See the neighborhood of Zichron Ya'akov.)

Salman, Eliyahu, Rabbi (1882 – 1966)
Bachar – Hacham Shalom **G12**

(See the neighborhood of Zichron Ya'akov.)

Neighborhoods and Villages with No Listing of Streets

'Arab e-Sawahira

This is a village in the southeastern part of the city, on the slope of the mountain on which is built Armon HaNatziv, and south of the neighborhoods of Jebel Mukabir and Talpiot Mizrah. The residents are Bedouin, and the neighborhood is named for their tribe – Sawahira. Through the village passes a winding road from east Jerusalem to Bethlehem, what was considered to be the "Burma Road" of the Jordanians until the Six Day War.

E-Turi (Abu Tor)

This is an Arab neighborhood, located in the southern part of the city below the Jewish neighborhood of Giv'at Hanania (the Hebrew name for Abu Tor) and near the old railroad station. The residents of the neighborhood are mostly refugees who came here after the War of Independence. From the neighborhood of Giv'at Hanania, a path descends, passing through the neighborhood of E-Turi and continuing to *Nahal Kidron* [the Kidron stream] and from there to *'Ir David* [the City of David] and the Old City (see the neighborhood of Giv'at Hanania/Abu Tor).

The streets of the neighborhood are named for its founders and for Arab leaders from the time of the prophet Muhammed.

'Issawiya

This is a village located in the northeastern part of the city, on the eastern slopes of Mount Scopus near Hadassah Hospital – Mount Scopus. Within the village are burial caves from the Second Temple period. Some think that this was the site of the priestly city of Nov (I Samuel 22:19), and according to another opinion, this was the site of the city of Laisha (Isaiah 10:30).

From the War of Independence until the Six Day War, when the IDF captured the entire area, the village was in the Israeli enclave of Mount Scopus, and this caused frequently repeated clashes between the village residents and the IDF soldiers.

Jebel Mukabir

This neighborhood is located in the southeastern part of the city, north of Talpiot Mizrah. According to an Arab legend, when the Caliph 'Omar ibn el-Khatab visited Jerusalem after it was conquered by the Arabs in 638 CE, he stood on the top of a mountain to the south of the city, on which today stands Armon HaNatziv, looked out over the city and cried out: "Allahu Akhbar (God is great)," and from here comes the name of the mountain and of the neighborhood. Jebel Mukabir means the mountain where a man calls out "Allahu Akhbar."

Lifta (*Neftoah*)

This is an Arab village, located in the northern part of the city, on the western approach to Jerusalem – today's Neftoah – on a tributary of *Nahal Sorek* [Sorek stream]. Lifta (*Mei Neftoah* in the sources) was a Biblical city on the northern border of the tribe of Judah: "The border was drawn from the top of the mountain to the *Mei Neftoah* spring, and from there to the cities of Mount 'Efron and from there it was drawn to *Ba'ala*, which is *Kiryat Ye'arim*" (Joshua 15:9). It is also mentioned in the description of the southern border of the tribe of Benjamin: "And the south side was from the far end of Kiryat Ye'arim, from there to the *Mei Neftoah* spring" (Joshua 18:15).

The village houses were built on the slope of the mountain in order not to use the arable farmland in the valley for this purpose. In the center of the village was a spring. Lifta was known for its *etrogim*, citrons of Lifta, that the Jews bought for the Sukkot festival. In addition, they would pick branches of the willow trees that grew by the spring to use as another of the four species for this festival.

During the attacks of 1936 and during the War of Independence, the Arabs of Lifta acted against the Jews nearby and even tried to halt traffic on the nearby highway, Jerusalem's lifeline to the rest of the country. After the IDF forces broke through to the besieged city, the Arabs of Lifta abandoned their homes, and the village was captured by the soldiers. After the village came under Israeli authority, new immigrants were moved into the village. After a few years these immigrants were moved to a different neighborhood, and since then the houses and the village have remained empty. Recently, a tunnel was built to ease the congestion of traffic entering and leaving the city. Today the abandoned village of Lifta is included in the neighborhood of Romema (see the neighborhood of Romema).

Sharafat

This is a village located in the southwestern part of the city, between the neighborhoods of Gonenim/Katamonim and Gilo, on top of a mountain. The Arabic name Sharafat is similar to the Hebrew name *Tzofim* [Scopus], and indeed from this village, located atop a mountain, it is possible to view the incredible panorama of Jerusalem. At the top of the village was found the tomb of Sith Badriya, a holy woman, the daughter of Sheikh Badr. Also in this village, an oak tree was found that is about eleven hundred years old and is thought to be the oldest and largest oak tree in the country, about thirty meters (one hundred feet) in height, and with a trunk measuring about two meters (over six feet) in diameter.

From the War of Independence until the Six Day War, the village was under Jordanian rule. Soldiers of the Arab Legion fortified themselves in the village and harassed the Jews who lived nearby, especially the residents of Gonenim/Katamonim. During the Six Day War, the village was captured and passed into Israeli control.

Silwan [*Kfar HaShiloah*] and Ras el-'Amud

The village is located on the south side of the Mount of Olives, sloping down to the Kidron stream. According to one opinion, the name of the village is a distortion of the name Siluwam, which appears in the New Testament, which is itself a Greek distortion of the ancient Hebrew name *Shiloah,* for the pool that is here. The Arabs write the name as "Salwa", which is similar to the Hebrew *shalva*, meaning tranquility, as the waters of the spring are thought to impart tranquility to those who drink of them.

In recent years the village has spread across the Mount of Olives and is called Ras el-'Amud. Next to the village, a Jewish village has been established, called *Kfar HaShiloah*.

In the Middle Ages, no one lived in this area except Christian monks and nuns, who lived there in caves, under very harsh conditions. At the beginning of the fifteenth century, according to the testimony of

Christian travelers, there were already Arabs living in the caves, farmers and shepherds. The Gihon spring was their source of water. In 1885 a group of Jews from Yemen moved into the area. They lived there a few years, as evidenced by the grooves for mezuzot on the doorways. During the War of Independence, the neighborhood Arabs harassed the convoys that traveled from the direction of the Dead Sea into Jerusalem.

North of the village are the ancient *'Ir David* [City of David] and the wall of the Old City, that were uncovered in archeological digs in the area; to the west is the Jewish Quarter; to the east is the Temple Mount; to the south is the spring of *'Ein Rogel*, the channel of the Kidron stream, and the Gihon spring whose waters flow through a tunnel to the *Shiloah.* Within the village boundaries or nearby are many historical-archeological sites: the 'Ir David excavations, burial caves carved into the rock, Jehoshafat's Cave, the cave of the prophet Isaiah, the tomb of Pharaoh's daughter, Hezekiah's Tunnel, the *Shiloah* Pool, the *Gihon* spring, the *'Ein Rogel* spring ("Bir Ayub" in Arabic – Job's Well – named for the prophet Job who was cured of his leprosy there; Jewish pilgrims to Jerusalem called the place *Beer Yoav*, after Yoav ben Tzruya, one of King David's warriors).

The streets of the village are named for streams and springs in the area.

Sur Bahir and Umm Tuba

Sur Bahir is a village located southeast of the neighborhood of Talpiot Mizrah and near Kibbutz Ramat Rahel. The meaning of the name is "a light-colored rock", named for the light-colored rock on which the village is built.

In ancient times, there was an aqueduct near the village that was built in the time of King Herod and brought water from Solomon's pools, south of the city, to the Temple Mount. It is possible to see the remains of the aqueduct on the upper part of the mountain on which Armon HaNatziv stands.

Until the Six Day War, Sur Bahir was under Jordanian jurisdiction, near the border with Israel. The Jordanians put up a fortified position there that faced toward Ramat Rahel. IDF soldiers called it the "Bell Post", because of its shape, and captured it in 1967.

From Sur Bahir starts a new road named Asher Wiener Road, which splits into two: going west, toward Derech Hevron and Derech Beit Lehem, and going east, toward the neighborhood of Talpiot Mizrah. Another road, called Sur Bahir Road after the name of the village, leads from Sur Bahir to Kibbutz Ramat Rahel.

The village further south, Umm Tuba, is today part of the village of Sur Bahir. This village was built by Arab refugees who came to this spot at the end of the War of Independence.

Umm Lison

This neighborhood is located southeast of Talpiot Mizrah and east of the village of Sur Bahir. In this neighborhood there are burial caves, from the days of the Romans and Byzantines, carved into the rock.

Neighborhoods That Were Built and No Longer Exist

Batei Nissan Bek

A neighborhood in the eastern part of the city, west of the Damascus Gate, called in Arabic "Bab el-'Amud", the Pillar Gate. It was founded in 1879 and named for Nissan Bek (a street in Mahanayim is named for him). Prominent families of the Volyn Hasidim settled in the neighborhood. Its main street was Rehov Montefiore. It was the only Jewish neighborhood built near the Damascus Gate and was totally destroyed during the War of Independence.

Batei Siebenbürgen

This neighborhood, which was located near Mea She'arim and the Mandelbaum Gate, east of Batei Kollel Ungarin/Nahlat Zvi, was established in 1908. It was a Kollel neighborhood built by devout Jews from Siebenbürgen ("seven fortresses", after the seven cities in the region) in Transylvania, between Hungary and Rumania, hence its name. During the War of Independence (1948), Jordanian forces penetrated into the neighborhood, the residents fled from their homes, and the neighborhood was destroyed in the course of the battles that raged there. The area remained under Jordanian rule until the Six Day War (1967). Batei Siebenbürgen was located near *Shefech HaDeshen*, where in ancient times the ashes remaining from the sacrifices in the Holy Temple were brought for disposal outside the city walls (Leviticus 4:12).

Beit Aharon

A small neighborhood spread along one street, which was swallowed up in nearby Rehavia. It was founded in 1931 on private property bordering Sha'arei Hesed. The founders were seven immigrants from America, headed by Aharon (Aaron) Jacobs, hence the name.

In the beginning, the street was called Aharon Street, but was later changed to HaRa"N Street, the acronym for **Ha**R**a**v **N**issim (ben Reuven Gironde), one of the outstanding rabbis and arbiters of Jewish law in fourteenth century Spain.

Beit HaMa'alot

This was not a neighborhood but a large residential building with several entrances along HaMa'alot Street, built in 1936 between King George and Shmuel HaNagid Streets. At the time, this was the largest building bloc in Jerusalem. It had seven stories, seven entrances, seven elevators and Sukkah balconies that did not overhang one another. The apartments were intended for well-educated religious families. Despite the fact that this was one large building and not really a neighborhood, special neighborhood regulations were published for Beit HaMa'alot.

Beit Yosef

This neighborhood, originally called Abu Tor, today called Giv'at Hanania, was founded in 1887 and located in the southern part of the city. It was named for Yosef Navon, the man who initiated the construction of the Jaffa-Jerusalem railroad, the main station for which was near the neighborhood. During the riots of 1929, the Jewish residents abandoned the neighborhood, and Arabs moved into their houses. Today Giv'at Hanania/Abu Tor is located on this site, and both Jews and Arabs live there.

Ben Tzion/Batei Bentzion

A neighborhood on the west side of the city south of the Giv'at Shaul neighborhood, it was founded in 1944-1946 and named for the purchaser of the land, Rabbi Dr. Shmuel Ben Tzion. Houses were built at 6 Korot Ha'Itim Street and 20 Ben Tzion Street, which are today part of the neighborhood of Kiryat Moshe. These two buildings were intended as housing for poor families. During the War of Independence, the building on Ben Tzion Street was used as a central defensive position that protected the area from Arab attacks. Today, most of the parcels of land have been appropriated from the Ben Tzion family for public use.

Eshel Avraham

A neighborhood on the eastern side of the city near the Damascus Gate and near the Batei Nissan Bek neighborhood that was destroyed and the neighborhood of Morasha/Musrara of today. This neighborhood was established in 1892, inspired by the Biblical verse that tells of the patriarch

Abraham: "He planted a tamarisk tree..." (Genesis 21:33). The verse means that our forefather Abraham stopped wandering from place to place and settled permanently in one place. Most of the residents of the neighborhood were Georgian Jews. The houses here were destroyed in the bloody attacks of 1929.

Giv'at Eliyahu

A neighborhood in the southern part of the city, next to Talpiot and close to Kibbutz Ramat Rahel, it was founded in the early 1920s and named for its proximity to the monastery of "Mar Elias", the prophet Elijah. Today the neighborhood has been swallowed up in Talpiot.

HaMekasher

A neighborhood on the west side of the city, located next to the entrance to Jerusalem, near the Egged bus garages and the neighborhood of Kiryat Moshe, and alongside Herzl Boulevard. It was founded in 1934. The houses there were built by bus drivers of HaMekasher, the cooperative public transportation service that operated in Jerusalem from World War I until its merger with the larger Egged bus cooperative.

Nahlat Yitzhak

A neighborhood in the eastern part of the city, at the foot of Mount Scopus next to the road going up to the Hadassah Hospital and the Hebrew University on Mount Scopus. It was founded in 1927 and named for its founder, Yitzhak Fuller, an immigrant from the United States. On the side toward the Old City is the Arab neighborhood of Wadi el-Joz. During the War of Independence (1948), fierce battles raged in the area that caused the destruction of the neighborhood, and the Jewish residents were forced to flee. In the Six Day War (1967), the IDF captured the area along with the rest of east Jerusalem.

Shoshanat Tzion

Residential housing that was supposed to have been built in 1930 on the west side of the city, between the neighborhoods of Kiryat Moshe and Beit HaKerem, at the end of Eli'ezer HaLevi Street, from the corner of HaBaron Hirsch Street to Rav Tza'ir Street. Immigrants from Persia-Iran wanted to build residential housing for themselves in the area, and even gave the future neighborhood a name, Shoshanat Tzion, commemorating their capital city Shushan, and to emphasize the city of Zion, the focus of their longing. It is told in our sources that, on one of the gates of the Second Holy Temple was inscribed a picture of the city of Shushan, as a mark of honor to Koresh (Cyrus), king of Persia, for allowing the Jews to rebuild Jerusalem and build the Second Holy Temple. With regard to the planned neighborhood, only two buildings were actually built by the original owners, and the rest of the land was sold for construction of a synagogue. Today the buildings are part of Kiryat Moshe.

Streets Named after Women

In the various neighborhoods there are streets named after women. Below the name of each neighborhood are noted the names of the streets that are so named, as follows:

Bab e-Zahara
E-Zahara – see page 102

Batei Perlman/'Ir Shalom
Dvora HaNevia – see page 120

Beit HaKerem
Ya'akovi, Rahel – see page 138

Beit Hanina
Mai Ziyada – see page 142
Shejrat a-Dur – see page 142

Christian Quarter *[HaRova' HaNotzri]*
Al-Sa'adiya – see page 154
St. Helena – see page 156

Dahiyet el-Barid
El-Kubatiye, Maryum – see page 160

E-Tur (Mount of Olives)
Rab'a el-'Adawiyeh – see page 168

German Colony *[HaMoshava HaGermanit]*/**RaMBa"M**
Rahel Imeinu – see page 180
Root [Ruth] – see page 180

Geulim/Bak'a
Ester HaMalca – see page 187
Miriam HaHashmonait – see page 188
Rivka – see page 189
Tzipora – see page 189
Ya'el – see page 189
Yocheved – see page 190

Gilo
HaAhot Yehudit – see page 193
HaGanenet (Hasia Sukenick) – see page 194
HaMehanechet (Hanna Miriam Spitzer) – see page 195
Tzvia (Lubetkin Cukierman VeYitzhak) – see page 200

Giv'at Hanania/Abu Tor
Avigayil – see page 207
Bat Sheva' – see page 207
Na'omi – see page 208
Tzruya – see page 208

Giv'at HaVradim/Shikun Rassco
Selma Lagerloff [Steps] – see page 210

Giv'at Massua
Ben Porat, Lea – see page 212
Kraus, Gertrud, Prof. – see page 212
Miss Landau (Rina Yehudit) – see page 213
Nurse Zelma (Meir) – see page 213

Giv'at Ram
Rahel Yanait (Ben-Zvi) – see page 221

Giv'at Shaul
Pu'a (Rakovsky) – see page 233

Gonen/Katamon HaYeshana
Freier, Recha – see page 237
Netiv Zahara Levitov – see page 239
Rahel Imeinu – see page 240

The Years the Neighborhoods Were Founded

The revolutionary idea of building Jewish neighborhoods outside the walls of the Old City was put into action less than 150 years ago, in 1860. Until then, Jews lived in crowded conditions within the walls of the Old City. There were many elements that promoted the expansion outside the walls and encouraged people to move there. On one hand, they included the *'aliya* of numerous Hasidim to the Holy Land at the end of the eighteenth century and the *'aliya* of *Perushim* (*mitnagdim*, opponents of the Hasidim) at the beginning of the nineteenth century. On the other hand, there were additional factors that encouraged the process: the great demand for housing, the increasingly crowded conditions, the poor sanitary conditions, and the high rent that the Jews of the Old City were required to pay to the Arab landlords. All these motivations sped up the process and gradually turned the desire into reality.

The construction of neighborhoods did not take place all at once, not at one time and not even in the framework of any special planning. The neighborhoods were built over many years, except for the years of the two world wars. Most of the land in the New City was in the hands of Christian institutions and churches. Jews without means succeeded in acquiring property from those institutions only through an association or with the assistance of various charitable philanthropists.

The first neighborhood that was built outside the walls of Old Jerusalem was Mishkenot Shaananim (1860), after which seven more neighborhoods were built that were also considered to be in the first group:

Mahane Yisrael/Shchunat HaMa'aravim (1868), Nahlat Shiv'a (1869), Beit David/Beit HaRav Kook (1872), Mea She'arim (1874), Even Yisrael (1875), Mishkenot Yisrael (1875), Beit Ya'akov (1877).

Most of the neighborhoods were founded before the establishment of the State starting in the time of Turkish rule (1860-1920), and during the British Mandate period (1920-1948) when many neighborhoods were founded in all parts of the New City. After the establishment of the State, from 1948 to 1967, new neighborhoods were built all over the city. After the Six Day War, neighborhoods were built with the political consideration of forming a belt of Jewish neighborhoods around the city, to protect it. The establishment of new neighborhoods has continued into the twenty-first century.

During the Period of Turkish Rule

1860	Mishkenot Shaananim
1868	Mahane Yisrael/Shchunat HaMa'aravim
1869	Nahlat Shiv'a
1872	Beit David/Beit HaRav Kook
1873	German Colony [*HaMoshava HaGermanit*] (see 1948)
1874	Mea She'arim
1875	Even Yisrael
	Mishkenot Yisrael
1877	Beit Ya'akov
1883	Ohel Moshe
	Mazkeret Moshe
1884	Batei Goral/Mishkenot HaTeimanim
1885	Kerem/Beit Avraham
	Kfar HaShiloah
1886	Batei Wittenberg/Sha'arei Moshe
1887	Mahane Yehuda
	Beit Yisrael
	Batei Perlman/'Ir Shalom
1888	Sukkat Shalom
1889	Sha'arei Pina
1890	Zichron Tuvia
	Sha'arei Tzedek
~1890	Shevet Tzedek/Shchunat HaPahim
	Wadi el-Joz
1891	HaBucharim/Batei HaBucharim
	Batei Kollel Ungarin/Nahlat Zvi
	Bnei Moshe/Neve Shalom
	Nahlat Shim'on
	Ohel Shlomo
	Knesset Yisrael
	Sha'arei Rahamim (Sha'arei Yeshu'a)
1892	Yemin Moshe
	Bak'a (see 1948)

	Batei Milner/Agudat Shlomo
	Batei Kollel Horodna/Damesek Eli'ezer
	'Ezrat Yisrael
	Sha'arei Shalom
1893	Even Yehoshu'a
	Nahlat Tzion
1894	Nahlat Zvi/ Shchunat HaTeimanim
	Sha'arei Yerushalayim
1897	Batei Kollel Minsk/ Beit HaLevi
1898	Batei Kollel Warsaw/Nahlat Ya'akov
~1900	Greek Colony *[HaMoshava HaYevanit]*
1902	Batei Werner/Ohalei Moshe
	Batei Broide/Ohalei Ya'akov
1903	Batei Naitin
1905	Batei Hornstein/Kollel Volyn
1906	Zichron Moshe
1907	Giv'at Shaul
1908	Ahva
	Yegiy'a Kapayim
	Nahlat Tzadok
1909	Sha'arei Hesed
1910	Batei Rand
1911	Batei Sa'idoff

During the British Mandate Period

~1920	Gonenim/Katamonim
1921	Rehavia
	Romema
	Bayit VaGan
	Ruhama
1922	Beit HaKerem
	Talpiot
1923	Komemiyut/Talbieh
	Kiryat Moshe

1924	Mekor Baruch
	Neve Ya'akov
	Nahlat Ahim/Nahlaot
1925	Mekor Haim
	Neve Shaanan
~1925	Sheikh Jarrah
1926	Geula
	Mahanayim
	Sanhedria
1927	Neve Betzalel (Shchunat HaOmanim)
1928	Beit Kollel Munkacs
	HaPo'alim
	Kiryat Shmuel
1929	Yefei Nof
	'Etz Haim/Wolfson
1931	Arnona
	Zichron Yosef (Shchunat HaKurdim)
	Tel-Arza
1933	Kerem Avraham
1934	Zichron Ahim
1935	Talpiot Tzafon
1937	Zichron Ya'akov
	Maimon (Shchunat HaPo'el HaMizrahi)
1938	Merhavia

After the Establishment of the State

1948	Gonen/ Katamon HaYeshana
	Giv'at Hanania/Abu Tor
	German Colony *[HaMoshava HaGermanit]*/ RaMBa"M
	Geulim/ Bak'a
	Giv'at Oranim
1949	Giv'at Ram
	Morasha/Musrara

	Manhat/Malha
	‘Ein Kerem
1951	Giv‘at HaVradim/Shikun Rassco
	Kiryat HaYovel
1953	‘Ir Ganim
1954	Dahiyet el-Barid
1955	Giv‘at Mordechai
1958	Kiryat Menachem
1960	Giv‘at Beit HaKerem
~1960	Kiryat Belz
~1961	Shikunei Shmuel HaNavi
1962	Nayot (HaShikun HaAnglo-Saxi)
1963	Neve Granot
	Kiryat Mattersdorf/Kiryat Sheva‘
1965	Kiryat Zanz

After the Six Day War

1969	Ramat Eshkol
1970	Giv‘at HaMivtar
	Kiryat Wolfson
	Ramat Denya
~1970	‘Ezrat Torah
1971	Gilo
	Giv‘at Shapira/French Hill
	Sanhedria HaMurhevet
	Pat
	Ramot Allon
1972	Talpiot Mizrah
	Kiryat Ta‘asiyot ‘Atirot Mada‘/Har Hotzvim
	Ma‘alot Dafna/Arzei HaBira
	Neve Ya‘akov
	Tzameret HaBira
1974	Ramat Sharett
1981	Har Nof

1982	Kiryat Aryeh
1984	Pisgat Zeev
1990	Kfar David-Mamilla
~1990	Giv'at HaMatos
	Ramat Beit HaKerem
1996	Giv'at Massua
	Ramat Shlomo/Rechess Shu'afat
1997	Homat Shmuel/Har Homa
2003	Holyland Park

Did You Know?

There are streets whose original names were changed to the names of Jewish heroes.

David HaMelech Street was previously named Julian Street, after a Catholic saint.

Heleni HaMalca Street was previously named Melisande Street, after a Crusader queen of Jerusalem in the twelfth century.

Yohanan MiGush Halav Street was previously named Tancred Street, after a Crusader warrior.

Shivtei Yisrael Street was previously named Saint Paul the Christian Street.

Straus Street was previously named Chancellor Street, after a British high commissioner.

Shlomtzion HaMalca Street was previously named Princess Mary Street, after a princess of the British royal family.

Shlomo HaMelech Street was previously named St. Louis Street, after a French king during the period of the Crusades.

Six neighborhoods in the city are named after Sir Moses Montefiore:

Ohel Moshe (1883)
Mazkeret Moshe (1883)
Bnei Moshe (1891)
Yemin Moshe (1892)
Zichron Moshe (1906)
Kiryat Moshe (1923)

Six neighborhoods are considered the garden neighborhoods of the New City of Jerusalem:

Rehavia (1921)
Bayit VaGan (1921)
Talpiot (1922)
Kiryat Moshe (1923)
Mekor Haim (1925)

Nine public parks (and even more) are spread throughout the city:

Giv'at Ram -	the Botanical Garden
	the Billy Rose Sculpture Garden
Yemin Moshe -	the Bloomfield Garden
Mid-Town -	Independence Park
	Gozlan Park (HaBustan)
	Daniel Garden
Sanhedria HaMurhevet -	Sanhedrin Park
Komemiyut/ Talbieh -	Liberty Bell Park
	the Rose Garden

In Geulim/ Bak'a the streets are named for the tribes of Israel. Which tribe did not have a street named after it?

Asher	Naftali
Dan	Reuven
Efraim	Shim'on
Gad	Yehuda
Levi	Yissachar
Menashe	Zvulun

A number of neighborhoods were given Hebrew names, but the names did not catch on with the public:

Geulim – Bak'a
Giv'at Hanania – Abu Tor
Gonen – Katamon HaYeshana
Gonenim – Katamonim
Morasha – Musrara
Manhat – Malha
Komemiyut – Talbieh

In Gilo several of the streets are named for the stones on the High Priest's breastplate. Which two stones do not have streets named for them?

Odem (carnelian)	Nofech (turquoise)	Leshem (jacinth)
Tarshish (chrysolite)	Topaz (topaz)	Shvo (agate)
Shoham (onyx)	Bareket (emerald)	Yahalom (diamond)
	Ahlama (amethyst)	

* The answer can be found in the Book of Exodus Chapter 28.

Which lane in the city is named after a dog?

* The answer can be found in the German Colony/RaMBa"M.

Which square in the city is named for cats?

* The answer can be found in Mid-Town.

In the neighborhood of Pisgat Zeev, a number of streets are named for signs of the Zodiac. Which four Zodiac signs do not have streets named after them?

Aquarius	Leo
Aries	Libra
Taurus	Sagittarius
Gemini	Capricorn

Mayors

(with the years of their term in office)

Daniel Auster
1948 – 1951

Gershon Agron
1955 – 1959

Teddy Kollek
1965 – 1993

Shlomo Zalman Shragai
1951 – 1952

Mordechai Ish Shalom
1959 – 1965

Ehud Olmert
1993 – 2003

Yitzhak Kariv
1952 – 1955

Uri Lupolianski
2003 –

Sites, Museums and Public Institutions

Sites		**Phone**
Arts & Crafts Lane [*Hutzot HaYotzer*]	Yemin Moshe	
Begin Heritage Center	Yemin Moshe	565-2020
Beit Yad LeVanim [Soldiers Memorial]	Giv'at Ram	624-8338
Ben-Zvi Institute [*Yad Ben-Zvi*]	Rehavia	539-8888
Biblical Zoo	Manhat/Malha	675-0111
Cardo	Jewish Quarter	
Christian Quarter Market	Christian Quarter	
Great Synagogue	Mid-Town	623-0628
Haas and Sherover Promenades	Talpiot Mizrah	
Heichal Shlomo	Mid-Town	624-7112
Jerusalem Mall (Malha)	Manhat/Malha	
Mahane Yehuda Market	Mahane Yehuda	
Military Cemetery	Mount Herzl	
Mosad HaRav Kook	Maimon – Kiryat Moshe	652-6231
Mount Herzl [*Har Herzl*]	Mount Herzl	
Mount of Olives [*Har HaZeitim*]	Mount of Olives	
Mount Scopus [*Har HaTzofim*]	Mount Scopus	
Shai 'Agnon House	Talpiot	671-6498
Supreme Court	HaKirya [Government Campus] Giv'at Ram	659-3666
Teddy Stadium	Manhat/Malha	678-8320
Valley of the Cross	Giv'at Ram	
Van Leer Institute	Komemiyut/Talbieh	560-5222
Via Dolorosa (Path of Sorrows)	Christian Quarter	
Western Wall Tunnels	Jewish Quarter	627-1333
Western Wall	Jewish Quarter	
Windmill	Yemin Moshe	629-2222
Yad Kennedy [Kennedy Memorial]	Kiryat Menahem	570-9926
Yad Sarah	Bayit VaGan	644-4444
Yad Vashem	Hill of Remembrance *[Har HaZikaron]*	644-3400
Zalman Shazar Center	Talpiot	565-0444
Zoharei Hama [Sundial] Synagogue	Mahane Yehuda	

Museums		**Phone**
Ammunition Hill Museum	Giv'at HaMivtar – Ramat Eshkol	582-8442
Armenian Museum	Armenian Quarter	628-2331
Beit HaRav Kook	Beit David/Beit HaRav Kook	623-2560
Bible Lands Museum	Giv'at Ram – Neve Granot	561-1066
Bloomfield Science Museum	Giv'at Ram	654-4888
Central Zionist Archives	Giv'at Ram	620-4800
Chamber of the Holocaust *[Martef HaShoa]*	Mount Zion	671-5105
Courtyard of the Old Yishuv	Jewish Quarter	628-4636
Herzl Museum	Mount Herzl	620-2330
Holocaust Martyrs' and Heroes' Remembrance Authority	Yad Vashem	644-3400
Israel Museum	Giv'at Ram – Neve Granot	670-8811
Museum of Islamic Art	Gonen/Katamon HaYeshana	566-1291
Museum of Italian Jewry	Mid-Town	624-1610
Museum of the Burnt House	Jewish Quarter	628-7211
Museum of Underground Prisoners (Hall of Heroism)	Russian Compound	623-3166
Nature Museum	German Colony	563-1116
Rockefeller Archeological Museum	Wadi el-Joz	628-2251
Second Temple Model	Giv'at Ram - Neve Granot	670-8811
Shrine of the Book	Giv'at Ram – Neve Granot	670-8862
Tax Museum	Mahane Yisrael – Mid-Town	625-8978
Ticho House Museum	Beit David/Beit HaRav Kook	624-5068
Tower of David Museum	Jaffa Gate	626-5333

Public Institutions		**Phone**
Bank of Israel	HaKirya [Government Campus], Giv'at Ram	655-2211
Central Bus Station	Romema	530-4933
HaKeren HaKayemet LeYisrael (JNF)	Mid-Town	1-800-350-550
Hebrew University	Giv'at Ram	658-5111
Hebrew University	Mount Scopus	588-2111
International Convention Center [*Binyanei HaUma*]	Giv'at Ram	655-8558
Jerusalem Theater	Komemiyut/Talbieh	560-5755
Jewish Agency	Mid-Town	620-2222
Keren HaYesod	Mid-Town	670-1811
Knesset	HaKirya [Government Campus], Giv'at Ram	649-6107
Municipality – Safra Square	Mid-Town	629-6666
National and University Library	Giv'at Ram	658-5039
President's Residence	Komemiyut/Talbieh	670-7211

Important Telephone Numbers

Emergency Services

Police	100
Magen David Adom	101
Fire Department	102
Information	144

Medical Services

Al-Muqased	E-Tur (Mount of Olives)	627-0222
Augusta Victoria	E-Tur (Mount of Olives)	627-9911
Bikur Holim	Mid-Town	646-4111
‘Ezrat Nashim	Giv‘at Shaul	531-6811
Hadassah Medical Center	‘Ein Kerem	677-7111
Hadassah Medical Center	Mount Scopus	584-4111
Magen David Adom (Red Magen David)	Romema	653-5027
MaTa”R Clinics	Talpiot	671-7111
Sha‘arei Tzedek Medical Center	Bayit VaGan	655-5111
TeRe”M (Emergency Medical Care)	Romema	652-1748
TeRe”M (Emergency Medical Care)	Talpiot	673-8550

Walking Tour Routes

Tour 1: Agrippas Street

(The street begins at King George Street and continues parallel to Yafo Road, passing ten neighborhoods in the area. Agrippas used to continue all the way to Shazar Boulevard, but today it ends at the intersection of Nissim Bachar and Beit Ya'akov Streets, where the name changes.)

Starting from King George, Even Yisrael is on the right (a neighborhood of one street from Agrippas to Yafo), then Sukkat Shalom and Mishkenot Yisrael on the left (the home of Rabbi Aryeh Levin), Mazkeret Moshe and Ohel Moshe on the left (both founded in the same year and named after Sir Moses Montefiore), the Mahane Yehuda Market on the right, Zichron Tuvya on the left, Mid-Town to the right, Zichron Yosef (Shchunat HaKurdim) on the left, and Nahlat Tzion on the left.

Tour 2: Betzalel Street

(The street starts at the intersection of Ben Yehuda and Mesilat Yesharim Streets and passes ten neighborhoods, ending at Ben-Zvi Boulevard.)

Starting from the western end of Ben Yehuda, the first neighborhood is Mid-Town, then Batei Kollel Munkacs on the right (one building), Batei Kollel Minsk/Beit HaLevi on the right (with the Mahane Yehuda Market further to the right), Knesset Yisrael on the right, Nahlat Ahim/Nahlaot to the left (the *Mekor Haim* Synagogue and Gerard Bachar Center), Nahlat Tzion on the right, Zichron Yosef on the right, Zichron Ahim on the left (with Sacher Park beyond), Sha'arei Rahamim to the left, and Zichron Ya'akov to the right.

Tour 3: Yafo Road

(The main thoroughfare and longest street in the New City of Jerusalem, it winds from the Jaffa Gate all the way to the entrance/exit of the city, and from there the road continues to the city of Jaffa on the Mediterranean coast, the port for the city of Jerusalem in ancient days. On its way through the city, the street passes fifteen neighborhoods.)

From the Jaffa Gate (the Tower of David and its museum) one first passes Kikar TZaHa"L, then the new municipality in Safra Square on the right, the Russian Compound on the right (courthouses, police headquarters, the Museum of the Underground Prisoners, Holy Trinity Church), Nahlat Shiv'a to the left (*Nahlat Ya'akov* Synagogue, the Tmol Shilshom Restaurant, Kikar Tzion), Beit David/Beit HaRav Kook on the right (Ticho House Museum, Rav Kook House), Mid-Town on the left (Ben Yehuda Pedestrian Mall, Independence Park), 'Ezrat Yisrael on the right (a neighborhood of one street between Yafo Road and HaNeviim – Bikur Holim Hospital), Even Yisrael on the left, the Mahane Yehuda neighborhood on the right and the Mahane Yehuda Market on the left (Yafo Road passes between the two; *Zoharei Hama* Synagogue, *'Etz Haim* Yeshiva, the Ministry of Health, Kikar HaHerut), Batei Kollel Horodna/Damesek Eli'ezer on the right, Ohel Shlomo on the right, Beit Ya'akov to the left (in the past it was the site of the station for the neighborhood carts of Jerusalem, for transportation of people and goods, now the site of a Bank Discount branch and the western end of the Mahane Yehuda Market), Mekor Baruch on the right (the Tahkemoni School, the Schneller Camp), Batei Sa'idoff on the left (a line of what were once small stores and workshops that are now abandoned), Sha'arei Tzedek on the left (named for Sha'arei Tzedek Hospital that was located on this site and was relocated to Bayit VaGan), Sha'arei Yerushalayim on the right, Romema on the right (the Broadcasting Authority for Israeli television, the Central Bus Station, Allenby Square, the International Conference Center), and the exit/entrance to the city.

Tour 4: Mea She'arim Street

(The street begins at Kikar HaShabbat, the intersection of Straus–Malchei Yisrael–Yehezkel, continues through the neighborhood of Mea She'arim and passes nine neighborhoods, ending at Shivtei Yisrael Street.)

Geula is on the left, to the north (Talmudical academies), Sha'arei Pina on the left (religious elementary schools and study halls), Batei Kollel Warsaw/Nahlat Ya'akov on the right (one long bloc of housing and two study halls), Nahlat Zvi/Shchunat HaTeimanim to the left (a synagogue named for Rabbi Shalom Shabazi), Beit Yisrael to the left (the Hasidei Karlin Yeshiva and the Mir Yeshiva), Mea She'arim on the right (the Mea She'arim market, *Mea She'arim* Yeshiva and the home of Rabbi Shmuel MiBarezhin Huminer, at 21 Honi HaMe'agel Street, one of the first to settle in the neighborhood), Batei Naitin and Batei Kollel Ungarin/Nahlat

Zvi on the left, Batei Perlman/'Ir Shalom to the right (a neighborhood of one street at the eastern end of Mea She'arim Street).

Tour 5: Malchei Yisrael Street

(The street begins at Sarei Yisrael, passes five neighborhoods on its route, and ends at Kikar HaShabbat.)

The first neighborhood is Mekor Baruch on the right (Tahkemoni School), then Kerem Avraham to the left (the Schneller Camp), Kerem/Beit Avraham to the right, Ahva to the right, and finally Geula on the left (Talmudical academies).

Tour 6: RaSH"I Street

(The street begins at Rehov HaHashmonaim, passes by six neighborhoods, and ends at Rehov Pines.)

The first neighborhood is Sha'arei Yerushalayim on the right (the Central Bus Station is just beyond), then Mekor Baruch on the left (Tahkemoni School, the Schneller Camp), the Mahane Yehuda neighborhood and market to the right, Kerem/Beit Avraham on the left, Ruhama to the right (*Sfat Emet* Yeshiva with the tomb of the Admor of Gur in the courtyard, and the Mahane Yehuda market beyond), and ending in Zichron Moshe on the right (the Laemel School, the deserted building of the Edison Theater, one of the first movie theaters in the city, Bikur Holim Hospital).

Glossary of Terms Used Frequently in the Text

Admor – acronym for **Ad**oneinu, **Mo**reinu Ha**R**av, meaning our master, teacher and rabbi; the title is used for important Hasidic rabbinic leaders.

Aggada – anecdotal material that fleshes out or provides background for Mishnaic law, found in Talmudic and homiletic texts.

'Aliya – literally "going up", the term used in Hebrew to denote immigration to Israel.

Amora/Amoraim – commentators on the words of the Tannaim (sages of the Mishna).

Beitar – acronym for Brit Yosef Trumpeldor, an organization of Trumpeldor's followers. OR a Jewish Zionist youth movement. OR a historical village near Jerusalem connected with the Bar Kochva rebellion against Rome in the second century CE.

Ben/ibn/bar – son of

Bible – in this book, the word refers to the Jewish Bible: five Books of Moses, Prophets and Writings.

Builders of Jerusalem/ builders of neighborhoods – initiators, supporters or founders of the neighborhoods built outside the walls of the Old City.

Derech – road

ETZe"L – acronym for **I**rgun **Tz**vai **L**eumi, an underground resistance organization operating in the Land of Israel during the British Mandate period.

Gemara – the part of the Talmud that contains the discussions of the Amoraim on the Mishna.

Halacha – Jewish religious law.

Hasidism – a mass movement founded by **HaBa**'al **Sh**em **T**ov (HaBE'SH"T), the principal point of their faith being prayer with intent and devotion.

Haskala – the Enlightenment movement in Jewish society which began in the 1770s, influenced at first by the general Enlightenment in Europe, and continued on its own distinct path until the early 1880s.

Kabbala – Jewish mysticism having roots as far back as the first century CE. Its more modern form is based on the Book of Zohar [brightness], a product of the thirteenth century Kabbala movement in Spain, but often ascribed to Rabbi Shim'on bar Yohai in the second century CE.

Kibbutz – agricultural collective

Kikar – square

LeH"I – acronym for **L**ohamei **H**erut **Y**israel, an underground resistance organization operating in the Land of Israel during the British Mandate period.

Midrash – study of the Torah not according to the literal meaning of the words but using homily (teaching a lesson), parable and anecdotes.

Mishna – codification of the Oral Law, the clarifications of the sages on the laws written in the Torah; compiled and arranged into six orders by Rabbi Yehuda HaNasi in the late second century CE.

Old Yishuv – the name used to designate the veteran Orthodox Jewish population of Jerusalem and the other holy cities (Tiberias, Hebron and Tzfat) going back before the early Zionist *'aliya* movements of the second half of the nineteenth century.

PaLMa"H – acronym for **Pl**ugat **Mah**atz. One of the fighting groups in the Land of Israel during the British Mandate period and the War of Independence.

Religious or rabbinical court – A court consisting of three rabbis acting as a tribunal to judge matters of religious law.

Sanhedrin – the name for the supreme court and legislative body of seventy-one scholarly rabbis who assembled in Jerusalem during the time of the Second Temple, and after its destruction met in other locations.

Talmud – the overall work which includes the Mishna, the Gemara and later commentaries called Tosafot (additions to the Oral Law that were added in the generation following Rabbi Yehuda HaNasi).

Tanna/Tannaim – the sages of the Second Temple period and the years following (end of the third century BCE until the generation after Rabbi Yehuda HaNasi), who began to shape the body of the Oral Law: Mishna, Tosefta, Baraita (Oral Laws developed after the codification by Rabbi Yehuda HaNasi) and Midreshei Halacha (legal interpretations based on Torah laws).

Temple Mount – another name for Mount Moriah, in Jerusalem, on which were built the First and Second Holy Temples (the First by King Solomon in the tenth century BCE, and the Second by ‘Ezra and Nehemia in the sixth century BCE).

Torah – refers to the five Books of Moses: Genesis, Exodus, Leviticus, Numbers, Deuteronomy. May also be used to refer to Jewish law arising out of these five books.

TZaHa"L [IDF] – acronym for **Tz**va **Ha**Hagana **L**eYisrael. The collective name for all the branches of the military in Israel, the Israel Defense Force.

Western Wall – the western side of the supporting wall, built by King Herod, to expand the area of the Temple Mount, and that remained after the destruction of the Second Holy Temple in 70 CE.

Yakir/Yekirat Yerushalayim – a title granted by the Jerusalem Municipality to honor a citizen of Jerusalem.

Yishuv – the collective Jewish population in the Land of Israel prior to the establishment of the State of Israel.

Bibliography

‘Amiram, Dr. Moshe, “‘Ein Kerem – Masa‘ el HaKfar HaKasum” [‘Ein Kerem – Journey to the Enchanted Village], Jerusalem, 2004.

Ben-Aryeh, Yehoshu‘a, “Yerushalayim HaHadasha BeReishita” [The New City of Jerusalem in Its Beginning], Jerusalem, 5739 (1979).

Benvenisti, David, “Rehovot Yerushalayim” [The Streets of Jerusalem], Jerusalem, 1984.

Central Office for Statistics, MMG Unit, Maps, “Eizorim Statistiim BiYerushalayim” [Statistical Areas in Jerusalem], Jerusalem, 1997.

Cohen, Meir, ed., “Yerushalayim – ‘Ir shel Shchunot” [Jerusalem – City of Neighborhoods], Jerusalem, 5756 (1996).

Even-Shoshan, Avraham, “Milon Even-Shoshan, Mehudash Ume‘udcan LiShnot HaAlpayim” [Even-Shoshan Dictionary, Renewed and Updated for the Twenty-first Century], Israel, 2003.

Feurst, Dr. Aharon, “Yerushalayim HaHadasha” [The New Jerusalem], Jerusalem, 5742 (1982).

Gellis, Ya‘akov, “Shchunot BiYerushalayim” [Neighborhoods in Jerusalem], Jerusalem, 5748 (1988).

Grayevsky, Pinhas ben Zvi, “Sefer HaYishuv, HaYishuv Ha‘Ivri MiHutz LeHomot Ha‘Ir” [The Book of the Yishuv, the Jewish Community Outside the City Walls], Jerusalem, 5699 (1939).

Jerusalem Municipality, “Shchunot HaBira” [The Neighborhoods of the Capital], published by the Department of Information and Public Relations, Jerusalem, 1980.

Jerusalem Municipality, City Archives, Minutes of the Committee on Street Names.

Kluger, Binyamin, “Yerushalayim Shchunot Saviv La” [Jerusalem, Neighborhoods All Around], Jerusalem, 5739 (1979).

Kroyanker, David, “Yerushalayim, Mabat Architectoni: Madrich Tiyulim BiShchunot u Vatim” [Jerusalem, an Architectural View: A Guide to Tours of Neighborhoods and Houses], Jerusalem, 1996.

Langbaum, Shlomit, “Mea She‘arim u Svivata” [Mea She‘arim and Its Surroundings], Jerusalem, 2004.

Mazar, Professor Binyamin, "Atlas LiTkufat HaTaNa"CH" [Atlas of the Biblical Period], Tel-Aviv, 1972.

Padan, Yehi'am, "Tel-Aviv – Yafo, Madrich HaRehovot" [Tel-Aviv – Jaffa, the Street Guide], Tel-Aviv – Jaffa, 2003.

Rivlin, Ya'akov Moshe, "Reishit HaYishuv HaYehudi MiHutz LaHomot" [The Beginning of the Jewish Community Outside the Walls], Jerusalem, 5738 (1978).

Rivlin, Yosef Yoel, "Mea She'arim" [Mea She'arim], Jerusalem, 5707 (1947).

Roth, Cecil, Encyclopedia Judaica, Jerusalem, 1972.

Vilnay, Dr. Zeev, "Yerushalayim, Birat Yisrael" [Jerusalem, Capital of Israel], Jerusalem, 1969.

—, "Entziklopediyat Vilnay LiYerushalayim" [Vilnay Encyclopedia to Jerusalem] (2 vols.), Jerusalem, 1993.

—, "Yerushalayim, Ha'Ir HaHadasha u Svivata, Dalet" [Jerusalem, the New City and Its Surroundings, Vol. 4], Jerusalem, 1976.

Zecharia, Shabtai, "Yerushalayim shel Mata, Shchunot Yerushalayim VeSipureihen" [The Earthly Jerusalem, the Neighborhoods of Jerusalem and Their Stories], Jerusalem, 2003.

Jerusalem Municipality Website, www.jerusalem.muni.il.

About the Author

CHANOCH SHUDOFSKY made *'aliya* in 1999, although his connection with Israel in general and Jerusalem in particular in particular extends over a period of more than one hundred thirty years. His great-grandfather, with his wife and children, made *'aliya* from Europe in 5631 (1871) and settled in the Old City. When the Mea She'arim Society was established in the year 5634 (1874), his great-grandfather and his family were among its first members, and he was among the first to build his home in the new neighborhood and move his family into it. In that very house, which is still standing in Mea She'arim, the author's mother was born. The author and his wife were married in Jerusalem and after a number of years realized their youthful dream to make *'aliya* and live in Jerusalem. They were also fortunate that their younger daughter was married in Jerusalem to an Israeli-born young man, and even their daughter's first-born daughter (the author's granddaughter) was born in Jerusalem. The connection the author feels to Jerusalem is a physical, mental and spiritual one – and it is deeply rooted and very solid.

Notes

Notes

Notes

Notes

Notes

Notes

Notes

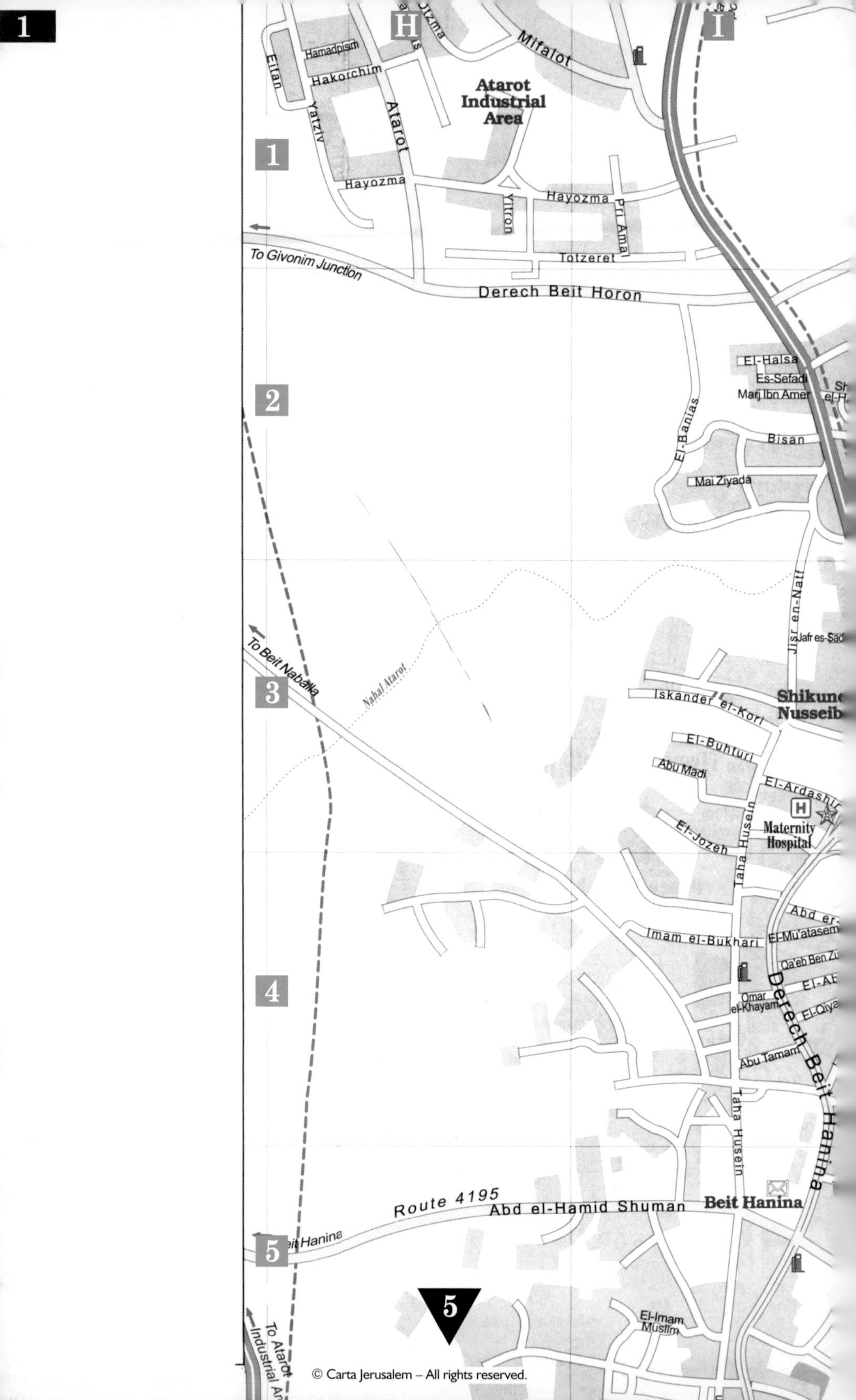
H
I
Hamadpisim
Eitan
Hakorchim
Yatziv
Atarot
Mifalot
Atarot
Industrial
Area
1
Hayozma
Hayozma
Yitron
Pri Amal
Totzeret
To Givonim Junction
Derech Beit Horon
El-Halsa
Es-Sefadi
Marj Ibn Amer
2
El-Banias
Bisan
Mai Ziyada
Jisr en-Naif
To Beit Naballa
Nahal Atarot
3
Iskander el-Kori
El-Buhturi
Abu Madi
El-Ardashir
Maternity
Hospital
El-Jozeh
Taha Husein
Imam el-Bukhari
El-Mu'atasem
Omar
el-Khayam
Abu Tamam
Derech Beit Hanina
4
Taha Husein
Route 4195
Abd el-Hamid Shuman
Beit Hanina
5
5
El-Imam
Muslim
To Atarot
Industrial Area

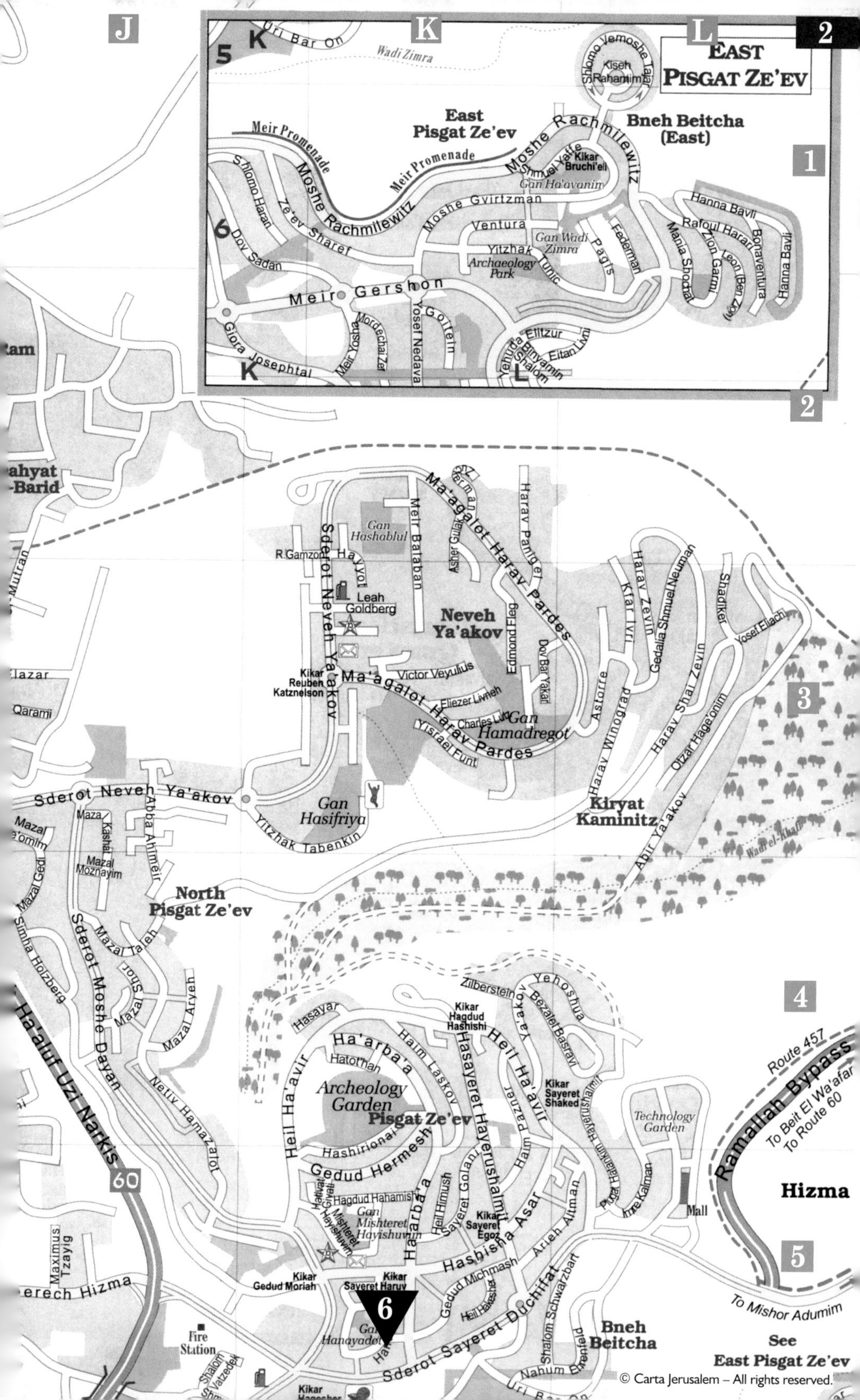
2
East Pisgat Ze'ev
East Pisgat Ze'ev
Bneh Beitcha (East)
Wadi Zimra
Uri Bar On
Meir Promenade
Moshe Rachmilewitz
Shlomo Haran
Ze'ev Sharef
Dov Sadan
Moshe Gvirtzman
Ventura
Yitzhak Tunic
Archaeology Park
Gan Wadi Zimra
Gan Ha'avanim
Kikar Bruchi'eli
Kiseh Rahamim
Pagis
Federman
Hanna Bavli
Rafoul Haran
Bonaventura
Mania Shochat
Zion Garmi
Leon (Ben Zion)
Meir Gershon
Giora Josephtal
Meir Yosha
Mordechai Zer
Yosef Nedava
Goitein
Elitzur
Eitan Livni
Yehuda Binyamin
Shalom
Neveh Ya'akov
Gan Hashablul
Meir Balaban
Sderot Neveh Ya'akov
Ma'agalot Harav Pardes
Harav Panigel
Edmond Fleg
Dov Bar Yakar
R.Gamzon
Leah Goldberg
Kikar Reuben Katznelson
Victor Veyufus
Eliezer Livneh
Charles Lutz
Gan Hamadregot
Yisrael Funt
Gan Hasifriya
Yitzhak Tabenkin
Harav Zevin
Kfar Ivri
Gedalia Shmuel Neuman
Shadiker
Yosef Eliach
Astorre
Harav Winograd
Harav Shai Zevin
Otzar Hage'onim
Abir Ya'akov
Kiryat Kaminitz
Wadi el-Khafi
North Pisgat Ze'ev
Abba Ahimeir
Mazal Kashat
Mazal Moznayim
Mazal Gedi
Mazal Taleh
Mazal Shor
Mazal Aryeh
Sderot Moshe Dayan
Simha Holzberg
Ha'aluf Uzi Narkis
60
Netiv Hamazalot
Maximus Tzayig
Derech Hizma
Fire Station
Pisgat Ze'ev
Archeology Garden
Hasayar
Ha'arba'a
Hatothan
Haim Laskov
Heil Ha'avir
Hasayeret Hayerushalmi
Kikar Hagdud Hashishi
Zilberstein
Yehoshua
Bezalel Basravi
Kikar Sayeret Shaked
Haim Pazner
Hashirionai
Gedud Hermesh
Hagdud Hahamishi
Gan Mishteret Hayishuvim
Heil Himush
Sayeret Golani
Kikar Sayeret Egoz
Hashisha Asar
Arieh Altman
Kikar Gedud Moriah
Kikar Sayeret Haruv
6
Gan Hanayadot
Gedud Michmash
Heil Hakesher
Sderot Sayeret Duchifat
Shalom Schwarzbart
Bneh Beitcha
Nahum Ehrenfeld
Technology Garden
Mall
Route 457
Ramallah Bypass
To Beit El Wa'afar
To Route 60
Hizma
To Mishor Adumim
See East Pisgat Ze'ev
3
4
5
J
K
L

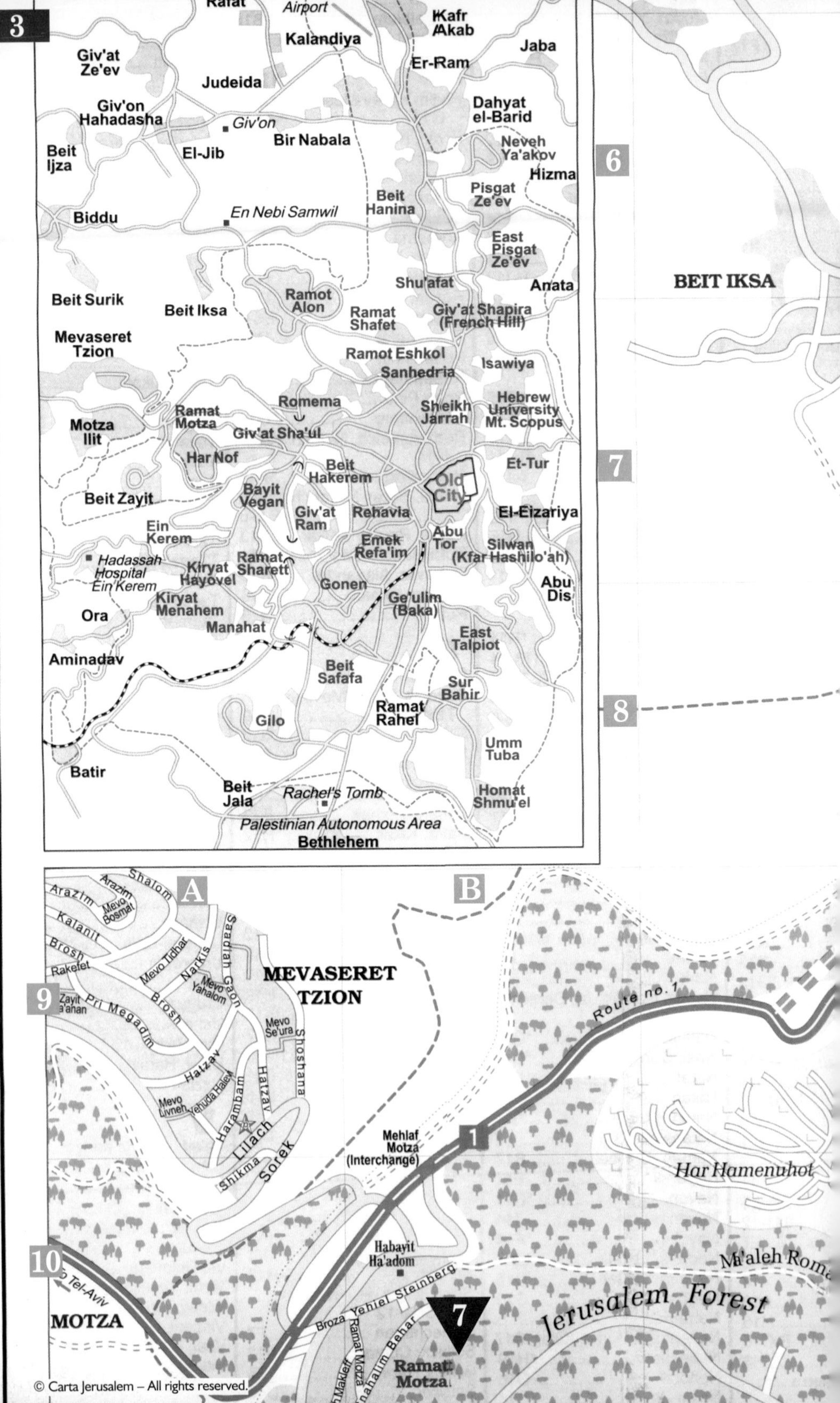
3
Rafat
Airport
Kafr Akab
Kalandiya
Jaba
Giv'at Ze'ev
Er-Ram
Judeida
Dahyat el-Barid
Giv'on Hahadasha
Giv'on
Neveh Ya'akov
Bir Nabala
Beit Ijza
El-Jib
Hizma
Pisgat Ze'ev
Beit Hanina
En Nebi Samwil
Biddu
East Pisgat Ze'ev
Shu'afat
Anata
Ramot Alon
Beit Surik
Beit Iksa
Ramat Shafet
Giv'at Shapira (French Hill)
Mevaseret Tzion
Ramot Eshkol
Isawiya
Sanhedria
Romema
Hebrew University Mt. Scopus
Sheikh Jarrah
Ramat Motza
Motza Ilit
Giv'at Sha'ul
Har Nof
Beit Hakerem
Et-Tur
Old City
Bayit Vegan
Beit Zayit
Giv'at Ram
Rehavia
El-Eizariya
Ein Kerem
Abu Tor
Emek Refa'im
Silwan (Kfar Hashilo'ah)
Hadassah Hospital Ein Kerem
Ramat Sharett
Kiryat Hayovel
Gonen
Abu Dis
Kiryat Menahem
Ge'ulim (Baka)
Ora
Manahat
East Talpiot
Aminadav
Beit Safafa
Sur Bahir
Ramat Rahel
Gilo
Umm Tuba
Batir
Beit Jala
Rachel's Tomb
Homat Shmu'el
Palestinian Autonomous Area
Bethlehem
6
7
8
BEIT IKSA
A
B
Shalom
Arazim
Mevo Bosmat
Kalanit
Brosh
Rakefet
Mevo Tidhar
Narkis
Saadiah Gaon
Mevo Yahalom
MEVASERET TZION
9
Zayit Ra'anan
Pri Megadim
Mevo Se'ura
Shoshana
Hatzav
Yehuda Halevi
Mevo Livneh
Harambam
Lilach
Shikma
Sorek
Route no. 1
1
Mehlaf Motza (Interchange)
Har Hamenuhot
10
Habayit Ha'adom
Ma'aleh Roma
to Tel-Aviv
Yehiel Steinberg
Broza
Ramat Motza
Nahalim Behar
Makleff
7
Jerusalem Forest
MOTZA
Ramat Motza

D
E
F
4
Ramat "Gimel"
Ramat Polin
Ramot Allon
Ramot "Beth"
Sderot Golda Meir
Sulam Ya'akov Park
Technological Park
Gan Ha'etz
Gan Hakipod
Gan Hashablul
Gan Truman
Ramot Forest
Route 9 under construction
Nahal Shmuel
Nahal Sorek
Nahal Romema
Kikar Binyamin Shehor
Kikar Harav Judah Eleazar
Kikar Shostakovich
Kikar George Minis
Kikar Jacobson
Kikar Mafkura
Kikar Golei Kafrisin
Kikar Benjamin Cohen
Kikar Ahi Eilat
Kikar Ha'ahim Rut
Avraham Recanati
Haro'eh
Ramot
Yitzhak Mirski
Shivat Tzion
Abba Hillel Silver
Henry Morgenthau
Harry Truman
Zondek
Derech Hahoresh
Aliyat Hano'ar
Yigal (Allon)
Asirei Tzion
Aharon Eshkoli
Nelson Glueck
Kadima
Mishol Hakitron
Mishol Moran
Mishol Hamargalit
Mishol Haya'ara
Ma'aleh Oranim
5
6
7
8
9
10
Mehlaf Golda (Interc...)
Sderot Ben Gurion
Sha'arei Yerushalayim
Mei Nefto'ah (Lifta)
Sacharov Gardens
Wholesale Market
Kikar Ezrat Nashim
Romema Ilit
Mattersdorf Kiryat Sheva
Kiryat Unsdorf
Harav Sorotzkin
Industrial Area
Panim Me'irot
Kikar Harav Klein
Kikar Elkashvili
Mehlaf Giv'at Sha'ul

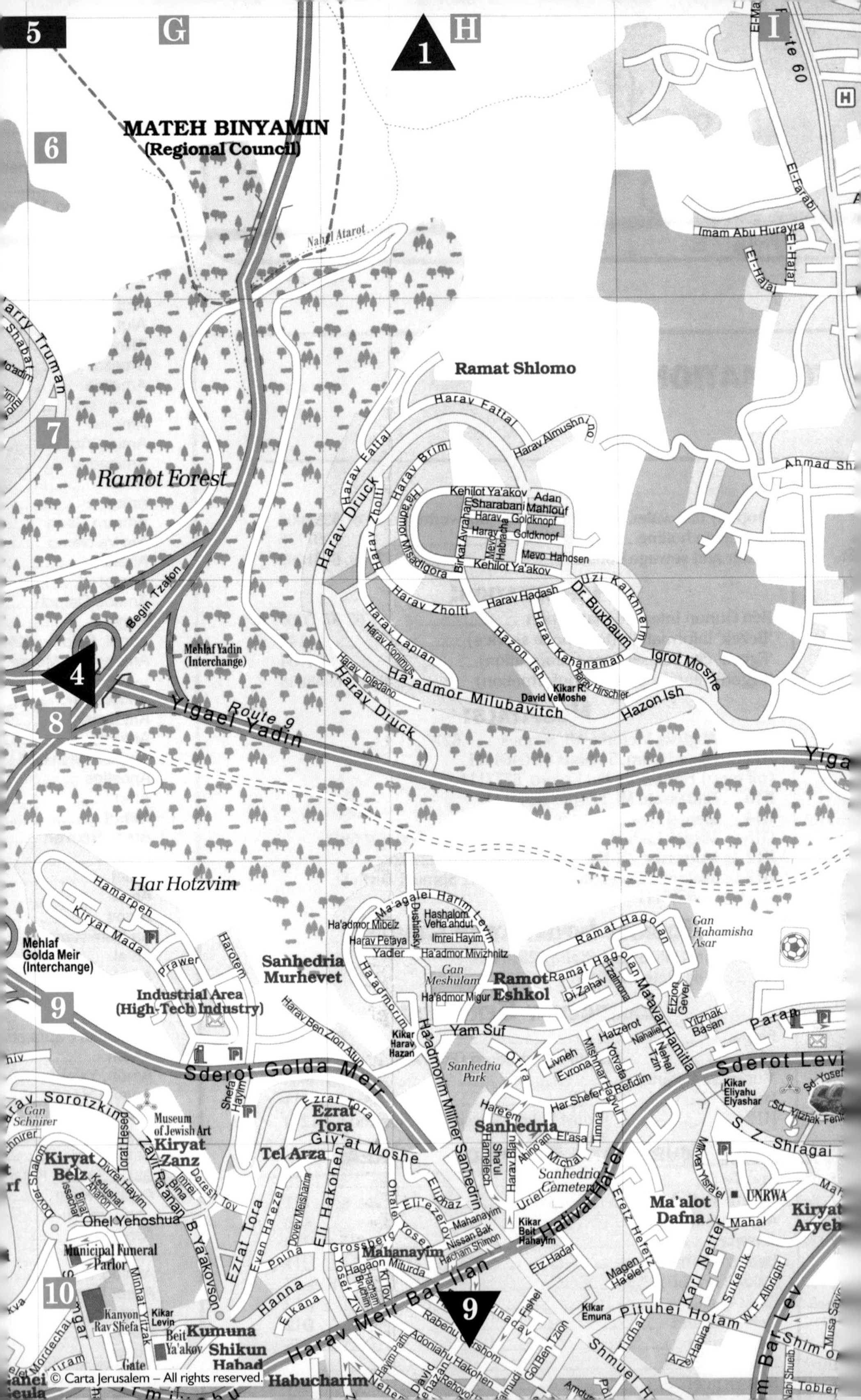

5
G
1
H
I
6
7
8
9
10
4
9
MATEH BINYAMIN
(Regional Council)
Nahal Atarot
Ramat Shlomo
Ramot Forest
Begin Tzafon
Mehlaf Yadin
(Interchange)
Route 9
Yigael Yadin
Harav Fattal
Harav Almushnino
Harav Brim
Harav Druck
Harav Zholti
Kehilot Ya'akov
Sharabani
Adan Mahlouf
Harav Goldknopf
Mevo Hahosen
Birkat Avraham
Ha'admor Misadigora
Harav Hadash
Uzi Kalkhheim
Dr. Buxbaum
Harav Kahanaman
Hazon Ish
Igrot Moshe
Harav Lapian
Harav Konimus
Harav Toledano
Ha'admor Milubavitch
Kikar R. David VeMoshe
Harav Hirschler
Imam Abu Hurayra
El-Hajaj
El-Farabi
Route 60
Ahmad Sh
Har Hotzvim
Hamarpeh
Kiryat Mada
Mehlaf Golda Meir (Interchange)
Harotem
Prawer
Industrial Area (High-Tech Industry)
Sanhedria Murhevet
Ma'agalei Harim Levin
Dushinsky
Hashalom Veha'ahdut
Ha'admor Mibelz
Harav Petaya
Yadler
Imrei Hayim
Ha'admor Mivizhnitz
Gan Meshulam
Ha'admor Migur
Ramot Eshkol
Ramat Hagolan
Gan Hahamisha Asar
Di Zahav
Ma'avar Hamitla
Etzion Gever
Yitzhak Basan
Paran
Harav Ben Zion Atun
Ha'admorim
Kikar Harav Hazan
Yam Suf
Sanhedria Park
Ofira
Livneh
Evrona
Hatzerot
Yotvata
Nahal Tzin
Refidim
Sderot Golda Meir
Sderot Levi
Kikar Eliyahu Elyashar
S. Z. Shragai
Museum of Jewish Art
Kiryat Zanz
Harav Sorotzkin
Gan Schnirer
Torat Hesed
Shefa Hayim
Ezrat Tora
Giv'at Moshe
Tel Arza
Eli Hakohen
Dovev Meisharim
Ha'admorim Miliner
Sanhedrin
Sanhedria
Har Shefer
Sanhedria Cemetery
Hatzvi
Timna
El'asa
Michal
Uriel
Harav Blau
Sha'ul Hamelech
Kiryat Belz
Divrei Hayim
Kedushat Aharon
Binat Issachar
Dover Shalom
Imrei Bina
Zayit Ra'anan
Doresh Tov
Ohel Yehoshua
B Yakovson
Even Ha'ezel
Eliphaz
Eli'ezer
Ohalei Yosef
Mahanayim
Nissan Bak
Hacham Shimon
Kikar Beit Hahayim
Hativat Har'el
Erez Hefetz
Ma'alot Dafna
UNRWA
Kiryat Aryeh
Mahal
Municipal Funeral Parlor
Pnina
Grossberg
Hagaon Miturda
Etz Hadar
Magen Ha'elef
Karl Netter
Sukenik
W.F. Albright
Hanna
Elkana
Kikar Levin
Kanyon Rav Shefa
Beit Ya'akov
Kumuna
Shikun Habad
Harav Meir Bar Ilan
Rabenu Gershom
Adoniahu Hakohen
Kikar Emuna
Pituhei Hotam
Shmuel H
Bar Lev
Habucharim
Geula
Mordechai

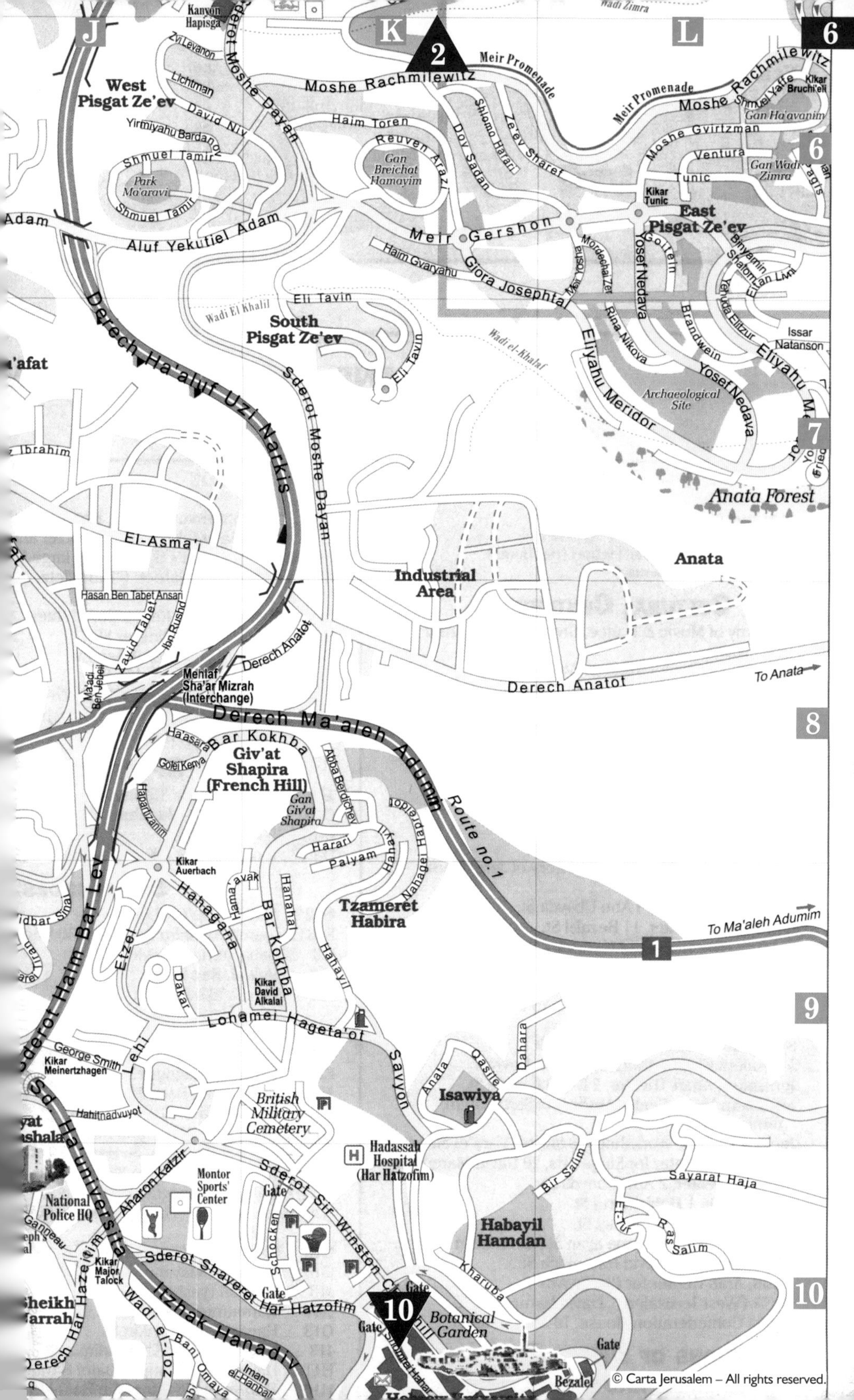

J
K
L
6
2
Kanyon Hapisga
Wadi Zimra
West Pisgat Ze'ev
Zvi Levanon
Lichtman
David Niv
Yirmiyahu Bardanov
Shmuel Tamir
Park Ma'aravi
Sderot Moshe Dayan
Moshe Rachmilewitz
Meir Promenade
Haim Toren
Reuven Arazi
Gan Breichat Hamayim
Dov Sadan
Shlomo Harari
Ze'ev Sharef
Moshe Gvirtzman
Shmuel Yaffe
Kikar Bruchi'eli
Gan Ha'avanim
Ventura
Tunic
Gan Wadi Zimra
Kikar Tunic
East Pisgat Ze'ev
Adam
Aluf Yekutiel Adam
Meir Gershon
Haim Gvaryahu
Giora Josephtal
Mordechai Zer
Yosef Nedava
Goitein
Binyamin Shalom
Yehuda Elitzur
Eitan Livni
Eli Tavin
Wadi El Khalil
South Pisgat Ze'ev
Wadi el-Khalaf
Rina Nikova
Brandwein
Issar Natanson
Eliyahu Meridor
Archaeological Site
7
Anata Forest
Derech Ha'aluf Uzi Narkis
Ibrahim
El-Asma'i
Hasan Ben Tabet Ansari
Zayid Tabet
Ibn Rushd
Industrial Area
Anata
Derech Anatot
To Anata
Menlaf Sha'ar Mizrah (Interchange)
Ma'adi Ben Jebeil
Derech Ma'aleh Adumim
8
Ha'asara
Bar Kokhba
Golei Kenya
Giv'at Shapira (French Hill)
Abba Berdichev
Gan Giv'at Shapira
Hapartizanim
Route no.1
Harari
Palyam
Hahayil
Nahagei Hapirdot
Kikar Auerbach
Hama'avak
Hanahal
Hahagana
Bar Kokhba
Tzameret Habira
Etzel
Dakar
Kikar David Alkalai
Midbar Sinai
To Ma'aleh Adumim
1
9
Sderot Haim Bar Lev
Lohamei Hageta'ot
Lehi
George Smith
Kikar Meinertzhagen
Savyon
Anata
Qasile
Dahara
Isawiya
Hahitnadvuyot
British Military Cemetery
Sd. Ha'universita
National Police HQ
Aharon Katzir
Montor Sports' Center
Sderot Sir Winston Churchill
Gate
Hadassah Hospital (Har Hatzofim)
Bir Salim
Sayarat Haja
Habayil Hamdan
El-Tur
Ras Salim
Kharuba
Schocken
Ganneau
Derech Har Hazeitim
Kikar Major Talock
Sderot Shayeret Har Hatzofim
Sheikh Jarrah
Itzhak Hanadiv
Wadi el-Joz
Bani Omaya
Imam el-Hanbali
10
Botanical Garden
Shmuel Hahar
Bezalel

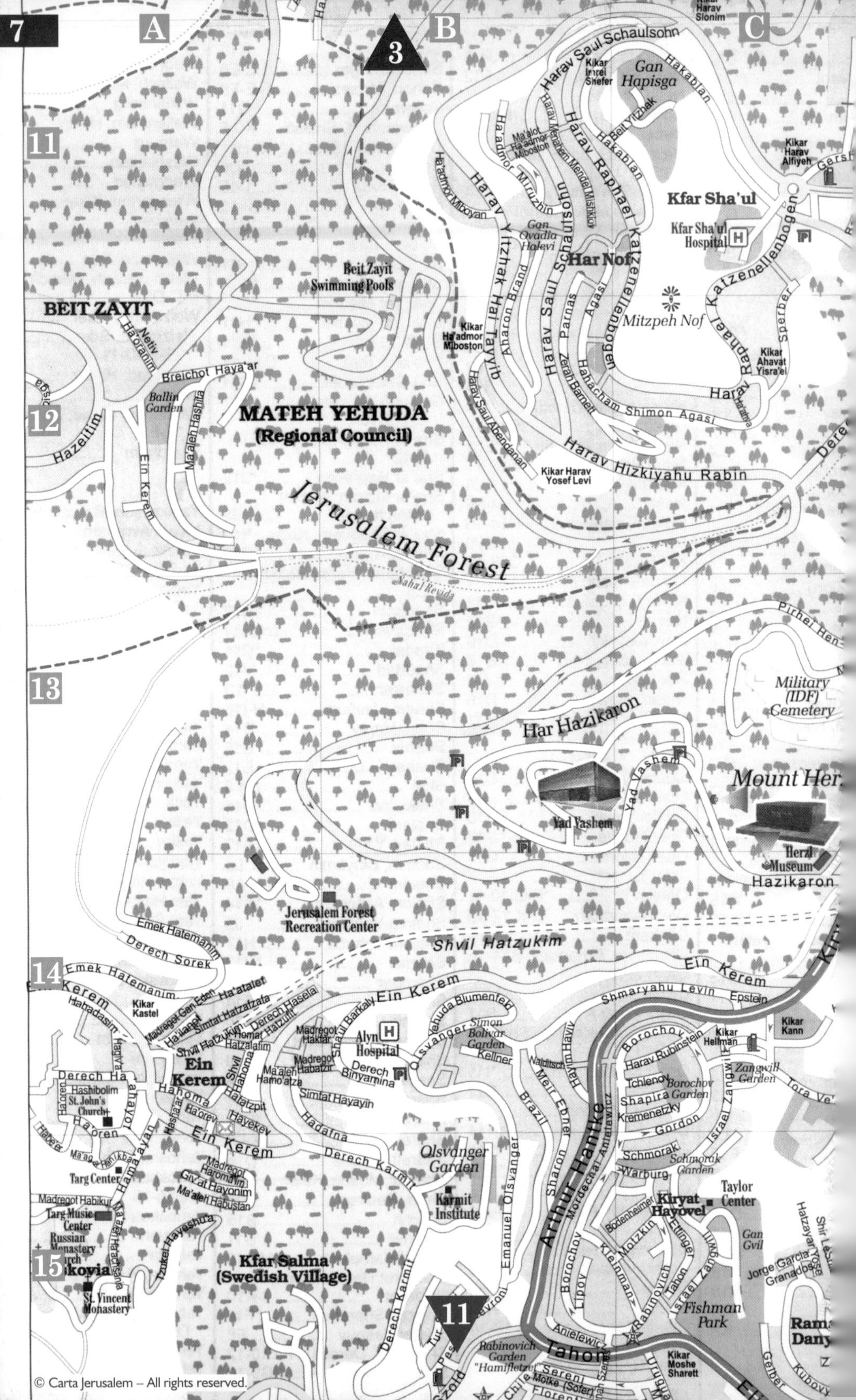
A
B
C
3
11
12
13
14
15
BEIT ZAYIT
MATEH YEHUDA
(Regional Council)
Jerusalem Forest
Nahal Revida
Beit Zayit
Swimming Pools
Neliv Haoranim
Breichot Haya'ar
Ballin Garden
Ma'aleh Hashita
Hazeitim
Ein Kerem
Harav Saul Schaulsohn
Gan Hapisga
Hakablan
Kikar Imrei Shefer
Beit Yitzhak
Ma'alot Ha'admor Miboston
Harav Menahem Mendel Mishkov
Harav Raphael Katzenellenbogen
Ha'admor Miruzhin
Ha'admor Miboyan
Harav Yitzhak Hai Tayyib
Gan Ovadia Halevi
Har Nof
Aharon Brand
Harav Saul Schaulsohn
Parnas
Agasi
Zerah Barnett
Hahacham Shimon Agasi
Kikar Ha'admor Miboston
Harav Saul Abendanan
Kikar Harav Yosef Levi
Harav Hizkiyahu Rabin
Kfar Sha'ul
Kfar Sha'ul Hospital
Mitzpeh Nof
Katzenellenbogen
Raphael
Sperber
Kikar Ahavat Yisra'el
Kikar Harav Alfiyeh
Kikar Harav Slonim
Pirhei Hen
Military (IDF) Cemetery
Har Hazikaron
Yad Vashem
Mount Herzl
Herzl Museum
Hazikaron
Jerusalem Forest Recreation Center
Emek Hatemanim
Derech Sorek
Shvil Hatzukim
Ein Kerem
Shmaryahu Levin
Epstein
Kikar Kastel
Madregot Gan Eden
Ha'atalef
Simtat Hatzafzafa
Derech Hasela
Ha'ilanot
Shvil Hatzukim
Homat Hatzuf
Hatzalafim
Shaul Barkaly
Madregot Haktar
Madregot Habatzir
Alyn Hospital
Derech Binyamina
Yehuda Blumenfeld
Simon Bolivar Garden
Olsvanger
Kellner
Naiditsch
Hayim Haviv
Meir Ebner
Brazil
Borochov
Harav Rubinstein
Kikar Hellman
Kikar Kann
Zangwill Garden
Tora Va'
Tchlenov
Borochov Garden
Shapira
Kremenetzky
Gordon
Israel Zangwill
Schmorak
Schmorak Garden
Warburg
Kiryat Hayovel
Taylor Center
Gan Gvil
Jorge Garcia Granados
Hatzayar Yosef
Shir Lashir
Ein Kerem
Hashibolim
St. John's Church
Ha'oren
Derech Ha'ahayot
Hama'ayan
Hahoma
Ma'aleh Hamo'atza
Simtat Hayayin
Hadafna
Derech Karmit
Olsvanger Garden
Karmit Institute
Emanuel Olsvanger
Sharon
Arthur Hantke
Mordechai Anielewicz
Targ Center
Madregot Haromanim
Giv'at Hayonim
Ma'aleh Habustan
Madregot Habikur
Targ Music Center
Russian Monastery
St. Vincent Monastery
Tzukei Hayeshua
Kfar Salma
(Swedish Village)
Derech Karmit
Lipov
Kleinman
Motzkin
Bodenheimer
Ettinger
Rabinovich
Israel Zangwill
Tahon
Fishman Park
Anielewicz
Rabinovich Garden
"Hamifletzet"
Tahon
Kikar Moshe Sharett
Sereni
Molke (Soter)
Chile
Florentin
Szold
Gelber
Kubovy

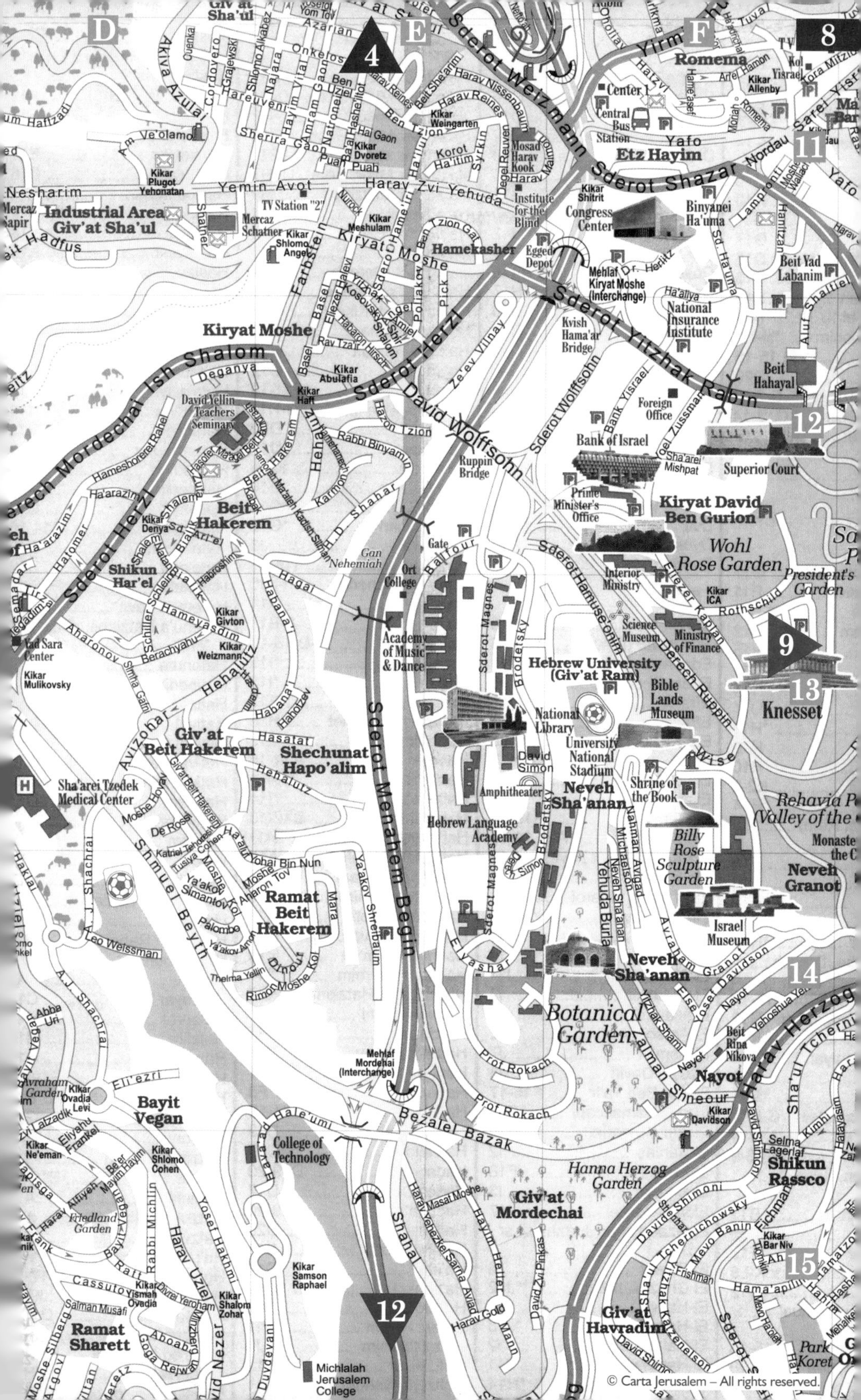
D
E
F
8
4
Giv'at Sha'ul
Azarian
Onkelos
Romema
Center 1
Central Bus Station
Yafo
Etz Hayim
Sderot Weizmann
Sderot Shazar
Nordau
Kikar Allenby
Yirmiyahu
11
Akiva Azulai
Cordovero
Am Ve'olamo
Kikar Plugot Yehonatan
Nesharim
Yemin Avot
Harav Zvi Yehuda
Industrial Area Giv'at Sha'ul
Mercaz Sapir
Beit Hadfus
Mercaz Schatner
TV Station "2"
Kikar Meshulam
Kikar Shlomo Angel
Kiryat Moshe
Hamekasher
Sherira Gaon
Hareuveni
Kikar Dvoretz
Kikar Weingarten
Harav Nissenbaum
Harav Reines
Ben Tzion
Hai Gaon
Korot Ha'itim
Syrkin
Degel Reuven
Mosad Harav Kook
Institute for the Blind
Kikar Shitrit
Congress Center
Binyanei Ha'uma
Egged Depot
Mehlaf Kiryat Moshe (Interchange)
Sderot Yitzhak Rabin
National Insurance Institute
Kvish Hama'ar Bridge
Beit Yad Labanim
Beit Hahayal
12
Kiryat Moshe
Sderot Herzl
Sderot Mordechai Ish Shalom
Derech Mordechai
Deganya
Kikar Abulafia
Kikar Haft
David Yellin Teachers Seminary
David Wolffsohn
Sderot Wolffsohn
Ze'ev Vilnay
Hazon Tzion
Rabbi Binyamin
Ruppin Bridge
Foreign Office
Bank of Israel
Sha'arei Mishpat
Superior Court
Prime Minister's Office
Kiryat David Ben Gurion
Wohl Rose Garden
President's Garden
Interior Ministry
Kikar ICA
Rothschild
Science Museum
Ministry of Finance
Derech Ruppin
9
13
Knesset
Hameshoreret Rahel
Ha'arazim
Beit Hakerem
Kikar Denya
Shikun Har'el
Kikar Givton
Kikar Weizmann
Hameyasdim
Aharonov
Hehalutz
Yad Sara Center
Kikar Mulikovsky
Gan Nehemiah
Ort College
Academy of Music & Dance
Balfour
Gate
Hagai
Habanai
Sderot Magnes
Brodetsky
Hebrew University (Giv'at Ram)
National Library
University National Stadium
Bible Lands Museum
Wise
Shrine of the Book
Billy Rose Sculpture Garden
Israel Museum
Rehavia Park (Valley of the Cross)
Monastery of the Cross
Neveh Granot
Giv'at Beit Hakerem
Shechunat Hapo'alim
Hasatat
Sha'arei Tzedek Medical Center
Avizohar
Moshe Hovav
De Rossi
Shmuel Beyth
David Simon
Amphitheater
Neveh Sha'anan
Hebrew Language Academy
Sderot Menahem Begin
Ramat Beit Hakerem
Ya'akov Shrenbaum
Mara
Leo Weissman
Elyashar
Botanical Garden
Neveh Sha'anan
Avraham Granot
Yosef Davidson
14
Harav Herzog
Nayot
Beit Rina Nikova
Kikar Davidson
Zalman Shneour
Prof. Rokach
Mehlaf Mordechai (Interchange)
Bezalel Bazak
Hale'umi
College of Technology
Bayit Vegan
Kikar Ovadia Levi
Eli'ezri
Kikar Ne'eman
Kikar Shlomo Cohen
Friedland Garden
Harav Uziel
Yosef Hakhmi
Rabbi Michlin
Kikar Samson Raphael
Shahal
Hanna Herzog Garden
Giv'at Mordechai
Hayim Hefetz
David Zvi Pinkas
Harav Gold
Shikun Rassco
Sha'ul Tchernichowsky
Mevo Banin
Fichman
Kikar Bar Niv
15
Giv'at Havradim
Park Koret
Cassuto
Kikar Yismah Ovadia
Kikar Shalom Zohar
Salman Musafi
Ramat Sharett
Bayit Vegan
Nezer
Duvdevani
12
Michlalah Jerusalem College

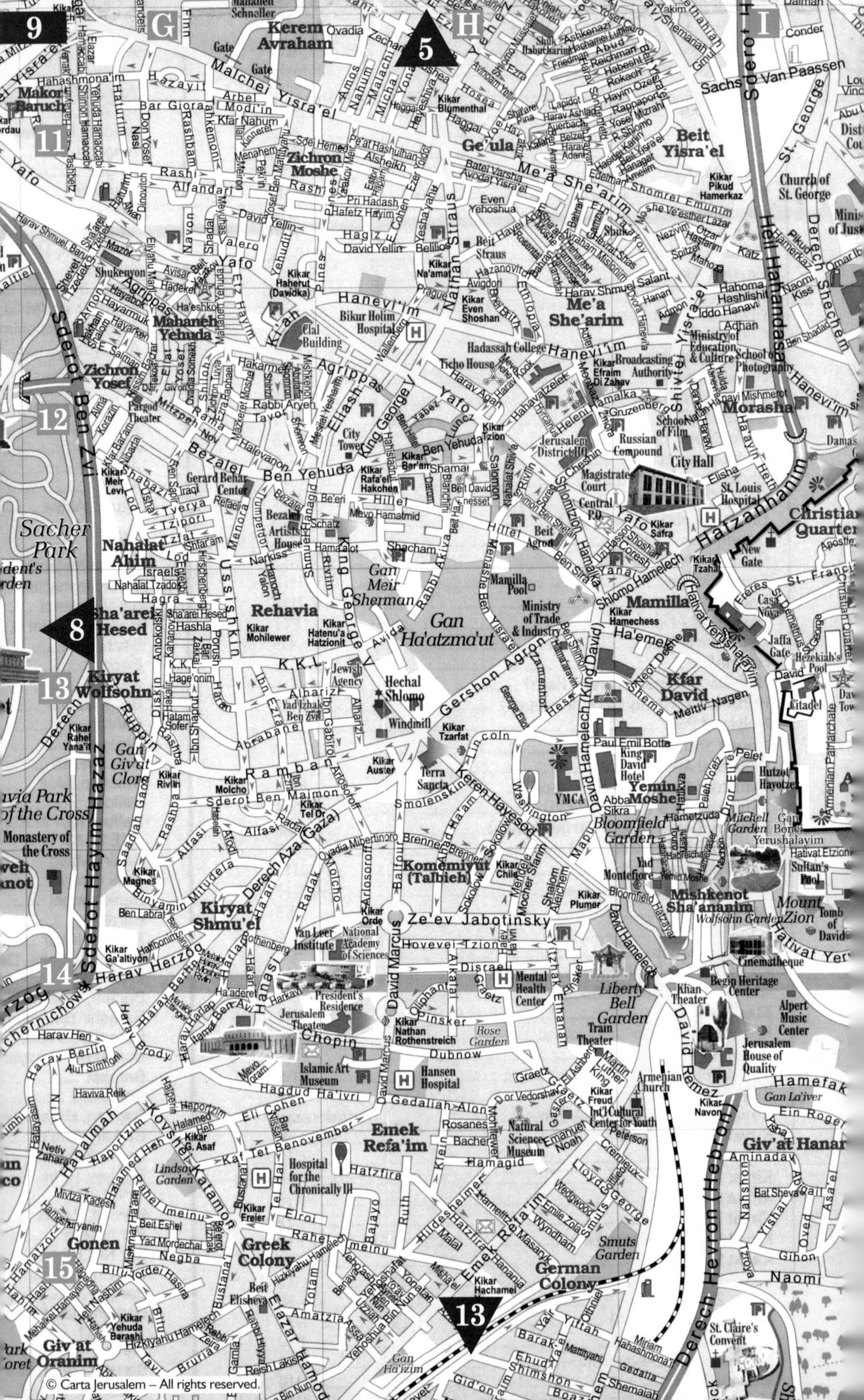
9
G
H
I
5
11
12
8
13
14
15
13
Mahaneh Schneller
Kerem Avraham
Makor Baruch
Zichron Moshe
Ge'ula
Beit Yisra'el
Church of St. George
Mahaneh Yehuda
Zichron Yosef
Me'a She'arim
Hadassah College
Ticho House
Bikur Holim Hospital
Clal Building
Broadcasting Authority
Ministry of Education & Culture
School of Photography
Morasha
Russian Compound
Jerusalem District HQ
City Hall
St. Louis Hospital
Magistrate Court
Central P.O.
Kikar Safra
Christian Quarter
New Gate
Sacher Park
Nahalat Ahim
Rehavia
Gan Meir Sherman
Gan Ha'atzma'ut
Mamilla Pool
Ministry of Trade & Industry
Mamilla
Jaffa Gate
Hezekiah's Pool
Citadel
Sha'arei Hesed
Kiryat Wolfsohn
Jewish Agency
Hechal Shlomo
Windmill
Kfar David
King David Hotel
YMCA
Terra Sancta
Yemin Moshe
Bloomfield Garden
Mitchell Garden
Gan Bonei Yerushalayim
Sultan's Pool
Mount Zion
Tomb of David
Mishkenot Sha'ananim
Wolfsohn Garden
Cinematheque
Begin Heritage Center
Komemiyut (Talbieh)
Kiryat Shmu'el
Van Leer Institute
National Academy of Sciences
President's Residence
Jerusalem Theater
Mental Health Center
Liberty Bell Garden
Khan Theater
Train Theater
Alpert Music Center
Jerusalem House of Quality
Islamic Art Museum
Hansen Hospital
Rose Garden
Armenian Church
Int'l Cultural Center for Youth
Natural Science Museum
Emek Refa'im
Hospital for the Chronically Ill
Lindsay Garden
Gonen
Greek Colony
German Colony
Smuts Garden
Giv'at Hanania
Gan La'iver
St. Claire's Convent
Giv'at Oranim
Gan Ha'izim
Gan Giv'at Clore
Monastery of the Cross
Derech Hevron (Hebron)
Sderot Ben Zvi
Sderot Hayim Hazaz
Harav Herzog
Jaffa
Hanevi'im
King George V
Ben Yehuda
Agrippas
Gershon Agron
Keren Hayesod
Ramban
David Hamelech (King David)
Ze'ev Jabotinsky
Derech Aza (Gaza)
Hatzanhanim
Hativat Yerushalayim
Malchei Yisra'el
Sderot Haim Bar Lev
Sachs
Van Paassen
Derech Shechem
Heil Hahandasa
Shivtei Yisra'el
Ussishkin
Emek Refa'im
Kovshei Katamon
Hapalmah
© Carta Jerusalem – All rights reserved.

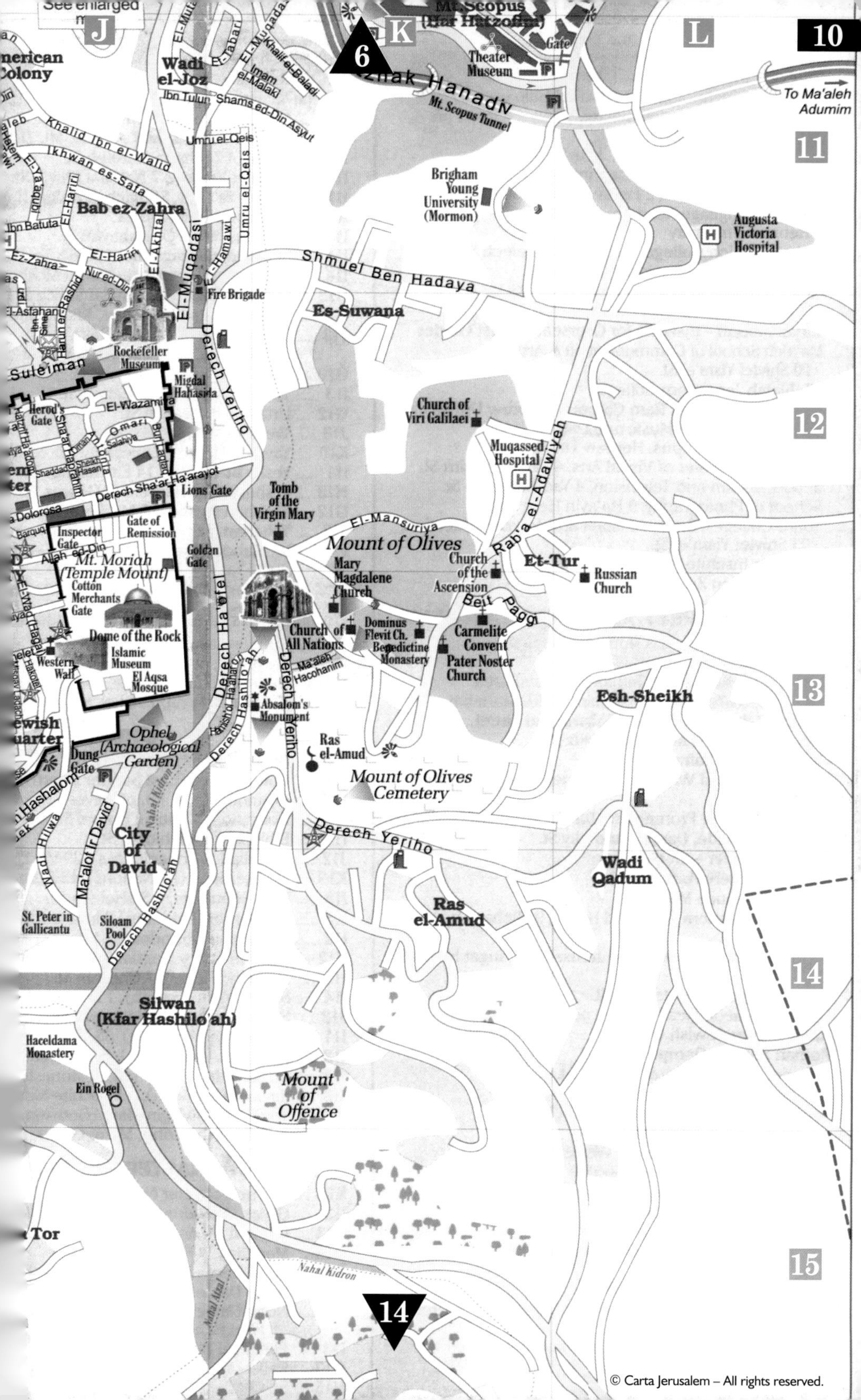
10
J
K
L
6
11
12
13
14
15
14
Mt. Scopus (Har Hatzofim)
Theater
Museum
Gate
Yitzhak Hanadiv
Mt. Scopus Tunnel
To Ma'aleh Adumim
American Colony
Wadi el-Joz
Bab ez-Zahra
Brigham Young University (Mormon)
Augusta Victoria Hospital
Shmuel Ben Hadaya
Es-Suwana
Fire Brigade
Rockefeller Museum
Migdal Hahasida
Derech Yeriho
Herod's Gate
Suleiman
Lions Gate
Derech Sha'ar Ha'arayot
Via Dolorosa
Church of Viri Galilaei
Muqassed Hospital
Tomb of the Virgin Mary
El-Mansuriya
Mount of Olives
Rab'a el-Adawiyeh
Church of the Ascension
Et-Tur
Russian Church
Mary Magdalene Church
Inspector Gate
Gate of Remission
Golden Gate
Mt. Moriah (Temple Mount)
Cotton Merchants Gate
Dome of the Rock
Islamic Museum
El Aqsa Mosque
Western Wall
Derech Ha'ofel
Church of All Nations
Dominus Flevit Ch.
Benedictine Monastery
Carmelite Convent
Pater Noster Church
Beit Paggi
Ma'aleh Hacohanim
Absalom's Monument
Esh-Sheikh
Ophel (Archaeological Garden)
Dung Gate
Jewish Quarter
Ras el-Amud
Mount of Olives Cemetery
Derech Yeriho
City of David
Wadi Qadum
Ras el-Amud
St. Peter in Gallicantu
Siloam Pool
Derech Hashilo'ah
Silwan (Kfar Hashilo'ah)
Haceldama Monastery
Ein Rogel
Mount of Offence
Nahal Kidron
Nahal Atzal

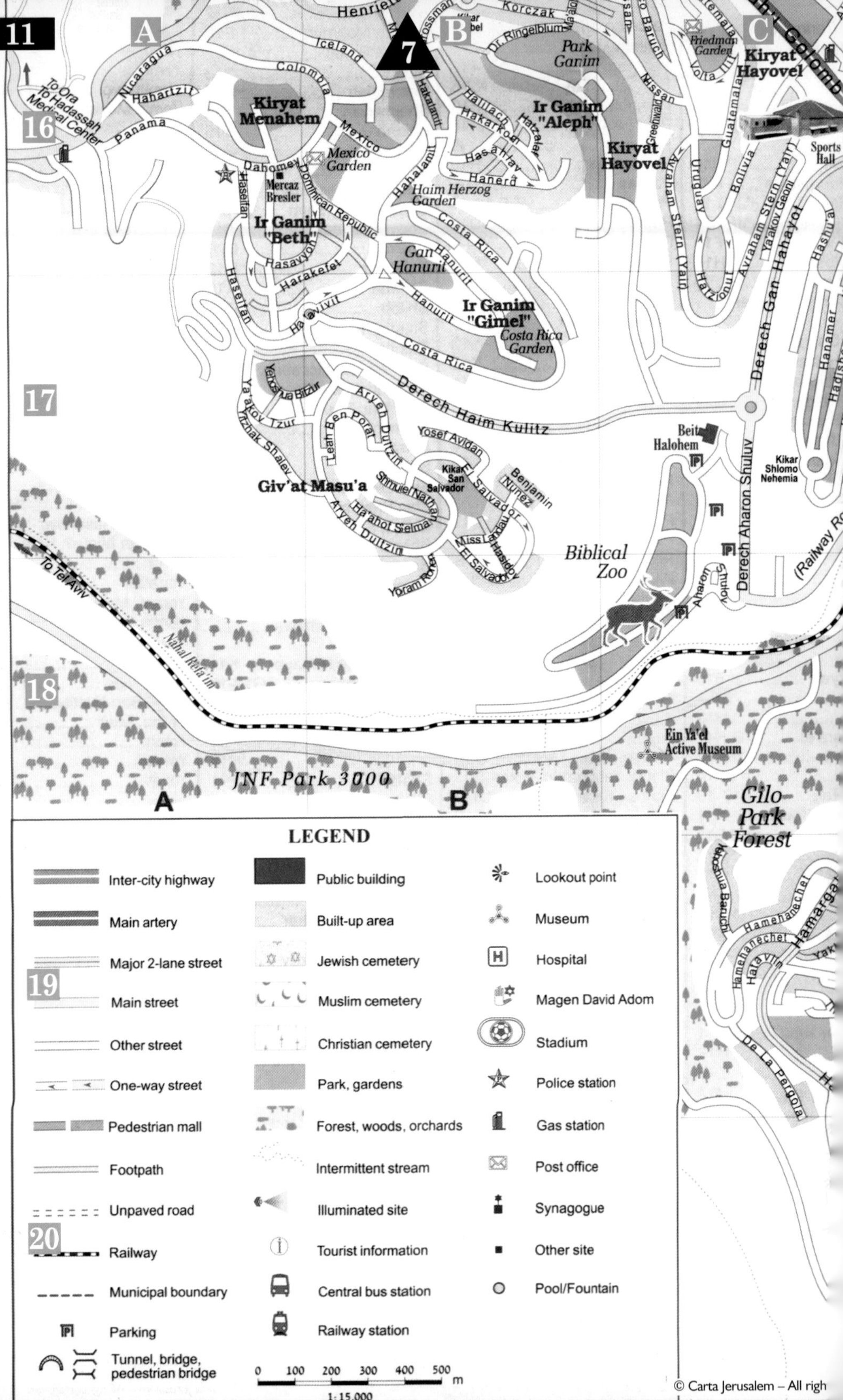

11
7
A
B
C
16
17
18
19
20
Henriet
Korczak
Kikar
Dr. Ringelblum
Park Ganim
Friedman Garden
Kiryat Hayovel
Iceland
Colombia
Nicaragua
Hahartzit
To Ora
To Hadassah Medical Center
Panama
Kiryat Menahem
Mexico
Mexico Garden
Dahomey
Mercaz Bresler
Dominican Republic
Haseifan
Ir Ganim "Beth"
Hasavyon
Harakefet
Hanurit
Hahalamit
Hallach
Hakarkom
Hatzalaf
Hasahlav
Hanerd
Ir Ganim "Aleph"
Kiryat Hayovel
Haim Herzog Garden
Costa Rica
Gan Hanurit
Ir Ganim "Gimel"
Costa Rica Garden
Nissan
Volta
Guatemala
Uruguay
Bolivia
Avraham Stern (Yair)
Yaakov Geoni
Hatzionut
Sports Hall
Derech Gan Hahayot
Hashu'al
Hanamer
Hadishon
Derech Haim Kulitz
Yehoshua Bitzur
Ya'akov Tzur
Yitzhak Shalev
Leah Ben Porat
Aryeh Dultzin
Yosef Avidan
Kikar San Salvador
El Salvador
Benjamin Nunez
Giv'at Masu'a
Shmuel Nathan
Ha'ahot Selma
Miss Landau
Hasidov
Yoram Rohen
Beit Halohem
Kikar Shlomo Nehemia
Derech Aharon Shuluv
Biblical Zoo
(Railway Ro
To Tel Aviv
Nahal Refa'im
Ein Ya'el Active Museum
JNF Park 3000
Gilo Park Forest
Yehoshua Bauchi
Hamehanechel
Hamargalit
Halavin
De La Pergola
LEGEND
Inter-city highway
Main artery
Major 2-lane street
Main street
Other street
One-way street
Pedestrian mall
Footpath
Unpaved road
Railway
Municipal boundary
Parking
Tunnel, bridge, pedestrian bridge
Public building
Built-up area
Jewish cemetery
Muslim cemetery
Christian cemetery
Park, gardens
Forest, woods, orchards
Intermittent stream
Illuminated site
Tourist information
Central bus station
Railway station
Lookout point
Museum
Hospital
Magen David Adom
Stadium
Police station
Gas station
Post office
Synagogue
Other site
Pool/Fountain
0 100 200 300 400 500 m
1:15,000
© Carta Jerusalem – All righ

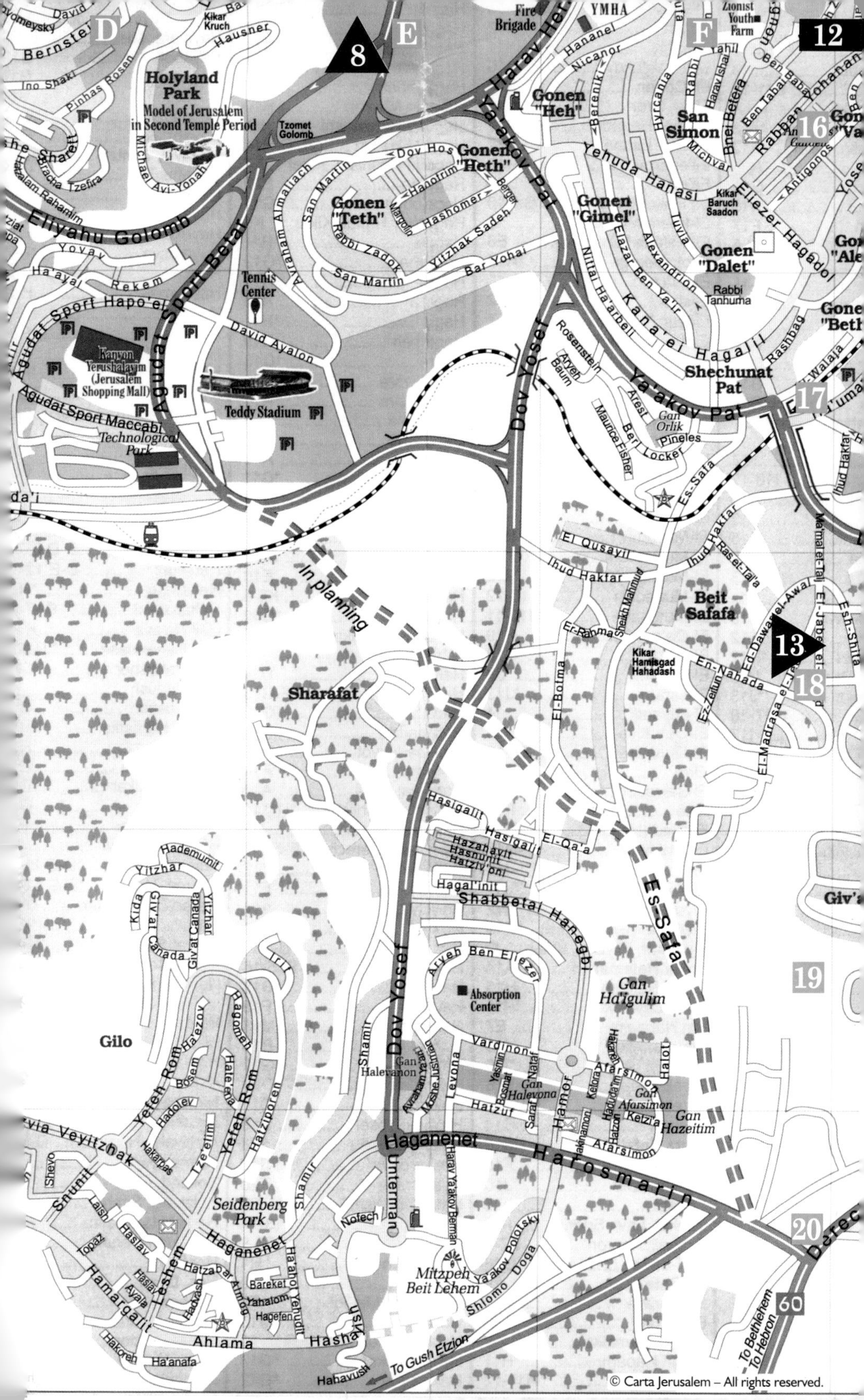

D
E
F
8
12
13
16
17
18
19
20
60
Holyland Park
Model of Jerusalem in Second Temple Period
Tzomet Golomb
Eliyahu Golomb
Gonen "Heh"
Gonen "Heth"
Gonen "Teth"
Gonen "Gimel"
Gonen "Dalet"
San Simon
Shechunat Pat
Tennis Center
Kanyon Yerushalayim (Jerusalem Shopping Mall)
Teddy Stadium
Technological Park
Agudat Sport Betar
Agudat Sport Hapo'el
Agudat Sport Maccabi
David Ayalon
Dov Yosef
Ya'akov Pat
Harav Herzog
In planning
Sharafat
Beit Safafa
Kikar Hamisgad Hahadash
Es-Safa
Gilo
Gan Ha'igulim
Absorption Center
Gan Halevanon
Gan Afarsimon
Gan Hazeitim
Seidenberg Park
Mitzpeh Beit Lehem
Haganenet
Harosmarin
Yehuda Hanasi
Eliezer Hagadol
Kana'ei Hagalil
Shabbetai Hanegbi
To Gush Etzion
To Bethlehem
To Hebron
Fire Brigade
YMHA
Zionist Youth Farm

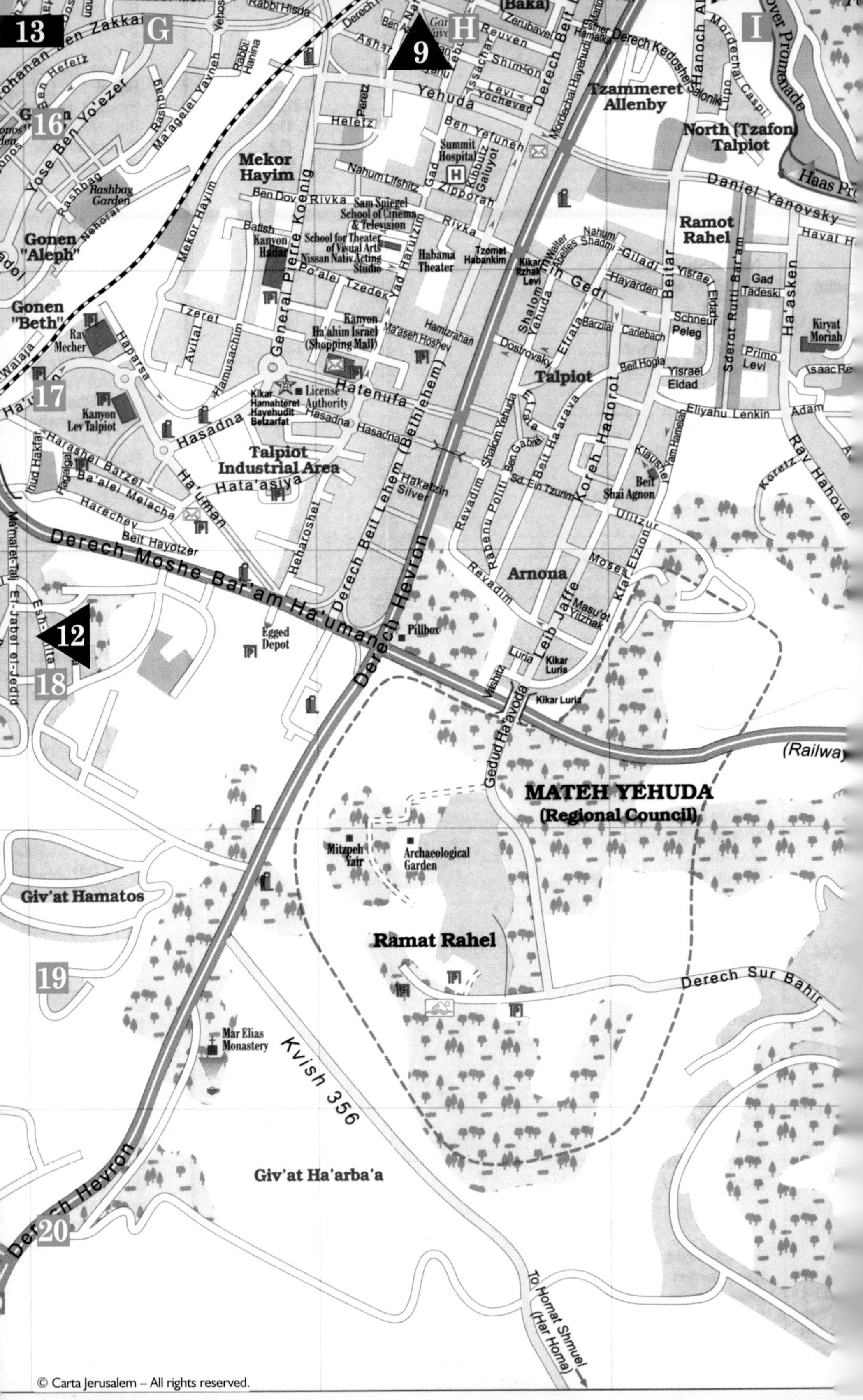

13
G
H
I
9
12
16
17
18
19
20
Mekor Hayim
Gonen "Aleph"
Gonen "Beth"
Rashbag Garden
Summit Hospital
Sam Spiegel School of Cinema & Television
School for Theater of Visual Arts
Nissan Nativ Acting Studio
Habama Theater
Tzomet Habankim
Kikar Itzhak Levi
Kanyon Hadar
Kanyon Ha'ahim Israel (Shopping Mall)
Kanyon Lev Talpiot
License Authority
Kikar Hamahteret Hayehudit Betzarfat
Talpiot Industrial Area
Talpiot
Tzammeret Allenby
North (Tzafon) Talpiot
Ramot Rahel
Kiryat Moriah
Arnona
Beit Shai Agnon
Kikar Luria
Egged Depot
Pillbox
MATEH YEHUDA
(Regional Council)
Mitzpeh Yair
Archaeological Garden
Ramat Rahel
Giv'at Hamatos
Mar Elias Monastery
Giv'at Ha'arba'a
Derech Hevron
Derech Beit Lehem (Bethlehem)
Derech Moshe Bar'am Ha'uman
Derech Sur Bahir
Kvish 356
Daniel Yanovsky
Haas Promenade
Derech Kedoshei Saloniki
Hatenufa
Hasadna
Hata'asiya
Ha'uman
General Pierre Koenig
Yad Harutzim
Po'alei Tzedek
Hamizrahan
Dostrovsky
Ein Gedi
Efrata
Beit Hogla
Korch Hadorot
Beit Ha'arava
Revadim
Rabenu Politi
Leib Jaffe
Kfar Etzion
Gedud Ha'avoda
Eliyahu Lenkin
Sderot Ruth Bar'am
Ha'askan
Rav Hahover
Yehuda
Ben Yefuneh
Rivka
Zipporah
Nahum Lifshitz
Heleitz
Yose Ben Yo'ezer
Ma'agelei Yavneh
Harechev
Beit Hayotzer
Hakatzin Silver
Heharoshet
El-Jabel el-Jedid
(Railway)
To Homat Shmuel (Har Homa)
© Carta Jerusalem – All rights reserved.

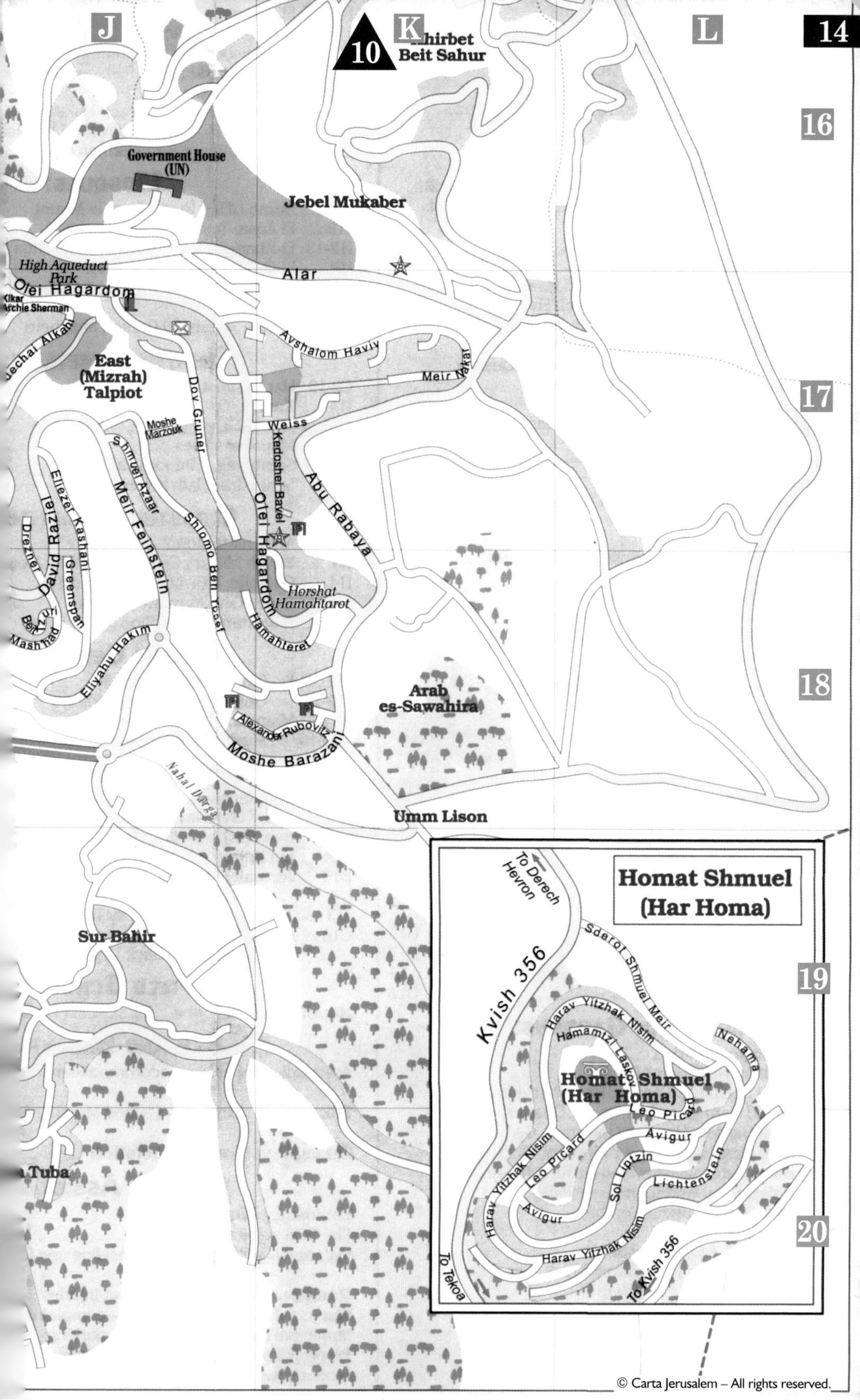
J
K
L
10
Khirbet Beit Sahur
16
17
18
19
20
Government House (UN)
Jebel Mukaber
High Aqueduct Park
Alar
Olei Hagardom
Kikar Archie Sherman
East (Mizrah) Talpiot
Avshalom Haviv
Meir Nakar
Dov Gruner
Moshe Marzouk
Weiss
Kedoshei Bavel
Abu Rabaya
Shmuel Azaar
Eliezer Kashani
David Raziel
Drezner
Greenspan
Meir Feinstein
Shlomo Ben Yosef
Olei Hagardom
Horshat Hamahtarot
Hamahteret
Eliyahu Hakim
Beit Mash'had
Tzuri
Arab es-Sawahira
Alexander Rubovitz
Moshe Barazani
Nahal Darga
Umm Lison
Sur Bahir
Tuba
Homat Shmuel (Har Homa)
To Derech Hevron
Kvish 356
Sderot Shmuel Meir
Harav Yitzhak Nisim
Hamamtzi Laskov
Nehama
Homat Shmuel (Har Homa)
Leo Picard
Avigur
Sol Liptzin
Lichtenstein
Leo Picard
Harav Yitzhak Nisim
Avigur
Harav Yitzhak Nisim
Harav Yitzhak Nisim
To Tekoa
To Kvish 356

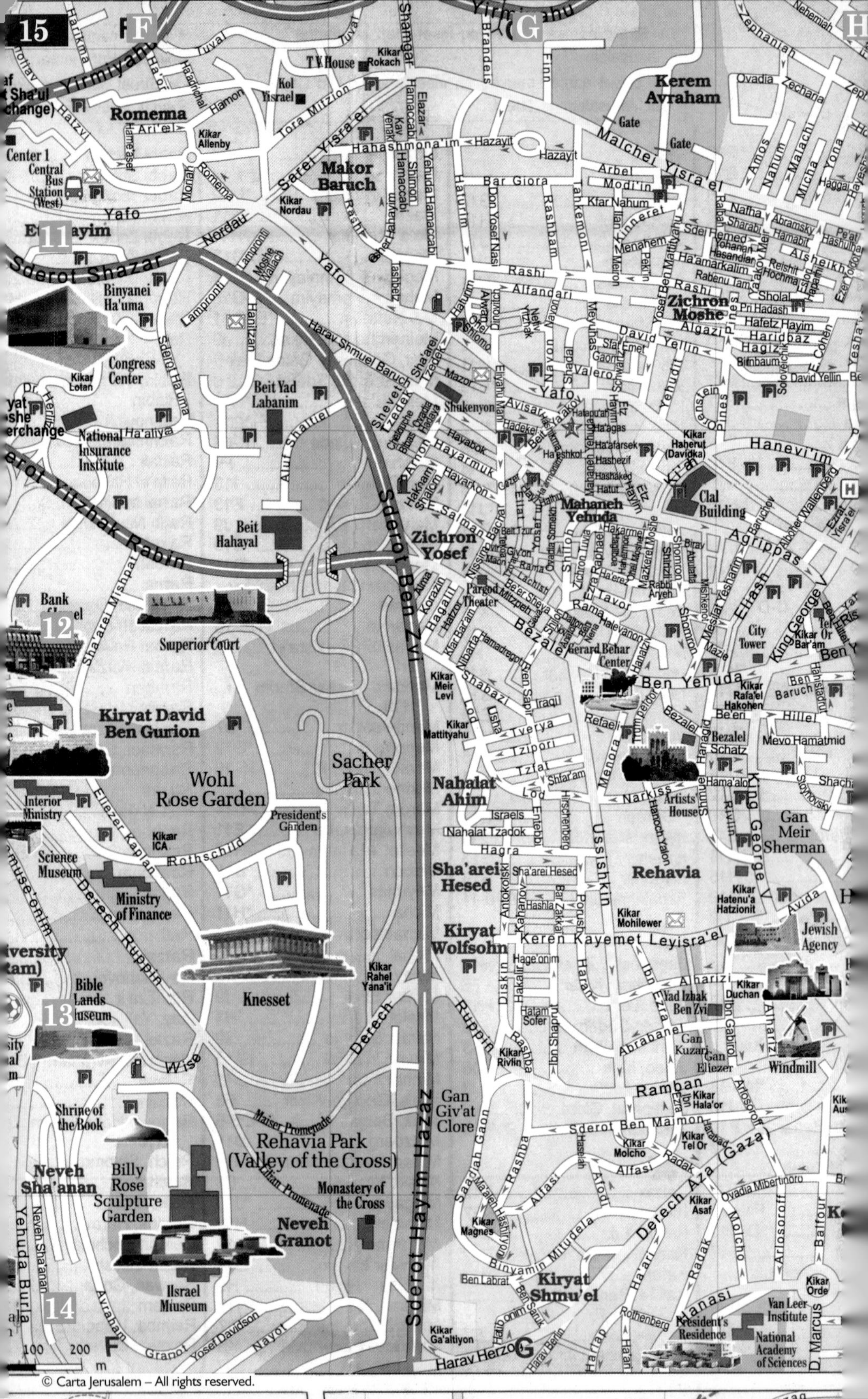
15
F
G
H
Romema
Kerem Avraham
Makor Baruch
Central Bus Station (West)
Center 1
Kikar Allenby
Kikar Rokach
T.V. House
Kol Yisrael
Kikar Nordau
Binyanei Ha'uma
Congress Center
Kikar Lotan
National Insurance Institute
Beit Yad Labanim
Beit Hahayal
Zichron Moshe
Zichron Yosef
Mahaneh Yehuda
Shukenyon
Kikar Haherut (Davidka)
Clal Building
Pargod Theater
City Tower
Gerard Behar Center
Bank of Israel
Superior Court
Kiryat David Ben Gurion
Wohl Rose Garden
Sacher Park
President's Garden
Interior Ministry
Science Museum
Ministry of Finance
Kikar ICA
Knesset
Kikar Rahel Yana'it
Bible Lands Museum
Shrine of the Book
Neveh Sha'anan
Billy Rose Sculpture Garden
Israel Museum
Rehavia Park (Valley of the Cross)
Maiser Promenade
Lilian Promenade
Monastery of the Cross
Neveh Granot
Gan Giv'at Clore
Nahalat Ahim
Sha'arei Hesed
Kiryat Wolfsohn
Rehavia
Artists' House
Bezalel Schatz
Gan Meir Sherman
Kikar Hatenu'a Hatzionit
Kikar Mohilewer
Jewish Agency
Kikar Duchan
Yad Izhak Ben Zvi
Gan Kuzari
Gan Eliezer
Windmill
Kikar Molcho
Kikar Tel Or
Kikar Asaf
Kikar Magnes
Kiryat Shmu'el
Kikar Ga'altiyon
President's Residence
Van Leer Institute
National Academy of Sciences
Kikar Orde
Sderot Shazar
Sderot Yitzhak Rabin
Sderot Ben Zvi
Sderot Hayim Hazaz
Yafo
Malchei Yisra'el
Sarei Yisra'el
Agrippas
Hanevi'im
King George V
Ben Yehuda
Keren Kayemet Leyisra'el
Ussishkin
Ramban
Derech Aza (Gaza)
Derech Ruppin
Eliezer Kaplan
Rothschild
Wise
Harav Herzog
Yehuda Burla
Avraham Granot
Yosef Davidson
Nayot
Sderot Ben Maimon
Alfasi
Radak
Arlosoroff
Balfour
D. Marcus
Hanasi
Narkiss
Bezalel
Rashba
Saadiah Gaon
Binyamin Mitudela
11
12
13
14
100
200
m
© Carta Jerusalem – All rights reserved.

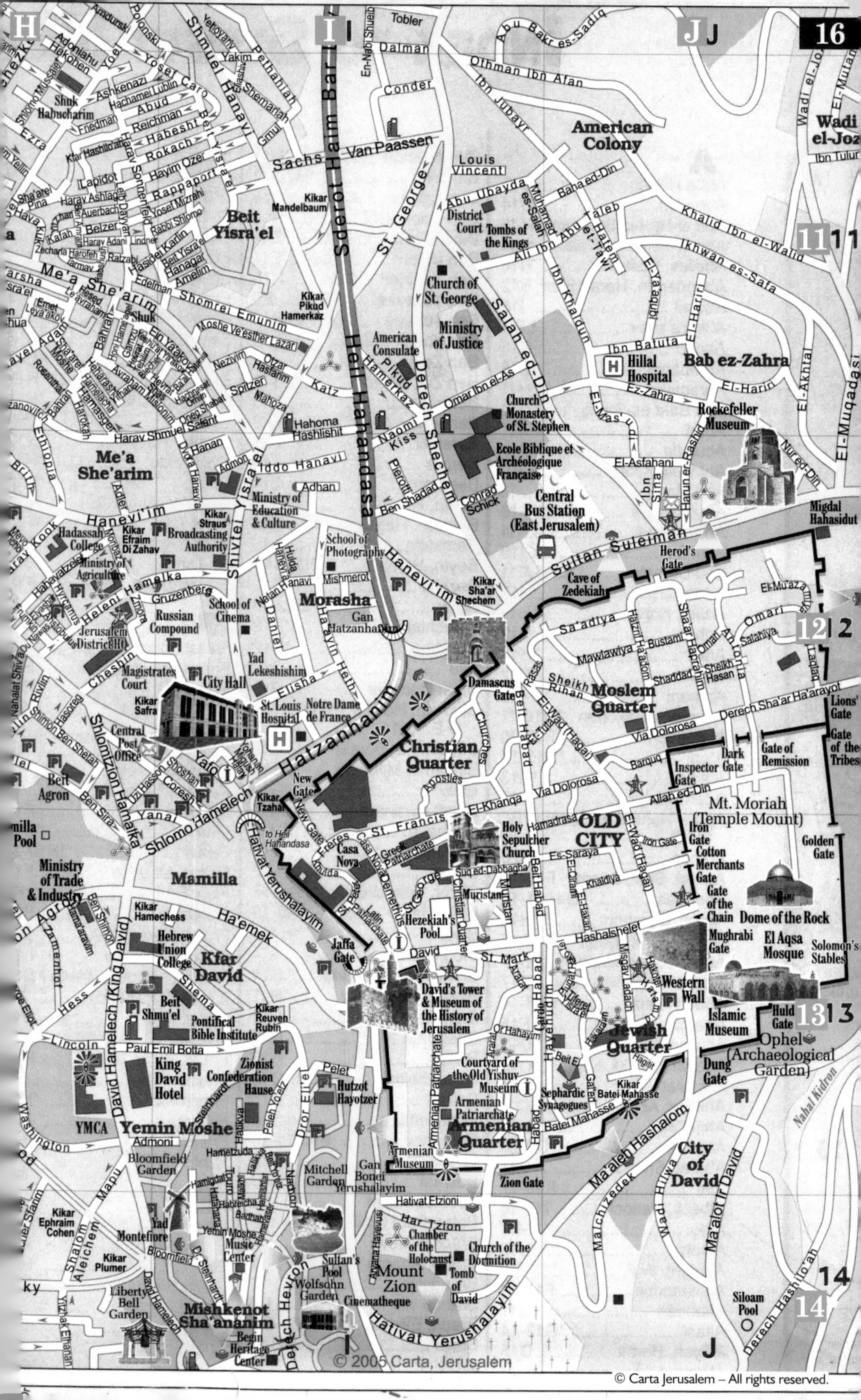
H
I
J
American Colony
Wadi el-Joz
Beit Yisra'el
Me'a She'arim
Shuk Habucharim
District Court
Tombs of the Kings
Church of St. George
Ministry of Justice
American Consulate
Hillal Hospital
Bab ez-Zahra
Rockefeller Museum
Church Monastery of St. Stephen
Ecole Biblique et Archéologique Française
Central Bus Station (East Jerusalem)
Ministry of Education & Culture
School of Photography
Morasha
Hadassah College
Broadcasting Authority
Ministry of Agriculture
School of Cinema
Russian Compound
Jerusalem District HQ
Magistrates Court
City Hall
Yad Lekeshishim
St. Louis Hospital
Notre Dame de France
Central Post Office
Beit Agron
Mamilla Pool
Mamilla
Ministry of Trade & Industry
Herod's Gate
Cave of Zedekiah
Damascus Gate
Moslem Quarter
Christian Quarter
New Gate
Lions' Gate
Gate of the Tribes
Gate of Remission
Inspector Gate
Dark Gate
Mt. Moriah (Temple Mount)
OLD CITY
Iron Gate
Cotton Merchants Gate
Gate of the Chain
Golden Gate
Dome of the Rock
Holy Sepulcher Church
Casa Nova
Hezekiah's Pool
Jaffa Gate
David's Tower & Museum of the History of Jerusalem
Mughrabi Gate
El Aqsa Mosque
Solomon's Stables
Western Wall
Islamic Museum
Huld Gate
Ophel (Archaeological Garden)
Jewish Quarter
Dung Gate
Kfar David
Hebrew Union College
Beit Shmu'el
Pontifical Bible Institute
King David Hotel
YMCA
Zionist Confederation Hause
Hutzot Hayotzer
Yemin Moshe
Courtyard of the Old Yishuv Museum
Sephardic Synagogues
Armenian Patriarchate
Armenian Quarter
Armenian Museum
Zion Gate
City of David
Nahal Kidron
Bloomfield Garden
Mitchell Garden
Gan Bonei Yerushalayim
Yad Montefiore
Music Center
Sultan's Pool
Wolfsohn Garden
Mount Zion
Chamber of the Holocaust
Church of the Dormition
Tomb of David
Cinematheque
Liberty Bell Garden
Mishkenot Sha'ananim
Begin Heritage Center
Siloam Pool
11
12
13
14
© 2005 Carta, Jerusalem